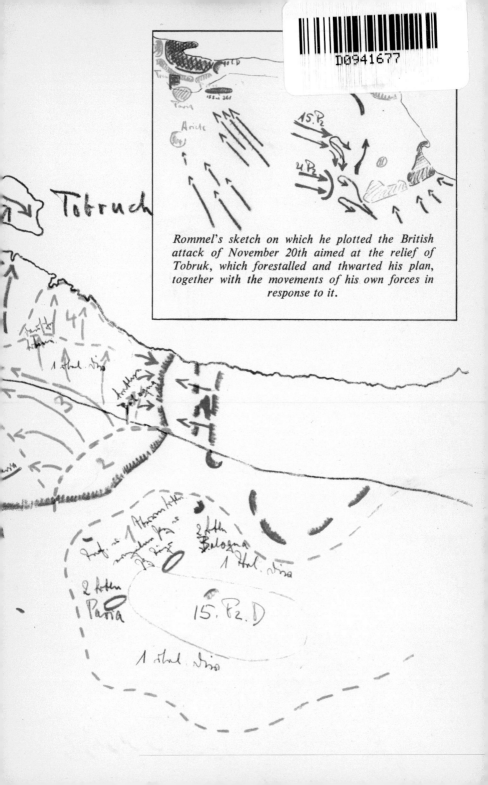

Rommel's sketch on which he plotted the British attack of November 20th aimed at the relief of Tobruk, which forestalled and thwarted his plan, together with the movements of his own forces in response to it.

ExLibris

THE BARCLAYS

THE ROMMEL PAPERS

Field Marshal Rommel and (right) General Fritz Bayerlein during the Battle of Alamein, November 1942

THE
ROMMEL
PAPERS

EDITED BY

B. H. LIDDELL HART

With the assistance of
LUCIE-MARIA ROMMEL
MANFRED ROMMEL
AND GENERAL FRITZ BAYERLEIN

Translated by
PAUL FINDLAY

NEW YORK
HARCOURT, BRACE AND COMPANY
1953

LIBRARY OF CONGRESS CATALOG CARD NO. 53-5656

PRINTED IN THE UNITED STATES OF AMERICA

Contents

PART THREE

THE WAR IN AFRICA—SECOND YEAR

PART FOUR

ITALY

PART FIVE

INVASION

LIST OF MAPS

Drawn by J. F. Trotter

LIST OF PLATES

INTRODUCTION

THE IMPACT that Rommel made on the world with the sword will be deepened by his power with the pen. No commander in history has written an account of his campaigns to match the vividness and value of Rommel's—which, for the most part, has now been retrieved from its various hiding places and put together in this volume.

No other commander has provided such a graphic picture of his operations and method of command. No one else has so strikingly conveyed in writing the dynamism of *Blitzkrieg* and the pace of *panzer* forces. The sense of fast movement and quick decision is electrifyingly communicated in many of the passages—Rommel carries the reader along with him in his command vehicle.

Great commanders have mostly been dull writers. Besides lacking literary skill in describing their actions, they have tended to be cloudy about the way their minds worked. In relating what they did, they have told posterity little about how and why. Napoleon was an exception, but the value of his account is impaired by a more than usual unscrupulousness in treating facts, and by his intentness to falsify the balance-sheet. Like Caesar's, his writing was not merely coloured but dominated by a propaganda purpose.

Rommel's narrative is remarkably objective, as well as graphic. In drafting it he certainly had, like most men who have made history, a concern for his place in history. But while he shows a natural desire for justification in his explanation of events, it is subordinate to his burning interest in the military lessons of the campaigns. His evidence stands up uncommonly well to critical examination, and checking by other sources. A number of errors of fact can be found in it, but fewer than in many of the official and personal narratives compiled with the advantage of post-war knowledge. There are some disputable interpretations, but not the purposeful distortions, for national or personal credit, which are all too often found in such accounts.

The clarity and high degree of accuracy which distinguish Rommel's picture of the operations are the more notable because of the confused impressions that are apt to be produced by fast-moving tank battles, especially in the desert. The clearness of Rommel's picture owes much to his way of command—his habit of getting right forward and seeking to be near the crucial spot at the crucial time. It also owes much to his prolonged self-training in observation, highly developed eye for spotting what was significant in a scene, and knack of registering it. His passion for taking photographs at every step of advance was a symptom of this characteristic—as it was with Lawrence, in the Arabian theatre of World War I.

There were marked resemblances between these two masters of desert warfare, whatever their differences in temperament, range of interest and philosophy. They were strikingly akin in their sense of time and space, instinct for surprise, eye for ground and opportunity, combination of flexibility with vision, and ideas of direct personal leadership. Another military link was in the application of mechanised mobility to desert warfare. Lawrence, who is popularly associated with camel-rides, was among the first to see how the new means of mobility could transform desert warfare, and had demonstrated this embryonically and in miniature, with a few armoured cars and aircraft. Rommel's exploitation of these potentialities on the grand scale would have delighted the Lawrence who was a connoisseur of military art and had a revolutionary bent.

Rommel, also, had an urge to express himself on paper as well as in action. That became evident—long before he became famous as a commander—from his extraordinarily vivid treatise on infantry tactics, inspired by his experiences as a young officer in World War I and by his reflections upon them. Most text-books on tactics are deadly dull, but he brought life into the subject. The more mobile operations of the next war, and his own greater role, gave him bigger scope—of which he took full advantage. He was a born writer as well as a born fighter. The same expressive gift and urge can be seen in the way he sketched on paper, with pencil or coloured chalks, the operations he planned or even imagined.

Throughout his activities in World War II he kept constantly in mind the project of a book to match the performance, and continually made notes for the purpose—notes that he developed into a narrative whenever he had a breathing space.

Death, under Hitler's decree, prevented him from completing the project, but what he had already drafted makes a book that has no peer among narratives of its kind. It may lack polish, but its literary power is very striking. Along with descriptive clarity it has dramatic intensity, while its value is much increased by the comments that accompany and illuminate its story. His section on " The Rules of Desert Warfare " is a masterly piece of military thinking, while the whole narrative is sprinkled with sage reflections, often with a fresh turn—about concentration in time rather than in space; about the effect of speed in outweighing numbers; about flexibility as a means to surprise; about the security provided by audacity; about the stultifying conventions of the " quarter-master " mind; about creating new standards and not submitting to norms; about the value of indirect rather than direct reply to the enemy's moves; about the way that air inferiority requires a radical revision of the rules of ground operations; about the unwisdom of indiscriminate reprisals and the folly of brutality; about the basic inexpediency of unprincipled expediency.

Until I delved into Rommel's own papers I regarded him as a brilliant tactician and great fighting leader, but did not realise how deep a sense of strategy he had—or, at any rate, developed in reflection. It was a surprise to find that such a thruster had been so thoughtful, and that his audacity was so shrewdly calculated. In certain cases, his moves may still be criticised as too hazardous, but not as the reckless strokes of a blind and hot-headed gambler. In analysis of the operations it can be seen that some of the strokes which miscarried, with grave results for him, came close to proving graver for his opponents. Moreover, even in failure his strokes made such an impression on them as to assure his army a chance of escape.

One of the clearer ways in which commanders can be measured is by the extent to which they impress the opposing side. By that measure Rommel's stature is very high. In centuries of warfare only Napoleon has made a comparable impression on the British, and that was not achieved purely in the military field, as it was in Rommel's case.

Moreover, Rommel became much more than a bogey to the British. Awe for his dynamic generalship developed into an almost affectionate admiration for him as a man. This was inspired primarily by the speed and surprise of his operations, but it was fostered by the way that he maintained in African warfare the decencies of the soldierly code, and by his own chivalrous behaviour towards the many prisoners of war whom he met in person. He became the hero of the Eighth Army troops who were fighting against him—to such an extent that it became their habit, when wanting to say that someone had done a good job of any kind on their own side, to describe it as " doing a Rommel ".

Such intense admiration for the enemy commander carried an underlying danger to the soldiers' morale. Thus the British commanders and headquarter staffs were compelled to make strenuous efforts to dispel " the Rommel legend ". It is a tribute to their sense of decency and his personal conduct that such counter-propaganda was not directed towards blackening his character but towards diminishing his military scale. In that respect, his ultimate defeats provided a lever—and it was hardly to be expected that his opponents would emphasise his crippling disadvantages in strength and supplies, or the significance of what he managed to achieve under such handicaps. Juster comparison and truer reckoning are left for history, which has a habit of correcting the superficial judgments that temporarily keep company with victory. Hannibal, Napoleon and Lee went down in defeat, yet rose above their conquerors in the scales of history.

In true judgment of performance, due account must be taken of the conditions and relative resources, together with the other factors that lie outside a commander's control. Only then can we properly estimate the quality of his performance. The outstanding feature of Rommel's numerous successes is that they were achieved with inferiority of resources and without any command of the air. No other generals on either side in World War II won battles under these handicaps, except for the early British leaders under Wavell—and they were fighting Italians.

Rommel's performance was not flawless, and he suffered several possibly avoidable reverses—but when fighting superior forces any slip may result in defeat, whereas numerous mistakes can be effectively covered up by the commander who possesses a big margin of superiority in strength. For all his audacity and rapidity of movement and decision, Rommel comes out well, on balance, from the test embodied in Napoleon's saying that " the greatest general is the one who makes the fewest mistakes."

That criticism, however, has too passive a note to fit the nature of war, and is apt to foster a dangerous caution. It would be more profoundly true to say: " the greatest general is the one who leads his opponent to make the most mistakes." By that test, Rommel shines even more brightly.

The best line of comparison between famous commanders of different eras lies through their art, which can be distinguished from changing technique. It is possible to make a comparative study of the use they made of the means at their disposal to achieve their effects—particularly their use of mobility, flexibility, and surprise to upset their opponents' mental and physical balance. It is even possible, with such as have disclosed their conceptions, to gauge how far their effects were a matter of calculation.

Here, above all, lies the instructive value of Rommel's papers—and the more so because his narrative was not revised in the light of postwar knowledge, while his letters frequently provide pre-event evidence of the way in which he approached his problems. It is in the approach, more than in the act, that a man reveals the bent of his thought, and the compass of his mind.

The Rommel Papers should go far to dispel the dust of controversy that has been stirred up, from various motives. Rommel's narratives were written long before he could have any idea of the controversy that would arise outside Germany, and could frame them to meet it; his letters to his wife have still more immediacy. It is remarkable how frank they are in comment in view of the fact that they were liable to be opened. From these conjoint sources the reader can get a clear view into Rommel's mind and the mainsprings of his action. The picture may naturally differ according to the individual reader's predisposition, but there is little obscurity about the personality itself, and its various facets.

Rommel was very human—apart from his extraordinary energy and his military genius. The " warts " are plainly self-revealed in his narratives and letters. Like most of the leaders of mankind he was in a state of immaturity. During his spell of greatest success his attitude had the boyishness that is captivating but dangerously unphilosophical, and his outlook had the limitations that make for success in leadership. In the earlier part of the war, his letters suggest that he tended to regard war as a great game—the game for which, in his country's service, he had trained himself with single-minded devotion. For maximum driving power, a commander must feel like that about war—and the most thrustful of them always have. Rommel had an unusual capacity for reflection, but his did not go beyond the military field until the last months of his life.

Like most forceful soldiers, too, he did not find it easy to be tolerant about contrary views, especially among those who were fighting on the same side. That is manifest in his biting comments on Halder and Kesselring in particular, which were certainly unjust on several counts. It should also be remembered that he was a sick man during the later stages of the African campaign, a condition which naturally tended to increase his aggravation and warp his view. But there was little malice in him—his explosiveness was an outlet—and he was unusually ready to repair an injustice when his anger passed. That can be seen, for instance, in the high tribute he pays to Kesselring in his final reflections. Moreover, his comments on the enemy—French, British and American—show a remarkable freedom from hatred and readiness to recognise their qualities.

Rommel's attitude to " the Fuehrer " and his long-continued loyalty are a puzzle only to those who do not understand the habit of mind produced by a professional soldier's early training, particularly in Germany, and are unable to imagine how things look from such a point of view. But the Papers make clearer two factors that for a time buttressed his soldierly loyalty. It is easy to perceive how Rommel's dynamism made him responsive to Hitler's and how the obstruction he suffered from the intermediate " top-hamper " with which he was in close contact made him feel more sympathetic to the distant Fuehrer. That continued while Rommel's reflectiveness was simply military. But the wide measure of independent authority he had in Africa, the larger problems with which he had to deal, and the deep impression made on him by the material superiority of the Allies, gradually widened the scope of his reflection— and thus paved the way for the momentous change of attitude that developed when he came back to Europe and into closer contact with Hitler. It would have been madness for him to have recorded on paper this process of change—indeed, some of his later letters show an obvious effort to disguise it—but there are a number of clues scattered through the pages. His son and closest associates have supplemented these with their evidence of how he was brought to the break-away, and the resolve to overthrow Hitler, which cost him his life.

The main importance of the papers lies, however, in the abundant light they shed on Rommel's military leadership. Their evidence confirms the judgment of the British soldiers who actually fought against him, and shows that their estimate was closer to the mark than the counter-propaganda designed to depreciate his formidable reputation. The " Rommel legend " clearly had a much better foundation than most. Save for his many narrow escapes from death or capture in battle, he owed less to luck than most commanders who have attained fame. Now that his actual conceptions and the workings of his mind are laid open for examination it becomes evident that his successes were earned, not accidental. They bear the hall-mark of military genius.

This is not the place for a biographical survey of Rommel's career—which has been ably and vividly presented in Desmond Young's book,[1] a valuable complement to this. But it may be worthwhile to epitomise the principal features of Rommel's generalship, and briefly discuss them in relation to the general experience of warfare.

In most fields, genius is associated with originality. Yet it has been rare among those who are usually acclaimed as the great masters of war. Most of them have gained their successes by using conventional instruments superlatively well, and only a few have sought new means and methods. That is strange, since history shows that the fate of nations has been repeatedly decided, and the most epoch-making changes in history determined. by change in weapons and tactics—especially the latter.

But such developments have usually been produced by some student of war with a fresh turn of mind, and by his. influence upon the progressively inclined soldiers of his time, rather than by the action of any top-level commander. In the history of war great ideas have been less numerous than great generals, but have had a more far-reaching effect. The distinction between the two is a reminder that there are two forms of military genius—the conceptive and the executive.

In Rommel's case they were combined. While the theory of *Blitzkrieg* —the new super-mobile style of warfare with armoured and motorised forces—had been conceived in England, long before he came on the stage, the quickness with which he grasped it and the way he developed it showed his fresh-mindedness and innate conceptive power. He became, next to Guderian, the leading exponent of the new idea. That was the more remarkable because he had had no experience of tanks until given command of the 7th Panzer Division in February, 1940, and then had less than three months to study the theory and master the problem of handling such forces before he was launched into action. His brilliant share in the panzer drives that produced the collapse of France led to his being given the opportunity of applying the new conception

[1] *Rommel* (Harpers, 1951).

in Africa and with the advantage of independent command—which Guderian was never allowed in Europe, fortunately for Germany's surviving opponents. Moreover, in Africa, Rommel demonstrated a subtler application of the theory, blending the defensive with the offensive and drawing the opposing tanks into baited traps, preparatory to his own lightning thrusts. In other respects, too, he made signal contributions to the new technique.

It is significant that Rommel was one of the few eminent commanders who have gained distinction as military thinkers and writers. More remarkable still is the fact that his chance to prove his powers as a commander came through the effect of his writings. For it was his book *Infanterie greift an* that first attracted Hitler's attention to him, and by the impression it made paved the way for his phenomenal rise.

Rommel was able to make the most of his chance because he also possessed executive genius. The extent to which he had it may best be realised by taking note of the qualities that the great commanders of history have shown—although the degree of each quality has varied in each case.

In earlier times, when armies were small and fought with short-range weapons, and when the battlefield rather than the theatre of war was the general's arena, the quality most prized in a commander was *coup d'œil*—an expressive term for the combination of acute observation with swift-sure intuition. All the Great Captains possessed in high degree this faculty of grasping instantly the picture of the ground and the situation; of relating one to the other, and the part to the whole. Rommel most clearly had this faculty. It had a renewed importance in Africa owing to the nature of fast-moving armoured warfare and the moderate scale of the forces in that theatre.

In recent times, as the range of weapons lengthened and armies became more extended as well as larger in scale, so the need increased for a faculty wider and deeper than *coup d'œil*—for insight. The power of penetrating, as Wellington aptly expressed it, into what was going on " at the other side of the hill "—behind the enemy's lines, and in the enemy's mind. In the present even more than in the past, a leader must have a deep understanding of psychology in general, and of the opposing commander's psychology in particular. The extent to which Rommel possessed this kind of insight, or psychological sense, can be seen in his Papers as well as in his operations.

Such a psychological sense is in turn the foundation of another essential, and more positive, element of military genius—the power of creating surprise, of producing the unexpected move that upsets the opponent's balance. For full effect, as history shows, it must be reinforced by an acute time-sense, and by the capacity to develop the highest possible degree of mobility. Speed and surprise are twin qualities. They are predominantly the " hitting," or offensive, qualities of true generalship. And their development, like that of the informative senses, depends on a faculty which may be best, and briefly, defined as creative imagination.

In power of producing the unexpected move, acuteness of time-sense, and capacity to develop a pitch of mobility that can paralyse opposition, it is hard to find a modern parallel to Rommel, except Guderian, the prime minister of *Blitzkrieg*. Later in the war, Patton and Manteuffel displayed similar qualities, but comparative assessment is difficult because of their more limited scope. So it is, also, when we go back into the past, where instruments were so different—although we know that Seydlitz, Napoleon, and Bedford Forrest were outstandingly gifted in achieving surprise through speed, and although a similar dynamism can be discerned in the great Mongol leaders such as Genghiz Khan and Sabutai. The secret of this combination has never been so clearly communicated as in Rommel's Papers.

In seeking to upset the enemy's balance, a commander must not lose his own balance. He needs to have the quality which Voltaire described as the keystone of Marlborough's success—" that calm courage in the midst of tumult, that serenity of soul in danger, which the English call a cool head." But to it he must add the quality for which the French have found the most aptly descriptive phrase—" *le sens du praticable.*" The sense of what is possible, and what is not possible—tactically and administratively. The combination of both these two " guarding " qualities might be epitomised as the power of cool calculation. The sands of history are littered with the wrecks of finely conceived plans that capsized for want of this ballast.

On this count, there is more question about Rommel's qualifications. Along with tremendous courage he had what is called the artistic temperament, and was apt to swing from exaltation to depression—as his letters show. Moreover, he was often criticised in German staff circles, including his own, for not taking sufficient account of supply difficulties, and attempting strategically more than was practicable administratively. In a number of cases the course of the operations tends to bear out such criticism. On the other hand, the Papers show that in the risks he took there was a deeper calculation than appeared on the surface. He demanded more than was possible by " Quartermasters' " standards as the most probable way of gaining great results under the new conditions of strategy. Although that strategic policy miscarried at times, it is remarkable how often he managed more than was possible administratively by any normal calculation—and in consequence achieved results that would not have been possible in any other way.

Finally, and beyond all the other qualities that mark a great commander, comes actual power of leadership. That is the dynamo of the battle-car and no skill in driving will avail if it is defective. It is through the current of great leadership that troops are inspired to do more than seems possible, and thus upset an opponent's "normal" calculations.

There is no doubt on this score of Rommel's qualification as a "Great Captain". Exasperating to staff officers, he was worshipped by the fighting troops, and what he got out of them in performance was far beyond any rational calculation.

B. H. LIDDELL HART

THE STORY OF THE ROMMEL PAPERS

By *Manfred Rommel*

WHEN MY father died, he left a considerable number of documents which had accumulated during his campaigns. There were army orders, situation reports, daily reports to the High Command; besides these official documents he left a number of volumes comprising his personal diary, and comprehensive notes on the French campaign of 1940 and on the war in the desert.

After the First World War my father published a book on infantry tactics, based largely on his own experiences. When he was writing that book he found he had preserved few of the essential documents, while his diary was hardly more helpful; there were great gaps during the most important periods, when he had been too occupied with fighting to have time for his diary.

My father undoubtedly intended to publish another book on the military lessons to be derived from his experiences in World War II, and this time he was determined not to be at the same disadvantage in the matter of contemporary records.

From the moment he crossed the frontier on 10 May 1940 he began to keep a personal account of his operations, which he generally dictated daily to one of his aides. Whenever a lull allowed, he prepared a more considered appreciation of what had taken place.

He preserved all his official orders, reports and documents. In addition there were hundreds of maps and sketches of his operations which he or his staff had drawn in coloured chalks, some being carefully and exactly finished off in drawing ink; there were also drafts for maps intended to illustrate his subsequent writings.

As events took a less favourable turn, my father became all the more anxious that an objective account of his actions should survive his possible death so that his intentions could not be misinterpreted. On his return from Africa he worked on his papers in great secrecy, dictating, or giving drafts for typing, only to my mother or to one of his A.D.Cs. On his return from France in August, 1944, he began to write an account of the Invasion, but he destroyed this when it became clear that he was suspected of complicity in the July 20 plot. On the other hand, some papers have survived which he would undoubtedly have burned had he had the time.

My father was an enthusiastic photographer. Here, again for the purposes of his book, he had gone back to Italy after the first World War to get photographs, which he needed for making tactical sketches, of the places where he had fought in 1917; but that had not been easy, for the Italians did not welcome German officers with cameras to their frontier territory. My father travelled as an " engineer " with my mother on a motor-cycle. For the book he planned to write on the Second World War he intended to be well provided with photographs and he took literally thousands, both in Europe and in Africa, including a large number in colour. He took photographs only when advancing, he once told me; " I don't photograph my own retreat."

Furthermore, he wrote to my mother almost daily and she had preserved about a thousand of his letters.

Only a proportion of all this material survived the various vicissitudes which it underwent.

During the months immediately preceding the outbreak of war, my father commanded the War Academy at Wiener Neustadt, about thirty miles south of Vienna. The academy was housed in an enormous old castle. When in 1943 British and American bomber squadrons started to raid the town and our home was in danger of being destroyed, we deposited some of my father's papers in the deep cellars of the castle; others we sent to a farm in south-west Germany. The rest we took with us when in the autumn of 1943 we moved from Wiener Neustadt to Herrlingen, five miles from Ulm in Wuerttemberg.

My father's death made my mother all the more anxious to save his papers, not only for personal reasons but so that, when history came to be written, the truth might be told. Already at the time of the funeral, an S.S. officer had tried to find out, in the course of conversation, what had become of my father's papers. We did not take the bait. Nonetheless, it appeared highly probable that an attempt would be made to take them from us.

My mother, therefore, immediately began to assemble all the papers in the house. I went to Wiener Neustadt to retrieve the documents which we had left in the castle cellars. One did not need to be very far-sighted at that time to realise that Soviet troops would, in due course, reach Vienna; and, as it turned out, six months later they stormed the castle after it had been reduced to a heap of rubble following stout resistance on the part of the German officer cadets in training there. Everything that was not nailed to the ground, was plundered.

With the help of my father's sister and of Captain Aldinger, his

A.D.C., my mother began to pack up all the papers ready for evacuation should the need arise. She intended to rely on dispersal, for while it was probable that one hiding place would be discovered, it was improbable that all would be.

In the middle of November, 1944, Captain Aldinger, who had stayed with my mother to help her clear up my father's affairs, was suddenly ordered by the town major of Ulm to present himself at the main railway station of that city. It was said that an officer on General Maisel's staff would be there and that he had certain matters to discuss with Captain Aldinger. It was General Maisel who had fetched my father away a month earlier. It was further intimated to Captain Aldinger that this officer had orders to proceed to Herrlingen afterwards.

The purpose of this visit was obscure to my mother and Captain Aldinger. Was an arrest planned? Or did they intend to carry out a house search for my father's notes? No one could tell.

The work of hiding the remaining papers was speeded up as much as possible. By the evening of the 14th November, with the exception of drafts and jottings for his personal notes, all that remained in the house were official war documents, marked " Secret ", which would, in any event, have to be given up.

On the morning of the 15th November, Aldinger left Herrlingen to go to Ulm. " I shall leave the car here," he said to my mother; " God knows whether I shall ever come back. Perhaps I shall be arrested right away. If not, I shall come back to Herrlingen at once."

My mother waited. When the afternoon came, she became seriously concerned about Aldinger's arrest. There was all the more danger that this might happen because, with the exception of my mother and myself, he was the only witness who knew the real cause of my father's death. Towards three o'clock the gate of our garden opened. Aldinger came in. He was alone and was carrying rather a bulky parcel under his arm which was wrapped in white paper. Mercifully my mother's fears had not materialised. The officer on Maisel's staff had handed over the baton and service cap which the two generals had taken from my father on the 14th October, after he died. They had taken these " trophies " to the Fuehrer's Headquarters and, as we found out afterwards, they were kept for a time in the desk of Schaub, Hitler's A.D.C. Immediately after my father's death, Captain Aldinger had repeatedly and vigorously protested, in the name of my mother, at this unheard-of behaviour and had now, against all expectations, been successful.

The majority of the documents had by this time been dispersed. They were hidden on two different farms in south-west Germany, in one case walled up in a cellar, in the other behind a heap of empty boxes in a cellar. A small box which contained some of my father's notes on the battle of Normandy was buried by a friend of ours between the walls of a bombed Stuttgart ruin in a part of the town which had been so pounded by numerous air attacks that it was no longer likely to be considered a worthwhile target. My father's diaries for 1943-44 were deposited in a hospital, while other material was sent to my aunt in Stuttgart. My mother retained in the house at Herrlingen the drafts of my father's notes which had formed the original manuscript on Africa, films taken by my father in the French campaign of 1940 and his personal letters.

Strangely enough, my mother was so preoccupied with the fear that the Nazi authorities might get hold of the papers that she never thought of the possibility that the Allies, who were now approaching, might show an equal interest.

During the second half of April 1945, the bombing became continuous. Hour by hour the American H.E. bombs crashed down on Ulm, which was burning night and day in many places. From the west and from the north the sound of artillery fire could be heard and day by day it became more menacing. The remnants of the German Army were streaming back weaponless through the valley in which Herrlingen lay, some on farm-carts, some on foot, all in perpetual fear of attack by U.S. fighter-bombers. The local Volksturm, comprising youngsters of fourteen and old men of sixty-five, was mobilised. Placards had been put up everywhere which read " Anyone who fails to defend Ulm against the enemy is a swine."

One day, it must have been the 20th April, my mother, looking out of her window, saw the American tanks approaching Ulm. Only when, on the following day, Allied soldiers set fire to parts of the neighbouring village on the false assumption that it was occupied by German partisans, and long columns of refugees from that village came streaming through Herrlingen, only then did my mother become anxious about the documents that were still in the house. She got the letters, notes and films ready so that she could take them with her at a moment's notice. Part of these she threw in an old trunk which, with the help of neighbours, she buried in the garden.

The American troops now occupied Herrlingen. Sentries were posted everywhere. It was impossible to bury any further material. Among the first Americans who came to see my mother was a Captain Marshall of the Seventh Army. He asked whether there were any documents in the house. In the confident belief that private letters would not be confiscated, my mother answered: "I have only the personal letters of my husband written to me." "Where are these letters? "asked Marshall.

He went with my mother down to the cellar. When he saw the folders containing the letters lying in a box, he said: " I will have to take them away. We shall want to have a look at them. I will bring them back in a few days."

Next my mother was told that the return of these letters would be delayed for a bit. A fortnight later Captain Marshall's interpreter came to my mother, and said: "The Captain is terribly sorry that we can't keep our promise but the Army has decided that these documents will have to be sent to Washington."

One day, in the middle of May, at eight o'clock in the morning, my mother was ordered to leave her house by nine. An American unit was to be billeted in our home. While my mother was still packing, American soldiers started to open the drawers and cupboards and to search. Numerous documents of my father's (drafts for notes on Africa and handwritten maps) which at the time were on the library shelves, in the desk and in the cellar have not been seen since. All my mother managed to do was to bring away on a small hand-cart a trunk containing my father's films, the manuscript of the African campaign, and the official history of the 7th Panzer Division's operations in France in 1940, of which only three copies had ever been made.

The papers which were evacuated to other places met with varied fates.

On the one farm in south-west Germany, some Americans appeared, announced that they belonged to the Counter Intelligence Corps and demanded to see the trunks which Field Marshal Rommel had had placed there. Unfortunately, some of these trunks and boxes had already been brought up from the cellar—in which they had been walled up—into the house itself. The Americans commandeered a chest and a trunk. The chest contained my father's documents, notes and sketches from the First World War—the material he had used in his book, *The Infantry in Attack*. The trunk contained my father's complete Leica equipment (a camera and twelve different accessories), personal effects and about 3,000 snapshots which my father had himself taken. He was particularly proud of his colour photographs, some of which had been taken with a certain amount of danger to himself. One, I remember, which was most impressive, showed Australian infantry attacking with bayonets. There were several thousand other photographs which he had collected from war reporters and soldiers between 1940 and 1944; some he had already captioned.

The Americans gave a receipt for the chest and the trunk. But American officers who subsequently came and tried to be helpful about the recovery of the trunks, and to whom we showed this "receipt," were doubtful whether these people had really been acting under official orders. There remained on this farm another box containing the personal diary of my father from 1940 to 1943 as well as notes on the French campaign of 1940; there were two further boxes with maps. The owner of the farm, a friend of my father, had denied, despite threats from the two C.I.C. people, that he had any further material. Subsequently, he did his best to see that at least these boxes remained in our possession. Even then, the box with my father's diaries and notes on France in 1940 was, in an unguarded moment, stolen from the loft by an unknown person. Whether he was pleased with what he found when he opened the box, is doubtful.

On the other farm, meanwhile, a Moroccan force had taken over. Cattle and poultry were slaughtered and open fires were burning in the farmyard. The whole place was thoroughly searched several times by Moroccans. Fortunately, none of them ever suspected that a further cellar existed behind a whole heap of empty boxes. It was in this way that the documents here were saved.

The papers which my aunt had kept for us and those that had been buried in the Stuttgart ruins also survived the German collapse.

When my mother had to leave her home, she found emergency accommodation in a small room in the neighbourhood. It was here that she made an inventory of the material that remained to her. The box which had been buried in the garden at Herrlingen was once again unearthed and removed to another place. The boxes on the farm, which had in the meantime been evacuated by its Moroccan occupiers, were fetched. Thus, when my mother eventually found new shelter in the Herrlingen school, she took all the material along with her.

When my mother learned that posthumous denazification proceedings were going to be taken against my father with the object of confiscating what effects he had left, she once again loaded up the small hand-cart and hid the documents away from where she was living. Fortunately, these new threats never materialised, though we heard of a case in which similar documents belonging to another officer were confiscated.

Encouraged by Brigadier Young, and by Captain Liddell Hart's undertaking to edit my father's papers, I eventually started to reassemble the documents from their various hiding places. In fact, it was possible to translate hurriedly a few passages and incorporate them as an Appendix to the biography of my father which Brigadier Young had written and which was by then already at press.

General Speidel, my father's former Chief of Staff, made repeated efforts to have my father's letters restored to my mother. Brigadier Young asked General Eisenhower to intercede with Washington for their recovery. Finally, through the efforts of Captain Liddell Hart, and after much protracted search, the letters were handed over to General Speidel by Colonel Nawrocky on behalf of the American Historical Division. It transpired that in Washington they had been filed, not under " ROMMEL ", but under " ERWIN ", my father's Christian name and the signature on the letters. Some are still missing, notably those written at the time of the Invasion. However, some other documents dealing with Normandy were subsequently returned to my mother.

With the return of the letters we felt we had recovered as many of my father's papers as had survived the destruction of war, in part carried out by my father for his own personal safety, and the looting which inevitably follows in the wake of war.

EDITORIAL NOTE

THE MAIN part of Rommel's papers deal with the North African campaign. The whole of his narrative is printed in this volume. The only part of the story he did not cover, as he would have done if he had lived, is the winter campaign of 1941-42. So a chapter on this has been provided by General Bayerlein—then Chief of Staff of the Afrika Korps—with the aid of Rommel's notes and letters as well as his own knowledge, from very close contact, of Rommel's views. Bayerlein's own exceptional experience and ability as a "Panzer leader" make this addition all the more interesting.

Rommel's story of the 1940 campaign is on the whole intensely exciting, but in some places it turns aside to deal with minor details of unit movement, while occasionally there is nothing of particular interest in the day's events. Such passages have been cut, as indicated in the text.

During the months he was in Italy, during 1943, Rommel did not conduct any active operations, but his diary contains a number of illuminating entries about the Italian *coup d'état* and the efforts to prevent Italy changing side. Manfred Rommel has woven these diary passages, and Rommel's letters at the time, into a short chapter.

Rommel did not live to write his story of the Normandy campaign, but he left a lot of notes and a number of other records, especially about his pre-invasion ideas and plans. General Bayerlein has pieced these together, and also incorporated in this chapter Rommel's letters of the period.

In a final chapter, Manfred Rommel relates the story of his father's death, and of the tense weeks that preceded the arrival of the executioners who came to carry out Hitler's decree.

The interest and value of these chapters and of Rommel's own narrative is much enhanced by his letters. For they convey the colour of his thought at the actual moment in the operations, and thus, besides their vividness, often provide an historical check on the recollected story in his subsequent narrative.

He wrote his wife almost every day, however hard pressed, although his letters were always rather short. They were usually written in the early hours of the morning, and sometimes when he was on the move in his armoured car or in a tank. The handwriting of the letters often has a shakiness caused by the movement of the vehicle—or the chill of the hours before sunrise.

While he had to be discreet in referring to operations in progress, it is remarkable how frank he often was in his comments, in view of the risk that his letters might be opened—either by the ordinary or the secret censorship.

Naturally, many of his letters were simply affectionate notes to his wife, but any that contained significant comments are incorporated in this volume.

Acknowledgments

IN THE first place, tribute is due to the excellent work of Manfred Rommel and General Bayerlein in the initial assembly and classification of the material. I was greatly impressed by their diligence and conscientiousness during all the months we worked jointly on the Papers. The first section recovered was Rommel's draft narrative of the African campaign, and this was published in Germany under the title of *Krieg Ohne Hass* (*War Without Hate*) with a number of footnotes by Manfred Rommel and by General Bayerlein. These footnotes have been kept in the present volume—where the full material is being published for the first time— while I have added numerous editorial notes to clarify points in the narrative and to provide an historical background, relating Rommel's actions and observations to those on the Allied side.

For the recovery of the letters and their restoration to Frau Rommel, grateful thanks are due to Major-General Orlando Ward, Chief of Military History, U.S.A., and to the initiative taken by Brigadier General S. L. A. Marshall, the eminent military analyst and historian, whose help I sought in the matter.

In the editing of *The Rommel Papers*, I would like to express my appreciation of the manifold help given by Mark Bonham Carter, Paul Findlay (the translator—but far more than that), and Ronald Politzer, as well as of Manfred Rommel and General Bayerlein. It was most refreshing and stimulating to have such discerning and able associates in the editorial task.

B. H. LIDDELL HART

Wolverton Park,
Buckinghamshire, August, 1952

Part One

FRANCE 1940

CHAPTER I

THE BREAK-THROUGH ON THE MEUSE

ON THE 10th May, 1940, Hitler launched his long-expected invasion of the West.[1] It achieved a lightning victory that changed the course of history, with far-reaching effects on the future of all peoples.

The decisive act in this world-shaking drama began on the 13th— when the Meuse was crossed by Guderian's panzer corps near Sedan and by Rommel's panzer division near Dinant. The narrow breaches were soon expanded into a vast gap. The German tanks, pouring through it, reached the Channel coast within a week, thus cutting off the Allied armies in Belgium. That disaster led on to the fall of France and the isolation of Britain. Although Britain managed to hold out behind her sea-ditch, rescue came only after a prolonged war had become a world-wide war. The price of that mid-May breakdown in 1940 has been tremendous, and remains immeasurable.

After the catastrophe, the breakdown was commonly viewed as inevitable, and Hitler's attack as irresistible. But appearances were very different from reality—as has become clear from post-war revelations.

Instead of having an overwhelming superiority in numbers, as was imagined, the German armies were not able to muster as many as their opponents did. The offensive was launched with 136 divisions, and was faced by the equivalent of 156—French, British, Belgian and Dutch. It was only in aircraft that the Germans had a big superiority, in numbers and quality. Their tanks were fewer than those on the other side— barely 2,800 against more than 4,000. They were also, on the average, inferior in armour and armament, although slightly superior in speed. The Germans' main advantage, besides that in airpower, lay in the speed with which their tanks were handled and the superior technique they had developed. Their panzer leaders had adopted, and put into practice with decisive effect, the new theories that had been conceived in Britain but not comprehended by the heads of the British and French armies.

[1]This introductory note is supplied by the Editor, Captain B. H. Liddell Hart. Elsewhere all his editorial comments apart from footnotes are set in italics.

Of the 136 German divisions, only 10 were armoured—but that small fraction, used as spearheads, virtually decided the issue of the campaign before the mass of the German Army came into action.

The brilliant result of these panzer thrusts obscured their small scale, and also the narrowness of the margin by which they succeeded. That success could easily have been prevented but for the paralysis, and all too frequent moral collapse, of the opposing commanders and troops in face of a tempo and technique of attack for which their training had not prepared them. Even as it was, the success of the invasion turned on a series of long-odds chances—and on the readiness of dynamic leaders like Guderian and Rommel to make the most of such chances.

The original plan for the offensive in the West had been on the lines of the pre-1914 Schlieffen plan, with the main weight on the right wing, where Bock's Army Group " B " was to advance through the plain of Belgium. But early in 1940 the plan was changed—following the proposal of Manstein for a more daring, and thus more unexpected, thrust through the hilly and wooded Ardennes country of Belgian Luxembourg. The centre of gravity was now shifted to Rundstedt's Army Group " A," which faced that sector. It was given seven of the ten German panzer divisions and the largest part of the infantry divisions.

The main drive for the Meuse was led by Kleist's Panzer Group, which was in the van of List's 12th Army. It had two spearheads, the stronger one being formed by Guderian's corps (of three panzer divisions), which made the decisive thrust near Sedan, while Reinhardt's corps (of two panzer divisions) on its right aimed for the crossing at Monthermh' Farther to the right, operating under Kluge's Fourth Army, Hot'ss. panzer corps drove through the northern Ardennes as cover for Kleiste flank and with the aim of getting across the Meuse between Givet and Namur. This secondary thrust had two spearheads of smaller scale, formed respectively by the 5th and 7th Panzer Divisions.

The 7th was commanded by Rommel. This was one of the four " light " divisions that had been converted into panzer divisions during the winter. It had only one tank regiment instead of the normal two, although this regiment was given three battalions instead of two— making a total of 218 tanks. More than half of these were Czech-built.[2]

[1]The 7th Panzer Division comprised:
> *Armour*
> > 25th Panzer Regiment (of 3 tank battalions)
> > 37th Panzer Reconnaissance Battalion
> *Motorised Infantry*
> > 6th Rifle Regiment
> > 7th Rifle Regiment
> > 7th Motor-cycle Battalion
> *Engineers*
> > 58th Pioneer Battalion
> *Artillery*
> > 78th Field Artillery Regiment (of 3 battalions, each of 3 four-gun batteries)
> > 42nd Anti-Tank Artillery Battalion

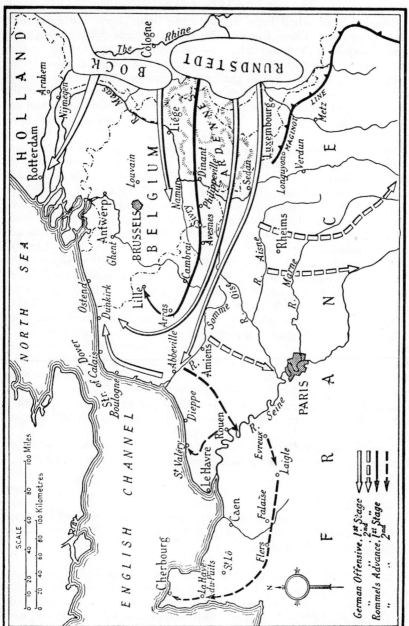

1. THE ADVANCE FROM THE RHINE TO CHERBOURG

The conversion had been made in the light of the lessons of the Polish campaign. There Rommel, himself an ardent infantryman, had come to recognise the potentialities of the tank arm. It was only on the 15th February that he had taken over command of the 7th at Godesberg, on the Rhine, but he learned the new technique, and adapted himself to it, with extraordinary quickness. He had always been a thruster in the infantry field, handling infantry as if they were mobile troops, and he revelled in the much greater scope for mobility offered by his new command.

On the opening day of the offensive, little resistance was met. The mass of the Belgian Army was concentrated to defend the plain of Belgium, where the chief cities lie, and the defence of the hilly and wooded region of Belgian Luxembourg, beyond the Meuse, was left to the special *Chasseurs Ardennais*, whose role was simply to impose as much delay as possible until the French came up to cover this wide flank approach to their own frontier. Such was the calculation on which the Belgian plan was based.

The French plan, however, was based on a more offensive concept. The First and Seventh Armies, which comprised the bulk of the French mechanised divisions, drove far forward into the plain of Belgium, together with the British Expeditionary Force. Meanwhile, the Ninth Army, forming the hinge of this manœuvre, made a shorter wheeling advance over the Belgian frontier to align itself along the Meuse from Meziéres to Namur. It consisted of seven infantry divisions (only one of which was motorised) and two cavalry divisions—these last being horse-mounted troops with mechanised elements. The cavalry were sent forward across the Meuse on the night of the 10th May, and next day pushed deep into the Ardennes, where they met the rapidly advancing panzer divisions, which had already overcome most of the Belgian defences there.

On the eve of the attack, during the last tense hours of preparation, Rommel wrote this brief letter to his wife, and then takes up the narrative:

9 May 1940

Dearest Lu,
    We're packing up at last. Let's hope not in vain. You'll get all the news for the next few days from the papers. Don't worry yourself. Everything will go all right.

In the sector assigned to my division the enemy had been preparing obstructions of every kind for months past. All roads and forest tracks had been permanently barricaded and deep craters blown in the main roads. But most of the road blocks were undefended by the Belgians, and it was thus in only a few places that my division was held up for any length of time. Many of the blocks could be by-passed by moving across country or over side roads. Elsewhere, all troops quickly set to work to deal with the obstructions and soon had the road clear.

At our first clash with French mechanised forces, prompt opening fire on our part led to a hasty French retreat. I have found again and again that in encounter actions, the day goes to the side that is the first to plaster its opponent with fire. The man who lies low and awaits developments usually comes off second best. Motor-cyclists at the head of the column must keep their machine-guns at the ready and open fire the instant an enemy shot is heard. This applies even when the exact position of the enemy is unknown, in which case the fire must simply be sprayed over enemy-held territory. Observation of this rule, in my experience, substantially reduces one's own casualties. It is fundamentally wrong simply to halt and look for cover without opening fire, or to wait for more forces to come up and take part in the action.

Experience in this early fighting showed that in tank attacks especially, the action of opening fire immediately into the area which the enemy is believed to be holding, instead of waiting until several of one's own tanks have been hit, usually decides the issue. Even indiscriminate machine-gun fire and 20 mm. anti-tank fire into a wood in which enemy anti-tank guns have installed themselves is so effective that in most cases the enemy is completely unable to get into action or else gives up his position. In engagements against enemy tanks also—which more often than not have been more heavily armoured than ours—opening fire early has proved to be the right action and very effective.

11 May 1940

DEAREST LU,

I've come up for breath for the first time to-day and have a moment to write. Everything wonderful so far. Am way ahead of my neighbours. I'm completely hoarse from orders and shouting. Had a bare three hours' sleep and an occasional meal. Otherwise I'm absolutely fine. Make do with this, please, I'm too tired for more.

Following up the retreat of the French 1st and 4th Cavalry Divisions, Rommel's advanced troops reached the Meuse in the afternoon of the 12th May. It was his aim to rush a crossing if possible on the heels of the French, and gain a bridgehead on the west bank. But the bridges at Dinant and Houx were blown up by the French—just as the leading tanks began to cross—and Rommel was thus compelled to mount a river-crossing assault with troops ferried over in rubber boats. This assault was launched early next morning, and suffered heavy casualties before it succeeded. Rommel writes:

On the 13th May, I drove off to Dinant at about 04.00 hours with Captain Schraepler. The whole of the divisional artillery was already in position as ordered, with its forward observers stationed at the crossing

points. In Dinant I found only a few men of the 7th Rifle Regiment.
Shells were dropping in the town from French artillery west of the
Meuse, and there were a number of knocked-out tanks in the streets
leading down to the river. The noise of battle could be heard from the
Meuse valley.

There was no hope of getting my command and signals vehicle down
the steep slope to the Meuse unobserved, so Schraepler and I clambered
down on foot through the wood to the valley bottom. The 6th Rifle
Regiment was about to cross to the other bank in rubber boats, but was
being badly held up by heavy artillery fire and by the extremely troublesome small arms fire of French troops installed among the rocks on the
west bank.

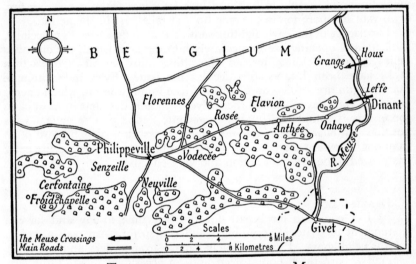

2.   THE BREAK-THROUGH ON THE MEUSE

The situation when I arrived was none too pleasant. Our boats were
being destroyed one after the other by the French flanking fire, and the
crossing eventually came to a standstill. The enemy infantry were so
well concealed that they were impossible to locate even after a long
search through glasses. Again and again they directed their fire into
the area in which I and my companions—the commanders of the Rifle
Brigade and the Engineer Battalion—were lying. A smoke screen in
the Meuse valley would have prevented these infantry doing much
harm. But we had no smoke unit. So I now gave orders for a number of
houses in the valley to be set alight in order to supply the smoke we
lacked.

Minute by minute the enemy fire grew more unpleasant. From up
river a damaged rubber boat came drifting down to us with a badly

wounded man clinging to it, shouting and screaming for help—the poor fellow was near to drowning. But there was no help for him here, the enemy fire was too heavy.

Meanwhile the village of Grange [1¼ *miles west of Houx (and the Meuse)*, *and 3 miles north-west of Dinant*] on the west bank had been taken by the 7th Motor-cycle Battalion, but they had not cleaned up the river bank as thoroughly as they should have done. I therefore gave orders for the rocks on the west bank to be cleared of the enemy.

With Captain Schraepler, I now drove south down the Meuse valley road in a Panzer IV to see how things were going with the 7th Rifle Regiment. On the way we came under fire several times from the western bank and Schraepler was wounded in the arm from a number of shell splinters. Single French infantrymen surrendered as we approached.

By the time we arrived the 7th Rifle Regiment had already succeeded in getting a company across to the west bank, but the enemy fire had then become so heavy that their crossing equipment had been shot to pieces and the crossing had had to be halted. Large numbers of wounded were receiving treatment in a house close beside the demolished bridge. As at the northern crossing point, there was nothing to be seen of the enemy who were preventing the crossing. As there was clearly no hope of getting any more men across at this point without powerful artillery and tank support to deal with the enemy nests, I drove back to Division Headquarters, where I met the Army commander, Colonel-General von Kluge and the Corps commander, General Hoth.

After talking over the situation with Major Heidkaemper and making the necessary arrangements, I drove back along the Meuse to Leffé [*a village on the outskirts of Dinant*] to get the crossing moving there. I had already given orders for several Panzer IIIs and IVs and a troop of artillery to be at my disposal at the crossing point. We left the signals vehicle for the time being at a point some 500 yards east of the river and went forward on foot through deserted farms towards the Meuse. In Leffé we found a number of rubber boats, all more or less badly damaged by enemy fire, lying in the street where our men had left them. Eventually, after being bombed on the way by our own aircraft, we arrived at the river.

At Leffé weir we took a quick look at the footbridge, which had been barred by the enemy with a spiked steel plate. The firing in the Meuse valley had ceased for the moment and we moved off to the right through some houses to the crossing point proper. The crossing had now come to a complete standstill, with the officers badly shaken by the casualties which their men had suffered. On the opposite bank we could see several men of the company which was already across, among them many wounded. Numerous damaged boats and rubber dinghies lay on the opposite bank. The officers reported that nobody dared show himself outside cover, as the enemy opened fire immediately on anyone they spotted.

Several of our tanks and heavy weapons were in position on the embankment east of the houses, but had seemingly already fired off almost all their ammunition. However, the tanks I had ordered to the crossing point soon arrived, to be followed shortly afterwards by two field howitzers from the Battalion Grasemann.[1]

All points on the western bank likely to hold enemy riflemen were now brought under fire, and soon the aimed fire of all weapons was pouring into rocks and buildings. Lieutenant Hanke[2] knocked out a pill-box on the bridge ramp with several rounds. The tanks, with turrets traversed left, drove slowly north at 50 yards' spacing along the Meuse valley, closely watching the opposite slopes.

Under cover of this fire the crossing slowly got going again, and a cable ferry using several large pontoons was started. Rubber boats paddled backwards and forwards and brought back the wounded from the west bank. One man who fell out of his boat on the way grabbed hold of the ferry rope and was dragged underwater through the Meuse. He was rescued by Private Heidenreich, who dived in and brought him to the bank.

I now took over personal command of the 2nd Battalion of 7th Rifle Regiment and for some time directed operations myself.

With Lieutenant Most I crossed the Meuse in one of the first boats and at once joined the company which had been across since early morning. From the company command post we could see Companies Enkefort and Lichter were making rapid progress.

I then moved up north along a deep gully to the Company Enkefort. As we arrived an alarm came in: " Enemy tanks in front." The company had no anti-tank weapons, and I therefore gave orders for small arms fire to be opened on the tanks as quickly as possible, whereupon we saw them pull back into a hollow about a thousand yards north-west of Leffé. Large numbers of French stragglers came through the bushes and slowly laid down their arms.

---

[1]In the Germany Army, units and formations were often called by the name of their commanders.

[2]*Note by Manfred Rommel.* Hanke was a prominent member of the Nazi Party and an official of Goebbels's Propaganda Ministry. He appears to have been very unpopular with the other officers on account of his high-handed behaviour, and Rommel finally removed him from the Staff after an incident in the Mess when he suggested that he had the power to have Rommel himself removed from his command. Rommel made a long report later to Hitler's Adjutant.

Later in the war, Hanke became Gauleiter of Silesia and achieved notoriety for his defence of Breslau to the last stick and stone However, when the devastated city finally capitulated, Hanke did not stay to meet the invading Red Army, but escaped in an aeroplane, leaving the population to the tender mercies of the Russian troops. He has never been heard of since.

Other accounts show that Rommel's intervention was even more crucial, and decisive, than he conveys. The German troops were badly shaken by the intensity of the defenders' fire when he arrived on the scene and organised the fresh effort, in which he himself took the lead. Fortunately for his chances, the French 18th Infantry Division, which was charged with the defence of the Dinant sector, was only in process of taking over the position after a lengthy march on foot, and was short of anti-tank guns, while the 1st Cavalry Division had not recovered from the tank-mauling it had received in the Ardennes. Thus the boldly led attackers were able to prise open the defence once they had gained sufficient space on the west bank to develop a manœuvring leverage.

I now went down with Most to the Meuse again and had myself taken back to the other bank, where I drove north with a tank and a signals vehicle to the 6th Rifle Regiment's crossing point. Here the crossing had meanwhile been resumed in rubber boats and was in full swing. I was told by Colonel Mickl, the commander of the anti-tank battalion, that he already had twenty anti-tank guns on the western bank. A company of the engineer battalion was busily engaged in building 8-ton pontoons, but I stopped them and told them to build the 16-ton type. I aimed to get part of the Panzer Regiment across as quickly as possible. As soon as the first pontoon was ready I took my 8-wheeled signals vehicle across. Meanwhile, the enemy had launched a heavy attack, and the fire of their tanks could be heard approaching the ridge of the Meuse bank. Heavy enemy shells were dropping all round the crossing point.

On arrival at Brigade Headquarters on the west bank I found the situation looking decidedly unhealthy. The commander of the 7th Motor-cycle Battalion had been wounded, his adjutant killed, and a powerful French counter-attack had severely mauled our men in Grange. There was a danger that enemy tanks might penetrate into the Meuse valley itself.

Leaving my signals lorry on the west bank, I crossed the river again and gave orders for first the Panzer Company, and then the Panzer Regiment to be ferried across during the night. However, ferrying tanks across the 120-yards-wide river by night was a slow job, and by morning there were still only 15 tanks on the west bank, an alarmingly small number.

At daybreak [*14th May*] we heard that Colonel von Bismarck had pressed through his attack to close on Onhaye [*3 miles west of Dinant*], where he was now engaged with a powerful enemy. Shortly afterwards a wireless message came in saying that his regiment was encircled, and I therefore decided to go to his assistance immediately with every available tank.

At about 09.00 hours the 25th Panzer Regiment, under the command of Colonel Rothenburg, moved off along the Meuse valley with the 30 tanks which had so far arrived on the west bank, and penetrated as far as a hollow 500 yards north-east of Onhaye without meeting any resistance. It transpired that von Bismarck had actually radioed "arrived" instead of " encircled "[1] and that he was now on the point of sending an assault company round the northern side of Onhaye to secure its western exit. This move, as had been shown by an exercise we had carried out earlier in Godesberg, was of the greatest importance for the next stages of the operation. Accordingly, five tanks were placed under von Bismarck's command for this purpose—not to make a tank attack in the usual sense, but to provide mobile covering fire for the infantry attack on the defile west of Onhaye. It was my intention to place the Panzer Regiment itself in a wood 1,000 yards north of Onhaye and then to bring all other units up to that point, from where they could be employed to the north, north-west or west, according to how the situation developed.

I gave orders to Rothenburg to move round both sides of the wood into this assembly area, and placed myself in a Panzer III which was to follow close behind him.

Rothenburg now drove off through a hollow to the left with the five tanks which were to accompany the infantry, thus giving these tanks a lead of 100 to 150 yards. There was no sound of enemy fire. Some 20 to 30 tanks followed up behind. When the commander of the five tanks reached the rifle company on the southern edge of Onhaye wood, Colonel Rothenburg moved off with his leading tanks along the edge of the wood going west. We had just reached the south-west corner of the wood and were about to cross a low plantation, from which we could see the five tanks escorting the infantry below us to our left front, when suddenly we came under heavy artillery and anti-tank gunfire from the west. Shells landed all round us and my tank received two hits one after the other, the first on the upper edge of the turret and the second in the periscope.

The driver promptly opened the throttle wide and drove straight into the nearest bushes. He had only gone a few yards, however, when the tank slid down a steep slope on the western edge of the wood and finally stopped, canted over on its side, in such a position that the enemy, whose guns were in position about 500 yards away on the edge of the next wood, could not fail to see it. I had been wounded in the right cheek by a small splinter from the shell which had landed in the periscope. It was not serious though it bled a great deal.

I tried to swing the turret round so as to bring our 37 mm. gun to bear on the enemy in the opposite wood, but with the heavy slant of the tank it was immovable.

The French battery now opened rapid fire on our wood and at any moment we could expect their fire to be aimed at our tank, which was in full view. I therefore decided to abandon it as fast as I could, taking the crew with me. At that moment the subaltern in command of the

---

[1]Translator's note: *eingetroffen* instead of *eingeschlossen*.

tanks escorting the infantry reported himself seriously wounded, with
the words: " Herr General, my left arm has been shot off." We clambered
up through the sandy pit, shells crashing and splintering all round.
Close in front of us trundled Rothenburg's tank with flames pouring out
of the rear. The adjutant of the Panzer Regiment had also left his tank.
I thought at first that the command tank had been set alight by a hit
in the petrol tank and was extremely worried for Colonel Rothenburg's
safety. However, it turned out to be only the smoke candles that had
caught light, the smoke from which now served us very well. In the
meantime Lieutenant Most had driven my armoured signals vehicle
into the wood, where it had been hit in the engine and now stood immobilised. The crew was unhurt.

I now gave orders for the tanks to drive through the wood in a
general easterly direction, a move which the armoured cars, which stood
at my disposal, were of course unable to follow. Slowly Rothenburg's
command tank forced its way through the trees, many of them tall and
well grown. It was only the involuntary smoke-screen laid by this tank
that prevented the enemy from shooting up any more of our vehicles.
If only the tanks had sprayed the wood which the enemy was believed
to be holding, with machine-gun and 37 mm. gunfire during their
advance, the French would probably have immediately abandoned their
guns, which were standing in exposed positions at the edge of the wood,
and our losses would almost certainly have been smaller. An attack
launched in the evening by the 25th Panzer Regiment was successful,
and we were able to occupy our assembly area.

A tight combat control west of the Meuse, and flexibility to meet the
changing situation, were only made possible by the fact that the divisional
commander with his signals troop kept on the move and was able to
give his orders direct to the regiment commanders in the forward line.
Wireless alone—due to the necessity for encoding—would have taken
far too long, first to get the situation reports back to Division and then
for Division to issue its orders. Continuous wireless contact was maintained
with the division's operations staff, which remained in the rear, and a
detailed exchange of views took place early each morning and each
afternoon between the divisional commander and his Ia.[1] This method
of command proved extremely effective.

*By his advance that day Rommel had created a breach which had momentous
consequences, particularly by its effect on the mind of General Corap, the commander
of the French Ninth Army.*

*Three crossings of the Meuse had been achieved on the 13th, Rommel's being
the first. In the afternoon, the leading troops of Reinhardt's panzer corps had got
across at Monthermé, and Guderian's at Sedan. But Reinhardt's gained only a
narrow foothold, and had a desperate fight to maintain it. Not until early on the
15th were they able to build a bridge over which his tanks could cross, and the exit*

[1] " Ia " is the operations side of the staff, and is also used for the officer in charge of it.

from Monthermé ran through a precipitous defile that was easy to block. Guderian's troops were more successful, but only one of his three divisions gained an adequate foothold, and at daybreak on the 14th only one bridge had been completed. The bridge was lucky to escape destruction, as it was repeatedly attacked by the Allied air forces. Guderian's troops had little support from the Luftwaffe on this second crucial day, but his anti-aircraft gunners put up such a deadly canopy of fire that they brought down an estimated 150 French and British aircraft, and effectively upset the bomb-aiming. By the afternoon, all three of Guderian's panzer divisions were over the river. Holding off heavy counter-attacks from the south he wheeled west towards the joint between the French Second and Ninth Armies, which began to give way under his fierce and skilfully manœuvred pressure.

That night the commander of the French Ninth Army made a fatal decision, under the double impact of Guderian's expanding threat to his right flank and Rommel's penetration in the centre of his front—wild reports conveyed that thousands of tanks were pouring through the breach there. Orders were issued for the abandonment of the Meuse, and a general withdrawal of the Ninth Army to a more westerly line.

On Rommel's front this intended stop-line ran along the railway east of Philippeville, and 15 miles behind the Meuse. It was penetrated by Rommel next morning, the 15th, before it could be occupied, and under his deep-thrusting threat the confusion of the withdrawal quickly developed into a spreading collapse. His renewed thrust also forestalled an intended counter-attack towards Dinant by the French 1st Armoured Division and 4th North African Division, which were just arriving on the scene. The former appeared on Rommel's right flank but ran out of fuel at this crucial moment, and only a small fraction of its tanks went into action. Rommel's advance swept past its front while it was at a standstill, and many of its tanks were subsequently captured before they could get away. Meantime, the North African Division was bowled over by the onrush of the panzers and the stream of fugitives.

Worse still, Corap's general withdrawal order had uncorked the bottleneck at Monthermé, where the right wing of the Ninth Army had hitherto blocked Reinhardt's panzer corps. Once a withdrawal began here, it quickly became a hopelessly confused retreat, and Reinhardt's leading troops were able to slip round the right flank of the Ninth Army—behind the back of the forces opposing Guderian—and then drove on westward many miles along an open path. By that evening, also, Guderian had overcome the last line of resistance that faced him, and broke through into open country. The breach in the French front was now 60 miles wide.

The significance of Rommel's story of the 15th May becomes all the clearer when set against the wider background of that decisive day.

My intention for the 15th May was to thrust straight through in one stride to our objective, with the 25th Panzer Regiment in the lead and with artillery and, if possible, dive-bomber support. The infantry was to follow up the tank attack, partly on foot and partly lorry-borne. The essential thing, to my mind, was that the artillery should curtain off both flanks of the attack, as our neighbouring divisions were still some way behind us. The 25th Panzer Regiment's route, which was marked out on the map, led round the outskirts of Philippeville [*18 miles west of Dinant*], avoiding all villages, and on to our objective, the district round Cerfontaine [*8 miles west of Philippeville*]. It was my intention to ride with 25th Panzer Regiment so that I could direct the attack from up forward and bring in the artillery and dive-bombers at the decisive moment. To simplify wireless traffic—over which highly important messages often arrived late, due to the necessity for encoding—I agreed a " line of thrust " with the Ia and artillery commander. Starting point for this line was taken as Rosée church and finishing point Froidchapelle church. All officers marked the line on their maps. If I now wanted artillery fire on, for instance, Philippeville, I simply radioed: " Heavy artillery fire immediate round eleven." The artillery commander was delighted with the new system.

At about 09.00 hours I met a Luftwaffe major who informed me that dive-bombers could be made available for my division that day. As the tanks were already starting to move I called for them immediately, to go into action in front of the attack. I then moved over to Rothenburg's tank and instructed my *Gefechtsstaffel*[1] to follow up the tank attack from cover to cover with their armoured car and signals vehicle.

After a brief engagement with enemy tanks near Flavion, the Panzer Regiment advanced in column through the woods to Philippeville, passing on the way numerous guns and vehicles belonging to a French unit, whose men had tumbled headlong into the woods at the approach of our tanks, having probably already suffered heavily under our dive-bombers. Enormous craters compelled us to make several détours through the wood. About 3 miles north-west of Philippeville there was a brief exchange of fire with French troops occupying the hills and woods south of Philippeville. Our tanks fought the action on the move, with turrets traversed left, and the enemy was soon silenced. From time to time enemy anti-tank guns, tanks and armoured cars were shot up. Fire was also scattered into the woods on our flanks as we drove past. Staff and artillery was kept closely informed of the progress of the attack by brief radio messages sent in clear, with the result that the artillery curtain functioned perfectly. The day's objective was soon reached.

With one of Rothenburg's panzer companies placed under my command, I then drove back over the tracks of the advance to establish contact with the infantry in the rear. On the high ground 1,000 yards west of Philippeville we found two of our tanks which had fallen out with mechanical trouble. Their crews were in process of collecting prisoners, and a few who had already come in were standing around. Now hundreds of French motor-cyclists came out of the bushes and, together with their

[1]The *Gefechtsstaffel*, to which Rommel refers throughout his campaigns, was a small headquarters group consisting of signals troops and a small combat team, together with the appropriate vehicles (including a wireless lorry), which always accompanied him in action.

officers, slowly laid down their arms. Others tried to make a quick getaway down the road to the south.

I now occupied myself for a short time with the prisoners. Among them were several officers, from whom I received a number of requests, including, among other things, permission to keep their batmen and to have their kit picked up from Philippeville, where it had been left. It was greatly to my interest that the Philippeville garrison should surrender quickly and without fighting, so I granted the requests.

My escorting panzer company now drove for Neuville [*2 miles south of Philippeville*], with the object of cutting off the French retreat from Philippeville to the south. On arriving at the company with Most, I found it involved in fighting near Neuville, with the action moving south and threatening to turn into a pursuit. I had no intention of pushing any farther south, and so gave orders for the battle to be broken off and for the company to continue eastward from Neuville. About 500 yards south of Vocedée we ran into part of Panzer Company Hüttemann, which joined up with us. On the southern edge of Vocedée we had a brief engagement with a considerable force of French tanks, which was soon decided in our favour. The French ceased fire and were fetched out of their tanks one by one by our men. Some fifteen French tanks fell into our hands, some of them damaged, others completely intact. It being impossible to leave a guard, we took the undamaged tanks along with us in our column, still with their French drivers. About a quarter of an hour later we reached the main Dinant-Philippeville road, where I met the leading troops of the Rifle Brigade, with 8th M.G. Battalion under command, who were following up the tank attack. I took several officers into my armoured car and with the whole column behind me, drove at high speed along the dusty road through the northern outskirts of Philippeville. [*Rommel had turned about, and was heading westward again.*]

En route I described the situation to the commanding officers and instructed them in their new tasks. At the rate we were driving (average about 40 m.p.h.) the dust-cloud behind us was enormous. Near Senzeille [*4 miles west of Philippeville*], we met a body of fully armed French motor-cyclists coming in the opposite direction, and picked them up as they passed. Most of them were so shaken at suddenly finding themselves in a German column that they drove their machines into the ditch and were in no position to put up a fight. Without delaying, we drove on at high speed to the hills west of Cerfontaine, where Rothenburg was standing with the leading units of the Panzer Regiment. On its arrival, the column was deployed as quickly as possible and without halting into the surrounding district. Looking back east from the summit of the hill, as night fell, endless pillars of dust could be seen rising as far as the eye could reach—comforting signs that the 7th Panzer Division's move into the conquered territory had begun.

The fact that the enemy had been able to infiltrate between the

Panzer Regiment and the Rifle Brigade during the afternoon had been solely due to the latter's delay in getting moving. The officers of a panzer division must learn to think and act independently within the framework of the general plan and not wait until they receive orders. All units had known the start time of the attack, and they should have formed up at that time.

Next day, the 16th May 1940, I received orders from Corps to stay at Divisional H.Q. The reason was unknown to me. It was about 09.30 hours before I at last received Corps' permission to move forward to the new H.Q. Shortly after my arrival the division received orders to thrust via Sivry through the Maginot Line and on that night to the hills around Avesnes.

This was not the Maginot Line proper, which ended near Longuyon, but its later westward extension—where the type of fortification was much less strong. But German accounts often draw no distinction between the original line and its extension.

Guderian's and Reinhardt's corps had encountered, and broken through, the Maginot Line extension shortly after crossing the Meuse, and were now racing westward behind it. But Hoth's corps, having crossed the Meuse farther north, in Belgian territory, had still to penetrate it in their south-westerly drive. Sivry is 12 miles west of Cerfontaine, and Avesnes 12 miles west of Sivry.

I had just discussed the plan for our attack on the Maginot Line with my Ia, when the Army Commander, Colonel-General von Kluge, walked in. He was surprised that the division had not already moved off. I described to him our plan. The intention was first to gain the frontier near Sivry, while, at the same time the Reconnaissance Battalion reconnoitred the Maginot Line over a wide front and the mass of the artillery moved into position round Sivry. Then the Panzer Regiment, under powerful artillery cover, was to move in extended order up to the French line of fortifications. Finally, the Rifle Brigade, covered by the tanks, was to take the French fortifications and remove barricades. Not until all this was accomplished was the break-through to Avesnes to be made, with the armour in the lead and the mass of the division following closely behind. General von Kluge gave complete approval to our plan.

Soon the leading battalion was moving rapidly forward towards Sivry, which was reached without fighting. Artillery and anti-aircraft went into position and received instructions to open fire immediately into certain areas on the other side of the frontier to see whether the enemy would reply. Meanwhile, the 25th Panzer Regiment arrived at Sivry and received orders to cross the frontier and take Clairfayts [*3 miles beyond*]. No enemy battery had replied to our artillery fire on their fortified zone.

I rode, as on the previous day, in the regimental commander's command tank. Soon we were across the French frontier and then the tanks rolled slowly on in column towards Clairfayts, which was now only a mile or so away. When a report came in from a reconnaissance troop

that the road through Clairfayts had been mined, we bore off to the
south and moved in open order across fields and hedges in a semi-circle
round the village. There was not a sound from the enemy, although
our artillery was dropping shells at intervals deep into their territory.
Soon we found ourselves among orchards and tall hedges, which slowed
up the advance. Rothenburg's tank was among the leading vehicles,
with Hanke, my aide-de-camp, following behind in a Panzer IV. His
orders were to open fire quickly on a sign from me and thus act as a
lead-gun for the rest. It had been very evident in the previous days'
fighting that frequently far too much time elapsed before the tank crews
opened fire on fleeting targets.

Suddenly we saw the angular outlines of a French fortification about
100 yards ahead. Close beside it were a number of fully-armed French
troops, who, at the first sight of the tanks, at once made as if to surrender.
We were just beginning to think we would be able to take it without
fighting, when one of our tanks opened fire on the enemy elsewhere, with
the result that the enemy garrison promptly vanished into their concrete
pill-box. In a few moments the leading tanks came under heavy anti-
tank gunfire from the left and French machine-gun fire opened over the
whole area. We had some casualties and two of our tanks were knocked
out. When the enemy fire had quietened down again, reconnaissance
established the existence of a very deep anti-tank ditch close beside the
enemy fortification, which had not so far opened fire. There were more
defence works in the enemy rear and the road from Clairfayts towards
Avesnes was blocked by high steel hedgehogs (anti-tank obstacles).

Meanwhile, elements of 25th Panzer Regiment had joined battle
with the enemy west and 2,000 yards south of Clairfayts; the artillery
had also opened a heavy fire at my orders and was laying smoke over
various sections of the Maginot Line. French artillery now began to
bombard Clairfayts and Sivry. Soon the motor-cyclists arrived with the
engineer platoon of the 37th Armoured Reconnaissance Battalion. Under
covering fire from tanks and artillery, infantry and engineers pushed
forward into the fortified zone. The engineer platoon began to prepare
the demolition of the steel hedgehog blocking the road to our advance.

Meanwhile, an assault troop of the Panzer Engineer Company overcame the concrete pill-box. The men crawled up to the embrasure and
threw a 6-pound demolition charge in through the firing slit. When,
after repeated summonses to surrender, the strong enemy garrison still did
not emerge, a further charge was thrown in. One officer and 35 men
were then taken prisoner, although they shortly afterwards overcame the
weak assault troop and escaped, after French machine-guns had opened
fire from another pill-box.

Slowly the sky darkened and it became night. Farms were burning
at several points in Clairfayts and farther west. I now gave orders for
an immediate penetration into the fortified zone, and a thrust as far as

possible towards Avesnes. Staff and artillery were quickly informed by wireless, and then it was time for us to climb into the command tank and get under way. Taking our place immediately behind the leading panzer company, we were soon rolling across the demolished road-block towards the enemy.

During the time that the sappers of the 37th Reconnaissance Battalion had been demolishing the steel hedgehogs, more violent fighting had broken out against anti-tank guns and a few field-guns located near a cluster of houses 1,000 yards west of Clairfayts. Round after round had been fired over open sights at our tanks and infantry standing near Clairfayts. Finally, the enemy guns had been silenced by a few rounds from a Panzer IV.

The way to the west was now open. The moon was up and for the time being we could expect no real darkness. I had already given orders, in the plan for the break-through, for the leading tanks to scatter the road and verges with machine and anti-tank gunfire at intervals during the drive to Avesnes, which I hoped would prevent the enemy from laying mines. The rest of the Panzer Regiment was to follow close behind the leading tanks and be ready at any time to fire salvoes to either flank. The mass of the division had instructions to follow up the Panzer Regiment lorry-borne.

The tanks now rolled in a long column through the line of fortifications and on towards the first houses, which had been set alight by our fire. In the moonlight we could see the men of 7th Motor-cycle Battalion moving forward on foot beside us. Occasionally an enemy machine-gun or anti-tank gun fired, but none of their shots came anywhere near us. Our artillery was dropping heavy harassing fire on villages and the road far ahead of the regiment. Gradually the speed increased. Before long we were 500—1,000—2,000—3,000 yards into the fortified zone. Engines roared, tank tracks clanked and clattered. Whether or not the enemy was firing was impossible to tell in the ear-splitting noise. We crossed the railway line a mile or so south-west of Solre le Château, and then swung north to the main road which was soon reached. Then off along the road and past the first houses.

The people in the houses were rudely awoken by the din of our tanks, the clatter and roar of tracks and engines. Troops lay bivouacked beside the road, military vehicles stood parked in farmyards and in some places on the road itself. Civilians and French troops, their faces distorted with terror, lay huddled in the ditches, alongside hedges and in every hollow beside the road. We passed refugee columns, the carts abandoned by their owners, who had fled in panic into the fields. On we went, at a steady speed, towards our objective. Every so often a quick glance at the map by a shaded light and a short wireless message to Divisional H.Q. to report the position and thus the success of 25th Panzer Regiment. Every so often a look out of the hatch to assure myself that there was still no resistance and that contact was being maintained to the rear. The flat countryside lay spread out around us under the cold light of the moon. We were through the Maginot Line! It was hardly conceivable. Twenty-two years before we had stood for four and a half long years before this self-same enemy and had won victory after victory and yet finally lost the war. And now we had broken through the renowned Maginot Line and were driving deep into enemy territory. It was not just a beautiful dream. It was reality.

Suddenly there was a flash from a mound about 300 yards away to the right of the road. There could be no doubt what it was, an enemy gun well concealed in a concrete pill-box, firing on 25th Panzer Regiment from the flank. More flashes came from other points. Shell bursts could not be seen. Quickly informing Rothenburg of the danger—he was standing close beside me—I gave orders through him for the regiment to increase speed and burst through this second fortified line with broadsides to right and left.

Fire was opened quickly, the tank crews having been instructed in the method of fire before the attack. Much of our ammunition was tracer and the regiment drove on through the new defence line spraying an immense rain of fire far into the country on either side. Soon we were through the danger area, without serious casualties. But it was not now easy to get the fire stopped and we drove through the villages of Sars Poteries and Beugnies with guns blazing. Enemy confusion was complete. Military vehicles, tanks, artillery and refugee carts packed high with belongings blocked part of the road and had to be pushed unceremoniously to the side. All around were French troops lying flat on the ground, and farms everywhere were jammed tight with guns, tanks and other military vehicles. Progress towards Avesnes now became slow. At last we succeeded in getting the firing stopped. We drove through Semousies. Always the same picture, troops and civilians in wild flight down both sides of the road. Soon the road forked, one going right to Maubeuge, which was now only about 10 miles away, and the other left down into the valley towards Avesnes. The road was now thick with carts and people, who moved off to the side of the tanks or had to be directed into the side by us. The nearer we came to Avesnes the greater was the crush of vehicles through which we had to fight our way. In Avesnes itself, which had been shelled by our artillery shortly before, the whole population was on the move, jammed between vehicles and guns on both sides of the road in front of our moving tank column. It was obvious that there were strong French forces in the town.

I did not have the column halted, but drove on with the leading battalion of tanks to the high ground west of Avesnes, where I intended to stop and collect up prisoners and captured equipment. On the way a scouting party of two tanks was detached in the southern outskirts of Avesnes and dispatched down the main road to the south. Some 500 yards outside the town on the road to Landrecies, we made a halt, marshalled our units and rounded up the French troops in the immediate neighbourhood. Here, too, farmyards and orchards beside the road were jammed full of troops and refugee carts. All traffic down the road from the west was halted and picked up. Soon a prisoner-of-war cage had to be constructed in the field.

Meanwhile, firing had started behind us in Avesnes—tank guns by the sound of it—and soon we saw flames rising, probably from burning tanks or lorries. We had lost contact with the tank battalion behind us and with the 7th Motor-cycle Battalion.

This did not yet cause me any concern, as, in the confusion of owner-less refugee carts, it was only too easy for a traffic jam to pile up. We had reached our objective and that was the main thing. However, the enemy in Avesnes—there must have been at least a battalion of tanks—made good use of the gap in the Panzer Regiment, and French heavy tanks soon closed the road through the town. The 2nd Battalion of the 25th Panzer Regiment at once tried to overcome the enemy blocking the road, but their attempt failed with the loss of several tanks. The fighting in Avesnes grew steadily heavier. Intermittent wireless contact was established between the 2nd Battalion and ourselves. The battle in Avesnes lasted until about 04.00 hours [*17th May*]. Finally, Hanke, who, on my orders, advanced from the west against the powerful enemy tanks with a Panzer IV, succeeded in disposing of the French tanks. Dawn was slowly breaking when the battle ended and contact was re-established with the 2nd Battalion.

Meanwhile, I had sent repeated signals to Corps through the divisional staff asking whether, in view of the success of our break-through of the Maginot Line, we should not now continue our advance over the Sambre. Receiving no reply—wireless contact had not been established—I decided to continue the attack at dawn with the object of seizing the Sambre crossing at Landrecies and holding it open. I issued orders by wireless to all other units to follow up the Panzer Regiment's advance to Landrecies [*11 miles west of Avesnes*].

At about 04.00 hours I moved off towards Landrecies with the leading battalion of Rothenburg's Panzer Regiment. The 7th Motor-cycle Battalion, which had now closed up, followed behind, and I was firmly convinced that behind them again the remaining units of the division would take part in the attack. The failure of the wireless had left me in ignorance of the exact position of the regiments and we had simply transmitted all orders into the blue.

As no supplies had come up during the night, we now had to be sparing with ammunition and drove westwards through the brightening day with guns silent. Soon we began to meet refugee columns and detachments of French troops preparing for the march. A chaos of guns, tanks and military vehicles of all kinds, inextricably entangled with horse-drawn refugee carts, covered the road and verges. By keeping our guns silent and occasionally driving our cross-country vehicles alongside the road, we managed to get past the column without great difficulty. The French troops were completely overcome by surprise at our sudden appearance, laid down their arms and marched off to the east beside our column. Nowhere was any resistance attempted. Any enemy tanks we met on the road were put out of action as we drove past. The advance went on without a halt to the west. Hundreds upon hundreds of French troops, with their officers, surrendered at our arrival. At some points they had to be fetched out of vehicles driving along beside us.

Particularly irate over this sudden disturbance was a French lieutenant-colonel whom we overtook with his car jammed in the press of vehicles. I asked him for his rank and appointment. His eyes glowed hate and impotent fury and he gave the impression of being a thoroughly fanatical type. There being every likelihood, with so much traffic on the road, that our column would get split up from time to time, I decided on second thoughts to take him along with us. He was already fifty yards away to the east when he was fetched back to Colonel Rothenburg, who signed to him to get in his tank. But he curtly refused to come with us, so, after summoning him three times to get in, there was nothing for it but to shoot him.

We drove through Maroilles [*8½ miles west of Avesnes*], where the street was so crowded that it was not easy for the people to obey our shouts of " A droit! " On we went, with the sun on our backs through the thin morning mist to the west. The road was now just as full of troops and refugees outside the villages. Our shouts of " A droit! " had little effect and progress became very slow, with the tanks driving through the fields alongside the road. At length we arrived at Landrecies, the town on the Sambre, where there was again a vast crush of vehicles and French troops in every lane and alley, but no resistance. We rolled across the Sambre bridge, on the other side of which we found a French barracks full of troops. As the tank column clattered past, Hanke drove into the courtyard and instructed the French officers to have their troops paraded and marched off to the east.

Still in the belief that the whole division was rapidly approaching Landrecies behind us, I continued the attack towards Le Câteau [*8 miles west of Landrecies*]. We drove through a long wood, which the enemy was using as an ammunition dump. Against the rising sun, the sentries were unable to identify us until we were on top of them. Then they surrendered. In Pommereuille, too, the French troops stationed in the village laid down their arms. I kept the advance going until the hill just east of Le Câteau, where we finally halted. It was 6.15 a.m. My first task was to assure myself that contact with the rear still existed, after which I intended to make another attempt to get in touch with Division Headquarters.

Rommel's division had advanced nearly 50 miles since the previous morning. The way he had driven on with his tanks during the night was a daring act. Then, and later, most commanders considered that, even in exploiting a victory, the continuation of a tank advance in the dark was too great a hazard.

On Rommel's left, the leading troops of Reinhardt's and Guderian's Panzer Corps were racing level with him. Early that day Guderian's left wing division reached the Oise at Ribemont, 20 miles south of Le Câteau. That was the breadth

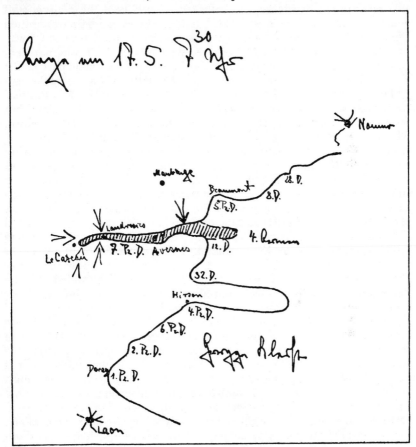

3. ROMMEL'S ADVANCE, 16TH-17TH MAY

Map drawn by Rommel showing his advance in the 24 hours to 7.30 a.m. 17th May—in relation to those of the neighbouring divisions and of von Kleist's Panzer Group. This map brings out the extraordinary depth, narrowness and audacity of his thrust—from Cerfontaine to Le Câteau.

of the swathe that had been cut by the tank torrents that were sweeping west towards the sea, across the rear of the Allied armies in Belgium. All attempts to block them proved too late, for each time that the French Command chose a new stop-line it was overrun by the German tanks before the slower-moving French reserves arrived, or before they settled into position.

It was now high time that the country we had overrun was secured by the division, and the enormous number of prisoners—approximately two mechanised divisions—was collected. I had kept the division staff constantly informed of our progress, but all messages had been transmitted blind from the Panzer Regiment's command tank and there was no way of telling whether they had been received. Even so, I was not very pleased when I heard shortly afterwards that only a small part of the Panzer Regiment and part of the Motor-cycle Battalion had come through as far as the hill east of Le Câteau. An officer was sent off to the rear immediately. Then I tried myself to drive back to establish contact, but soon came under anti-tank gun fire from Le Câteau and had to return. Meanwhile, Rothenburg with part of Panzer Battalion Sickenius had been in action with French tanks and anti-tank guns on the hill east of Le Câteau, but had soon disposed of them. I returned to the Panzer Battalion, which had meanwhile formed a hedgehog, and waited there until the arrival of part of the Motor-cycle Battalion under Captain von Hagen. I now felt the situation in front of Le Câteau to be secure, and, still in the belief that the rest of the division had almost closed up, ordered Rothenburg to hold his position with the aid of the Motor-cycle Battalion which was placed under his command. I then started back in my signals vehicle, with a Panzer III as escort, to bring up and deploy the rest of the division. On the way we came across several stranded vehicles belonging to the Motor-cycle Battalion and Panzer Regiment, whose crews told us that it was wise to go carefully in Landrecies as a number of our vehicles had been fired on there, by enemy tanks. I then drove on [*eastwards*] at high speed to Landrecies, where the Panzer III, which was in the lead, lost its way in the town. When at last we reached the road to Avesnes, we saw a German vehicle standing in the road a hundred yards ahead, where it had been shot up by enemy guns. There must have been a French tank or anti-tank gun somewhere around, but we had no time for a long palaver and so—through! As we drove past, wounded motor-cyclists shouted frantically to us to take them along. I could not help them, unfortunately—there was too much at stake. Both vehicles crossed the danger zone at top speed and won through to the Maroilles road. Then the escorting Panzer III dropped out with mechanical trouble.

Vehicles now stood everywhere, all over and across the road. Alongside the road there were French officers and men bivouacked close beside their weapons. But they had apparently not yet recovered from the fright which the German tanks had spread and so we put them on the march so far as we could by shouts and signs from the moving vehicle. There were no German troops to be seen. On we went, at top speed, through Maroilles. East of the village we suddenly discovered a Panzer IV, which had been stranded by mechanical trouble and had its 75 mm. gun in working order. We sighed with relief. A Panzer IV was a strong protection at such a moment.

There were now French troops everywhere, on both sides of the road, most of them bivouacked beside their vehicles. There was no chance, unfortunately, of getting them on the march as prisoners as we had no men to form an escort. Where we did manage to get them moving, they marched only so long as our armoured car was with them, and then vanished into the bushes the moment we drove on ahead.

I gave the Panzer IV orders to hold the hill east of Maroilles and to send any prisoners who came from the west on to the east. Then we drove on, but had only gone a few hundred yards when the driver reported that he had to stop for petrol. Fortunately, he still had several full cans aboard. Meanwhile, I was informed by Hanke that he had heard from the crew of the Panzer IV that the village beyond had been reoccupied by the enemy. There could be no question of tackling French tanks and anti-tank guns with my lightly armoured vehicle, so I drove back to the Panzer IV with the idea of making wireless contact from there with all parts of the division and organising a quick move into the territory we had overrun. Fortunately, there was no sound of fighting anywhere in the vicinity.

I had barely arrived back at the Panzer IV when a motor rifle company appeared on the horizon, travelling fast down the road from Marbaix [5 miles west of Landrecies]. There now being a hope that further detachments would be following in the wake of this company, I drove off again in the direction of Avesnes, but found nothing.

A short distance east of Marbaix a French car came out of a side-turning from the left and crossed the road close in front of my armoured car. At our shouts it halted and a French officer got out and surrendered. Behind the car there was a whole convoy of lorries approaching in a great cloud of dust. Acting quickly, I had the convoy turned off towards Avesnes. Hanke swung himself up on the first lorry while I stayed on the cross-road for a while, shouting and signalling to the French troops that they should lay down their arms—the war was over for them. Several of the lorries had machine-guns mounted and manned against air attack. It was impossible to see through the dust how long the convoy was, and so after 10 or 15 vehicles had passed, I put myself at the head of the column and drove on to Avesnes. Shortly before the town we had to make a detour across country where the road was closed by burning vehicles.

At length we arrived at the south-west entrance to Avesnes, where we found part of the Battalion Paris [the commander's name] installed near the cemetery. Without halting, Hanke led the lorry convoy on to a parking place and there disarmed the enemy troops. We now found that we had had no less than 40 lorries, many of them carrying troops, behind us.

Staff H.Q. of the division arrived in Avesnes at about 16.00 hours, and now unit after unit began to move into the territory we had overrun during the night and early morning. In the course of this move, the 2nd Battalion of the Artillery Regiment successfully prevented 48 French tanks from going into action just north of Avesnes. The tanks stood formed up alongside the road, some of them with engines running. Several drivers were taken prisoner still in their tanks. This action saved the 25th Panzer Regiment an attack in their rear by these tanks.

The 7th Panzer Division's losses during the break-through of the Maginot Line extension (on the 16th/17th May) are given in the division's official history as 35 killed and 59 wounded. In the division's sector the prisoners taken were approximately 10,000 men, together with 100 tanks, 30 armoured cars and 27 guns.

The account concludes, " The division had no time to collect large numbers of prisoners and equipment."

After settling the layout of the division between Le Câteau and the French frontier west of Sivry, I took an hour and a half's rest. Shortly after midnight orders came in for the attack to be continued next day, the 18th May, towards Cambrai. At about 07.00 hours next morning the adjutant of the 25th Panzer Regiment arrived at headquarters and reported that a powerful enemy force had established itself in Pommereuille Wood [*midway between Landrecies and Le Câteau*]. He had managed to break through from west to east in an armoured car under cover of night. The 25th Panzer Regiment, which was still holding its position east of Le Câteau, urgently needed petrol and ammunition and the commander had instructed him to get them brought up as quickly as possible.

At about 08.00 hours I put the remaining panzer battalion on the march for Landrecies and Le Câteau with orders to push through to the regiment and get the ammunition and petrol up to it. The 37th Armoured Reconnaissance Battalion was to follow up behind. With Most and Hanke, I later caught up with the Panzer Battalion in the wood half a mile east of Pommereuille, and found them in action against French tanks which were barring the road. Violent fighting developed on the road and there was no chance of outflanking the enemy position on either side. Our guns seemed to be completely ineffective against the heavy armour of the French tanks.

The French tanks had from 40 mm. to 60 mm. of armour whereas even the German medium tanks had only 30 mm., and the light tanks had even less protection.

We stood for some time watching the battle from close range, until I finally decided to take the battalion south through the wood via Ors [*4 miles south-west of Landrecies*]. We again came up against the French in the northern outskirts of Ors and progress became slow while we fought our way forward. For some unknown reason the Panzer Regiment's ammunition and petrol column did not follow up behind the battalion. It was midday before we finally reached Rothenburg's position. He reported that his force had held the position against heavy enemy tank attacks, but that he was now incapable of further movement and in urgent need of petrol and ammunition. Unfortunately, I was not at that moment in a position to help him.

The necessary forces were now dispatched to Pommereuille to open the shortest road to Landrecies. Meanwhile, French heavy artillery had begun to lay down a heavy barrage on our hedgehog position. Their fire was accurate and part of the position had to be vacated. Confident that the fighting at Pommereuille would soon be decided in our favour, I now gave orders for the Panzer Regiment to form up for their attack on Cambrai. By 15.00 hours the situation had cleared up sufficiently for the attack to open.

The passages that follow in Rommel's narrative have more detail than significance, and may therefore be summarised. The ammunition and petrol column which had been left south-east of Pommereuille Wood did not reach 25th Panzer Regiment's two battalions located near Le Câteau until some hours later. By the time these tanks had filled up with ammunition and petrol, the one Panzer Battalion which Rommel had brought up was already far ahead on the road to Cambrai.

I now gave orders to the reinforced Battalion Paris to secure the roads leading from Cambrai to the north-east and north as quickly as possible. Led by its few tanks and two troops of self-propelled A.A. guns, the battalion advanced over a broad front and in great depth straight across the fields to the north-west, throwing up a great cloud of dust as they went. Tanks and A.A. guns scattered fire at intervals into the northern outskirts of Cambrai. The enemy in Cambrai, unable in the dust to see that most of our vehicles were soft-skinned, apparently thought that a large-scale tank attack was approaching the north of the town and offered no resistance.

Nothing could have been more futile than the way that the French Command used its armoured forces. It had 53 tank battalions compared with the Germans' 36. But all the German battalions were formed into divisions (of which they had ten) while nearly half the French were infantry-support units. Moreover, even their seven divisions of armoured type were used piecemeal.

Before the war the only French armoured formations had been the so-called " light mechanised division " (200 tanks), of converted cavalry. The French had three of these, which were employed for the advance into Belgium. There were also four " armoured " divisions (of 150 tanks only) which had been formed during the winter. These four were thrown separately and successively against the seven German armoured divisions (averaging 260 tanks apiece) that drove across the Meuse like a vast phalanx. The 1st French Armoured Division was directed towards Dinant, but ran out of fuel and was overrun—as already related. The 3rd was directed against Sedan, but distributed to support the infantry there; the fragments were swamped by Guderian's three divisions. The 4th (under de Gaulle), recently formed and still incomplete, went into action against Guderian's flank as he swept on towards the Oise, but was brushed aside. The 2nd was spread along a 25-mile stretch of the Oise, and Guderian's two leading divisions quickly burst through this thin string of static packets.

The three French mechanised divisions from Belgium were assembling just north of Cambrai, and although two of them had been mauled in their fight with Hoeppner's Panzer Corps in the Belgian plain they were still a powerful force. They were ordered to strike south towards Cambrai and St. Quentin on the 19th, but the order was not executed—as a considerable proportion of the tanks had been detached to aid the infantry at various places.

As for the British, they had only ten tank units in France, and these were all split up among the infantry divisions. The first armoured division was not embarked for France until after the German offensive had started.

CHAPTER II

CLOSING THE TRAP

The fast going of the break-through drive ended, for Rommel, with the capture of Cambrai. For on the 16th May the imperilled Allied armies in Belgium had at last started to withdraw from their far advanced line in Belgium, and on the 18th the right wing of the German Panzer forces had been engaged with forces that the French First Army had sent back to cover its rear. The terrific momentum of the Panzer drive had brushed aside these intervening forces in the last lap, from Le Câteau to Cambrai, but the increasing opposition and flank threat caused concern in the higher commands on the German side. So, while Guderian's and Reinhardt's corps pursued the westward drive, Hoth's corps (including Rommel's division) on the right wing was held back until infantry reinforcements began to arrive on the scene and take over the protection of the northern flank.

Rommel's account of the next two days can be briefly summarised. After covering the stretch between Le Câteau and Cambrai, he paused to reorganise and get up supplies, as well as to give his troops a chance to sleep and recover their energy. He planned to continue the advance on the evening of the 19th, with the aim of reaching the high ground south-east of Arras.

In the late afternoon he was discussing the plan with his staff at Divisional H.Q. when the Corps Commander, General Hoth, suddenly appeared and ordered a postponement, on the ground that the troops were too exhausted by their efforts of the past days. Rommel did not share Hoth's opinion. " The troops have been twenty hours in the same place," he said, " and a night attack during moonlight will result in fewer losses." So Hoth let him have his way.

The attack towards Arras began at 01.40 hours (on the 20th), and Rommel accompanied the tank spearhead, which at 06.00 hours reached Beaurains (2½ miles south of Arras). But the motorised rifle regiments had not followed the tank spearhead closely as intended, so Rommel drove back in an armoured car to hurry them forward—only to find that the French had meanwhile infiltrated into his line of communication. For the next few hours he was in an extremely tight corner, until the situation was restored by the arrival of an infantry regiment with artillery. These troops were then put on the defensive south of Arras, news having come through that a number of French and British divisions had assembled around that city.*

On the 21st the 7th Panzer Division was to advance round the flank of Arras

towards the north-west, with the S.S. Division Totenkopf on its left flank, while
the 5th Panzer Division advanced east of Arras. While again screening his exposed
flank with artillery, Rommel this time put his Armoured Reconnaissance Battalion
in between the Panzer Regiment, forming the spearhead, and the Rifle Regiments
behind—in order to maintain communications and hold the road open. These
precautions were well justified, as his account shows.

At about 15.00 hours I gave the Panzer Regiment orders to attack.
Although the armour had by this time been seriously reduced in numbers,
due to breakdowns and casualties, this was a model of what an attack
should be. When I saw the weight of it I was convinced that the 7th
Panzer Division's new thrust into enemy territory would be as successful
as all the other actions of the preceding days. I had actually intended to
accompany the tanks again myself, together with Lieutenant Most, my
dispatch riders, armoured car and signals vehicle, and to conduct
operations from there by wireless, but the infantry regiments were so
slow in backing up that I drove straight off back to chase up the 7th Rifle
Regiment and get it to hurry. It was nowhere to be found. A mile or
so north of Ficheux we eventually came across part of the 6th Rifle
Regiment, and driving alongside their column, turned off with them
towards Wailly. Half a mile east of the village we came under fire from
the north. One of our howitzer batteries was already in position at the
northern exit from the village, firing rapid on enemy tanks attacking
southward from Arras.

This attack had been hurriedly organised by the Allied commanders in an
attempt to break the net that was swiftly closing round their armies in Belgium.
For the purpose, the British 5th and 50th Divisions were rushed south to Arras,
together with the 1st Army Tank Brigade (infantry tanks), while the French
planned to co-operate with two mechanised divisions and two infantry divisions.
The attack took longer to mount than had been reckoned, and was launched before
its mounting could be completed. For on the 20th Guderian's Corps raced into Amiens
in the morning and reached the sea near Abbeville that night, thus cutting the Allied
armies' supply lines—a deadly stroke.

Under pressure of the emergency, the British commander decided to start his
attack without waiting any longer for the French. But, as delivered, the British
attack boiled down to a matter of two tank battalions (the 4th and 7th R.T.R., with
74 tanks in all) supported by two infantry battalions. Part of the French 3rd Light
Mechanised Division (70 tanks) co-operated on its right flank.

As we were now coming under machine-gun fire and the infantry
had already taken cover to the right, Most and I ran on in front of the
armoured cars towards the battery position. It did not look as though
the battery would have much difficulty in dealing with the enemy tanks,
for the gunners were calmly hurling round after round into them in
complete disregard of the return fire. Running along behind the battery
lines, we arrived at Wailly and then called up the vehicles. The enemy

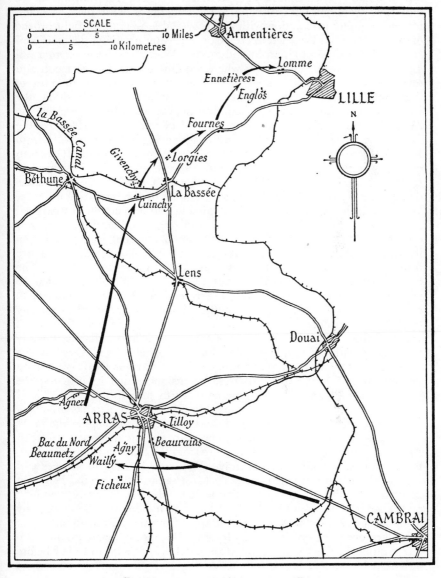

4. Battles round Arras and Lille

tank fire had created chaos and confusion among our troops in the village and they were jamming up the roads and yards with their vehicles, instead of going into action with every available weapon to fight off the oncoming enemy. We tried to create order. After notifying the divisional staff of the critical situation in and around Wailly we drove off to a hill 1,000 yards west of the village, where we found a light A.A. troop and several anti-tank guns located in hollows and a small wood, most of them totally under cover. About 1,200 yards west of our position, the leading enemy tanks, among them one heavy, had already crossed the Arras-Beaumetz railway and shot up one of our Panzer IIIs. At the same time several enemy tanks were advancing down the road from Bac du Nord and across the railway line towards Wailly. It was an extremely tight spot, for there were also several enemy tanks very close to Wailly on its northern side. The crew of a howitzer battery, some distance away, now left their guns, swept along by the retreating infantry. With Most's help, I brought every available gun into action at top speed against the tanks. Every gun, both anti-tank and anti-aircraft, was ordered to open rapid fire immediately and I personally gave each gun its target. With the enemy tanks so perilously close, only rapid fire from every gun could save the situation. We ran from gun to gun. The objections of gun commanders that the range was still too great to engage the tanks effectively, were overruled. All I cared about was to halt the enemy tanks by heavy gunfire. Soon we succeeded in putting the leading enemy tanks out of action. About 150 yards west of our small wood a British captain climbed out of a heavy tank and walked unsteadily towards us with his hands up. We had killed his driver. Over by the howitzer battery also—despite a range of 1,200 to 1,500 yards—the rapid fire of our anti-tank and anti-aircraft guns succeeded in bringing the enemy to a halt and forcing some of them to turn away.

We now directed our fire against the other group of tanks attacking from the direction of Bac du Nord, and succeeded in keeping the tanks off, setting fire to some, halting others and forcing the rest to retreat. Although we were under very heavy fire from the tanks during this action, the gun crews worked magnificently. The worst seemed to be over and the attack beaten off, when suddenly Most sank to the ground behind a 20 mm. anti-aircraft gun close beside me. He was mortally wounded and blood gushed from his mouth. I had had no idea that there was any firing in our vicinity at that moment, apart from that of the 20 mm. gun. Now, however, the enemy suddenly started dropping heavy gunfire into our position in the wood. Poor Most was beyond help and died before he could be carried into cover beside the gun position. The death of this brave man, a magnificent soldier, touched me deeply.

Meanwhile, violent and costly fighting had been going on in the region of Tilloy-Beaurains-Agny. Very powerful armoured forces had thrust out of Arras and attacked the advancing 1st Battalion of the 6th

Rifle Regiment, inflicting heavy losses in men and material. The anti-tank guns which we quickly deployed showed themselves to be far too light to be effective against the heavily armoured British tanks, and the majority of them were put out of action by gunfire, together with their crews, and then overrun by the enemy tanks. Many of our vehicles were burnt out. S.S. units close by also had to fall back to the south before the weight of the tank attack. Finally, the divisional artillery and 88 mm. anti-aircraft batteries succeeded in bringing the enemy armour to a halt south of the line Beaurains-Agny. Twenty-eight enemy tanks were destroyed by the artillery alone, while the anti-aircraft guns accounted for one heavy and seven light.

While this heavy fighting had been going on round the 6th and 7th Rifle Regiments, Rothenburg's 25th Panzer Regiment had reached its objective in a dashing advance, and then waited in vain for the arrival of the Reconnaissance Battalion and the Rifle Regiments. At about 19.00 hours I gave orders for the Panzer Regiment to thrust south-eastwards in order to take the enemy armour advancing south from Arras in the flank and rear. During this operation, the Panzer Regiment clashed with a superior force of heavy and light enemy tanks and many guns south of Agnez. Fierce fighting flared up, tank against tank, an extremely heavy engagement in which the Panzer Regiment destroyed seven heavy tanks and six anti-tank guns and broke through the enemy position, though at the cost of three Panzer IVs, six Panzer IIIs and a number of light tanks.[1]

This action brought the enemy armour into such confusion that, in spite of their superior numbers, they fell back into Arras. Fighting ceased at nightfall. Meanwhile, the situation north-west of Wailly had been fully restored.

This attack was the one serious counter-stroke made by the entrapped armies before the end came. Small as was its scale, it gave the Germans a shock.

That was due to the tough skins of the tanks rather than to any deep penetration by the attack. The British here employed slow but heavily armoured infantry tanks —" Matildas." They had in all 58 of the small Mark Is, armed only with machine-guns, and 16 of the later and larger Mark IIs with a 2-pounder gun. Even the Mark IIs' maximum speed was only 15 m.p.h., but they had 75 mm. (3 inches) of armour, and proved impervious to the ordinary 37 mm. German anti-tank guns, while even artillery shells often bounced off them. The French cavalry tanks, Somuas, were faster and more thinly armoured—although not so thinly as the German.

The British tank advance—which was not in superior numbers—had been handicapped by having little infantry support, less artillery support, and no air support. It was largely these deficiencies which had brought it to a halt, after a very promising start, and then caused its withdrawal.

[1] The official history of the 7th Panzer Division states that the Division's losses on this day were 89 killed, 116 wounded and 173 missing. That was four times the loss suffered during the break-through into France.

But its mental and moral effect on the German higher commands was very marked—and out of all proportion to material results. Discussing the 1940 campaign after the war, Field-Marshal von Rundstedt said: " A critical moment in the drive came just as my forces had reached the Channel. It was caused by a British counter-stroke southward from Arras on May 21. For a short time it was feared that our armoured divisions would be cut off before the infantry divisions could come up to support them. None of the French counter-attacks carried any serious threat as this one did." Kluge and Kleist were particularly affected. Kluge was inclined to stop any further advance westward from Arras until the situation there had been cleared up. Kleist, too, became nervously cautious. Thus when Guderian turned north from Abbeville on the 22nd—driving towards Boulogne, Calais and Dunkirk—his advance was slowed down by Kleist's restrictive orders.

Then, on the 24th, Guderian's and Reinhardt's corps were halted by Hitler's order when they were barely 10 miles from Dunkirk—the only remaining port through which the British Army could escape from the trap. But that fateful order was only issued after Hitler had visited Rundstedt, who was naturally influenced by the cautious views of Kluge and Kleist. When the halt order was lifted two days later, on the 26th, the chance of preventing the British Army's escape had faded—as it had been allowed time to establish a shield round the port.

23 *May* 1940

DEAREST LU,

With a few hours' sleep behind me, it's time for a line to you. I'm fine in every way. My division has had a blazing success. Dinant, Philippeville, break-through the Maginot Line and advance in one night 40 miles through France to Le Câteau, then Cambrai, Arras, always far in front of everybody else. Now the hunt is up against 60 encircled British, French and Belgian divisions. Don't worry about me. As I see it the war in France may be over in a fortnight.

24 *May* 1940

Close in front of Bethune. I'm in splendid form. On the go all day of course. But by my estimate the war will be won in a fortnight. Lovely weather—if anything too much sun.

26 *May* 1940

A day or two without action has done a lot of good. The division has lost up to date 27 officers killed and 33 wounded, and 1,500 men dead and wounded. That's about 12 per cent casualties. Very little compared with what's been achieved. The worst is now well over. There's little likelihood of any more hard fighting, for we've given the enemy a proper towsing. Food, drink and sleep are all back to routine. Schraepler is back already. His successor was killed a yard away from me.

*On the 22nd and 23rd May Rommel pushed forward round the western outskirts
of Arras, and under pressure of this outflanking threat the British forces there were
withdrawn on the night of the 23rd to the canal line (18 miles to the north) that
ran through La Bassée and Bethune to the sea at Gravelines, south-west of Dunkirk.
On the 24th came Hitler's order that the panzer forces were to halt on this canal
line. Rommel spent the next two days in reorganising his division, parts of which
had been badly mauled by the British tank attack on the 21st.*

*Hitler's cancellation of the halt order on the 26th coincided with the British
decision to withdraw to the sea at Dunkirk. The larger part of the forces holding
the canal line were already being drawn away northward to reinforce the line in
Belgium, where Bock's Army Group was developing an ever-increasing pressure—
under which the Belgian Army collapsed, and capitulated, on the following day.*

*As soon as the halt order was lifted, Rommel was quick to renew his northward
thrust, which was directed on Lille—with the aim of cutting off the Allied forces
that were still covering the city and lying east of it.*

*During this phase of the campaign the Allied commanders, having had their
lines of communication severed, naturally tended to be over-conscious of the difficulties
of their situation. But from " the other side of the hill " things looked different,
as Rommel's account serves to make clear. The difficulty he met in forcing the
passage of the La Bassée canal is the more notable, particularly in comparison with
the crossing of the Meuse, because of the very thin defence. Only one British
battalion was holding the sector he attacked.*

According to air reports which came in to my headquarters on the
afternoon of the 26th May, the enemy had been observed north of the
canal withdrawing towards the north-west. I immediately requested
permission from Corps to drive a bridgehead over the canal that evening.
It was soon granted.

I remained with the troops on the canal all the evening. The 37th
Reconnaissance Battalion, although suffering severely from the activities
of snipers, succeeded, with artillery help, in pushing armoured patrols
through as far as the canal, but strong enemy resistance prevented the
creation of a bridge-head. The 7th Rifle Regiment, however, achieved
a notable success that evening by getting elements of both its battalions
across the La Bassée canal, which was blocked by immense numbers of
sunken barges. After eliminating a number of enemy machine-gun nests,
both battalions established themselves on the northern bank. Apart from
a few casualties at the crossing point caused by flanking fire from British
machine-gun posts to the west, the creation of the bridge-head at this
point seemed to have caused no great difficulty and there was now good
reason to expect that the battalions would establish a strong position on
the northern bank during the night.

Early next morning, the 27th May, I drove to the crossing point at
Cuinchy to see for myself how things were going. Snipers were still very
active, mainly from the left, and a number of men had been hit, including
Lieutenant von Enkefort, though his was no more than a graze. The

Engineer Battalion had constructed a number of pontoons in a small harbour just off the canal, sufficient to build a bridge. However, they had built the 8-ton type instead of the long 16-tonners, as the latter would have been too difficult to manœuvre through the litter of submerged or semi-submerged barges which was blocking the canal. The sappers had already tried to blast a way through with explosives, but with little success, due to the unwieldiness of the sunken barges.

Prospects did not look too good for the attack across the canal. Elements of the 2nd Battalion, 7th Rifle Regiment, had crossed in rubber boats and were now located on the opposite bank in bushes close to the canal. The battalion had not, however, as I had wished, extended its hold deeper on the north bank and dug itself in, nor had it taken the village of Givenchy. It had also omitted to clean up the enemy for a few hundred yards along the north bank to the west, and to get anti-tank guns and heavy weapons across and dig them in. The fire protection of the heavy company on the south bank was also inadequate. Things were probably much the same with the 1st Battalion [*which had gained a bridge-head a little to the east*].

I now ordered 635th Engineer Battalion, which had newly been placed under command, to construct a 16-ton bridge in the sector held by Battalion Cramer near the demolished bridge at Cuinchy.

Then, under my personal direction, 20-mm. A.A. guns and later a Panzer IV were turned on the enemy snipers, who were maintaining a most unpleasant fire from the left and picking off our men one by one. I had every house from 300 to 600 yards west of 2nd Battalion's bridging point demolished and the bushes swept with fire—after which we had some peace. I was able to see for myself how effective our fire had been when we moved back again across the canal two days later. The British had installed themselves in a lock-house from which, judging by the number of empty cartridges I found there, they had maintained a steady fire in the flank of my troops. A few of our shells had wiped out the occupants of the building. Numerous blood-covered bandages and the body of a British soldier lay in the cellar.

While these nests were being engaged, and the sappers were con-structing a ramp on the northern bank and with great effort manœuvring across the first pontoons, a report came in that a strong force of enemy tanks from La Bassée had attacked the 7th Rifle Regiment's eastern bridge-head and thrown Battalion Cramer back across the canal. The enemy tanks, which included several British heavies,[1] were now standing on the northern bank and spraying the southern bank with machine-gun and shell fire. We could hear the enemy fire a few hundred yards away

[1] By " British heavies " Rommel evidently means the Matilda, Infantry Tank Mark II, which weighed 26 tons—and was also " heavy " in the sense of being slow compared with the German medium tanks Panzer III (20 tons and 22 m.p.h.) and Panzer IV (22 tons and 20 m.p.h.). But the British tank brigade was now reduced to one composite company of sixteen tanks, which included only a single Mark II.

to our right and there was a grave danger that the enemy tanks would push on to the west along the canal bank and attack the Battalion Bachmann, which still had no anti-tank weapons, apart from anti-tank rifles, on the northern bank, and also had no depth. If the enemy exploited his chance, he could be at the western crossing point in a few minutes.

The situation was extremely critical. I drove the sappers on to their utmost speed and had the pontoons lashed roughly together, in order to get at least a few guns and tanks across. With so many sunken barges and other obstacles jammed in the canal, it was impossible for the bridge to take a straight course, and its structure consequently had little strength. As the first Panzer III lumbered across, several pontoons gave noticeably, and it was touch and go whether or not the tank would slither bodily into the canal. While it was crossing, I sent off a Panzer IV 50 yards to the east along the high bank on our side of the canal, with orders to open fire immediately on the enemy tanks attacking from La Bassée. The fire of this Panzer IV brought the leading enemy tank to a halt. Shortly afterwards the Panzer III on the northern bank joined in, and a few minutes later a howitzer which had been manhandled across. This soon brought the enemy tank attack to a standstill.

Work was now started on strengthening the 16-ton bridge and before long a steady flow of vehicles began to move one by one across it. First to cross were field guns, anti-tank and 20 mm. anti-aircraft guns, then elements of the 25th Panzer Regiment interspersed with an 88 mm. anti-aircraft battery. All this time, the 2nd Battalion of 7th Rifle Regiment was extending its bridgehead north of the canal. Finally, with artillery support, it took the commanding village of Givenchy. Battalion Cramer was brought up in its wake to the western crossing point, where later the whole Rifle Regiment crossed on foot to attack the enemy near Canteleux. This action resulted, towards midday, in a widening of the bridgehead to the line Canteleux-Givenchy, and the capture, after a fierce resistance, of a large number of British prisoners. The newly-won territory on the north bank now steadily filled up with artillery and anti-aircraft guns. At about noon Heidkaemper wirelessed that my presence was urgently required at Divisional H.Q. as, by a Corps order, the 5th Panzer Brigade (General Harde) had been placed under my command for the attack on Lille. Soon after I arrived, General Harde came in with his regiment commanders and reported the location, etc., of his brigade.

These were the tanks of the 5th Panzer Division which, being one of the pre-war formations, had a Panzer brigade of two regiments, each of two tank battalions, whereas Rommel's division had only one Panzer regiment of three battalions. At the start of the campaign it had 324 tanks compared with Rommel's 218.

I now drove off with General Harde to the bridge near Cuinchy, which was finished by the time we arrived. Traffic across it was already in full swing, although the steepness of the ramps at either end prevented the flow from being very rapid. The rifle brigade was already across on the north bank, but without its vehicles. The 25th Panzer Regiment was standing ready to attack in the neighbourhood of Givenchy and a large force of artillery and light and heavy A.A. was in position on the northern bank. Several enemy batteries were maintaining an unpleasantly heavy fire on our bridgehead position. The area held by our forces on the northern bank was now far too constricted and I gave the 25th Panzer Regiment orders to widen the bridgehead by an attack on Lorgies [*2 miles north on the canal*]. At about 15.00 hours, the 5th Panzer Brigade began to move across the Cuinchy bridge. The steep angle of the approaches prevented the crossing from proceeding as quickly as we should have liked. Several of the heavy vehicles stuck on the ramps and had to be towed off. I could not agree to General Harde's proposal that in these circumstances the attack should be postponed, and gave orders for the brigade to move off punctually at 18.00 hours with such of its tanks as had then arrived on the northern bank.

The 25th Panzer Regiment had meanwhile made a long lunge forward and reached the neighbourhood of Lorgies. During this advance, the regiment had become involved in heavy and costly fighting against a powerful defensive front, which they had finally succeeded in penetrating. The enemy batteries, which had hitherto been dropping shells into our bridgehead, now withdrew at top speed before the advancing German tanks. The panzer regiment's attack moved on, and by its fire smashed a visible breach in the enemy front, through which the division, reinforced by Panzer Brigade Harde, then moved. With the tanks fighting their way across country, progress was sufficiently slow for the infantry to follow in extended order over a wide front. Soon Panzer Regiment Werner on the right came up level and other units of 5th Panzer Brigade followed them up. I was extremely impressed by the large numbers of spick-and-span tanks which the 5th Panzer Brigade possessed, far larger than the tank strength of my division.

Dusk was already far advanced when I reached a barn half a mile east of Fournes and caught up with Rothenburg's command vehicle on the road to Lille. Fighting in Fournes itself [*10 miles south-west of Lille*] seemed to be already over. About half a mile away to the east, the leading units of 5th Panzer Brigade could be seen in process of regrouping. Despite the onset of night I now gave the 25th Panzer Regiment orders to continue their attack and to close the western exit from Lille and the road to Armentières. The regiment was to form a hedgehog in the neighbourhood of Lomme [*on the western edge of Lille*] and await the arrival of reinforcements which I would send them.

Rothenburg asked whether I would not like to accompany the attack myself, but in view of the difficulty of handling the division in the situation at that time I was forced to decline. Wireless was practically unusable again and it seemed to me more important that I should detail the rest of my force, personally if possible, to its positions round our final objective at Lomme and see to it that they did in fact get there. I had also to ensure that substantial reinforcements for the 25th Panzer Regiment arrived by daybreak, and to organise their supply of ammunition and petrol—not an easy task. I wanted at all costs to avoid the Panzer Regiment being placed a second time in the difficult situation in which it had been outside Le Câteau.

Wireless contact with General Harde proving impossible, I tried to get orders to him via the divisional staff, to make an immediate advance to Englos in the wake of the 25th Panzer Regiment. However, I was unable to get the main body of the brigade on the move and the attack on Englos had to proceed, first with only a company and later with a battalion. It was unfortunately impossible for me to drive straight across country in the darkness and deliver the orders myself, as my *Gefechtsstaffel* was not fully equipped with cross-country vehicles. In any case, it would have exposed us to the danger of being taken for a British scouting party and fired on by one of the 5th Panzer Brigade's detachments of tanks which were scattered about the country.

27 May 1940

DEAREST LU,

I'm very well. We're busy encircling the British and French in Lille at the moment. I'm taking part from the south-west. I'm all right for washing, etc. Guenther [*Rommel's batman*] takes good care of that. I've taken a lot of photographs.

7th Panzer Division.   *27-5-40*
Adjutant.

MY DEAR FRAU ROMMEL,

May I be permitted to inform you that the Fuehrer has instructed Lieut. Hanke to decorate your husband on his behalf with the Knight's Cross.[1]

Every man of the division—myself particularly, who has the privilege of accompanying the General—knows that nobody has deserved it more than your husband. He has led the division to successes which must, I imagine, be unique.

[1]*Note by Manfred Rommel.* In the Second World War the following decorations for gallantry were awarded:
  (a) Iron Cross First and Second Class. (The First Class was mostly conferred on officers.)
  (b) German Cross in Gold. (Intermediate grade between the Iron Cross First Class and the Knight's Cross; approx. 3,000 awarded.)
  (c) Knight's Cross to the Iron Cross. (1,500 to 3,000 awarded.)
  (d) Oakleaves to the Knight's Cross. (250 to 300 awarded.)
  (e) Oakleaves with Swords. (80 to 100 awarded.)
  (f) Oakleaves with Swords and Diamonds. (Approx. 30 awarded.)
Later in the war these decorations were also awarded for command achievements.

The General is now up with the tanks again. If he knew that I were writing you, *gnädigste Frau*, he would immediately instruct me to send you his most heartfelt greetings and the news that he is well.

I beg you to accept my apologies that I write impersonally on a typewriter, but my arm is not yet well enough after my wound for me to write legibly.

May I close with the kindest regards from all members of the staff, and remain, *meine gnädigste Frau*,

Your obedient servant,

SCHRAEPLER

Meanwhile, Rothenburg had advanced through the night far to the north. His path was marked by the glare of burning vehicles shot up by his force. I now gave orders for the reinforced 6th and 7th Rifle Regiments to be deployed in depth for defence of the newly-won territory. 37th Reconnaissance Battalion was to come forward to Fournes and remain at my disposal. When the orders were out I went off to Fournes to supervise their execution. Massive stone barricades and deep trenches rendered movement through Fournes extremely difficult. Several convoys had driven up abreast of each other, and it was some time before the tangle could be straightened out. I had most of the convoys moved off the road into the fields alongside, where they were to wait until an orderly flow of traffic had been established. Amongst it all I found part of the 25th Panzer Regiment's petrol and ammunition column, to which I gave instructions to move off to the side of the road and await my orders. It was my intention to take these vehicles forward to 25th Panzer Regiment in the latter part of the night, covered by 37th Reconnaissance Battalion.

At about midnight I met the commander of the Reconnaissance Battalion, Major Erdman, on the western outskirts of Fournes and told him to expect an early alert and start next morning, the 28th May. I then quartered myself with my immediate staff in a house on the western outskirts of Fournes. At 01.40 hours [*28th May*] a wireless signal came in from Rothenburg to the effect that he had reached his objective near Lomme. With this, Lille was sealed off to the west, and I immediately had the Reconnaissance Battalion alerted and the Panzer Regiment's petrol and ammunition column brought up to the north-west boundary of Fournes, with the intention of pressing on to Lomme before morning if possible. The whole convoy—Reconnaissance Battalion and supply column—moved off at about 03.00 hours. After a détour to the west to avoid Fort Englos, I decided to take the road through Ennetières. In the darkness we drove past large numbers of enemy lorries, armoured vehicles and guns, mostly in the ditch, where they had apparently been abandoned by their crews in panic. When, as dawn was breaking, we found ourselves approaching the Lille-Armentières road with still no sign of Rothenburg's tanks, we began to feel thoroughly uncomfortable, for daylight was almost on us and any moment might find us under shell fire. At last we found the first of our tanks. Rothenburg was delighted at the increase in his strength in front of Lille, and even more over the arrival of the ammunition and petrol. He reported briefly on the night's fighting. The attack had first driven straight up the Fournes-Lille road. Then, after crossing the railway, the regiment had swung north, shortly afterwards coming up against enemy tanks and a strong motorised force. The enemy tanks and lorries had been wiped out in a short but sharp engagement, many of their crews seeking salvation in flight. The Panzer Regiment had then pushed on to Lomme and occupied the western exits from Lille.

I now regrouped the troops round Lomme into a planned defence. Shortly afterwards fierce fighting developed at the western outlet from Lille, with enemy units trying to break out to the west with tank and artillery support.

Part of the Reconnaissance Battalion and a heavy company were now placed on the defensive on either side of the Lille-Armentières road. During the early hours of the morning, it seemed to us that the enemy forces facing us west of Lille were growing steadily stronger and so I sent out an urgent call for heavy artillery fire.

I now decided to pull 6th and 7th Rifle Regiments out of their previous positions south of Englos and Fournes and to incorporate them in the general defence line north and south of Lomme.

Orders to this effect had just been issued, when a hail of shells suddenly began to fall round the Panzer Regiment's command post, which was also serving as Divisional H.Q. Even as they began we had the feeling that they were our own shells, and immediately sent up green flares. I tried to get to the radio to order the cease fire, but the fire was so thick that it was not easy to reach the signals lorry, which was standing behind the house. There was no doubt that they were our own shells, probably 150 mm., with whose effect we were only too familiar. I was just making a dash for the signals vehicle, with Major Erdman running a few yards in front, when a heavy shell landed close by the house door near which the vehicle was standing. When the smoke cleared, Major Erdman, commander of 37th Reconnaissance Battalion, lay face to the ground, dead, with his back shattered. He was bleeding from the head and from an enormous wound in his back. His left hand was still grasping his leather gloves. I had escaped unscathed, though the same shell had wounded several other officers and men. We continued to send up flares and try by radio to get the fire stopped but it was a long time before the last shell came down. We later discovered that the mistake had been caused by inaccurate transmission of fire orders by an intermediate signals point. The fire had come from the heavy battery of a neighbouring division.

In blocking the roads running west from Lille, Rommel had helped to trap nearly half the French First Army. After failing to break out, the trapped divisions were driven to surrender on the 31st.

Meanwhile, the bulk of the British, with what remained of the French First and Seventh Armies, had managed to reach Dunkirk—where a defensive bridgehead had now been formed, and covered by a belt of inundations in the low ground. That water-barrier proved a good protection except against the very harassing air attacks. The defence held out long enough to enable 338,000 troops, including 120,000 French, to be evacuated by sea to England between the 26th May and the 4th June. Only a few thousand were captured—belonging to the French rearguard which gallantly covered the last stage of the embarkation. But during the three weeks' whirlwind campaign the Germans had taken over a million prisoners altogether, at a cost to themselves of only 60,000 casualties.

The Belgian and Dutch Armies had been wiped off the slate. The French had lost 30 divisions—nearly one-third of their total strength, and including the most mobile part of it. They had also lost the help of 12 British divisions, for although the personnel had escaped across the Channel, most of their equipment had been left behind, and months would pass before they could be rearmed. Only 2 British divisions remained in France, although 2 more that were not fully trained were now sent over.

It was a grim situation that faced General Weygand, who had replaced Gamelin as Allied Commander-in-Chief on the 20th May. He was left with 66 divisions, mostly depleted, to hold a front that was longer than the original. The new front ran from the sea, near Abbeville, along the Somme and the Aisne to link up with the still untouched Maginot Line. Not much could be done to fortify this " Weygand Line," as it was called, in the very short time before the Germans struck afresh—after bringing up the mass of their marching divisions, which had taken little fighting part in the first offensive.

Rommel's division was given a few days' rest after its coup at Lille in cutting off the French retreat to the sea. Then it moved south for the final stage of the campaign.

29 May 1940

DEAREST LU,

Now that the Lille fighting is over (we were again the first in front of the western gates) we've come out to rest behind the front.

On the 26th May, Lieutenant Hanke, acting for the Fuehrer, ceremonially decorated me with the Knight's Cross and gave me the Fuehrer's best regards. $3\frac{1}{2}$ hours later my division, with three Panzer regiments under command, thrust against western Lille, which they reached by midnight. An hour and a half's sleep and I then took fresh troops, with ammunition and petrol for the tanks, up to the front line. Unfortunately one of my battalion commanders was killed by our own fire.

Now we'll probably get a few days' rest. Perhaps France will give

Crossing the Somme bridges under shell-fire

The tank that blocked the bridge [*see page* 47]

"*From 12 o'clock onwards, heavy enemy artillery began to bombard the area of our Somme crossing.*" *June 5th, 1940.* [*Rommel's own photograph*]

"*We had reached the coast of France.*" *June 10th, 1940.* [*Rommel's own photograph*]

up her now hopeless struggle. If she doesn't we'll smash her to the last corner. I'm fine in every way. My very best wishes to you for your birthday. There's a frightful lot to do. My Thuringians [*the home station of Rommel's division was in Thuringia*] have lost a lot of equipment on the road and in enemy tank attacks and this must be put right as soon as possible. Meanwhile, we are making do with French guns.

2 June 1940

Ordered to the Fuehrer to-day. We're all in splendid form. More to-morrow.

3 June 1940

The Fuehrer's visit was wonderful. He greeted me with the words: " Rommel, we were very worried about you during the attack." His whole face was radiant and I had to accompany him afterwards. I was the only division commander who did.

4 June 1940

We're off again to-day. The six days' rest has done a lot of good and helped us to get our equipment more or less back into shape.

The new move won't be so very difficult. The sooner it comes the better for us. The country here is practically untouched by war. It all went too fast. Would you cut out all the newspaper articles about me, please. I've no time to read at the moment, but it will be fun to look at them later.

CHAPTER III

THE BREAK-THROUGH ON THE SOMME

5 June 1940   3.30 a.m.

DEAREST LU,

To-day the second phase of the offensive begins. In an hour we shall be crossing the canal [*the Somme is canalised on this part*]. We've had plenty of time and so everything, so far as can be foreseen, is well prepared. I shall be observing the attack from well back in the rear. A fortnight, I hope, will see the war over on the mainland. Masses of post coming in every day. The whole world sending its congratulations. I've opened nowhere near all the letters yet. There hasn't been time.

The offensive was opened by Bock's Army Group on the right wing, along the Somme. Rundstedt's Army Group, facing the Aisne, did not join in until four days later. Bock was given three of the five panzer corps; two of them, forming Kleist's group, were used for a pincer stroke on the Amiens-Péronne sector, while Hoth's corps struck on the extreme right between Amiens and Abbeville. The two other panzer corps were grouped under Guderian—promoted after his decisive drive to the Channel—and were moved back eastward to the sector of the Aisne near Rethel, south-west of Sedan. Each panzer corps consisted of two panzer divisions and one motorised infantry division.

The extreme right wing thrust reached the Seine south of Rouen (70 miles distant) during the night of the 18th June thanks largely to a swift cut-through by Rommel's division after two days' tough fighting—and got across the Seine on the heels of the retreating troops. But the main right wing stroke, by Kleist's Panzer group, made slower progress and met increasingly stiff resistance as it pushed in the direction of Paris. By contrast, Guderian's group made a rapid advance after the Aisne had been crossed in the attack launched there on the 9th June. So Kleist's group was switched eastward to back up the break-through on the Aisne, which became the decisive stroke. For Guderian's group, turning south-east, raced on to the Swiss frontier, thus cutting off the retreat of the French right wing in the Maginot Line. By this time resistance was collapsing everywhere, and the French had been driven to appeal for an armistice on the night of the 16th June.

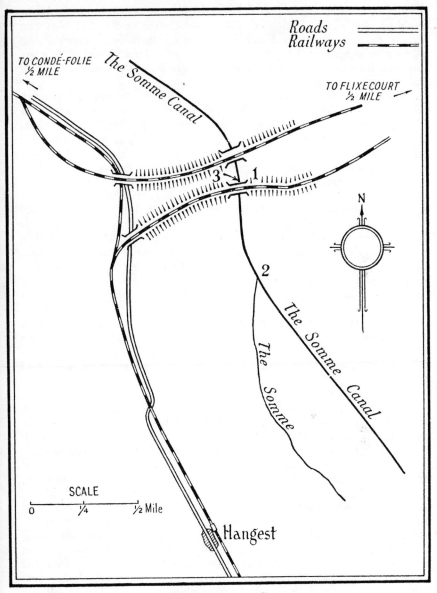

Roads
Railways

TO CONDÉ-FOLIE
½ MILE

The Somme Canal

TO FLIXECOURT
½ MILE

N

3 1

2

The Somme Canal

The Somme

SCALE
0   ¼   ½ Mile

Hangest

5. CROSSING THE SOMME

Fig. 1 shows the position of the tank blocking the railway bridge.
Fig. 2 shows the junction of the Somme Canal and the River Somme.
Fig. 3 shows the shell burst. See photographs facing page 42.

While Guderian's exploitation of the break-through on the Aisne had been decisive, Rommel's thrust on the other flank had started the collapse. That fact adds all the more significance to his account of the opening and development of the attack across the Somme. His division operated as a spearhead in the crossing itself, as well as in the exploitation.

Rommel's stroke was launched on the sector between Longpré and Hangest. Here there was a flat and marshy " no-man's land " of nearly a mile between the German position on the north bank of the Somme and the French position on the slopes south of the river. Across the stretch ran two railway tracks, carried on separate bridges over the river, then along embankments through the riverside meadows, and over the Hangest-Longpré road by two more bridges.

The French had blown up the bridges which carried roads across the Somme at Hangest and near Longpré, but not the two railway river-bridges nor even the two railway road-bridges, which lay so close to their own front. They paid heavily for these omissions—due originally to their own plans for taking the offensive. As a deterrent to any belated attempt to demolish these bridges, Rommel kept them under artillery and machine-gun fire by day and night prior to launching his attack on the 5th June, and succeeded in capturing all four intact early that morning. Once the rails had been taken up, his tanks and other vehicles were able to pass over the river and marshy belt with far less delay than if bridges and causeways had had to be built.

To overcome such a multiple obstacle in this way was an extraordinary feat. If the French had destroyed even the final pair of bridges, over the road, the capture of the bridges over the river would have been of little avail. In a theoretical staff exercise, what Rommel here achieved would hardly have been credited as a practical possibility.

At about 04.15 hours I drove with Lieut. Luft and my signals staff to the artillery command post, where we watched the opening of the all-important attack across the Somme. The preparatory barrage, which started punctual to the minute, made an extraordinarily impressive sight from our excellent vantage point. The flash of our shell-bursts seemed to be everywhere and there was little to be heard of enemy counter-fire.

This being so, we drove to 2nd Battalion 6th Rifle Regiment's bridging point, where news reached us at about 05.00 hours that the railway and road bridges had fallen intact into our hands. Part of the Engineer Battalion was already hard at work on the railway bridge, unbolting rails and clearing away sleepers, in order to prepare the way for the division to cross with its vehicles. On the other side of the river, the Rifle Regiment, under Colonel von Unger, was moving smoothly forward. We heard occasional short bursts of machine-gun fire. I now left my signals vehicle on the north bank, giving the crew instructions to be the first vehicle to cross, and walked over the Somme bridges with Lieutenant Luft. The signals vehicle crossed at 06.00 hours, followed shortly afterwards by artillery and anti-aircraft units and the 25th Panzer

Regiment.   The crossing went somewhat slowly, as there was still a considerable number of rails and sleepers to be cleared away.

Meanwhile, I drove forward with my signal troop towards the fighting. We had some difficulty in getting the vehicles up the steep slopes, which were devoid of any kind of road or track. I walked a few steps into the cornfield with Lieutenant Luft and L.-Cpl. Heidenreich in order to observe the two battalions of 6th Rifle Regiment through the glasses. We were a few hundred yards from our vehicle, when a French soldier's head suddenly appeared out of the cornfield in front of us and disappeared again as quickly.

Heidenreich walked across and found a wounded Frenchman, still with a machine-gun beside him. Close by we found more French troops, some dead, others wounded. Our barrage had apparently dealt heavily with the enemy positions.

Meanwhile, the leading vehicles of the Panzer Regiment and the artillery and anti-aircraft units were arriving on the steep slopes south-west of the Somme. Colonel Rothenburg, who had crossed with his adjutant in advance of his regiment, received orders to follow up 6th Rifle Regiment along a wide valley to a point behind Hill 116 where they were to take up position for an attack on Le Quesnoy [5 *miles beyond the Somme*]. French machine-gun fire several times forced us to take cover during the briefing.

Traffic across the bridge had now ceased again. A Panzer IV had shed its right track and was blocking the entire passage and preventing any other tanks or vehicles from passing. Attempts were being made to drag the tank bodily forwards, with little success as the sleepers were jamming in the rubber rollers and pushing the ballast along in front of them. A good half-hour was lost while the Panzer IV was pulled and pushed across the bridge, by other tanks. Then the crossing gradually began to move again.

By nine o'clock the attack to the south-west had made good progress. To eliminate the enemy force in Hangest, which had long been preventing us from bridge-building there, a whole panzer battalion was launched against the western outskirts of the village. Their orders were merely to shoot up the enemy in the western outskirts, without becoming involved in a fight for the village itself, which was to be cleaned up later by an armoured engineer company which was being sent up for that purpose. We watched the battalion approach closer and closer to the village and very soon heard their fire. Then the tanks turned off up the hill to the west, but only a few surmounted the topmost ridge. Most of them stuck on the hill. This route up the steep side of the hill was not very well chosen. The crews, who dismounted from their tanks, were suddenly fired on by enemy machine-guns and suffered casualties in the coverless terrain. Meanwhile, a detachment of self-propelled guns under Captain von Fischer came up and bombarded the western outskirts of Hangest.

All other troops were directed into the bridgehead position with orders to take up position in preparation for the forthcoming attack.

The cleaning up of Hangest was still giving a lot of trouble and I finally put in the Motor-cycle Battalion under Captain von Hagen. The battalion formed up in extended order for an attack on foot, and was on the point of moving off when I drove back to them again to give a further quick order to Captain von Hagen. Before I could do so, my armoured command vehicle was fired on by machine-guns from Hangest. The bullets clanged against its armoured walls but fortunately did not penetrate, though direct hits were scored on the aerial and machine-gun mounting. An N.C.O. in the 8-wheeled armoured signals lorry behind us was too slow getting his head down and was seriously wounded. The enemy in Hangest continued to cover the road with fire for some time, but finally the Motor-cycle Battalion attacked and reached its objective.

From 12 o'clock onwards, heavy enemy artillery began to bombard the area of our Somme crossing and shells fell thick and fast on both sides of the road over which the division was slowly but steadily moving forward. The hills west of the Somme and the hollows in which we were forming up for the attack were also the target of intermittent heavy shelling. Though casualties were light, the effect on morale of the heavy gunfire was not inconsiderable. The bridgeheads west of the Somme continued to fill with units of all arms and soon became overcrowded.

At midday, I was informed by Heidkaemper that the 5th Panzer Division's attack would not be starting until 16.00 hours and that the 2nd Motorised Division had so far only gained 2,000 yards of ground. In these circumstances I also ordered the attack to be resumed at 16.00 hours.

Orders were for the 25th Panzer Regiment to attack through the 6th Rifle Regiment to Le Quesnoy. The 37th Armoured Reconnaissance Battalion, following behind the Panzer Regiment, was to protect the rear of both its flanks, and to open fire in passing on all likely looking woods on either side of the route. The 7th Rifle Regiment was to follow up in its carriers. The orders for the artillery and A.A. were first to cover the division as it debouched from the assembly area and then to leap-frog forward behind the moving attack. After the attack, the territory which had been overrun was to be occupied by the infantry and was to have artillery, anti-tank and anti-aircraft units positioned in it in depth in such a manner that the maximum artillery support could be provided against any attack, whether from the west, south or east.

I was able to give these orders verbally, undisturbed by the enemy artillery fire, which was still dropping intermittently into our territory. At 16.00 hours sharp, the tanks moved to the attack. The various arms worked in such perfect co-ordination that it might have been a peacetime exercise. The French colonial troops opposing us, who were dug in in the small woods on the southern slopes of hills 116 and 104 with large numbers of field and anti-tank guns, defended themselves desperately. However, the tanks and Reconnaissance Battalion poured such a hail of fire into the woods as they passed that the enemy fire was at first not too heavy. I rode in my command vehicle with Luft near the rear of the tank column and had good radio contact throughout with Heidkaemper and the regiments. From time to time enemy fire clanged against the vehicle's armoured sides and forced us to get our heads down. In the northern outskirts of Le Quesnoy a fierce battle developed. The Panzer Regiment mopped up the enemy in its usual style, in spite of the fact that they had installed themselves very skilfully round the outskirts of the village.

This was particularly true of the wall round Château le Quesnoy, which was held by a battalion of coloured troops. Stones had been wrenched out all along the wall to make loopholes from which large numbers of machine and anti-tank guns poured their fire into the oncoming tanks. But even here they had no success, for the rapid fire of our tanks, particularly the shells of the Panzer IVs, soon smashed the enemy forces. While one battalion of tanks moved round Le Quesnoy to the west, Rothenburg took the main body forward close alongside the wall. The armoured cars, following up behind, then held the enemy in check long enough to allow the leading infantry units to come up.

Firing and fighting without a break, the tanks rolled round both sides of Le Quesnoy and came out on the wide and coverless plain to its south. On they went through fields of high-grown corn. Any enemy troops who were sighted were either wiped out or forced to withdraw. Large numbers of prisoners were brought in, many of them hopelessly drunk. Most of the prisoners were coloured troops. Our objective for the day, as set by Corps, being the country east of Hornoy, I decided to continue the attack at 19.25 hours through Montagne-le-Fayel and Camps Amienois. Orders were quickly issued. A large concentration of enemy troops in the Bois de Riencourt was destroyed by the fire of the Panzer Regiment's tanks as they drove past. Over to our left, a giant pillar of smoke belched up from a burning enemy petrol tanker and numerous saddled horses stampeded riderless across the plain. Then heavy enemy artillery fire from the south-west crashed into the division, but was unable to halt its attack. Over a broad front and in great depth, tanks, anti-aircraft guns, field guns, all with infantry mounted on them, raced across country east of the road. Vast clouds of dust rose high into the evening sky over the flat plain.

A Corps order arrived refusing authority for the advance through Montagne-le-Fayel [*8 miles beyond the Somme*] because of the danger the division would run of attack by our own dive-bombers. I therefore gave orders, verbally and by radio, for the advance to be halted and all units to dig in in the area they had reached. This involved us in heavy fighting against strong enemy forces, principally on our right flank. Enemy tanks also put in an appearance, but they were soon disposed of either by the 88 mm. A.A. guns, the anti-tank guns, or the tanks. Enemy-held territory, south and east, and also west of our position, was heavily shelled for some time by every gun we could bring to bear, which took away their taste for attack. At 21.10 hours I passed back a message through the divisional staff: " All quiet forward, enemy in shreds." Then I drove back to headquarters.

I left headquarters very early next morning, the 6th June, with Hanke as escort, to drive up to the commander of the 25th Panzer Regiment. Heavy fighting had developed at several points late the previous evening and during the night, against enemy tanks and coloured troops. One A.A. battery had lost several 88 mm. guns in action against enemy artillery. It was 09.00 hours before I could get the regiment and battalion commanders together to brief them for the day's operations.

The attack began at 10.00 hours. We followed close behind the Panzer Regiment. The division, in extended order, over a 2,000-yard front and a depth of 12 miles, moved as if on an exercise. In this formation we advanced up hill and down dale, over highways and byways straight across country. The vehicles stood up to it well, even those which were not meant for cross-country work. With the tanks clashing every so often with enemy forces, the attack moved forward slowly enough for the infantry to follow up and maintain close contact.

Hermilly was captured by men of 7th Rifle Regiment after a fierce fight. The Panzer Regiment moved on south over a broad front and crossed the Caulières-Eplessier road [*20 miles beyond the Somme*] without fighting. Several unsuspecting civilians driving down the road were halted. Immense dust-clouds could be seen approaching in the rear, a sign that 6th Rifle Regiment's troop carriers were coming up in area formation.

On the 7th June Rommel swept forward more than 30 miles, a thrust which split the French Tenth Army that was defending the sector from Amiens to the sea. Two British divisions, the 51st (Highland) and the 1st Armoured, were in this army—the 51st being on the coastal flank.

At about nine o'clock I left Divisional H.Q. at Camps with Schraepler to drive via Poix to Eplessier. On the main road to Poix we met numerous horse-drawn columns and guns of the 6th Division. Poix itself had suffered considerably from bombardment, and sandbag barricades had been constructed by the French on all the roads. However, there did not seem to have been any serious fighting. The place was still burning at many points.

In Eplessier I had a brief meeting with the Corps Commander. After a few words of thanks and praise for the 7th Panzer Division's deeds south of the Somme, and a brief explanation of future plans, General Hoth gave his agreement to the attack which had been ordered for the

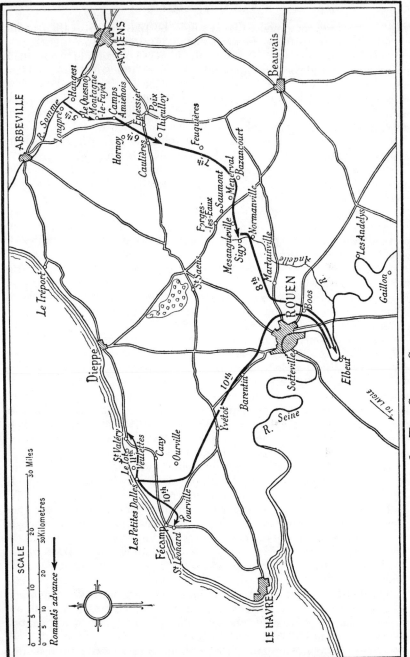

6. THE SOMME-SEINE BREAK-THROUGH

7th June. He even thought that it might be possible, with the existing
enemy situation, to thrust forward that day as far as Rouen.

We then drove on to Hill 184 south of Thieulloy la Ville, from which
point the left-hand column had been ordered to launch its attack at 10.00
hours. On the way we overtook the 6th Rifle Regiment and the 37th
Reconnaissance Battalion. At Point 184 I had another brief discussion
with Rothenburg and stressed the main points to be observed during the
day's advance; avoidance of villages—most of which were barricaded—
and all major roads; movement straight across country, thereby ensuring
a surprise appearance in the flank and rear of the enemy.

*Such a general cross-country advance was rarely attempted by the Allied
armoured forces in 1944-45. Many of the delays they suffered might have been
avoided by fuller use of this method of movement.*

The tanks moved off.

After some early delays, caused by mistakes in the route and too slow
correction from the map, the Panzer Regiment's attack flowed smoothly
forward.

The advance went straight across country, over roadless and trackless
fields, uphill, downhill, through hedges, fences and high cornfields. The
route taken by the tanks was so chosen that the less cross-country-worthy
vehicles of the 37th Reconnaissance Battalion and the 6th Rifle Regiment
could follow in their track-prints.

We met no enemy troops, apart from a few stragglers, but plenty of
indications in the shape of military vehicles and horses standing in open
country that they had left shortly before our arrival. Four French soldiers
were picked up near Feuquières. One of them, in spite of being severely
wounded, maintained his fire on our tanks right up to close quarters.
Fleeing civilians, and also troops, were on all the roads. Sometimes we
even surprised refugee lorries in open country, their occupants, men,
women and children, underneath the vehicles, where they had crawled
in mortal fear. We shouted to them, as we passed, to go back home.

East of Villers two enemy infantry guns and a light tank opened fire
on our tanks. They were quickly disposed of. Their crews, or those of
them who were still alive, fled into the wood.

From Bazancourt onwards our way led first along field paths and then
straight across country to the hills of Menerval, which we reached at
17.30 hours without any further fighting. In farms which we passed, the
people were hastily packing up, throwing bedding out of upper storey
windows into the yard, and would soon have been on the road if we had
not arrived.

In other farms carts stood packed high and ready harnessed; in others
again women and children took to their heels on sighting us and all our
shouting could not persuade them to return home. The only exception
was on Menerval Hill, where we found a farmer who had formerly been
a prisoner-of-war in Germany. He came up to us at once with his entire

family, shook hands and went off to the cellar to fetch cider for the thirsty German troops. He had, he said, got to know the Germans, and had no fear of them.

While the 25th Panzer Regiment now took possession of the hills round Menerval [*45 miles beyond the Somme*], the 37th Reconnaissance Battalion was ordered to reconnoitre west and south-west as far as the River Andelle [*7 miles beyond Menerval*], on either side of Sigy, and to get its main force up to Mesangueville, as its next objective.

After satisfying myself that the Panzer Regiment had occupied the important hills round Menerval, I drove to Captain Schultz's panzer company, which had been ordered to thrust forward into the wooded country west of Saumont as far as the main track intersection. The appearance of German troops on the main road from Paris to Dieppe near Saumont [*near Forges-les-Eaux*] had already sealed the fate of many French vehicles. By the time I arrived well over 40 vehicles had been picked up and traffic was still arriving from both directions. Panzer Company Schultz had also had great success in the woods east of Saumont, where a large ammunition depot had been captured. After fierce fighting at some points, they had taken 300 prisoners in quick time, including the supply staff of a French Army Corps, and captured 10 fighting vehicles and 100 lorries. As we drove back along the main Dieppe-Paris road we passed a German tankman bringing in a French tractor with a tank trailing behind it. The young soldier's face was radiant, full of joy at his success. We drove back to the new Division Headquarters, which had been erected by the staff in Marcoquet. It was, as usual, difficult to make our way back over the narrow, dusty roads, past the long approaching columns, and it was dark before we reached headquarters. When we arrived we found the Intelligence Officer, Major Ziegler, interrogating a number of French and British officers in the courtyard. Prisoners and booty for that day were tremendous and mounting hourly. Our losses were insignificant.

7 June 1940

DEAREST LU,

Your birthday was a thoroughly successful day. We laid about us properly. More and more signs of disintegration on the other side. We're all very, very well. Slept like a top.

The Andelle was now held, thinly, by British troops. To meet the emergency caused by the German break-through, an improvised force of nine infantry battalions (made up from lines-of-communication troops) had been hastily stretched along a 60-mile line from Dieppe to the Seine, to cover Rouen. It had no artillery and few anti-tank guns but the 1st Armoured Division, then refitting in rear, scraped up a brigade with 90 tanks to support the centre of the line. Rommel pierced the Andelle line next day at a point between the two main fractions of this armoured brigade—

which then withdrew southward and succeeded in slipping across the Seine at Gaillon before it was trapped.

On the 8th June, I called up the Ia at Corps shortly after 06.00 hours, informed him of the position and made a proposal for the attack which was planned on Rouen. I suggested that the 7th Panzer Division should push forward to a point some 4 miles east of Rouen and feign a direct assault on the city by artillery fire, after which the mass of the division would switch to the south-west with the object of seizing the Seine bridges at Elbeuf [*15 miles south-west of Rouen*] by a *coup de main* and cutting off the Seine bend.

After receiving the Ia's agreement, I drove quickly off with my escort officers to Menerval church, where I instructed the commanders to meet me at 08.30 hours for verbal briefing. To enable me to force the pace I took the leading battalion under my personal command. We moved off at 10.30 hours. Low-flying enemy air attacks on the battalion had little success to show for their efforts: the defence was too strong. We drove through the southern outskirts of Argeuil, finding no sign of enemy troops in the town. Now the main body of the division received orders to move off, and things went on fast as far as Sigy, where the Panzer Company, which had meanwhile taken the lead, was met with enemy fire, to which it gave an immediate and powerful reply.

During this brief engagement, the enemy blew the bridge over the river Andelle. We had observed the whole action from a point a few hundred yards away. The howitzer battery, which was close behind us, was now quickly pulled up forward and brought into action in the open. A motor-cycle company came up and anti-aircraft guns went into position. The roads were cleared and vehicles went into cover near a railway embankment. Meanwhile, I reconnoitred the chances of getting tanks across the river, and found a point 400 yards south of Sigy where it could probably be forded. Part of the Panzer Company was immediately brought up and sent across the river in support of the infantry who had already crossed to the other side.

Although there was over three feet of water near the eastern bank, the first tanks crossed without any trouble and soon overtook the infantry. However, when the first Panzer II attempted it, its engine cut out in midstream, leaving the crossing barred to all other vehicles. Meanwhile, several British soldiers had waded across to us with their hands up, and, with their help, our motor-cyclists started in to improve the crossing. Great pieces of the demolished railway bridge near by were thrown into the deepest part of the ford. Willows alongside the river were sawn down and similarly used to improve the passage across the ford. One of the Panzer IIIs which had already crossed was brought back to tow out the Panzer II.

At that moment I received a wireless signal saying that Lieut. Sauvant's reconnaissance troop had succeeded in preventing enemy preparations to blow the road and railway bridges in Normanville. Sauvant had both bridges firmly in his hands and was creating a bridgehead across the river with his reconnaissance troop.

At this good news, I at once broke off the action at Sigy and switched all forces south at top speed to cross the Andelle at Normanville. The division's assault group crossed the bridge and continued the advance to the west. Sigy was taken from the west at 14.00 hours with the capture of 100 British prisoners.

The route we now took by-passed, as far as possible, all villages. Good results had been achieved in the past few days by attacking away from the roads. The 25th Panzer Regiment's attack started punctually. At first we found no enemy troops in the small villages through which we passed. After some time we discovered that enemy dispatch riders and cars were suddenly travelling in our tank column. Here and there we heard isolated shots.

Towards 20.00 hours, one company of the Panzer Regiment was dispatched down the Rouen road to take the crossroad 5 miles east of the city and provide protection for the artillery and anti-aircraft units which were being sent there. My intention was to cause alarm among the enemy forces round Rouen by firing a long-range barrage, and thereby deceive them as to my true plans, which were to seize the Seine bridges at Elbeuf later that evening. The Panzer Company arrived at the cross-road by 20.00 hours, but the left-hand column did not come as well forward as I would have liked—the tail of the column had apparently become involved in fighting around Martainville—and we were consequently unable to get a quick deployment of the heavy artillery and anti-aircraft guns round the crossroad.

This seems to have been a brush with the tail of the British scratch force, which was retreating southward across Rommel's line of advance. The way he had repeatedly encountered British forces during this first short campaign, and the way their tracks crossed his, was a foreshadowing of future years.

With the day slowly fading, I waited in vain for the column to come up, until eventually part of the 7th Rifle Regiment came through. Apparently the right-hand column had also become involved in fighting and sometimes the noise of battle came so dangerously close that we were forced to leave the road and take to the bushes. Then prisoners began to be brought in from all sides and occasional enemy vehicles were discovered in concealed parking places. At long last, just before total darkness, a message came in that the right-hand column had arrived at the cross road 5 miles east of Rouen and established contact with the left-hand column. We now drove off quickly to the 25th Panzer Regiment to give orders for the thrust to the Seine bridges. About 15 minutes later, the left-hand column, consisting of the 25th Panzer Regiment and the 7th Motor-cycle Battalion, moved off as vanguard on the march to the Seine. We rode with the signals troop close behind the Panzer Regiment.

Soon it was completely dark. We passed a stranded enemy tank, which appeared to have lost a track and been abandoned by its crew.

While crossing the main road from Rouen to Pont St. Pierre in the eastern outskirts of Boos, the tail of the 25th Panzer Regiment's column was fired on at a range of about 100 yards, by an enemy tank or anti-tank gun. Probably the tank crews were unable to hear the gunfire and bursting shells above the noise of their engines, for at the end of a minute not one of our tanks had replied and the whole column was still proceeding steadily on its way to the south-west. The enemy gun was thus able to loose off some ten or fifteen rounds at us without being fired on in reply. It was extraordinary that none of our tanks was hit. To make the tank crews aware of this threat to their right flank, I sent orders to the commander of the nearest armoured car to open fire on the enemy with tracer. This soon brought the tanks into action and silenced the enemy gun. Then we went on our way through the night.

We had great difficulty in the darkness and with our inadequate maps in following the route. The noise of our passage as we drove through villages wakened people from their sleep, and brought them rushing out into the street to welcome us—as British. We drove past an enemy anti-aircraft battery. There was still light in the guardroom and the sentries paid us honours as we passed. It was not until next morning that we discovered that several anti-aircraft guns had stood ready for action a few yards away. We turned south at Les Authieux and reached the village of Sotteville at midnight—the first German troops to reach the Seine.

Tank brakes ground and screeched on the winding road. An occasional light flared up on the other side of the river. Lights were also burning at several points along the railway line running through the Seine valley. There were no enemy troops to be seen and everything looked set for the success of our dash for the Seine bridges. They were only nine miles away.

Radio communication had failed—the usual business at night time—and we had long been out of touch with the divisional staff and our other columns. The tank column rolled closer and closer to Elbeuf down the Seine valley. As we drove under a railway bridge a woman rushed out of a house on the right of the road, ran over to my staff car, and catching me by the arm, asked anxiously if we were British. She was sadly disappointed at the reply. I now had the Panzer Regiment halted and the Motor-cycle Battalion, reinforced by five Panzer IIIs, brought up into the lead past it. The motor-cyclists were to go on ahead and send out storming parties, each supported by several tanks, to seize the two bridges across the Seine at Elbeuf. They were then to keep a firm grasp of the bridges and hold them open. It took some time to filter the battalion forward past the Panzer Regiment and form it up with its tanks. We were still out of touch with the rest of the division.

The clock now crept on to 01.30 hours as we waited tensely for news of the storming parties. They must have long ago reached the Elbeuf bridges. Shortly after two I started for Elbeuf at the head of the 25th Panzer Regiment to see for myself how the enterprise had gone. I knew that dawn would be on us in 1½-2 hours and that it might then be inadvisable to be caught standing in column on the Seine valley road, for the enemy probably had artillery in position on the south bank of the Seine. I therefore wanted to get the main body of my troops at all costs on to the hills on one side or the other of the Seine by dawn.

In Elbeuf, we found a wild confusion of our vehicles in the narrow streets north of the Seine and I was forced to go forward on foot to get to the head of 7th Motor-cycle Battalion. There I found that the storming parties had still not yet made their attempt on the bridges, although the battalion had already been in Elbeuf well over an hour. I was informed that when the battalion had entered Elbeuf, they had found the bridges carrying a lively traffic of civil and military vehicles. An officer also told me that there had already been shooting near the bridges.

The situation was confused and prospects of success were pretty slim now that the battalion had stood in the town for a whole hour only a few hundred yards away from the bridges. But there might still be a chance, I thought, and I gave the battalion commander orders to launch his assault on the two bridges immediately. Under cover of the darkness I took myself up closer to the bridge. Civilians stood around in the streets and there were sandbag barricades at the crossroads, on one of which lay a dead French soldier. More valuable minutes slipped by while the storming parties were forming up. At last the first party moved off; it was shortly before 03.00 [*9th June*]. But they never reached the bridge, for the enemy blew it before they had gone a hundred yards. The same happened a few minutes later with the second storming party. Further heavy detonations followed from west and east, from close at hand and farther distant. The French had blown all the Seine bridges.

I was extremely angry over the failure of our enterprise. I had no idea where the main body of the division was. We had behind us the many enemy-held villages we had driven through during the night, and as dawn broke saw two captive observation balloons in the sky near Rouen. It was beginning to look as though we were in for a fight. I therefore decided to pull back out of the elongated peninsula into which we had advanced. The troops moved off quickly. Fortunately, the Seine basin lay shrouded in mist and we had no need to fear enemy fire from the opposite bank.

9 June 1940

DEAREST LU,
    Two glorious days in pursuit, first south, then south-west. A roaring success. 45 miles yesterday.

10 June 1940 5 a.m.

We'll soon be at the sea between the Somme and the Seine. I'm in fine form although I'm on the go the whole time. Our successes are tremendous and it looks to me inevitable that the other side will soon collapse.

We never imagined war in the west would be like this. There's been no post from you for several days.

The division now began to clean up the territory we had overrun. Rouen had meanwhile fallen to the 5th Panzer Division. Late that afternoon my division was instructed to prepare for a thrust to Le Havre, and the confirming Corps order arrived in the evening. The plan was for us to make a quick thrust through to the coast in order to cut off the escape of two or three British and French infantry divisions and one or two tank battalions through the port of Le Havre. The 25th Panzer Regiment now received orders to move first into the district south-west of Pissy. The Armoured Reconnaissance Battalion was to occupy the eastern outskirts of Yvetot [*22 miles north-west of Rouen*] as soon as possible and then probe towards the sea. I intended to follow up the Reconnaissance Battalion with the mass of the division as quickly as possible and then thrust on to the sea.

This meant that, after reaching the Seine, Rommel had to make a right-angled turn to the north-west, after his south-westerly drive from the Somme to the Seine.

At 07.30 hours [*10th June*] I drove round the north of Rouen to Barentin, giving orders by radio on the way for the division to join up with me. Road demolitions were reported by the Reconnaissance Battalion east of Yvetot. They were also repeatedly reporting the capture of British prisoners both with and without vehicles. A civilian, who maintained that he had left Le Havre at five o'clock that morning, was brought to me for interrogation. To my questions, which were interpreted to him by a French-speaking officer, he replied that on the previous day he had seen only a few British soldiers sitting about in cafés, and no formations or units. The roads had been prepared for demolition at various points a week before, but they were not mined, and it was possible to zig-zag past the obstructions. The man, who said he wanted to get through to Paris, gave the impression of being reliable. So it seemed that there was no need for the moment to worry about an enemy threat from Le Havre. I had the man's statement passed back by wireless. After filling up with petrol, the Panzer Regiment moved off to Yvetot at 09.20 hours; at the same time I gave the Reconnaissance Battalion orders to reconnoitre immediately up towards Veulettes [*on the coast, 20 miles north of Yvetot*].

These orders had just been issued, when a radio signal came in from Major Heidkaemper informing us that a powerful enemy motorised column had been reported moving west out of the forest north of St.

British and French prisoners at St. Valéry. June 11th, 1940. [*Rommel's own photograph*]

The surrender at St. Valéry. Extreme right, General Fortune, commander of the 51st Highland Division. The bareheaded figure is the liberated Luftwaffe pilot referred to in the text. [*Photograph taken with Rommel's camera*]

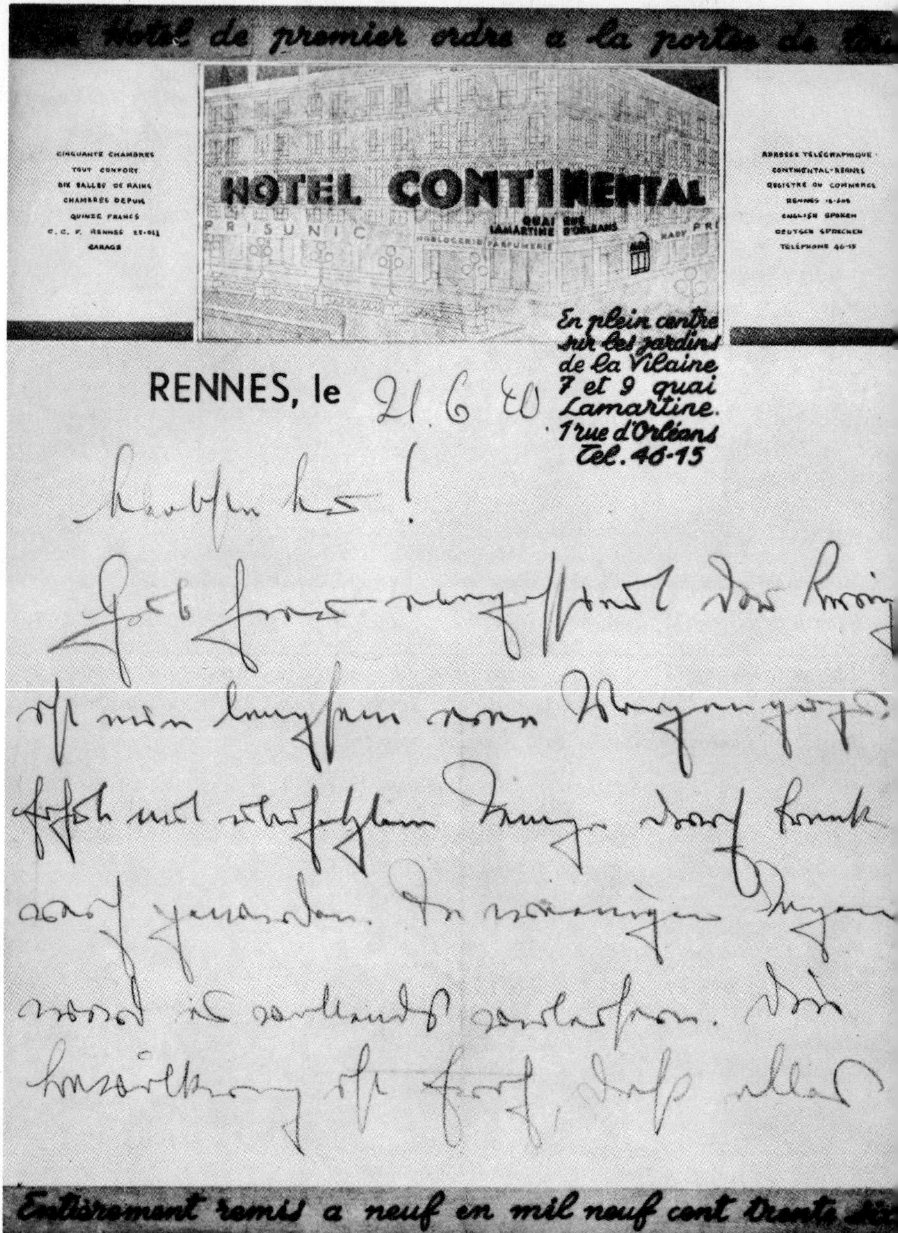

Hotel de premier ordre a la portée de

CINQUANTE CHAMBRES
TOUT CONFORT
SIX SALLES DE BAINS
CHAMBRES DEPUIS
QUINZE FRANCS
C.C.F. RENNES 21-011
GARAGE

HOTEL CONTINENTAL
QUAI LAMARTINE
RUE D'ORLÉANS

ADRESSE TÉLÉGRAPHIQUE
CONTINENTAL-RENNES
REGISTRE DU COMMERCE
RENNES 16-608
ENGLISH SPOKEN
DEUTSCH SPRECHEN
TÉLÉPHONE 46-15

En plein centre sur les jardins de la Vilaine 7 et 9 quai Lamartine 1 rue d'Orléans Tel. 46-15

RENNES, le 21.6.40

Entièrement remis a neuf en mil neuf cent trente

Rommel's letter to his wife, June 21st, 1940

[*See page 85*]

Saëns, and that, by all calculations, this force must be just about arriving at Yvetot. The Reconnaissance Battalion was accordingly given orders to close the main St. Saëns-Yvetot road immediately and to open fire as early as possible on the enemy force moving down it. I also had one heavy and one light A.A. battery brought up past the Panzer Regiment, and drove off with them at high speed towards Yvetot. I arrived at the road fork east of the town shortly before 10.00 hours and the A.A. batteries came in one after the other a few minutes later. They went straight into position at top speed and received orders to lay down a heavy fire on the road, on which a large number of enemy vehicles could already be seen.

When the Panzer Regiment appeared in sight of Yvetot at about 10.30 hours, I had the Reconnaissance Battalion launched against the crossroad two miles east of Ourville, closely followed over the same road by the Panzer Regiment. I positioned my signals troop immediately behind the first tanks. All other units of the division received orders by radio to make a further quick move forward. There were now two columns driving up the road, sometimes side by side, the tanks on the left and the Reconnaissance Battalion on the right. Wherever the ground was in any way suitable, the tanks took a track alongside the road. The division now went all out for the sea at an average speed of 25-40 m.p.h. I had already issued orders through H.Q. for all units to increase their speed to the maximum. No enemy force worthy of our notice had so far been sighted.

As we approached the main Cany-Fécamp road a dispatch rider from the Reconnaissance Battalion reported that Captain von Luck had found enemy lorry columns on the main road and was rounding them up. We at once drove up to the road to find that while single enemy vehicles had already got away to the west, there were others halted on the road to the east. It had every appearance of being a considerable formation. I at once gave orders to the leading tanks, which were just then arriving, and the armoured cars and light A.A. guns to open fire immediately on the enemy standing on the road. After a short time large numbers of British and French troops came running along the road to us. A quick interrogation revealed that it was the beginning of 31st French Division, which was to have embarked at Fécamp that afternoon. There were also some scattered British troops among them. The enemy column was quickly broken up and, while armoured cars and A.A. guns took the road beyond them under fire, the van of the division moved on again at high speed to the sea. With my signals section I drove on in advance of the regiment through Les Petites Dalles and down to the water [*10 miles east of Fécamp, and 6 miles west of Veulettes*].

The sight of the sea with the cliffs on either side thrilled and stirred every man of us; also the thought that we had reached the coast of France. We climbed out of our vehicles and walked down the shingle beach to the water's edge until the water lapped over our boots. Several dispatch riders in long waterproof coats walked straight out until the water was over their knees, and I had to call them back. Close behind us Rothenburg came up in his command tank, crashed through the beach wall, and drove down to the water. Our task was over and the enemy's road to Le Havre and Fécamp was closed.

Shortly afterwards the Brigade Commander, Colonel Fuerst, arrived with the commander of a French artillery regiment and several French officers. The French colonel was extremely impressed by the speed of our advance, but beyond that there was nothing to be had out of him.

A report now came in from the Reconnaissance Battalion to the effect that they were under heavy enemy pressure on the hill east of Fécamp. After briefly discussing the essentials of the situation with Heidkaemper, I drove off to Fécamp, to find that the Reconnaissance Battalion had meanwhile succeeded in getting the situation under control. A storming party under the command of Lieut. Sauvant had captured a coast defence battery which had been heavily shelling the battalion. We drove on towards the captured battery, but left our vehicles and walked the last 200 yards, as enemy guns were still firing from the western side of the town and the hills to its south. From the captured gun position we had an excellent view over the town and harbour, which apparently still contained strong enemy forces.

With the arrival of the two panzer companies and the Motor-cycle Battalion which had been sent to the aid of the Reconnaissance Battalion, I decided to push forward through the eastern outskirts of Fécamp to the hills south of the town. I wanted to prevent the enemy units still in the town from escaping to the south, and to get possession of the port at the earliest possible moment. This move led to a number of clashes with the enemy and we were more than once forced to change our plan. Finally, we bore off through Tourville with the intention of making a quick run up the main road from the south to St. Leonard. We had no time to lose, for it was already 22.00 hours. During the descent to Tourville, we received a tremendous welcome from the people of a workers' settlement, who apparently took us for British. Just south of Tourville, we drove through a road-block at the same moment as some British motor-cyclists rode up to it from the direction of Fécamp. The British stared a moment, then swung round and made off back as fast as they could go. The crew of my command car wanted to open fire, but I stopped them, because we were, for one thing, very short of time and, even more important, it would have given away our détour to the enemy around us and raised the alarm. A civilian whom we met on the road pointed north and said there were still plenty of British troops to be found up there. Shortly afterwards the leading tank fired a few rounds from its gun. I had no idea of the cause and, hearing no enemy fire, walked up forward, to find that the fire had been aimed at an enemy road-block. With less than an hour to darkness, and a pitch-black night ahead I could no longer enter into a slow probe forward but was compelled to demand that the tanks plunge forward at their top speed to St. Leonard, either on the road or alongside it. I led them myself for some way along the darkening village street. Not a shot was fired. Out in the open country again, we saw that the British had driven their vehicles off the road and concealed themselves behind bushes and hedges. A few of them were winkled out and taken along by the infantry and tanks following up behind. We had no time to halt, however, but pushed quickly on to St. Leonard. The motor-cyclists behind us had a short but successful clash with the British.

Captain von Hagen now received orders to occupy both roads from Fécamp leading south through St. Leonard with six tanks, bar them to traffic and establish an all-round defence. This was achieved without fighting. A bad traffic jam occurred on the road, however, when the motor-cyclists started to filter past both panzer companies just as the latter were turning for the trip back. I had given the panzer companies orders to return to their regiment that night once the Motor-cycle Battalion had reached St. Leonard. Knowing that it might be extremely important for me to be at Division H.Q. early next morning, I decided to drive back with the tanks.

We began the return journey at 23.00 hours. With the road still solidly blocked by the Motor-cycle Battalion, only one panzer company could leave with us. We drove behind the third tank. On the way we passed a number of enemy vehicles, which had apparently driven into the Motor-cycle Battalion's convoy in the darkness; their crews had been taken prisoner. Some of them looked as though they had put up a fight for it first. Suddenly anti-tank gunfire opened from a village just ahead, and the leading tank was hit in a track. The enemy gun then began to fire rapid along the road close over our heads. Without replying to the fire, the tanks in front of us drove straight up on the embankment on both sides of the road. The leading tank remained where it had been hit. My vehicle was now left standing only 150 yards away from the enemy gun, with round after round whistling a hairsbreadth overhead—not a comfortable situation. When, after two or three minutes of this our tanks had still not opened fire, I jumped down from my vehicle and ran to the Panzer II standing on the embankment left of the road, where I also found the commander of the leading tank. I told him what I thought of him for not having opened fire immediately and for having left his tank. Then I ordered the Panzer II to open fire at once, with both tank-gun and machine-gun, on the enemy anti-tank position, in order to give the whole column a chance of getting away to the left out of the cutting through which the road ran at this point.

When fire was at last opened, the Panzer II's 20 mm. shells and tracer ammunition caused such a firework display that the enemy ceased fire, as I had expected. We now managed to get my command truck up

the embankment, but it was too steep for the staff car and the armoured
cars and dispatch riders, and so I sent them back to spend the night with
the Motor-cycle Battalion.

Then we drove off with the Panzer Company. It was no easy task
in the pitch black night to find our way across country, in which we
might at any moment run into another enemy force, and required the
utmost vigilance.

11 June 1940

DEAREST LU,

Over 60 miles in the pursuit yesterday, reached the sea west of
Dieppe and cut off several divisions (French and British). Took two
ports, overcame batteries, bombarded warships—some severely
damaged. I didn't get back this morning until 3 a.m. To-day we're
bathing and sleeping.

Next day [*11th June*] the division moved out of Veulettes at about
noon, with the Panzer Regiment and part of 6th Rifle Regiment, to
advance along the coast to St. Valéry. [*This is St. Valéry-en-Caux, 6 miles
east of Veulettes and 20 miles west of Dieppe.*] I took my *Gefechtsstaffel* and
drove with the Panzer Regiment. On the hills a mile east of Veulettes
the enemy met us with heavy artillery and anti-tank gunfire, and we
bore off to the south-east. But the enemy fire grew in violence and
heavy batteries joined in, so that all movement was frequently pinned
down. Every lull in the fire was used to drive closer to the enemy. The
rifle company, which was equipped with armoured troop-carriers, did
not, however, follow up the attack, which the 25th Panzer Regiment,
despite the enemy fire, carried closer and closer to the enemy. Near Le
Tot the British had built a fortified line and resistance was heavy. So
tenacious was the enemy defence that hand-to-hand combat developed
at many points. Meanwhile, the 25th Panzer Regiment had thrust
forward to the high ground immediately north-west of St. Valéry and was
using every gun to prevent the embarkation of enemy troops. We drove
up as far as the Panzer Regiment with the *Gefechtsstaffel* and then walked
some distance farther on to get a look at the situation round St. Valéry.
British troops could be seen moving about among the port installations
and there were more troops with guns and vehicles in the northern part
of the town.

Elements of the Panzer Regiment and dispatch riders of my staff
did their best to summon the enemy, who were now only a few hundred
yards away, to give themselves up. In the course of the next few hours
we did, in fact, succeed in persuading about a thousand men to surrender
in the northern part of St. Valéry, including many officers. Most of them
were French and there were comparatively few British. Among the
latter there was one naval officer who had spent a long time haranguing

his men on the mole and apparently succeeded in dissuading them from surrendering. Finally, we opened up on this officer with machine-guns from the cliff about 200 yards away, without, as we found later, hitting him. For half an hour he lay as if dead behind a heap of stones, but then decided it was better to surrender. He spoke fluent German and, when accused by Major Schraepler of being to blame for so many of his men being wounded, replied: " Would you have acted differently in my situation? "[1]

That evening I sent a large number of German-speaking prisoners into St. Valéry itself, which was still full of enemy troops, to call on them to surrender by 21.00 hours and march under cover of white flags to the hills west of St. Valéry. It was mainly the British, though there were some French officers also, who turned down all idea of capitulation and sent our negotiators back empty handed. They kept their men hard at it building barricades and getting large numbers of guns and machine-guns into position all round St. Valéry and especially in the port area. Probably the British were hoping to resume their embarkation during the night.

In these circumstances, therefore, the concentrated fire of the division, including the Panzer Regiment and the Reconnaissance Battalion, which had been brought up in the meantime, was unleashed at 21.00 hours. A Panzer IV smashed the strong barricade on the mole, in which numerous guns had been positioned, and left it in flames. Fires were soon blazing everywhere. After a quarter of an hour, I had the whole division's fire directed on to the northern part of the town, where, as we saw next day, the effect was particularly devastating. The tenacious British, however, still did not yield.

Despite the violence of the fighting that afternoon, the division's casualties had been small. One very sad loss was Major Kentel, one of the 25th Panzer Regiment's battalion commanders, who had been mortally wounded by a shell splinter. Meanwhile, the infantry had arrived on the hills west of St. Valéry and at nightfall the tanks were withdrawn from the forward line, and light and heavy A.A. guns went into position. The infantry were ordered to maintain a harassing fire all night to prevent the enemy embarking his troops.

After returning to my H.Q., I discussed the situation with Heidkaemper. There was good reason to expect that the enemy would attempt a break out in strength during the night, either to the west or south-west. Heidkaemper had prudently taken all necessary counter measures to meet this, but it was doubtful whether they could be effective in time. To satisfy myself that a break-out attempt could be held, I drove off at

[1]This officer has been identified by the Admiralty as Commander (now Rear-Admiral) R. F. Elkins, C.V.O., O.B.E., at that time Naval Liaison Officer with 51st (Highland) Division. He figures on the extreme left of the top photograph taken by Rommel page 58. He did not long remain a prisoner, however, but escaped four days later and was back in England by the end of June, 1940.

06.30 hours next morning, the 12th June, to the threatened sectors of the front. Driving across country, I saw troops everywhere entrenched in depth. Anti-tank and anti-aircraft units were also in position. To enable me to deal with any break-out attempt quickly and effectively, I gave orders at 07.00 hours for the main body of the Panzer Regiment to move off immediately and remain at my disposal.

After visiting the Rifle Regiments, I was informed by radio that the enemy were attempting to make their way out in small boats under cover of warships to a number of transports which were lying one to two thousand yards off shore east of St. Valéry.

At about 10.00 hours the Panzer Regiment reached its old position of the previous day, where a violent duel had meanwhile taken place between an 88 mm. A.A. battery and an enemy warship, in which two of our guns had been lost by direct hits. About 1,000 yards north-east of St. Valéry an enemy transport was just steaming out to sea. Our A.A. battery had ceased fire. I at once had fire reopened on the enemy transport from an 88 mm. gun close by, although the mounting of this gun had been hit and it no longer stood firmly on all four feet. The crew worked splendidly and shells were soon falling hard by the ship. However, the damage to the mounting made it impossible to apply the necessary corrections. Meanwhile, the gun had come under fire from a British auxiliary cruiser lying 1,000 yards off shore. A smoke screen which I had laid to cover the gun from the warship's fire, proved very effective. Our gun crew, however, had no success with the enemy transport. Dive-bombers had already been called up by radio. Shortly afterwards I met a forward observer from a 100 mm. battery and instructed him to take the enemy auxiliary cruiser under fire immediately. At 10.40 hours the ship was set alight by several hits, and beached by her crew.

Meanwhile, I had brought up my *Gefechtsstaffel* past the wood north-west of St. Valéry as far as the first houses of the town. Rothenburg had orders to take the Panzer Regiment down the roads leading into the valley, steadily closer to the town, which was still burning at many points. The tanks, concealed by the undergrowth, rolled slowly down the narrow winding roads, nearer and nearer to the first houses, until finally they entered the western quarter of the town. I went on foot beside the tanks with Colonel Rothenburg and Lieut. Luft and we reached the western mole of the inner harbour without fighting. Fifty to a hundred yards away from us on the opposite side stood a number of British and French soldiers, irresolute, with their rifles grounded. Close beside them were numerous guns, which appeared to have been damaged by our bombardment. Fires were blazing all over the farther side of the town and there was war material lying about everywhere, including large numbers of vehicles. The Panzer Regiment's tanks rolled on steadily yard by yard to the south, with their guns traversed east, past rows of captured vehicles parked on the western side of the harbour. Meanwhile, we tried to persuade the enemy troops facing us to lay down their arms and walk across a narrow wooden bridge towards us. It was some minutes before the British could bring themselves to it. At first they came across singly, with long intervals between each man, then gradually the file began to thicken. Our infantry now went across to the other side to receive British and French prisoners on the spot.

While the tanks were moving round the southern side of the harbour towards the eastern quarter of the town, I followed the infantry across the narrow bridge to the market square. The town hall and many buildings round it were either already burnt out or still burning. Barricades, which the enemy had constructed out of vehicles and numerous guns, had also felt the effect of our fire. French and British troops were now streaming in from all sides to the market square, where they were formed up into columns and marched off to the west. The infantry were cleaning up the town house by house and street by street.

Shortly afterwards an N.C.O. reported to me that a high ranking French general had been taken prisoner on the eastern side of the town and was asking to see me. A few minutes later the French General Ihler came up to me wearing an ordinary plain military overcoat. His escort officer fell to the rear as he approached. When I asked the General what division he commanded, he replied in broken German: " No division. I command IX Corps."

The General declared himself ready to accept my demand for the immediate capitulation of his force. He added, however, that he would not have been standing there surrendering if his force had had any ammunition left.

The General's aide-de-camp, who spoke German, told us that the number of divisions involved was five, including at least one British. I now required the Corps Commander to return to his headquarters and issue orders, through his own command channels, for his troops to surrender and march off immediately with prominent white flags in the direction of St. Valéry. I wanted to ensure that our troops were able to see from a distance that the enemy had laid down their arms.

I then requested the General to present himself with his staff in the market square of St. Valéry and agreed to his request that he should be allowed his own vehicle and kit. Orders were issued to the artillery to cease all fire on St. Valéry and district and to fire only on shipping. The 5th Panzer Division, which had been reported in action at 11.40 hours against enemy tanks in the neighbourhood of Manneville [*2 miles south-east of St. Valéry*], was notified of the enemy surrender at St. Valéry. During the next few hours no less than twelve Generals were brought in as prisoners, among them four divisional commanders. A particular joy for us was the inclusion among them of General Fortune, commander of the 51st British Division, and his staff. I now agreed divisional boundaries with my neighbour, General Cruewell, commander of the 2nd Motorised Division. Meanwhile, the captured Generals and staff officers had been assembled in a house south of the market place. A German Luftwaffe lieutenant, who had just been liberated from captivity, was made responsible for the guard. He was visibly delighted by the change of role.

Particularly surprising to us was the *sang froid* with which the British officers accepted their fate. The General, and even more, his staff officers, stalked round laughing in the street in front of the house. The only thing that seemed to disturb them was the frequent photographing and filming they had to endure by our Propaganda Company and some other photographers.

The captured generals were now invited to an open air lunch at a German field kitchen, but they refused with thanks, saying that they still had supplies of their own. So we ate alone. There were still arrangements to be made for transporting away the prisoners, especially the numerous officers, for salvaging the equipment, securing the coast and evacuating St. Valéry. At about 20.00 hours we returned to Divisional H.Q. at Château Auberville.

It was impossible at that stage to estimate the total of prisoners and booty. 12,000 men, of whom 8,000 were British, were transported off by the 7th Panzer Division's vehicles alone. The total number of prisoners captured at St. Valéry is said to have numbered 46,000 men.

12 June 1940

DEAREST LU,
The battle is over here. To-day one corps commander and four division commanders presented themselves before me in the market square of St. Valéry, having been forced by my division to surrender. Wonderful moments! "

14 June 1940

On to Le Havre and inspected the town. It all went without bloodshed. We're now engaging targets out to sea with long-range artillery. Already set one transport alight to-day.

You can imagine my feelings when 12 Generals of the British and French Armies reported to me and received my orders in the market place of St. Valéry. The British General and his division were a particular source of joy. The whole thing was filmed and will no doubt be in the news reels.

Now we're getting a few days' rest. I can't think that there'll be any more serious fighting in France. We've even had flowers along the road in some places. The people are glad that the war is over for them.

16 June 1940

Before setting off south this morning (05.30 hours) I received your dear letter of the 10th, for which my heartfelt thanks. To-day we're crossing the Seine in the second line and will, I hope, get a good step forward on the southern bank. With the fall of Paris and Verdun, and a wide break-through of the Maginot Line near Saarbruecken, the war seems to be gradually becoming a more or less peaceful occupation of all France. The population is peacefully disposed, and in some places very friendly.

CHAPTER IV

PURSUIT TO CHERBOURG

After a brief pause to rest and reorganise, Rommel's division was switched back to the Seine south of Rouen. Crossings had been made there on the 9th June, on the heels of the French Tenth Army, which was so badly shaken that the Germans were able to get across this wide water-line with little fighting. The Tenth Army then fell back westwards to the line of the Risle, whereas its neighbour retreated southward. To exploit the fresh split in the French front, the leading German infantry corps pressed their advance southwards towards the Loire, while Rommel's division was brought down behind them on the 16th June and then launched westward next day on a drive for Cherbourg.

On the night of the 16th the French Tenth Army had begun a fresh step back, and the remaining British troops serving with it were ordered to withdraw to Cherbourg for re-embarkation to England—as resistance was already collapsing. That order was given in the nick of time for them, as the sector they had been holding lay south of the route of Rommel's drive next morning, and they only just succeeded in reaching Cherbourg before they were cut off.

On the 17th June 1940, the division resumed its advance south of the Seine, in the first place into the Laigle district. The 7th Panzer Division had instructions to push through as far as the Nonant-Sées road. After arriving at this road, the division was to be reinforced by the Brigade Senger and was then to strike on and capture the French naval port of Cherbourg. Air reconnaissance had reported the presence in Cherbourg of either warships or transports and it was therefore highly probable that embarkation was in progress there.

The advance was made in two columns, neither of which at this stage met any serious resistance. A few road-blocks were eliminated, a number of prisoners made and several tanks captured. As soon as I heard that the head of both columns had reached the Nonant-Sées road, I gave orders for the attack to be continued round the flank of Sées. Routes were as follows:

For the right-hand column, via Maroques, round the south of Ecouché, then along the main road to Briouze and from there past the south side of Flers to Landissacq.

For the left-hand column, via Macé, Méhéran, St. Brice, Le Ménil to La Chapelle.

I drove with my *Gefechtsstaffel* in the left-hand column. Things went fairly fast as far as Montmerrei, where 20 French soldiers were taken prisoner at about 13.00 hours. The column then pushed on towards Bouce. In Francheville I received a report that enemy tanks were holding the entry into Bouce and closing the road, although our reconnaissance troops had not so far been fired on. Since our column contained nothing more than armoured cars, I ordered an immediate diversion to the north. We now came across small groups of French troops all along the route, whom we had no difficulty in making our prisoners. Among them were several carloads of French officers, one of whom spoke German and was accordingly now used as an interpreter. Dense clouds of dust were stirred up by our passage over the side roads. Soon the head of the column clashed with enemy motor-cyclists, whom they quickly eliminated by their fire. Close behind the motor-cyclists, however, we met a French column on the march. They were taken completely by surprise at our appearance and did not seem very anxious to fight. Negotiations opened between Captain von Luck [*commander of 37th Armoured Reconnaissance Battalion*] and the French captain. I soon went forward myself to find out what had caused the halt.

The French captain declared that Marshal Pétain had made an armistice proposal to Germany and had instructed the French troops to lay down their arms. I had the French captain informed, through our interpreter, that we had heard nothing of this armistice and that I had orders to march on. I added that we would not open fire on any French troops who surrendered and laid down their arms. I then requested the French captain to free the road for our advance and have his column moved off to the fields alongside it and ordered to lay down their arms and fall out. The French captain still seemed to hesitate as to whether or not he should do this. Anyway, it took too long to get the French troops into their parking place and so I gave my column orders to move on. We now drove on past the French column, which stood on the road with its guns and anti-tank guns still limbered up. The French captain looked a trifle disconcerted as we passed, but his men seemed to be quite satisfied with this solution. We met more French troops behind this column and beckoned to them with white handkerchiefs, calling out that the war was over for them. The advance went on at a speed of 25 to 30 m.p.h. The next villages we came to were full of French coloured troops, with their guns and vehicles parked in orchards and farmyards. We drove past at top speed, waving, but not otherwise bothering about them. In this way we got through without fighting. After overtaking more convoys of brand-new American-built vehicles, we reached the neighbourhood of Montreuil [*40 miles west of Laigle, and 12 miles W.S.W. of Argentan*] at about 17.30 hours, where I ordered an hour's rest for a meal, and, above all, to refill our tanks.

Since there seemed to be little further need to worry about serious resistance, I decided to continue the advance at 18.40 hours, with Cherbourg, which was still 140 miles[1] away, as the objective. Our right-hand column, consisting of the 7th Motor-cycle Battalion and part of the 25th Panzer Regiment, had met with enemy resistance in the neighbourhood of Ecouché between 16.00 and 17.00 hours, but this action now seemed to be over. I also decided to make the rest of the journey over main roads via Flers, Coutances and Barneville to Cherbourg, and to take the whole division forward in one column.

This was an indirect approach, as Coutances lies close to the west coast of the Cotentin Peninsula. Not until reaching this point did Rommel turn north up the west coast route to Cherbourg.

Details of the new objective and route were transmitted by radio to the different parts of the division, although the messages did not get through to one or two units.

At 18.40 hours the 37th Armoured Reconnaissance Battalion began the advance to Cherbourg. They had orders to keep up the pace. We reached the main road in a few minutes, where we found Panzer Company Hanke, which I ordered to join up with us. The right-hand column now received orders by radio to follow the left via Flers to Cherbourg.

We now raced on at top speed towards Flers. There were French troops encamped on both sides of the road, and we waved to them as we drove by. They stared in wonderment when they saw a German column racing past. Nowhere was there any shooting. For the next few hours we went steadily on at about 30 m.p.h. motoring in perfect formation through one village after the other. A short halt was made in Flers, due to difficulty in finding the right road. Crowds of people in the streets, both troops and civilians, looked on curiously and without taking up any kind of hostile attitude, at our hurried progress through the town.

In the western outskirts of Flers we passed a large square crowded, as usual, with French soldiers and civilians. Suddenly a civilian a few yards from the column ran towards my car with drawn revolver, intending to shoot, but French troops pulled him up short and prevented him carrying out his purpose. We drove on. I now had the whole division behind me and was anxious to get to Cherbourg as quickly as possible. I was very conscious of the fact that the territory we were crossing was full of French troops, though their fighting value was probably low. It looked indeed as though Pétain's request for an armistice was already common knowledge here. I was also under no illusions that the mass of the division would be able to keep up our speed, but reckoned that any units that fell behind would be able to catch up in a few hours. The Reconnaissance Battalion raced steadily on, with never a stop. We had already been driving for more than twelve hours. One French town after another was left behind us without a shot being fired. Night fell,

[1]It was actually about 130 miles by the route which Rommel took.

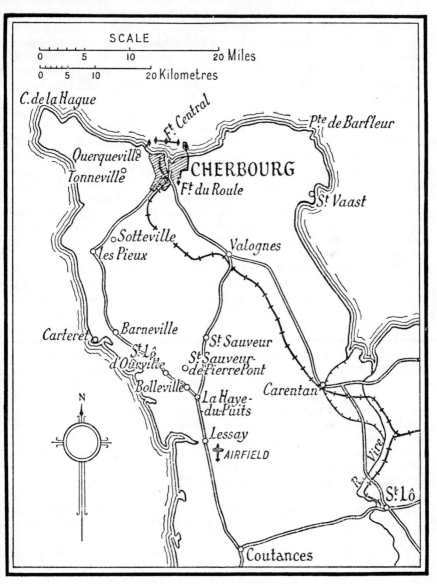

7. THE DRIVE INTO CHERBOURG

revealing enormous fires burning to our right front, probably coming from petrol and oil stores set alight by the enemy on the Lessay airfield [*30 miles north of Coutances, and 34 miles south of Cherbourg*]. As usual after nightfall, radio contact now failed. I knew that Senger's brigade, which was on our right, had not yet come up and supposed it to be in the neighbourhood of Falaise [*i.e. 130 miles behind*]. This did not alter my decision, however, for I thought I would be able to cope with Cherbourg alone.

After it had grown quite dark two officers reported to me, having overtaken the column in a car. In the darkness I failed at first to recognise their dust-covered faces, but they turned out to be Captain Kolbeck and Lieut. Hausberg from the Fuehrer's H.Q. Hausberg informed me that he had been posted to my division and I immediately installed him as aide-de-camp. Kolbeck had not been posted to me, but had merely taken this opportunity of getting a trip to the front. I now sent Captain Stollbrueck, my escort officer, back over our road on a motor-cycle to ensure that everybody was following and to hand each regiment its orders for the attack on Cherbourg. We would be there, barring obstacles, in three hours.

On we raced without a stop into the dark night. It was about midnight when the Reconnaissance Battalion drove across the market square of La-Haye-du-Puits [*5 miles north of Lessay*]. There was a surprising number of men in working clothes standing in the square and behind them a number of lorries laden with material. They were mainly civilian workmen, there were few troops, although several French officers could be seen hurrying busily around. One of them ran through the column directly in front of my car and vanished into a doorway. We drove on. As we passed the church I noticed a heavy French lorry carrying a gun of 88 to 100 mm. calibre standing beside it. Still without halting, the leading vehicles of the Reconnaissance Battalion, under Lieut. Isermayer, bore off as ordered on the secondary road to Bolleville and then drove at a smart pace onwards. I was just turning over in my mind the detailed deployment of the division in front of Cherbourg, when the head of the column suddenly ran up against a defended roadblock and came under very heavy artillery and machine-gun fire. The leading vehicles were hit and three went up in flames. Lieut. Isermayer, who had been riding in the first vehicle, was seriously wounded in the head and lay unconscious beside his burning vehicle.

By all appearances, the road-block was held by a considerable enemy force. The moon was now up but I still did not like the idea of attacking immediately with tired troops and without artillery and tanks. I therefore gave the Reconnaissance Battalion orders to break off the action and not to move against the enemy position until daybreak.

Rommel's division had covered more than 150 miles since morning, and more than 100 miles since its early evening halt to refuel. This far exceeded any day's advance which had ever been made in warfare.

Then I drove back with my signals troop to La Haye-du-Puits. We still had no contact with the infantry regiment behind us. On arrival at La Haye-du-Puits, I took my stand by the church with Kolbeck, Hausberg, a few dispatch riders, an armoured car and a signal lorry. The heavy lorry we had seen on our way through, with the gun aboard, was no longer in its old place. The labour column had also disappeared from the market square.

A car coming up the main road from Cherbourg was halted. Its occupant, a French naval officer, told us that he was an engineer officer and that he had instructions to supervise a labour column building barricades at this point against the German advance. I told him to return to Cherbourg and report that he had come too late.

A few minutes later a number of British officers returning in a car from sea bathing in the south were halted and taken prisoner. Then Colonel von Unger arrived with the 6th Rifle Regiment. I now issued orders for the next morning's attack on the enemy road-block. I was satisfied that we would be able to break through the enemy positions three miles north-west of La Haye-du-Puits and resume our dash for Cherbourg during the morning.

At daybreak [*on the 18th June*] I drove forward to the 6th Rifle Regiment with Hausberg. I had already given orders during the night for French officers to be sent across to the enemy at dawn, with a demand for an immediate surrender. When we arrived von Unger was already in negotiation with the enemy. The French officers had gone into the enemy positions, which were in an extremely commanding situation, and we could see some of the garrison standing beside their strong-points with rifles grounded. Through the glass we could also see guns and machine-guns off to the right beside St. Sauveur church. [*This was St. Sauveur-de-Pierre Pont, not the larger village of St. Sauveur-le-Vicomte, which lies 4 miles north-east, on the main road.*] The road leading to the enemy position was blocked at the bridge by a barricade of tree trunks.

The forward troops of the 6th Rifle Regiment were standing on either side of the road, also with their rifles grounded, but with the difference that, whereas the French had fixed positions close beside them, our men stood in the open country or on the road entirely without cover. If shooting had started suddenly, our troops would inevitably have suffered heavy casualties. I was very angry at this lack of forethought and ordered the officers concerned to reorganise their units immediately.

Shortly afterwards von Unger returned with the French officers and reported that the troops opposite had no knowledge of Pétain's armistice proposal and did not believe it. They were not prepared to lay down their arms and allow us to move on. These negotiations had cost us valuable time and I therefore sent across a French officer once again to deliver a summons to the enemy to lay down their arms by 08.00 hours, failing which I would attack.

Preparations for the attack were now pushed ahead as quickly as possible. Meanwhile, Heidkaemper had arrived and reported on the division's night march to La Haye-du-Puits, which, it seemed, had by no means gone smoothly. Due to incorrect marking of roads in Vire with the " DG 7 "[1] sign, part of the division had gone off in error to St. Lô [*17 miles east of Coutances*]. No serious fighting had so far occurred in the rear, but part of the column, including the divisional staff, had been attacked by enemy tanks from out of a cornfield. Casualties had been suffered, both dead and wounded, and several of our vehicles had been set alight. In addition, one of the aides-de-camp, Lieut. Luft, had narrowly escaped being taken prisoner during the night by either British or French troops.

Since there had been no fighting of any note in the territory through which we had come, it was fair to expect that the rest of the division would close up with us during the morning, or at any rate, during the day. It was therefore now possible to proceed with my plan for an immediate attack on Cherbourg. At 08.00 hours, we found that the enemy at St. Sauveur had suddenly disappeared. When we broke into the enemy positions they were deserted, except for a few wounded and one dead. An artillery and machine-gun barrage was now laid down on the enemy's rear areas, while the leading battalion of the 6th Rifle Regiment completed the occupation of the enemy positions, which were tremendously strong. At the same time work went actively forward in removing the obstructions across the stream and across a deep cutting farther to the north. Baulks of timber had to be dragged out of the railings on either side of the bridge, where they had been anchored with heavy chains. We also had to get through a 100-yard long barricade formed by numerous poplar trees, three feet or so in diameter, laid across the road. The engineers did some good work here with motor-driven saws.

At about 09.00 hours the leading company of the 6th Rifle Regiment, which was equipped with armoured troop-carriers, moved off as vanguard on the road to Cherbourg. About a mile and a quarter north-east of St. Lô d'Ourville, the leading platoon, with which I and my signals troop were travelling, suddenly came under heavy flanking fire from a hill to the right. Shortly afterwards an enemy battery joined in from the neighbourhood of St. Lô [*d'Ourville*], but by that time our men had jumped from their vehicles and taken cover. A wounded man lay a few yards in front of us behind the parapet of a bridge. The enemy fire was now lively both from our right and from the front. Our own fire, on

---

[1]Rommel had the roads over which his division advanced marked with the sign " DG 7 " (*Durchgangstrasse* 7). This was contrary to normal German practice and he was taken to task for it later. See page 85.

the other hand, was very slow in answering and, in order to get it moving, I ordered the machine-gun crew of my armoured car to open fire immediately into the bushes on the right of the road. At the same time the commander of an anti-tank gun was given orders from me to open fire as quickly as possible on the nearest houses and bushes to our right. Lieut. Hausberg took charge of all the machine-gunners and riflemen near by and got them into position.

While this fire was pouring into the unseen enemy, the first field howitzer came into action, firing over open sights 150 yards behind us. The weight of our fire soon silenced the enemy on the hill, whereupon the 2nd Battalion of the 6th Rifle Regiment attacked the hill and took it.

After this short but violent action, the division resumed its march to Cherbourg in the same order as before. Our speed through Barneville to Les Pieux—at times only 6 to 10 m.p.h.—was too slow for me and I several times had to make my presence felt to get it increased, for the longer we took getting to Cherbourg, the more chance the enemy in the intervening territory or in the port itself had to prepare for our arrival. The telephone system was still everywhere intact and there was little doubt that the Cherbourg garrison would be well informed about our movements.

As we dropped down into the valley at Barneville, we could see the sea on our left and some large buildings on the hills south of Barneville which looked to us like barracks. There was, however, no sign anywhere of enemy troops. Instead, we found a number of civilians at the entrance to Barneville engaged in clearing away some partially constructed road-blocks. We saw more of this on our way to Les Pieux [*12 miles south-west of Cherbourg*], which we reached at 12.15 hours. Nowhere did we have to go into action. Where we did come across enemy troops we found them quite ready to lay down their arms.

The column bore off at Les Pieux without halting and drove at a smart pace steadily closer to Cherbourg. Several captive balloons were hanging in the sky over the port and it was not long before one of the forts began to drop shells on the rear of our column. Now we were going to see fighting. The leading unit halted a few minutes later, although there was no firing yet up in front. I accordingly drove forward along the column with my *Gefechtsstaffel*, to find out why we had stopped, and found the rifle company's armoured vehicles halted 100 yards short of a strong road-block, where negotiations were in progress with the enemy garrison, who gave every sign of being ready to surrender. Von Unger came across to me and reported. French troops were already on their way across to us with white flags when suddenly a 75 mm. shell landed among us, closely followed by a second. Hostilities had opened.

Everyone at first dived for cover, although one or two courageous drivers did try to get their vehicles into shelter—successfully in many cases, as, for instance, with the drivers of my *Gefechtsstaffel*, who, despite the fire, drove off up a side road until they were concealed from the enemy. The leading vehicles of the 6th Rifle Regiment were already in flames from the enemy shell-fire. My troops had unfortunately again made the bad mistake of diving straight for cover instead of immediately replying to the enemy fire with their machine-guns.

In order to get fire to bear as quickly as possible, I ordered the machine-gunner of my armoured car to open fire at once in the general direction of the enemy, and had orders given to the nearest platoon commander to lead his platoon to an immediate attack on the road-block. But with enemy shells falling all round and a hail of splinters whistling about our ears, it was not easy to get the infantry to leave cover once they had found it and advance against the enemy. L.-Cpl. Heidenreich and my driver L.-Cpl. Koenig particularly distinguished themselves by their cool courage in this situation. They swept the infantry forward, although it was still a long time before the machine-gunners opened fire—due apparently to the fact that they had not seen the enemy and had probably not been trained to open fire immediately at the spot where the enemy was thought to be.

In the meantime von Unger had been given orders from me to push forward with his leading battalion round the right flank to Cherbourg. Captain Kolbeck had already received instructions from me to hurry back to the rear and bring a troop of artillery into action as quickly as possible.

As there was no more for my small staff to do up in the forward line, and my most important job was to get the rest of the division into action as quickly as possible, I took myself off to the rear with Lieut. Hausberg and L.-Cpl. Heidenreich. The driver and operator of my signals lorry had to remain with their vehicle. Enemy shell-fire was now incessant on and along the road, forcing us to make several wide détours, during which we had to be constantly on the alert for a clash with enemy infantry.

When, about half an hour or so later, we at last got back to the road over which we had advanced, several motor-cyclists came riding up and prepared themselves to move on to the front. We now continued our journey by motor-cycle. A few hundred yards farther on we met Lt.-Col. Kessler, commander of the 1st Battalion, 78th Artillery Regiment. I ordered him to deploy his batteries on both sides of the road and to lay down the heaviest barrage he could on the heights round Cherbourg and above all, on the port installations. We then went on at top speed farther to the rear. The 1st Battalion of the 6th Rifle Regiment received orders from me to launch an attack on the hill 1,000 yards west of the Port Militaire. Shortly afterwards I met the commander of a 37 mm. anti-aircraft battery and took him forward myself with his battery to the point where Kessler's battalion was already in position. His orders were to open rapid fire immediately on the heights round Cherbourg and the docks.

Kessler's battalion had already opened fire. A few minutes later the rapid fire of the 37 mm. guns was also tearing into Cherbourg and the enemy hastily hauled down his balloons. The situation seemed to be developing in our favour.

From my command post, which I had installed in a farmhouse on the main road, all sound of infantry fire from the north had ceased. L.-Cpl. Heidenreich managed to get my transport section out of the front line and back to me unharmed. They had been in action against 40 British soldiers, who had come on them suddenly from the rear and opened fire. However, the signals corporal finally succeeded in disposing of the enemy with his machine-gun and forcing them to surrender.

Radio contact had now been established with Major Heidkaemper. The situation, which had appeared to be going so well, took a sudden turn against us shortly before 16.00 hours, when within a few minutes of each other, many of Cherbourg's forts opened a tremendous barrage with guns of all sizes, including super-heavies, into the area which we were holding and through which we had made our advance. British warships also joined in with heavy naval guns. I was extremely glad that the 6th Rifle Regiment had left its vehicles and deployed. The positions occupied by the artillery battalion and A.A. battery came in for particularly heavy attention and casualties soon began to mount. My command post, too, was so seriously threatened that we found it advisable to shift out into the open country along a hedge 500 yards to the west, where, although overlooked by the enemy, we were far better off than in the buildings with heavy shells falling all round.

One thing to be thankful for was that the radio was working. The rapid fire of the forts lasted about an hour. I realised that things could be very difficult for us if the enemy were to mount a strong infantry attack from Cherbourg, and therefore devoted all my efforts to bringing up reinforcements—above all, the 7th Rifle Regiment and the 25th Panzer Regiment.

On hearing that the divisional staff had arrived in Sotteville [9 miles south-west of Cherbourg], I decided to conduct further operations from there. We drove off soon after, keeping 300 yards spacing between vehicles because of the enemy shell-fire.

Driving at top speed, we succeeded in getting our few vehicles back along the road to Divisional H.Q. at Château Sotteville without loss. The 7th Rifle and the 25th Panzer Regiments arrived soon afterwards, also the whole of the Division's light artillery and A.A. units. There was, however, no hope of the heavy artillery getting into action before the late evening. They had been unable to maintain the speed of the pursuit over the 210-mile stretch to Cherbourg.

It was now decided to adhere to our original plan of attack, which was to launch the 7th Rifle Regiment, reinforced by tanks, through Hainneville to Querqueville [on the north coast, 3 miles west of Cherbourg].

With the hills south of Querqueville in our hands it would be easy to command the port and town of Cherbourg with artillery fire. Then the eastern front of the Cherbourg defences could be cut off later by the Brigade Senger. There was now no hope of this brigade arriving before the following day.

Not having had any sleep since the previous morning, I took an hour's rest at about 17.00 hours. During that time the commanders of the 7th Rifle and the 25th Panzer Regiments came in, and after being quickly briefed on the situation, received their orders for the attack. Rothenburg drew attention to the fact that the terrain, criss-crossed as it was with hedges and sunken roads, was extremely unfavourable for tanks. Despite his objections I gave orders for a reinforced company of the 25th Panzer Regiment to be attached to the battalions of the 7th Rifle Regiment for the attack on Querqueville. The approach route was to be through Tonneville.

Shortly after the commanders had gone, a number of highly important maps were brought in, to which I gave immediate and careful study. It seemed that the château in which we had taken up our quarters belonged to the Commandant of Cherbourg, and a whole collection of maps of the Cherbourg fortifications had been found in his secret drawers. They included maps of the defended zone south of Cherbourg and, above all, one map showing the zones of fire of all the light and heavy batteries in and around the fortress. I studied this map very carefully and came to the conclusion that it would be unwise to proceed with the attack through Tonneville, for which orders had just been issued, as the enemy would be able to cover it with the combined fire of several forts. Meanwhile, a welcome signal had come in from Paris's Battalion to the effect that it had achieved its task of capturing Hill 79, just west of the Rédoute du Tot. I therefore decided to send the Rifle Regiment round the western side of Hill 79 for its attack on Querqueville and amended my orders accordingly. I intended to accompany the regiment forward on its approach march myself that evening, in order to satisfy myself of its deployment on the ground.

With my *Gefechtsstaffel*, I overtook the regiment at 21.00 hours and then moved forward behind the tanks which formed its spearhead. Every village we passed was crowded with French sailors and refugees from Cherbourg, but we met no resistance. It was already growing dark. Just south of Hainneville we passed a large concrete structure fenced in with wire and a high wall, apparently a defence installation. A little farther north I ran my *Gefechtsstaffel* under some trees, from which point I was able to watch the deployment of the 7th Rifle Regiment, which proceeded smoothly. The concrete structure turned out to be part of an underground tank system.

Meanwhile, my dispatch rider had taken a look round the neighbourhood and discovered a point from which a view of the naval dockyard could be obtained from about 2,000 yards away. In the last gleam of daylight we saw the defence works on the outer and inner moles, and the naval harbour, which contained only small ships. The rest of the harbour was empty, the British having apparently already gone. [*The last troopship had left at 16.00 hours.*] While we were looking out over Cherbourg, the long column of the 7th Rifle Regiment moved up behind us through Hainneville and occupied the positions assigned to them on the hills south of Querqueville and round Hainneville. Light and heavy A.A. batteries followed up the Rifle Regiment and took up position at a point where they could prevent the escape of ships from the harbour. The enemy forts around us were silent and it was soon completely dark. Our position was now so strong that we were certain of being able to force the enemy to capitulate next day.

It was midnight by the time I arrived back at Divisional H.Q. During the night, Lt.-Col. Froehlich disposed the whole of the divisional artillery, plus a heavy battalion from the Brigade Senger, in front of Cherbourg in such a manner that, when dawn broke, they would be able to launch a concentrated fire of both heavy and light artillery on the various defensive nests and forts.

Next morning, the 19th of June, I drove up forward shortly before 06.00 hours, with Captain Schraepler and Lieut. Hausberg. Numerous prisoners were being sent into Cherbourg from various points of the front, with leaflets printed in French calling for an unconditional surrender. In the area just south of the Rédoute du Tot I met part of the 6th Rifle Regiment under Lt.-Col. Jungk. I left my *Gefechtsstaffel* at the edge of the wood as I felt that it would be dangerous, with the enemy so close, to take the vehicles out of cover.

We now walked forward in a north-easterly direction beside some low bushes. A dispatch rider followed on foot behind my two escort officers and myself. As we made our way forward, we suddenly found the men of a machine-gun platoon lying beneath the bushes. I asked the platoon commander why his men were not in position and received the reply that he had not so far been able to find a suitable field of fire. I ordered him to get his platoon into position immediately in the front line. I was just about to look for the battalion command post, which we were told was farther forward, when shells suddenly started to fall behind us, apparently from our own artillery. We dived straight for cover in a trench to our right, but not before a shell had killed the dispatch rider, Ehrmann, and wounded the signals officer, an N.C.O. and a second dispatch rider. I was positive that the shells had come from our own artillery and gave orders for no gun to fire without my express authority. The order was transmitted by radio. It turned out later that the fire had not come from the divisional artillery, but from an 88 mm. A.A. battery.

Jungk now received orders to work his way forward with the leading troops of the battalion alongside the bushes up to the outskirts of Cherbourg. The enemy seemed to be offering no further resistance. As on the previous evening, there were sailors everywhere, and hordes of civilians streamed down every road out of Cherbourg and even across country in order to escape the approaching battle. I issued orders by radio for the exodus to be halted and the civilians sent back into Cherbourg, for we had no intention of bombarding the town, but only the military targets, such as the forts and the fortified naval dockyard, around it.

We then drove over to the 7th Rifle Regiment's command post in Hainneville, but found that Col. von Bismarck was not there. On the way we came across a heavy A.A. battery which had been completely blocking the road with its guns and vehicles for hours past and was still not in position. I said a few straight words to the numerous officers who were with the battery and ordered them to take up position alongside the road immediately and get all their vehicles away off the road.

At the northern edge of Hainneville I received a message that Lieut. Durke had just been killed by artillery fire from Fort Central and accordingly issued orders by radio for concentrated fire to be opened on the fort. Fire was opened within a few minutes. We had excellent observation from the 7th Rifle Regiment's command post, and were able to send back a few small corrections which soon directed the fire into the centre of the fort. Finally, it became so accurate that three out of four shells were direct hits, and the fort ceased fire. In order to put its open gun positions out of action, I had a heavy A.A. battery brought up with orders to take a hand in the heavy artillery's next shoot on Fort Central —which was timed for 11.00 hours—and to destroy its superstructure by direct fire.

Shortly afterwards Major von Paris informed me that the garrison of the Rédoute des Couplets, 10 officers and 150 men, had just surrendered. We could see the prisoners standing under guard over to our right. I immediately went over to the Rédoute, where I expected to get an excellent view across the Cherbourg defences. We drove the first part of the way in our combat vehicles, and then went on foot up the last 500 yards to the fort standing on its commanding height. We penetrated through the forward trenches into the inner part of the fort, where we found part of the 6th Rifle Regiment and the forward artillery observers. The observation posts, which were intact and equipped with excellent glasses, gave a view over the whole of the port and town.

I had just sent a radio message to Major Heidkaemper informing him of the progress of the attack, when Col. Fuerst arrived from the eastern side of Querqueville with the news that Col. von Bismarck was in negotiation there with a deputation from the town. This was probably a direct result of the division's leaflets calling on the garrison to surrender.

So it seemed that negotiations were starting. I took myself off at once to a point half a mile north of the Rédoute des Couplets. The naval dockyard was still held by enemy forces, who were apparently not yet inclined to surrender, so fire was opened on anything moving in the area. By this time all fire had ceased from the forts out to sea. Fort Querquevilel had refused to surrender, but the Commandant had informed us that the fort would not open fire unless we did. He would only surrender, however, on orders. Fort Central was silent.

At 12.15 two civilian cars drove out of the town. Their occupants, a Deputy of the Chamber in Paris and the Cherbourg Prefect of Police, were unfortunately not in a position to announce the surrender of the fortress, but declared themselves ready to make urgent representations to that end to the Commandant, who, they said, was in the naval dockyard. They wished at all costs to avoid the bombardment and hence the destruction of their town. I told them to drive back into the town and effect an immediate surrender through the agency of the Chief of Staff. I gave them until 13.15 hours. They hoped to be back by then to bring me the answer personally.

During their journey back, the two cars were fired on from the naval dockyard and their occupants had to alight and crawl for some distance along the ditch running alongside the road. I did not hear of this, of course, until later. At 13.15 hours the answer still had not arrived, and so dive-bombers, punctual to the minute, swooped down and released their bombs on the sea forts, scoring a direct hit on Fort Central. The artillery also opened fire. I went back as quickly as possible to the Rédoute des Couplets to watch the effect of our fire from that excellent observation point.

A storm of shells now descended on the naval dockyard, and flames were soon shooting up from its extensive arsenals and sheds. Tremendous clouds of smoke showed the existence of major conflagrations. Meanwhile, the Rifle Regiments had been given orders to occupy the town during this bombardment. When the whole naval dockyard was concealed under a pall of flame and smoke, I had the fire switched to Fort Querqueville in order to bring the garrison there to an early surrender.

During this bombardment, of which I had an excellent view from my command post, a number of French naval officers appeared in the Rédoute des Couplets to negotiate the surrender of the fortress. I had the officers brought up to my observation tower, mainly in order to let them see the tremendous effect of our artillery fire. Among them was the Commandant of Fort Querqueville, a naval officer with a long black beard. He was horrified when he saw his fort shrouded with smoke, and asked me why we were bombarding it—it had already ceased fire. " That may be," I replied. " But it has not surrendered."

The negotiations for the surrender went ahead fairly quickly. The French spokesman—a captain—who was apparently invested with some powers, asked for our terms in writing. I accordingly dictated the following:

" I have taken cognisance of the fact that the fortress of Cherbourg is prepared to surrender, and have given orders for an immediate cease-fire. I require the garrison of each fort to hoist a white flag as a sign of surrender and then to march off along the road from Cherbourg to Les Pieux. Personal kit may be carried, including essential rations. I require that N.C.O.s shall be instructed to take charge of the men. Officers will assemble in the Préfecture Maritime. They will be permitted their batmen. All weapons will be unloaded and stacked in an orderly manner in the forts."

The formal surrender was fixed to take place at 17.00 hours in the Préfecture Maritime. After the French delegates had declared their agreement with the conditions, and given their assurance that they would be carried out, I gave orders for the cease-fire and then drove off with my *Gefechtsstaffel* to Cherbourg.

In the Préfecture Maritime, the staff of the fortress had already transmitted the surrender conditions to all establishments. As there was over an hour to wait until the official ceremony, I drove through Cherbourg with Heidkaemper to inspect the town and port. We visited first the British port area and the harbour railway station. In their haste to get their ships away, the British had left all their vehicles standing in the extensive harbour area and hundreds of lorries were parked there and in the adjacent quarter of the town. The material was practically new and most of the lorries intact.

We now found our way to the seaplane base, which had not been touched by the bombardment, and then returned to the Préfecture, where we found the commanding officers of 7th Panzer Division assembled on one side of the courtyard and the officers of the Cherbourg garrison, including the commandants of the various forts, on the other. After a quick exchange of salutes with my officers, I addressed the senior French officer, through the interpreter, in roughly the following terms:

" As Commander of the German troops at Cherbourg, I take note of the fact that the fortress has surrendered and wish to express my pleasure that the surrender has taken place without bloodshed among the civilian population."

The French Chief of Staff then had me informed, on behalf of the officers, that the fortress would not have surrendered if sufficient ammunition had been available.

Meanwhile, we discovered that the commandant of Cherbourg was not there, nor, what was worse, the senior officer of the station—the admiral commanding the French Channel Fleet. Accordingly, the division's liaison officer, Captain von Platen, was sent off to fetch the gentlemen from their headquarters, which was housed in a château heavily protected by anti-tank guns and barricades. When they arrived

I had the interpreter repeat to them the words I had already addressed to the French Chief of Staff. Admiral Abrial said that the surrender of the fortress had taken place without his agreement, to which I replied that I took note of his statement. This concluded the capitulation of Cherbourg.

Meanwhile, all forts which could be reached from the land had been occupied by our troops and cleaning up began in the town and forts. With Heidkaemper I visited Fort de Roule, which stood on a hill commanding the town and harbour. A road-block, which we met on the way, was quickly disposed of by the 8-wheeled armoured signals lorry. It pushed an enormous half-burnt-out lorry in front of it like a football and so cleared the road.

The Commandant of the fort and his deputy had been killed the day before by a German shell, while standing on the walls of the fort. I went into the casemates, which still contained their garrisons. The French troops saluted mutely.

I then went on to Fort Querqueville, where I found the aerodrome untouched, although the fourteen aircraft standing in its spacious hangars were all more or less damaged. I was surprised to see how little damage our shell-fire had caused in the fort. In the Commandant's house, which stood in the middle of the open square, not even the window panes were broken. The shell pits in the masonry of the fort were some 12-16 inches deep and the garrison had apparently come to no serious harm.

The British forces with the French Tenth Army had escaped by the narrowest margin. It had been an even closer shave for them than for the main B.E.F. at Dunkirk three weeks before.

Lieut.-General Sir Alan Brooke, who had landed at Cherbourg on the 13th to take overall command, came to the conclusion next day that the French position was hopeless, and, after securing the British Government's agreement, made arrangements to evacuate all the British troops still left in France, including the two fresh divisions that had just been landed. But the withdrawal of " Norman Force," the troops already operating with the French Tenth Army, was deferred. The main elements of this were now the 157th Infantry Brigade (of the 52nd Lowland Division), which was then in the front line south of Laigle, and the 3rd Armoured Brigade (of the 1st Armoured Division), which was in reserve. Lieut.-General J. H. Marshall-Cornwall, who took command of " Norman Force " on the 15th, issued orders for its immediate withdrawal to Cherbourg when he learned on the following night that the Tenth Army was starting a general retirement towards Brittany.

The British troops set off at midnight and reached Cherbourg within 24 hours, after having " moved 200 miles by roads encumbered by columns of troops and refugees." That fact was remarkable proof of the value of motorised mobility for escape purposes. It was found that the direct road to Cherbourg through Carentan was already mined, so the British tank column was diverted to the west-coast route through Lessay. Then at La Haye-du-Puits a further westward diversion was made via Barneville and Les Puits, as the main road was already mined and blocked. In taking the same roundabout approach a few hours later, Rommel chose the route that gave him a clear passage, without any diversion. That calculation of the advantages of the indirect approach, as the line of least expectation, showed his insight and foresight.

General Marshall-Cornwall's report of the last phase ended: " In order to protect the embarkation at Cherbourg, I had asked for a fresh battalion of the 52nd Division to be left to occupy a covering position some 20 miles to the south. This, combined with the 5 French battalions of the Cherbourg garrison, ought to have provided ample security, and I had hoped to continue the embarkation until the 21st in order to remove all the stores and mechanised vehicles. The enemy, however, again upset our calculations by the speed with which he followed up our rapid withdrawal. At 9 a.m. on the 18th, a column of 60 lorries, carrying motorised German infantry, reached the covering position near St. Sauveur. Finding resistance there, they turned west to the sector held by French troops, and succeeded in penetrating the position by the coast road. The French made little attempt to resist, and I had to make the decision at 11.30 to complete the evacuation by 3 p.m. The covering battalion (5th Bn. K.O.S.B.) was withdrawn between 12 noon and 3 p.m. and the last boat left at 4 p.m. All weapons were removed, except one 3.7 inch A.A. gun, which broke down and was rendered unserviceable, and one static Bofors gun which could not be removed in the time. Two anti-tank guns also had to be abandoned during the withdrawal. When the last troopship left, the Germans had penetrated to within 3 miles of the harbour."

The casualties of Rommel's 7th Panzer Division during the six weeks' campaign were 682 killed, 1,646 wounded, and 296 missing, while its loss in tanks was only 42 totally destroyed. Its captures amounted to 97,648 prisoners, together with 277 field guns, 64 anti-tank guns, 458 tanks and armoured cars, over 4,000 lorries, over 1,500 cars, and over 1,500 horse-drawn vehicles.

On the 20th, immediately after the capture of Cherbourg, Rommel wrote to his wife:

I don't know whether the date's right, I've rather lost count of time after the last few days.

The division made the assault on Cherbourg in one stride over a distance of 220 to 230 miles and took the powerful fortress despite a strong defence. There were some bad moments for us, and the enemy was at first between 20 and 40 times our superior in numbers. On top of that they had 20 to 35 forts ready for action and many single batteries. However, by buckling to quickly we succeeded in carrying out the Fuehrer's special order to take Cherbourg as fast as possible. . . .

With the capture of Cherbourg, the war in the West was over for 7th Panzer Division and the division was now ordered south. Rommel wrote from Rennes:

Rennes 21 June 1940

DEAREST LU,

Arrived here safely. The war has now gradually turned into a lightning tour of France. In a few days it will be over for good. The people here are relieved that it's all passing off so quietly.

25 June 1940

At last the armistice is in force. We're now less than 200 miles from the Spanish frontier and hope to go straight on there so as to get the whole Atlantic coast in our hands. How wonderful it's all been. Something I ate yesterday upset me but I'm better again already. Billets middling.

8 July 1940

France's war with the British Fleet is something quite unique. It's good for France to be working in with the victors. The peace terms will be so much the more lenient for her.

Anxiety about Russian expansion comes out clearly in Rommel's letter of 30th June 1940:

Russia's demands on Rumania are pretty stiff. I doubt whether this suits us very well. They're taking all they can get. But they won't always find it so easy to hold on to their spoils. . . .

Note by MANFRED ROMMEL: *During the advance of the 7th Panzer Division, my father had introduced several new techniques on his own account, with, as will be remembered, considerable success. Firstly, his method of command had been something other than orthodox, secondly he had introduced his " line of thrust," and finally he had, against all instructions, sign-posted all his communication roads with the sign " DG 7," to enable units following behind to close up quickly and to facilitate supply traffic.*

There was, of course, trouble from his superiors and criticism from others concerning these independent experiments. He defended himself fiercely and with success. Even Major Heidkaemper, his Ia, took the side of the critics in some questions, a fact which made him particularly angry. On the 13th June Heidkaemper submitted a memorandum to my father in which he complained that contact had been broken between the staff and the divisional commander, and that the practical conclusion to be drawn from this fact was that the commander should stay farther to the rear. In fact, the principal cause of the crisis which had arisen was that the unit commanders had not been sufficiently familiar with my father's technique of command. He had had far too little opportunity of exercising his division as a formation and with its full complement of weapons. The result, especially at the beginning of the campaign, was a need for repeated makeshift measures, until finally, towards the end, operations went more or less smoothly.

After receiving Heidkaemper's memorandum, my father wrote the following letter to my mother:

I'm having a lot of trouble with my Ia just at the moment. He's sent me a long screed about his activities on the 18th May. I shall have to have him posted away as soon as I can. This young General Staff Major, scared that something might happen to him and the Staff, stayed some 20 miles behind the front and, of course, lost contact with the fighting troops which I was commanding up near Cambrai. Instead of rushing everything up forward, he went to Corps H.Q., upset the people there and behaved as if the command of the division were no longer secure. And he still believes to this day that he performed a heroic deed. I'll have to make a thorough study of the documents so as to put the boy in his place.

Heidkaemper was actually on quite good terms with Rommel, who wrote, only a few days later, after his first wave of indignation had subsided:

The Heidkaemper affair was cleared up yesterday and has now been finally shelved. I have the feeling that it's all going to be all right now. I went and saw Hoth and we had a long talk about the whole thing. I'm glad there's peace in the camp again. However, it was necessary to assert my authority.

During the next few months life for Rommel was much the same as for most other German officers who were taking part in the occupation of France at that time. A few extracts from letters which he wrote at the beginning of 1941 give some idea of the life he was leading and what was in his mind. With so much material available, it is only possible to include a selection of letters from this period.

6 Jan. 1941

I received a whole pile of post yesterday, including your letters of the 21st and 23rd December. It looks as though the mails are gradually getting right again. This afternoon we saw the film *The Queen's Heart* (Mary Stuart), which I thoroughly enjoyed. We're expecting distinguished visitors to-morrow to inspect our quarters. We're not exactly comfortable. The wine growers round here probably spent their lives in the same miserable hovels a thousand years ago as they do to-day—primitive sandstone block buildings with flat roofs and sharply-curved tiles, just like those the Romans used. A lot of the villages haven't even got piped water and are still using wells. None of the houses are built for the cold. The windows don't shut and the draught whistles straight through them. However, I suppose things will soon be better. . . .

8 Jan. 1941

The visit passed off very well yesterday. It was intensely interesting to me to see what primitive lives the people round here are still leading and how poverty-striken some of the billets are. The troops made a very good impression everywhere. I'm intending to take my leave at the beginning of February. A lot of things will probably have been cleared up by then. I'm not surprised that our Allies aren't having things all their own way in North Africa. They probably thought that war was easy and now they've got to show what they can do. They began just the same in Spain, but fought very well later on. . . .

17 Jan. 1941

Nothing new here. I spend most evenings with my officers talking over the May 1940 war diary, which seems to impress them all.

The British Mediterranean Fleet has had to take some hard knocks. Let's hope we see more of this sort of thing.

Part Two

THE WAR IN AFRICA

FIRST YEAR

CHAPTER V

GRAZIANI'S DEFEAT—CAUSE AND EFFECT

IN A speech made by the Duce in February 1941, he said that between 1936 and 1940, Italy had sent to Libya an army of 14,000 officers and 327,000 men, and supplied it with great stores of material. His words sounded very grand and impressive, but the harsh truth was that this army fell a long way short of the standard required by modern warfare. It was designed for a colonial war against insurgent tribesmen, such as Graziani had had to wage against the Senussi and the Negus. Its tanks and armoured vehicles were too light and their engines under-powered. Their radius of action was short. Most of the guns with which the artillery units were equipped dated from the 1914-18 war and had a short range. The army had too few anti-tank and anti-aircraft guns and even its rifles and machine-guns were of obsolete pattern or otherwise unsuitable for modern warfare.

But its worst feature was the fact that a great part of the Italian Army consisted of non-motorised infantry. In the North African desert, non-motorised troops are of practically no value against a motorised enemy, since the enemy has the chance in almost every position, of making the action fluid by a turning movement round the south. Non-motorised formations, which can only be used against a modern army defensively and in prepared positions, will disturb him very little in such an operation. In mobile warfare, the advantage lies as a rule with the side which is subject to the least tactical restraint on account of its non-motorised troops. It follows then that the decisive disadvantage of the Italian Army *vis-à-vis* the British was that the greater part of it was non-motorised.

Graziani's Army was set in motion in September 1940, at a time when the British had nothing in Egypt capable of halting the Italians before Alexandria. Starting from the Bardia area, the Italian divisions moved across the Egyptian frontier at Sollum and then along the coast to Sidi Barrani. The weak British holding forces did not stand to fight a decisive action, but skilfully fell back to the east before the advancing Italians. After reaching Sidi Barrani, Graziani did not continue his advance, but chose instead to fortify the territory he had gained and lay a communication road along the coast; then he went on to assemble stores and reinforcements and to organise water supplies. From this new base he intended to continue the offensive towards the east.

If quartermasters and civilian officials are left to take their own time over the organisation of supplies, everything is bound to be very slow. Quartermasters often tend to work by theory and base all their calculations on precedent, being satisfied if their performance comes up to the standard which this sets. This can lead to frightful disasters when there is a man on the other side who carries out his plans with greater drive and thus greater speed. In this situation the commander must be ruthless in his demands for an all-out effort. If there is anyone in a key position who appears to be expending less than the energy that could properly be demanded of him, or who has no natural sense for practical problems of organisation, then that man must be ruthlessly removed. A commander must accustom his staff to a high tempo from the outset and continually keep them up to it. If he once allows himself to be satisfied with norms, or anything less than an all-out effort, he gives up the race from the starting-post and will sooner or later be taught a bitter lesson by his faster-moving enemy and be forced to jettison all his fixed ideas.

Weeks and months passed, but Graziani still stood fast at Sidi Barrani. The British, who commonly possess a good combination of brains and initiative, were given time to prepare themselves to meet a further Italian advance and to organise the defence of Egypt. Forces were assembled all over the British Empire and, above all, modern, mechanised troops with numerous tanks were brought into Egypt. The British tanks were far superior in quality to the Italian.

Although the British Army was far smaller in numbers than the Italian it was better equipped, had a better and more modern air force, faster and more up-to-date tanks, longer-range artillery, and, what was most important, its striking columns were fully motorised. The British Fleet dominated the western Mediterranean, and the Italian Battle Squadron and Cruiser Groups did not put to sea to sweep away the numerically inferior British ships. Finally—and this was of immense importance throughout the African campaign—the British possessed a railway along the coast as far as Mersa Matruh, with connections through to the Egyptian railway system, over which material could be brought to the front. Egypt could be looked upon as an arsenal for war material of all kinds.

At the end of November, General Wavell suddenly launched a surprise attack. [*It was actually launched on 9th December.*] His air force struck first. Every British aircraft that could take the air, from the oldest to the newest, dropped its bomb load on the Italian positions at Sidi Barrani and the forward airfields. Simultaneously, the guns of British warships thundered from the sea and covered Sidi Barrani and the coast road with their heaviest shells.

In the light of a full moon, an outflanking attack was then launched against the Italian positions at Sidi Barrani by a striking force made up of British, Australians, French, Poles and Indians, all units fully motorised. After a short fight, strong Italian positions 15 miles south of Sidi Barrani were overrun and 2,000 Italians found their way into British prison camps.

The larger part of the striking force was British, and the bulk of the remainder was Indian. The ground troops comprised the 7th Armoured Division, the 4th Indian Division (partly British), and two British infantry brigades—a total of 31,000 men. The Italian force in the forward zone was about 80,000 but had only 120 tanks compared with 275 British—of which 35 were the heavily-armoured Matildas of the 7th Battalion, Royal Tank Regiment.

The initial attack was against the Nibeiwa camp, and here 4,000 prisoners were taken—not 2,000 as Rommel says. The 4th Indian Division, spearheaded by the 7th R.T.R., then continued its attack northward against the Italian positions in the Sidi Barrani area.

The British motorised column now divided, one part continuing the attack to the north against the Sidi Barrani area, while the other moved off west far into the rear of the Italians.

This second part was the 7th Armoured Division, which in fact moved independently from the start.

At the same time waves of British infantry accompanied by infantry tanks advanced from the east against the Italian positions at Sidi Barrani in co-ordination with the outflanking columns attacking from the rear. Again the thunder of British naval guns mingled with the fury of the battle. It all swept over the Italians like a storm, and at the end of a brief action, the three Italian infantry divisions at Sidi Barrani had been wiped out.

Wavell continued his offensive. Soon he came up with a Black Shirt Division, which laid down its arms after a short battle in which the Italians had fought with great courage. On the 16th December, Wavell reached the Libyan frontier and defeated Graziani's troops at Capuzzo. The light Italian tanks simply split apart in the British fire. Maletti, the gallant commander of the Italian Armoured Corps in Africa, was killed in action and 30,000 Italians were taken prisoner. The Tenth Italian Army had virtually ceased to exist.

The total bag in this battle was over 38,000 prisoners, 400 guns and 50 tanks —at a cost of barely 500 British casualties.

The British successes were obviously having an almost paralysing effect on the Italians. They withdrew to their strongholds at Bardia and Tobruk and waited to see what the enemy would do next.

On the 19th of December, Wavell's forces appeared in front of Bardia and began to lay siege to the fortress. Under cover of R.A.F. bombs and the shells of the Royal Navy, the superb Australian infantry stormed the fortress and forced 20,000 Italians to surrender. The Italian Commandant successfully escaped to Tobruk.

Only the 7th Armoured Division followed up the Italian rout, and " appeared in front of Bardia," as the 4th Indian Division had been dispatched to the Sudan at the end of the Sidi Barrani battle. The siege-assault on Bardia was thus delayed until the arrival of a fresh infantry division, the 6th Australian. The assault was at last launched on January 3rd, again spearheaded by the Matilda tanks of the 7th Battalion R.T.R. By the third day the fortress was completely captured—45,000 prisoners and 462 guns being taken.

The British Army continued its advance to the west and on the 8th January 1941 enveloped Tobruk. Despite its tremendously strong defences, its garrison of 25,000 men and powerful artillery formations with their plentiful supply of stores, this first-class stronghold only managed to hold out for a fortnight, after which the defence collapsed in an attack mainly conducted by infantry tanks. The Italian troops had no real means of defence against the heavily-armoured British vehicles.

Tobruk was actually enveloped on the 6th January by the 7th Armoured Division, but the 6th Australian Division was not completely assembled and ready to deliver the assault until a fortnight later. The attack opened on the 21st, and by early next morning all resistance had been overcome. Nearly 30,000 prisoners were taken, with 236 guns.

After the fall of Tobruk, the British moved farther into Cyrenaica, fighting short actions at Derna and Mechili. In spite of the difficult terrain in Cyrenaica, which offered excellent opportunities for defence, the British northern column, with Australians in the lead, made rapid progress. Benghazi was in British hands as early as the 7th February. Meanwhile, a powerful British armoured column had pushed forward through Msus, apparently unnoticed by the Italians. The column struck the coast road 30 miles south-west of Benghazi and brought to battle the remainder of Graziani's army, which was retreating down the road. The action, which was fought on either side of the Via Balbia, ended with the destruction of over 100 Italian fighting vehicles; 10,000 Italian troops marched into British prison camps.

In this battle, near Beda Fomm, the total captures were 20,000 men, 216 guns and 120 tanks, mainly of the new (Italian) cruiser type. The British force consisted of part of the 7th Armoured Division, and amounted to only 3,000 men, while it had no more than 32 cruiser tanks available. But the Italian tanks were retreating along the road in small packets, and these were broken up in turn by the British tanks, which skilfully manœuvred to gain flanking fire-positions. The Italian infantry and other troops offered little resistance when their protecting tanks were destroyed.

On the 8th February, leading units of the British Army occupied El Agheila and thus stood on the frontier between Cyrenaica and Tripolitania. Graziani's army had virtually ceased to exist. All that remained of it was a few lorry columns and hordes of unarmed soldiers in full flight to the west. The realisation that their arms were of no avail against the British had cast fear and trepidation into the Italian Army. They had lost 120,000 men in prisoners alone—not counting their dead and wounded —also 600 armoured vehicles and almost the whole of their artillery, vehicles and stores. The Italian Air Force in Africa had suffered an annihilating defeat at the hands of the R.A.F., and lost most of its aircraft and ground organisation.

The aggregate figures that Rommel gives for the British captures are closer to the mark than those he gives for the various battles. The total during the campaign was just over 130,000 prisoners, 1,300 guns, and 400 tanks (excluding armoured cars and machine-gun carriers.)

If Wavell had now continued his advance into Tripolitania, no resistance worthy of the name could have been mounted against him—so well had his superbly planned offensive succeeded.

To delay Wavell's advance, the Italians mined the road between El Agheila, Arco dei Fileni, and Sirte and destroyed several bridges across the wadis. These demolitions offered little obstruction to the enemy as they could easily be by-passed. A weak Italian rearguard force, consisting of one reinforced artillery regiment, stood at Sirte. Thousands of stragglers collected at Homs and the remainder of the Italian forces in Tripolitania moved into the outer environs of Tripoli and into the Tripoli defence line itself—a semi-circle 12 miles out of the city centre— for defence of the port. This defence line, which was constructed in sandy soil, consisted of a wide and deep anti-tank ditch with walls partially reinforced because of the loose sand, field positions protected by wire entanglements, and occasional observation towers of light concrete construction, which could be seen for miles. In comparison with Tobruk and Bardia, the defence works round Tripoli were totally inadequate. They could possibly have been defended with some hope of success against insurgent Senussi or Arab tribesmen, but never against the British.

However, the enemy stopped his advance, probably thinking that Tripoli would sooner or later fall into his hands like a ripe plum. No doubt he wanted time to assemble stores and organise supplies before going on. But in doing so, he gave the Axis powers the chance to prepare for a resumption of the struggle.

The advance was stopped by the British Government in order to dispatch an expeditionary force to Greece, under the belief that a powerful flank threat to Germany could be created in the Balkans. Early in January Mr. Churchill had pressed the Greeks, who were already at war with Italy, to accept the aid of a British contingent. But General Metaxas, who was then head of the Greek Government, had declined the proposal on the ground that it was likely to provoke a German invasion without providing a strong enough force to check such an invasion.

This polite rebuff coincided with the capture of Tobruk, so the British Government decided to allow Wavell to continue his advance in North Africa and capture the port of Benghazi. That fresh step forward was duly achieved, and the remains

*of the Italian Army in Cyrenaica were wiped out. But in the meantime General
Metaxas had died, on the 19th January, and Mr. Churchill then renewed his offer
to the Greek Government which, this time, was persuaded to accept it. Hence the
British Government ordered Wavell to halt the advance in Africa, leave only a
minimum force to hold conquered Cyrenaica, and prepare to send the largest possible
force to Greece.*

*The Balkan venture was short lived. The British force began to land in Greece
on the 7th March, the Germans invaded Greece on the 6th April, and the British
were driven to re-embark before the end of the month. That costly disaster was
followed in May by an even quicker expulsion from Crete, at the hands of a German
airborne force.*

*General O'Connor, the executive commander of the victorious advance in North
Africa, had been eager to push on from Benghazi to Tripoli, and was convinced
that he could have carried out this fresh bound with little delay for replenishment of
supplies. Many other officers who were concerned in the planning shared his view.
Rommel confirms it.*

When a commander has won a decisive victory—and Wavell's victory
over the Italians was devastating—it is generally wrong for him to be
satisfied with too narrow a strategic aim. For that is the time to exploit
success. It is during the pursuit, when the beaten enemy is still dispirited
and disorganised, that most prisoners are made and most booty captured.
Troops who on one day are flying in a wild panic to the rear, may, unless
they are continually harried by the pursuer, very soon stand in battle
again, freshly organised as fully effective fighting men.

The reason for giving up the pursuit is almost always the quartermaster's growing difficulty in spanning the lengthened supply routes
with his available transport. As the commander usually pays great
attention to his quartermaster and allows the latter's estimate of the
supply possibilities to determine his strategic plan, it has become the
habit for quartermaster staffs to complain at every difficulty, instead
of getting on with the job and using their powers of improvisation, which
indeed are frequently nil. But generally the commander meekly accepts
the situation and shapes his actions accordingly.

When, after a great victory which has brought the destruction of the
enemy, the pursuit is abandoned on the quartermaster's advice, history
almost invariably finds the decision to be wrong and points to the
tremendous chances which have been missed. In face of such a judgment
there are, of course, always academic soldiers quick to produce statistics
and precedents by people of little importance to prove it wrong. But
events judge otherwise, for it has frequently happened in the past that a
general of high intellectual powers has been defeated by a less intelligent
but stronger willed adversary.

The best thing is for the commander himself to have a clear picture
of the real potentialities of his supply organisation and to base all his
demands on his own estimate. This will force the supply staffs to develop

their initiative, and though they may grumble, they will as a result produce many times what they would have done left to themselves.

The gravest results of the Italian defeat were to their morale. The Italian troops had, with good reason, lost all confidence in their arms and acquired a very serious inferiority complex, which was to remain with them throughout the whole of the war, for the Fascist state was never able to equip its men in North Africa properly. Psychologically, it is particularly unfortunate when the very first battle of a war ends with such a disastrous defeat, especially when it has been preceded by such grandiose predictions. It makes it very difficult ever again to restore the men's confidence.

CHAPTER VI

THE FIRST ROUND

AFRICAN MISSION

As A result of the strained situation in France at the end of 1940,[1] I had to break off my Christmas leave before it was up and drive quickly back over the snow-covered and icy roads to Bordeaux, where my division was then stationed. Nothing, however, came of the scare and we did not go into action.

Weeks of intensive training followed. I intended to make up for my spoiled Christmas by taking some leave at the beginning of February, but it was again abortive, for on my second evening at home I was informed by an adjutant from the Fuehrer's H.Q. that I was to cut short my leave and report to Field Marshal von Brauchitsch and the Fuehrer immediately.

On the 6th February Field Marshal von Brauchitsch inducted me into my new task.

In view of the highly critical situation with our Italian allies, two German divisions—one light and one panzer—were to be sent to Libya to their help. I was to take command of this German Afrika Korps and was to move off as soon as possible to Libya to reconnoitre the ground.

The middle of February would see the arrival of the first German troops in Africa; the movement of the 5th Light Division would be complete by mid-April and of the 15th Panzer Division at the end of May.

The basic condition for providing this help was that the Italian Government should agree to undertake the defence of Tripolitania in the Gulf of Sirte area, on a line running south from about Buerat, in order to secure the necessary space for the employment of the German Luftwaffe in Africa. This represented a departure from the previous Italian plan, which had been limited to holding the Tripoli defence line.

---

[1] The German Command had reports of a possible revolt in the unoccupied zone of France. It was planned in that case to enter and occupy the whole South of France the moment any such rising occurred.

Rommel talking with Major-General Gambier-Parry, commander of the British 2nd Armoured Division, who was captured with his headquarters at Mechili. The bare-headed officer with dark glasses is Colonel Younghusband, his G.S.O.1. [Photograph taken with Rommel's camera]

The Fieseler Storch used by Rommel [Rommel's own photograph]

Tracks south of Tobruk, Summer 1941

Another type of desert terrain photographed by Rommel during a reconnaissance

The Italian motorised forces in North Africa were to be placed under my command, while I myself was to be subordinate to Marshal Graziani.

In the afternoon I reported to the Fuehrer, who gave me a detailed account of the situation in Africa and informed me that I had been recommended to him as the man who would most quickly adapt himself to the altogether different conditions of the African theatre. The Fuehrer's chief adjutant, Colonel Schmundt, was to accompany me for the first stage of my tour of reconnaissance. I was advised to start by assembling the German troops in the area round Tripoli so that they could go into action as one body. In the evening the Fuehrer showed me a number of British and American illustrated papers describing General Wavell's advance through Cyrenaica. Of particular interest was the masterly co-ordination these showed between armoured land forces, air force and navy.

6 Feb. 1941

DEAREST LU,
    Landed at Staaken 12.45. First to Ob.d.H. [*C.-in-C. of the Army*], who appointed me to my new job, and then to F. [*Fuehrer*]. Things are moving fast. My kit is coming on here. I can only take barest necessities with me. Perhaps I'll be able to get the rest out soon. I need not tell you how my head is swimming with all the many things there are to be done. It'll be months before anything materialises.
    So " our leave " was cut short again. Don't be sad, it had to be. The new job is very big and important. . . .

7 Feb. 1941

    Slept on my new job last night. (It's one way of getting my rheumatism treatment.)[1] I've got a terrible lot to do, in the few hours that remain, getting together all I need.

On the morning of the 11th February I reported to General Guzzoni, Chief of Staff of the Commando Supremo [*in Rome*], where the plan to shift the defence of Tripolitania into the Gulf of Sirte met with complete approval. Instructions were given to General Roatta, Chief of Staff of the Italian Army, to accompany me to Libya. In the afternoon I flew on to Catania [*in Sicily*] where I met General Geissler, the Commander of the X Luftwaffe Korps. The latest news from Africa was very grave. Wavell had taken Benghazi, destroyed the last Italian armoured division south of the town and was about to advance into Tripolitania. In fact no further serious resistance by the Italians was to be expected. It was not impossible that the next few days would see the arrival of the leading

---

[1]Rommel suffered from rheumatism and had been advised some time before to undertake a cure in Egypt.   His wife was thus able to deduce that his new job was in Africa.

British troops in the outer environs of Tripoli. As the first German division would not be complete in Africa until the middle of April, its help would come too late if the enemy continued his offensive. Something had to be done at once to bring the British offensive to a halt.

I therefore asked General Geissler to attack the port of Benghazi that night and to send bombers next morning to attack the British columns south-west of the town. General Geissler would not at first hear of it—apparently the Italians had asked him not to bomb Benghazi, as many Italian officers and civil officials owned houses there. I had no patience with this, and so Colonel Schmundt communicated with the Fuehrer's H.Q. that night and received authority to go ahead. A few hours later the first German bombers took off on their mission to cripple the British supply traffic to Benghazi.

At about 10 o'clock next morning [*12th February*], our reconnaissance party took off from Catania, heading for Tripoli. Flying low across the water, we met numerous flights of German Junkers on the way back from Tripoli, probably engaged on supply duties for the German Air Force already in Africa. We landed at about midday at Castel Benito, south of Tripoli. Lieut. Heggenreiner, Liaison Officer of the German General in Rome[1] to the Italian High Command in North Africa, received us with the news that Marshal Graziani had given up the High Command and handed over to his Chief of Staff, General Gariboldi. Heggenreiner briefly put me in the picture concerning the set-up of the Italian forces in Africa and described some very unpleasant incidents which had occurred during the retreat, or rather the rout which it had become. Italian troops had thrown away their weapons and ammunition and clambered on to overloaded vehicles in a wild attempt to get away to the west. This had led to some ugly scenes, and even to shooting. Morale was as low as it could be in all military circles in Tripoli. Most of the Italian officers had already packed their bags and were hoping for a quick return trip to Italy.

At about 13.00 hours I reported to General Gariboldi and put him in the picture concerning my mission. He showed little enthusiasm for the plan to establish a defence in the Sirte. With the help of a map I explained to him the outline of my scheme for defending Tripolitania. Its main features were—not a step farther back, powerful Luftwaffe support and every available man to be thrown in for the defence of the Sirte sector, including the first German contingents as soon as they landed. It was my belief that if the British could detect no opposition they would probably continue their advance, but that if they saw that they were going to have to fight another battle they would not simply attack—which would have been their proper course—but would first wait to build up supplies. With the time thus gained I hoped to build

---

[1] General von Rintelen, German Military Attaché in Rome and the representative of the German Supreme Command with the Italian Supreme Command.

up our own strength until we were eventually strong enough to withstand the enemy attack.

Gariboldi looked very dubious about it all. He was extremely discouraged by the defeat and advised me to have a look at the Sirte country first, because, having only just arrived, I could hardly be expected to have any idea of the difficulties of this theatre. I impressed on him as strongly as I could that we could only come to their help if they really made up their minds to hold the Sirte. " It won't take me long to get to know the country," I added. " I'll have a look at it from the air this afternoon and report back to the High Command this evening."

I had already decided, in view of the tenseness of the situation and the sluggishness of the Italian command, to depart from my instructions to confine myself to a reconnaissance and to take the command at the front into my own hands as soon as possible, at the latest after the arrival of the first German troops. General von Rintelen, to whom I had given a hint of my intention in Rome, had advised me against it, for, as he put it, that was the way to lose both honour and reputation.

That afternoon, our H.E. 111 carried Colonel Schmundt and myself over the soil of Africa. After seeing the field fortifications and the deep anti-tank ditches east of Tripoli, we flew across a belt of sand which had the appearance of being difficult country for either wheeled or tracked vehicles and of thus forming a good natural obstacle in front of Tripoli. The flight continued over the hilly country between Tarhuna and Homs —not, as far as we could see, particularly suitable territory for motorised forces. The level plain between Homs and Misurata, on the other hand, looked ideal for that purpose. The Via Balbia stretched away like a black thread through the desolate landscape, in which neither tree nor bush could be seen as far as the eye could reach. We passed Buerat, a small desert fort with a few huts and a landing stage. Finally, we circled over the white houses of Sirte and saw Italian troops in position east and southeast of the village.

Apart from the salt marshes between Sirte and Buerat, which only extended a few miles to the south, there was not a single break, such as a ravine or deep valley, anywhere in the landscape. The flight confirmed me in my plan to fortify Sirte and the country on either side of the coast road and to reserve the motorised forces for the mobile defence.

When we met General Gariboldi that evening to report on the results of our reconnaissance, General Roatta had already arrived and brought the Duce's new directive. Nothing more was now put in the way of my plan.

Next day, the X Italian Corps, consisting of the Brescia and Pavia Divisions, was to move forward to the Sirte-Buerat area and establish a defence. In its wake, the Ariete, which at that time possessed only 60 tanks of completely obsolete design (they were far too light and had once been used to chase the natives round Abyssinia), was to take up position west of Buerat. For the time being these were all the forces we could muster. The movement of even these formations was a headache for the Italian High Command, for they did not have enough transport for the lift and the road from Tripoli to Buerat was 250 miles long.

We could not therefore expect these Italian formations to arrive at the front very quickly, which meant that the only force we had immediately available with which to hold up the enemy—apart from the weak Italian garrison at Sirte—was the German Luftwaffe. The Luftwaffe Commander Afrika—General Froehlich — was accordingly asked to undertake this task, after it had been impressed on him how vitally important it was for the future of the African theatre. The commander of X Luftwaffe Korps was asked to provide support. With the limited forces available to them they did all they could, day and night, to help us out of our predicament, and not without success, for General Wavell's army remained at El Agheila.

A few days later I flew to Sirte to inspect the Italians holding the line there. They amounted to perhaps one regiment of troops and were well led by Major Santa Maria and Colonel Grati. This unit was the only force we had immediately available to oppose the British and our anxiety about the situation will be easily understood. The rest of our troops were standing nearly 200 miles away to the west.

At my insistence, the first Italian division was put on the march for Sirte on the 14th of February. On the same day the first German units— 3rd Reconnaissance Battalion and an anti-tank battalion—arrived in Tripoli harbour. With the situation so dangerous, I pressed for their rapid disembarkation, and asked that it should be continued throughout the night, by lamplight. The danger of enemy air attack simply had to be accepted.

The all-night unloading of this 6,000-ton transport was a record for the port of Tripoli. The men received their tropical kit early next morning, and by eleven o'clock were fallen in on the square in front of Government House. They radiated complete assurance of victory, and the change of atmosphere did not pass unnoticed in Tripoli. After a short march past, Baron von Wechmar [*commanding the 3rd Reconnaissance Battalion*] moved off with his men to Sirte and arrived at the front 26 hours later. On the 16th, German reconnaissance troops, working with Santa Maria's column, made their first move against the enemy. I now took over command at the front. Colonel Schmundt had returned to the Fuehrer's H.Q. several days before.

14 Feb. 1941

DEAREST LU,

All going as well as I could wish. I hope to be able to pull it off.

I'm very well. There's nothing whatever for you to worry about.
A lot to do. I've already had a thorough look round.

17 Feb. 1941

Everything's splendid with me and mine in this glorious sunshine.
I'm getting on very, very well with the Italian Command and
couldn't wish for better co-operation.

My lads are already at the front, which has been moved about
350 miles to the east. As far as I am concerned they can come now.

Through my daily flights between Tripoli and the front, I came to
know Tripolitania very well from the air and formed a great admiration
for the colonising achievement of the Italians. They had left their mark
all over the country, particularly round Tripoli, Tarhuna and Homs.

Day by day now, more columns of Italian and German troops moved
up to the front. Despite Italian advice to the contrary, the Afrika Korps'
Quartermaster (Major Otto), a first-class man, organised supplies along
the coast by small ships, thus considerably easing the pressure on our
lorry columns. The Italians had unfortunately never built a railway
along the coast. It would now have been of immense value.

To enable us to appear as strong as possible and to induce the
maximum caution in the British, I had the workshops three miles south of
Tripoli produce large numbers of dummy tanks, which were mounted
on Volkswagen [*the German People's Car*] and were deceptively like the
original. On the 17th February the enemy was very active and I feared
that he would continue his offensive towards Tripoli. This impression
was strengthened on the 18th, when we established the presence of further
British units between El Agheila and Agedabia. To give them in turn
an impression of activity on our part, I decided to push forward 3rd
Reconnaissance Battalion, reinforced by the Battalion Santa Maria and
with 39th Anti-tank Battalion under command, as far as the Nofilia
area, with instructions to make contact with the enemy.

On the 24th February, the first clash occurred between British and
German troops in Africa. Two enemy scout cars, a lorry and a car were
destroyed, and three British soldiers, including an officer, taken prisoner,
with no casualties on our side. Meanwhile, the movement of further
units of the 5th Light Division to the front proceeded as planned.

We were still rather suspicious about the British moves and to clarify
the situation, General Streich, commander of the 5th Light Division—who
had taken over command at the front—advanced up to the defile of
Mugtaa on the 4th March and closed it with mines. He saw nothing of
the enemy.

This move gained us a sector of some importance and materially
strengthened our position. The salt marsh known as Sebcha el Chebira
extends here 20 miles south of the Via Balbia and is impassable to

vehicles except at a few points, which we very soon mined. An enemy frontal attack against the narrows would have been comparatively easy to beat off, and an outflanking movement, which would have involved him in a long march over sandy and difficult country, was not very likely. At Mugtaa we were already some 500 miles east of Tripoli. For our coastal supply traffic we had gained the small port of Ras el Ali—like all those places with high-sounding names, this was in reality a desolate and miserable hole—to which the quartermasters very soon began sending stores.

5 March 1941

DEAREST LU,

Just back from a two-day journey—or rather flight—to the front, which is now 450 miles away to the east. Everything going fine.

A lot to do. Can't leave here for the moment as I couldn't be answerable for my absence. Too much depends on my own person and my driving power. I hope you've had some post from me.

My troops are on their way. Speed is the one thing that matters here. The climate suits me down to the ground. I even " overslept " this morning till after 6. . . .

. . . A gala performance of " Victory in the West "[1] was given here to-day. In welcoming the guests—there were a lot, some with ladies—I said I hoped the day would come when we'd be showing " Victory in Africa." . . .

Our operations against Mugtaa resulted in a British withdrawal eastward and we now supposed their main body to be lying round Agedabia and along the coast to Derna.

The British forces had been reduced in number, and quality, to a greater extent than Rommel realised. At the end of February the illustrious 7th Armoured Division had been sent back to Egypt to rest and refit. Its place had been taken by half of the 2nd Armoured Division, raw from home—the other half having been sent to Greece. The 6th Australian Division had also been replaced by the 9th Australian Division, but part of this was kept back at Tobruk because of maintenance difficulties farther forward. Besides lacking experience, the new formations had also been stripped of much equipment and transport for the benefit of the expedition to Greece. Moreover, O'Connor had gone back to Egypt and been relieved by a commander, General Neame, who was without experience of mechanised desert warfare.

In taking such risks for the sake of giving " maximum support " to the Greek venture, Wavell based himself on the belief that the " Italians in Tripolitania could be disregarded and that the Germans were unlikely to accept the risk of sending large bodies of armoured troops to Africa in view of the inefficiency of the Italian Navy." He was correct in his general estimate of the attitude of the German High

[1]Film of the 1940 French campaign, made by German propaganda companies.

Command, and also in his detailed estimate that only the equivalent of " one armoured brigade " (i.e. the 5th Panzer Regiment) had been landed. On normal reasoning Wavell was justified in his conclusion of the 2nd March: " I do not think that with this force he (the enemy) will attempt to recover Benghazi." But such reckoning did not allow for a Rommel.

Enemy attempts to strangle our supplies by naval action in the Mediterranean and air attack against Tripoli achieved no great success at this stage. On the 11th March, the 5th Panzer Regiment completed its disembarkation in Tripoli; this force with its—for those days—up-to-date equipment made a tremendous impression on the Italians.[1]

On the 13th March, I moved my H.Q. up to Sirte in order to be closer to the front. My original intention was to fly to Sirte in a Ghibli[2] aircraft with my Chief of Staff. After taking off, however, we ran into sandstorms near Tauorga, whereat the pilot, ignoring my abuse and attempts to get him to fly on, turned back, compelling me to continue the journey by car from the airfield at Misurata. Now we realised what little idea we had had of the tremendous force of such a storm. Immense clouds of reddish dust obscured all visibility and forced the car's speed down to a crawl. Often the wind was so strong that it was impossible to drive along the Via Balbia. Sand streamed down the windscreen like water. We gasped in breath painfully through handkerchiefs held over our faces and sweat poured off our bodies in the unbearable heat. So this was the Ghibli. Silently I breathed my apologies to the pilot. A Luftwaffe officer crashed in a sandstorm that day.

On the 15th of March, a mixed German and Italian force, under the command of Count Schwerin, moved out from Sirte towards Murzuch [*about 450 miles to the south*]. The Italian High Command had asked us to undertake this operation because General de Gaulle's troops in southern Libya were beginning to become a nuisance. As far as we were concerned, however, the main purpose of the move was to gain experience of long marches and in particular to test the suitability of our equipment for African conditions. Shortly afterwards the whole of the Brescia Division arrived in the line at Mugtaa and the 5th Light Division was freed for mobile employment.

On the 19th March I flew to the Fuehrer's H.Q. to report and obtain fresh instructions. The Fuehrer made me a retrospective award of the Oakleaves[3] for the 7th Panzer Division's actions in France. The C.-in-C. of the Army [*von Brauchitsch*] informed me that there was no intention of striking a decisive blow in Africa in the near future, and that for the

[1]The 5th Panzer Regiment was equipped with 120 tanks, but of these only 60 were medium tanks (Panzer III and IV). In addition, the Italian Ariete Division advanced with 80 tanks—all that were serviceable at the time.

[2]The name of an Italian aircraft. Ghibli is also the Arabic word for sandstorm, in which sense it is used later in this passage.

[3]See footnote on page 39.

present I could expect no reinforcements. After the arrival of the 15th Panzer Division at the end of May, I was to attack and destroy the enemy round Agedabia. Benghazi might perhaps be taken. I pointed out that we could not just take Benghazi, but would have to occupy the whole of Cyrenaica, as the Benghazi area could not be held by itself. I was not very happy at the efforts of Field Marshal von Brauchitsch and Colonel-General Halder to keep down the numbers of troops sent to Africa and leave the future of this theatre of war to chance. The momentary British weakness in North Africa should have been exploited with the utmost energy, in order to gain the initiative once and for all for ourselves.

In my opinion it was also wrong not to risk a landing in England in 1940-41. If ever there was a chance for this operation to succeed it was in the period after the British Expeditionary Force had lost its equipment. From then on the operation became steadily more difficult to undertake, and undertaken it eventually had to be, if the war against Britain was to be won.

Before my departure, I had instructed the 5th Light Division to prepare an attack on El Agheila for the 24th March, with the object of taking the airfield and small fort, and driving out the present garrison. A short time before, the Marada Oasis, some distance to the south, had been occupied by a mixed Italian and German force. This force now had to be maintained and our supply columns were being constantly molested by the British from El Agheila.

Accordingly, after my return to Africa, 3rd Reconnaissance Battalion took the fort, water points and airfield at El Agheila in the early hours of the 24th March. The garrison, which consisted of only a weak force, had strongly mined the whole place and withdrew skilfully in face of our attack.

After our capture of El Agheila, the British outposts—as we learnt from the Luftwaffe—appeared to fall back to the defile at Mersa el Brega.

26 March 1941

Dearest Lu,
    Spent our first day by the sea. It's a very lovely place and it's as good as being in a hotel in my comfortable caravan. Bathe in the sea in the mornings, it's already beautifully warm. Aldinger and Guenther [*Rommel's A.D.C. and batman respectively*] living in a tent close by. We make coffee in the mornings in our own kitchen. Yesterday an Italian General, Calvi de Bergolo, made me a present of a bournous. It's a magnificent thing—blue-black with red silk and embroidery. It would do well for you as a theatre cloak. . . .
    Little fresh from the front. I have to hold the troops back to prevent them bolting forward. They've taken another new position,

20 miles farther east. There'll be some worried faces among our Italian friends.

THE RAID THROUGH CYRENAICA

The defile at Mersa el Brega was the first objective for the attack which we were due to launch in May on the enemy forces round Agedabia. After the British had been driven out of El Agheila, they established themselves on the commanding heights at Mersa el Brega and south of the salt marsh at Bir es Suera, and began to build up their position. It was with some misgivings that we watched their activities, because if they had once been allowed time to build up, wire and mine these naturally strong positions, they would then have possessed the counter-part of our position at Mugtaa, which was difficult either to assault or to outflank round the south. The country south of the Wadi Faregh, some 20 or 30 miles south of Mersa el Brega, was extremely sandy and almost impassable for vehicles. I was therefore faced with the choice of either waiting for the rest of my troops to arrive at the end of May—which would have given the British time to construct such strong defences that it would have been very difficult for our attack to achieve the desired result—or of going ahead with our existing small forces to attack and take the Mersa el Brega position in its present undeveloped state. I decided for the latter. It was, in fact, fair to expect that an attack by even our relatively weak forces would give us the defile. The Mersa el Brega position was just as well suited for our purpose as that at Mugtaa and would at the same time provide us with a suitable assembly and forming-up area for the May attack. A further argument in favour of an immediate move was that our water supply had recently been so bad that it was essential to open up new wells. An operation against Mersa el Brega would give us access to plentiful water-bearing land.

On the 31st March our attack moved forward against the British positions at Mersa el Brega, and a fierce engagement took place in the early hours of the morning with British reconnaissance troops at Maaten Bescer. In the afternoon, troops of the 5th Light Division attacked the Mersa el Brega position proper, which was stubbornly defended by the British. Our attack came to a halt.

I spent the whole day on the battlefield with Aldinger and my Chief of Staff, Lieut.-Col. von dem Borne, and in the afternoon reconnoitred the possibility of attacking north of the coast road. The 8th M.G. Battalion was put in at this point late in the evening and in a dashing attack through rolling sandhills, succeeded in throwing the enemy back to the east and taking possession of the Mersa el Brega defile.

The 5th Light Division's success was not reported to Corps until the morning. The British had apparently beaten a somewhat precipitate

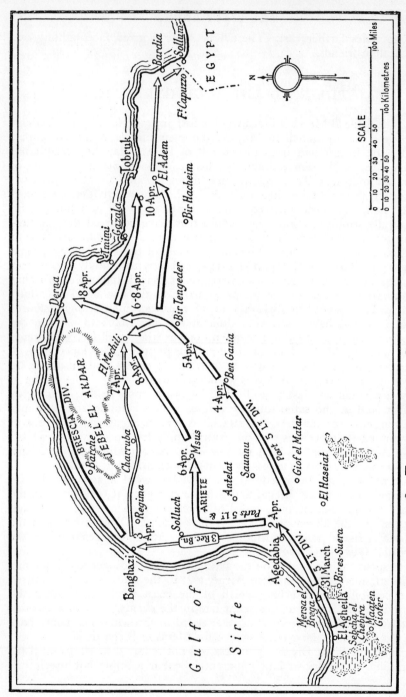

8. THE THRUST INTO CYRENAICA, APRIL 1941

retreat, and 50 Bren-carriers and about 30 lorries had fallen into our hands. For the 1st April, I ordered our forces to close up in the area Mersa el Brega and Maaten Giofer.

Luftwaffe reports clearly showed that the enemy was tending to draw back and this was confirmed by reconnaissance patrols which General Streich had sent out. It was a chance I could not resist and I gave orders for Agedabia to be attacked and taken, in spite of the fact that our instructions were not to undertake any such operation before the end of May. Accordingly, on the 2nd of April, the 5th Light Division moved forward on either side of the Via Balbia to Agedabia. The enemy minefields gave us little trouble. The Italians followed along the coast road. Agedabia was taken in the afternoon after a short action and our forward units then pushed on rapidly to the Zuetina area. Meanwhile, 5th Panzer Regiment, which formed the main weight of our attack south of the Via Balbia, ran up against British tanks and a skirmish developed. Soon seven enemy tanks were burning on the battlefield. We lost only three. In this action the enemy used a very effective camouflage in the form of Arab tents, which enabled them to come into action unexpectedly.

By the time evening came we had occupied the country round Agedabia up to a point 12 miles to the east. The Italians closed up again. On the 3rd April I shifted my forward H.Q. to Agedabia and watched the enemy's movements. He was now withdrawing generally and seemed to be evacuating Cyrenaica. Apparently he was under the impression that we were extremely strong, an impression in which our dummy tanks had probably played a big part.

Wavell became anxious about the risks he had taken from the moment Rommel's advanced force retook El Agheila. Neame was instructed to fall back on a position near Benghazi if he was pressed, and given permission to evacuate the port if necessary. Immediately after the capture of Agedabia on the 2nd April, hurried orders were given for the abandonment of Benghazi, and a retreat eastward, with the idea of keeping the forces intact. But in the confusion of the retreat they soon disintegrated.

During the morning, a report came in that a force of 20 enemy tanks was located some 20 miles north of Agedabia and I instructed Lieut. Berndt[1] to check its accuracy. He drove up the Benghazi road as far as Magrun, identified them as abandoned Italian tanks and came back.

By this time we had taken 800 British prisoners. The British apparently intended to avoid, in any circumstances, fighting a decisive action; so, that afternoon, I decided to stay on the heels of the retreating enemy and make a bid to seize the whole of Cyrenaica at one stroke. With this intention, I immediately put an advance party of the Ariete, under the command of Colonel Fabris, on the march for Ben Gania and gave orders to the 5th Light Division to push 3rd Reconnaissance Battalion forward

[1]Alfred Ingemar Berndt, an official of the Propaganda Ministry attached to Rommel's force.

along the Via Balbia towards Benghazi. General Streich had some misgivings on account of the state of his vehicles, but I could not allow this to affect the issue. One cannot permit unique opportunities to slip by for the sake of trifles.

I had been told by the Italian General, Zamboni, that the track from Agedabia to Giof el Matar was an absolute death-trap, and he had done his best to dissuade me from sending troops through Cyrenaica over that route. However, I placed more faith in my own observation and set off with my A.D.C., Lieut. Aldinger, in the direction of Giof el Matar. After 12 miles we reached the head of the Italian Reconnaissance Battalion Santa Maria, which was attached to Fabris's force. The battalion was advancing, extremely well deployed in area formation. The ground was quite good for driving and caused us no particular difficulty.

On returning to my H.Q. at about 16.00 hours, I learnt that the 5th Light Division were saying they needed four days to replenish their petrol. This seemed to me to be utterly excessive and I immediately gave orders for the division to unload all its vehicles and send them off at once to the divisional dump at Arco dei Fileni, whence they were to bring up sufficient petrol, rations and ammunition for the advance through Cyrenaica inside 24 hours. It meant the division being immobilised for 24 hours but with the enemy withdrawing, this was a risk we could afford to take.

Meanwhile, it was becoming increasingly clear that the enemy believed us to be far stronger than we actually were—a belief that it was essential to maintain, by keeping up the appearance of a large-scale offensive. Of course I was not at that moment in any position to press hard after the enemy with my main force, but it looked as though we should be able to maintain enough pressure with our advance troops to keep him on the run. In 24 hours' time I hoped to be able to move up stronger forces, which I intended to concentrate on the southern flank, with the object of pushing through Ben Gania to Tmimi, thereby cutting off and putting out of action as many British troops as possible.

That evening I drove north to see how things were going with 3rd Reconnaissance Battalion, which had been sent off in the direction of Benghazi. On coming up with them in the region of Magrun I was informed by von Wechmar that he had not so far made any contact with British troops. He had been informed by an Italian priest, who had come out from Benghazi to meet them, that the enemy had already left the town. At von Wechmar's request I immediately sent the battalion forward to Benghazi.

On our way back to Agedabia we came across a German vehicle which was apparently manned by British officers. We did not bother to stop, assuming that they would be picked up by 3rd Reconnaissance

Battalion, which is what in fact did happen. We heard later that the Tommies had ambushed a German driver north-west of Agedabia and taken his vehicle in the hope of making their way through to their own troops in Cyrenaica. After their gallant attempt one could almost have wished them success. However, they were unlucky.

On my return to H.Q. I met the Italian Commander-in-Chief, General Gariboldi, who was by no means pleased about the course of the action to date, and berated me violently, principally because our operations were in direct contradiction to orders from Rome. He added that the supply situation was far too insecure to enable anyone to take responsibility for such an operation, or for its consequences. He wanted me to discontinue all action and undertake no further moves without his express authority.

I had made up my mind to stand out from the start for the greatest possible measure of operational and tactical freedom and, what is more, had no intention of allowing good opportunities to slip by unused. As a result the conversation became somewhat heated. I stated my views plainly and without equivocation. General Gariboldi wanted to get authority from Rome first. But that way days could go by unused; I was not going to stand for it, and said that I intended to go on doing what I felt I had to in whatever situation might arise. This brought the argument to a climax. At that very moment, a signal arrived—*deus ex machina*—from the German High Command, giving me complete freedom of action, and settling the argument exactly as I wanted it.

Von Wechmar's battalion moved into Benghazi during the night of the 3rd April, amid great jubilation from the civil population. The British had set fire to all their stores.

3 April 1941

DEAREST LU,

We've been attacking since the 31st with dazzling success. There'll be consternation amongst our masters in Tripoli and Rome, perhaps in Berlin too. I took the risk against all orders and instructions because the opportunity seemed favourable. No doubt it will all be pronounced good later and they'll all say they'd have done exactly the same in my place. We've already reached our first objective, which we weren't supposed to get to until the end of May. The British are falling over each other to get away. Our casualties small. Booty can't yet be estimated. You will understand that I can't sleep for happiness.

Early next morning, a detachment of the Brescia to the strength of one reinforced regiment set out for Benghazi in order to free 3rd Reconnaissance Battalion for further operations. The main body of the 5th Light Division was to move forward through Ben Gania, and its leading battalion, under Count Schwerin's command, was strengthened. The Ariete was detailed to push forward over the same route as far as Bir Tengeder and then to turn off north to take El Mechili. Speed was now everything. We wanted at all costs to bring some part of the British force to battle before they had all managed to withdraw from Cyrenaica and thus escape the danger threatening them.

On the 4th April, I visited Benghazi with the Chief of Staff and Aldinger and sent off the Reconnaissance Battalion, strengthened by a Panzer company, through Regima and Charruba to Mechili. In the afternoon I flew in a Junkers—there being no Storch serviceable—over Ben Gania and towards Tengeder. Columns were rolling eastwards along the track raising great pillars of dust. I thought I could identify our leading units 12 miles east of Gania.

That evening, the enemy's dispositions appeared to be roughly as follows:

Small bodies of their troops were located east of Ben Gania, while other British forces continued to hold Msus. During the evening 3rd Reconnaissance Battalion had made contact with a weak enemy force at Regima and thrown it back. The British main body was in full retreat and was evacuating Cyrenaica.

4 April 1941

DEAREST LU,

Congratulations have come from the Fuehrer for the unexpected success, plus a directive for further operations which is in full accord with my own ideas. Our territory is expanding and now we can manœuvre.

Next morning [*5th April*] I alerted the *Kampfstaffel*[1] of the Afrika Korps at 04.00 hours and put it on the march for Ben Gania. I intended, as soon as the situation permitted, to go up to the forward units myself, take over command and personally lead the advance on Tmimi or Mechili.

I now took a look from my Storch at the progress of the advance to Ben Gania and, after my return, talked over with Major Schleusener how best to get up the heavy supply columns. We had some doubts about using the rather difficult road through Ben Gania and decided that we might get supplies up through Solluch to Mechili.

The Luftwaffe reported that the British retreat was continuing. At about midday I ordered Colonel Olbrich to move forward immediately with a strong force of armour, consisting of 5th Panzer Regiment and 40

---

[1]The *Kampfstaffel*, not to be confused with the *Gefechtsstaffel* (see note on page 15) was a unit formed for the protection of the Corps or Army headquarters. It was normally of company strength at Corps level and battalion strength at Army. During the course of the African campaign the *Kampfstaffel* came to be used more and more as a combat group for special tasks.

Italian tanks, through Magrun and Solluch to Msus, destroy the enemy there and go on to Mechili.

5 *April 1941*

DEAREST LU,

Off at 4 this morning. Things are happening in Africa. Let's hope the great stroke we've now launched is successful. I'm keeping very fit. The simple life here suits me better than the fleshpots of France. How are things with you both? . . .

At about 14.00 hours that afternoon I took off in a Junkers and flew to Ben Gania. After landing, I heard from the Luftwaffe that there were no longer any British to be seen in the area of Mechili and to its south. Schwerin's column thereupon received the order: " Mechili clear of enemy. Make for it. Drive fast. Rommel." The remainder of our forward troops were also switched to Mechili. I myself flew off with Aldinger in the afternoon to take over personal command of the leading units. Towards evening we flew back to look for the 5th Light Division's columns, which we discovered making good speed to the north-east. Shortly afterwards we also found my *Generalsstaffel*,[1] I now sent the Storch back and drove up the track in my " Mammoth "[2] to Ben Gania in order to get my own idea of the difficulty of the march. Two and a half hours later, completely covered in dust, we reached the airfield where I was informed that the 5th Light Division had been switched to Mechili. Shortly afterwards, Lieut. Schulz arrived back from a recon- naissance flight and reported that Mechili and its surroundings were now held by strong British forces. Earlier in the day Major Heymer had been sent on a mission with two aircraft to mine the tracks east of Mechili. He had not yet returned. My Ic,[3] Captain Baudissin, had been shot down in a H.E. III and taken prisoner by the enemy.

It was now night and too late to fly back to Agedabia. In view of the new and rather less favourable situation, I decided to drive up to the 5th Light Division and take over command of the operation myself.

We drove at first with headlights. Every now and again we had to pick our way past minefields, which we located by the burning vehicles standing at their edges. At about midnight, our long and brilliantly lit column, winding its way through the desert, was suddenly attacked by British aircraft. No damage was suffered, however, and we went on our way, this time without lights. At about three in the morning we

[1]Another term for the *Gefechtsstaffel*.

[2]Rommel's armoured command vehicle which had been captured from the British near Agheila.

[3]In the German Army, " Ic " is the Intelligence branch of the General Staff. The term is also used, as here, to denote the chief representative of that branch on the staff of any formation, high or low.

reached the head of the 5th Light Division's column, where we found the commander. The column halted and we discovered that we had missed our route. According to the speedometer reading we should have been in Bir Tengeder long before. There was nothing in sight.

Shortly afterwards two German aircraft flew over from the north, a Henschel and a Storch. They recognised us and landed in spite of the rough and stony ground. It was Major Heymer and his men—their task accomplished. After landing on the airfield at Mechili just before nightfall and mining the tracks leading to the east, they had lain all night a few yards away from their aircraft, keeping watch on the British traffic. When morning dawned, they had discovered that British troops had taken up position close beside them, but had managed to reach their aircraft in a sharp sprint and take off unmolested. For the rest, they reported that Mechili was strongly held, with heavy vehicle traffic to the east. There was now no time to lose, otherwise the bird would be flown. As we were still about 12 miles from Mechili I instructed Lieut. Behrend to push forward at top speed with his small combat team to the Mechili-Derna track and close it at a suitable point. Lieut.-Col. Ponath, of whose force there were unfortunately only 15 vehicles with us, was dispatched to Derna, where he was to close the Via Balbia to both directions. Soon Count Schwerin arrived with part of his force and he too received orders to block the tracks leading out of Mechili to the east.

At about 07.30 hours, Lieut. Schulz landed at Corps H.Q. and reported the presence of 300 British vehicles at Mechili. General Streich also arrived shortly afterwards and I informed him of my intentions. Then I drove off with my staff to Count Schwerin's command post. On the way we saw numerous British tank tracks in the sand, all going east.

Unfortunately, we were unable to launch the attack we had planned on Mechili on the 6th April—with Fabris's force attacking from the east and Schwerin's from the south and south-east—as Fabris did not arrive in the hills east of Mechili until the evening. I had no reports at all that evening from a large part of the Corps, distances having become too great for wireless communication.

Colonel Olbrich's column reported to my Ia [*operations chief*], who was still in Agedabia, that sandstorms and shortage of petrol had badly held up their progress through Msus. In spite of these delays they succeeded in taking Msus in the late evening, and continued their march on towards Mechili. At about 02.00 hours on the 7th April, Fabris's column reported that they were completely out of petrol and were unable to get their artillery into position. All petrol reserves held by Divisional H.Q. were immediately collected together—35 cans in all—and at 03.00 hours, I set off with my *Gefechtsstaffel* to get the artillery into position before daybreak. In the pitch darkness, however—there were not even any stars—we completely failed to find the column. Even when we repeated our attempt next morning, we still had a great deal of trouble before we eventually found it. Among other vicissitudes, we ran into the rear of a British outpost of several Bren-carriers. Although we had only three vehicles, and only one of those was armed with a machine-gun, we drove at top speed towards the enemy, raising a great cloud of dust which prevented them seeing how many vehicles we had behind us. This obviously rattled the enemy troops who hurriedly abandoned their position.

After we had supplied the Italian vehicles with petrol, the force moved forward in area formation towards Mechili. Soon we came in sight of Fort Mechili. Large numbers of enemy vehicles were parked there and through glasses we were easily able to pick out the men standing about in groups. I led Fabris's column to a point two miles north-east of Mechili, where we halted and took up position. At first, the enemy showed no sign of putting up a defence, and I sent Lieut. Grohne across under a flag of truce with a summons to the British commander to surrender. Of course he refused.

Unfortunately, we had seen no sign yet of Olbrich's force. He should have arrived at Mechili long ago, and I took off in my Storch later that morning to look for him. We flew at 2,000 feet across the sandy plain and soon approached the hills near Mechili. West of the fort I suddenly saw long black columns of vehicles, which I took for Olbrich's. Several men laid out a landing cross between the vehicles. At the last moment I suddenly spotted the flat helmets of British troops. We immediately banked and made off, followed by machine-gun fire from the British troops. We were lucky to get away practically unscathed, with only one hit in the tail. After that episode, we flew on west at a great height. Some 15 to 20 miles south-west of Mechili, we saw a number of small vehicles travelling east. Their German markings could be clearly identified. I landed and found part of 3rd Reconnaissance Battalion, which I immediately put on the right road. After taking off again I discovered several columns of German and Italian tanks 15 to 20 miles farther south. I landed and pitched into them for being so slow. Apparently the leading vehicles, while crossing a dried-out salt marsh, had seen what appeared to be a wide stretch of water away to the east and turned back. It was, of course, only a mirage—a common enough occurrence in that district. I now ordered them to press on forward as fast as they could.

After returning to H.Q. I waited in vain for the arrival of Olbrich's force. Finally, in the afternoon I took off in my Storch to look for them again. Black smoke was rising from the hill at Mechili—probably a British vehicle on fire. At one point we crossed a new track on which British vehicles were streaming off to the south-east. The Tommies took cover when they saw the Storch, but did not open fire. There was nothing to be seen anywhere and it was obvious that Olbrich's force had once again lost its way. But where? There were tracks in the salt marsh, but these soon vanished in the stony country. I was extremely angry and decidedly worried, because the decision in eastern Cyrenaica depended entirely on the early arrival of this force. The sun had already gone down and we knew that it would be dark in an hour and a half. We now flew north. At last I saw plumes of dust on the horizon. Grown wary after the incident with the British landing cross, we flew cautiously up to the column. German vehicles they were, however, and we landed near Colonel Olbrich's staff. I was extremely angry about the unnecessary détour they had made—due, it is true, to their ignorance of the road—and ordered them to get on as fast as they could. Flying by watch and compass, we eventually found my H.Q. again and landed successfully in spite of the darkness. During my absence British low-flying aircraft had shot up an airstrip and set fire to several Junkers.

8 April 1941

DEAREST LU,

I've no idea whether the date is right. We've been attacking for days now in the endless desert and have lost all idea of space or time. As you'll have seen from the communiqués, things are going very well.

To-day will be another decisive day. Our main force is on its way up after a 220-mile march over the sand and rock of the desert. I flew back from the front yesterday to look for them and found them in the desert. You can hardly imagine how pleased I was. It's going to be a " Cannae ", modern style.

I'm very well. You need never worry.

Our attack was now due to be launched on the following morning. At about 06.00 hours on the 8th April, I flew off in my Storch to the front east of Mechili in order to follow the course of action. Flying at about 150 feet, we approached a Bersaglieri battalion which had been brought up by Colonel Fabris the previous day. The Italians had apparently never seen a Storch before and were so completely bewildered by our sudden appearance over their heads that they fired on us from all directions. At the range of 50 to 100 yards, it was a miracle that we were not shot down, and it did not speak well for Italian marksmanship. We swung round immediately and soon put a fold in the ground between our allies and ourselves. Having no wish to be shot down by my own Italians I had the aircraft climb to 3,000 feet, from where we observed the situation in safety. The attack on Mechili was obviously making progress. A large column of enemy vehicles was on the move from Mechili to the west and we flew on in the hope of finding Olbrich's force, which must at last be coming up. But there was still no sign of them. We did sight an 88-mm. gun with its crew a mile or two west of the British. Thinking we would find more of our troops there, we came in to land and taxied in to a sandhill, where the Storch piled up. The gun commander reported that his gun had been attacked and shot up by tanks the previous day. There were none of our troops about in the neighbourhood and he had sent a man off in a truck to make contact with our own forces. I asked him whether he could at least fire on the approaching dust cloud, which was being raised by British vehicles. At first he said he could, but then he discovered that the man who had gone off in the truck had taken the firing-pin. The British vehicles, driving in area formation, were getting steadily closer and it was obviously high time for us to be off if we were not to find our way to Canada! Luckily, the gun crew still had another lorry left and we drove off in it to the south-east, where we shortly found a salt marsh which I recognised from my flights of the previous day. From there, we eventually found our way back to Corps H.Q.

Immediately on my return I sent Major Heymer off with a Henschel to look for Olbrich and his men, and bring them in at long last to Mechili. Meanwhile, more and more of the Ariete were arriving and were immediately put on the march to Mechili. As nothing was yet known about the progress of the attack, which had been going on since morning, I set off for Mechili with a small staff, to see for myself. It is impossible to take the correct decisions without accurate knowledge of the situation. We had not gone far before we found ourselves in a violent sandstorm and were forced to stop for a while on the next hill. Driving on compass bearing through the raging sand, we at length succeeded in finding our way to Mechili airfield. From there we groped our way along the telegraph wire steadily closer to Mechili, which had meanwhile been taken by our troops. As we heard later from General Streich, all British attempts to break out to the east—they had made several during the morning—had collapsed in the fire of the German and Italian artillery. The attack which our infantry had launched with the few German tanks and A.A. guns, had been successful. Meanwhile, Olbrich and his force had arrived.

At about 12.00 hours, I received a report from Lieut.-Col. Ponath, who was barring the Via Balbia at Derna, that prisoners and booty were mounting hourly, but that his fighting strength was now greatly weakened and he urgently required reinforcements. I immediately sent off Schwerin's and Olbrich's forces to Derna. The remainder of the 5th Light Division was to hold the captured territory at Mechili. The Ariete was also to assemble there for the present.

Schwerin's force moved off to Derna at about midday and I followed shortly afterwards with my *Fuehrungsstaffel*[1] and the anti-aircraft platoon. Just beyond the fort we ran into a sandstorm, which scattered the column so badly that it was some time before it could be marshalled again. Despite this delay, we managed, by fast driving, to reach Derna by 18.00 hours, where Ponath reported the capture of 800 prisoners, including to

[1] The *Fuehrungsstaffel* consisted of the staff branches "Ia" (operations) and "Ic" (intelligence). It was normally sited statically in the forward operations area while Rommel himself exercised command on the move with his *Gefechtsstaffel* (see note, page 15).

my great joy, almost the whole of the British staff. Among them were General P. Neame, C.-in-C. British Troops in Egypt and Transjordan, and General O'Connor, the man who had so roughly handled the Italian Army. They had been rounded up and taken prisoner by motor-cycle troops.[1] The Brescia had already arrived in Derna from Benghazi, largely thanks to the energetic intervention of General Kirchheim, who had accompanied their advance.

General von Prittwitz, commander of the 15th Panzer Division, part of which had just arrived in Africa, was now instructed to take command of the pursuit force and follow up the British to Tobruk. The 3rd Reconnaissance Battalion, 8th M.G. Battalion and 605th Anti-Tank Battalion were put under his command. Not all this force had arrived yet, of course, but the machine-gun battalion had already refuelled and was ready to continue the pursuit.

The re-conquest of Cyrenaica was now complete.[2] However, it still seemed to me very important to remain on the enemy's heels, and, by keeping the pressure up, persuade him to continue his retreat. Even though—judging by experience to date—we could not expect to split off and destroy any major part of the enemy army, we would have an excellent spring-board in the Marmarica for a possible summer offensive against Alexandria, quite apart of course from the high propaganda and psychological value that the reconquest of the Italian colony would have, especially among the Italians. There was now a good hope that normal supply traffic would soon be established along the coast road.

Several of our units had unfortunately gone astray during the raid through the desert. We organised search parties to find and bring in all stragglers and had the desert combed by aircraft. A large fire, giving out dense clouds of smoke, was kept going in Mechili.

10 April 1941

DEAREST LU,

After a long desert march I reached the sea the evening before last. It's wonderful to have pulled this off against the British. I'm well. My caravan arrived at last early this morning and I'm hoping to sleep in it again.

[1]O'Connor had been sent up to take over command from Neame, but with characteristic consideration had preferred to act as adviser until the battle was over. The car in which the two were travelling ran into a German patrol, when unescorted, and both were captured.

[2]In speaking of Cyrenaica, Germans and Italians apply that term to the western part of the country, and describe the area east of Gazala as the Marmarica.

FIRST LESSONS

Probably never before in modern warfare had such a completely unprepared offensive as this raid through Cyrenaica been attempted. It had made tremendous demands on the powers of improvisation of both command and troops, and in some cases commanders had been unable to reach their objectives. One thing particularly evident had been the tendency of certain commanders to permit themselves unnecessary delays for refuelling and restocking with ammunition, or for a leisurely overhaul of their vehicles, even when an immediate attack offered prospects of success. The sole criterion for a commander in carrying out a given operation must be the time he is allowed for it, and he must use all his powers of execution to fulfil the task within that time. I had not demanded too much on the march to Mechili; this was shown by the fact that commanders who had used their initiative had achieved what I asked. A commander's drive and energy often count for more than his intellectual powers—a fact that is not generally understood by academic soldiers, although for the practical man it is self-evident. Later in the campaign, when I had had a chance to establish closer relations with the troops, they were capable at all times of achieving what I demanded of them.

Later on our advance came in for some criticism on grounds of higher strategy. When General Paulus came to Africa he said that our rapid and unplanned advance through Cyrenaica had caused the British to withdraw their troops from Greece, a move which had been entirely contrary to the intentions of the High Command.[1]

To this I would point out: first, I knew nothing of the High Command's plan for Greece, and, in any case, doubt very much whether we could have trapped the British in Greece, assuming that they were in the south-west at the time of the German attack. They were, as a rule, always able to get their troops away by sea very quickly when it came to the point. I need only quote Dunkirk, Andalsnes and, not least, Greece itself, where the Royal Navy managed to get away to North Africa or Crete by far the majority of the Empire troops known to have been there at the time the German offensive opened.

[1]General Paulus was then *Oberquartiermeister I* at O.K.H.—a post best defined as Deputy Chief of the General Staff. He was mistaken in his view that Rommel's rapid advance in Cyrenaica led to the withdrawal of the British force from Greece. That was due to the effect of Yugo-Slavia's rapid collapse under *Blitzkrieg* attack and the threat to the British force's exposed western flank in Greece. As soon as this happened, the Greek authorities suggested that the force should be evacuated in order to spare Greece from devastation. The British Commander and the Government promptly concurred. General Wilson hurriedly retreated southward to the Peloponnese peninsula, resisting the temptation to make a heroic stand at Thermopylae, while the Navy hastened to the rescue. Three-quarters of the force were safely brought away, although nearly 12,000 were left behind along with most of the equipment.

Secondly, it is my view that it would have been better if we had kept our hands off Greece altogether, and rather created a concentration of strength in North Africa to drive the British right out of the Mediterranean area. The air forces we employed in Greece should have been used for the protection of convoys to Africa, and every possibility of gaining shipping space in the Mediterranean should have been exploited to the full.   Malta should have been taken instead of Crete.   Powerful German motorised forces in North Africa could then have taken the whole of the British-occupied Mediterranean coastline, which would have isolated south-eastern Europe.   Greece, Yugoslavia and Crete would have had no choice but to submit, for supplies and support from the British Empire would have been impossible.   The price in casualties of this scheme—which would not only have achieved our aims in south-east Europe, but would also have secured the Mediterranean area and the Near East as sources of oil and bases for attack on Russia—would not have been much greater than the price we did in fact have to pay in Greece, Yugoslavia, Crete and North Africa in the summer of 1941.   But our superiors had inhibitions about undertaking any major operation in a theatre of war where supplies had to be brought up by sea, and the circles where obsolete and outdated ideas were held in reverence fought tooth and nail, both then and later, against any such operation.

The experience which I had gained during this advance through Cyrenaica formed the main foundation for my later operations.   I had made heavy demands throughout the action, far more than precedent permitted, and had thus created my own standards.   One is forced again and again to re-learn the fact that standards set by precedent are based on something less than average performance, and, for that reason, one should not submit to them.

The British had been completely deceived as to our real strength. Their moves would have been very astute, if they had in fact really been attacked by a force as strong as they had supposed.   They had not accepted a decisive battle with their weak forces at Agedabia but had pulled back in order to concentrate their strength.   The capture of Mechili was a coup; the enemy had probably not reckoned on our using the route through Ben Gania or on our appearing as early as we did in front of Mechili.   Thus their troops were taken completely by surprise and were probably again deceived as to our true strength by the dust-clouds which were deliberately stirred up by our troops.   Similarly, the enemy forces still in Cyrenaica had probably not reckoned on our making such a rapid advance to Derna.   Hence it was principally our speed that we had to thank for this victory.   Incidentally, it is of interest to note here that about twelve months later the British did make the mistake of accepting battle at Agedabia with partial forces.

Wavell was obviously intending to maintain his hold on Tobruk and to supply it by sea, assuming, that is, that our first attacks on the fortress did not succeed. I knew that we should then find ourselves in an extremely unpleasant situation, both tactically and strategically, which would become particularly difficult if the British launched an attack on the Sollum front. Either—so the British commander's thinking probably ran —we would pull back to the level of Tobruk, in which case he would always have this powerful fortress as a support for his defence, or we would continue to hold the Sollum front, in which event we would be exposed to a threat from all sides and thus be diverted from further operations on Tobruk.

The following account shows what heavy restraints this situation did in the event impose on our conduct of operations.

ASSAULT ON TOBRUK

On the 9th April we had a great deal to do to complete the administrative arrangements for our supplies and for bringing up more troops. A report came in that the enemy had concentrated strong contingents of troops round Tobruk and was loading material into ten transports in the harbour. Unfortunately, the Luftwaffe was fully occupied in bringing up its aircraft and could only put a very few machines in the air. When the commander of the Brescia arrived at about midday I informed him of my intentions, which were for the Brescia and, later, the Trento to attack Tobruk from the west, raising a great cloud of dust in the process and tying down the enemy strength, while at the same time the 5th Light Division made a sweep through the desert round the south of Tobruk in order to attack it from the south-east.

Early in the afternoon, Aldinger and I arrived in Tmimi, where our advance troops were located, and I informed General von Prittwitz of the plan for Tobruk.

Meanwhile, I imagined that the 5th Light Division was on the march for Tmimi. It was now of the utmost importance to appear in strength before Tobruk and get our attack started as early as possible, for we wanted our blow to fall before the enemy had recovered his morale after our advance through Cyrenaica, and had been able to organise his defence of Tobruk. I therefore flew off in the direction of Mechili to meet the 5th Light Division, but after 30 miles was forced by a rising Ghibli to break off the flight and return to Derna. After waiting for the sandstorm to abate a little I took off again and arrived in Mechili at 16.30 hours, and found the whole of the 5th Light Division still there. They had imagined they could allow themselves a couple of days for maintenance work on their vehicles. This was far from being my idea and I ordered the division to move on through Tmimi that night and to be in the Gazala area, which was to be their starting point for the attack on Tobruk, by daybreak.

In the early hours of the 10th April, I drove off in the direction of Tobruk and found 3rd Reconnaissance Battalion 30 miles west of the fortress. Unfortunately, they had not yet started their switch to the right for their outflanking attack. I now ordered General von Prittwitz to launch his attack immediately astride the road to Tobruk and 3rd Reconnaissance Battalion to move up through Acroma to El Adem. I then drove off towards Tobruk again and found the leading troops of the machine-gun battalion in attack ten miles from Tobruk. Heavy British artillery fire from Tobruk soon brought their attack to a halt. We had at that time no real idea of the nature or position of the Tobruk defences. The air shimmered and a sandstorm began to blow up; soon the visibility, which had so far been good, closed right down and I drove back. At about midday, Count Schwerin reported to me at a point some 25 miles west of Tobruk that General von Prittwitz had been killed a few hours earlier by a direct hit from an anti-tank gun.

To the 5th Light Division I gave orders, after they were relieved by the Brescia, to thrust forward to the Via Balbia east of Tobruk and close the fortress in. Meanwhile, the Ariete had been located at Bir Tengeder and ordered forward to El Adem.

As the situation was rather confused I spent next day at the front again. It is of the utmost importance to the commander to have a good knowledge of the battlefield and of his own and his enemy's positions on the ground. It is often not a question of which of the opposing commanders is the higher qualified mentally, or which has the greater experience, but which of them has the better grasp of the battlefield. This is particularly the case when a situation develops, the outcome of which cannot be estimated. Then the commander must go up to see for himself; reports received second-hand rarely give the information he needs for his decisions.

We first jolted in our Mammoth down a freshly made track running south from Acroma, and then turned east to approach the Tobruk-El Adem road about $2\frac{1}{2}$ miles north of El Adem. British tanks and armoured cars were moving about on a ridge in front of us—apparently El Adem had not yet been taken by 3rd Reconnaissance Battalion. On the high ground north-east of El Adem, we discovered a tented camp, which the enemy had already abandoned. British artillery was heavily shelling elements of the 5th Light Division standing on the road, and soon their shells began to fall near us. I met Lieut.-Col. Count Schwerin on the Tobruk-El Adem road and instructed him to close on Tobruk from the east and prevent any attempts at a break-out. Then I drove back to Acroma to bring up more forces. There was now nothing to be seen of German troops anywhere on the south-west front of Tobruk. The roof of the Mammoth made an excellent observation tower and gave us a wide view over the whole country—necessary in that dangerous corner where it would have been only too easy for a British scouting party to have picked us up. At last I found the staff of the 5th Light Division. Soon afterwards 5th Panzer Regiment came up with 20 tanks and the machine-gun battalion; they were immediately sent in to attack Tobruk from the south-east. I now went forward again into the assembly area. Scattered British artillery fire was falling at a few points. The attack seemed to be meeting more difficulties in the open desert than I had anticipated.

During the afternoon 3rd Reconnaissance Battalion reported the capture of El Adem and I instructed them to continue the pursuit to Bardia. Other forces were now coming in steadily.

On the 11th April, the envelopment of Tobruk was complete and the first attack began. Stukas attacked the defence works, the layout of which was still completely unknown to us. More troops arrived on the 12th April and it was decided to open the first major attack on the stronghold that afternoon. Bardia was taken that day by 3rd Reconnaissance Battalion.

The Brescia Division, which had meanwhile taken over the western front of Tobruk, opened the attack in the afternoon. The 5th Light Division was not too happy about its orders for the attack and raised a number of objections which I had to brush aside. It was a day of driving sand and there was no need to concern ourselves about aimed British artillery fire. The 5th Light Division's attack finally got under way at about 16.30 hours. I drove north in my Mammoth behind the tanks. Enemy artillery scattered shells over the area as the tanks approached, but caused few casualties. The 5th Panzer Regiment halted when they arrived at the break-in point and, of course, came under heavy artillery fire. Finally, the tanks were brought to a standstill in front of an anti-tank ditch, which we were not then in a position to blow in. Tobruk's defences stretched much farther in all directions, west, east and south, than we had imagined. We had still not been able to get hold of any of the plans of the defences, which were held by the Italians.

After the failure of this attack, I decided to renew the attempt a few days later when more artillery and the Ariete had arrived. In no circumstances was the enemy to be allowed time to complete the organisation of his defence.

For the 13th I ordered a reconnaissance raid by the 5th Light Division in which the reconnaissance groups were, if possible, to penetrate to the crossroad inside the Tobruk defences and blow in the anti-tank ditch. To divert the attention of the enemy command, the Brescia Division was to pin down the enemy west of the fortress by fire, and, by raising as much dust as possible, to simulate the existence of large-scale assembly areas.

After the failure of the previous raid on Tobruk, the 5th Light Division had lost confidence in itself and was unwarrantedly pessimistic about my plan to open our main attack on the 14th. The division's command had not mastered the art of concentrating its strength at one point, forcing a break-through, rolling up and securing the flanks on either side, and then penetrating like lightning, before the enemy has had time to react, deep into his rear.[1] My estimate of the enemy at that time was that we had a good chance of executing such an operation with the forces we had. All it wanted was a little initiative and some realistic thinking to find a way. Unfortunately, I had not had the opportunity of training my formations personally before the raid through Cyrenaica, otherwise we would have measured up much better to the tasks which faced us at Tobruk.

There being still no sign of the Ariete, which was to back up the 5th Light Division's attack, I set off myself to bring it up. I met the head of the [*Ariete*] division 22 miles west of El Adem and ordered its commander, General Baldassare, to take his force into the area north of El Adem.

At about 18.00 hours, 8th Machine-Gun Battalion began its raid under the excellent leadership of Lieut-Col. Ponath. Its objective, as already said, was to demolish the anti-tank ditch and create a bridgehead in the British defence zone. The supporting fire of the German and Italian artillery concentrations was well placed. The 18th A.A. Battalion's batteries, under the personal command of Major Hecht, brought the enemy strong points under direct fire, obviously with considerable success. The progress of our tanks and anti-tank troops seemed to me somewhat on the slow side. The British were scattering the country here and there with artillery fire, but we were suffering no great losses. Evening came and we had still received no definite reports as to whether the demolition of the anti-tank trench had been successful. It was, however, clear that Ponath had broken into the British positions, formed a bridgehead and thus created the conditions for the next day's attack.

Meanwhile, the position on the Sollum front had become more or less stabilised. Sollum and Capuzzo had been taken and the British were keeping fairly quiet.

14 April 1941   03.00

DEAREST LU,
    To-day may well see the end of the Battle of Tobruk. The British were very stubborn and had a great deal of artillery. However, we'll bring it off. The bulk of my force is now out of the desert after a fortnight of it. The lads stuck it magnificently and came through the

[1]Rommel here succinctly describes the combined features of the " *Blitzkrieg* " method that was executed with such decisive effect by the German armoured forces in the opening campaigns of the war. It could not be better epitomised in a sentence. To find an expressive name for it is more difficult—*Blitzkrieg* (lightning war) is too vague. When setting forth the compound idea in 1920 I christened it the " expanding torrent," which perhaps comes nearer to conveying the combination of concentration—initial penetration—lateral expansion—exploitation by deep penetration.

battle, both with the enemy and nature, very well. We've even got water again.

Start time for the 5th Light Division's attack was now fixed for 00.30 hours on the 14th. Artillery Regiment Grati and 18th A.A. Battalion were instructed to work in closest co-operation with the 5th Light Division. I advised the division to be sure to secure the flanks of its penetration and to bring the artillery up quickly.

The attack opened punctually to time, with heavy artillery support. Ponath soon reported that he was making good progress. At daybreak I drove up to a point about 100 yards south of the wire to see for myself how the operation was developing. The attack seemed to be well under way and light signals were rising in the north. Suddenly British shells began to fall in our neighbourhood and we were forced to withdraw after the aerial of our signals vehicle had been cut through by a splinter. Unfortunately, there was nothing to be seen of the force which should have been covering the flanks, although a penetration had obviously been made through the enemy positions west of the road. I therefore drove straight off to the Ariete and ordered them to follow up.

On returning to Corps H.Q. at about 09.00 hours, I found a report from the 5th Light Division saying that their attack had come to a standstill, caused by the fact that their penetration of the enemy line had been too narrow. Shortly afterwards General Streich and Colonel Olbrich arrived at my H.Q. Olbrich reported that he had already had his tanks at a point two and a half miles south of the town, but they had then come under a murderous British fire and had withdrawn to the level of Corps H.Q. He added that a large part of the infantry had probably been lost. I was furious, particularly at the way that the tanks had left the infantry in the lurch, and ordered them forward again immediately to open up the breach in the enemy line and get the infantry out. I hoped to get the attack moving again after the arrival of the Ariete, and immediately drove back to them to see that they were carrying out my orders. Unfortunately, nothing had yet been done. I spurred the division on to the utmost speed.

When I returned to the 5th Light Division at about midday, I found that practically nothing had been done because of the heavy enemy fire. In these circumstances I had no choice but to abandon the attack on Tobruk for the moment, and to try to establish contact with Ponath's battalion and fight a way out for them.

I then drove off to the Ariete for the third time and informed them of my decision. I ordered them to take over the sector south of Ras el Madauer, adjoining the 5th Light Division, and accompanied them forward myself at about 17.00 hours. South-east of Gasr el Glecha they received a few rounds of artillery fire from Tobruk. The confusion was indescribable. The division broke up in complete disorder, turned tail and streamed back in several directions to the south and south-west. Their commander, General Baldassare, was away with me at the time reconnoitring the ground north of Gasr el Glecha; with night coming on, he had the greatest difficulty in getting his division under control again and moving it forward into its allotted position.

We were unable to establish contact with Ponath's battalion on the night 14-15 April. A large part of the battalion had been wiped out. Lieut.-Col. Ponath himself, who had received the Knight's Cross for his exploits during the advance through Cyrenaica, had been killed.

When the Panzer Army Afrika eventually broke into Tobruk, on the 20th June of the following year, and took possession of the British positions south of the road fork 3 miles south of the town, I found there the remains of several German tanks which had been put out of action by British artillery and anti-tank guns on the 14th April 1941. They had reached the hill and thus gained the most important point of the Tobruk defences.[1] Had the 5th Light Division been in a position to secure its two flanks and thus allow the artillery and the Ariete to follow through the breach, Tobruk would probably have fallen on the 14th or 15th April 1941.

16 April 1941

DEAREST LU,

The battle for Tobruk has quietened down a bit. The enemy is embarking, so we can expect the fortress to be ours very shortly. Then we'll probably come to a stop. Nevertheless, our small force has achieved a tremendous amount, which has put a different picture on the whole campaign in the south.

On the move a lot and very busy.

My plan now was to take the hill, Ras el Madauer, using elements of the Ariete and Trento and several German companies attacking under strong artillery support.

At 17.00 hours on the 16th April, I launched the armoured battalion of the Ariete (6 medium and 12 light tanks) against hill 187. We accompanied the attack on its left flank. Instead of halting south of the hill and then dismounting and observing the country through glasses, the Italians drove to the highest point of hill 187 and then proceeded to halt. It was not many minutes of course before British artillery opened fire on the hill, whereupon the Italians promptly retired at top speed and halted, confused and undecided, in a wadi. I tried to get the Italian tank commander to advance in open order on Ras el Madauer, but without success.

All this while Lieut. Berndt was observing the advance of the Italian

---

[1] Rommel was mistaken here. Olbrich's tanks never, in fact, reached this point. Chester Wilmot—who was the Australian Broadcasting Commision's war correspondent, and in Tobruk during the siege—has told me that the wrecked German tanks which Rommel saw had been towed there by the British for use as targets in anti-tank gun practice shoots.

infantry. Progress at first was in perfect order, but suddenly the Italians turned and fled in a wild rout to the west. I instructed Berndt to take an armoured car and drive to the Italians as fast as he could to find out what was wrong. All sound of battle had ceased. Half an hour later Berndt reappeared and reported that he had been told by an Italian infantryman that the enemy was attacking with tanks. After moving on a few hundred yards to the east, he had seen a British scout car herding away a company of Italians with their hands up and had at once opened fire on the scout car in order to give the Italians a chance to run. They had run—towards the British lines. Finally, a British armoured vehicle had taken them over.

I now drove off with three anti-tank guns in order to save what was left. I was unable to persuade the Italian tank crews to come with us. Under Berndt's command, the anti-tank gunners succeeded in shooting up several British Bren-carriers. However, the Italian battalion, which had had no effective anti-tank weapons, had meanwhile been rounded up and carried off by the enemy. My Adjutant, Major Schraepler, who had accompanied the first wave of the Italians, had managed to escape capture. He said that the Italians had advanced in too dense a mass. He was now holding the heights round Acroma with what was left of the Italians, and I sent him two more rifle companies to make up his strength.

The reason for attacking the Ras el Madauer was because the British were in a position there to threaten our supply route through Acroma. So a further attempt was to be made on the 17th. The Ariete, although they had not yet seen any action, now had only 10 tanks left out of the 100 odd with which they had started the offensive. The remainder had fallen out, due to engine failure or some other mechanical trouble. It made one's hair stand on end to see the sort of equipment with which the Duce had sent his troops into battle.

But again nothing went right in our next attack. The attacking force had instructions to advance from one dip in the ground to the next, waiting each time until supporting fire had first been secured. But the company commanders ignored their instructions and made a blind dash straight for the enemy. The Ariete's armour was led by Lieut. Wahl, an interpreter on the 5th Light Division's staff. Contrary to their orders to remain behind the infantry, they pushed on far ahead and soon vanished out of sight. There was no means of communicating with them and their location was unknown. Meanwhile, the leading infantry reached the wire in front of Ras el Madauer without meeting any opposition of consequence.

Suddenly at about 13.00 hours, a single tank appeared north of the summit of Ras el Madauer, moving towards our line with its gun trained on us. In the dust it was impossible to see if there were any more following it. Fearing that the enemy was again using tanks in an attempt to destroy my infantry, who were defenceless against armour, I quickly brought up my three anti-tank guns. More tanks had meanwhile been sighted. An exchange of fire developed and two tanks were hit, which, to our great consternation, turned out shortly afterwards to be Italians. Lieut. Wahl did not return; he had obviously pushed his tank right forward into the enemy positions and been shot up. The infantry attack had also come to a standstill in the enemy wire. All further attempts to penetrate into the British positions failed. It was now finally clear that there was no hope of doing anything against the enemy defences with the forces we had, largely because of the poor state of training and useless equipment of the Italian troops. I decided to break off the attack until the arrival of more troops.

On the 19th April, I drove to Bardia, where I found that the fortress had not been occupied by my troops. Vast quantities of Italian war material—mainly vehicles and hundreds of guns which had been left behind by Marshal Graziani's army—lay on either side of the road. I decorated Lieut.-Col. von Wechmar with the Knight's Cross. I also gave orders for Bardia to be occupied immediately by a German company. As it happened, the British sent a sizeable sabotage group into the fortress that night, all 56 of whom, including a regular major, were taken prisoner.

On the way back, we were twice attacked by British ground-strafing aircraft about 10 miles west of Bardia. Corporal Eggert, the driver of my cross-country vehicle, was killed; the vehicle received 25 hits. My dispatch rider, Private Kanthak, was also killed. The driver of the Mammoth was wounded by a bullet which came through the visor. Leaving Berndt with the damaged vehicles, I climbed into the driving seat of my Mammoth and drove myself. The road was in a frightful state. I wanted to get back to H.Q. that night and turned off south before Tobruk with the object of by-passing it through the desert. It was a pitch-black night and we tried to navigate by the stars, but the sky eventually clouded over so that I was forced to give up the attempt and wait till morning.

The plans of the Tobruk defences had now at last arrived from the Italian High Command. They included detailed maps of the layout of the fortifications and plans showing the construction of individual defence works. From these plans it appeared that the defences consisted of two lines of strong-points, not in the usual form of concrete pill-boxes with loop-holes, but completely sunk into the ground. The outer belt was surrounded by an anti-tank ditch, covered with thin boarding disguised by a layer of sand and stones on top, so that it could not be detected even at the shortest distance. Each defence work had a diameter of about 90 yards and consisted of several heavily concreted dugouts, each holding 30 to 40 men. The individual dugouts were inter-connected by a communications trench, which had emplacements for machine-guns, anti-tank guns and mortars at each angle. As with the anti-tank ditch, the communications trench, which was 8 feet deep, was covered with boards topped lightly with earth and could therefore easily be opened up at any point. Each work was surrounded by strong wire entanglements and all were inter-connected by barbed wire. The second defence line, which lay two to three thousand yards behind the first, was of similar design, but without the anti-tank ditch.

It was now my endeavour to pull the motorised troops out of the investing front round Tobruk in order to make them available for mobile use. I accordingly asked the Commando Supremo to send me two further static divisions.

I continued, in the days ahead, to work on a plan for attacking Tobruk, especially as we now had some idea of the form and layout of its defences. ·I intended to instal the main body of the Brescia Division in fixed positions on Tobruk's eastern front, thus freeing 2nd M.G. Battalion, and to use part of the Trento Division to occupy Bardia and, if possible, Sollum, in order to release the Battalion Knabe. The main attack was to be made by the 15th Panzer Division—as much of it as had arrived in Africa—reinforced by units of the Ariete; the line of the attack was to be through Ras el Madauer into the rear of the fixed defences. Simultaneous with the main attack, the 5th Light Division was to mount a secondary attack on the south-east front. I had hopes of launching the attack at the end of April or the beginning of May.

21 April 1941

Dearest Lu,

Things are slowly quietening down and I'm at last able to collect my thoughts after three weeks of offensive. It's been very hectic for the last few weeks. We're hoping to pull off the attack on Tobruk very soon now.

We're lying at the moment in a rocky hollow, widely dispersed on account of the very active British aircraft. Froehlich is doing some tidying up over on the other side. But the strengths are fairly equal and there's some doubt as to whether the British are not bringing in new forces every day.

But before many days had passed we suffered a new reverse. On the morning of the 22nd the enemy overran Battalion Fabris on Hill 201 and then moved on towards Acroma. I immediately alerted the 15th Panzer Division, part of which had now arrived, and ordered it to occupy the Via Balbia east of Cantoniera 31 [*road maintenance depot, 31 km. from Tobruk*]. Soon machine-gun fire was reported from in front of Acroma. At this news I drove across there as fast as I could go. We overtook 605th Anti-tank Battalion on the way and took them along with us. On arrival, we heard that the enemy had actually taken prisoner the greater part of Fabris's staff, after which the six British tanks which had made the attack had moved on into the Italian gun positions, destroyed the guns and captured the crews. The six Italian tanks which had been put there to protect the position, and which should have been perfectly capable of engaging and driving off the enemy tanks, had been sent back by Colonel Fabris. I immediately took a combat group to the Fabris Battalion's positions, where we found vehicles and motor-cycles still burning; the guns of two batteries seemed to be still quite serviceable. Needless to say, I was not very pleased at this curious behaviour in face of the enemy.

Meanwhile, feverish training was going on among the forces detailed for the attack, as it has become only too evident that the training of our infantry in position warfare was nowhere near up to the standard of the British and Australians. This we now intended to correct. On my inspections, both German and Italian troops made a very good impression. I soon gave up my plan for the 5th Light Division to attack on the southeast side of Tobruk, as the division had little taste for the project, because of the open terrain and lack of cover.

Major Schraepler, Rommel's Adjutant, to Frau Rommel:

22 April

MY DEAR FRAU ROMMEL,

I realise that there is a possibility that it may cause you a shock to receive a letter bearing my name as sender; nevertheless, I am taking this risk in order to give you the assurance that all is well with your esteemed husband.

He will have had little time for writing during the past few days, as they have been very full for him, and very worrying too. His endeavour and the desire of every one of us to be not only in, but far beyond Tobruk, is at the moment impossible to realise. We have too few German forces and can do nothing with the Italians. They either do not come forward at all, or if they do, run at the first shot. If an Englishman so much as comes in sight, their hands go up. You will understand, Madam, how difficult this makes the command for your husband. I am certain, however, that by the time this letter arrives you will not have much longer to wait for the special communiqué announcing the capture of Tobruk, and then things will begin to move again.

We are now located in a rocky ravine, where enemy aircraft will find it difficult to spot us. We also have some German fighters here now, which keep the British bombers and low fliers away. Field Marshal Milch has promised your husband still further support.

Though we do not live as well as we did in France, we are still not doing badly. Captured British stores provide an improvement to the army rations. You may rest assured, Madam, that Guenther

Rommel on the Via Balbia, April 1941, in the Mammoth, a British armoured command vehicle captured during Rommel's first advance through Cyrenaica. Left, Lt.-Col. von dem Borne, his Chief of Staff at the time

Rommel's Main Headquarters on the Via Balbia, photographed from his Storch

Rommel's Advanced Headquarters near Tobruk photographed from his Storch

Rommel outside his caravan

looks after your husband very well within the limits of what can be done. I am very glad that your husband has an Italian caravan, which at least offers him some comfort and quiet, and protection against the cold nights. The Italians are past masters at such amenities; others we will provide for ourselves in Cairo.

The latest issue of *Das Reich* to arrive contained an article on your husband, which you will no doubt have already read. Your husband was very angry about it and wrote the word " Nonsense " in the margin. I have discussed it with Berndt, the Deputy *Reichspressechef* who is serving here on Corps staff. All Germany knows of the tremendous achievements of your husband, and there is no need for a paid hack to write untrue statements about them.

(Signed: Schraepler.)

23 April 1941

DEAREST LU,

Heavy fighting yesterday in front of Tobruk. The situation was highly critical, but we managed to restore it. There's little reliance to be placed on the Italian troops. They're extremely sensitive to enemy tanks and—as in 1917—quick to throw up the sponge. Newly arrived German units have now made the situation rather more secure.

I had a meeting with Gariboldi and Roatta yesterday. Minister Terruzzi was also present. I was ceremonially awarded the Italian " Medal for Bravery." I am also supposed to be getting the Italian " Pour le Mérite." What a trivial business it all is at a time like this. I've been able to have my sleep out during the last few days, so now I'm ready for anything again. Once Tobruk has fallen, which I hope will be in ten days or a fortnight, the situation here will be secure. Then there'll have to be a few weeks' pause before we take on anything new.

How are things with you both? There must be a whole lot of post lying at the bottom of the Mediterranean.

P.S.—Easter has slipped by unnoticed.

25 April 1941

Things are very warm in front of Tobruk. I shan't be sorry to see more troops arrive, for we're still very thin on the long fortress front. I've seldom had such worries—militarily speaking—as in the last few days. However, things will probably look different soon.

. . . Greece will probably soon be disposed of and then it will be possible to give us more help. Paulus is due to arrive in a few days. The battle for Egypt and the Canal is now on in earnest and our tough opponent is fighting back with all he's got.

The attack on Ras el Madauer was opened at about 18.30 hours on the 30th April by our Stukas. Sirens screaming, they swooped down on the enemy positions and the hill was soon hidden by a thick pall of smoke and dust. Our artillery opened fire on the break-in points—with good effect, as far as we could see. The attack on the outer defence line was completely successful, the enemy line being penetrated to a depth of up to two miles immediately north and south of the Ras el Madauer. The enemy fought with remarkable tenacity. Even their wounded went on defending themselves with small arms fire and stayed in the fight to their last breath. At about 21.00 hours the commanding hill of Ras el Madauer was attacked in the rear and taken by Battalion Voigtsberger. The enemy put up a heavy defensive barrage, but it was directed mainly at the point of our feint attacks on the roads leading from Derna and El Adem towards Tobruk. Unfortunately, a few forts and strong points continued to hold out all night, and our attacking force foolishly allowed itself to be drawn into a fight for these points before pushing on with its main attack. This should really have been a job for a few storming parties. It is a great mistake to allow oneself to be diverted from the main line of one's plan by relative trivialities.

The Ariete was now put on the march with orders to close up on the Kirchheim Group during the night. Driving east to Kirchheim's H.Q. next morning [1st May], I met part of the Ariete, which should have moved into the captured positions long before. As I stopped at Kirchheim's H.Q., the Italian force was just halting, unloading its weapons and ammunition and going into position.

I was extremely annoyed and charged Major Appel with the task of getting the Italians forward. He made a great effort, but did not achieve much. With British artillery fire sweeping the whole area, the Italians crept under their vehicles and resisted all their officers' attempts to get them out again.

Shortly afterwards a batch of some fifty or sixty Australian prisoners was marched off close beside us—immensely big and powerful men, who without question represented an élite formation of the British Empire, a fact that was also evident in battle. Enemy resistance was as stubborn as ever and violent actions were being fought at many points. All the same, I continued for some time to think that we would be able to maintain our attack and take Tobruk. The only question was whether we had enough troops to go on feeding the attack long enough. After a while I went off to the attacking front, riding part of the way and walking the rest, in order to get a picture of the situation for myself. On arrival I gave orders for the captured positions to be occupied immediately, in order to guard against unpleasant surprises.

But next day [2nd May] it became obvious that we were not strong enough to mount the large-scale attack necessary to take the fortress, and I had no choice but to content myself with what we had achieved, namely, the elimination of the threat to our supply route from enemy positions on the Ras el Madauer. It was now impossible to contemplate anything more for the present than isolated operations against individual strong points.

The next few days brought several British counter-attacks against the captured sector, which were beaten off with little result. Many of the British troops engaged in these attacks were depressed and in poor spirits because of water shortage, their ration being under a pint a day.

6 May 1941

DEAREST LU,

There was too much doing yesterday for me to write. We've had several days of Ghibli, which has left us all quite limp. It seems to be gradually getting better now.

Paulus has now gone, although Froehlich has just phoned to say that he couldn't fly because of the Ghibli. Water is very short in Tobruk, the British troops are getting only half a litre [*just under a pint*]. With our dive-bombers I'm hoping to cut their ration still further.

The heat is getting worse every day and it's a relief when night comes. One's thirst becomes almost unquenchable.

In this assault we lost more than 1,200 men killed, wounded and missing. This shows how sharply the curve of casualties rises when one reverts from mobile to position warfare. In a mobile action, what counts is material, as the essential complement to the soldier. The finest fighting man has no value in mobile warfare without tanks, guns and vehicles. Thus a mobile force can be rendered unfit for action by the destruction of its tanks, without having suffered any serious casualties in man-power. This is not the case with position warfare, where the infantryman with rifle and hand grenade has lost little of his value, provided, of course, he is protected by anti-tank guns or obstacles against the enemy's armour. For him enemy number one is the attacking infantryman. Hence position warfare is always a struggle for the destruction of men—in contrast to mobile warfare, where everything turns on the destruction of enemy material.

The high casualties suffered by my assault forces were primarily caused by their lack of training. Even in the smallest action, there are always tactical tricks which can be used to save casualties, and these must be made known to the men. It frequently happened that dash was used where caution was really needed, with, of course, casualties as the result. On the next occasion, when boldness really was required, the men would be over-cautious. In these small-scale infantry tactics in particular, what is wanted is a maximum of caution, combined with supreme dash at the right moment.

The captured Ras el Madauer positions lay under continuous British artillery fire. Our defence works were shallow—the ground was too rocky to dig in far—with the result that the troops were forced to remain motionless all day, exposed defenceless to thousands of flies. Many men had dysentery and the conditions were frightful. To disperse the enemy artillery fire, we installed dummy tanks—mainly in the sector held by the Brescia—and these did in fact soon draw heavy fire from the British artillery. Unfortunately, the troops had no idea of how to use such devices, which must be kept continually moving and not be left standing for a fortnight on the same spot. I made repeated visits to the front to try to inculcate in the troops some up-to-date ideas in position warfare appropriate to the conditions they were facing.

The Italians had acquired a very considerable inferiority complex, as was not surprising in the circumstances. Their infantry were practically without anti-tank weapons and their artillery completely obsolete. Their training was also a long way short of modern standards, so that we were continually being faced by serious breakdowns. Many Italian officers had thought of war as little more than a pleasant adventure and were, perforce, having to suffer a bitter disillusionment.

One thing that worked very seriously against us was the fact that the Luftwaffe in Africa was not subordinate to the Afrika Korps. As a result, fighter and ground-strafing groups were used more in a strategic role than tactically in support of the ground forces. It would have been far better for the cause as a whole if the Luftwaffe Commander Afrika had been responsible for the tactical requirements of the Afrika Korps while X Luftwaffe Corps took care of the strategic tasks.

The supply situation was none too good, due to the fact that the Italian transport fleets were still arriving at Tripoli and making too little use of Benghazi. This meant a tremendous strain on our road transport. The German quartermasters had, it is true, wasted no time in organising coastal shipping, but here again, far more could have been done with a little more activity on the part of the Italians.

Little came of the operations planned against individual British strong-points, as the Axis forces, despite all their training, were still not up to these difficult tasks.

BATTLE ON THE FRONTIER

The siege of Tobruk stood or fell by the maintenance of our Sollum positions. It was therefore necessary to apportion out the tasks of the German-Italian forces in North Africa, as follows:

One force to keep Tobruk securely closed in and hold the line against any break-out attempt by the enemy garrison.

A second force to hold the line at Sollum and at the same time provide a mobile defence against any enemy turning movement in the area bounded by Bir Hacheim, Gazala, Sollum and Sidi Omar, in order to prevent the enemy operating against the rear of our forces round Tobruk.

Non-motorised troops, of which—unlike the British—we had a great number, could only be employed with any prospect of success in the following ways:

In the investing front round Tobruk.
In holding the static Sollum-Sidi Omar line.
In holding Bardia.

This meant that the main weight of the fighting in any British attack from the east had to be carried by our motorised forces. The purpose of occupying a number of fixed positions was merely to deny certain operations to the enemy. The motorised forces could not be given any second task, and consequently could not at one and the same time be earmarked for the mobile defence and be committed in the siege of Tobruk.

Accordingly it was our aim, firstly to hold the fixed positions detailed above with adequate non-motorised forces, and secondly to hold ready a motorised force strong enough to provide adequate opposition to any enemy offensive concentration against our Tobruk front, and at the same time to beat off an attack by the British motorised forces located east of Sollum. To this end the motorised forces in the static lines were to be relieved by non-motorised troops.

Our dispositions at the middle of May were far from fulfilling these requirements. The Sollum front was not yet fully manned by infantry; in fact, all it consisted of was a few light combat groups holding something in the nature of an outpost line. A surprise attack by the Herff force had brought us the Halfaya Pass, but fortification of this or of the Sollum Pass had hardly begun.

In these circumstances, we looked forward with no little anxiety to the attack which we were shortly expecting the British to launch on Sollum.

To prepare for the worst I had already given instructions for a line to be constructed at Gazala. The defences were to be laid out in a similar manner to those at Tobruk, which had shown themselves so admirably suited to meet modern methods of attack. But how to withdraw the non-motorised German and Italian forces to that line remained, of course, a problem.

In the early hours of the 15th May, the British launched an attack on our forces near Sollum. While our strong points on the Halfaya Pass and along the frontier were attacked frontally, British armour moved forward from the Habata area along the escarpment, first to the north-west and then to the north, towards Capuzzo. The troops holding the strong points and the mobile units of Herff's force both suffered considerable losses and our forces were pressed steadily back to the north.

This attack was launched by Wavell with the idea of catching Rommel unawares before the expected arrival of the 15th Panzer Division, and in the hope of driving him back west of Tobruk. The attack was carried out by General Gott with the 7th Armoured Brigade (comprising some 55 tanks) and the 22nd Guards Brigade.

I accordingly sent a Panzer battalion reinforced by A.A. guns, under the command of Lieut.-Col. Kramer, to Herff's assistance. The two forces, Herff's and Kramer's, were to join up during the night 15-16 May west of Sidi Azeiz. Our air reconnaissance and the units holding the Sollum-Bardia line had formed the impression that the British intended to concentrate their troops south of Sidi Azeiz, in order to sweep aside Herff's force on the morning of the 16th and then completely unhinge our Sollum-Bardia front by a further thrust to the north. My intention, therefore, in uniting Herff's and Kramer's forces, was to prevent this British move being driven home.

Herff's force drove towards Kramer's during the night in order to ensure that the enemy had no opportunity of tackling the two forces separately in the morning. But the two formations missed each other and, on the morning of the 16th, Kramer arrived in the Sidi Azeiz area alone. Contrary to expectations, however, the enemy had meanwhile withdrawn to the south and obviously broken off his attack.

This is an example of how different things look when viewed from " the other side of the hill." The British 7th Armoured Brigade had pushed on to Sidi Azeiz, but was pulled back when news came that Capuzzo, which lay on its rear flank, had been recaptured by a German counter-attack—which Rommel does not mention. Disconcerted by the fact that the Germans had shown greater strength than had been expected, the British Command decided to withdraw the whole force, leaving a garrison at the Halfaya Pass. For it was deemed best to await a special convoy that, on Churchill's bold initiative, was being rushed out by the short but hazardous Mediterranean route, carrying 180 Matilda and 100 cruiser tanks. By the time this big reinforcement had arrived, the 15th Panzer Division had also arrived—on the other side—so that the prospective advantage disappeared.

During the next few days, the British moved back to their starting line and the situation once again stabilised. Our garrison at Halfaya had been overpowered and the British were now holding the pass. Hence on the 18th May we were, with that exception, virtually back where we had started.

The Halfaya and Sollum Passes were points of great strategic importance, for they were the only two places between the coast and Habata where it was possible to cross the escarpment—of anything up to 600 feet in height—which stretched away from Sollum in a south-easterly direction towards Egypt. The Halfaya positions gave an equal command over both possible roads. In any offensive from Egypt, therefore, possession of these passes was bound to be of the utmost value to the enemy, as they offered him a comparatively safe route for his supplies. If, on the other hand, he were to attempt to attack Bardia without holding them, he would be thrown back on a supply route through Habata which would be vulnerable to attack and harassing action by us.

The British began to fortify the captured positions at Halfaya after the 17th May and deployed strong combat groups made up of tanks, artillery and anti-tank guns in the territory they had captured. But we were by no means prepared to leave the British in possession of the Halfaya Pass and I soon instructed the Herff force to organise a move to recapture it.

23 May 1941

DEAREST LU,

I haven't had a chance to write until this afternoon, after getting back from Sollum and Bardia.

We left at 5 a.m. yesterday and have been riding in the Mammoth through the endless landscape ever since, part of the time over desert tracks (sand roads worn out with driving—terribly hard on the vehicles) and part on the Via Balbia. I've come back from my trip to the front very impressed. Command is good up there and we have fresh forces standing by in case we're not left in peace. Overnight we formed a laager (five vehicles) in the desert. Even my A.D.C.s did watch, without my knowing it. You see how well I'm guarded.

Three assault groups moved into position in front of the [*Halfaya*] Pass on the evening of the 26th May, and our attack opened on the morning of the 27th. The British were soon driven out and fled in panic to the east, leaving considerable booty and material of all kinds in our hands. Our losses were comparatively insignificant.

The German recapture of the Halfaya Pass seriously hampered the British offensive when it was launched in mid-June.

In the period following these actions we made strenuous efforts to strengthen our Sollum-Halfaya-Bardia front. The construction of the Halfaya Pass positions was pushed ahead with the utmost vigour and several strong points were built along the Egyptian frontier. During an inspection of the Bardia defence area I found vast quantities of material lying in the defences where it had been left by Graziani's army. This material was just waiting to be used, and I therefore gave immediate instructions for all unclaimed Italian guns to be collected up and used to strengthen the Sollum-Halfaya-Sidi Omar front. A substantial number of these guns was put in order by one or two of our German workshops and then installed in the strong points. But the Italian High Command did not agree at all, and General Gariboldi had me informed, through

Heggenreiner, that the guns were Italian property and were only to be used by Italians. They had been perfectly content up till then to stand by and watch this material go to wrack and ruin, but the moment the first guns had been made serviceable on our initiative, they began to take notice. However, I was not to be put off.

In constructing our positions at Halfaya and on Hill 208 great skill was shown in building in batteries of 88 mm. guns for anti-tank work, so that with the barrels horizontal there was practically nothing to be seen above ground. I had great hopes of the effectiveness of this arrangement.

This significantly showed that the Germans not only knew how to exploit the offensive potentialities of the long-disputed theory of armoured warfare but had also grasped the idea of the defensive counter to it. Rommel was the first Panzer leader to demonstrate the modern version of the " sword and shield " combination, and prove the value of the " defensive-offensive " method in mobile mechanised warfare. The effectiveness of his offensive strokes was greatly aided by the skilful way he laid defensive traps for his opponents' attacks—blunting the edge of their " sword " on his " shield."

One very great problem was the maintenance of our troops at Sollum-Halfaya-Bardia. With the Via Balbia barred by the British at Tobruk, all supplies for the troops east of Gambut had to be carried through the open desert round the south of the fortress. The lorry routes which the troops had marked out had become so badly worn and widened at each side that driving was almost impossible. Light vehicles had become embedded in the dust at many points, and even lorries had the utmost difficulty in grinding their way through. It was a good effort for a column to get round Tobruk in a day. I repeatedly pressed the Italian higher authorities to have a by-pass road built, but for the moment, with little success. They quite saw the necessity for the road but it occurred to nobody to make a real assault on the job.

A further trial for us was that the Italians were still carrying the bulk of our supplies to Tripoli and making very little use of Benghazi. Tripoli was over 1,000 miles from the front. Bearing in mind that 1,500 tons of supplies, including water and rations, had to be carried up to the front every day, even for normal activity, it is easy to understand that our transport could not cope indefinitely with a route of that length. With no authority over the people responsible for shipping in the Mediterranean, however, it was very difficult for us to do anything about it.

As a result of Italian loss of prestige after Graziani's defeat, a number of Arab tribes had begun to get restive. This was not helped by the fact that Italian troops occasionally took liberties with the Arab women, a thing which Arabs particularly resent. I was forced to send an urgent request to the Italian High Command, asking them to see to it that the Arabs were treated with sufficient respect to avoid an armed uprising close behind our front.

At about this time officers and men of the Trento Division were responsible for several excesses against the Arab population, with the result that the Arabs killed a number of Italian soldiers and kept the Italians away from their villages by armed force. There are always people who will invariably demand reprisals in this sort of situation—for reasons, apart from anything else, of expediency. Such action is never expedient. The right thing to do is to ignore the incidents, unless the real culprits can be traced.

Our greatest worry was still the difficult strategic situation caused by our dual task of having to maintain the siege of Tobruk and at the same time be ready for major British attacks from Egypt. We would thus have given a lot to have driven the British out of Tobruk. We had hoped that when Crete fell the Luftwaffe would be able to get such a stranglehold on British sea traffic to Tobruk that the enemy would find it impossible to maintain the fortress. But the Luftwaffe formations that were released from service in Greece and Crete were not sent to North Africa.

I also asked for German submarines and motor torpedo boats to be sent into the Mediterranean to provide an alternative weapon against British seaborne traffic to Tobruk. The Italian Navy was quite incapable of coping with the task. Their submarines—of which they had the largest fleet in the world before the war—were so full of technical defects, that they were almost completely unusable for war in the Mediterranean. Their motor torpedo boats, which would have had a very good base at Bardia as Balbo had constructed it, were not seaworthy enough for the job.

One day, General Gause of the OKW[1] arrived with a large staff to reconnoitre the possibilities of employing bigger forces in Africa for an offensive against Egypt, and to prepare the ground for them. General Gause had received explicit instructions not to place himself under my command, but did in fact do so after I had told him categorically that the command of all troops in Africa was vested in me alone.

As a result of his discussions with the Italian authorities, Gause had gained the impression that it would be difficult to persuade them to agree to further German forces being shipped to North Africa, for they feared that the German element would then gain a preponderance in the theatre and be in a position of advantage *vis-à-vis* their own.

26 May 1941

DEAREST LU,

Yesterday evening I received a considerable rocket from Brauchitsch, the reason for which completely passes my comprehension. Apparently the reports I send back, stating the conditions as they exist, don't suit their book. The result will be that we'll keep our mouths shut and only report in the briefest form. However, we had $\frac{3}{4}$ litre of Bavarian beer last night to console us.

[1]OKW (Oberkommando der Wehrmacht)—Supreme Command of the Armed Forces.

Otherwise things have grown quiet, both here and on the front near Sollum. Though of course one can never know whether it isn't the calm before some new attack.

29 May 1941

Von dem Borne [*then Rommel's Chief of Staff*] is to take this letter with him to-morrow and I hope it will reach you earlier than usual. I've had a major rocket from the OKH[1]—to my mind unjustified—in gratitude for our previous achievements. But as with the " Line of Thrust " in 1940,[2] I'm not going to take it lying down, and a letter is already on its way to v. B. [*von Brauchitsch*].

For your peace of mind, I've kept very well so far and the situation has also shown a noticeable change for the better. The heat, it's true, is almost unbearable and it's a good thing to stay indoors during the hottest part of the day.

2 June 1941

It was 107° here yesterday, and that's quite some heat. Tanks standing in the sun go up to as much as 160°, which is too hot to touch.

My affair with the OKH is under way. Either they've got confidence in me or they haven't. If not, then I'm asking them to draw their own conclusions. I'm very intrigued to know what will come of it. It's easy enough to bellyache when you aren't sweating it out here.

11 June 1941

Borne is back, with partially satisfactory results. They were mad at me in the OKH because my reports had gone to the OKW as well. But that was Rintelen's fault who was acting in accordance with his duty. I've had no reply to my letter to B.

---

[1]O.K.H. (Oberkommando des Heeres)—Army High Command, subordinate to the OKW.

[2]See pages 15 and 85.

CHAPTER VII

THE BRITISH SUMMER OFFENSIVE, 1941

After its failure, this offensive was described as merely a reconnaissance in force, and the British public were kept in the dark about its originally ambitious aims—to " destroy " Rommel's forces and gain a " decisive victory " in North Africa. Its code-name " Battleaxe " epitomised the conception. Wavell began to have doubts as the time approached, not only because of the arrival of the 15th Panzer Division but also on technical grounds. In a report on the 28th May he said: " Our infantry tanks are really too slow for a battle in the desert, and have been suffering considerable casualties from the fire of the powerful enemy anti-tank guns. Our cruisers have little advantage in power or speed over German medium tanks." But he still hoped to " succeed in driving the enemy west of Tobruk."

The offensive was directed by General Beresford-Peirse, and carried out by a force comprising the 7th Armoured Division, 4th Indian Division, and 22nd Guards Brigade. There is a wide variation in the figures given in different British reports as to the number of tanks used—they range from 170 to 250. Rommel, it will be seen, says that the 15th Panzer Division had 80 tanks available to meet the British attack, but shows that they were reinforced by the tanks of the 5th Light Division. In other German records the total is given as 150, of which only 95 were Panzers III or IV. No Italian tanks were in action.

At the beginning of June there were many signs that a major British attack on our Tobruk[1] front was to be expected at about the middle of the month. Two British divisions had concentrated opposite the 15th Panzer Division's positions. (15th Panzer Division had meanwhile been transferred to the Sollum-Bardia-Halfaya sector, although its Rifle Brigade was still holding the line on the Ras el Madauer.) The bulk of the 5th Light Division was already in reserve south of Tobruk.

Unfortunately, our petrol stocks were badly depleted, and it was with some anxiety that we contemplated the coming British attack, for we knew that our moves would be decided more by the petrol gauge than by tactical requirements.

[1]It would seem likely, by the context, that Rommel made a slip here and intended to write the *Sollum* front. This front, which covered the forces investing Tobruk, was 70 miles to the east.

At about 21.00 hours on the 14th June, I alerted the Sollum front. Several of the 5th Light Division's units and some Italian were put on the march for new positions, with instructions to hold themselves in readiness to intervene on the Sollum front.

The expected enemy attack came at 04.00 hours on the 15th. They advanced over a wide front, both in the coastal plain and on the plateau, and forced back our outposts south-east and south of Sollum. The first reports we received from Sollum were fairly optimistic. But the enemy rapidly gained ground and from 09.00 hours onwards a tank attack was already in progress on Capuzzo. The 15th Panzer Division had orders not to launch its counter-attack until the situation had clarified.

Meanwhile, the 5th Light Division's combat group had been alerted and its advance troops had already arrived south of Gambut. At 11.00 hours all other available units of the 5th Light Division were alerted and put on the march towards Sollum.

The enemy was meanwhile concentrating very powerful forces between Sidi Omar and Capuzzo, obviously with the intention of destroying the 15th Panzer Division by a concentric attack to the north. To be ready for any eventuality, I ordered the garrison of Bardia to man the eastern and western exits from the fortress. Unfortunately, there were not enough troops available to man the whole of Bardia's defences.

Meanwhile, the British were making repeated attacks on the Halfaya Pass from both sides in an attempt to open the road. But Major Bach and his men fought magnificently. The British force engaged in this attack was soon describing its position as serious and complaining of heavy casualties.

In the afternoon and evening of this first day of battle, the British enveloped Capuzzo and began to mount attacks against the southern front of Bardia.[1] Late in the evening Capuzzo was stormed by British troops. A violent tank battle developed between 80 tanks of 8th Panzer Regiment (15th Panzer Division) and some 300 British tanks which pressed stubbornly northwards.

Rommel overestimates the British tank strength in the same way that the British overestimated his.

The 15th Panzer Division, together with a panzer battalion of the 5th Light Division, which had meanwhile come up in support, had orders to take up positions south of Bardia during the night for a renewed counter-attack to the south. In view of the tremendous strength of the British, there was of course no certainty that this attack would achieve any decisive success.

The main force of 5th Light Division had orders to launch an attack on the morning of the 16th from a point west of Sidi Azeiz towards Sidi Suleiman, with the object of getting through to the Halfaya Pass,

---

[1]Actually the bulk of the British armour penetrated only a few miles north of the line Capuzzo-Musaid during this battle.

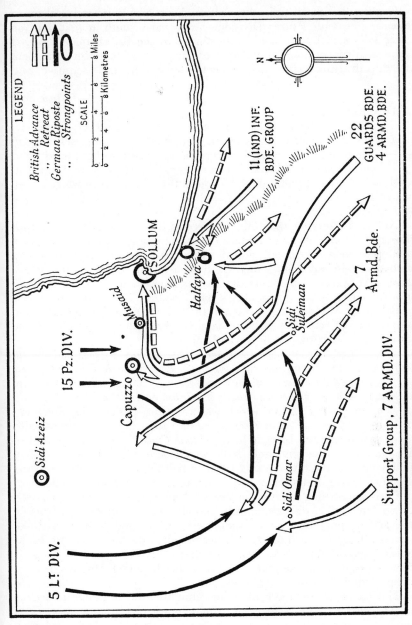

LEGEND

British Advance
      "   Retreat
German Riposte
      "   Strongpoints

SCALE

8 Miles

8 Kilometres

Sidi Azeiz

5 Lt. Div.

15 Pz. Div.

Capuzzo

Musaid

SOLLUM

Halfaya

11 (IND.) INF.
BDE. GROUP

Sidi
Suleiman

Sidi Omar

7
Armd. Bde.

22

GUARDS BDE.
4 ARMD. BDE.

Support Group, 7 ARMD. DIV.

9.   THE BRITISH OFFENSIVE, JUNE 1941—BATTLEAXE

cutting the British off from their supply bases and thus forcing them to retreat. The 15th Panzer Division was to move south at first light on either side of Capuzzo in order to pin down the British main force. I planned to concentrate both armoured divisions suddenly into one focus and thus deal the enemy an unexpected blow in his most sensitive spot.

16 June 1941

DEAREST LU,

There was heavy fighting in our eastern sector all day yesterday, as you will have seen long ago from Wehrmacht communiqués. To-day —it's 2.30 a.m.—will see the decision. It's going to be a hard fight, so you'll understand that I can't sleep. These lines in haste will show you that I'm thinking of you both. More soon—when it's all over.

At 05.00 hours on the 16th, the second day of the battle, the 15th Panzer Division launched its attack on Capuzzo, and a violent and heavy tank battle soon developed. For all its efforts, however, the division was unable to gain any telling success. Soon Musaid also fell into British hands. At about 10.30 hours the Panzer Division reported that it had been forced to break off its attack on Capuzzo. The enemy remained unshaken. Of the 80 tanks which 15th Panzer Division had taken into battle, only 30 remained; the remainder were either burnt out on the battlefield or awaiting recovery and repair.

The British force at Capuzzo was the 22nd Guards Brigade and the 4th Armoured Brigade—which here consisted of the 4th and 7th R.T.R. They were equipped with Matilda tanks, of which they had 90. Rommel had met these two tank battalions in his first encounter with the British at Arras in May 1940.

The 5th Light Division, which was attacking toward Sidi Suleiman from the area west of Sidi Azeiz, was also soon heavily engaged with 7th British Armoured Brigade [*equipped with Cruiser tanks*] 6 miles west of Sidi Omar. The violent tank battle which ensued was soon decided in our favour and the division succeeded in fighting its way through to the area north-east of Sidi Omar and continuing its advance on Sidi Suleiman. This was the turning point of the battle. I immediately ordered the 15th Panzer Division to disengage all its mobile forces as quickly as possible and, leaving only the essential minimum to hold the position north of Capuzzo, to go forward on the northern flank of the victorious 5th Light Division towards Sidi Suleiman. The decisive moment had come. It is often possible to decide the issue of a battle merely by making an unexpected shift of one's main weight.

The enemy seemed unwilling to relinquish the initiative so easily, and concentrated the bulk of his armour north of Capuzzo in order to launch a heavy attack early next morning against the element of 15th Panzer Division still left in the north, with the object of forcing a break-through. To impose my plans on the enemy from the outset, I ordered the 5th Light and 15th Panzer Divisions to get their attack on Sidi Suleiman moving at 4.30 a.m., i.e. before the probable start time of the enemy attack.

Next morning, the 17th June, the 5th Light Division set off at the appointed time and after a headlong advance reached the neighbourhood of Sidi Suleiman at 06.00 hours. The 15th Panzer Division had become involved in heavy fighting against an armoured force which the British had sent to parry the danger menacing their army. But it soon reached its objective. Great numbers of destroyed British tanks littered the country through which the two divisions had passed.

This operation had obviously taken the British completely by surprise. In wireless messages which we intercepted they described their position as very serious. The commander of 7th Armoured Division sent a request to the Commander-in-Chief of the desert force to come to his headquarters. It sounded suspiciously as though the British commander no longer felt himself capable of handling the situation. It being now obvious that in their present bewildered state the British would not start anything for the time being, I decided to pull the net tight by going on to Halfaya. Accordingly, at about 09.00 hours, orders were issued for the 5th Light and 15th Panzer Division to push on to Halfaya and prevent any break-through of British armour from the north. The British were seriously in trouble over petrol and ammunition and I hoped to be able to force them into a stand-up fight and destroy their whole force.

The enemy wireless was repeatedly reporting lack of ammunition. Soon they set fire to their stores at Capuzzo and withdrew, leaving the desert littered with vehicles abandoned for lack of petrol. They complained bitterly of their high tank casualties.

The 5th Light and 15th Panzer Divisions reached the Halfaya Pass shortly after 16.00 hours. There they turned and advanced side by side to the north. This was a very unfortunate move, as its result was to squeeze out the pocket instead of closing it and preventing the enemy's escape. Thus the enemy was able to pour back east unmolested through the vast gap between Sidi Omar and Halfaya. I was furious at this missed opportunity. The two divisions should have deployed in front of the enemy as soon as they reached Halfaya, thus bringing him to battle and preventing his escape. In that way we might have raked in a large portion of his offensive power.

Rommel is mistaken. The main body of the British striking force had already withdrawn to the south between the Halfaya Pass and the head of the Afrika Korps column.

Thus the three-day battle of Sollum was over. It had finished with a complete victory for the defence, although we might have dealt the enemy far greater damage than we actually had done. The British had lost, in all, over 220 tanks and their casualties in men had been tremendous. We, on the other hand, had lost only about 25 tanks totally destroyed.

Although two-thirds of the British tanks were out of action by the end of the battle, the number destroyed or captured was 87 (58 " I " tanks and 29 cruisers), besides 500 men killed or captured. They took 570 prisoners, and claimed to have knocked out nearly 100 enemy tanks. Here, again, it can be seen how each side is apt to overestimate the other's loss, particularly in a fast-moving battle.

18 June 1941

DEAREST LU,

The three-day battle has ended in complete victory. I'm going to go round the troops to-day to thank them and issue orders. I'm leaving at six, so please be content with this brief note for the moment.

23 June 1941

I've been three days on the road going round the battlefield. The joy of the " Afrika " troops over this latest victory is tremendous. The British thought they could overwhelm us with their 400 tanks. We couldn't put that amount of armour against them. But our grouping and the stubborn resistance of German and Italian troops who were surrounded for days together, enabled us to make the decisive operation with all the forces we still had mobile. Now the enemy can come, he'll get an even bigger beating.

THE BATTLE OF SOLLUM—A REVIEW

Wavell's strategic planning of this offensive had been excellent. What distinguished him from other British army commanders was his great and well-balanced strategic courage, which permitted him to concentrate his forces regardless of his opponent's possible moves. He knew very well the necessity of avoiding any operation which would enable his opponent to fight on interior lines and destroy his formations one by one with locally superior concentrations. But he was put at a great disadvantage by the slow speed of his heavy infantry tanks, which prevented him from reacting quickly enough to the moves of our faster vehicles. Hence the slow speed of the bulk of his armour was his soft spot, which we could seek to exploit tactically.

Rommel's high tribute to Wavell is significant. For immediately after this battle, Churchill, who was deeply disappointed with the outcome, decided to replace Wavell by Auchinleck as Commander-in-Chief. It will be seen that Rommel's diagnosis of the main factor in the British failure corresponds with forebodings that Wavell had expressed on the 28th May when cautioning the authorities at home against counting too much on a decisive success.

The enemy's plan had been extremely simple, but simple plans are in most cases more menacing than complex ones. With the German and Italian holding forces in the Sollum-Halfaya sector tied down frontally, the British had planned to move their assault brigades round the escarpment and then to the north. The Halfaya Pass was to be taken by an attack from both sides, the success of which must have seemed certain to the British after their experience in May. Once the road through the passes was opened, the British had intended to concentrate their forces and move on to the north, thus unhinging our whole Sollum-Halfaya position. Most probably they would then have gone all out for Tobruk and tried to raise the siege.

In this battle, the British used large numbers of their Mark II [*Matilda*] tanks, which were too heavily armoured to be penetrated by most of our anti-tank weapons. However, the gun which they carried was far too small and its range too short. They were also only supplied with solid, armour-piercing shell. It would be interesting to know why the Mark II was called an infantry tank, when it had no H.E. ammunition with which to engage the opposing infantry. It was also, as I have already said, far too slow. In fact, its only real use was in a straight punch to smash a hole in a concentration of material.

In the winter battles 1941-42, the enemy Mark VI Cruiser tank made its first appearance. With its tremendous speed—more than 40 m.p.h.—this was an extremely useful tank. But its gun was again too small, and it could not make up for its lack of calibre—and thus of range—by the heavy armour it carried. Had this tank been equipped with a heavier gun, it could have made things extremely unpleasant for us.

The British Mark VI cruiser was the type better known by its name, the "Crusader." Rommel's high opinion of it, apart from its 2-pounder gun, is worthy of note—since disappointment with its inadequate gun-power led to sweeping criticism of it on the British side, and to its good qualities being under-valued. Rommel is mistaken in saying that it first appeared in the winter—50 were used in "Battleaxe" in June.

Its 2-pounder gun had a penetration of 44 mm. at 1000 yards, which was slightly better than either the 50 mm. Kwk. gun in the Panzer III or the short 75 mm. in the Panzer IV. It had 49 mm. of armour on the turret front, compared with 35 mm. on the Panzer III and IV, though thinner elsewhere. But the frequency of mechanical trouble when it first appeared tended to aggravate dissatisfaction with it on other scores.

The crucial position in this battle was the Halfaya Pass, which Captain Bach and his men held through the heaviest fighting. Major Pardi's artillery battalion also rendered distinguished service in this action, thus showing that Italian troops could give a good account of themselves when they were well officered. Had the British been able to take the Halfaya Pass as they had planned, the situation would have been very different.

They would have been able to thrust both to the front and the rear along the coast, and would have been in a position to make better tactical use of their armour in all circumstances. The armoured units which they threw against our striking force in the area north of Sidi Omar failed to prevent the advance of the 5th Light Division and 15th Panzer Division, and thanks to the excellent co-ordination between our anti-tank, armoured and A.A. forces, were themselves destroyed. We could have annihilated the greater part of the British force north of Sidi Suleiman if our commanders had been alive to their opportunity and had acted on their own initiative.

When the German attack was launched from north of Sidi Omar, Wavell was prevented by the slowness of his infantry tanks from shifting his main weight at that moment from Capuzzo to the point of the Axis attack. There was nothing for him but a quick retreat, which he executed with the minimum of casualties to the British forces.

The garrisons holding the strong points on our Sollum front also had a great share in the Axis victory. Some of them succeeded in beating off every enemy attack, while others fought on to the last breath.

This battle made a great impression on our superior commands. General Roatta, who arrived in Africa some time later, informed me that the Italian High Command realised the necessity of considerably reinforcing the Axis forces in North Africa. The German element was to be brought up to four mechanised divisions and the Italian to an armoured corps of three divisions, with a further two to three motorised divisions. Their zeal unfortunately did not last long.

If these reinforcements had in fact come to Africa in the autumn of 1941, with their supplies guaranteed, we could have beaten off the British winter offensive in the Marmarica—assuming that is, that Auchinleck would have begun it at all in those circumstances. We would have been strong enough to destroy the British in Egypt in the spring of 1942, and could have advanced into Irak and cut off the Russians from Basra. This would have been a very heavy blow strategically both for Britain and Russia.

28 June 1941

DEAREST LU,

You need not worry yourself any more about my health. I'm doing fine. Our place is much healthier, lying 600 feet above sea level. Besides, I've got the advantage of my four walls. Aldinger was sick for a few days, but he's now getting better. There's a lot of work.

3 July 1941

A quite atrocious heat, even during the night. One lies in bed, tossing and turning and dripping with sweat.   The news of the victories in Russia is very good to hear.   It's all quiet here so far. But I'm not being taken in.   Our stubborn friends on the other side will be back sooner or later.   The first congratulations on my promotion to Panzer General are coming in.   Of course I've heard nothing official yet, but I understand it's been announced on the radio.

5 July 1941

I usually spend a lot of time travelling; yesterday I was away eight hours.   You can hardly imagine what a thirst one gets up after such a journey.   I'm hoping that my flight (to the Fuehrer's H.Q.) will come off in about a fortnight.   It's no good going until the Russian affair is more or less over, otherwise there'll be scant regard for my interests.

I was glad to hear that Manfred is now getting on in mathematics. It's all a matter of the method of teaching.   I'm also very pleased about his other successes in school.

I'm managing, by dint of keeping the place dark and " shooting a lot of them down," to keep my office fairly clear of mosquitoes. I'm even having an occasional bang while writing.

21 Aug. 1941

Nothing to report of importance.   Had another visit from the Italian C.-in-C. yesterday; purely " comradely ", however.   On the official level I've been disagreeing with a number of things which have been done and have said so through Calvi, so this visit was probably a goodwill gesture.   I've got a number of visitors to-day. We're having chicken and I'm not going to miss it in spite of my diet.   This perpetual mush loses its fascination after a time.   I'm very pleased about my new appointment.   [*Rommel had just been appointed Commander of the Panzer Group Afrika.*]   Everybody else in that position is a Colonel-General.   If things here go as I should like them, I, too, will probably get that rank after the war's over.

26 Aug. 1941

I was unable to write yesterday—on the road all day.   I returned to my new H.Q. in the evening and moved into my two rooms. Bagged two more bugs, alas, this morning—although they were outside the net.   There are endless swarms of flies and my flycatcher is going to come in very useful.

27 Aug. 1941

Nothing new.   The heat's frightful, night time as well as day time. Liquidated four bugs.   My bed is now standing in tins filled with water and I hope the nights will be a little more restful from now on. Some of the others are having a bad time with fleas. They've left me alone so far.

28 Aug. 1941

. . . As to my health, I'm feeling absolutely right. Everything's working again. I'm getting on famously with my new Chief of Staff [*Gause*]—which is of tremendous importance to me. Unfortunately the bugs are still about—four in the last twenty-four hours. But I hope to win this campaign also.

29 Aug. 1941

A ferocious heat! We're going off some time to bathe. Otherwise nothing new. There's a lot of blather about an imminent attack by the British, but it's probably pure gossip. They're scraping together troops for Iran. Their communications with Russia through Siberia are very shaky, because of Japan's attitude, so there only remains the route across the Persian Gulf. This also looks a very doubtful proposition. Probably they'll come too late.

A night without bugs! Maybe I have killed the last of the Mohicans. I've even mastered the flies in my rooms.

30 Aug. 1941

We've settled in very well in our new place. I've been free of the bugs ever since I had petrol poured over my iron bedstead, and set light to. They must have been in the framework. We had a quick bathe yesterday, but the sea water is too warm to refresh.

A caravan is supposed to be on the way for me, but it seems to have sunk. A pity, but it can't be helped.

31 Aug. 1941

It's damned hot again, so hot that one steams even in the early morning. Otherwise there's nothing doing, except that the Italian High Command is dissatisfied at having so little say in things here. They mess us about over all manner of petty details, but we don't take any of it lying down. Maybe they're working for a real bust-up, in order to get me, or perhaps the whole German force, out of the way. I for one wouldn't be sorry to have a change of theatre.

10 Sept. 1941

I went out shooting last evening with Major von Mellenthin and Lieutenant Schmidt. It was most exciting. Finally, I got a running gazelle from the car. We had the liver for dinner and it was delicious.

We have a distinguished visitor coming to-day—Major Melchiori, a close confidant of the Duce. I'm hoping for a lot from this visit, as the feeling towards us is not particularly friendly at the moment. Things have changed! However, we take good care of ourselves and don't always mince our words. All for now, our visitor's arriving.

29 Sept. 1941

The last few days have been exciting. A large shipment arrived for us at Benghazi. It took 50 hours to unload. All went well. You can imagine how pleased I was. With things as they are in the Mediterranean it's not easy to get anything across. For the moment we're only stepchildren and must make the best of it. Anyway, they're making good progress in Russia and our time will come again.

The wind's howling outside, although there is no Ghibli. Guenther's doing fried potatoes this evening and I'm looking forward to it after being off my food for a few days.

6 Oct. 1941

Unable to write yesterday, my stomach struck work again. We had a fowl the evening before last which must have come from Rameses II's chicken run. For all the six hours' cooking it had it was like leather, and my stomach just couldn't take it.

7 Oct. 1941

My stomach is completely back in order and I'm rushing around in fine fettle. What do you think of my leave plans? I should be able to get away to Rome for a week at the beginning of November. I've got a lot of business to clear up there. I'll have to come back for the battle, of course, and we must hope that supplies work all right, so that we can really get down to it. Then I'll be able to take my leave at the end of November. I know it's not a very good time for leave and it won't be easy for me to get used to the cold. However, it's the best time for things here. Of course supplies might upset everything and cause a long postponement.

9 Oct. 1941

I received some nice news from Voggenreiter[1] yesterday. He says that royalties for the large edition (50,000) will not be less than 25,000 marks. At the same time Mittler und Sohn notified me of a credit of 1021.5 marks![2] That really is something to be going on with.

And now there are all these special communiqués from the East. I wonder if Britain won't soon begin to get cold feet. A lot of work

[1]Rommel's publisher.

[2]Rommel refers here to his book *Infanterie greift an* which sold 400,000 copies in Germany before and during the war.

here. Gambarra's[1] coming to-day, but it's doubtful whether his news will be very pleasant.

10 Oct. 1941

A fairly stormy meeting yesterday, to be continued to-day. Not much to show for it. The things one has to put up with! I'm keeping very fit—touch wood—lively from morning to night.

12 Oct. 1941

Wonderful news from Russia! After the conclusion of the great battles, we can expect the advance east to go fast and thus remove all possibility of the enemy creating any significant new forces. The British workers seem to be getting thoroughly rebellious. . . .

Britain would be only too pleased to attack, but she has neither the troops nor the equipment to make a major landing in Europe. They'll be too late for Russia if they choose the only road left open to them, through India, and an attack in Libya would be a risky business and would not have any direct effect on things in Russia. Once we've taken T. [*Tobruk*], there'll be precious little hope for them here.

13 Oct. 1941

I hope we meet all right on the 1st November. Inquire about the trains please and let me know exactly when you'll be getting to Rome. Then I'll arrange things so that I can be there on time. I'm hoping the situation will permit me to stay until the 15th. But you must bring along a civilian outfit for me (brown suit).

24 Oct. 1941

DEAR MANFRED,

You'll be getting more letters from me now that you're alone in the house.

Everything is going as planned here. I visit the troops every day, most of them are by the sea. Occasionally we bathe. The water is still very warm, and the heat pretty bad during the day, but it's so cool at night now, that I need two blankets. My new home is nicely furnished. The wall is covered with all different maps, especially of Russia, on which every advance we make is immediately marked in.

28 Oct. 1941

DEAR MANFRED,

We had the Ghibli again yesterday. Sometimes the dust-clouds were so thick you could only see two to three yards. It seems to be better to-day.

[1] Italian Corps Commander.

It's only a few days now before I take off to fly across the water. I'm very pleased to be seeing Mummy again in Rome and am only sorry that you, young man, can't be with us. But it couldn't be helped. I am certain to get some leave this winter and then we'll have a good prowl round together. There's not much hunting here where I am now. Some of the officers have shot cheetahs, which have their homes in the stony wadis. Occasionally one comes across a bustard, a fox, a jackal or even a gazelle. The camel thorn bushes are now growing faintly green and have got tiny flowers. Last night the British bombarded us from the sea. Dive-bombers and torpedo-bombers sank one or two of their cruisers and we've had peace since. All for to-day.

No further German divisions beyond the original two were sent from Europe in 1941 (nor during the first half of 1942), but one extra division was formed in Africa from a number of independent units there. This division, which was called the 90th Light, had no tanks and comprised only four infantry battalions, but was relatively strong in fire-power, having three field artillery battalions, an anti-tank battalion, and a battalion of 88 mm. dual-purpose (A.A. and A.Tk.) guns.

The 5th Light Division was renamed the 21st Panzer Division, but without any change in organisation and equipment. Both this and the 15th Panzer Division had only two tank battalions and three infantry battalions.

After Rommel's command was raised to the status of a Panzer Group in August, Lieut.-General Cruewell was appointed commander of the Afrika Korps (with Colonel Bayerlein as Chief of Staff). Only the two Panzer divisions were included in the Afrika Korps.[1] Besides the Africa Korps and the 90th Light Division, Rommel also had under him six Italian divisions—the Ariete and Trieste (forming the XX Motorised Corps); the Pavia, Bologna and Brescia (forming the XXI Infantry Corps) which were investing Tobruk; and the Savona, which was garrisoning Bardia.

[1]Each of the two panzer divisions comprised:
A panzer regiment of 2 battalions (each of 4 companies).
> Companies had an establishment of 21 tanks apiece—the total of the regiment, including command and signal tanks, being 194.
> One company of each battalion, however, was still in Germany when the British autumn offensive, " Operation Crusader," was launched in November, 1941. By the spring of 1942 the 4th company of each battalion had been sent to Africa, and the proportion of medium tanks was increased. In August, 1942, the (nominal) establishment of a regiment was reduced to 180 tanks.
A Motorised Infantry Regiment of 3 battalions (each of 4 companies).
An Artillery Regiment of 3 battalions (each of 3 batteries, and each battery of 4 guns). One battalion was heavy—with 150 mm. howitzers.
An Anti-Tank Battalion (of 3 companies, each with 12 anti-tank guns).
An Armoured Reconnaissance Battalion (with 30 armoured cars).
Engineers and other troops.
The establishment (planned strength) of the panzer division in personnel was approximately 12,500—and in anti-tank guns, 120.

CHAPTER VIII

THE WINTER CAMPAIGN, 1941-2

By Lieut.-General Fritz Bayerlein

UNFORTUNATELY THERE is no connected account written by Rommel for the next period of the war in Africa—the winter of 1941-42. As a proper appreciation of the tactical and strategical problems in Africa, and of Rommel's generalship, is impossible without this part of the story, it has been thought necessary for a summary of operations during this period to be compiled from the available documents. I have been all the more ready to undertake this task as I was myself in the centre of events, having arrived in the desert from the mud of the early Russian winter shortly before the beginning of the British autumn offensive, with a thorough practical schooling in mobile warfare behind me, which I had acquired in the European theatre under that master of the art, General Guderian. The account which follows has, therefore, been compiled partly from my own experience during the Libyan campaign and partly from the documents available to me.

The German-Italian operations in the spring of 1941 and the rapid conquest of Cyrenaica which had resulted had left the whole world gasping. The reconquered Italian territory had been held against heavy British counter-attacks and its defence strengthened by the construction of the Sollum-Bardia line. On the other side of the picture, we had failed, despite all efforts, to take Tobruk and thus acquire a supply port close to the front—for Benghazi was about 300 miles away and Tripoli about 1,000. The British had been quick to appreciate the decisive importance of Tobruk and were defending it with the utmost tenacity. Important German and Italian forces were now tied up in the siege. But far worse was the fact that all future operations were bound to be determined by the situation at Tobruk. Were the enemy to launch simultaneous attacks from Egypt and Tobruk, Rommel's position could not fail to become extremely critical. The weak Axis forces had insufficient depth to allow them to operate freely; their supply lines were continually threatened, and a serious danger existed of their fighting units being squeezed into the confined space between the sea, the Sollum and the Tobruk fronts, and there surrounded and destroyed by a superior and skilfully led enemy.

Rommel was in no doubt that the British would exploit this opportunity towards the end of the year and that it was essential to forestall them by taking Tobruk before they had the chance. In any attack on Tobruk, however, he had to reckon with the possibility of a British relieving attack in the rear of his assault force; to meet it he would be forced to deploy the mass of his mobile forces between Capuzzo and Bir el Gobi. Rommel did not expect the British to launch a major attack until they thought the Middle East free of the danger of a German offensive through the Caucasus, when they would be able to draw off major forces for employment on the Egyptian front sufficient to ensure the success of their plan. With the adverse turn which our operations in Russia had taken, this situation could be expected to arise by about November.

During September the siege front round Tobruk was strengthened and suitable jump-off points for the attack were taken. The transportation across the Mediterranean of the necessary reinforcements, arms and supplies for the attack required a substantial increase in the level of Italian shipments to Africa. But these remained, as usual, far below the promises given us by the High Command, which had themselves been regarded as an absolute minimum. The result was that by the end of September only a third of the troops and a seventh of the supplies which we needed had arrived. This was a terrible handicap in our race for time with the British, and forced us to postpone our attack until November; even then we had to be content with inadequate forces and material.

As time was pressing, Rommel reported to the High Command at the beginning of November that he had enough troops in position to open the offensive and that he thought it essential, even if the necessary supplies had not all arrived, to mount the attack in the second half of November, by which time all other preparations would be ready. But the High Command failed to appreciate the situation and were apprehensive. In their reply they drew attention to the British superiority in the air and proposed that the attack should be put off until the following year. Rommel could not let it go at that and replied the same day that with the present state of shipping in the Mediterranean, he feared that any lengthy postponement would only result in the balance of strength swinging even further against us. He therefore regarded it as vital to strike at the earliest possible moment. The High Command thereupon gave approval for the operation to be undertaken at the time proposed.

The assault proper was to be made by the 90th Light Division, 15th Panzer Division and two Italian infantry divisions. As a covering force Rommel moved the Italian Motorised Corps Gambarra (the Ariete Armoured Division and Trieste Motorised Division) and the 21st Panzer Division into the area south and south-east of Tobruk between Bir Hacheim, Gasr el Arid and Got el Hariga, where they were to form a mobile defence against any relieving attacks which the enemy might mount either on the rear of the Tobruk assault force or on the Sollum front. This move was complete by the 16th November. The siege of Tobruk was maintained by the Italian Brescia and Trento Divisions.

Rommel's tank strength at that time comprised 260 German and 154 Italian tanks. Of the German tanks, 15 were Panzer I, 40 were Panzer II, 150 were Panzer III (50 per cent of which were still equipped with the 37-mm. gun), and 55 were Panzer IV.

During the night 17-18 November, British Commandos, in a raid of great audacity, tried to wipe out what they supposed to be Army Headquarters in Beda Littoria—200 miles behind our front—as a prelude to their offensive. The place they attacked was actually occupied at the time by the Quartermaster staff, who lost two officers and two other ranks.

It is interesting to note that Rommel had in fact formerly had his H.Q. in this house. He himself had had the first floor and his A.D.C.s the ground floor. The British must have received knowledge of this through their Intelligence Service.

The British Commandos answered the sentry in German. Although they did not know the password, the sentry did not fire, thinking they were Germans who had lost their way. The British were wearing no insignia which might have identified them as enemy. Suddenly one of them drew his pistol and shot the sentry. They pressed quickly into the house, fired a volley into the room on the left of the entrance door, killing two Germans, and tried to get up to the first floor. Here, however, they were met by German bullets. One British officer was killed and a German fatally wounded. The remainder of the British Commandos withdrew.

THE BRITISH ATTACK

In the middle of October, our Army intelligence circular notified all formations that with large quantities of enemy war material and strong contingents of troops steadily pouring into Egypt, there was a grave danger that the British would soon launch a major offensive. Even before this, in September, a move by the South African and New Zealand Divisions from the Nile Delta to Mersa Matruh had been detected by

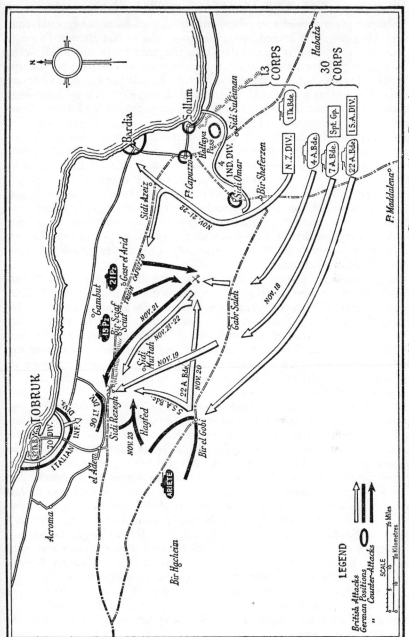

10. The British Offensive, November 1941—Crusader (1st Phase)

LEGEND

British Attacks
" German Positions
" Counter-Attacks

SCALE

our interception service and afterwards confirmed by prisoner interrogation. However, the armed reconnaissance which 21st Panzer Division made in the middle of September into the area south of Sidi Barrani brought back no evidence of an impending attack. No supply dumps capable of supporting a major offensive were seen in the Egyptian frontier area. The enemy's approach march and deployment passed unnoticed by our reconnaissance. His concealment of his preparations was excellent. The wireless silence which he imposed prevented our interception service detecting his approach march into the assembly areas. Our air reconnaissance—operating, it is true, with far too few aircraft—failed to spot his troop movements, probably because he only moved by night and laid up during the day under the protection of excellent camouflage. Moreover, as luck would have it, torrential rain put all our airfields out of commission on the 18th November and no air reconnaissance was flown that day. But air reconnaissance failed just as badly on the southern flank, where the British had established large supply dumps. Ground reconnaissance was equally ineffective. As a result the attack achieved complete tactical surprise.

From captured papers we later learned the dispositions of the British Eighth Army for their attack. Its aim was to destroy the German-Italian forces, relieve Tobruk and then exploit victory by an advance to occupy Tripolitania. XXX Corps, on the desert flank, was to advance on Tobruk from the frontier with the bulk of the British armour. The task of XIII Corps, on the coast, was first to pin down the garrisons of the Sollum front while the armoured manœuvre was in progress, then to advance northward to cut off these garrisons and then to move west to support XXX Corps.

This offensive, called "Crusader," began on the 18th November with a long approach march, by the main force, that passed wide round the flank of the German-Italian fortified position near Sollum, on the coast route. The attacking force comprised the equivalent of seven divisions, including the Tobruk garrison, and was opposed by three German and seven Italian. But such figures give a false impression, and all the more so because the issue mainly turned on armour and air-power. The British had five brigades of armour, while Rommel had the equivalent of two German and one Italian. In number of tanks the British total was 724, with some 200 in reserve (which were sent up at the rate of about forty a day). Rommel's strength at the start was 414 (including 154 Italian). He had some fifty under repair but had no reserve of new tanks. In the air the British predominance was much greater, as in aircraft fit for action they had close on 1,100 against 120 German and about 200 Italian. The initial advantage was multiplied by surprise.

Rommel himself was in Rome during the first part of November. He had gone there to win sanction for his plan of an early attack on Tobruk, and stayed on to spend his birthday, the 15th, with his wife—flying back to Africa just before the British advance began.

It was not until the afternoon of the 18th November, when operations were already under way, that the Panzer Group realised that the enemy had launched an offensive. Our outposts were forced back from the Bir el Gobi—Sidi Omar line by superior enemy forces. A statement given by a British soldier captured at Sidi Suleiman on the 17th November, provided us with a detailed account of the enemy's forces and plans, so detailed in fact that we at first doubted its veracity. Subsequent developments confirmed it in every detail.

In the circumstances, Rommel decided not to go ahead with the attack on Tobruk. The enemy had beaten him to it. He immediately ordered the Afrika Korps to launch an attack against the British masses moving north through Gabr Saleh.

Considerable controversy has occurred since as to whether Rommel was right in calling off the attack on Tobruk in order to deal with the enemy offensive first. Our covering force might indeed have sufficed to hold off the enemy attack until after Tobruk had fallen and this would have been of the greatest advantage for us, for we could then have operated in the Marmarica with far greater ease and freedom than we were, in the event, able to do with the strong Tobruk garrison in our backs. But would the British have allowed us time to capture Tobruk undisturbed? This was not just a matter of audacity and daring; it was a gamble, which General Rommel refused to undertake.

The British armour advanced towards the Tobruk area in three columns, and struck our covering screen on the 19th November. The left column reached Bir el Gobi, forcing back the Ariete Division after a hot fight. The right column was checked by part of the 21st Panzer Division, and then driven back on Gabr Saleh. Meanwhile, the centre column had penetrated to the airfield at Sidi Rezegh, and established itself on the escarpment, barely 10 miles from the Tobruk perimeter.

On the 20th the Afrika Korps continued and developed its pressure on the enemy's right flank, and destroyed many tanks in the day's fighting. Both our divisions won through to the area Gabr Saleh-Sidi Omar, a good base for an attack on the rear of the enemy's centre column. Rommel's plan, taking into account our inferior strength and the limited usefulness of the Italians, was to concentrate his mobile formations into one compact force, and defeat the enemy formations one after the other, until finally the entire British striking force had been destroyed.

The British obliged by throwing their armoured brigades into the battle in separate units. This enabled us to gain a series of partial successes, and eventually led to victory in one of the greatest armoured battles of the campaign, in which the bulk of the enemy's armour was destroyed. In these actions, which are among the most interesting of the African war, the tactics were developed which were to bring such success later. They provide an illuminating picture of Rommel's generalship and that of his subordinate commanders.

Rommel returned to Africa on 18th November. Two days later he wrote to his wife:

20 Nov. 1941

DEAREST LU,

The enemy offensive began immediately after my arrival. The battle has now reached its crisis. I hope we get through it in good order. It will probably all be decided by the time this letter arrives. Our position is certainly not easy.

I'm as well as can be expected.

On the morning of the 21st November, the Afrika Korps moved to the attack against the rear of the British armour. By evening, after heavy fighting, it gained the escarpment near Bir Sciaf-Sciuf south of the Trigh Capuzzo, where it took up position for a mobile defence to meet the enemy's renewed attack.

On the previous night, a minor sortie of the Tobruk garrison from the south-east sector was followed by a heavy attack supported by 50 infantry tanks. The enemy broke through the investing front, and over-ran the artillery positions of the Bologna Division. Although the position was restored this sector of the front remained a continual source of anxiety for us.

For the 22nd November Rommel ordered " mobile operations " south of the Trigh Capuzzo. On the previous night General Cruewell had led the 15th Panzer Division out to the east, completely unobserved by the enemy, and regrouped them in depth up against the enemy's long flank. While the 21st Panzer Division attacked the Sidi Rezegh airfield and threw the enemy back to the south, the 15th Panzer Division drove into the flank and rear of the enemy force attacking Bir Sciaf-Sciuf. Pushing on during the night, they overran the headquarters of the British 4th Armoured Brigade, captured the commander and disrupted the brigade.

That day no attacks were made from Tobruk. Farther east the enemy launched an outflanking movement aimed at the rear of the Sollum front. Our strong points held, but Fort Capuzzo was taken by the New Zealanders.

THE TANK BATTLE OF *TOTENSONNTAG*[1]

Orders for the 23rd November were the destruction of the enemy's main striking force by a concentric attack of all German-Italian mobile forces.

That day Rommel was unable for the first time to issue his orders

[1]Memorial Sunday. The German day of remembrance for those who died in the First World War.

verbally and so the Afrika Korps received a lengthy wireless signal which would have taken far too long to transcribe and decode. General Cruewell could not wait and, knowing Rommel's general plan, felt compelled to act on his own initiative. Accordingly, he left his H.Q. at Gasr el Arid at about 05.30 hours to lead his troops personally in the forthcoming decisive battle. Half an hour later, his whole headquarters staff together with almost the entire paraphernalia of command was surprised by the New Zealanders, who had come up from Sidi Azeiz unobserved, and taken prisoner after a heroic defence. General Cruewell and I escaped this fate by a hairsbreadth.

On the morning of the 23rd, German-Italian dispositions were as follows :

The 15th Panzer Division was reorganising after its success near Bir Sciaf-Sciuf. The 21st Panzer Division was deployed for defence in the Sidi Rezegh area. The Italian Ariete and Trieste Divisions were assembled round Bir el Gobi.

The enemy armour was thought to be lying on the extensive desert plateau of Sidi Muftah and Bir el Haiad, divided up into several combat groups.

General Cruewell's plan was to attack the enemy in the rear, but he first intended to join up with the Ariete, who were moving up from Bir el Gobi, in order to bring all the available armour to bear in one united effort. At about 07.30 hours, the 15th Panzer Division moved to the south-west where they discovered and immediately attacked a strong force of enemy armour round Sidi Muftah. Violent tank fighting developed. More enemy groups with vast vehicle parks, numerous tanks and guns were discovered north of Hagfed el Haiad and General Cruewell accordingly embarked on an even wider outflanking movement. By the early afternoon, after continuous fighting, he reached a point south-east of Hagfed el Haiad, deep in the enemy's rear.

The Ariete's assault spearheads had meanwhile arrived with 120 tanks and General Cruewell now launched the combined German and Italian armoured forces northwards into the enemy's rear, with the object of bottling him up completely and forcing him back against the 21st Panzer Division's front at Sidi Rezegh.

The attack started well, but soon came up against a wide artillery and anti-tank gun screen, which the South Africans had formed at a surprising speed between Haiad and Muftah. Guns of all kinds and sizes laid a curtain of fire in front of the attacking tanks and there seemed almost no hope of making any progress in the face of this fire-spewing barrier. Tank after tank split open in the hail of shells. Our entire artillery had to be thrown in to silence the enemy guns one by one. However, by the late afternoon we had managed to punch a few holes in the front. The tank attack moved forward again and tank duels of tremendous intensity developed deep in the battlefield. In fluctuating fighting, tank against tank, tank against gun or anti-tank nest, sometimes in frontal, sometimes in flanking assault, using every trick of mobile warfare and tank tactics, the enemy was finally forced back into a confined area. With no relief forthcoming from a Tobruk sortie, he now saw his only escape from complete destruction in a break-out from the ring surrounding him.

At one moment during this confused battle, the Afrika Korps' Mammoth, containing General Cruewell and his staff, was suddenly ringed round by British tanks. The German crosses on the sides of the vehicle, which had been originally captured from the British, were not easy to identify. The hatches were shut. The British tankmen, who had fortunately fired off all their ammunition, had no idea whom they had met. A number of them left their Mark VI, walked across to the Mammoth and knocked on the armour plate, whereupon General Cruewell opened the hatch and found himself looking into the face of a British soldier, to the great astonishment of both. At that moment gunfire started to spray into the neighbourhood. The occupants of the Mammoth threw themselves flat on the thin wooden flooring, but the vehicle escaped undamaged. A German 20-mm. anti-aircraft gun had opened fire on the dismounted British tank crews, who promptly jumped back into their tanks and disappeared as fast as they could to the south, thus releasing the staff of the Afrika Korps from a highly precarious situation.

The wide plain south of Sidi Rezegh was now a sea of dust, haze and smoke. Visibility was poor and many British tanks and guns were able to break away to the south and east without being caught. But a great part of the enemy force still remained inside. Twilight came, but the battle was still not over. Hundreds of burning vehicles, tanks and guns lit up the field of that *Totensonntag*. It was long after midnight before we could get any sort of picture of the day's events, organise our force, count our losses and gains and form an appreciation of the general situation upon which the next day's operations would depend. The most important results of this battle were the elimination of the direct threat to the Tobruk front, the destruction of a large part of the enemy armour and the damage to enemy morale caused by the complete ruin of his plans.

After these reverses, the commander of XXX Corps, General Norrie, decided to withdraw what remained of his forces southward to the Gabr Saleh area. Two-thirds of his tanks had been lost, and the remaining 150 were badly dispersed.

23 Nov. 1941

DEAREST LU,

The battle seems to have passed its crisis. I'm very well, in good humour and full of confidence. Two hundred enemy tanks shot up so far. Our fronts have held.

THE RAID INTO EGYPT

General Cruewell's conduct of the battle had been masterly; on the morning of the 24th November he reported to Rommel on the ring road —Rommel did not yet know the full details of the action south of Tobruk —that the enemy had been smashed at Sidi Rezegh, and that only a part of his force had escaped destruction. This fact strengthened Rommel in the decision he had already taken to strike to the south-east deep into the enemy's rear. Rommel explained his plan in the following words: " The greater part of the force aimed at Tobruk has been destroyed; now we will turn east and go for the New Zealanders and Indians before they have been able to join up with the remains of their main force for a combined attack on Tobruk. At the same time we will take Habata and Maddalena and cut off their supplies. Speed is vital; we must make the most of the shock effect of the enemy's defeat and push forward immediately and as fast as we can with our entire force to Sidi Omar."

Rommel's intention was to exploit the disorganisation and confusion which he knew must exist in the enemy's camp, by making an unexpected and audacious raid into the area south of the Sollum front. He hoped to complete the enemy's confusion and perhaps even induce him to pull back into Egypt again. Our entire mobile force was to take part in the operation.

A weak holding force, scraped together from different formations and put under the command of the artillery commander, General Boettcher, was placed south of Tobruk to deal with any further enemy attempts to raise the siege. Italian infantry remained at Bir el Gobi and the siege of Tobruk was maintained by the same forces as hitherto. This decision of Rommel's—probably the boldest he ever made—has been severely criticised by certain German authorities, who were for ever incapable of understanding the African theatre, but has been praised and admired by the enemy.

It would, of course, have been possible for him to have first disposed finally of the enemy remnants who had been fortunate enough to escape destruction south of Tobruk; but this would have taken a great deal of valuable time. He therefore judged it better to take the enemy unawares by going for his Sollum front and at the same time striking a blow at his most sensitive spot—his life-line of supply. Accordingly, at midday on the 24th November, the Afrika Korps and the Ariete Division started on their long desert trek towards Sidi Omar, which they reached in the evening after a wild drive in complete disregard of the British threat to their flanks. Rommel, who was at the head of the column, led the 21st Panzer Division straight through the 4th Indian Division into the Sidi Suleiman district in order to seal off the Halfaya front to the east. The 15th Panzer Division was ordered to attack Sidi Omar. One mixed combat group was assembled to take the supply centre at Maddalena, while another was to destroy the camps round Habata, the terminus of the desert railway. There is no doubt that these moves would have seriously upset the enemy's supply, but they could never have caused it to collapse altogether, and the story put about by a number of writers that " the whole fate of the Eighth Army hung by a single thread, which Rommel was unable to cut " is entirely without foundation.

On the 24th November, the issue of orders took place late in the afternoon near Bir Sheferzen, east of Graziani's wire fence. Rommel then drove off to 21st Panzer Division and personally put them at the Halfaya Pass. On the way back to Sidi Omar his one and only vehicle broke down with engine trouble. It was pure luck that as dusk was falling, the Afrika Korps' Mammoth, containing General Cruewell and his battle staff, came by. " Give us a lift," said Rommel, who, with Gause, was shivering with cold. The Mammoth, now carrying all the most senior officers of the Panzer Group, drove on to the wire fence. Unfortunately, no way through it could be found, and it was impossible to make one. Finally, Rommel grew impatient. " I'll take over myself," he said, and dismissed the A.D.C., who had been directing the vehicle up till then. But this time even Rommel's legendary sense of direction did not help. To make matters worse they were in an area completely dominated by the enemy. Indian dispatch riders buzzed to and fro past the Mammoth, British tanks moved up forward and American-built lorries ground their way through the desert. None of them had any suspicion that the highest officers of the German-Italian Panzer Group were sitting in a captured command vehicle, often only two or three yards away. The ten officers and five men spent a restless night.

During the days that followed, Rommel continued to drive from one unit to another, usually through the British lines, in order to deal with the continually recurring crises. On one occasion he went into a New Zealand hospital, which was still occupied by the enemy. By this time no one really knew who was captor and who captive—except Rommel, who was in no doubt. He inquired if anything was needed, promised the British medical supplies and drove on unhindered. He also crossed an air strip occupied by the British, and was several times chased by British vehicles, but always escaped.

Meanwhile, the 21st Panzer Division, contrary to its original instructions, but following an order wrongly transmitted to it by the Army's rear operations staff, had moved through the Halfaya position on to Capuzzo and become involved in dangerous and costly fighting with the New Zealanders. The attack made by units of the Afrika Korps on Sidi Omar miscarried, and it soon became apparent that the enemy was everywhere still far stronger than might have been expected after our victories. He had recovered from the shock very quickly and the situation had been saved—as we discovered later—by the personal intervention

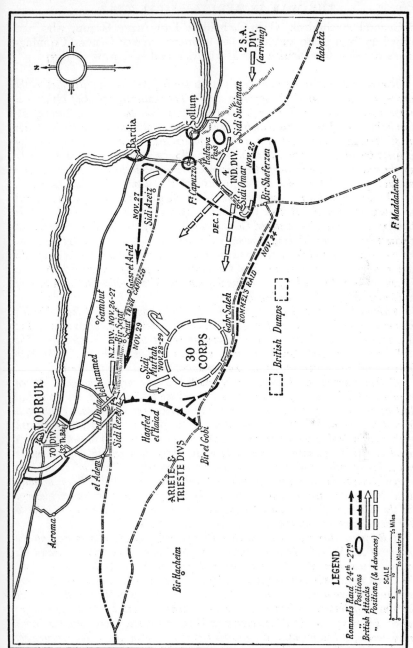

LEGEND

Rommel's Raid 24th–27th
   ,,   Positions
British Attacks
   ,,   Positions (& Advances)

SCALE
0   5   10   20 Miles
0   10   20 Kilometres

British Dumps

11. CRUSADER (2ND PHASE)

2 S.A.
DIV.
(arriving)

Habata

Sollum

Bardia

Sidi Suleiman

Halfaya
Pass

4
IND. DIV.

NOV. 25

Sidi Omar

Bir Sheferzen

F. Maddalena

Ft. Capuzzo

NOV. 27

Sidi Azeiz

DEC. 1

Gasr el Arid

Gabr Saleh

ROMMEL'S RAID

NOV. 24

°Gambut

Bir Sciaf

N.Z. DIV. NOV. 26–27

Scuti Trigh Capuzzo

NOV. 29

Sidi
Muftah
NOV. 28–29

30
CORPS

el Duda
Belhammed

Sidi Rezegh

TOBRUK

70 DIV.

(32) (h.Bde)

el Adem

Hagfed
el Haiad

Bir el Gobi

ARIETE &
TRIESTE DIVS

Acroma

Bir Hacheim

of General Auchinleck, C.-in-C. Middle East Army Group, who had rushed up from Cairo and at the last moment reversed General Cunningham's decision to evacuate the Marmarica and withdraw to Egypt.

Rommel's daring stroke came very close to proving decisive—by its effect on the mind of the commander of the opposing army. The shattering defeat of his armour in the battle around Sidi Rezegh led Cunningham on the 23rd to contemplate abandoning the offensive and withdrawing over the frontier to reorganise his forces out of Rommel's reach. By such a timely withdrawal he could reckon on keeping his army in being, whereas by continuing the offensive in the existing conditions he ran the risk of having it completely destroyed. But his inclination to retreat was overruled by Auchinleck, who arrived at this crucial moment by air from Cairo.

The next day, Rommel launched the Afrika Korps on its strategic raid. As it burst through into the British rear area it spread confusion and panic. This alarming news naturally increased Cunningham's anxiety. If the decision to persist or retreat had rested with him, Rommel's deep advance might have settled the issue. But on the 26th Auchinleck, after returning to Cairo, came to the conclusion that he must reinforce his order to continue the offensive by giving the Eighth Army a different commander, and replaced Cunningham by Ritchie—the Deputy Chief of the General Staff at his own headquarters.

Auchinleck's intervention and resolution brought victory out of defeat. Yet his decision was basically more of a gamble than Rommel's raid, because it staked the survival of the Eighth Army on a continuance of the British offensive. The misdirection of the 21st Panzer Division, as well as the firm resistance of the New Zealand and 4th Indian Divisions, was an important factor in the issue.

As things turned out, Rommel's raid resulted in more forfeit than gain. When the raid started, he had almost won the battle. When the raid ended, the scales had tilted against him. But the margin was very narrow, not only psychologically but physically. For in his south-easterly drive to the frontier—aimed at the British supply sources behind it—he actually passed the two field supply depots on which the whole British advance depended. These two huge dumps, each some six miles square, lay 15 miles south-east and south-west respectively of Gabr Saleh, and only the 22nd Guards Brigade was available to defend them. The Afrika Korps actually passed through the water point on the northern edge of the more easterly dump. But the existence of these two vital supply sources was not discovered—thanks to good concealment, and control of the air on the British side.

If Rommel, after his success at Sidi Rezegh, had pushed south to mop up the remains of XXX Corps, he would have found the dumps—and probably sealed his victory. It was ironical that in pursuing the bigger aim he missed the bigger target. The course he actually took might be condemned by cautiously conventional doctrine, but it was in accord with the classic ideas of generalship as applied by the " Great Captains " of history. When a similar course was followed by the Panzer forces the year before against the Allied armies in Western Europe, under more precarious circumstances, it had produced the greatest victory of modern times. Its miscarriage, this time in Africa, was due partly to the human factors already mentioned—

Auchinleck above all—but it was also a demonstration of the big part that chance plays in the issues of war.

BACK TO TOBRUK

Rommel had notified his Ia, Lieut.-Col. Westphal, of his decision to strike for Sidi Omar in the early morning of the 24th November. Westphal wanted to raise objections, and in particular to draw attention to the fact that the British were reassembling their troops south of Bir el Gobi. But Rommel permitted no discussion, pulled General Gause, his Chief of Staff, into the car and drove off to Sidi Omar.

Before they had gone far the accompanying wireless vehicle stuck fast in the desert. Rommel drove on without it and the operations staff at headquarters could no longer reach him by wireless. So when the British, freshly organised after Auchinleck's assumption of command, advanced on the now practically denuded area of Sidi Rezegh, Westphal tried desperately to make contact with Rommel. Several aircraft were sent out to look for him, but they did not return. The situation south of Tobruk grew steadily more tense, and finally Westphal decided to take matters into his own hands and recall the 21st Panzer Division to Sidi Rezegh.

When Rommel heard of this order he regarded it at first as an enemy trick, but soon found out that it was genuine. An A.D.C. of Rommel's, Lieut. Voss, gives the following account of his return to H.Q.:

" Rommel was at first furious at Lieut.-Col. Westphal's independent action in recalling 21st Panzer Division to El Adem. On returning to headquarters he greeted nobody but stalked silently into the command vehicle and looked at the situation maps. Behind him stood Gause. We tried to signal to Gause that he should talk to Rommel and explain Westphal's decision. But it was not necessary, for Rommel suddenly left the vehicle saying that he was going to lie down. Nobody dared go to the vehicle where Rommel was sleeping, to report on the situation. Next morning, however, to everybody's relief, the General made no further mention of the incident. He was as friendly as ever and work at headquarters continued smoothly."

Although the British 7th Armoured Division and the South Africans had undoubtedly been very badly mauled, the New Zealanders, the Indians, the Guards Brigade and the Tobruk garrison were all fully intact and active. In these circumstances, Rommel was compelled to give up the operations against the supply centres at Maddalena and Habata [*in the desert, 25 miles south of Buqbuq*], as these long-range and time-consuming raids could no longer take the enemy by surprise and would have meant a wanton dispersal of our strength. He now concentrated all his mobile forces against the New Zealanders. On the 25th November heavy fighting flared up again at Tobruk, where our holding force was caught between pincers, one coming from the south-east and the other from the fortress itself. By mustering all their strength, the Boettcher Group succeeded in beating off most of these attacks, and the only enemy penetration was brought to a standstill by an Italian counter-attack.

In view of this critical situation, Rommel immediately broke off operations on the Sollum front and brought all his formations back as quickly as possible to the main centre of the battle at Tobruk.

27 Nov. 1941

Dearest Lu,

The battle has now been raging in the desert round Tobruk and in front of Sollum since the 19th. You will have heard from the communiqués more or less how it has gone. I think we're through the worst and that the battle will be of decisive importance to the whole war situation.

I'm very well. I've just spent four days in a desert counter-attack with nothing to wash with. We had a splendid success.

It's our 25th wedding anniversary to-day. Perhaps it'll run to a special communiqué. I need not tell you how well we get on together. I want to thank you for all the love and kindness through the years which have passed so quickly. I think, with gratitude to you, of our son, who is a source of great pride to me. With his splendid gifts he should go far.

All for now. Our next move is already beginning.

On the 28th November, while the 21st Panzer Division raced along on either side of the coast road to Gambut and gained the country south of Zafraan, 15th Panzer Division drove down the Trigh Capuzzo with its flank constantly threatened by mobile forces. After fighting its way up the escarpment and for the Jebel, the division found itself in the evening once again on the old battleground at Sidi Rezegh.

A wireless signal from Rommel summoned the commander of the Afrika Korps to the Panzer Group's forward H.Q., which was said to be located near Gambut. After searching for a long time in the darkness they finally discovered a British lorry, which General Cruewell's command car approached with great caution. Inside it, to his good fortune, were no British troops, but Rommel and his Chief of Staff, both of them unshaven, worn with lack of sleep and caked with dust. In the lorry was a heap of straw as a bed, a can of stale water to drink and a few tins of food. Close by were two wireless trucks and a few dispatch riders. Rommel now gave his instructions for next day's operations.

His plan was to surround the New Zealand division, which had meanwhile joined hands with the Tobruk garrison, and thus close the ring round Tobruk again. For this operation he gathered together every available formation and put the main weight of his attack on the western flank in order to prevent the New Zealanders withdrawing into Tobruk.

29 Nov. 1941

Dearest Lu,
    The battle seems to be developing well. The decision will probably come to-day. I'm full of confidence.
    In haste.

The 21st Panzer Division—whose commander, General von Ravenstein, had been taken prisoner by the New Zealanders—closed the ring from the east and at the same time defended itself against heavy relieving attacks from the south. In the evening the 15th Panzer Division, moving north, took the important ridge of El Duda, but it was lost again during the night.

30 Nov. 1941

Dearest Lu,
    The battle is still going on and will need all our efforts if we are to win it. Prospects are good, but the troops are dead tired after twelve days of it. I'm in good form, very lively and ready for anything. The British have captured von Ravenstein. All for to-day.

On the morning of the 30th November, powerful enemy armour and massed infantry advanced against our southern screen, but their attacks were unco-ordinated and we were able to repulse them all along the line. The 15th Panzer Division, on the other hand, in spite of many attempts, failed to take Belhammed or make contact with the 90th Light Division, which would have cut the pocket off from Tobruk.
    It was not finally sealed off until the following day, when, after all attempts at relief from the south and east had been beaten off, a concentric attack was launched which resulted in the destruction of the greater part of the New Zealand Division.
    Thus the British garrison was once again locked up in Tobruk. The enemy, moreover—as we learnt from an intercepted wireless message— had suffered such heavy losses that he now intended temporarily to break off the battle.
    But Rommel could not allow his troops the rest they so badly needed. The Sollum front was having to fight hard to defend itself against the Indians, the supply line was being continually molested and Bardia was seriously threatened. He therefore dispatched two mixed combat groups of the Afrika Korps along the Trigh Capuzzo and the coast road, respectively, to open our lines of communication. He placed the bulk of the German and Italian mobile forces south-east of Tobruk where,

while being supplied and refitted, they could be sent quickly either to the Sollum front or to the south against the British main force.

The enemy formations carried out their reorganisation and re-grouping on either side of the Trigh el Abd, covered by a deep screen of armoured cars along the line Sidi Muftah—Capuzzo.

With the enemy so much better off for supplies than we were, we could expect him soon to be ready to resume his offensive. However, the battle had reached a temporary conclusion and the army reported to the High Command on its victories:

" In the continuous heavy fighting between the 18th November and the 1st December, 814 enemy armoured fighting vehicles and armoured cars have been destroyed, and 127 aircraft shot down. No estimate can yet be given of the booty in arms, ammunition and vehicles. Prisoners exceed 9,000, including three generals."

Not until later did we learn that the enemy had meanwhile made a change in the command of the Eighth Army. General Ritchie had replaced General Cunningham.

2 Dec. 1941

DEAREST LU,

Yesterday we succeeded in destroying the remains of one, or perhaps two, British divisions in front of Tobruk, which has made the situation a little easier. But the British won't give up, if I know them. However, we are now fighting under better conditions than before and will pull it off for certain.

The attack of our two mixed combat groups on Bardia-Sollum mis-carried. On the 4th December, the army gained a clear picture of the enemy's dispositions. A new force was being formed round Bir el Gobi, obviously with the intention of thrusting round our flank deep into our rear and unhinging the siege front round Tobruk. Rommel decided to attack this force immediately and with all his mobile formations, before it had had time to complete its preparations.

Our forces had now become too weak to maintain the ring round Tobruk, and Rommel had preparations made to give up the eastern part of the siege front. During the night 4-5 December the Afrika Korps moved westwards through the corridor between El Duda and Sidi Rezegh—now only two miles wide—to its assembly area at El Adem. The attack on Gobi was due to be made in conjunction with the Italian Motorised Corps coming up from the north-east, but with the Italians neither assembled nor in a fit state to attack, the Afrika Korps had to strike the blow alone, which they did at midday on the 5th December. The Korps first came up against the British Guards Brigade—newly arrived in the battle—and then the refitted brigades of 7th Armoured Division. In spite of this they advanced by evening to a point 10 miles north-west of Gobi. Meanwhile, the British had launched an attack from Tobruk, and taken the hill line Duda-Belhammed. This finally forced us to give up the eastern part of the Tobruk front.

At midday on the 5th December, a Commando Supremo Staff officer, sent by the Duce, arrived at Army H.Q. and informed us that no reinforcements for the Panzer Group could be expected to arrive before the beginning of January. Nothing could be done until that date except to cover the barest essentials of rations and ammunition. This information did not make us any more cheerful.

Auchinleck managed to send up two more infantry brigades, and two armoured car regiments. Moreover, the 1st Armoured Division had just arrived from England and was moved up close to the frontier for intense desert training; it would thus provide additional insurance against any further panzer raid.

On the evening of the 5th December, Rommel had the following appreciation to consider: " The Afrika Korps' attack has inflicted no decisive damage on the enemy at Gobi, largely because of the absence of the Italian Motorised Corps. It is to be expected that the enemy force in the Gobi area will be further reinforced by fresh formations and will soon go over to the attack itself in superior strength. Events at Tobruk have shown that there, too, the enemy still disposes of battle-worthy formations. Nevertheless, there still appears to be a chance of gaining a decision, by launching all the remaining German and Italian panzer and motorised divisions in a concerted attack against the British at Gobi. If this fails to destroy a substantial part of the enemy's force, then, in view of our own heavy losses in men and material, we shall have to consider breaking off the battle and withdrawing to the Gazala position, and later evacuating Cyrenaica altogether."

The Afrika Korps launched their attack on the 6th December, once again alone. The Italians reported that their troops were exhausted and no longer fit for action. The enemy fell slowly back on Bir el Gobi, but it was no longer possible to destroy, or even outflank and envelop any material part of their force. There was in fact a serious danger of our own force being outflanked round both sides by the superior enemy.[1] In spite of this, the attack was resumed on the 7th December, again without success. Our casualties were heavy.

In view of the great numerical superiority of the enemy and the condition of our own troops, Rommel now decided to give up Tobruk completely and beat a fighting retreat to the Gazala position. It was a painful decision to have to take, for the German troops had fought successfully and inflicted very heavy losses on the enemy. But to have stayed any longer at Tobruk would merely have led to the steady

---

[1]Cruewell, who realised that the destruction of the enemy could only be achieved with the co-operation of the Italians, repeatedly wirelessed: " Where is Gambarra? " But Gambarra did not appear on the battlefield. Cruewell's signal later became a stock witticism with the troops in Africa.

attrition of our already weakened forces, and thus ultimately to the loss of Libya.

Letter written by L-Cpl. Guenther, Rommel's batman

6 Dec. 1941

DEAR FRAU ROMMEL,

The General went off to his command post very early again this morning. I am to send you his warmest greetings and to inform you that the General is still in good health and that all is well with him.

The new fighting is making very heavy demands on the General; he has no time to spare.

We left our house a fortnight ago and have moved several times since then. Now to-day we have landed up once again in a small wadi, where aircraft will not find us very easily. Our vehicles are well camouflaged and now have quite a look of the desert about them. We have still got the two chickens, the General has no doubt told you about them. They are even managing to find something green here. [*Rommel had been presented with a number of chickens, which at Guenther's special request had not been killed, but were being taken along as mascots.*]

It is very quiet to-day compared with the past weeks. We are no longer in range of the enemy artillery, which used to fire very frequently all round and behind us. So it is very pleasant again not to have the shells whizzing all round. Now I will close. I wish you the very best and send the warmest greetings on behalf of the General to you and your son.

HERBERT GUENTHER
L-Cpl.

9 Dec. 1941

DEAREST LU,

You will no doubt have seen how we're doing from the Wehrmacht communiqués. I've had to break off the action outside Tobruk on account of the Italian formations and also the badly exhausted German troops. I'm hoping we'll succeed in escaping enemy encirclement and holding on to Cyrenaica. I'm keeping well. You can imagine what I'm going through and what anxieties I have. It doesn't look as though we'll get any Christmas this year. It's only a fortnight away.

RETREAT FROM CYRENAICA

During the night 7-8 December, with the defence of Tobruk's western front maintained, the Afrika Korps and the Italian Motorised Corps disengaged from the enemy. Elements of the non-motorised Italian XXI Corps and 90th Light Division were already arriving in the Gazala position. Our main danger during the withdrawal was to the southern flank, where the enemy could outflank us without difficulty, and the Afrika Korps was accordingly detailed to cover the flank of the whole force. However, the enemy attempted nothing so ambitious, but limited himself to thrusts against our front, all of which were beaten off. The Sollum front—now 120 miles from the main force—was still holding out, in spite of the fact that there was now no land route through to them for supplies.

A substantial force was now put in to protect the weakest and most dangerous point on the German-Italian side, the bottleneck at Agedabia, where it would have been a simple matter for the enemy to cut the life-line of the whole Axis Army.

Withdrawing a step at a time, fighting isolated and sometimes very troublesome actions as they went, all troops reached the Gazala Line by the 12th December, without the enemy having succeeded, during the withdrawal, in cutting off any sizeable detachments of troops or inflicting any serious casualties.

Rommel's decision found no agreement with his Italian superiors, and an interesting sidelight on this situation is given in the following entry in his diary:

" I also received a visit from Excellency Bastico in a ravine south-east of Ain el Gazala bay, where we established our H.Q. on the 12th December. He is very upset about the way the battle is going and is particularly worried about the Agedabia area, to which he wants to move an Italian division as quickly as possible. It worked up to a very stormy argument, during which I told him, among other things, that I was not going to stand for any of my Italian divisions being taken from me and redisposed by him. I would have no option but to make the retreat through Cyrenaica with the German forces alone, leaving the Italians to their fate. I added that I was quite certain that we for our part would be able to fight our way through, but that the Italians would not manage it without our help. In short, I did not intend to have a single Italian soldier removed from my command. Excellency Bastico thereupon became more amenable."

12 Dec. 1941

Dearest Lu,

Don't worry about me. It will all come out all right. We're still not through the crisis. It'll probably go on for another couple of weeks yet. But I still have hopes of holding on here. I'm now living in a proper house complete with " hero's cellar " [*a dugout or shelter*]. I spend the days with the troops.

Happy Christmas to you and Manfred. I hope to be with you shortly afterwards.

On the 13th December, a strong enemy infantry attack broke through XX Italian Motorised Corps's line and enemy reconnaissance forces reached Bir Temrad, 12 miles behind our front.

13 Dec. 1941

DEAREST LU,

The situation has been made extremely critical by the failure of a major Italian formation. However, I hope to be able to hold on. Otherwise, I'm very well, in fixed quarters.

Simultaneously enemy armour [*4th Armoured Brigade*] was enveloping the Afrika Korps positions on the desert flank. The enemy's frontal break-through was temporarily checked by a successful counter-attack, but he was strong enough to renew it. Beyond that, there was obviously a danger that the enemy armour might push through to the desert cross-roads at Mechili, stop our supplies and cut off our retreat through Cyrenaica. It was no use concealing the fact that the strength of the Axis forces was at an end and Rommel reported to the High Command: " After 4 weeks of uninterrupted and costly fighting, the fighting power of the troops—despite superb individual achievements—is showing signs of flagging, all the more so as the supply of arms and ammunition has completely dried up. While the Army intends to maintain its hold on the Gazala area during the 16th December, retreat through Mechili-Derna will be unavoidable, at the latest during the night of the 16th, if it is to escape being outflanked and destroyed by a superior enemy."

The Italian High Command was horrified over this plan. On the 16th December General Cavallero appeared at Army H.Q. and had several conferences with Rommel. The diary entry reads as follows:

" At my meeting at 15.15 hours with General Cavallero, I stated that as things had developed, there was only one possibility open to me, namely, to break off the action south of the Ain el Gazala bay and near Tmimi during the night and withdraw our troops to Mechili and Tmimi respectively. The enemy had enveloped the whole of this front and the only escape route left to us was a narrow strip through Tmimi. The Italian troops now had little fight left in them. Cavallero raised no objections at the time.

" However, at 23.00 hours he appeared at my H.Q. again, this time accompanied by Field-Marshal Kesselring, Excellency Bastico and

General Gambarra. In a voice charged with emotion, he demanded that the order for the retreat should be withdrawn. He did not see the necessity for it, and in any case feared political difficulties for the Duce if Cyrenaica were lost. Kesselring backed him up strongly and said that it was completely out of the question for him to give up the airfield at Derna. I stood my ground and said that it was too late to alter my decision. The orders had been issued and were in some cases already being executed. Unless the Panzer Group wanted to face complete destruction, it had no choice but to fight its way back through the enemy during the night. I fully realised that this would mean the eventual loss of Cyrenaica and that political difficulties might result. But the choice I was faced with was either to stay where I was and thus sacrifice the Panzer Group to destruction—thereby losing both Cyrenaica and Tripolitania—or to begin the retreat that night, fight my way back through Cyrenaica to the Agedabia area and at least defend Tripolitania. I could only choose the latter. Excellency Bastico and Gambarra behaved so violently in my room that evening, that I was finally obliged to ask Bastico how he, as Commander-in-Chief of the North African forces, proposed to handle the situation. Bastico evaded the question, and said that as Commander-in-Chief it was not his business; he could only say that we ought to keep our forces together. Finally, the delegation left my H.Q. having accomplished nothing."

On the evening of the 16th December the Afrika Korps and the Italian Motorised Corps, all under the command of General Cruewell, began their withdrawal across the southern edge of the Cyrenaican mountains to El Abiar, while the Italian non-motorised infantry formations marched back through Cyrenaica [*i.e. the coastal strip*].

20 Dec. 1941

DEAREST LU,

We're pulling out. There was simply nothing else for it. I hope we manage to get back to the line we've chosen. Christmas is going to be completely messed up.

I'm very well. I've now managed to get a bath and a change, having slept in my coat most of the time for the last few weeks. Some supplies have arrived—the first since October. My commanding officers are ill—all those who aren't dead or wounded.

22 Dec. 1941

Retreat to A———![1] You can't imagine what it's like. Hoping to get the bulk of my force through and make a stand somewhere. Little ammunition and petrol, no air support. Quite the reverse with the enemy. But enough of that. . . .

[1]Agedabia.

23 Dec. 1941

Operations going satisfactorily to-day, so far as it's possible to tell in the morning. It looks as though we'll succeed in extricating ourselves from the envelopment and getting the main body back. It'll be a great Christmas treat for me if it does come off. How modest one becomes! It's no good turning to the Italian High Command of course. They would have been roped in long ago with all their force.

25 Dec. 1941

I opened my Christmas parcel in my caravan yesterday evening and was very pleased with the letters from you and Manfred and the presents. Some of it, like the bottle of champagne, I took straight across to the Intelligence truck where I sat over it with the Chief, the Ia and Ic. The night passed quietly. But the Italian divisions give us a lot of worry. There are shocking signs of disintegration and German troops are being forced to the rescue everywhere. The British were badly disappointed at Benghazi in neither cutting us off, nor finding petrol and rations. Cruewell has been made a full Panzer General. He really deserves it. I'm up at the front every day, regrouping and organising our forces. I hope we now succeed in making a stand.

P.S.—I don't think I've told you yet that Schraepler met with a fatal accident (run over by the Mammoth).

By the 25th December, the retreat to Agedabia was complete, without the enemy having exploited a single one of the many chances which he had had for outflanking the German forces. The non-motorised German-Italian troops moved into improvised defence lines on either side of the town, while the Afrika Korps and the Italian Motorised Corps took up positions round Agedabia for a mobile defence.

There was one more major " victory " to record before the retreat was over—on the 19th December a convoy from Italy arrived in Benghazi carrying two German panzer companies, artillery batteries and supplies. These were the first ships carrying arms which had arrived since the beginning of the British offensive in mid-November. Part of the convoy had been sunk during the crossing and two panzer companies and one battery lost.

It remains a mystery why the British did not outmarch us through the excellent driving country of the desert and finally cut off our retreat at the critical point, i.e. Agedabia. Fortunately for us, this danger, of which Rommel was all the time afraid, did not materialise.[1]

[1]The British follow-up was greatly handicapped by the difficulties of maintaining supplies as the line of supply became increasingly stretched. In consequence, the follow-up forces not only had to be reduced, but dwindled as the advance continued. The re-equipped 22nd Armoured Brigade formed the main armoured element, but was twice

Even so, the threat of our flank being turned by a wide hook through the desert was still with us at Agedabia, which was operationally a weak position. In view of the condition of our troops—particularly the Italians —and the deficiencies in our supply it did not seem very advisable to make a long stay at Agedabia, but rather to limit ourselves to fighting a delaying action there, and then, when the moment seemed right, to pull back the bulk of our force to Mersa el Brega. Rommel reported in these terms to the Commando Supremo and they, after long deliberation, were eventually forced to agree that whereas we might lose everything if we stayed at Agedabia, Tripolitania at least could be successfully defended if we pulled back to Mersa el Brega. However, the time for this retreat had not yet come.

Our defence at Agedabia was centred on the Afrika Korps. As the position itself was incapable of withstanding a major attack, the only way to defend it was by movement and counter-attack. Meanwhile, the enemy had already pushed forward very close to our front, so that we could expect both a frontal assault on our line and a hook round our desert flank. On the 27th December, the 22nd British Armoured Brigade, recently refitted and again up to full fighting strength,[1] moved forward through El Haseiat, while other troops launched a frontal attack at Agedabia. In three days of tank fighting, the enemy was outflanked, forced to fight on a reversed front, and finally surrounded. Some thirty of his tanks succeeded in escaping east, as petrol shortage checked the completion of our success. Under the impress of this defeat the elements of the Support Group and Guards Brigade which had mounted the frontal attack, also withdrew to the north-east. Thus the immediate danger to the Agedabia position was over. Rommel immediately made use of this breathing space to evacuate the position and retire by stages without enemy pressure into the Mersa el Brega line. The withdrawal began on the 2nd January with the departure of the Italian infantry. The mobile formations moved last and all troops were ready for action in the Brega line by the 12th January.

While these successful actions were being fought, the situation on the Halfaya-Bardia front, where the garrisons—now 450 miles away from the main body—were still maintaining a heroic resistance, had visibly deteriorated. On the 30th December, the enemy launched a decisive attack on Bardia with powerful artillery, air and naval support and gained a deep penetration over a wide front in our defences. The last of our ration and ammunition dumps fell into enemy hands, and the Com-

held up for lack of petrol. It is clear that Rommel's supply system was far better adapted to rapid and long-range movement than the British. Auchinleck himself emphasises that Rommel was " greatly helped by the remarkable elasticity of his supply organisation."

[1]That is not correct. It had been made up to a strength of 130 tanks, but of these many had broken down in the long desert march from Gazala. In the battle that followed 65 were destroyed.

mandant, with Army's approval, asked for terms. The fortress was finally handed over on the 2nd January.

In the Halfaya sector the starving garrison held out until the 17th January, when, having exhausted its stores and being cut off from its last water supply, it was forced to surrender. Superb leadership was shown by the Italian General de Georgis, who commanded this German-Italian force in its two months' struggle.

As a result of the fall of these frontier garrisons, Rommel's loss, which had been about the same as the British (18,000), during the battle, became much larger in the end. Some 4,000 Germans and 10,000 Italians were captured at Bardia, Sollum and Halfaya.

The British had suffered a much heavier loss of tanks in the battle, but through Rommel's retreat they were able to recover and repair a large proportion so that their permanent loss was only 278, while Rommel's was about 300 (including the Italian tanks).

30 Dec. 1941

Dearest Lu,

Heavy fighting yesterday, which went well for us. Their new attempt to encircle us and force us back against the sea has failed.

I'm back in Army H.Q. again. Kesselring and Gambarra are coming to-day. Gause will be flying off afterwards to Rome. They've got absolutely no idea there of the difficulties here in Africa and are all going about their normal daily round of business or pleasure.

Rain is falling and the nights are bitterly cold and windy. I'm keeping fit—sleeping all I can. You will no doubt understand that there's no chance whatever of my leaving here at the moment.

All for now, must go to the Chief [*Chief of Staff*].

31 Dec. 1941

My thoughts to-day, the last day of the year, are more than ever with you two, who mean the happiness of this earth to me.

Almost superhuman exertions lie behind my gallant troops. The past three days' fighting, in which we have been on the attack, has cost the enemy 111 tanks and 23 armoured cars. The difficulties under which this success has been scored beggar description. Anyway, it was a good finish for 1941 and gives hope for 1942.

I'm well. One cockerel and one hen have accustomed themselves to this gipsy existence and run loose round the truck. They belong half to Gause.

All the best to you both for 1942.

5 Jan. 1942

Everything going as planned so far. Maybe better times are coming, in spite of everything. Gause was with the Fuehrer yesterday.

I would have liked him to have spent a fortnight in Rome with his wife. He was very exhausted after all he has had to go through at my side. Our Ia (Lieut.-Col. Westphal) is bearing up, although he had to go and get jaundice in the middle of it all. Kesselring was here yesterday. We're gradually getting more stuff across. He's doing very good work over Malta.

10 Jan. 1942

Yesterday's letter was also dated the 10th. One has no feeling for time here.

Operations going as planned so far. Our mines and Luftwaffe are making things difficult for the enemy pursuit. To think that we've got our force back 300 miles to a good line, without suffering serious harm, and in spite of the fact that the bulk of it is non-motorised! That our " unemployed " generals are grousing all the time doesn't surprise me. Criticism doesn't cost much.

The Afrika Korps goes into the second line to-day, for the first time since the 18th November. Cruewell's got a very bad dose of jaundice and it's doubtful if he'll stick it out. I'll soon be the only one of the German officers who's seen the whole thing through from start to finish. The nights are bitterly cold and damp. I wrap myself up in woollens as much as I can. My stomach's all right. Guenther sees to it that I eat well. I'm on the move from morning to night seeing that everything is going properly with the troops. It's very necessary. Best wishes to you and our son.

14 Jan. 1942

All going as planned here. The clash must come very soon now, but I have the greatest confidence that we'll survive it. Kesselring is coming to-day, so I won't be able to go to the front until 9.30. The Japanese victories are quite tremendous. The British will be out of eastern Asia in a few weeks. They'll look all the more for victories in North Africa, but they're going to be very disappointed. My troops are back in good fettle again.

17 Jan. 1942

The situation is developing to our advantage and I'm full of plans that I daren't say anything about round here. They'd think me crazy. But I'm not; I simply see a bit farther than they do. But you know me. I work out my plans early each morning, and how often, during the past year and in France, have they been put into effect within a matter of hours? That's how it should be and is going to be, in future.

19 Jan. 1942

The sun's quite warm here now at midday, just like on a fine spring day at home. The troops are already sunbathing. A few quiet days have done a lot of good. Gause has written from Rome. The Fuehrer apparently approved of all I'd done and was full of praise and admiration. Supplies have now improved, so you'll understand the Wehrmacht communiqués for the next few days. I'm so pleased at this new turn I can hardly sleep at night. But as you know that's always been the same when I've been particularly looking forward to something.

Much to do and discuss.

20 Jan. 1942

6.30 hours. As usual, a few lines to you. I wish you were in as good spirits as I am. The British may attack to-day, but I'm ready for them. So you'll understand why I'm cheerful. Weeks of frightful hardship and anxiety lie behind us and are forgotten—by the troops also.

By the time this letter arrives you will long ago have heard how the battle's gone from the Wehrmacht communiqués. The preparations are taking me all my time. Cruewell is not quite back on form yet and I'm doubtful whether he'll be able to keep going with us for long. I should be very sorry if there had to be a change. I myself am very well.

21 Jan. 1942

The Army launches its counter-attack in two hours' time. After carefully weighing the pros and cons, I've decided to take the risk. I have complete faith that God is keeping a protective hand over us and that He will grant us victory.

THE COUNTER-STROKE

On 5th January, a convoy of ships carrying 55 tanks and 20 armoured cars, as well as anti-tank guns and supplies of all kinds arrived safely in Tripoli. This was as good as a victory in battle, and Rommel immediately began to think of taking the offensive again. His plans for the reconquest of Cyrenaica were already prepared.

On the 20th January—by which time the Afrika Korps had 111 serviceable tanks at the front and 28 in the rear, while the Italian Motorised Corps disposed of 89—Rommel launched his counter-stroke. The plan was for the Afrika Korps to make an outflanking drive along the Wadi el Faregh, starting from the southern sector of the front, while the Italians, together with a German combat group, attacked frontally.

Bad going delayed the Afrika Korps's move round the flank, with the result that the enemy managed to escape encirclement.

Rommel's diary for the 21st January, 1942, remarks:

" I had maintained secrecy over the Panzer Group's forthcoming attack eastwards from Mersa el Brega and informed neither the Italian nor the German High Command. We knew from experience that Italian Headquarters cannot keep things to themselves and that everything they wireless to Rome gets round to British ears. However, I had arranged with the Quartermaster for the Panzer Group's order to be posted up in every Cantoniera [*Road Maintenance Depot*] in Tripolitania on the 21st January—the day the attack was due to take place. Excellency Bastico in Homs learnt of our intentions through this, of course, and was furious that he had not been told before. He reported to this effect to Rome, and so I was not surprised when Cavallero turned up in person at Mersa el Brega a few days later."

On the 22nd of January, Agedabia was taken and the enemy retired in disorder. The Afrika Korps then pushed forward to the line Antelat-Saunnu and enveloped a combat group of the British 1st Armoured Division, which lost 117 tanks and armoured cars, 33 guns, numerous vehicles and thousands of prisoners. But the pocket was not completely closed and a large part of the enemy force managed to get away to the north. During the pursuit to Msus, another 98 armoured fighting vehicles and 38 guns were destroyed in a concentric attack.[1] The supply centre of Saunnu, with large stores of war material, fell to the Afrika Korps.

22 Jan. 1942

DEAREST LU,

I wonder what you have to say about the counter-attack we started at 08.30 yesterday? Our opponents are getting out as though they'd been stung. Prospects are good for the next few days. You can guess how we'll react. I'm very well, except that I could bear to sleep a little better. Though the sleepless early morning hours are very productive for me at the moment.

On the 23rd January, General Cavallero appeared at Army H.Q. to remonstrate with Rommel about the independent action of the Panzer Army[2]. Rommel's diary entry says of this meeting:

" General Cavallero brought directives from the Duce for future

[1]In tanks, the 1st Armoured Division lost 70 out of its initial strength of 150 in the first fight, and more than half the remainder on the way to Msus. It also lost during the retreat 30 field guns, 30 anti-tank guns, and 25 light anti-aircraft guns.

[2]The " Panzergruppe Afrika " was made the " Panzerarmee Afrika " on the 22nd January 1942. It included all the Italian troops at the front, which then consisted of:

XX Corps (Ariete Armoured Division and Trieste Motorised Division),
XXI Corps (Pavia, Trento, and Sabratha Infantry Divisions),
X Corps (Bologna and Brescia Infantry Divisions).

operations. Everything indicates that Rome is anything but pleased
with the Panzer Army's counter-attack, and would like to put a stop
to it as soon as possible by issuing orders. During the discussion Cavallero
said: 'Make it no more than a sortie and then come straight back.'
I was not standing for this and told him that I had made up my mind
to keep at the enemy just as long as my troops and supplies would allow;
the Panzer Army was at last getting under way again and its first blows
had struck home. We were first going to drive south and destroy the
enemy south of Agedabia; then we would move east and later north-east.
I could always fall back to the Mersa el Brega line if things went wrong,
but that was not what I was after; my aims were set much higher.
Cavallero implored me not to go on with it. I told him that nobody
but the Fuehrer could change my decision, as it would be mainly German
troops who would be engaged. Finally, after Kesselring had made some
attempt to back him up, he went off growling. I kept General von
Rintelen behind so as to give him at least a glimpse of the battlefield
next day. He had spent practically all his time sitting in Rome and I
wanted to instil in him some understanding of the needs of this theatre.

" Cavallero took his revenge by holding back part of the Italian Corps
in the Mersa el Brega area and part in Agedabia, so that it was more or
less removed from my command. In spite of this, the German troops
retook Cyrenaica."

25 Jan. 1942

DEAREST LU,

Four days of complete success lie behind us. Our blows struck
home. And there's still one to come. Then we'll go all modest again
and lie in wait for a bit. The foreign press opinion about me is
improving again. Cavallero arrived and wanted to whistle me
straight back on orders from the Duce. But the Duce's directive,
which was given to me in writing, reads differently and, at least, left
me greater freedom.

27 Jan. 1942

Everything O.K. here. We're clearing up the battlefield, collecting
up guns, armoured cars, tanks, rations and ammunition for our own
needs. It will take some time. It's chilly again and rainy, though
the rain has its advantages, as it prevents the British getting their
planes off the ground from their airfields in Cyrenaica.

Gause will be back on 1st February. But he'll never be quite
the same. It was all rather much at once. I'm more used to such
things.

We're getting on fine with the Italian Corps now. They're very
sick that they couldn't come along with us. But that's their own fault.

Rommel could not risk continuing the pursuit to Mechili as the threat to his rearward communications from the Benghazi area was too great. So, on the 28th January, he launched a surprise attack on Benghazi itself. The fortress was first sealed off to the north and then to the south, and by the 29th was in our hands. The vast quantities of vehicles, arms and material which fell into our hands served to equip and motorise many of our own units.

After this victory, Rommel decided to embark on a long-range thrust to the east.

Two mixed combat groups, neither very strong, attacked frontally through Cyrenaica and retook this great territory by the 6th February [*i.e. exclusive of the Marmarica district in the east*]. During this time the Afrika Korps and the Italian Motorised Corps were lying idle round Msus and Agedabia. If only we could have thrown these two formations forward at the same time through Tengeder and Mechili, we could probably have overrun and destroyed a great part of the enemy's force.

Thus the enemy was able to get the bulk of his forces back safely to the Gazala - Bir Hacheim - Tobruk area, where they began with the construction of large-scale defence works. The Axis Army similarly went over to defence, holding the eastern edge of Cyrenaica between Mechili and Temrad. The German-Italian motorised formations were deployed behind the front for use in a mobile role.

This concluded the winter fighting. Both sides now prepared for the approaching decisive battle of the summer.

4 Feb. 1942

DEAREST LU,

On the move since the 2nd. But we have got Cyrenaica back. It went like greased lightning. I hope to be home in 10 days and to get quite a bit of leave. But there's still a lot to do until then.

7 Feb. 1942

It's quiet again on our front, which now extends for 300 miles (from the left to the right wing). It's particularly pleasing to have got Cyrenaica back again. I'm hoping the situation will stabilise sufficiently in the next week for me to get away for a while. I've been given a new order, by the way (a star on the chest to match the one I've already got round my neck).

10 Feb. 1942

... Trouble with Rome, who don't agree with the way I'm running things and would be best pleased to see us get out of Cyrenaica again.

23 Feb. 1942

... The Italians have taken an Army Corps off me because I'm not sitting as far back as they would like me to. They'll be sorry for it.

THE WINTER FIGHTING IN REVIEW

The British autumn offensive had as its aims the destruction of the German-Italian forces in the Marmarica, the conquest of Libya, and the occupation, in conjunction with the Free French, of the North African coast as the base for an attack on southern Europe. Its military objectives were therefore set high.

The assembly of the offensive force took place under the cover of very clever camouflage, and was greatly favoured by the weather. It achieved, in consequence, complete surprise. But, however skilful and ingenious the enemy's preparations for the offensive, their execution of it was not so effective. Even at the outset the dispositions of the enemy formations were designed to set them on divergent courses. They should have been first concentrated on Sidi Rezegh and then thrust forward in echelon formation. Better still would have been a thrust at Acroma in order simultaneously to cut off our supplies.

The Sollum front, on the other hand, only needed watching and there was no need to use two divisions to attack it. The 4th Indian Division was tied up there for fully two months. In effect the main offensive force consisted of only one division containing the bulk of the armour, with a second division as cover for the flank, and the decisive blow was thus struck by only a fraction of the total force engaged in the offensive. Contrary to the principle that one can never be strong enough at the centre of gravity and must concentrate everything at that point, every attack was made by part only of the Eighth Army, and even the main offensive force, already too weak for its purpose, was thrown into battle dispersed.

The result of these tactics of dispersal was that the British formations were either badly battered or destroyed one after the other and disappeared from the theatre while the battle was still in progress. The British Command did not once, during the whole of this battle, succeed in conducting operations with a concentration of its forces at the decisive point. This fundamental mistake was one of the reasons why victory escaped them. Their unwieldy and rigidly methodical technique of command, their over-systematic issuing of orders down to the last detail, leaving little latitude to the junior commander, and their poor adaptability to the changing course of the battle were also much to blame for the British failures.

Immobility and a rigid adherence to pattern are bad enough in European warfare; in the desert they are disastrous. Here everything is in flux; there are no obstructions, no lines, water or woods for cover; everything is open and incalculable; the commander must adapt and reorientate himself daily, even hourly, and retain his freedom of action. Everything is in motion; he must be constantly on the alert, all the time on the edge of capture or destruction by a more cunning, wide-awake or versatile enemy. There can be no conservatism in thought or action, no relying on tradition or resting on the laurels of previous victory. Speed of judgment, and action to create changing situations and surprises for the enemy faster than he can react, never making dispositions in advance, these are the fundamentals of desert tactics.

The merit and value of the desert soldier can be measured by his physical capacity, intelligence, mobility, nerve, pugnacity, daring and stoicism. A commander of men requires these same qualities in even greater measure and in addition must be outstanding in his toughness, devotion to his men, instinctive judgment of terrain and enemy, speed of reaction and spirit. In General Rommel these qualities were embodied in rare degree, and I have known no other officer in whom they were so combined.

The British soldier fought very well in the desert, even though he may not have attained the *élan* of the German attack. Their officers fought with tremendous courage and self-sacrifice. Rommel himself often expressed his high admiration for his adversary and once said, on seeing a number of them as prisoners, that he would be happy to lead such men into battle.

The actions in North Africa during the winter of 1941-42 left no doubt that the decisive part in desert warfare is played by the tank, principally because the desert contains no obstacles for it and no limitations on its use.

Hence the extent of either a victory or a defeat can be measured by the number of tanks destroyed. But it is not only the quantity of tanks which matters, even more important is their technical performance, manœuvrability and the range and calibre of the tank guns. For the main thing in the open desert is to bring the enemy under effective fire and start hitting him before he is in a position to hit back. What matters is to be " farther away from the enemy than he is from you." For a long time the British Matilda tank was feared because its heavy armour made it difficult to kill. But it was slow and had a short, small-calibre gun. At the end of 1941 the German Panzer III and Panzer IV were still superior to enemy types in range and calibre of guns and, in some measure, manœuvrability. This advantage was held until May 1942, when our opponents found an answer with the Grants and Lees, and later the Shermans. Much of the German success in the winter battles must be put down to the superiority of their tanks.

The principles that apply for the tank gun apply equally to the artillery. A long arm is decisive—and here the British had the best of it. It was not pleasant to be exposed to the fire of their 25-pounder guns at extreme range and to be unable to make an effective reply. But the Germans had one weapon—the 88-mm. dual-purpose (anti-tank and anti-aircraft) gun—which was always envied for its versatility; and remained unequalled in this respect. This gun—regarded by the British, so prisoners told me, as an unfair weapon against tanks—contributed in no small measure to the German successes. The infantry on either side played a comparatively unimportant part in the mobile fighting, and it was only in the position warfare on the Sollum front, that they had any significant share.

Given equal leadership, equal training, equal supply conditions and air force, the primary decisive factors in desert warfare are the number and manœuvrability of the tanks and the range of their guns; after that comes the number of field-guns and their range; and then, finally, the number of anti-tank guns, their range and calibre.

If either side is inferior in these arms, the quality of their troops and command must make up for the disadvantage. But there is no compensating for the lack of an air force or for shortage of supplies.

21 March 1942

DEAREST LU,

I went to Cruewell's birthday party yesterday. Everything went very nicely. He's going on leave in a few days and will probably have a course of treatment. I hope he comes back, it wouldn't be so easy to replace him here. His deputy is a real cold fish. Everything is green in Cyrenaica now; even places which are usually desert are covered with a green carpet. It's pleasantly warm at sea level, but there's a lot of wind and it's downright cold up here where we are, 2,500 feet up. There's a great deal to do, although our position seems to be fairly well secured.

26 March 1942

Nothing to report. Supply difficulties, particularly getting the stuff up overland, are still a great headache. The new Army Chief of Staff came to see us yesterday. Gambarra has been given a command back in Italy—in other words he's in disgrace. The new man makes a good impression.

29 March 1942

It should be Sunday to-day. It's 10 days since I flew back from home. I'm getting about a lot and putting on the pressure everywhere to get the most urgent jobs done. I got thoroughly sunburnt yesterday, but we have the right ointment.

31 March 1942

I couldn't write yesterday, we were " moving." We're glad to be in a new place and I'm pleased to be nearer the front and not to have to spend so much time travelling. It's also very lovely up here, as the flowers are still all in full bloom. I've made a colour film and will send it home shortly.

I suppose it will soon all be green at home. Before they left my new " house " the British wrote on the door: " Keep clean, we'll be back soon! " We'll see about that.

9 April 1942

Kesselring came yesterday. His news—so far as it concerns our allies—wasn't very cheerful. They're just riddled with bureaucracy in anything and everything, and on top of that there's a complete lack of understanding of the demands of modern warfare. The whole tempo of the supply organisation is completely inadequate. And that with Malta neutralised as never before.

With us everything's O.K.—apart from some minor mishaps with an Italian formation. The next three weeks are going to be very busy.

10 April 1942

I'm getting another visitor from the Reich on Sunday—an Admiral from the O.K.W. It would be a good thing if a few more of the gentlemen from home came to see us. A lot of Easter parcels have arrived. Amorous letters piling up from all manner of females. A shell splinter came through the window recently and landed in my stomach after going through my overcoat and jacket. All it left was a multi-coloured bruise the size of a plate. It was finally stopped by my trousers. The luck of the devil!

25 April 1942

Just another line before we move off to the south through a real moon landscape. Dawn has a fantastic beauty in this country of flat-topped mountains. Temperature is around zero. But it will soon warm up.

I had a couple of lively meetings yesterday, with Weichhold and General Barbassetti—Gambarra's successor. I'm told that Gambarra went because he declared in the presence of some officers that all he wanted was to live till the day when it would be granted him to lead an Italian army against us Germans. What a fool!

All for to-day.

27 April 1942

Kesselring will be here this afternoon. I'm very anxious to hear his news. To-morrow Bastico is coming to present me with another Italian decoration. I can't say I'm terribly thrilled about it. More troops would suit me better.

28 April 1942

Unable to write to-day until the evening. Kesselring was here this morning. Nothing much new to report. Plenty of plans are being made in Rome, but whether they'll come to anything I very much doubt. I've already spoken plainly on this point at the Fuehrer's H.Q. It all went off amicably with Bastico. He presented me, in the name of the King, with the new Colonial Order. A large silver star, even bigger than the previous one, plus a red sash with small order. This really is enough.

12 May 1942

Nothing much to report. Heat and lots of dust. The main road is a sea of pot-holes with the amount of traffic on it.

There's a certain nervousness on our front. The British are expecting us and we them. One day the two forces will measure their strength. You'll hear about it soon enough from the papers. We're all hoping that we'll be able to bring the war to an end this year. It will soon have lasted three full years.

Part Three

THE WAR IN AFRICA

SECOND YEAR

CHAPTER IX

GAZALA AND TOBRUK

THE BUILD UP

AFTER[1] THE conclusion of our counter-offensive, which had led at the beginning of 1942 to the reconquest of Cyrenaica, serious difficulties arose over supplies.

The blame for this—apart from the scant attention given to the African theatre of war by the German High Command, who failed to recognise its immense importance—lay with the half-hearted conduct of the war at sea by the Italians. The British Navy, in contrast, was very active in the early part of 1942, and the R.A.F. was also extremely troublesome.

The German High Command, to which I was subordinate, still failed to see the importance of the African theatre. They did not realise that with relatively small means, we could have won victories in the Near East which, in their strategic and economic value, would have far surpassed the conquest of the Don Bend [*in Southern Russia*]. Ahead of us lay territories containing an enormous wealth of raw materials; Africa, for example, and the Middle East—which could have freed us from all our anxieties about oil. A few more divisions for my Army, with supplies for them guaranteed, would have sufficed to bring about the complete defeat of the entire British forces in the Near East.

But it was not to be. Our demands for additional formations were refused on the grounds that with the huge demand for transport which the eastern front was making on Germany's limited productive capacity, the creation of further motorised units for Africa was out of the question.

It was obvious that the High Command's opinion had not changed from that which they had expressed in 1941, namely, that Africa was a " lost cause " and that any large-scale investment of material and troops in that theatre would pay no dividends. A sadly short-sighted and misguided view! For, in fact, the supply difficulties which they were so anxious to describe as " insuperable " were far from being so. All that

[1]Rommel's own narrative starts again here.

was wanted was a real personality in Rome, someone with the authority and drive to tackle and clear away the problems involved. No doubt it would have led to friction in certain Italian circles, but this could have been overcome by an authority unencumbered with other political functions. Our Government's weak policy towards Italy seriously prejudiced the German-Italian cause in North Africa.

The heavy burden which the eastern front was placing upon German material resources was certainly not to be underestimated, particularly after our Eastern Army had lost the great part of its equipment in the winter of 1941-42. Nevertheless, I am firmly convinced that, bearing in mind the tremendous possibilities offered by the North African theatre, some less important sectors could have been found which could have spared us a few mechanised divisions.

Basically, however, there was no understanding of the situation, and thus no will to do anything.

The consequences were very serious. With only three German divisions, whose fighting strength was often ludicrously small, we kept the British Army busy in Africa for eighteen long months and gave them many a trouncing, until our strength finally ran out at Alamein. After the loss of Africa an increasing number of German divisions had to be employed against the British and Americans, until finally some 70 divisions were thrown into the fighting in Italy and France—whereas in the summer of 1942, given six German mechanised divisions, we could have smashed the British so thoroughly that the threat from the south would have been eliminated for a long time to come. There is no doubt that adequate supplies for these formations could have been organised if the will had been there. Afterwards, in Tunisia—when, of course, it was too late—it became perfectly possible to double our supplies; but by that time the fact that we were up to our necks in trouble had penetrated even to the mainland.

After March 1942, during which month only 18,000 tons reached the Panzer Army in Africa out of a total supply requirement of 60,000 tons, the situation changed—thanks to the initiative of Field-Marshal Kesselring, whose air force succeeded in attaining air superiority over the Mediterranean during the spring of that year. The heavy Axis air raids against Malta, in particular, were instrumental in practically neutralising for a time the threat to our sea routes. It was this fact which made possible an increased flow of material to Tripoli, Benghazi and Derna— the reinforcement and refitting of the German-Italian forces thereupon proceeded with all speed.

Nevertheless, it was obvious that the British Eighth Army could still be reinforced more rapidly than our own. The British Government was making tremendous efforts to provide them with all the material they could lay their hands on. Large convoys were arriving one after the other in the Egyptian ports, bringing war material from Britain or America round the Cape. Naturally, this 12,000-mile voyage, which the British transports could make at the most only once or twice a year, must have made very heavy demands on the enemy staffs, who were having to cope with the immense difficulties caused by our U-boat warfare. In spite of this, the British Navy and Mercantile Marine were able to maintain supplies to the British forces in the Near East on a scale far superior to our own, even over this huge distance. Moreover, the British could get all the petrol they wanted, and more, from the refineries in the Near East.

It was rarely that the British supply ports received the serious attention of German bombers. From these ports the enemy could feed supplies to the front over three different routes:

1. By a well-laid railway line running from the Suez area to the outer perimeter of Tobruk.
2. By sea. The British Navy had created an admirable coastal shipping organisation and had the use of Tobruk, one of the best ports in North Africa.
3. By road. They had the coast-road and abundant transport at their disposal.

Even more important, however, was the fact that on the British side there were men with great influence and considerable foresight, who were doing all they could to organise the supply service in the most efficient manner possible. In this respect, our adversary benefited from a number of factors:

1. North Africa was the principal theatre of war for the British Empire.
2. The British Government regarded the fighting in Libya as of decisive influence in the war.
3. The British had in the Mediterranean a powerful and first-class Navy and Air Force of their own, while we had to deal with the unreliable Italian naval staff.
4. The entire British Eighth Army, down to the last unit, was fully motorised.

The ordinary British infantry formations were not "fully" motorised in the true sense of the term—of being always mounted in their own vehicles. The bulk of the personnel were merely "lifted" from place to place as and when troop-carrying transport could be provided from the pool. Such formations were not tactically mobile, and the fact of having to be carried in relays, instead of simultaneously, was a limitation on their strategic mobility.

It was clear to us that the British would try to destroy our army with all the means at their disposal as soon as they felt themselves strong enough to do so. Our southern flank lay wide open and they had a large choice of possible operations to choose from.[1] A constant threat would hang over our supply lines. Retreat, if we were forced into it by the danger of being outflanked, would be fraught with tremendous difficulties, due to the fact that most of my Italian divisions were non-motorised. But the British were not to have the chance of exploiting their opportunities, for I had decided to strike first.

The basic British plan for the defence of the Marmarica was shaped by a desire to impose on the attacker a form of warfare more to the liking of their own command than manœuvring in the open desert. The technical execution of the plan was first rate.

But the premises from which they approached the problem were false. In any North African desert position with an open southern flank, a rigid system of defence is bound to lead to disaster. The defence must be conducted offensively for it to be successful. Naturally, fortified lines can be of very great value in preventing the enemy from undertaking particular operational moves. But the manning of such lines must not, under any circumstances, be at the expense of the forces required for the mobile defence.

The British dispositions in the Marmarica were as follows:

A heavily mined defence line stretching away to the south from the coast near Gazala was held by 50th British and 1st South African Divisions. From the southern end of this line a deep belt of mines extended down as far as Bir Hacheim. This place, which represented the southern bastion of the British Gazala front, was built up as a fortress, with its defence positions embedded in extensive minefields. It was garrisoned by the 1st Free French Brigade.

The whole line had been planned with great skill. It was the first time that an attempt had been made to build a line of this kind so far into the desert. Some 500,000 mines lay in the area of these defences alone.

On a track intersection some miles east of the centre of the Gazala line lay the strong-point "Knightsbridge",[2] held by the British 201st Guards Brigade.

The area round El Hatian and Batruna was strongly fortified to cover the southern approaches of Tobruk. The El Adem "box", as this was called, was held by units of 5th Indian Division. Tobruk itself acted as a supply base and as a fixed support for the whole Gazala line. Since 1941 the British had been pushing ahead with improvements in the Tobruk defences[3], mainly in the form of extensive minefields throughout

[1] The outflanking potentialities were handicapped, however, not only by the superior gun-power of the German tanks but also by the superior leadership and training of their armoured formations—as Auchinleck frankly pointed out in his note of 21st March, 1942.

[2] Rommel, it will be noted, adopts the name that the British gave to this pivotal point of their defence.

[3] This is not quite correct. Since the relief of Tobruk in December, 1941, the development of it as a fortress had slipped into the background, and most of the earlier work went out of order before Midsummer, 1942.

the defended area. These defences were garrisoned by the reinforced
2nd South African Division.

All fortified points were provided with powerful artillery, infantry
and armoured car units, and abundant supplies. The entire line was
remarkable for the extraordinary degree of technical skill which had gone
into its construction. All defence positions and strong-points conformed
to the most modern requirements of warfare. Countless numbers of mines
had been laid—over a million in the Marmarica positions. And judging
by the 150,000 or so which were later picked up by my men in the British
rear areas, even more mining had been planned.

Besides the fully motorised forces I have mentioned, the British had
a mobile reserve in position behind the main defence works, consisting
of powerful armoured and mechanised formations (1st and 7th Armoured
Divisions and several independent armoured brigades and battalions).

Although the basic British defence plan was essentially a " second-
best solution", particularly in view of the complete motorisation of their
forces, the skilful construction of their defence works made their line a
very tough nut for us to crack.

*The basic defect in the British dispositions was that they had been planned
primarily with a view to an offensive—under pressure from the War Cabinet at
home. They were better suited to provide a pivot for an attack westwards, than
to meet an attack by Rommel. Moreover, the vast accumulation of supplies in the
forward base at Belhammed (just north of Sidi Rezegh) weighed on the minds of the
British commanders, making them hesitate to manoeuvre their armour in any way
that might uncover their base.*

THE BALANCE OF FORCES

At the beginning of the battle, the German-Italian Panzer Army consisted of two German and one Italian armoured divisions, together with
one German and one Italian motorised division. In additions, four non-
motorised Italian infantry divisions and one non-motorised German rifle
brigade were held under the command of the German-Italian Army High
Command. During the battle, a further Italian armoured division—the
Littorio—was sent to us by the Commando Supremo. Thus we had in all,
three German divisions, one German brigade and seven Italian divisions,
although only three of the Italian divisions were motorised—and hence
of use in mobile warfare. Many German and all Italian units were well
below strength; the 90th Light Division, for instance, went into battle
with a company strength of only fifty men. This low man-power was
particularly serious with the Italians—so much so, in fact, that an Italian
motorised division rated rather as a brigade and an infantry division as
a regiment.

At the beginning of the battle the British had under command four motorised infantry divisions, two armoured divisions and four independent mechanised brigades. In addition, by the middle of July they received a further four divisions and a number of independent armoured units. All these forces were motorised and up to full establishment. Since the British armoured divisions, unlike our own, were undiluted—that is to say, they consisted exclusively of armoured[1] units—the relative strengths at the beginning of the battle showed a 6 to 9 ratio to our disadvantage. We went into battle with 320 German and 240 Italian tanks. The British brought against us, in all, approximately 900. Tank reinforcements received by the enemy during the battle were out of all proportion to ours.[2]

Up to May of 1942 our tanks had in general been superior in quality to the corresponding British types. This was now no longer true, at least not to the same extent. The American-built Grant tank, which appeared for the first time in the summer battles, undoubtedly had a match in our long-barrelled Panzer IV, but only four of these latter were on African soil during our offensive. There was, in any case, no ammunition available for them, so that they were in fact unable to take any part. Our short-barrelled Panzer IV was also clearly superior to the Grant in speed and manœuvrability. Nevertheless, the Grant had the advantage, as it could shoot up the short-barrelled Panzer IV at a range where the latter's shell was unable to penetrate the heavy armour of the American

---

[1]This is not correct. The pattern of the British armoured division had recently been changed, and now comprised one armoured brigade (of 3 tank units and 1 motor infantry unit) and one lorried infantry brigade (of three battalions)—although an additional armoured brigade was sometimes attached.

[2]On the British side, the forces which took part in the original battle were:
INFANTRY DIVISIONS—50th, 1st and 2nd South African, 5th Indian.
BRIGADE GROUPS—3rd Indian Motor, 1st Free French.
ARMOURED DIVISIONS— { 1st (with 2nd and 22nd Armoured Brigades, and 201st Guards Motor Brigade); 7th (with 4th Armoured Brigade, and 7th Motor Brigade).
ARMY TANK BRIGADES—1st and 32nd (infantry tanks).

In addition the recently re-equipped 1st Armoured Brigade had just arrived, and was to have been given to the 7th Armoured Division so that each division might have two armoured brigades. That promised a big advantage as the German panzer divisions had only one apiece. But the 1st Armoured Brigade was not quite ready for action when the battle opened, and was used instead to replace casualties in the other three armoured brigades.

It can thus be seen that Rommel understates the number of armoured formations that opposed him, while his broad use of the term "motorised" confuses the distinction between the different types of formation. His figure of 900 tanks on the British side is roughly correct, counting the replacements that came into action during the battle.   In the initial stage the British superiority in *number* of tanks was not very large. But the Grant type, of which about 200 were available, had a stronger punch than any of Rommel's, while all his 240 Italian tanks and his 50 Panzer IIs counted for little in a tank v. tank battle.

Rommel's chief asset in meeting such adverse tank odds lay in his 88-mm. guns, but he had only 48 of these. Even at Alamein in October the total was only 70.

tank. We had forty short-barrelled Panzer IVs as against 160 British Grants.

The main armament of our panzer formations was the Panzer III, which, with its 50-mm. gun—of which by far the majority were short-barrelled—was even less of a match for the Grant. Those British tanks which were still armed with a 40-mm. gun—a large proportion of the older British types had meanwhile been supplied with a 75-mm.[1]—were inferior to the Panzer III. The 240 Italian tanks were no sort of match for the British and the troops had long talked of them as " self-propelled coffins".

It was the same with the artillery, in which the British had a superiority of 8 to 5.

As far as the air is concerned, it would probably be safe to say that apart from a few fluctuations to either side, the German-Italian Air Force held the balance with the R.A.F., at any rate at the beginning of the battle. Things were very different later.[2]

So it will be seen that taken as a whole the Panzer Army was faced by British forces of considerably greater strength. Compared with what was to come during the British winter offensive 1942-43, of course, the balance of power was quite tolerable—even though only three German and three Italian divisions were fit to be used in the offensive, while the remainder, due to their lack of mobility, had to remain almost entirely in the background. A further factor was that the two weak Italian motorised divisions, due to their poor armament, could only be used under German protection.

RULES OF DESERT WARFARE

Of all theatres of operations, it was probably in North Africa that the war took on its most advanced form. The protagonists on both sides were fully motorised formations, for whose employment the flat and obstruction-free desert offered hitherto undreamed-of possibilities. It was the only theatre where the principles of motorised and tank warfare, as they had been taught theoretically before the war, could be applied to the full—and further developed. It was the only theatre where the pure tank battle between major formations was fought. Even though the struggle may have occasionally hardened into static warfare, it remained —at any rate, in its most important stages (i.e. in 1941-42 during the Cunningham-Ritchie offensive, and in the summer of 1942—Marmarica

[1]This is not correct—Rommel must have been misinformed.

[2]The British first line strength was actually 604, while the German-Italian was only 542. But 120 of the 351 Axis fighters were of the Messerschmitt 109 class, which was superior to the Hurricanes and Kittyhawks on the British side.

battles, capture of Tobruk)—based on the principle of complete mobility.

In military practice, this was entirely new, for our offensives in Poland and the West had been against opponents who, in all their operations, had still had to take account of their non-motorised infantry divisions and had thus had to suffer the disastrous limitation in their freedom of tactical decision which this imposes, especially in retreat. Often they had been forced into actions quite unsuited to the object of holding up our advance. After our break-through in France, the enemy infantry divisions had simply been overrun and outflanked by our motorised forces. Once this had happened they had had no choice but to allow their operational reserves to be worn away by our assault groups, often in tactically unfavourable positions, in an endeavour to gain time for the retreat of their infantry.

Non-motorised infantry divisions are only of value against a motorised and armoured enemy when occupying prepared positions. If these positions are pierced or outflanked, a withdrawal will leave them helpless victims of the motorised enemy, with nothing else to do but hold on in their positions to the last round. They cause terrible difficulties in a general retreat—for, as I have indicated, one has to commit one's motorised formations merely to gain time for them. I was forced to go through this myself during the Axis retreat from Cyrenaica in the winter of 1941-42, when the whole of the Italian infantry and a considerable part of the German, including the majority of what was to become 90th Light Division, were without vehicles and had either to be carried by a shuttle service of lorries, or to march. It was only the gallantry of my armour that enabled the retreat of the Italo-German infantry to be covered, for our fully motorised enemy was in hot pursuit. Similarly, Graziani's failure can be attributed mainly to the fact that the greater part of the Italian Army was delivered up helpless and non-motorised in the open desert to the weaker but fully motorised British formations, while the Italian motorised forces, although too weak to oppose the British successfully, were nevertheless compelled to accept battle and allow themselves to be destroyed in defence of the infantry.

The British forces—in contrast to ours—were all fully mobile, and the war in Africa was, in fact, waged almost exclusively by mobile forces. Out of this pure motorised warfare, certain principles were established, principles fundamentally different from those applying in other theatres. These principles will become the standard for the future, in which the fully-motorised formation will be dominant.

The envelopment of a fully-motorised enemy in the flat and good-driving terrain of the desert has the following results:

(a) For a fully-motorised formation, encirclement is the worst tactical situation imaginable, since hostile fire can be brought to bear on it from all sides; even envelopment on only three sides is a tactically untenable situation.

(b) The enemy becomes forced, because of the bad tactical situation in which the encirclement has placed him, to evacuate the area he is holding.

The encirclement of the enemy and his subsequent destruction in the pocket can seldom be the direct aim of an operation; more often it is only indirect, for any fully-motorised force whose organisational structure remains intact will normally and in suitable country be able to break out at will through an improvised defensive ring. Thanks to his motorisation, the commander of the encircled force is in a position to concentrate his weight unexpectedly against any likely point in the ring and burst through it.[1] This fact was repeatedly demonstrated in the desert.

It follows therefore that an encircled enemy force can only be destroyed

(a) when it is non-motorised or has been rendered immobile by lack of petrol, or when it includes non-mobile elements which have to be considered;

(b) when it is badly led or its command has decided to sacrifice one formation in order to save another;

(c) when its fighting strength has already been broken, and disintegration and disorganisation have set in.

Except for cases (a) and (b), which occurred very frequently in other theatres of war, encirclement of the enemy and his subsequent destruction in the pocket can only be attempted if he has first been so heavily battered in open battle that the organic cohesion of his force has been destroyed. I shall term all actions which have as their aim the wearing down of the enemy's power of resistance " battles of attrition." In motorised warfare, material attrition and the destruction of the organic cohesion of the opposing army must be the immediate aim of all planning.

Tactically, the battle of attrition is fought with the highest possible degree of mobility. The following points require particular attention:

(a) The main endeavour should be to concentrate one's own forces in space and time, while at the same time seeking to split the enemy forces spatially and destroy them at different times.

(b) Supply lines are particularly sensitive, since all petrol and ammunition, indispensable requirements for the battle, must pass along them. Hence, everything possible must be done to protect

[1]The first part of this comment is well founded, but the conclusion goes too far. A break-out can be made very difficult if the commanders in the encircling force really understand the defensive side of modern mobile warfare.

one's own supply lines and to upset, or better still, cut the enemy's. Operations in the enemy's supply area will lead immediately to his breaking off the battle elsewhere, since, as I have indicated, supplies are the fundamental premise of the battle and must be given priority of protection.

(c) The armour is the core of the motorised army. Everything turns on it, and other formations are mere auxiliaries. The war of attrition against the enemy armour must therefore be waged as far as possible by the tank destruction units. One's own armour should only be used to deal the final blow.

(d) Reconnaissance reports must reach the commander in the shortest possible time; he must take his decisions immediately and put them into effect as fast as he can. Speed of reaction decides the battle. Commanders of motorised forces must therefore operate as near as possible to their troops, and must have the closest possible signal communication with them.

(e) Speed of movement and the organisational cohesion of one's own forces are decisive factors and require particular attention. Any sign of dislocation must be dealt with as quickly as possible by reorganisation.

(f) Concealment of intentions is of the utmost importance in order to provide surprise for one's own operations and thus make it possible to exploit the time taken by the enemy command to react. Deception measures of all kinds should be encouraged, if only to make the enemy commander uncertain and cause him to hesitate and hold back.

(g) Once the enemy has been thoroughly beaten up, success can be exploited by attempting to overrun and destroy major parts of his disorganised formations. Here again, speed is everything. The enemy must never be allowed time to reorganise. Lightning regrouping for the pursuit and reorganisation of supplies for the pursuing forces are essential.

Concerning the technical and organisational aspect of desert warfare, particular regard must be paid to the following points:

(a) The prime requirements in the tank are manœuvrability, speed and a long-range gun—for the side with the bigger gun has the longer arm and can be the first to engage the enemy. Weight of armour cannot make up for lack of gun-power, as it can only be provided at the expense of manœuvrability and speed, both of which are indispensable tactical requirements.

(b) The artillery must have great range and must, above all, be capable of great mobility and of carrying with it ammunition in large quantities.

(c) The infantry serves only to occupy and hold positions designed either to prevent the enemy from particular operations, or to force him into other ones. Once this object has been achieved, the infantry must be able to get away quickly for employment elsewhere. It must therefore be mobile and be equipped to enable it rapidly to take up defence positions in the open at tactically important points on the battlefield.

It is my experience that bold decisions give the best promise of success. But one must differentiate between strategical or tactical boldness and a military gamble. A bold operation is one in which success is not a certainty but which in case of failure leaves one with sufficient forces in hand to cope with whatever situation may arise. A gamble, on the other hand, is an operation which can lead either to victory or to the complete destruction of one's force. Situations can arise where even a gamble may be justified—as, for instance, when in the normal course of events defeat is merely a matter of time, when the gaining of time is therefore pointless and the only chance lies in an operation of great risk.

The only occasion when a commander can calculate the course of a battle in advance is when his forces are so superior that victory is a foregone conclusion; then the problem is no longer one of " the means " but only of " the method". But even in this situation, I still think it is better to operate on the grand scale rather than to creep about the battlefield anxiously taking all possible security measures against every conceivable enemy move.

Normally, there is no ideal solution to military problems; every course has its advantages and disadvantages. One must select that which seems best from the most varied aspects and then pursue it resolutely and accept the consequences. Any compromise is bad.

It is in the light of all these considerations that the plan which I and my staff had worked out should be read. It should be regarded as the best possible solution under the most favourable circumstances. The fate of my army was in no way tied up with the success of this particular plan —for, following my usual principles, I reckoned throughout with the possibility that things might not all go as we wanted them. But even in that event, the situation at the start of the battle would be—as far as could be foreseen—by no means unfavourable. We looked forward to the battle full of optimism, trusting in our troops, with their superb tactical training and their experience in improvisation.

The opening move of the offensive was to be a frontal attack by the Italian infantry divisions in the Gazala line against the 50th British Division and the South Africans. A powerful force of artillery was detailed to support the attack. Tanks and lorries were to be driven in circles day and night behind the front, to simulate the existence of tank assembly areas.

The British command was to be made to expect our main attack in the north and centre of the Gazala line. We hoped to persuade them to deploy their armour behind the infantry positions in this sector. The idea of a German frontal attack against the Gazala position could not appear so very far fetched to the British command, as it was quite within the bounds of possibility that we would prefer it to the risky right hook round Bir Hacheim. If we failed to mislead the British into concentrating the whole of their armour in this sector, then we hoped that they would send at least part of it up there and thus split their striking power.[1]

During daylight all movement of my motorised forces was to be directed towards the point of the Italian infantry's attack. They would then move into their assembly area after nightfall. The striking force was to consist of the Africa Korps (15th and 21st Panzer Divisions), XX Italian Motorised Corps (Trieste and Ariete Divisions) and the 90th Light Division reinforced by three reconnaissance regiments. The beginning of the advance, which was to be an outflanking movement round Bir Hacheim, was fixed for 22.00 hours. From Bir Hacheim the Afrika Korps and XX Italian Motorised Corps were to push on through Acroma to the coast, with the object of cutting off and destroying the British divisions in the Gazala line and the armoured units behind it.

The task of the 90th Light Division, with the three reconnaissance battalions, was to push into the El Adem—Belhammed area in order to prevent the withdrawal of the Tobruk garrison and the movement of reinforcements into the Acroma area, and in addition to cut the British off from the extensive supply dumps they had established in the area east of Tobruk. To enable the 90th Light Division to feign the presence of massed armour in the area, they were to be provided with several dust-raisers (lorries carrying aero engines and propellers, which by stirring up great clouds of dust were intended to suggest the approach of powerful armoured forces). We hoped to keep the British forces in that area from intervening in the Acroma battle so long as our armoured formations were trying to force a decision.

Following on the destruction of the British forces in the Marmarica,

[1]A long advisory letter that Auchinleck wrote to Ritchie on the 20th May, nearly a week before the battle opened, shows that Auchinleck thought it more likely that Rommel would attempt a break-through in the centre, but reckoned with either alternative. Moreover, the letter urged Ritchie to keep both armoured divisions together and complete, placing them astride the Trigh Capuzzo ready for a concentrated flank counter-stroke against Rommel's armour when this was clearly committed in one direction or the other. But Ritchie, while positioning the 1st Armoured Division just south of the Trigh Capuzzo, put the 7th Armoured Division (the weaker of the two) ten miles farther south—on the exposed desert flank round which Rommel delivered his right hook. This disposition, and separation, turned out badly. On the first morning (the 27th May) the 7th Armoured Division was overrun and broken up while isolated. One of the two armoured brigades of the 1st Armoured Division was belatedly sent to reinforce the 7th, but itself became engaged in a lone fight, and suffered heavily.

it was our intention to make a quick conquest of Tobruk. My freedom of operation was limited by the Duce to the area up to the Egyptian frontier.

It had actually been intended that Malta should be taken by Italo-German parachute and airborne forces before the offensive started, but for some unaccountable reason our High Command abandoned this scheme.[1] My request to have this pleasant task entrusted to my own army had unfortunately been refused in the previous spring.

And so, in view of the steady increase of British strength, we fixed the date of the attack for the 26th May, 1942.

STRUGGLE FOR THE INITIATIVE

26th May to 15th June, 1942

During these first three weeks the battle of attrition was waged in the Western Desert in its most violent form. It began very badly for us, but in the fluctuating fighting which followed we succeeded—partly by attacks with limited objectives, partly in defence—in smashing the British formations one by one, despite the courage with which they fought.

In view of the superior strength of the British force this victory of my German-Italian troops came as a complete surprise to world opinion, and the measures taken by my adversary, Lieut.-General Ritchie, became the subject of severe criticism. But was it in fact true that the British defeat was the result of their commander's mistakes?

After the battle I came upon an article by the British military critic, Liddell Hart, which ascribed the shortcomings of the British command during the African campaign to the British generals' close associations with infantry warfare. I had the same impression. The British command had not drawn the correct conclusions from their defeat of 1941-42.

Prejudice against innovation is a typical characteristic of an Officer

---

[1]After the plan had been worked out for this " Operation Hercules", Mussolini went to Berchtesgaden for a conference with Hitler at the end of April. Here it was agreed that the attack on Malta should be launched early in July, after Rommel's offensive in Africa—which was to be halted, so that the weight of the Luftwaffe could be switched against Malta. But soon after this agreement Hitler showed renewed doubts, and in discussion with his staff brought up a series of arguments against the operation—that the Italians could not keep anything secret; that they had not got the fighting spirit for such a difficult venture; that they would not be punctual in arriving to support the German parachute troops; that their Navy would not face the British, and were thus likely to leave the German troops stranded without supplies.

So, on the 21st May, he decided that the preparations were only to be continued on paper, and that the operation was in any case to be dropped if Rommel succeeded in taking Tobruk. For he argued that supply ships could then be sent to Tobruk via Crete, by-passing Malta. While that argument proved fallacious, his doubts of the Italian Navy were borne out by the extreme caution it showed in the months that followed.

Corps which has grown up in a well-tried and proven system. Thus it was that the Prussian Army was defeated by Napoleon. This attitude was also evident during this war, in German as well as British officer circles, where, with their minds fixed on complicated theories, people lost the ability to come to terms with reality. A military doctrine had been worked out to the last detail and it was now regarded as the summit of all military wisdom. The only military thinking which was acceptable was that which followed their standardised rules. Everything outside the rules was regarded as a gamble; if it succeeded then it was the result of luck and accident. This attitude of mind creates fixed preconceived ideas, the consequences of which are incalculable.

For even military rules are subject to technical progress. What was good for 1914 is only good to-day where the majority of the formations engaged on both sides, or at least on the side which is attacked, are made up of non-motorised infantry units. Where this is the case the armour still acts as the cavalry, with the task of outrunning and cutting off the infantry. But in a battle fought between two fully-motorised adversaries, quite different rules apply. I have dealt with this already.

However praiseworthy it may be to uphold tradition in the field of soldierly ethics, it is to be resisted in the field of military command. For to-day it is not only the business of commanders to think up new techniques which will destroy the value of the old: the potentialities of warfare are themselves being continually changed by technical advance. Thus the modern army commander must free himself from routine methods and show a comprehensive grasp of technical matters, for he must be in a position continually to adapt his ideas of warfare to the facts and possibilities of the moment. If circumstances require it, he must be able to turn the whole structure of his thinking inside out.

I think that my adversary, General Ritchie, like so many generals of the old school, had not entirely grasped the consequences which followed from the fully motorised conduct of operations and the open nature of the desert battlefield. In spite of the good detailed preparation of his plans, they were bound to go wrong, for they were, in essence, a compromise.

26 May 1942

DEAREST LU,

By the time you get this letter you will have long ago heard from the Wehrmacht communiqués about events here. We're launching a decisive attack to-day. It will be hard, but I have full confidence that my army will win it. After all, they all know what battle means. There is no need to tell you how I will go into it. I intend to demand of myself the same as I expect from each of my officers and men. My thoughts, especially in these hours of decision, are often with you.

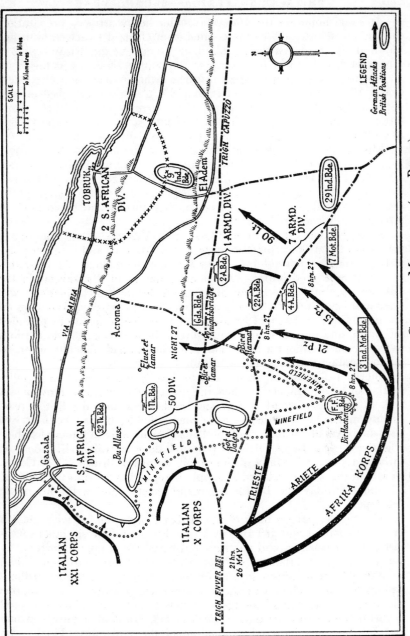

12. ROMMEL'S ATTACK AT GAZALA, MAY 1942 (1ST PHASE)

At 14.00 hours on the 26th May, after heavy artillery preparation, the Italian infantry under the command of General Cruewell launched a frontal attack against the Gazala line. To deceive the British—who, as I have said, were to be led to expect the main Axis thrust at this point and on this assumption to bring up their armour—one panzer regiment of the Afrika Korps and one of Italian XX Corps was attached to each of the assault formations. These regiments were to return to their parent formations in the evening. The British outposts in front of the Gazala line offered little resistance and withdrew to their main defences.

Meanwhile, the striking group, consisting of the Afrika Korps, 90th Light Division and XX Italian Corps, was gathering in its appointed assembly area. During the evening, part of this force moved off towards the point of the Italian attack and, after being observed as intended, by the British evening air reconnaissance, they turned and raced back at top speed to the assembly area.

At 20.30 hours I ordered "Operation Venezia", and the 10,000 vehicles of the striking force began to move. My staff and I, in our place in the Afrika Korps's column, drove through the moonlit night towards the great armoured battle. Occasional flares lit up the sky far in the distance—probably the Luftwaffe trying to locate Bir Hacheim. I was tense and keyed-up, impatiently awaiting the coming day. What would the enemy do? What had he already done? These questions pounded my brain, and only morning would bring the answers. Our formations rolled forward without a halt. The drivers often had difficulty in maintaining contact with the vehicle ahead.

Shortly before daybreak we took an hour's rest some 10 or 12 miles south-east of Bir Hacheim; then the great force started to move again and, in a swirling cloud of dust and sand, thrust into the British rear. Enemy minefields and decoys gave some trouble, but an hour or two after daybreak all formations of the Panzer Army were in full cry for their objectives. 90th Light Division reported their arrival at El Adem as early as 10.00 a.m. Many of the supply dumps of British XXX Corps, for whom this area had acted as supply base, had fallen into their hands. At about midday the British command reacted and a furious battle developed.

Meanwhile, panzer units of the Afrika Korps collided with the 4th British Armoured and 3rd Indian Motor Brigades some six miles south-east of Bir el Harmat, and an armoured battle flared up. Unfortunately our panzer units attacked without artillery support, although I had constantly been at pains to impress on them not to do so until our artillery had opened fire. There was also a British surprise awaiting us here, one which was not to our advantage—the new Grant tank, which was used in this battle for the first time on African soil. Tank after tank, German and British, was shattered in the fire of the tank-guns. Finally, we succeeded in throwing the British back to the Trigh el Abd, although at the cost of heavy casualties. The British, however, soon came back to the attack.

When at around midday I and my staff attempted to get through to the 90th Light Division at El Adem, our column was attacked by British tanks and we were forced to turn back. Contact between the 90th Light Division and the Afrika Korps was broken. Trying to fight our way back to the Afrika Korps, we suddenly found ourselves confronted by a British battery, probably en route from the Bir Hacheim area to Tobruk. Although the staff did not represent much in the way of fighting power, we attacked the British on the move and rounded them up. They seemed to have been taken completely by surprise.

In the afternoon, heavy tank fighting flared up some five miles northeast of Bir el Harmat, south of the Trigh Capuzzo. 1st British Armoured Division joined in the battle, its powerful armoured units attacking mainly from the north-east. The British armour, under heavy artillery cover, poured their fire into the columns and panzer units of the Afrika Korps, which were visible for miles. Fire and black smoke welled up from lorries and tanks, and our attack came to a standstill. Again my divisions suffered extremely serious tank losses. Many of our columns broke into confusion and fled away to the south-west, out of the British artillery fire. The Afrika Korps, while maintaining its defence to the east, fought its way step by step to the north. The battle raged on in the camel-thorn-studded plain until nightfall, by which time the mass of the Afrika Korps had thrust through to a point some eight miles south and south-west of Acroma. Unfortunately, most of the lorry columns had been parted from the panzer divisions and part of the infantry had also been unable to follow. Contact had been broken within my staff. Lieut.-Col. Westphal, my Ia, had pushed on with a number of signals lorries to the Afrika Korps, whereas I myself, with the rest of the army staff, was located at nightfall about two miles north-east of Bir el Harmat.

Looking back on the first day's fighting, it was clear that our plan to overrun the British forces behind the Gazala line had not succeeded. The advance to the coast had also failed and we had thus been unable to cut off the 50th British and 1st South African Divisions from the rest of the Eighth Army. The principal cause was our underestimate of the strength of the British armoured divisions. The advent of the new American tank had torn great holes in our ranks. Our entire force now stood in heavy and destructive combat with a superior enemy.[1]

[1]This is a sidelight on how differently a situation is apt to look when viewed from " the other side of the hill." Under the shock of the losses suffered in encountering the new Grant tanks, the Germans did not fully appreciate the extent of the opening advantage they had gained in disrupting a large proportion of the British armoured force. The effect on the British side was seen in the lack of any really strong and well-directed effort to exploit the weakness and precariousness of the attacker's situation. Thus Rommel had a respite to reorganise, and was then enabled to profit by the tactical advantages of the defensive—when ably conducted—towards wearing down the British

Certainly we had seriously mauled the brigades which the British had thrown against us south-east of Bir el Harmat. The 3rd Indian Motor Brigade had suffered such heavy losses that it was unable to make any further appearance during the whole of the battle. It was also to be a long time before the 7th Armoured Division recovered from the blows it had been dealt that day.

But I will not deny that I was seriously worried that evening. Our heavy tank losses were no good beginning to the battle (far more than a third of the German tanks had been lost in this one day). The 90th Light Division under General Kleeman had become separated from the Afrika Korps and was now in a very dangerous position. British motorised groups were streaming through the open gap and hunting down the transport columns which had lost touch with the main body. And on these columns the life of my army depended.

However, in spite of the precarious situation and the difficult problems with which it faced us, I looked forward that evening full of hope to what the battle might bring. For Ritchie had thrown his armour into the battle piecemeal and had thus given us the chance of engaging them on each separate occasion with just about enough of our own tanks. This dispersal of the British armoured brigades was incomprehensible. In my view the sacrifice of the 7th Armoured Division south of Bir el Harmat served no strategical or tactical purpose whatsoever, for it was all the same to the British whether my armour was engaged there or on the Trigh Capuzzo, where the rest of the British armour later entered the battle. The principal aim of the British should have been to have brought all the armour they had into action at one and the same time. They should never have allowed themselves to be duped into dividing their forces before the battle or during our feint attack against the Gazala line. The full motorisation of their units would have enabled them to cross the battlefield at great speed to wherever danger threatened. Mobile warfare in the desert has often and rightly been compared with a battle at sea—where it is equally wrong to attack piecemeal and leave half the fleet in port during the battle.

The plan for next day was to concentrate forces for an attack to the north. I intended to disengage the 90th Light Division, which was under heavy enemy pressure in the El Adem area, and join it up with the Afrika Korps in the west in order to increase our striking power.

superiority of numbers. It was by his skilful " trapping " defence in the following days that he paved the way for another, and more decisive, offensive stroke. Like most dynamic soldiers, he was inclined to despise defence, but when circumstances compelled him to adopt it he showed an instinctive grasp of its subtle technique, and in that lay the foundation of his victories.

His practice aptly fulfilled the maxim of the famous pugilist, Jem Mace: " Let 'em come to ye, they'll beat theirselves "—a maxim that was more explicitly defined by another great boxer in a later generation, Kid McCoy: " Draw your man into attack—and get him so that he has both hands out of business and you have one hand free."

At dawn on the 28th May, I took a look round the horizon through glasses to see what was going on in the neighbourhood. North-east of us, there were British forces moving in a north-westerly direction. We still had no contact with the various separate parts of the Panzer Army. Shortly after dawn, British tanks opened fire on my command post, which was located close beside the *Kampfstaffel* and our vehicles. Shells fell all round us and the windscreen of our command omnibus flew into fragments. Fortunately, we were able to get away in our vehicles out of range of the British fire. During the morning I drove to XX Italian Motorised Corps and ordered them to push northwards in the wake of the Afrika Korps.

The 90th Light Division was unable to carry out its orders to join up on the east of the Afrika Korps and reinforce its striking power, as it was being repeatedly attacked by powerful British forces. About 100 British tanks were engaged in the fighting. Large numbers of R.A.F. aircraft showered bombs on the division, and several of its units soon became split away. To enable it to meet further enemy attacks, the division was forced to form a hedgehog some six miles east of Bir el Harmat.

Fortunately, we at least managed to form a defensive front during the morning, for the protection of our columns. The front was composed of elements of the Afrika Korps and was located north-east of Bir el Harmat.

Things were also very serious with the Afrika Korps. The enemy had now concentrated practically the whole of his available armour north of the Trigh Capuzzo and was launching attack after attack on the Afrika Korps. News had come in from Westphal during the morning. He had had to order the Italians to attack the Gazala line in order to prevent the British and South Africans located there from joining in the battle. The attack, which went in about midday, made good progress near Eluet el Tamar against the resistance of weak British forces.

I was now becoming uneasy and, wishing to make contact with the two panzer divisions, set out in the afternoon with my Chief of Staff, General Gause, to try to find a negotiable route to the Afrika Korps; a signal had meanwhile come in from it with the alarming news that part of the 15th Panzer Division was out of action for lack of ammunition. It was therefore vitally important to get up its supply columns. By late afternoon we managed to push forward with several vehicles and anti-tank guns to a hill about ten miles north of Bir el Harmat, from where we could see the Afrika Korps. It was a typical picture of a desert battle. Black smoke clouds rolled up to the sky, giving the landscape a curious sinister beauty. I decided to use this route to take the supply columns up to the Afrika Korps early next morning.

On our way back to Battle H.Q. we had a brush with one British and one Italian column! The latter also took us for hostile and opened a wild fire, which we escaped by a quick withdrawal. After dark we made our way through a lane which the Italians had cleared through the minefields, as far as the area south-west of Bir el Harmat, where we met our own troops and heard that the British had overrun my staff during our absence. Several British tanks had been shot up by *Kampfstaffel* Kiehl, but other British columns had penetrated right through to the Afrika Korps' supply units, causing great confusion and destroying a number of petrol and ammunition lorries. Order was restored and we succeeded in re-occupying our old positions during the night.

Late that evening, I formed up the supply columns ready to take them up myself to the Afrika Korps next morning. In view of the small amount of cover we could expect to find, this journey through a district dominated by enemy formations promised to be a decidedly risky affair.

Fortunately, however, the 90th Light Division was able to disengage from the British during the night and take up a position near Bir el Harmat. In addition, the Ariete was put in to stop the gap between the 90th Light and the Afrika Korps. These new dispositions made the supply columns' route far safer. We set off for the Afrika Korps at daybreak [*29th May*] and all went smoothly.

On arrival on the battlefield, we found that the Afrika Korps had just been attacked from the north and east by British armour. Shortage of petrol and ammunition had been severely limiting their freedom of action, but now this situation could at last be eased. I set up my command post in the area during the afternoon.

Now that contact had been fully restored between all parts of the Army, I was at last able to obtain a comprehensive picture of the situation.

We had now succeeded in concentrating our forces on both sides of the Trigh el Abd and had established a firm defence line. But the German-Italian units had suffered heavily. Our supply route had been virtually cut through by British motorised units south of Bir Hacheim. The Italian infantry assault on the Gazala line had penetrated as far as the main British positions and then come to a standstill in front of well-constructed defence works. Their commander, General Cruewell, had been shot down in his Storch and was missing. Later I heard that he had been taken prisoner by the British. Nor was he the only one of our generals to be put out of the fight that day, for General von Vaerst, commander of the 15th Panzer Division, had been wounded and forced to leave the battlefield. The British had now assembled their 2nd, 4th and 22nd Armoured Brigades and, with 201st Guards Brigade, were throwing them in concentric counter-attacks against our front.

In this situation it was far too hazardous to continue our attack to the north, as we had originally planned. I drew my conclusions accordingly. The main thing now was to open up a secure supply route for our striking force, and I therefore decided to move units of 90th Light Division and an element of the Afrika Korps against the minefields from the east. To cover this move the remainder of the force was to go over to the defensive on a shortened front. As soon as the penetration of the Gazala defences had been made I intended to pinch out Bir Hacheim, the southern bastion of the British line.

I made this plan on the certain assumption that, with strong German motorised forces standing south of the coast road, the British would not dare to use any major part of their armoured formations to attack the Italians in the Gazala line, for a counter-attack by my panzer divisions would have put them between two fires. On the other hand, I hoped that the presence of the Italian infantry in front of the 1st South African and 50th British Divisions would continue to persuade the overcautious British command to leave those formations complete in the Gazala line. It seemed highly improbable to me that Ritchie would order these two infantry divisions to attack the Italian infantry corps without support from other formations, for such an operation would not have fulfilled the normal British demand for what they supposed to be 100 per cent certainty. Thus I foresaw that the British mechanised brigades would continue to run their heads against our well-organised defensive front and use up their strength in the process. The defence was to be conducted with the maximum of elasticity and mobility.

Orders for these operations went out on the evening of the 29th of May.

At first light on May 30th the respective divisions moved into their appointed positions and put themselves on the defensive. During these moves, we established the presence of strong British forces, including armour, in the Ualeb area. It was the reinforced 150th Brigade of 50th British Division. [*The 1st Army Tank Brigade had been sent to support it— and in the outcome shared its fate.*] Meanwhile, elements of X Italian Corps had succeeded in crossing the British minefield and establishing a bridge-head east of it, although the lanes through the British mines lay under heavy British artillery fire, which had an extremely upsetting effect on our columns. Nevertheless, contact was established at noon between the striking force and X Italian Corps, and a direct supply route was opened to the west. During the day the British brigade in Got el Ualeb was surrounded.

In the afternoon, I drove through the minefield to X Italian Corps H.Q. for a meeting with Field Marshal Kesselring, the commander of X Italian Corps, and Major von Below (Adjutant to the Fuehrer), during which I informed them of my further plans. With the Afrika Korps screening the British minefield against all attacks from the north-east, we were first going to clean up the whole of the southern part of the Gazala line and then to resume the offensive. In the course of this operation, we intended to destroy the 150th British Brigade in Ualeb and then the 1st Free French Brigade in Bir Hacheim.

The enemy was very hesitant in following up our movements. The withdrawal of the German-Italian formations had evidently come as a complete surprise to him, and, in any case, the British command never reacted very quickly. During the morning we established the presence of British assembly areas east and north of our front, with 280 tanks in the former and 150 in the latter, and we expected the British to launch their major blow at any moment. Nothing happened during the morning, however, except a few attacks on the Ariete, which the Italians beat off, and a number of even weaker thrusts on the rest of the front. Fifty-seven British tanks were shot up that day.

In the afternoon I personally reconnoitred the possibilities for an attack on Got el Ualeb, and detailed units of the Afrika Korps, 90th Light Division and the Italian Trieste Division for an assault on the British positions next morning.

The attack was launched on the morning of the 31st May. German-Italian units fought their way forward yard by yard against the toughest British resistance imaginable. The defence was conducted with considerable skill and, as usual, the British fought to the last round. They also brought a new 57-mm. anti-tank gun [*the 6-pounder*] into use in this action. Nevertheless, by the time evening came we had penetrated a substantial distance into the British positions.

31 May 1942

Dearest Lu,

I'm well. The great crisis of the battle is over and so far we've done well. But the next few days are still going to be hard. Cruewell has, unfortunately, fallen into British hands, complete with Storch, but I'm still hoping to hack a way out for him.

On the following day the defenders were to receive their quietus. After heavy Stuka attacks, the infantry again surged forward against the British field positions. I went forward with them, accompanied by Colonel Westphal, who was unfortunately seriously wounded in a surprise British mortar attack and had to be taken back to Europe, so that I had to do without him in the days ahead. This was a grave loss to the Panzer Army, for whom he had always been an outstandingly important man, because of his great knowledge, experience and ready decision. However, the attack went on. Piece by piece the elaborate British defences were won until by early afternoon the whole position was ours. The last British resistance was quenched. We took in all 3,000 prisoners and destroyed or captured 101 tanks and armoured cars, as well as 124 guns of all kinds.

At about this time there fell into our hands an order issued by the 4th British Armoured Brigade to the effect that German and Italian prisoners were to be given nothing to eat or drink until they had been interrogated. We found this very disturbing, for measures of this kind could only result in the war between the British and Germans, already tragic enough, being intensified to a deplorable bitterness. Evidently the British command were of the same opinion, for they withdrew the order at our intervention.

In the late afternoon of June 1st, after the fall of Got el Ualeb, British reconnaissance units attacked the front which was screening our position to the east and south-east. A violent artillery barrage followed, mainly on my command post, and my Chief of Staff, General Gause, was wounded by a small splinter. Thus two of my most important assistants had been put out of the fight on the same day. I decided to appoint the Chief of Staff of the Afrika Korps, Colonel Bayerlein, as Chief of the Army Staff.

1 June 1942

Dearest Lu,

The battle is going favourably for us; about 400 tanks have been shot up. Our losses are bearable.

Got el Ualeb having fallen, it was now the turn of Bir Hacheim, which was to be surrounded and stormed next day. British and French raiding parties from the fortress were constantly attacking our line of communications and this had to be stopped.

VICTORY IN THE DESERT

On the night 1-2 June, the 90th Light Division and the Trieste moved against Bir Hacheim. They crossed the minefields without heavy casualties, thus shutting off the fortress from the east.

After our summons to surrender had been rejected, the attack opened at about midday. The Trieste from the north-east and the 90th Light from the south-east advanced against the fortifications, field positions and minefields of the French defenders. With our preliminary barrage there began a battle of extraordinary severity, which was to last for ten whole days. I frequently took over command of the assault forces myself and seldom in Africa was I given such a hard-fought struggle. The French fought in a skilfully planned system of field positions and small defence works—slit trenches, small pill-boxes, machine-gun and anti-tank gun nests—all surrounded by dense minefields. This form of defence system is extraordinarily impervious to artillery fire or air attack, since a direct hit can destroy at the most one slit trench at a time. An immense expenditure of ammunition is necessary to do any real damage to an enemy holding a position of this kind.

It was a particularly difficult task to clear lanes through the minefields in face of the French fire. Superhuman feats were performed by the sappers, who suffered heavy casualties. Working under the cover of smoke-screens and artillery fire, they were frequently forced to sap their way direct through to the mines. Our victory was in a great measure due to their efforts.

Under non-stop attacks by our Luftwaffe (from the 2nd June up to the capture of the last French positions on the 11th, the Luftwaffe flew 1,300 sorties against Bir Hacheim) the French positions were attacked in the north by mixed assault groups drawn from various formations and in the south by the 90th Light Division. Attack after attack came to a halt in the excellent British defence system.

During the first few days of our attack on Bir Hacheim the mass of the British forces kept astonishingly quiet. Their only move was on the 2nd June against the Ariete, who resisted stubbornly. After a counter-attack by the 21st Panzer Division, the situation quietened down again. British raiding parties from the area south of Bir Hacheim were continually harrying our supply traffic, to our great discomfort. Mines were laid on the desert tracks and attacks made against our supply columns. The British Motorised Group " August " particularly distinguished itself in this work. We were forced to use armoured cars and self-propelled guns for convoy protection.

The Afrika Korps took advantage of the lull to make good some of its heavy material losses by repairs. On June 2nd they had only 130 serviceable tanks left, as against 320 at the beginning of the battle. Now the number slowly began to rise again.

3 June 1942

DEAREST LU,

The battle continues, though we're in such a favourable position that I've got no more serious worries. I think we'll pull it off all right and reach our objectives.

We could feel that there was something brewing. It was obvious that the British would soon launch an attack, either against the line held by our armour in the north or against our force investing Bir Hacheim in the south.[1] During the night 4-5 June we moved the 15th Panzer Division into position south of Bir el Harmat, where it would be able to strike

---

[1] Auchinleck had expressed anxiety about the way that Rommel was being allowed time to consolidate the wedge in the British position. He had also been urging the early delivery of an indirect counterstroke, aimed at the enemy's supply route. But Ritchie considered this too hazardous. He felt that he must keep enough armour near Acroma to protect his own rear, and that his total did not suffice to provide for a stroke at the enemy's rear at the same time. (He had some 400 tanks still available, whereas Rommel had only 130 German tanks, and about 100 of the relatively ineffective Italian M.13s.)

Ritchie, therefore, preferred to mount a direct assault on the enemy salient. This proved very costly, and turned out disastrously. The British superiority in tank strength withered in the repeated attempts to overcome the enemy by direct assault. By the 6th June it had fallen to 170. Thus the way was smoothed for a decisive thrust by Rommel's armour—which had suffered very little in the meantime.

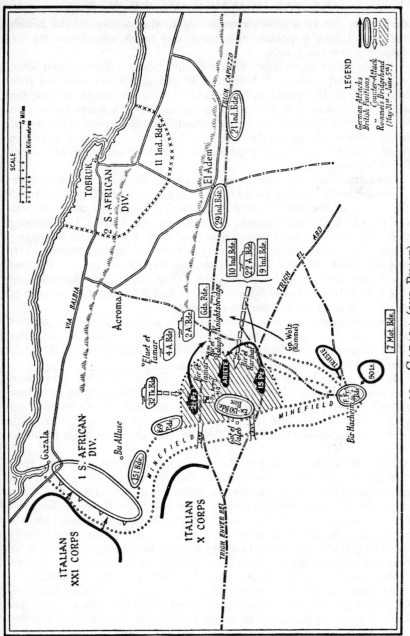

13. GAZALA (2ND PHASE)

LEGEND

German Attacks
British Positions
" Counter-Attack
Rommel's Bridgehead
(May 31st – June 5th)

either north-east or south-east according to the location of the British attack. Just how important this move was to be was shown on the morning of the 5th June.

Shortly before 06.00 hours, after an hour's heavy artillery preparation, the British 2nd and 22nd Armoured Brigades, together with the 10th Indian and 201st Guards Brigade, advanced to the attack against the Ariete. As a feint, they put down smoke and fired a heavy barrage in the 21st Panzer Division's sector, which adjoined the Ariete to the north. Shortly afterwards an attack was also launched at that point by the 4th Armoured Brigade and 42nd Royal Tank Regiment with the object of dividing our forces.

Rommel was mistaken about several points here. The initial attack from the east was delivered by the 10th Indian Infantry Brigade. After it had captured Aslagh Ridge, the 22nd Armoured Brigade passed through to continue the attack, and was followed by the 9th Infantry Brigade. They soon ran into trouble. The converging attack from the north was delivered by the 32nd Army Tank Brigade—employing two units, the 7th and 42nd R.T.R.—and part of the 69th Infantry Brigade. This attack miscarried. It was not until a later stage that the 2nd and 4th Armoured Brigades were used—to retrieve the situation. Their attack became disjointed, and failed to save the 10th Indian Infantry Brigade, with four supporting regiments of artillery, from being overwhelmed while isolated.

Thus the British attack was even more of a piecemeal affair than Rommel imagined. As for its consequences, Auchinleck's dispatch expressed the judgment: " This unsuccessful counter-stroke was probably the turning point of the whole battle."

In face of the heavy British pressure—their forces in this sector were several times stronger than ours—the Ariete fell right back to the Army artillery lines, where the British attack came to a halt under concentrated artillery fire. Meanwhile, to relieve the pressure on the Italians, 8th Panzer Regiment of 15th Panzer Division had thrust through to Bir et Tamar.

From these positions, the Panzer Army, with its northern flank secured, moved to the counter attack. Combat Group Wolz, which had been deployed as Army reserve six miles north-east of Bir Hacheim, thrust forward under my command into the rear of the British at Knightsbridge. The 15th Panzer Division drove into battle on our left. Its task was to close the British in from the south. Soon the guns of our tanks were firing from three sides into the British, who fought back in their usual way with extreme stubbornness but far too little mobility. By the evening, more than fifty British tanks lay shot up on the battlefield.

At about six o'clock next morning the mass of 21st Panzer Division, which had hitherto been firmly held down by British attacks, was also able to move and launched an attack to the east. And now at last the British slowly began to give ground in the fierce tank fighting. Combat Group Wolz closed the Trigh Enver Bei to the west and thus forced the

British units into the fire of the attacking Axis forces. Soon the Wolz Group came under heavy attack from the east and, after being out-flanked by the enemy in the south, had to withdraw during the night to Bir el Harmat.

Once again, the Axis troops had fought superbly. The British, under pressure from three sides, had suffered very heavy losses. Some 4,000 British troops, mainly from 201st Guards and 10th Indian Brigades, marched into our prisoner-of-war camps on the 5th and 6th of June. The newly arrived 10th Indian Brigade had been wiped out.

This defeat had done considerable damage to the enemy's offensive power. As I had foreseen, the British command had decided against committing any major force from the two divisions in the Gazala line to form a second point of pressure on the 21st Panzer Division. Nor had any units of the 2nd South African Division been committed. In a moment so decisive they should have thrown in all the strength they could muster. What is the use of having overall superiority if one allows one's formations to be smashed piece by piece by an enemy who, in each separate action, is able to concentrate superior strength at the decisive point?

After this British defeat we no longer expected any major relieving attack on our forces round Bir Hacheim, and hoped to get on with our assault undisturbed.

Meanwhile, there had been a pause in the fighting in front of the French positions. Now, at 11.00 hours on the 6th June, the 90th Light Division resumed its attack against General Koenig's troops. The assault spearheads succeeded in approaching to within half a mile of the Ridotta[1] Bir Hacheim, but there the attack came to a halt again. A hail of fire tore across the rocky and coverless ground into the ranks of our attacking troops and the attack had to be called off in the evening. The noose round Bir Hacheim was drawn still tighter. Weak relieving attacks made on the 90th Light Division by the 7th British Motor Brigade were beaten off.

That night, the 6-7 June, the 90th Light Division cleared several lanes through the mines in their sector and assault groups approached under cover of darkness to within storming distance. Combat Group Wolz was detailed to support the attack. On the morning of the 7th June, after an artillery and air bombardment, the infantry stormed straight for the French positions. Yet for all their dash, this attack too, was broken up by the fire of all arms. Only in the north were a few penetra-tions made. This was a remarkable achievement on the part of the French defenders, who were now completely cut off from the outside world. To tire them out, flares were fired and the defences covered with machine-gun fire throughout the following night. Yet, when my storming parties went in next morning, the French opened fire again with un-

[1]Ridotta—a small desert fort.

diminished violence. The enemy troops hung on grimly in their trenches and remained completely invisible.

8 June 1942

Dearest Lu,
 The past two days have been particularly lively, but also successful. You will already have seen from the Wehrmacht communiqués how things are going. The fighting will last another fortnight, but I hope to be through the worst of it by then.
 I thought of you in the heat of the tank battle on the 6th June [*Frau Rommel's birthday*] and hoped that my greeting from Africa arrived punctually on the day.

On the 9th June I drew a further combat group from the Afrika Korps to support the attack on Bir Hacheim. From early morning onwards, waves of our infantry surged once more against the enemy defences. At about midday the 90th Light Division, which had hitherto only been giving support by their heavy weapons to the combat group attacking in the north, joined in the assault from their positions in the south. Continuously exposed to the fire of the French, who fought grimly to the end, our storming parties suffered grievous casualties. However, by eight o'clock that night they worked their way forward to within about 220 yards of the Ridotta Bir Hacheim. During the day, Ritchie made a weak diversionary attack against the 90th Light Division's covering units south of Bir Hacheim, using motor battalions and an armoured regiment of the 4th Armoured Brigade. We had no difficulty in beating it off.
 Meanwhile, we had several times had trouble with Kesselring. He was being severely critical of the slow progress of our attack on the French. What mainly upset him was the fact that he had had to keep Luftwaffe formations continuously employed over Bir Hacheim, where they had suffered severe losses. [*On one day alone, the R.A.F. shot down very nearly 40 dive-bombers.*] He insisted that an immediate attack should be launched on the French by all our armoured formations. This was completely out of the question, for tanks cannot be sent into minefields which are protected against clearance by strong-points. Moreover, Ritchie would not have remained inactive on the other fronts while this was going on. Such a move would have led to disaster. We did our best to pacify Kesselring, who probably had little idea of the difficulties we were up against.
 Next day, the 10th June, the Afrika Korps' combat group, under the command of Colonel Baade, succeeded at long last in breaking into the main enemy position north of Bir Hacheim. The attack took place under very heavy artillery fire and air attack, with the French desperately defending every single nest of resistance and suffering terrible casualties

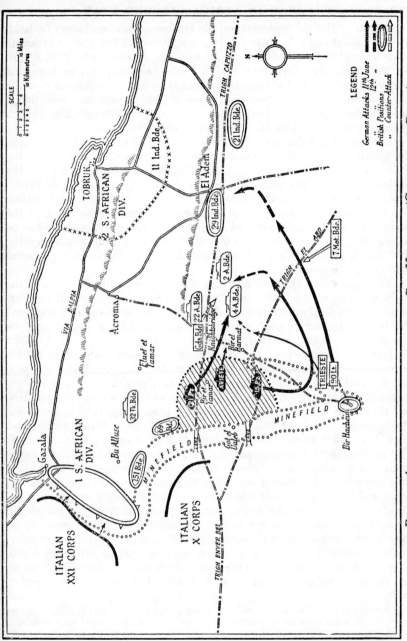

14. Rommel's Eastward Thrust after Bir Hacheim (Gazala 3rd Phase)

as a result. After this penetration, Bir Hacheim could no longer be held.

We now thought it likely that the enemy would bring up a relieving force to enable the French garrison to stage a break-out. Part of 7th British Motor Brigade which had hitherto been engaged in harassing our supply routes, had already been sighted by our reconnaissance on the march towards Bir Hacheim. To arm myself against any situation I ordered the 15th Panzer Division to move to Bir Hacheim. The French garrison was to be given its quietus next day.

But the French did not oblige, for in spite of all our security measures, the greater part of the garrison broke out during the night under the leadership of their commander, General Koenig, and disappeared in the darkness away to the west, where they joined up with the 7th British Motor Brigade. Later we discovered that the instructions for sealing the ring round the fortress had not been properly carried out at the point where the break-out had been made. Once again it had been shown that, however desperate the situation, there is always something that can be done by a resolute commander who is not just prepared to throw in his hand.

The 90th Light Division was thus able to occupy Bir Hacheim in the early morning of the 11th June. Some 500 French soldiers fell into our hands, the majority of them wounded. Later in the morning I inspected the fortress for which such a bitter struggle had been waged and the fall of which we had awaited with such impatience.[1]

Now our forces were free. Despite all the courage which the British in the Ualeb position and the French in Bir Hacheim had displayed, Ritchie had been badly mistaken if he had thought to wear down my forces by these pitched battles. Certainly we had suffered heavy casualties, but they were in no way comparable with those of the British, for in the strong-points which we had surrounded thousands of British troops had been compelled to surrender through lack of water and ammunition. For psychological reasons alone, the sacrifice of whole formations to the enemy is generally a mistake.[2] Even though considerable advantage may sometimes be gained for other formations by ordering troops to resist to the end, one should still think twice before taking such a decision, for the confidence of the ordinary soldier—so vitally important to the Army Commander—is liable to become undermined. The men will no longer obey the command's orders with the necessary care-free equanimity, because they will fear that if a crisis arises they may be left in the lurch.

On the afternoon of the 11th June, I put the Bir Hacheim force on the move to the north in order to seek a final decision without further delay.

[1]*Note by General Bayerlein.* The defence works round Bir Hacheim included, among other things, some 1,200 nests, combat positions, etc., for infantry and heavy weapons.

[2]Rommel's line of thought here may have been accentuated by his reflections on what happened in the previous winter when he fell back westwards, leaving large garrisons in the frontier position to be cut off and captured.

In the evening, the 15th Panzer and 90th Light Divisions with 3rd and 33rd Reconnaissance Battalions, all under my command, reached an area six to ten miles south and south-west of El Adem. To parry this danger, Ritchie moved the 2nd British Armoured Brigade from a point south of Acroma into the neighbourhood of Bir Lefa. After a violent battle with the concentrated British armour, which fought under strong artillery support, we succeeded in taking the area round El Adem and south of the Trigh Capuzzo before noon on the 12th of June. El Adem itself was occupied by the 90th Light Division. The British suffered considerable tank losses and left 400 prisoners in our hands. The 29th Indian Brigade defended itself stubbornly in the El Adem box.

On the same morning [*12th*] a combat group of the 21st Panzer Division also drove east, thus steadily pressing together the British armour, which, squeezed between the two German panzer divisions, no longer possessed full freedom of movement. Into this area, which was already extremely confined, Ritchie now brought up the 32nd Army Tank Brigade from out of the Gazala line. A continuation of the 15th Panzer Division's attack north-westwards now held out promise of great success. The initiative was ours.

In the morning I set off with my *Kampfstaffel* to a ridge south-east of El Adem, where I observed the course of the battle between the 90th Light Division and the Indians. Incessant British bomber attacks were giving the 90th Light Division a bad time. Later I tried to get through to the 15th Panzer Division, but our vehicles were heavily fired on from the north and south and pinned down in the open for several hours. It was afternoon before I reached the 15th, whom I then accompanied in their attack to the west. During the evening we were bombed by some of our own Stukas. They were being chased by British fighters and, lame ducks that they were, were forced to drop their bombs on their own troops for the sake of some extra speed. However, the three of us— Bayerlein, the driver and I—escaped once again without a scratch.

I spent the next day [*13th June*] with the Afrika Korps whose 15th Panzer Division was cleaning up the escarpment to the west, while the Italian Trieste and Ariete Divisions were pressing the British into the area north of the Trigh Capuzzo. The 21st Panzer Division, too, began to move during the evening and thrust east in a raging sandstorm, which at times brought visibility to zero. The slaughter of British tanks went on. One after the other of the 120 or so which they probably now had left remained lying on the battlefield. A murderous fire struck from several sides into the tightly packed British formations, whose strength gradually diminished. Their counter-attacks decreased steadily in momentum.

Unfortunately, the 90th Light Division was unable for several hours to carry out its orders to join up on the east of the 15th Panzer Division, as the British were attacking on all sides and forcing the division to fight for its life. It was afternoon before it was able to disengage and, evading a strong British column, move into its new position.

The Guards Brigade evacuated Knightsbridge that day, after it had been subjected all the morning to the combined fire of every gun we could bring to bear. This brigade was almost a living embodiment of the virtues and faults of the British soldier—tremendous courage and tenacity combined with a rigid lack of mobility. The greater part of the armoured force attached to the Guards Brigade was destroyed, either during that day or on their retreat in the following night.

My intention now was to bring the whole of my motorised force, both German and Italian, into action during the next day or two, in a bid to break through to the sea. The British divisions from the Gazala line, which were already beginning to move east along the coast road, were to be flung back to the west and destroyed. Kesselring's aircraft were already over their columns and the Via Balbia stood in flames.

It was clear that there was going to be very heavy fighting during the next day or so as the British seemed to be determined to hold on to the Acroma position in order to keep a retreat road open for the troops in the Gazala line. It looked as though Ritchie would sacrifice his last tank to that end.

By the evening of the 13th the British strength in this decisive area was reduced to about 70 tanks. Although Rommel had also lost heavily, he had now a superiority of more than two to one in tanks fit for action—and being in possession of the battlefield he was able to recover and repair many of his damaged tanks, while Ritchie could not.

The battle, which had begun so badly for us, was now taking an increasingly favourable turn. All this we owed to the courage of the German and Italian soldiers.

During the night of the 13th both divisions of the Afrika Korps were deployed west of the Trigh Bir Hacheim ready for an attack to the north. The Italian Ariete and Trieste Divisions were to act as a screen for their eastern flank. The 90th Light Division moved off to the east to put itself in a position for a quick grab at the Tobruk approaches.

Next morning [*14th*] the German panzer divisions moved off and rolled northwards. Full speed was ordered, as British vehicles were now streaming east in their thousands. I rode with the tanks and constantly urged their commanders to keep the speed up. Suddenly we ran into a wide belt of mines. Ritchie had attempted to form a new defence front and had put in every tank he had. The advance halted and our vehicles were showered with British armour-piercing shells.

I at once ordered the reconnaissance regiments to clear lanes through the minefields, a task which was made easier by the violent sandstorm which blew up towards midday. Meanwhile, I ordered our 170-mm. guns to open fire on the Via Balbia. The thunder of our guns mingled with the shock of demolitions. The British and South Africans were blowing up their ammunition dumps in the Gazala line.

Late in the afternoon, the 115th Rifle Regiment moved to the attack against Hill 187. In spite of violent counter-fire from British tanks, artillery and anti-tank guns the attack steadily gained ground. Towards five o'clock the British fire, to which my own vehicle had also for some hours been exposed, slowly began to slacken. Enemy resistance crumbled and more and more British troops gave themselves up. Black dejection showed on their faces.

By evening the British barrier was pierced. After violent and successful fighting—its success could be measured in the hulks of 45 British tanks lying on the battlefield—the German panzer divisions gained the area west of Acroma. The way to the Via Balbia was now virtually open.

The 1st British Armoured Division was no longer in a fit state for action and left the battlefield during the night.

Its remaining tanks were transferred to the 4th Armoured Brigade (of 7th Armoured Division). This armoured brigade—the only one left—was thereby made up to a strength of about 60 tanks.

That same night, units of the 50th British Division succeeded in breaking through the Italians of X Corps and escaping to the south. Although we shot up 400 vehicles and took several hundred prisoners, yet British troops to the strength of about a brigade managed to get away. After the break-through, the British commander took his troops in small columns through our supply zone, where they were able to do considerable damage on the way. It would have been right, in fact, for both British divisions to have broken through at this point. At least it would have enabled them to get away in a better condition than was possible along the Via Balbia. But an even more important reason was the fact that the British armoured brigades would not have had to let themselves be pulverised in the tactically hopeless position at Acroma, but would have remained in the fight. As it was, the destruction of the British armour— its remnants were now streaming back into Egypt—cost Ritchie his last chance of taking any further effective part in events in the Marmarica.

After the fall of Got el Ualeb and Bir Hacheim, the British command ought to have realised that there was nothing more to be gained by holding on to the northern part of the Gazala line. There had been no point in sacrificing the 1st French Brigade unless the time thus gained had been used to move the two British divisions in the Gazala line into the Acroma-Gazala area for mobile defence against the expected advance of my motorised forces. With their 300 guns and 200 to 300 light armoured vehicles and Bren-carriers they would have tilted the scales heavily in the British favour. My Italian divisions, with their antediluvian weapons and worse still, without vehicles, could never have been sent forward into the open desert, unless with considerable German motorised support. There would have been no danger from that side.

In the early hours of the 15th of June, units of the 15th Panzer Division thrust across the Via Balbia to the sea. Contrary to my express instructions, however, the detachment they left to bar the Via Balbia was only seven tanks strong. The British and South Africans of course had no difficulty in shooting up these few vehicles and breaking through the barrier; thus several more units escaped to the east, most of them in wild flight. Shortly afterwards the breach was finally closed. Meanwhile, the pursuit had been joined by the Italian divisions and the German brigade from the Gazala line.

15 June 1942

Dearest Lu,

The battle has been won and the enemy is breaking up. We're now mopping up encircled remnants of their army. I needn't tell you how delighted I am. We've made a pretty clean sweep this time. Of course it's cost us some sad losses here and there. Gause and Westphal have been wounded. Gause will be back in three to four weeks, Westphal in a month or two. My health has stuck it all right. I've been living in my car for days and have had no time to leave the battlefield in the evenings. Perhaps we will now see each other in July after all.

I had already withdrawn the 21st Panzer Division from the Acroma district during the morning, and dispatched it eastwards through El Adem with the 90th Light Division and a reconnaissance group. The attack on the El Adem box, with its strong points Batruna and El Hatian, rolled past me in area formation, and a violent exchange of fire soon blazed up between our tanks and the Indians defending the box. That evening Batruna was stormed with the capture of 800 prisoners and numerous guns and other war material. Despite heavy British bomber attacks the division reached Sidi Rezegh before night, where their advance came to a temporary standstill under heavy British counter-fire. The 90th Light Division, in spite of many attempts, did not succeed that day in taking El Hatian, the main position in the El Adem box.

Meanwhile, the remnants of the British Eighth Army had retired to the Egyptian frontier area. Tobruk and El Hatian obviously had the task of tying down our forces long enough to enable a defence line to be constructed on the Egyptian frontier.

I was convinced that major organisational weaknesses must still exist in the Tobruk defences, because part of the 2nd South African Division had made a stand at Acroma. So the main thing now was to attack and take Tobruk while confusion and depression were still rife among the garrison and while our victory in the desert was still having its effect on the British soldier's morale. Once again speed was vital.

THE SECOND BATTLE FOR TOBRUK

Tobruk was one of the strongest fortresses in North Africa. In 1941, with magnificent troops in its garrison, it had presented us with immense difficulties. Many attacks had collapsed in its defences and much of its outer perimeter had literally been soaked in blood. Often the battle had raged round a square yard at a time. We were no strangers to Tobruk.

We intended this time to attack and storm the fortress according to the plan which we had finally evolved in 1941 but which had been forestalled by Cunningham's offensive. Under this plan a feint attack was first to be launched in the south-west to conceal our true design and pin down the garrison at that point. The formations assigned to make the main assault were to arrive on the scene unexpectedly. To this end they were to move on eastwards past Tobruk in order to give the impression that we intended to lay siege to the fortress as in 1941. Then they were to switch back suddenly to the south-eastern front of the fortress, deploy for the assault during the night and, after a heavy dive-bomber and artillery bombardment, launch their assault at dawn and overrun the surprised enemy.

To every man of us, Tobruk was a symbol of British resistance and we were now going to finish with it for good.

On the morning of the 16th June, I drove up to the Via Balbia and then along it to the west. Fighting at Gazala had finally ceased and another six thousand British troops had found their way into our prison camps. Evidence of the British defeat could be seen all along the road and verges. Vast quantities of material lay on all sides, burnt-out vehicles stood black and empty in the sand. Whole convoys of undamaged British lorries had fallen into our hands, some of which had been pressed into service immediately by the fighting troops, while others were now awaiting collection by the salvage squads. Apparently the British had taken off some of their units by sea. Soon we met our troops advancing eastwards from the Gazala line. They received orders to push on as fast as they could up to the western edge of Tobruk and were provided with lorry columns to carry their men up to the front by shuttle service. Quick regrouping for the investment of Tobruk was now the most urgent necessity.

One of the first lessons I had drawn from my experience of motorised warfare was that speed of manoeuvre in operations and quick reaction in command are decisive. Troops must be able to carry out operations at top speed and in complete co-ordination. To be satisfied with norms is fatal. One must constantly demand and strive for maximum performance, for the side which makes the greater effort is the faster—and the faster wins the battle. Officers and N.C.O.s must continually train their troops along these lines.

In my view the duties of a commander are not limited to his work with his staff. He must also concern himself with details of command and should pay frequent visits to the fighting line, for the following reasons:

(a) Accurate execution of the plans of the commander and his staff is of the highest importance. It is a mistake to assume that every unit officer will make all that there is to be made out of his situation; most of them soon succumb to a certain inertia. Then it is simply reported that for some reason or another this or that cannot be done—reasons are always easy enough to think up. People of this kind must be made to feel the authority of the commander and be shaken out of their apathy. The commander must be the prime mover of the battle and the troops must always have to reckon with his appearance in personal control.

(b) The commander must be at constant pains to keep his troops abreast of all the latest tactical experience and developments, and must insist on their practical application. He must see to it that his subordinates are trained in accordance with the latest requirements. The best form of " welfare " for the troops is first-class training, for this saves unnecessary casualties.

(c) It is also greatly in the commander's own interest to have a personal picture of the front and a clear idea of the problems his sub-ordinates are having to face. It is the only way in which he can keep his ideas permanently up to date and adapted to changing conditions. If he fights his battles as a game of chess, he will become rigidly fixed in academic theory and admiration of his own ideas. Success comes most readily to the commander whose ideas have not been canalised into any one fixed channel, but can develop freely from the conditions around him.

(d) The commander must have contact with his men. He must be capable of feeling and thinking with them. The soldier must have confidence in him. There is one cardinal principle which must always be remembered: one must never make a show of false emotions to one's men. The ordinary soldier has a sur-prisingly good nose for what is true and what false.

The Indians were still holding on in El Hatian. On the 16th June, the 90th Light Division, despite all the courage they displayed, were again unable to extend the wedges in the defence system which assault teams had made the evening before. As with all other British defence systems in the Marmarica, this position had been constructed with great technical skill and according to the most up-to-date ideas. Following the example of Bir Hacheim, a part of the garrison (consisting of 29th Indian Brigade) broke out during the night and withdrew to the south.

The Mammoth is used to haul a captured British gun

Digging a way through the sand hills for Rommel's caravan

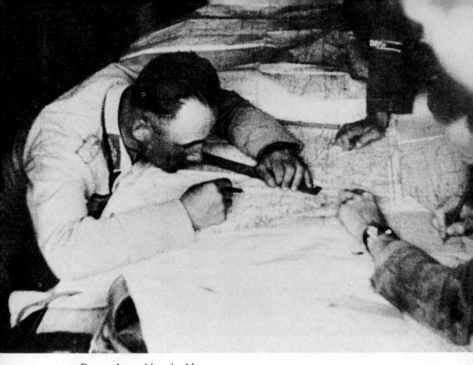

Rommel working in his caravan

Left to right: Field Marshal Kesselring, General Froehlich, General Gause, Field Marshal Rommel, General Cruewell

The Indians simply concentrated their weight on one sector, opened fire with every weapon and then broke out, thus showing once again the difficulty of effectively enveloping a fully-motorised enemy whose structure of command has remained intact.

The remainder of the Indians in El Hatian surrendered on the evening of 17th July. Some 500 prisoners and considerable quantities of war material fell into our hands.

The powerful forts of El Duda and Belhammed had already been captured the day previously by the Afrika Korps. The moment that El Hatian fell I sent the 90th Light Division against several other British strong points which were still holding out in that area. They were surrounded and stormed.

The whole of the Afrika Korps with the Ariete were now put on the march to Gambut and the area to its south. We wanted, as I have already said, to divert British attention from Tobruk and at the same time gain the necessary freedom of movement in our rear for the Tobruk attack. Primarily, however, this advance was directed against the R.A.F. who, with their short time of flight from neighbouring bases, were being unpleasantly attentive. We intended to clear them off their airfield near Gambut and keep them out of the way during our assault on Tobruk.

So now my army was moving east again. The Ariete, who had instructions to maintain touch with the Afrika Korps, fell behind from the start and lost contact. I went off to look for them but very soon ran into a tank battle. Shells whistled backwards and forwards and we were not sorry to escape from that unfriendly neighbourhood. Soon afterwards we succeeded in making contact with the Ariete by radio and moved them up to the main body.

At about 19.30 hours that evening [*the 17th*] I switched the 21st Panzer Division to the north and rode with my *Kampfstaffel* about two miles in front of the van of the division. A slight fracas blew up south of Gambut and a few Foreign Legionaries were taken prisoner. Finally, after some trouble with extensive British minefields, we arrived at Gambut with the leading troops at around 22.00 hours. The main body remained lying before the minefields all night.

At dawn on the 18th June, British aircraft again appeared over the 21st Panzer Division, which was moving on northwards. The road and railway were reached shortly before 04.30. This railway, which the British had built during the past few months, ran from Mersa Matruh to the outer perimeter of Tobruk. We crossed it, demolishing some of the track on the way. The 4th Rifle Regiment had already taken 500 prisoners on the road during the night and this figure was now steadily increasing. On the airfields, which the British had not evacuated until the last moment, we captured 15 serviceable aircraft and considerable quantities of oil and petrol, which we found very useful.

On arriving back that night at Army H.Q., we found life being made unpleasantly hazardous by the activities of a British 25-pounder battery, which began to shell our position. I sent Captain Kiehl with the *Kampfstaffel* to drive it off, which he did, but the British promptly selected another site and began to honour us with their attentions again. I soon became bored with this and shifted my H.Q. back to El Hatian, where the staff of British XXX Corps had formerly been housed.

Mopping up of the area between Tobruk and Gambut was completed on 18th June and the necessary moves carried out to close in Tobruk. An excellent piece of organisational work was now done in building up supplies for the assault. During our advance we had found some of the artillery depots and ammunition dumps, which we had been forced to abandon during the Cunningham offensive in 1941. They were still where we had left them, and were now put to good use.

The Afrika Korps moved into its new position on the afternoon of 19th June, while the 90th Light Division thrust east to take possession of British supply dumps between Bardia and Tobruk. The movement of this division was particularly important to increase still further British uncertainty about our true intentions. In addition the Pavia Division and Littorio Armoured Division, units of which were just arriving, were to screen the attack on Tobruk to the west and south.

We had the impression that evening that our movements had only been partially and inaccurately observed by the enemy, and there was therefore every chance that our attack would achieve complete surprise. Outside the fortress of Tobruk, there was no British armour of any consequence left in the Western Desert and we could therefore look forward with great hopes to the forthcoming enterprise.

In spite of the hard time we had been through, the army was on its toes and confident of victory. On the eve of the battle every man was keyed up and tense for attack.

THE CONQUEST OF TOBRUK

The Tobruk garrison was of approximately the same strength as it had been in 1941, and consisted of the following troops of the British Empire:

2nd South African Infantry Division, reinforced.
11th Indian Brigade.
2nd Battalion, Guards Brigade.
Several infantry tank regiments, under command 32nd Army Tank
  Brigade.
Artillery strengthening to the extent of several artillery regiments.

This is not quite correct.   The 2nd South African Division had only two infantry brigades instead of three. On the other hand, the 201st Guards Brigade had two battalions and part of a third under its command. The 32nd Army Tank Brigade had two battalions of infantry tanks. There was no additional artillery apart from the 4th Anti-Aircraft Brigade.

Although this force corresponded in numbers to the 1941 garrison, it could not be expected to put up such a stubborn and well-organised resistance, for the bulk of the troops had already given us battle and were tired and dispirited. The British command, moreover, which never was very quick at reorganising, had been given no time to build up its defensive machine.

Besides this force in Tobruk, Ritchie still had available five infantry divisions of which three had been very badly mauled; the other two had been freshly brought up. His two armoured divisions had been virtually wiped out in the recent fighting, but were now receiving reinforcements and replacements from the Nile Delta.

One more word about the Tobruk defences.

Tobruk, hemmed in on its eastern and western sides by rocky and trackless country, extends out to the south into a flat and sandy plain. It had been extremely well fortified by the Italians under Balbo, and full account had been taken of the most modern weapons for the reduction of fortifications. The numerous defence positions running in a belt round the fortress were sunk in the ground in such a manner that they could only be located from the air. Each defence position consisted of an underground tunnel system leading into machine and anti-tank gun nests. These nests, of which most of the defence positions had a considerable number, waited until the moment of greatest danger before throwing off their camouflage and pouring a murderous fire into the attacking troops. Artillery could not take them under direct fire because of the lack of apertures on which to take aim. Each separate position was surrounded by an anti-tank ditch and deep wire entanglements. In addition the whole fortified zone was surrounded at all points passable to tanks by a deep anti-tank ditch.

Behind the outer belt of fortifications, most of which was several lines in depth, were powerful artillery concentrations, field positions and several forts. The majority of the defence works were protected by deep minefields.

The feint attack in the south-west was to be executed by XXI Italian Corps, who were provided with several tanks in support. The group making the main attack consisted of the Afrika Korps and XX Italian Corps. Before the attack was opened the main attack sector, south-east of the fortress, was to be bombed by the entire German-Italian Air Force in Africa. Once the infantry had succeeded in reducing the fortified lines, the Afrika Korps was to press on over the crossroads to the harbour and open up the Via Balbia to the west. Following up the Afrika Korps,

XX Italian Corps was to capture the British defence works and thrust through to the Ras el Madauer in the rear of the South Africans.

20 June 1942

DEAREST LU,

Only two hours' sleep last night. This is the really decisive day. Hope my luck holds. I'm very tired, though quite well otherwise.

My assault force moved into its assembly areas on the night of the 19th June. At 05.20 hours several hundred aircraft hammered their bombs on the break-in point south-east of the fortress. I watched the effect of this attack. Great fountains of dust plumed up out of the Indian positions, whirling entanglements and weapons high into the air. Bomb after bomb tore through the enemy wire.

As soon as the aircraft had finished, the infantry of the Afrika Korps (15th Rifle Brigade) and XX Italian Corps moved forward to the assault. Lanes had been cleared through the mines the night before. Two hours later the German storming parties had succeeded in driving a wedge into the British defences. One position after another was attacked by my " Africans " and captured in fiercest hand-to-hand combat.

The engineers had the anti-tank ditch bridged by 08.00 hours. The exploits of the engineers that day merited particular praise. It is difficult to conceive what it meant to do work of this kind under heavy British fire. Now the way was open and we unleashed the armour.

At about 08.00, I drove with my *Gefechtsstaffel* through the Ariete's sector and into the 15th Panzer Division's. Riding in an armoured troop-carrier, I went through as far as the lanes through the minefields, which lay under heavy British artillery fire. Considerable traffic jams were piling up as a result of this fire and I sent Lieut. Berndt up immediately to organise a smooth flow of traffic. Half an hour later, I crossed the anti-tank ditch with Bayerlein and examined two of the captured positions. Meanwhile, the Afrika Korps was becoming the target of British tank attacks from outside the fortress and a violent tank battle flared up, in which the artillery on both sides joined. Towards 11.00 hours, I ordered the Ariete and Trieste, who, after overcoming the anti-tank ditch, had come to a halt in the British defended zone, to follow up through the Afrika Korps's penetration. The German attack moved steadily on and the Afrika Korps, after a brief action in which 50 British tanks were shot up, reached the crossroad Sidi Mahmud at about midday. We held the key to Tobruk.

I now accompanied the Afrika Korps's advance onward from the crossroad. A furious fire beat into the attacking troops from the Fort Pilastrino area and several nests on the Jebel descent. Several British ships weighed anchor and made as if to leave harbour, apparently attempting to get their men away by sea. I at once directed the A.A.

and artillery on to this target and six ships were sunk. Most of the men aboard them were picked up.

The advance continued and we soon reached the descent into the town, where we came up against a British strong-point which fought back with extraordinary stubbornness. I sent Lieut. von Schlippenbach with a summons to the garrison of 50 men to surrender. Their only answer was a withering fire on our vehicles. Eventually, our outrider, Corporal Huber, covered by six anti-aircraft men, succeeded in approaching the strong-point and putting the garrison out of action with hand grenades.

Pilastrino offered to capitulate in the evening and a Stuka attack on the fort was called off. Fort Solaro was stormed by my men and another gunboat sunk in the harbour. By nightfall two-thirds of the fortress was in our hands; the town and harbour had already been captured by the Afrika Korps in the afternoon.

At 05.00 hours on the 21st of June, I drove into the town of Tobruk. Practically every building of the dismal place was either flat or little more than a heap of rubble, mostly the result of our siege in 1941. Next I drove off along the Via Balbia to the west. The staff of the 32nd British Army Tank Brigade offered to surrender, which brought us 30 serviceable British tanks.[1] Vehicles stood in flames on either side of the Via Balbia. Wherever one looked there was chaos and destruction.

At about 09.40 hours, on the Via Balbia about four miles west of the town, I met General Klopper, G.O.C. 2nd South African Infantry Division and Garrison Commandant of Tobruk. He announced the capitulation of the fortress of Tobruk. He had been unable to stave off the defeat any longer, although he had done all he could to maintain control over his troops.

I told the General, who was accompanied by his Chief of Staff, to follow me in his car along the Via Balbia to Tobruk. The road was lined with about ten thousand prisoners of war.

On arrival at the Hotel Tobruk, I talked for a while with General Klopper. It seemed that he had no longer been in possession of the necessary communications to organise a break-out. It had all gone too quickly. I instructed the South African general to make himself and his officers responsible for order among the prisoners, and to organise their maintenance from the captured stores.

21 June 1942

DEAREST LU,
    Tobruk! It was a wonderful battle. There's a lot going on in the fortress area. I must get a few hours' sleep now after all that's happened. How much I think of you.

[1]These must have been tanks under repair in the workshops, and were not surrendered by the brigade staff proper. Only a few tanks remained in action with the brigade after its desperate fight the previous day, and the brigade commander ordered these to be destroyed that night prior to an attempt to escape on foot in small parties.

The capture of Tobruk, which had taken place without interference from outside, marked the conclusion of the fighting in the Marmarica. For every one of my " Africans", that 21st of June, was the high point of the African war. I had the following Order of the Day issued by the Panzer Army:

" Soldiers!

The great battle in the Marmarica has been crowned by your quick conquest of Tobruk. We have taken in all over 45,000 prisoners and destroyed or captured more than 1,000 armoured fighting vehicles and nearly 400 guns. During the long hard struggle of the last four weeks, you have, through your incomparable courage and tenacity, dealt the enemy blow upon blow. Your spirit of attack has cost him the core of his field army, which was standing poised for an offensive. Above all, he has lost his powerful armour. My special congratulations to officers and men for this superb achievement.

Soldiers of the Panzer Army Afrika!

Now for the complete destruction of the enemy. We will not rest until we have shattered the last remnants of the British Eighth Army. During the days to come, I shall call on you for one more great effort to bring us to this final goal.

ROMMEL."

Next day Rommel heard by wireless from Hitler's headquarters that in reward for his victory he had been made a Field-Marshal. He was forty-nine. He was so busy in the days that followed that he quite forgot to change his shoulder badges to those of his new rank—two crossed batons. It was only after he had reached El Alamein that he was reminded of this by Field-Marshal Kesselring, who gave Rommel a pair of his own badges. Rommel received his actual baton when he saw Hitler in Berlin in September. He remarked to his wife at the time: " I would rather he had given me one more division."

CHAPTER X

PURSUIT INTO EGYPT

In winning our victory at Tobruk we, too, had expended the last of our strength, for the weeks of very heavy fighting against an enemy superior in both men and material had left their mark on my forces. Now, however, with the vast booty that had fallen to us, including ammunition, petrol, food, and war material of all kinds, a build-up for a further offensive was possible.

Rome had assured me several times that supplies to Africa could only be guaranteed in adequate quantities if the ports of Tobruk and Mersa Matruh were in our hands. This strengthened my resolve to exploit the weakness of the British after the battle of Tobruk by thrusting forward as far as I could into Egypt.

But that was not the main reason for my decision. I was determined at all costs to avoid giving the British any opportunity of creating another new front and occupying it with fresh formations from the Near East. The Eighth Army was now extremely weak, with a core of only two fresh infantry divisions; its armoured formations, which had been rushed up in great haste from the Egyptian hinterland, could not possibly have any striking power worth mentioning. All in all, the proportion of our strength to the British, in comparison with what it had been, was highly encouraging. Our intention was to overtake the Eighth Army's formations by a lightning thrust forward and bring them to battle before they had been able to join up with other formations from the Middle East. If we could once succeed in destroying the tattered remnants of the Eighth Army which had escaped from the Marmarica battles, plus its two fresh divisions—and this was by no means impossible—then the British would have nothing left in Egypt capable of opposing our advance to Alexandria and the Suez Canal.

It was a plan with a chance of success—a try on. The existence of my army would in no way be jeopardised, for, with things as they were, we would be quite capable of looking after ourselves whatever the outcome.[1]

[1]It is interesting to observe that Rommel repeatedly defends himself against the criticism that he made a practice of gambling. He was evidently sensitive to that criticism. In general, his journal provides much evidence that his plans were carefully thought out, and that their boldness was based on deep calculation.

This move into Egypt has since been the subject of criticism in some quarters. It has been said that the supply line from Benghazi to El Alamein was too long for the supply columns to maintain for any length of time, and that the British derived great advantage from their short supply route from Port Said to the front.

Against this, there is the following to be said:

(a) British superiority would have had an even greater effect at Sollum than at El Alamein. For at Sollum they would have been able to outflank our line by wide sweeps into the desert and, with their armoured brigades—which, by the time of the Alamein battle were superior to ours not only in numbers, which they had been before, but above all in quality—to smash our motorised divisions. Moreover, the chances of withdrawing our non-motorised infantry from Sollum would have been even worse than from El Alamein. These non-motorised formations, which made up the bulk of my army at El Alamein, would have been completely ineffective at Sollum, where the enemy would not have had to break through their line, but could quite simply and without effort, have gone round it. They would then have become either easy prey for the British or mere ballast during the retreat.

(b) Nor would there have been any worthwhile improvement in our supply position at Sollum, for with our front so far west, instead of the ports of Tobruk and Mersa Matruh being within range of the British bombers it would have been Tobruk and Benghazi. Thus Benghazi would, for all practicable purposes, have been closed to the larger ships, which would have meant a lengthening of the overland supply line to Tripoli, a distance which our available transport was completely inadequate to cover. The British supply position, on the other hand, would have hardly been affected, for they had the railway, ample vehicle space for road transport, and well-organised coastal shipping all at their disposal.[1]

[1]*Note by General Bayerlein*. Rommel's argument was on the whole correct. One must add, however, that a build-up would have taken Montgomery far longer at Sollum than at El Alamein. There is no doubt that this would have meant a postponement, not only of the Eighth Army's offensive, but also of Anglo-American operations in North-west Africa, for it can hardly be supposed that the Allies would have landed in North-west Africa before Montgomery had first tied down Rommel's army by his attack. It is nevertheless extremely doubtful whether, with supply conditions as bad as they were, the time gained would have given the Panzer Army an advantage which would have made up for the disadvantages (as described by Rommel) of the Sollum position compared with that at El Alamein.

General Westphal, in his book *The German Army in the West* (Cassell), expresses the view that it would have been better to call off the offensive at Sollum and move the German-Italian air force engaged in Africa, to Catania for use in the capture of Malta. This can hardly be upheld. Quite apart from the fact that Malta would probably even then not have been attacked—the OKW and the Commando Supremo had already had eighteen

It is, of course, true that our supply columns were faced with serious difficulties as a result of our advance into Egypt. But the same effort should have been demanded from the supply staffs in Rome as from every tankman or infantryman, tired out as they were with weeks of fighting. Thus, supply by sea should have been improvised immediately to ports in the forward zone on the scale which had always been promised for this occasion. The top Italian authorities could have done this at any time. When I gave orders for the advance into Egypt, I was assuming that the fact of final victory in Egypt being now within reach would spur even the Italian Commando Supremo into some sort of effort.

On the strength of all these and other similar arguments, I requested the Duce, immediately after the capture of Tobruk, to lift the restrictions on the Panzer Army's freedom of operation and allow us to advance into Egypt. Permission was granted, whereupon orders went out immediately to all formations concerned to prepare for the march.

Our approach march for the thrust across the Egyptian frontier went without a hitch. In spite of the strain of the previous weeks, the troops were in high spirits and the superb morale of the Panzer Army was once again evident. My forces began to move east on the 22nd June. I myself crossed the frontier on the 23rd, well behind the 90th Light Division, which had thrust a long way ahead. Heavy smoke clouds were rising far over to the east; the British had evacuated the frontier area. The mass of the Eighth Army, as we learnt from captured documents, had been ordered to take up positions at Mersa Matruh. The supreme requirement now, and for several days, was speed.

23 June 1942

DEAREST LU,

We're on the move and hope to land the next big punch very soon. Speed is the main thing now. The events of the past weeks lie behind me like a dream. Gause is back again. He still looks thoroughly exhausted, but he just couldn't stick it any longer back at the rear. I'm very well, sleeping like a log.

On the 24th June I rode with the 90th Light Division's column and hour after hour urged them on to ever greater speed. Unfortunately, the Afrika Korps ran badly short of petrol that day and was immobilised for several hours. Luckily, we found a considerable quantity of British petrol

months in which to do it (*see also footnote on page 203—L.H.*)—the withdrawal of the German-Italian air force, which had suffered heavy losses in the Marmarica battle, was impossible unless one was prepared to vouchsafe the British complete command of the air immediately after the fall of Tobruk. Rommel has actually given clear enough reasons for his plan in his account. There is, however, one further point which should perhaps be mentioned, namely, that in the summer of 1942 the OKW supplied the 7th and 10th German Panzer Divisions with tropical equipment and prepared them for Africa. This must have led Rommel to believe that he could count on his German armoured force being doubled. The two divisions were later sent to Russia.

at Habata railway station where we were able to salvage a large part of the store, even though it was already burning. In spite of the difficulties, our advance continued to make good progress and by next day we had already reached a point 30 miles west of Mersa Matruh.

My formations were being repeatedly assailed by heavy R.A.F. bomber attacks. Our own Luftwaffe was re-grouping at the time and could not put up any fighters. The Afrika Korps, with its 50 remaining tanks, was the most frequent target of the R.A.F.'s attacks. An astonishingly high proportion of our transport now consisted of captured British vehicles and it was, in fact, no longer possible at any distance to distinguish us from the British. Thus, *Kampfstaffel* Kiehl, with its " British Look ", managed to coax up numerous British stragglers and put them in the bag—to their intense disgust when they found out their mistake.

The Italians were also having their difficulties. On the 25th June the Ariete and Trieste had a grand total of 14 tanks, 30 guns and 2,000 infantry between them! The Littorio was immobilised for hours on end by lack of petrol and simply could not keep up. Heavy demands were made on the supply services' powers of improvisation. British air attacks on our eastward-moving columns continued right into the night. Sortie after sortie was flown by the 200 multi-engined and 360 single-engined aircraft which Ritchie still had available in western Egypt.

On the morning of the 26th June, swarms of British aircraft continued the attack and succeeded in destroying a supply column, which caused the Afrika Korps a serious petrol shortage for a time. In spite of these difficulties, we managed that day to reach a point some 10 miles south-west of Mersa Matruh. The remnants of the British 1st and 7th Armoured Divisions fell back from this area, leaving only reconnaissance units behind. We did not expect any great British resistance here, but thought they would merely try to delay us long enough to enable them to get away the equipment of their numerous airfields and supply installations in the area round Mersa Matruh and El Daba.

Our intention was to bring the British to battle at this point and attempt to destroy a major part of their infantry. To this end we planned to envelop the fortress of Mersa Matruh with its powerful garrison inside and then take it by storm. To provide the necessary elbow room for this attack the British armour was to be driven back by a quick thrust to the east and thus prevented from taking any hand in operations round the fortress.

26 June 1942

DEAREST LU,

We've made a good move forward in the last few days and are hoping to launch our attack on the enemy remnants to-day. For days now I've been camping out in the car with Gause. Food has been good all the time but washing has suffered. I've had my headquarters by the sea for the past twenty hours and bathed yesterday and to-day. But the water doesn't refresh, it's much too hot. A lot to do. Cavallero and Rintelen are coming to-day, probably to put the brakes on, so far as they can. These beggars don't change!

On the same day, the 26th June, it became clear that Ritchie intended to make a preliminary stand on the line Mersa Matruh—Bir Khalda.[1] However, after the Afrika Korps had thrown the British reconnaissance units back into their line, 90th Light Division moved up, broke through the northern part of the line and in a quick dash reached the coast road in the evening and closed it to both directions.

Mersa Matruh was now successfully enclosed. This fortress was fortified in similiar strength to that of Tobruk, but its defences had not been constructed with anything like the same skill. Many mines— probably about 200,000—had been laid in its outer environs. Inside the fortress lay the mass of the New Zealand and 10th Indian Divisions, together with units of the 50th British and 5th Indian Divisions. Thus the greater part of the British infantry was locked up in this place.[2]

Meanwhile the Afrika Korps under General Nehring, and XX Italian Corps, whose brave and efficient commander, General Baldassare, had fallen to British fire the day before, collided with a concentration of British armour in the area north of Khalda. American medium tanks, most of them freshly brought up from Egypt, launched attack after attack against our formations. The battle lasted until late evening, by which time 18 American tanks lay shot up on the field. Lack of petrol and ammunition unfortunately prevented us from exploiting this success.

27 June 1942

DEAREST LU,

We're still on the move and hope to keep it up until the final goal. It takes a lot out of one, of course, but it's the chance of a life-time. The enemy is fighting back desperately with his air force.

P.S.—Italy in July might still be possible. Get passports!

Thus the British motorised forces had again been heavily defeated

[1] It had been the intention, as Rommel deduced, to defend Mersa Matruh. Indeed, it was planned as the final stand. But on the evening of the 25th Auchinleck took over direct control of the Eighth Army from Ritchie. He brought with him Major-General E. E. Dorman-Smith, his Deputy Chief of the General Staff, to act as his principal staff officer in the measures he now took to deal with the crisis. The first decision was that the plan of standing at Mersa Matruh should be discarded and that the Eighth Army should be kept mobile. This reversal of the previous decision was fortunate, as can be seen from Rommel's account of his plans to cut off and wipe out the remains of the Eighth Army.

[2] This is not correct. The garrison had been thinned out, and the New Zealand Division was posted 20 miles south of Mersa Matruh.

and there was now no chance of their giving any appreciable assistance to the troops locked up in Mersa Matruh. In these circumstances it seemed very unlikely that the British command, after their experience in Tobruk, would give us the opportunity of destroying what was left of their infantry in western Egypt, for this would have finally opened our road to Alexandria. So we had to expect that the fully motorised British infantry would try to break out through the ring round Mersa Matruh, which on the 27th June was by no means firmly closed, in order to gain the open desert and make off for the east. Many of their vehicles did actually try to get away through the open southern sector soon after the fortress was shut in.

To hamper the break-out of further enemy forces, I ordered units of the Brescia and Pavia, which had meanwhile been brought up in supply lorries, to move as fast as they could round to the south of Mersa Matruh. However, with their poor equipment and transport, this move went terribly slowly. Other Italian formations had already occupied the area round the west and south-west of the fortress. All units holding the line were ordered to maintain the utmost vigilance during the night.

The New Zealand Division under General Freyberg, an old acquaintance of mine from previous campaigns, did in fact concentrate in the night and break out in the south. A wild mêlée ensued, in which my own headquarters, which lay south of the fortress, became involved. *Kampfstaffel* Kiehl and units of the Littorio joined in the fighting. The firing between my forces and the New Zealanders grew to an extraordinary pitch of violence and my headquarters was soon ringed by burning vehicles, making it the target for continuous enemy fire. I soon had enough of this and ordered the headquarters and the staff to withdraw to the south-east. One can scarcely conceive the confusion which reigned that night. It was pitch-dark and impossible to see one's hand before one's eyes. The R.A.F. bombed their own troops, and, with tracer flying in all directions, German units fired on each other.

In the early hours of the morning, several hundred more New Zealand vehicles broke out through great gaps on the south-east side of our front. It is in fact extremely difficult in desert warfare to improvise a long front capable of withstanding the attack of a force which has retained its cohesion and is able, thanks to motorisation, to focus its strength suddenly.[1]

At 05.00 hours next morning, the 28th June, I drove up to the break-out area where we had spent such a disturbed night. There we found

---

[1] Rommel has not got the picture clear—probably owing to the confusion he describes, His troops had driven through between the main position at Matruh and the outlying position of the New Zealanders at Minqa Quaim, and portions of them had then enveloped the New Zealanders' area on the 27th. But that night the 4th New Zealand Brigade, deployed for assault with bayonets fixed, broke through on foot by moonlight. The remainder of the division, loaded on transport, followed them through the gap or slipped out by a southerly circuit. Freyberg himself had been severely wounded during the day and the break-out was directed by Brigadier Inglis.

a number of lorries full of the mangled corpses of New Zealanders who had been killed by British bombs. Although the main body of the British had now moved off towards Fuka, Mersa Matruh was still being defended by units of the 10th Indian, New Zealand and 50th British Divisions. reinforced with additional artillery and a newly arrived regiment of 4th British Armoured Brigade. British units—now dispersed and less well organised—were still making constant attempts to slip out of the ring.

The troops at Matruh might have got away before the road was barred, but part of their troop-carrying transport had been taken away in order to make the New Zealand Division fully mobile for its flank-covering role. Nevertheless, most of them managed to break out or slip out the following night, though they had to abandon much of their ammunition and equipment. The fact that part of them were unable to get away underlines Rommel's point about the value of completely motorised formations, although he is mistaken in describing the British as such.

At about 17.00 hours, the 90th Light Division, 580th Reconnaissance Regiment, *Kampfstaffel* Kiehl and those units of XX and XXI Italian Corps that had arrived moved to the assault. In spite of stubborn British resistance the 90th Light Division's attack went forward well. The bitter struggle lasted all night, with groups of British vehicles, large and small, trying the whole time to break away. Most of them were shot up. In some places the British set fire to their vehicles with the bodies of their comrades inside and tried to get away on foot. We had little difficulty in the moonlit night in rounding most of them up. Enormous fires raged in the fortress zone of Mersa Matruh.

29 June 1942

Dearest Lu,

Now the battle of Mersa Matruh has also been won and our leading units are only 125 miles from Alexandria. There'll be a few more battles to fight before we reach our goal, but I think the worst is well behind us. I'm fine.

Some actions make demands on one's strength to the point of bodily exhaustion, but there are quieter periods when one gets a chance to recover. We're already 300 miles east of Tobruk. British rail and road system in first-class order!

At last, early next morning, the 29th June, the 90th Light Division from the east, and *Kampfstaffel* Kiehl and 580th Reconnaissance Regiment from the south forced their way into the fortress. Firing gradually died away and finally ceased. The booty was enormous. Besides the large supply dumps, war material of all kinds, approximating in all to the equipment of a whole division, fell into our hands. Forty enemy tanks were destroyed and 6,000 British troops marched into our prison camps.

Our men had once again fought with extraordinary courage. Unfortunately, the New Zealanders under Freyberg had escaped. This division, with which we had already become acquainted back in 1941-42, was among the élite of the British Army, and I should have been very much happier if it had been safely tucked away in our prison camps instead of still facing us.

The last fortress port in the Western Egyptian desert was now ours, and the British had once again suffered heavy losses. Nevertheless, they had been able to get the great bulk of their infantry back to the El Alamein position, where work on the development of the defences had been going ahead at top speed for some time past. The position was already occupied by a number of fresh units. Immediately after the fall of Mersa Matruh, therefore, I set my troops on the march again. We planned to get through to the Alamein line and overrun it while it was still incomplete and before the retreating remnants of the Eighth Army had had time to organise its defence. This line was the last bastion on which the British could oppose our advance. Once through it, our road was clear.

So the forces at Mersa Matruh moved off east again as soon as the fortress had fallen. The Italian infantry was also put on the march with its leading elements directed on Fuka. Then our vehicles, too, resumed their eastward drive. As we were passing the airfield Bir Teifel Fukasch, machine-gun bullets suddenly spurted into the dust around us. I immediately drove to Colonel Marcks, the fine commander of the 90th Light Division, and instructed him to take a column round in an arc to the south. However, it soon transpired that it was the Littorio who had fired on us, thinking that we were British troops on the run. Friend and foe were no longer distinguishable, for both sides were using mainly British vehicles.

Towards midday we learned from radio interception that the British were leaving Haneish. I immediately gave orders for the retreating Tommies to be picked up, and a considerable number of prisoners was brought in as a result. Several miles south-east of Fuka the 90th Light Division suddenly came under British artillery fire from the south-east, which was apparently being directed by scout cars. The vehicles were driven off by a few guns which we quickly brought into position, after which the artillery fire slowly died away. The march went on. A few miles farther on we stumbled across several belts of mines which had been laid between minefields on either side of the road. The crash of bursting mines came from beneath the wheels of our leading vehicles. After I and a few others had cleared away the mines the column moved off again. At nightfall we halted about six miles west of El Daba. Gigantic explosions could be heard from the east—an unwelcome sound, for it meant that the British were blowing up their dumps, which we could have put to good use.

There are always moments when the commander's place is not back with his staff but up with the troops. It is sheer nonsense to say that maintenance of the men's morale is the job of the battalion commander alone. The higher the rank, the greater the effect of the example. The men tend to feel no kind of contact with a commander who, they know, is sitting somewhere in headquarters. What they want is what might be termed a physical contact with him. In moments of panic, fatigue or disorganisation, or when something out of the ordinary has to be demanded from them, the personal example of the commander works wonders, especially if he has had the wit to create some sort of legend round himself.

The physical demands on the troops during this period approached the limits of endurance. This placed a particular duty on the officers to provide a continual example and model for their men.[1]

30 June 1942

Dearest Lu,

Mersa Matruh fell yesterday, after which the Army moved on until late in the night. We're already 60 miles to the east. Less than 100 miles to Alexandria!

On the morning of the 30th June I found that advance elements of the 15th Panzer Division had already reached a point far beyond El Daba. Great booty had fallen to the Afrika Korps, including a British 150-mm. battery, which they had immediately put back into action again. Unfortunately, the Italians were in trouble again, and it was almost midnight before they arrived in the area west of El Alamein.

While on a tour of reconnaissance, I came across a couple of lorries and a Russian gun[2] at the southern end of Telegraph Track;[3] one of the lorries was still fully loaded and there were loaded tommy-guns and rifles lying close by. It seemed that the British had surprised the gun team in their sleep and taken them prisoner. In El Daba, we found a large ration store by the roadside and set up headquarters in one of its huts. Fighter-bomber attacks, however, soon decided me to move farther east. But there again we soon heard the guns of British low-flyers, which

[1] *Note by General Bayerlein.* The value that Rommel placed on the personal example of the officer is shown by an address which he gave as Director of the Military School in Wiener Neustadt at the passing out parade of a 1938 class of cadets:

" Be an example to your men, both in your duty and in private life. Never spare yourself, and let the troops see that you don't, in your endurance of fatigue and privation. Always be tactful and well mannered and teach your subordinates to be the same. Avoid excessive sharpness or harshness of voice, which usually indicates the man who has shortcomings of his own to hide."

[2] A large number of Russian 76 mm. guns, captured on the Eastern Front, had been sent to Africa and were used by Rommel both as field guns and as anti-tank guns.

[3] A desert track, lined with telegraph wires and poles, which ran south behind the front from Sidi Abd el Rahman to the Qattara Depression.

had apparently already settled in on their new airfields. So we moved on a second time. Unfortunately, several of our vehicles had been burnt out.

During the afternoon I talked over the forthcoming attack on the El Alamein line with several of my generals and chiefs-of-staff. We decided that the attack should go in at 03.00 hours next morning. Meanwhile my " Africans " were moving into their assembly areas. On the same afternoon I drove on to the east through a violent sandstorm and met Colonel Bayerlein, who, on his way to the Army H.Q., had driven right through the columns of the British 7th Armoured Division, which we had broken through.

I again discussed the next day's attack. In the evening it became clear that we would not be able to keep to the time-table we had planned, as the formations taking part in the attack had been badly held up, partly by the retreating British and partly by the unforeseen difficulty of the country.

CHAPTER XI

THE INITIATIVE PASSES

CHECK AT ALAMEIN

My Panzer Army had now been five weeks in battle against superior British forces. For four of those weeks the fighting had raged backwards and forwards in the foreground of Tobruk. We had succeeded, partly by attacks with limited objectives, partly in defence, in wearing down the British forces. After the fall of Knightsbridge and Gazala we had stormed Tobruk. The British had retired first to Mersa Matruh and then to El Alamein.

This series of engagements had brought the strength of my Army to the point of exhaustion. With our reserves of material—including the immediately usable booty—beginning to run out, it was only the men's amazing spirit and will to victory that kept them going at all. Not only had no replacement material arrived, but, with an almost unbelievable lack of appreciation of the situation, the supply authorities had actually sent only three thousand tons to Africa during June, as compared with our real requirement of sixty thousand tons, a figure which was never in fact attained. Captured stores had certainly helped to tide us over the expected crisis in our supply situation after the fall of Tobruk, but it was urgently necessary that this should have been followed up by adequate supplies from our own sources.

In Rome one excuse after the other was found for the failure of the supply organisation which was supposed to maintain my army. It was easy enough back there to say: " It can't be done ", for life and death did not depend on finding a solution. If everybody had pulled together in a resolute search for ways and means, and the staff work had been done in the same spirit, the technical difficulties could without any doubt have been overcome.

The following are the detailed reasons why our supply failed:

(a) Many of the authorities responsible for supply did not put their best effort into it, simply because they themselves were not directly threatened by the urgency of the situation. Peace reigned in Rome and there was no immediate danger of disaster there, even if the problems were not solved. There were many, too, who did not realise that the African war was approaching its climax. Some did realise it, but for some inexplicable reason did not intensify their efforts. I knew the type well. Whenever difficulties arose they declared that our maintenance was a completely insoluble problem and proved it with rows of statistics. These people lacked any kind of practical ingenuity and initiative. They should have been packed off home before it was too late, and replaced by others who could do it.

(b) The protection of our convoys at sea was the responsibility of the Italian Navy. A great part of its officers, like many other Italians, were not supporters of Mussolini and would rather have seen our defeat than our victory. Hence they sabotaged wherever they could. The correct political conclusions, however, were not drawn from this.

(c) Most of the higher Fascist authorities were too corrupt or too pompous to do any good. Frequently, too, they wanted as little as possible to do with the whole African war.

(d) Those who did give of their best to get supplies to us were unable to make any headway in the maze of over-organisation which existed in Rome.

When it is remembered that in modern warfare supplies decide the battle, it is easy to see how the clouds of disaster were gathering for my army.

The British, on the other hand, were sparing no effort to master the situation. They organised the move of fresh troops into the Alamein line with admirable speed. Their leading men had clearly realised that the next battle in Africa would determine the situation for a long time to come, and were looking at things very cool-headedly. The peril of the hour moved the British to tremendous exertions, just as always in a moment of extreme danger things can be done which had previously been thought impossible. Mortal danger is an effective antidote for fixed ideas.

Later on even our supply authorities in Rome suddenly found it possible to ship supplies across to Tunis in quantities which we had never before seen in Africa, and that at a time when the greater part of the shipping which we had had in the summer of 1942 had been sunk, and when the British had a very different grip on the Mediterranean from that which they had wielded during our advance to El Alamein. But it was then too late, for the enemy's shipments of supplies, always far higher than ours, had meanwhile been multiplied several times over.

Up to this time my staff and I had been just about able to manage, largely by drawing on the abundance of material we had captured. Up to 85 per cent of our transport still consisted of captured enemy vehicles, and continued to do so, even after this time. My troops had at all times given of their best. But it had repeatedly been the superiority of certain German weapons over the British equivalents that had been our salvation. Now there were already signs, in the new British tanks and anti-tank guns, of a coming qualitative superiority of British material. If this were achieved, it would clearly mean the end for us.

For that reason alone, therefore, it was essential to do everything possible to bring about a British collapse in the Near East before any considerable shipments of arms could arrive from Britain or the United States. And so there followed during July a series of violent and bloody battles in front of El Alamein, the main feature of which was continuous round-the-clock bombing by the R.A.F. We succeeded in taking several fortified works of the Alamein line and advancing a few miles beyond them to the east. But there our attack came to a halt and our strength failed. We were met by greatly superior British armoured formations thrusting against our front. Our chance of over-running the remainder of the Eighth Army and occupying Eastern Egypt at one stroke was irretrievably gone.

On the 1st July, as we had foreseen the previous evening, the Afrika Korps was late in mounting its attack on the Alamein line. The attack at first made good progress.

At 02.30 hours I drove to the front from my command post south of El Daba to observe the course of operations. The coast road lay under heavy shell-fire from British artillery. During the morning two British bomber formations unloaded their gifts alongside the *Gefechtsstaffel* and our vehicles. I first went to the Afrika Korps command post and brought the army artillery into action against the British guns. I had already, at one o'clock that morning, asked the Luftwaffe to put everything it had into the battle that day. Now the British artillery fire slowly died away. Under relay bomber and low-flyer attack, we set up our command post at Hill 31 on the " Alarm " track. [*A desert track running close behind the front length of the front and giving rapid access to all troops in the main fighting zone.*] Batteries close by were receiving particular attention from the British aircraft. At about 09.00 hours the 21st Panzer Division ran up against the strong-point Deir el Shein, which was stubbornly defended by the 8th Indian Division, fresh from Iraq.

This was the 18th Indian Infantry Brigade Group—not the complete division.

Once again extensive enemy minefields caused great difficulty. The division's advance came to a halt and violent fighting flared up.

At about midday we observed the development of the battle to our south between the 21st Panzer Division and the Indians. British artillery fire fell round my *Gefechtsstaffel*. The *Kampfstaffel*, which was in position north-west of us, was heavily shelled and several vehicles were burnt out.

The 90th Light Division also reported that their attack had gone in at 03.20 hours. It had made smooth progress at first but had then come to a halt at about 07.30 hours before the fortress front of Alamein which was very strongly built up.

Not until the division moved farther south did its attack begin to flow forward again, at about midday. Slowly the division forced its way into the area south-east of El Alamein. [*There is very soft sand in this area.*] Here it formed a defensive front to the north and south and, at about 16.00 hours, renewed the attack with the object of breaking through to the coast road and thus closing in the Alamein fortress and either destroying its garrison or forcing it to break out. This was a deadly threat for the British and they threw in every gun they could muster, showering our attacking front with a hail of shells. Gradually the tempo of the attack slowed until finally our troops were pinned down in terrific British artillery fire. An S O S came in from the 90th Light Division calling for artillery, as the divisional artillery was no longer battleworthy. I at once sent in *Kampfstaffel* Kiehl south of the division and drove up myself in an armoured car to get a view of the situation and make my decisions. However, heavy British artillery fire soon forced us to turn back.

At 16.00 hours a report came in from Nehring [*Commander of the Afrika Korps*] saying that the Afrika Korps had stormed the greater part of the Indian strong-point Deir el Shein. In the evening the battle at this point was over. Two thousand Indians had been taken prisoner and 30 British guns destroyed or captured.

Late in the afternoon I decided to put everything I could into supporting the southern flank of the 90th Light Division's break-through attempt. Accompanied by my *Gefechtsstaffel*, I joined up with *Kampfstaffel* Kiehl. Furious artillery fire again struck into our ranks. British shells came screaming in from three directions, north, east and south; anti-aircraft tracer streaked through our force. Under this tremendous weight of fire, our attack came to a standstill. Hastily we scattered our vehicles and took cover, as shell after shell crashed into the area we were holding. For two hours Bayerlein and I had to lie out in the open. Suddenly, to add to our troubles, a powerful British bomber force came flying up towards us. Fortunately, it was turned back before it reached us by some German fighters who had been escorting a dive-bomber raid. Despite the heavy British anti-aircraft fire our dive-bombers returned to the attack again and again and fires were soon blazing in the attack area. When, towards evening, the British fire at last began to slacken, I ordered my *Gefechtsstaffel* to get out as fast as they could and return to our old headquarters. The *Kampfstaffel* was to maintain its hold on the area we had reached.

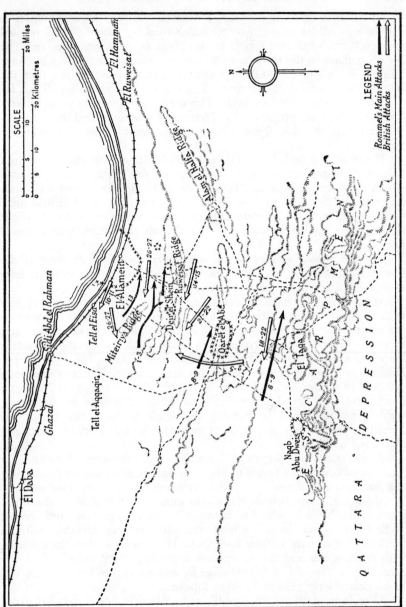

15. The Battle of Alamein, July 1942

At 21.30 hours that evening, I ordered the 90th Light Division to continue its attack through to the coast road by moonlight. I wanted to open the road to Alexandria at this point as quickly as possible. The British defence in the threatened sector was strengthening hour by hour. During the night the Luftwaffe commander reported to me that the British Fleet had left Alexandria. This determined me to go all out for a decision in the next few days. The British no longer seemed to trust their luck and were preparing for a retreat. I was convinced that a break-through over a wide front by my forces would result in complete panic.

However, the 90th Light Division's night attack was also forced to a halt, with heavy artillery and machine-gun fire raking the 1,300 men which were still left to it. To its north the division faced well-built concrete fortifications and to its east a strong system of British field defences. It proved completely impossible to make more than a slight advance against these defences, even though the attack was resumed next day.

The field defences south of the Alamein fortress were far from strong at this time, while disconnected and lacking in depth. Rommel's disappointment at being checked doubtless accounts for his impression of them.

Meanwhile, the Afrika Korps continued its attack on the 2nd July with a thrust to the north-east. Their object was to break through to the coast some eight miles east of El Alamein and then take the fortress by storm. The British at first fell back to the south but shortly afterwards launched a heavy attack on our open southern flank. The 15th Panzer Division was pulled out to parry this attack and its armour was soon involved in violent fighting with the British. The 21st Panzer Division's units were also forced increasingly on to the defensive in the sandy, scrubby country, until by evening the whole of the Afrika Korps was locked in violent defensive fighting against a hundred British tanks and about ten batteries.

This, too, is an exaggerated impression—probably increased because two squadrons of Grants were thrown in here. The German attack was not pushed hard, and prisoners taken during these critical days were obviously very tired men.

More and more British tanks and guns were arriving at the front. General Auchinleck, who had meanwhile taken over command himself at El Alamein, was handling his forces with very considerable skill and tactically better than Ritchie had done. He seemed to view the situation with decided coolness, for he was not allowing himself to be rushed into accepting a " second best " solution by any moves we made. This was to be particularly evident in what followed.

After three days vainly assaulting the Alamein line, I decided that I would call the offensive off for the moment after the next day's attack. Reasons for my decision were the steadily mounting strength of the enemy, the low fighting strength of my own divisions, which amounted by that time to no more than 1,200 to 1,500 men, and above all the terribly strained supply situation.

3 July 1942

DEAREST LU,

One loses all idea of time here. The struggle for the last position before Alexandria is hard. I've been up in the front area for a few days, living in the car or a hole in the ground. The enemy air force gave us a bad time. However, I hope to manage it. Heartfelt thanks for your many dear letters.

A mountain of post is arriving. And Boettcher [*Rommel's secretary*] is not here yet. He's probably with the caravan 450 miles away to the west.

At about midday on the 3rd July, after hours of British artillery bombardment round my H.Q., which was located close by the attack spearhead, I sent the Afrika Korps forward once more against the British line. After an initial success, the attack finally became pinned down in concentric defensive fire. On the same day, signs of disintegration began to show amongst the Italians. An attack by the New Zealanders against the Ariete, which had been detailed to protect the Panzer Army's southern flank, met with complete success. Twenty-eight out of thirty guns were lost to the enemy; 400 men were taken prisoner and the remainder took to their heels in panic.

This reverse took us completely by surprise, for in the weeks of fighting round Knightsbridge, the Ariete—covered, it is true, by German guns and tanks—had fought well against every onslaught of the British, although their casualties had not been light. But now the Italians were no longer equal to the very great demands being made of them.

The resulting threat to our southern flank meant that the Afrika Korps' intended knock-out attack now had to be carried on by the 21st Panzer Division alone, and the weight of the attack was consequently too small. The 90th Light Division joined up with them later, but was equally unable to force a decision. The attack came to a standstill.

In these circumstances a continuation of the attack next day would have resulted in nothing more than a useless attrition of our strength. However valuable a breathing space might be to the British command, we had to give the troops a few days' rest and try to carry out an extensive refit. We intended to return to the attack as soon as possible.

As it was highly probable that the next few days would bring British counter-attacks, the Panzer Army's formations were regrouped for defence along the line we had reached.

4 July 1942

DEAREST LU,

Unfortunately, things are not going as I should like them. Resistance is too great and our strength exhausted. However, I still hope to find a way to achieve our goal. I'm rather tired and fagged out.

5 July 1942

We're going through some extremely critical days. But I'm hoping to see them through. Gause is in trouble again with concussion (shell burst) and Bayerlein will probably have to replace him for a while. Our build-up of strength is very slow. It's not easy to have to hold on like this, only 60 miles from Alexandria. But it, too, will pass.

It was now our intention to withdraw the motorised and armoured units from the front one by one for reorganisation and refit, and to replace them by the Italian infantry divisions, most of which unfortunately were still in the rear areas. The 21st Panzer Division was taken out of the line on the 4th of July. The British, thinking apparently that this was the start of a withdrawal, followed up and broke through our line over a width of four thousand yards; 40 British tanks then thrust on to the west.[1] The situation was highly unpleasant for there was neither anti-tank nor artillery ammunition available for the defence. Artillery Command reported that all batteries had exhausted their ammunition. Luckily, one effective battery was found with the Zech Group, and this succeeded in bringing the British advance to a halt with its last few rounds. I immediately gave orders for the extensive use of decoys, including dummy tanks and 88-mm. A.A. guns, to take away the British taste for further attacks. Then we set about stocking up a few batteries with ammunition. Fortunately, we found 1,500 rounds of artillery ammunition in the captured British strong-point Deir el Shein, which at least enabled us to keep a few batteries of 25-pounders (captured British guns) in action. The Italians still had stocks, and so we were able to regard the crisis as over for the moment.

Unfortunately, the refit of our formations made very slow progress, due to the fact that for some unaccountable reason the few ships engaged on the Africa run were still not arriving at Tobruk or Mersa Matruh but at Benghazi or Tripoli. This meant that all supplies had to be carried by transport columns or our few coastal vessels over a distance of either 750 or 1,400 miles. This, of course, was more than we could manage.

British activity during this period was confined to small-scale sector attacks, which were all effectively beaten off. Gradually, the Italian infantry arrived in the line and took over from our motorised forces. One striking feature of this period was the astonishing amount of ammunition which the British expended in their preliminary barrages. Thus, during the night 7-8th July, British guns fired ten thousand rounds into a three-

[1]Most of these " 40 tanks " were, in fact, armoured cars. Auchinleck's three armoured car regiments had been grouped under the command of 2nd Armoured Brigade, which was rechristened a " light armoured brigade." The part that broke through penetrated almost to Daba.

mile sector of the 15th Panzer Division. Then, in the pitch-dark night,
British infantry worked their way forward as far as our outpost line and
suddenly flung explosive charges into the defence posts. This attack had
been preceded by all-day tank thrusts against my exhausted troops, who
had lain all the time in their trenches and foxholes exposed to the full
blaze of the sun. By these tactics the British did actually succeed in taking
part of our line in this sector. When they tried to move on, however,
they were thrown back by a spirited counter-attack of the sector reserve.

On the 8th July we drew up the following statement of the total
strength of the Panzer Army:

GERMAN TROOPS: The Afrika Korps, with 15th and 21st Panzer
Divisions, having a total of 50 tanks. Each division included a
rifle regiment (strength about 300 men and 10 anti-tank guns)
and an artillery regiment of seven batteries.

90th Light Division, consisting of four infantry regiments, with
an overall strength of 1,500 men; also 30 anti-tank guns and two
batteries.

Three reconnaissance battalions with, in all, 15 armoured cars,
20 armoured troop-carriers and three captured batteries.

The Army artillery, consisting of eleven heavy and four light
batteries, and the Army A.A. Artillery with 26 88-mm. and 25 20-
mm. guns.

ITALIAN TROOPS: XX Motorised Corps, containing two armoured
and one motorised divisions, with a total of 54 tanks and eight
motor battalions (overall strength of the motor battalions 1,600
men). Also 40 anti-tank guns and six light batteries.

Elements of X and XXI Italian Corps consisting in all of eleven
infantry battalions—each of about 200 men—and thirty light and
eleven heavy batteries. Four more heavy batteries were held by
the Italian Army Artillery.[1]

Thus it will be seen that my formations no longer merited the title
of divisions. On the Italian side, this low fighting strength was by no
means the result of battle; it had been more or less the same throughout
the campaign. Only in the motorised and armoured divisions had any
major losses been incurred.

Meanwhile, I had gained a detailed knowledge of the strength of the
Alamein line and discovered its weakest sector, where we intended to

[1] *Note by General Bayerlein.* At full establishment the tank and anti-tank gun strength
of these formations would have been: Afrika Korps (15th and 21st Panzer Divisions):
371 tanks, 246 anti-tank guns. 90th Light Division, 220 anti-tank guns. XX Italian
Motorised Corps (Ariete, Littorio and Trieste Divisions), 430 tanks, 120 anti-tank
guns.

launch a heavy blow on the New Zealanders on the 9th July, capture their position and use it as a base for a break-through.

During the night of the 8th a fighting reconnaissance group of the 21st Panzer Division penetrated into Qaret el Abd, which was held by the New Zealanders. Next morning the Panzer Army, with the 21st Panzer Division, Littorio Armoured Division and 90th Light Division, advanced against the southern sector of the British front, broke through it and thrust onward up to the level of the previous point of penetration in the centre of the front. The New Zealanders withdrew, their movement covered by units of the 5th Indian Division and elements of the 7th Armoured Division.[1] Meanwhile, the 21st Panzer Division had been able to occupy the whole of Qaret el Abd after its evacuation by the New Zealanders. Early in the afternoon, I met General von Bismarck, commander of the 21st Panzer Division, in Qaret el Abd and discussed our further plans. It was our intention to strike on from this point far to the east and thus bring about the fall of the Alamein line.

Qaret el Abd itself lay in extremely favourable terrain and was fortified with well-built concrete strong-points, gun emplacements and extensive minefields. The New Zealanders had left behind quantities of ammunition and equipment, and we were at a loss to understand why they had given the position up. I decided to bring my headquarters forward during the night and set it up in Qaret el Abd, where I intended to spend the night in one of the concrete fortifications. It was a quiet night. Seeing that the 5th Indian and 7th Armoured Divisions had been thrown back by our striking force during the day, we planned to thrust on next day with all our strength.

Next morning, the 10th July, we were awakened at about 05.00 hours by the dull thunder of artillery fire from the north. I at once had an inkling that it boded no good. Presently came the alarming news that the enemy had attacked from the Alamein position and overrun the Sabratha Division, which had been holding a line on either side of the coast road. The enemy was now in hot pursuit westwards after the fleeing Italians and there was a serious danger that they would break through and destroy our supplies. I at once drove north with the *Kampfstaffel* and a combat group of the 15th Panzer Division and directed them on to the battlefield. The attack from Qaret el Abd had to be cancelled, since the portion of our original striking force now left in the south was too weak to execute the thrust to the east.

Meanwhile, the battle on the coast had soon run its course. The Sabratha Division had been nearly annihilated and many of the batteries which had been alloted to it had been lost. It seemed that certain of the

---

[1]The withdrawal was ordered to avoid the risks of holding on to an isolated position. There was no real penetration of the " Alamein line "—nor, in fact, any " line " in the normal military sense of the term. It was also hoped that the withdrawal might disconcert Rommel and put him off his stride.

battery commanders had not fired on the approaching enemy because they had had no orders. The Italians had left their line, many of them in panic, and, with no attempt at defending themselves, sought the open desert, throwing away arms and ammunition as they ran. It was primarily the Panzer Army's staff, led at the time by Lieut.-Col. von Mellenthin, whom we had to thank for bringing the British attack to a halt. Machine and anti-aircraft guns had been hurriedly collected together and with the help of part of the 328th Infantry Regiment of 164th Light Division, which was just on its way up to the front, an improvised defence line had been formed about three thousand yards south-west of Army H.Q.

At about midday the forces which had been drawn off from the southern front moved forward against the flank of the British salient, but their attack came to a standstill in terrific British artillery fire from El Alamein. Next day, the 11th July, the British continued their attack south of the coast road, using powerful artillery and air support, and several more Italian units, this time of the Trieste, were overpowered and taken prisoner. Increasing numbers of troops had to be drawn off from the southern front and thrown into the fighting south of the coast road. Soon the whole of the Army artillery was brought into action, after which the British attack slowly petered out.

This British drive along the coast had brought about the destruction of the bulk of the Sabratha and a large part of the Trieste, and important sectors of country had fallen into enemy hands. We were forced to the conclusion that the Italians were no longer capable of holding their line. Far too much had already been demanded of them by Italian standards and now the strain had become too great.[1]

There were splendid Italian officers who made tremendous efforts to sustain their men's morale. Navarrini (XXI Italian Army Corps) for example, for whom I had the highest regard, did everything he could. I shall return to this question of the Italian forces in a later chapter.

There could be no question of launching any large-scale attack in the immediate future. I was compelled to order every last German soldier out of his tent or rest camp up to the front, for, in face of the virtual default of a large proportion of our Italian fighting power, the situation was beginning to take on crisis proportions.

THE FRONT BECOMES STATIC

Day by day now, reinforcements and fresh formations were flowing to the Eighth Army, and the British troops were once again firmly

[1]Auchinleck was aiming to produce a crack by striking at Rommel's soft spot—his Italian troops and their morale. Dorman-Smith, Auchinleck's chief assistant in this crucial phase, was an ardent advocate of the indirect approach. Two years earlier he had helped to devise the plan through which Graziani's army was taken in rear and overthrown at Sidi Barrani.

in the hands of their commander. With the abandonment of our offensive plans which the conditions had forced on us, we finally had to give up all idea of fighting it out with the British in the Alamein line while their formations were all still suffering under the impact of the Eighth Army's great losses during the summer battle. For the British commander was now in a position to press on at full speed with the replenishment and refitting of his beaten army. It had proved impossible to follow up our success in the Marmarica to final victory.

The front had now grown static and the British Command was in its element, for the modern form of infantry battle and static warfare was its strongest point. Local attacks carried forward under the protection of infantry tanks and artillery were the British speciality. The Alamein line abutted on the sea in the north and in the south opened out into the Qattara depression—a flat plain of loose sand studded with numerous salt marshes and hence completely impassable for motor vehicles. The line could not be turned, and as a result the war took on a form of which both sides possessed great experience and theoretical knowledge and in which neither could produce any revolutionary technique which would come as an innovation to the other. In static warfare, victory goes to the side which can fire the more ammunition.

My endeavour at El Alamein had been to escape from this rigid, static warfare—in which the British were masters and for which their infantry and tank crews had been trained—and to gain the open desert in front of Alexandria, where I could have exploited our definite tactical superiority in open desert warfare; but I had not succeeded. The British had brought my formations to a halt.

During the past few days the British Command had been showing considerable enterprise and audacity. They had learnt that Italians who were suffering from the apathy of sheer exhaustion were easy meat. It was therefore probable that they would continue their attacks.

To repair the unpleasant situation which had resulted from the rout of the Sabratha, and to eliminate the threat to our southern front caused by the British positions west of El Alamein, I decided to launch the 21st Panzer Division against the El Alamein fortress. The attack (on the 13th July) was to be supported by every gun and every aeroplane we could muster. The division was first to cut the fortress area off from the east in a lightning advance, and then to break into it.

12 July 1942

DEAREST LU,
    The very serious situation of the past few days is slowly being overcome. But the air is still electric with crisis. I hope to make another step forward to-morrow.

13 July 1942

To-day is to be another decisive day in this hard struggle. Things are already on the move all over the desert. This short but heartfelt greeting to you and Manfred.

But the attack miscarried, not even reaching the line of the 9th Australian Division, which had taken over the fortress area from the 1st South African several days before. The reason for this failure—apart from the heavy enemy artillery fire and their extremely well-constructed line, which included many dug-in tanks—was probably that the 21st Panzer Division's infantry had not assembled for the attack in the Italian line but in an area two or three thousand yards behind it. As a result the British gunners had been able to lay their guns on the attacking troops early in the operation and bring them to a halt by concentrated fire before they had passed our own lines.

In the evening I decided to break off the action. I was in an extremely bad humour, for a heavy sandstorm had been blowing all day, which had robbed the British of all visibility. How well this could have served us! We had indeed missed a unique opportunity.

This remark is hard to understand, and would seem to spring from emotion rather than reason. Failure was almost inevitable in view of the way the general situation had changed to Rommel's disadvantage.

14 July 1942

Dearest Lu,
My expectations for yesterday's attack were bitterly disappointed. It achieved no success whatever. However, the blow must be borne and we're going forward with fresh courage to new operations. Physically I'm very well. I'm wearing shorts for the first time to-day —it's pretty hot. The battle in the East[1] is going splendidly, which gives us courage to hang on here.

I again ordered the 21st Panzer Division forward on the following day, the 14th July. The objective this time was the position which the Sabratha had given up west of El Alamein, which was now being strongly fortified by the Australians. The attack went in after heavy air bombardment. But the infantry was too late again and failed to take full advantage of the effects of the preliminary bombing. Heavy British air attacks pounded our vehicle formations and the British artillery again came into action with every gun. With the sun at their backs, our units fought their way forward from south to north as far as the area between the road and railway, where the attack came to a halt. Fierce fighting followed with the Australians, whom we knew only too well from the time of the

[1]The German offensive, launched at the end of June, with the aim of capturing Stalingrad and the Caucasus oilfields.

Tobruk siege, and lasted well into the night. We had originally intended to continue this attack next day, but now a new and more serious set-back forced us to a different course.

That night, the 14-15th July, the British—mainly the 1st Armoured Division—attacked on the Ruweisat Ridge, and gained a penetration into the X Italian Corps's positions. Soon afterwards they succeeded in breaking through the Brescia Division and penetrating as far as the German tank and gun positions, where their leading troops were halted in severe hand-to-hand fighting. Early next morning, they continued their attack and succeeded in taking Ruweisat Ridge, from which point their main force struck off in a westerly direction. Part of this force turned east again into the rear of the Brescia and Pavia, with the result that the bulk of these two formations fell prisoner that morning to the British.

Nor was this all, for our own line south-east of Deir el Shein collapsed; our anti-aircraft detachments were soon overrun, because of their reluctance to fire into the swarms of Italians who had already been taken prisoner. Still in the early morning the British broke into Deir el Shein itself, and it was only with the utmost difficulty that the worst calamity —the loss of this strong-point—could be prevented by the reconnaissance regiments and a combat group of the Afrika Korps.

I immediately broke off 21st Panzer Division's attack in the north and brought them into the Afrika Korps's assembly area south-west of Deir el Shein.

The Panzer Corps's counter-attack was launched in the afternoon and gained ground slowly against a stubbornly resisting adversary. By evening the penetration had been sealed off. 1,200 British prisoners were taken in that day's fighting.

Next day, the 16th July, the British attacked again, but this time only locally. After intensive artillery preparation, the Australians attacked in the early hours of the morning with tank support and took several strong-points held by the Sabratha [i.e. what remained of it]. Many of the prisoners which they took in this action were sent back to our own lines. The rest they carried off to the rear. Under the concentric fire of the German-Italian artillery and the terrific effect of our mobile A.A., the enemy soon relinquished the territory he had gained, leaving behind a considerable number of dead and wounded.

After touring the front at 05.00 hours and becoming involved in a violent British artillery barrage and an R.A.F. bombing attack, I con-ferred with the Corps Commanders at the Afrika Korps H.Q. that morning on how to maintain command of the difficult situation. Our deliberations were badly interrupted, for no less than nine bombing raids took place between six in the morning and three in the afternoon in the immediate vicinity of the conference.

The night of the 16th was quiet; yet when I arrived at the operations vehicle at about six next morning, wireless messages were coming in one after the other. The Australians had attacked from El Alamein again, this time towards the south-west. They had soon penetrated our line in the Trento's and Trieste's sectors and had taken a large number of Italians prisoner. Now they were trying to roll up our front to the south.

17 July 1942

DEAREST LU,

Things are going downright badly for me at the moment, at any rate, in the military sense. The enemy is using his superiority, especially in infantry, to destroy the Italian formations one by one, and the German formations are much too weak to stand alone. It's enough to make one weep.

We had been planning an attack in the central sector to retake the territory which had been lost during the British assault on the Italian Corps, but this, of course, now had to be abandoned, for the German troops we had assembled for it had to move north at top speed to seal off this new penetration. Soon the Australian attack began to lose way in front of a line quickly improvised by German units. My " Africans " counter-attacked in the afternoon and re-occupied our old position in the evening. The enemy made similar attacks on the Trento elsewhere but suffered a sharp rebuff under the fire of Italian artillery and heavy air attacks.

On that day every last German reserve had to be thrown in to beat off the British attacks. Our forces were now so small in comparison with the steadily growing strength of the British that we were going to have to count ourselves lucky if we managed to go on holding our line at all. Field-Marshal Kesselring and Count Cavallero arrived at my head-quarters at about 16.00 hours that afternoon. Cavallero, typically, set about belittling our supply difficulties again, just as I had been stressing how serious they were. A long wrangle followed, until Kesselring and I finally asked for concrete decisions. This conversation made very clear again just how near the bottom of the barrel we were, and how little we could rely on the help of the Italian authorities. Cavallero promised that barges would now be used to build up the army's supplies and that the railway to the front would soon be put back into service. More Italian formations were promised. After our experience in the past we were sceptical—rightly, as the future showed.

18 July 1942

DEAREST LU,

Yesterday was a particularly hard and critical day. We pulled through again. But it can't go on like it for long, otherwise the front will crack. Militarily, this is the most difficult period I've ever been through. There's help in sight, of course, but whether we will live to see it is a question. You know what an incurable optimist I am. But there are situations where everything is dark. However, this period too, will pass.

During the next four days the front was more or less quiet, the British undertaking no major attacks. It was the calm before the storm. On the 19th and 20th July, we detected British assembly areas in the central sector of the front, in which Auchinleck was concentrating masses of tanks and artillery.

On the night of the 21st the storm broke. Waves of British infantry surged against the 15th Panzer Division's sector and broke into their line. The penetration was sealed off, however, and 500 British were taken prisoner. As a result of the immense casualties which the Italians had recently suffered our line was now very thinly manned, even though we had shortened it by withdrawing to a line on the level of the captured strong-points, Deir el Shein and Qaret el Abd. We had virtually no reserves.

An attack had also been launched on the northern front by a strong force of Australians supported by tanks. This attack gained ground yard by yard towards the south-west against fierce resistance by the German-Italian infantry.

Then, at about 08.00 hours [22nd], the main British attack was launched in the central sector by a force comprised of the 2nd New Zealand, 5th Indian and 1st Armoured Divisions, together with 23rd Army Tank Brigade, which had arrived from Britain only that month. Supported by over a hundred tanks, the British troops surged against our line at Deir el Shein and farther south. South of the strong-point they overran our positions, after the German-Italian infantry holding them had fought to the end, and by nine o'clock were already dangerously far behind our front. Finally, the tank spearhead came to a standstill on the Steinpiste [Stony Track], where a sizeable number of British tanks was shot up. Then the 21st Panzer Division's armour rolled forward and threw the British back. More and more British tanks were hit.

With the situation so critical in the central sector, an increasing number of formations had to be drawn off from the southern end of the front. The battle, which we fought with the maximum of mobility and which demanded the use of our very last reserves, raged the whole of that day. Gradually the force of the British attack was blunted. In the evening the Australians attacked in the north again, but without any notable success. Their advancing infantry were pinned to the ground by our defensive fire and the tanks which broke through were soon destroyed by my mobile formations.

When evening came, our defence had scored an undoubted success. 1,400 British prisoners had been taken and 140 enemy tanks put out of action. [The figure of tanks destroyed is approximately correct]. Most of the damaged British tanks lay in territory which we controlled and thus could not be salvaged by the enemy's recovery services.

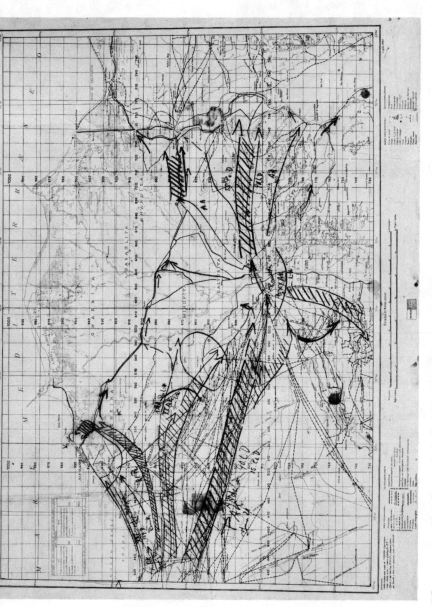

The map on which Rommel chalked his intended movements should he break through at Alamein [See Appendix]

Obstacles on the shores of France, Spring 1944

But our losses were also not negligible, especially in view of our low man-power. Something more than three weak infantry battalions had been lost and, although the armour had come through without any serious casualties, we were still very worried and regarded the prospect of further British attacks with considerable disquiet.

But the British apparently thought better of it and were probably suffering equal exhaustion. Next day was quiet again, except in the air, where our Luftwaffe attacked the enemy with everything it had. Before the enemy's attack, the Panzer Army's sappers had been feverishly laying minefield after minefield and this work was now resumed. Mines from all sources, British, German and Italian, were dug into the sand and soon several sectors were protected by minefields of considerable strength.

After the fighting of the 22nd July, I had the following signal transmitted to all troops: " I send all ranks my special appreciation of their gallant action during our victorious defence of 22nd July. I am positive that any further enemy attacks will meet with the same reception."

Meanwhile, replacement infantry units had been slowly trickling into our lines for several weeks past and the very large gaps in the ranks of our formations were being gradually filled—not all, unfortunately, by " fit for tropical service " troops. Elements of the 164th Infantry Division had been flown across from Crete, but had brought neither heavy weapons nor vehicles. Several units of an Italian parachute division—excellent troops by their appearance—also arrived at the front. All this while the army was working at feverish speed to strengthen its line. Yet, in spite of all these improvements in the situation we could not regard the immediate danger as over until an adequate operational reserve had been built up behind the front.

26 July 1942

DEAREST LU,

A fairly quiet day yesterday. Went down to the great [*Qattara*] Depression—a fantastic sight. It lies far below sea level. Our territory is slowly filling up again. The worst of our troubles are disappearing.

On the moonlit night of the 26th July, the Australians attacked again, this time in brigade strength. Their objective was the German line west of the Alamein-Abu Dweis track. The assembly had been made in all secrecy, and the assault, which was preceded by a violent R.A.F. bombing attack, consequently achieved a considerable measure of surprise. Despite the curtain of fire which was at once put down by the German-Italian artillery, the Australians succeeded in penetrating our front and wiping out the greater part of one German battalion. However, a dashing counter-attack by Combat Group Briehl, 3rd Reconnaissance Regiment and *Kampfstaffel* Kiehl eventually smashed in the Australian wedge, and threw the enemy back to his own line with heavy losses.

The central sector of our line was also attacked by the newly re-plenished 50th British Division, and part of an Italian battalion was overrun. A counter-attack by the 200th Infantry Regiment and a combat group of the Afrika Korps succeeded here, too, in throwing the enemy back to his own line.

The attack here was delivered by the 69th Infantry Brigade (of the 50th Division), which was to have been followed up by the 1st Armoured Division. But the com-mander was not satisfied that a sufficiently wide gap had been cleared in the minefield by the South African engineers, and his delay in advancing spoilt the prospects of the attack as a whole. The 69th Infantry Brigade was temporarily cut off, and suffered heavily before it was extricated.

The British had again suffered heavy casualties—a thousand prisoners and 32 tanks—and their command now lost all taste for further attacks. The German-Italian front had shown itself to be no longer penetrable by forces of the size they were committing. It was now certain that we could continue to hold our front, and that, after the crises we had been through, was at least something. Although the British losses in this Alamein fighting had been higher than ours, yet the price to Auchinleck had not been excessive, for the one thing that had mattered to him was to halt our advance, and that, unfortunately, he had done.

Rommel's final sentence is the final verdict on Auchinleck's achievement in these crucial weeks. The opening sentence, however, is not so correct. Auchinleck had not " lost all taste for further attacks," although some of his subordinates had. Reviewing the results he " most reluctantly concluded " that the Eighth Army was not capable of pursuing the offensive successfully without fresh reserves and fuller training. It had suffered over 13,000 casualties during the July struggle at Alamein, but had taken over 7,000 prisoners (including more than a thousand Germans). The price would have been lower, and the gains greater, if the execution of the plans had been more skilled. Even as it was, the difference in the total loss on either side was not large—and Rommel was less able to afford the loss. His account makes it clear how perilously close he was to defeat in July. Moreover, his frustration in itself was fatal.

RETROSPECT

So ended the great campaign of the summer. It had begun with a fantastic victory. But, after the capture of Tobruk, the immense strength of the British Empire had begun to tell again. There had only been a few days during which we could have hoped to conquer Alamein and take the Suez Canal area. While we, on our side, had had to fight every new action with the same formations, the British had been able to take their battered divisions out of the line for refitting, and to throw in fresh formations fully equipped and up to full battle strength. My troops had remained in the fight. Their numbers had grown continually smaller, while losses from dead, wounded and sick had steadily increased. Again and again, it had been the same battalions, carried for the most part in captured vehicles, who had driven up to the British line, leapt from their lorries and stormed through the sand up to the enemy. Again and again, it had been the same tank crews who had ridden their tanks into battle and the same gunners who had pushed their guns into position. The deeds performed in these weeks by both officers and men had reached the limit of human endurance.

I had made tremendous demands on my forces, and spared neither the men, the officers nor myself. I knew that the fall of Tobruk and the collapse of the Eighth Army was the one moment in the African war when the road to Alexandria lay open and virtually undefended, and my staff and I would have been fools not to have gone all out to seize this unique opportunity. If success had depended, as in times gone by, on the strength of will of my men and their officers, then we would have overrun Alamein. But our sources of supply had dried up—thanks to the idleness and muddle of the supply authorities on the mainland.

And then the power of resistance of many of the Italian formations had collapsed. The duties of comradeship, for me particularly as their Commander-in-Chief, compel me to state unequivocally that the defeats which the Italian formations suffered at El Alamein in early July were not the fault of the Italian soldier. The Italian was willing, unselfish and a good comrade, and, considering the conditions under which he served, had always given far better than the average. There is no doubt that the achievement of every Italian unit, especially of the motorised forces, far surpassed anything that the Italian Army had done for a hundred years. Many Italian generals and officers won our admiration both as men and soldiers.

The cause of the Italian defeat had its roots in the whole Italian military and state system, in their poor armament and in the general lack of interest in the war shown by many of the leading Italians, both officers and statesmen. This Italian failure frequently prevented the realisation of my plans.

In general terms, the defects which existed in the Italian armed forces arose from the following causes:

The Italian command was, for the most part, not equal to the task of carrying on war in the desert, where the requirement was lightning decision followed by immediate action. The training of the Italian infantryman fell far short of the standard required by modern warfare. His equipment was so utterly bad, that for that reason alone, he was unable to stand his ground without German help. Perhaps the best example of the inferior quality of the Italian armament—apart from the grave technical defects of their tanks, with their short-range guns and under-powered engines—was to be found in the artillery, with its low mobility and short range. Their supply of anti-tank weapons was totally inadequate. Rations were so bad that the Italian soldier frequently had to ask his German comrade for food. Particularly harmful was the all-pervading differentiation between officer and man. While the men had to make shift without field-kitchens, the officers, or many of them, refused adamantly to forgo their several course meals. Many officers, again, considered it unnecessary to put in an appearance during battle and thus set the men an example. All in all, therefore, it was small wonder that the Italian soldier, who incidentally was extraordinarily modest in his needs, developed a feeling of inferiority which accounted for his occasional failure in moments of crisis. There was no foreseeable hope of a change for the better in any of these matters, although many of the bigger men among the Italian officers were making sincere efforts in that direction.

During the march to El Alamein, I had wanted above all else to avoid another mutual build-up of material taking place on any line west of Alexandria. I had not wanted the British to have another chance of re-equipping, for I knew very well that we would then have an enemy to tackle whose material superiority would be even greater than it had been in the Marmarica, and who would also have learnt from his defeats during the summer. But the main thing I had wanted to avoid was the war settling down at El Alamein into mechanised static warfare with a stabilised front, because this was just what the British officers and men had been trained for. The good points of the British soldier, his tenacity, for instance, would have the maximum effect and the bad points, such as his immobility and rigidity, none at all.

But we had failed in these intentions and the future did not look very bright.

We had, of course, dealt the British severe losses. Between the 26th of May and the 20th of July, 60,000 British, South Africans, Indians, New Zealanders, French and Australians had found their way into our prisoner-of-war camps. My men had destroyed well over 2,000 British tanks and armoured vehicles. The equipment of an entire British offensive army lay destroyed in the desert and thousands upon thousands of their vehicles were now being used by my troops.

But our losses had also been heavy. On the German side alone, 2,300 officers and men had been killed, 7,500 wounded and 2,700 taken prisoner. Of the Italian forces, over 1,000 officers and men had been killed, more than 10,000 wounded and some 5,000 taken prisoner. Needless to say, the losses of material had also been very considerable.

Thus after immense victories, the great summer campaign had ended in a dangerous lull.

2 Aug. 1942

Dearest Lu,

All quiet, except for intense air activity against my supply lines. I'm thankful for every day's respite we get. A lot of sickness. Unfortunately many of the older officers are going down now. Even I am feeling very tired and limp, though I have got a chance to look after myself a bit just at the moment.

Unfortunately, the British railway from Tobruk to the front is not yet in operation. We're waiting for locomotives.

Holding on to our Alamein position has given us the severest fighting we've yet seen in Africa. We've all got heat diarrhœa now, but it's bearable. A year ago I had jaundice and that was much worse.

5 Aug. 1942

Trouble with supplies. Rintelen does little in Rome and constantly lets himself be done in the eye, for the Italian supplies are working excellently.

10 Aug. 1942

Kesselring was here yesterday. We reached agreement over what is to happen. Now it's a question of making full use of the few weeks to get ready. The situation is changing daily to my advantage.

The (nominal) establishment of the German forces at the end of August, 1942 was:

Afrika Korps:	25,000 men;
	371 tanks;
	246 anti-tank guns;
	72 artillery pieces;
	5,600 other vehicles (including 600 tracked).
90th Light Division:	12,500 men;
	220 anti-tank guns;
	24 artillery pieces (the balance was not sent to Africa).
	2,400 vehicles (including 250 tracked).
Army Artillery:	3,300 men;
	56 artillery pieces;
	1,000 vehicles (of which 100 were tracked).
164th Infantry Div.:	11,500 men;
	45 anti-tank guns;
	36 artillery pieces.

(It was intended to convert this into a " light " division, but the required increase of anti-tank guns and motor transport was not provided; the actual vehicle-strength was only about 300, including captured British vehicles.)

CHAPTER XII

RACE AGAINST TIME

AFTER THE temporary cessation of our attack on the Alamein line and the successful repulse of the enemy's counter-attack, a calm set in over the front. Both sides sought to use the breathing space to refit their forces and bring up fresh troops. Once again we were in a race to reorganise.

All efforts of the Panzer Army were directed towards an early resumption of the offensive, for its success during the summer had, as expected, struck fear and dismay into the Allied camps in New York and London. It was therefore obvious that the Anglo-Americans would spare no effort to prevent a further advance by the Panzer Army to Alexandria. But their shipping from Britain or America required two to three months for the journey round the Cape to North Africa and we therefore had a few weeks' grace before the immense reinforcements which they had no doubt planned for the Eighth Army after the fall of Tobruk, could reach African soil. We reckoned on mid-September as the arrival date of the Eighth Army's reinforcements (other than normal routine replacements) from Britain and America. The balance of strength would then go so heavily against us that our chances of mounting an offensive would be gone for good. So we intended to strike first.

There were other reasons why we had to get our attack launched as quickly as possible. Every day that went by the British laid more and more mines on their front. An outflanking move round the main Alamein position, which was what we were planning, first required a breakthrough in the southern part of the British front, and the difficulties facing such a project were growing steadily greater. The decisive element in our plan was speed and surprise—we had to make our thrust through the British line and win through to the open country beyond as quickly as possible in order to present the unsuspecting enemy with what amounted to an accomplished fact. If we were first to have to spend a long time overcoming strong British defences this element of surprise would be gone.

Moreover, with the Near East and India close at hand, the British would soon be in a position to face us at El Alamein with forces of very considerable strength. Fresh troops would be brought up to the enemy

front from India, Syria and Iraq. Equipment could be found for them
by combing out every available supply dump and using the regular
shipments as they arrived in Egypt. We estimated that by the 20th of
August, counting both the new and the reorganised units, the British
would have 70 infantry battalions, 900 tanks and armoured vehicles,
550 light and heavy guns and 850 anti-tank guns available for action.[1]

Already, at the end of July-beginning of August, the 50th British and
1st South African Divisions were back at the front, almost entirely
replenished. Soon afterwards the 10th Indian Division was also battle-
worthy again, after reorganisation with units from other formations.
Several large convoys had arrived in Suez during July and air reconnaissance had reported the arrival of several hundred thousand tons of
shipping.

Thus a strenuous effort was going to be necessary in the field of supply
if we were to keep pace with the steadily growing strength of the Eighth
Army. But it was in this very question of supply that a serious crisis was
upon us. The causes of this crisis and its effects were as follows:

Since the end of July, the R.A.F. had shifted the main weight of
its activity to our lines of communication between the African ports and
the front, where they were shooting up our transport columns and sinking
one barge and coastal vessel after the other. No ship lying in the harbours
at Bardia and Mersa Matruh, and frequently even at Tobruk, was safe
from the attentions of the British bombers. Our Luftwaffe had its hands
full at the front, where British air-power was also steadily increasing, and
could only supply very meagre forces for the protection of the coast road
and coastal waters. Thus, at the beginning of August, the R.A.F. sank
three coastal vessels in Bardia harbour on one day alone. The coastal
waters were also being harassed by British naval forces.

In the absence of Italian escort destroyers, the bulk of our supply
ships were having to run into Benghazi or Tobruk, a fact which made
very heavy demands on our road transport. To make matters worse,
Tobruk was heavily attacked by British bombers on the 8th of August,

---

[1]This estimate was approximately correct—counting the forces refitting behind the
front and those disposed for the defence of the Nile Delta. The front was held by 5
divisions (including 1 armoured), but in the rear there were 6 more divisions (including
3 armoured) as well as several independent brigades. Two of these divisions were
brought up to the front before the end of August.

By that time the British had on the Alamein front about 480 tanks, 230 armoured
cars, 300 medium and field guns, 400 anti-tank guns. (Rommel's tank strength had
been built up by then to a total of 229 German tanks, and 281 Italian.)

Meanwhile the War Cabinet had appointed General Alexander to replace Auchinleck
as Commander-in-Chief, Middle East, and General Montgomery had taken over
command of the Eighth Army.

Rommel had 4 German and 8 Italian divisions (2 of each being armoured). A com-
parative reckoning of the two sides in number of divisions is, of course, no true comparison.
Rommel's were being made up to strength much more slowly than the British, and his
Italian divisions were too poorly equipped to be reckoned on the same terms as the
British or German—apart from the question of fighting spirit.

and its capacity reduced by 20 per cent through the destruction of its principal wharf. This hit us very hard.

During the early part of August the supplies we received barely covered our daily requirements. Replenishment was hardly to be thought of and a build-up out of the question. The vehicle situation was particularly worrying; the bad state of the roads and the continual heavy demands we were having to make on our transport were resulting in a steady 35 per cent of our vehicle strength being in for repair. As some 85 per cent or so of our transport still consisted of vehicles of British or American manufacture, for which we had no great stocks of spares, it is easy to imagine the difficulties our repair shops were having to contend with.

The units of the 164th Division and Italian Folgore Parachute Division which were just then arriving, possessed no vehicles of their own and were thus becoming a load on the transport columns of other formations.

Our endeavour now was to have all captured vehicles gradually withdrawn from the transport units and replaced by new or repaired vehicles of our own manufacture. Standing ready in Italy, some of them for a year past, were upwards of 2,000 lorries and nearly 100 guns of all kinds awaiting transport across to the German forces. Owing to various troubles with our heavy shipping at that time, the transport of this material to Africa was proceeding desperately slowly. A further 1,000 vehicles and 120 tanks were held on call for us in Germany.

Of the German element of the Panzer Army, 17,000 men had been in action in Africa ever since the beginning of the campaign, and all of them had suffered more or less severely from the effects of the African climate. It was in most cases, only their enthusiasm and remarkable *esprit de corps* which had kept them with the Panzer Army. But now it was time for the majority of them, if they were to avoid serious damage to their health, to leave Africa and return to Europe. Much as I regretted losing these battle-tried veterans, I was forced to ask for their relief, since by far the majority of them were, with the best of intentions, no longer usable in a crisis. The German divisions (now numbering four) were short of a further 17,000 men, caused by death, sickness, wounds and, above all, the very low unit strength with which they had started. Hence, our problems were also very serious in the field of personnel. [*General Bayerlein estimates the German fighting strength at this time at 34,000 men.*]

Nevertheless, the worst difficulties were with bulk supply. Here there existed serious weaknesses of organisation which worked heavily against us. Control of shipping across the Mediterranean lay in the hands of the Commando Supremo. The only German office which could exercise an influence on supply matters was under the charge of General von Rintelen, who had been German Military Attaché in Rome for years. Field Marshal Kesselring and Admiral Weichhold were only called in on questions concerned with the air and sea protection of convoys and ports.

The only influence which the Panzer Army Command could exercise on the supply question was the production of a " priority list," that is to say a list showing the order in which the material stored in Italy should be brought to Africa—if at all.

We had no influence whatever over the shipping lists, the ports of arrival or—most important—the proportion of German to Italian cargoes. In theory this was supposed to be a ratio of 1:1; in fact, it moved steadily to the German disadvantage. A good example was the case of the Pistoia Division. This division, which was scheduled to arrive in mid-September and was intended for use in Libya instead of at the front, was shipped across with two-thirds of its men and between three and four hundred of its vehicles at the beginning of August, although only 60 vehicles had then arrived for 164th Division, which already had units in the line. Then again, while many of the Italian units in the Alamein line were being refitted at an astonishing speed and were exchanging their vehicles one after the other for new ones from Italy, not one German replacement vehicle left Italy for the Panzer Army up to the beginning of August.

It is always a bad thing when political matters are allowed to affect supply or the planning of operations. Where these two questions are concerned, any ill-feelings deriving from other fields must be swept ruthlessly aside and all efforts must be concentrated, regardless of all other considerations, to the one purpose of military victory.

The Panzer Army contained approximately two Germans for every one Italian (82,000 to 42,000). The following shows what proportion of supplies for the two forces were shipped across the Mediterranean by the Commando Supremo during the month of August:

For the German element of the Panzer Army: 8,200 tons (32 per cent of requirements);

For the Italian element of the Panzer Army, the Italian troops in Libya and the civilian population: 25,700 tons (800 tons of which were for civilian needs).

For the German Luftwaffe: 8,500 tons.

These figures speak for themselves.

The Panzer Army fought for its interests by every means open to it, without, however, achieving any improvement. It invariably finished in a battle of words. When, for instance, we protested against the dispatch of the Pistoia to Africa, the Italians produced the story that it had been done with shipping newly brought up from the Ægean. In the circumstances at that time, one might have thought that they would have put every ship they could lay their hands on at the service of the Panzer Army, to enable it to continue its fight against the British.

Cavallero, who from time to time visited the front, often promised to have all manner of things put right. But it just as frequently happened that on his next visit he would say with a laugh that he had made many a promise in his time and not all of them could be kept.

The unloading of shipping in Africa was also a terribly leisurely affair. It was only too often a triumph of antiquated ideas, lack of initiative and a total absence of any sort of technical ingenuity. Thus we found it completely impossible to get the port capacity of Tobruk increased—600 tons a day was all it could handle, with the result that ships were kept far too long in the harbour exposed to the danger of destruction by British bombers. We made repeated demands for increased port construction, the building of unloading facilities in neighbouring inlets by Italian labour, the provision of larger quantities of Italian dock equipment and stronger air defences for Tobruk—all, of course, with little success.

We had built tremendous hopes round the captured British military railway from Tobruk to El Daba, and had supposed that large-scale railway traffic would soon be organised to the front, thus greatly relieving the pressure on our road transport. But here, too, nothing immediate was done.

The cause of the trouble—as I have already said—lay in the over-organisation and muddle which characterised the Italian supply staffs.

Probably General von Rintelen had too many diplomatic ties rising out of his duties as Attaché to be able to apply himself really effectively to the service of our cause. He was also considerably inferior in rank and authority to the Italians with whom he had to deal. Another factor responsible for a great deal of our difficulty was the political relationship between Germany and Italy, which prevented us drawing the Italian command's attention, frankly and openly, to their weaknesses and demanding that they be put right. Instead of bringing matters to open discussion, a course which would have been far more in keeping with a true alliance than this continued insincerity, it was thought better to keep up outward pretences by declaring all the time that everything was in order—meanwhile, losing battles. This attitude of the German Government limited Herr von Rintelen's scope, and his military rank was not high enough to allow him to protest on matters of such high policy.

It follows then that what was needed was a single authority to control the organisation and protection of all sea traffic in Mediterranean and North African waters, with full powers of command over all Axis land, sea and air forces concerned in the operation and with the particular function of giving support to our demands. I therefore proposed to the High Command that the control of Mediterranean shipping should be vested in Field Marshal Kesselring, with special powers. In making this suggestion, I had the following considerations in mind:

Field Marshal Kesselring had a personal interest in helping us at Alamein; he had considerable strength of will, a first-class talent for diplomacy and organisation, and a considerable knowledge of technical matters.

Kesselring had the Luftwaffe and Goering behind him and could thus command sufficient support at the highest level to enable him to tackle questions of high policy in relation to Italy.

This suggestion, unfortunately, was not acted upon either early enough or in the form in which I wanted it.

The consequences of all these weaknesses were very serious. The fact that the German formations of the Panzer Army consumed, between the 1st and 20th August, almost double the supplies that were brought across the Mediterranean in the same period, tells its own story. The result was an even further diminution of our already meagre stocks. At the end of this period the German forces were below strength to the extent of 16,000 men, 210 tanks, 175 troop-carriers and armoured cars, and—at a low estimate—1,500 other vehicles.[1] If we had not had the big British dumps in the Marmarica and Western Egypt to fall back on we should never have been able to exist at all. Rations were miserable and so monotonous that we were sick of the sight of them. The petrol and ammunition situation was as serious as ever, and we were having to exercise the strictest economy. We were frequently compelled to put a complete ban on all forms of harassing fire merely in order to save ammunition. The British, on the other hand, were able to exercise the full weight of their material superiority and hammered away with their artillery for hours on end at our troops, who were forced to endure frightful hardships in the heat and desolation of their positions.

During the month of August, no effort should have been spared to provide an adequate build-up of petrol and ammunition on African soil. That this was not done I have already made clear. The refitting of our German formations also left much to be desired. Despite the high Italian supply quotas, even the infantry units of XX Italian Motorised Corps, which were to be a very important factor in the offensive which the Duce was always demanding from us, were short of half their vehicles; thus only four of their ten motor battalions were mobile, the rest being completely valueless in the open desert. Of the 220 tanks which this corps now possessed, at least half of them threatened to break down after the shortest run, due to their worn-out engines and inexperienced drivers.

On the British side, we had to expect that a large convoy of well over 100,000 tons, laden with a cargo of the very latest weapons and war material for the Eighth Army, would arrive in Suez at the beginning of September. The Panzer Army was therefore insistent on launching its offensive before that date. Because of the general shortage of supplies, planning had to be limited to striking a blow at the Eighth Army in the

[1]In enumerating these deficiencies, Rommel counted in his actual strength the captured British vehicles that he was using.

Alamein line and taking possession of the territory around Alexandria and Cairo. But the date of the attack had to be postponed again and again, for it depended on the arrival of large quantities of petrol and ammunition, without which an offensive was impossible.

The Panzer Army put every form of pressure it could on the supply authorities to provide it with the necessary build-up in time. But not the least thing was done, although it was never at any time impossible. Probably it was thought in Rome that victory in Africa was already in the bag. However, at the end of August, Cavallero informed me that tankers had been dispatched to get to us in time for the offensive. If these were sunk, other ships, which were already assembled, would sail at once under appropriate escort. Kesselring promised the Panzer Army that in an emergency his transport squadrons would fly across 500 tons of petrol a day. Cavallero said he would use submarines and warships for the carriage of the most urgent material.

24 Aug. 1942

DEAREST LU,

I was unable to write again yesterday. I'm now well enough to get up occasionally. But I'll still have to go through with the six weeks' treatment in Germany. My blood pressure must be got properly right again some time or other. One of the Fuehrer's doctors is supposed to be on his way. I'm certainly not going to leave my post here until I can hand over to my deputy without worrying. It's not yet known who is coming. I'm having another examination to-day. It's some comfort to know that the damage can probably all be cleared up. At the rate we've been using up generals in Africa— five per division in eighteen months—it's no wonder that I also need an overhaul some time or other.

Lieutenant Alfred Ingemar Berndt to Frau Rommel

Egypt   26 Aug. 1942

DEAR FRAU ROMMEL,

You'll no doubt be surprised at hearing from me from Africa. . . . The reason for my letter is to inform you about the state of the Marshal's health. Your husband has now been 19 months in Africa, which is longer than any other officer over 40 has stood it so far, and, according to the doctors, an astonishing physical feat. After the rigours of the advance, he has had to carry the immense responsibility of the Alamein front, anxiety for which has for many nights allowed him no rest. Moreover, the bad season has come again.

All this has, in the nature of things, not failed to leave its mark, and thus, in addition to all the symptoms of a heavy cold and the digestive disturbances typical of Africa, he has recently shown signs of exhaustion which have caused great anxiety to all of us who were aware of it. True, there is no immediate danger, but unless he can get a thorough rest some time, he might easily suffer an overstrain which could leave organic damage in its train.

The doctor who is treating him, Professor Dr. Horster of Würzburg University—one of the best-known stomach specialists in Germany—is constantly available to him for medical advice and to watch over his health. The Fuehrer has been informed, and it has been agreed that he will receive a long period of sick leave in Europe once the future of this theatre has been decided. Until that time, we will do everything we can to make his life easier and to persuade him to look after himself. We prepare and keep handy everything he needs for his health. I have installed a small kitchen and obtained a good cook. Fresh fruit and vegetables arrive by air daily. We fish, shoot pigeons, obtain chickens and eggs, etc., in order to keep his strength up.[1]

This sort of " mothering " is not of course particularly easy with the Marshal and he has to know as little about it as possible. Being the man he is, he would deny himself any extra rations.

I must ask you, Madam, not to misunderstand this letter. But a long medical report has gone to the O.K.W., and I know from experience that this will open the door for all sorts of rumours about the Marshal's health, as things of this kind get round very quickly. I wanted, therefore—there being nobody else to do it—to let you have a clear picture of the situation before you are caused anxiety by uninformed rumours of this kind. There is no cause for worry. All he needs is a lengthy rest in Europe at some time in the fairly near future, and that is already arranged. He must sleep peacefully again, have less worries and relax physically and mentally, although that will no doubt not be easy with such a restlessly active spirit.

It is certain that the Fuehrer will have need of our Marshal for other tasks, equally important and great, and for that the Marshal must be kept in health. Purely as a precaution, therefore, we attach

[1]*Note by General Bayerlein.* Professor Horster, who was Rommel's medical adviser in North Africa, and was on very close terms with him, was one day called by Gause to carry out an examination of the Field Marshal. Rommel was having frequent attacks of faintness at the time, but was trying with all his strength to remain on his feet. After the examination, Professor Horster and General Gause jointly sent off a signal in approximately the following words:

" Field Marshal Rommel suffering from chronic stomach and intestinal catarrh, nasal diphtheria and considerable circulation trouble. He is not in a fit condition to command the forthcoming offensive."

Rommel considered that the only man who could take his place was General Guderian and asked the OKW to appoint Guderian commander of the Panzer Army on an acting basis. Back came the reply the same evening: " Guderian unacceptable." Rommel thereupon decided to command the battle himself and Horster sent a further telegram to the OKW shortly before the offensive was due to open:

" C-in-C's condition so far improved that he can command the battle under constant medical attention. Nevertheless, essential to have a replacement on the spot."

greater importance to anything concerning *his* health than one would normally do.

I ask you, Madam, not to worry. As for his personal safety, I shall, in the event of further operations, once again do everything possible to safeguard it, for every one of us, officers and men, would be ready to die for the Marshal. . . .

27 Aug. 1942

DEAREST LU,

Kesselring is coming to-day for a long talk over the most acute of our problems. He, too, often has a tough job in Rome. He gets plenty of promises, but few are kept. His over-optimism concerning these blighters has brought him bitter disappointments.

All quiet here so far. The British artillery sometimes do some excited shooting and send a few thousand rounds over into our territory. But we've " thinned out " and so their effect is minimised.

29 Aug. 1942

Tension is growing here. Conferred yesterday with the Commanding Generals. General Vaerst is back and has taken over his division again. He commanded particularly well and with great dash back in the January fighting. He was, of course, wounded very early in the great May battle. My health is now very good again and I hope to stand up well to the lively days ahead. Gause will be staying at H.Q. this time and Westphal will come with me. I can't see Gause keeping it up much longer. He's been having constant headaches ever since that day at the beginning of June when the British gave us such a terrible pounding with their bombs and artillery. I hope it will be better for him in Europe.

THE NEW BREAK-THROUGH PLAN

At the end of August, 1942, the British dispositions in the Alamein line were roughly as follows:

The northern sector was held by the 5th Indian, 50th British and 9th Australian Divisions, with the 1st South African Division behind them on the coast, all under command of XXX Corps.

In the southern sector, under the command of XIII Corps, the 7th Armoured Division was in the line with the reconnaissance units. Holding the line to the north of the 7th Armoured Division was the 2nd New Zealand Division. Behind the centre and southern parts of the front were the 1st Armoured and, as we later discovered, the 10th Armoured Division.[1]

[1] Rommel is here mistaken on several points, and apparently unaware of others:
  i. The 50th Division was not in the line. One of its brigades was brought up on the third day of the battle (2nd September).

The Panzer Army's plan was as follows:

The motorised group of the Panzer Army, consisting of the Afrika Korps, XX Italian Motorised Corps and 90th Light Division, was to move into its assembly areas in the southern part of the front, taking all possible precautions against observation. The armour was to move to its new positions a quarter at a time and there deploy under camouflage, the movement extending over a period of several days. With the armour in position, the wheeled vehicles were to be shifted to the assembly area in one bound, being replaced in their old positions by supply vehicles. No effort was to be spared to keep our intentions concealed.

As is shown by the enemy dispositions given above, only small British forces lay in the southern part of the front. Our reconnaissance had consistently reported that only weakly mined defences existed in the south, which would be comparatively easy to penetrate. These positions were to be taken in a night attack by the German and Italian infantry, and the enemy thrown back by armoured formations following immediately behind. Then, in a headlong thrust to the east, the Afrika Korps and part of the Motorised Corps were to win through before morning as far as the area south-west of El Hammam, 25 to 30 miles from their starting point.

While X Italian Corps, which was holding the southern part of our front, stood on the defensive, partly in its present and partly in the newly captured positions, the 90th Light Division with part of XX Italian Corps was to cover our flank at the level of the British El Alamein line and east of it, and ward off all British attacks, which we anticipated

ii. The 1st South African Division was in the centre of the XXX Corps sector—which stretched from the sea to the Ruweisat ridge.

iii. The 1st Armoured Division was not in this battle.

iv. The 10th Armoured Division (in XIII Corps) had two armoured brigades under its command, while the 7th was left with only a light armoured brigade.

v. There was also an independent armoured brigade, the 23rd, so placed that it could support either of the two corps.

vi. The XIII Corps also included the 44th Division, which was posted on the Alam Halfa ridge.

vii. There was nothing directly behind the 7th Armoured Division on the southern part of the front. The 10th Armoured and 44th Division were posted behind the 2nd New Zealand Division—i.e. behind the northern part of the XIII Corps sector.

As Alexander clearly puts it in his dispatch: " The plan was to hold as strongly as possible the area between the sea and Ruweisat ridge, and to threaten from the flank any enemy advance south of the ridge from a strongly defended prepared position on the Alam el Halfa ridge." It was a plan of indirect counter to Rommel's characteristic out-flanking move. It had been devised by Dorman-Smith and adopted by Auchinleck. On taking over the Eighth Army Montgomery had " accepted this plan in principle", with Alexander's approval, while seeking to strengthen the rear flank position at Alam Halfa as additional infantry became available. In the event this proved superfluous, and the 44th Division was not engaged. The flank menace from the concentrated mass of British armour caused Rommel to turn north to tackle it, abandoning his intended wider move. His assault on the well-sited position of the British armour was a failure.

would probably be fairly heavy in this area in the early stages of the operation.

At dawn, the motorised group [*primarily the Afrika Korps*] was to thrust north up as far as the coast, and then east through the British supply area where a decision was to be sought in open battle. The appearance of our motorised group in the British supply area would probably draw off their motorised forces, and leave them with insufficient to overcome the defence of the 90th Light Division and thus cut off the motorised group before the latter had had time to react effectively to such a move. We placed particular reliance in this plan on the slow reaction of the British command and troops, for experience had shown us that it always took them some time to reach decisions and put them into effect. We hoped, therefore, to be in a position to present the operation to the British as an accomplished fact.

Things were then to move fast. The decisive battle was on no account to become static. With large British forces pinned down by repeated minor attacks by the German-Italian infantry left in the Alamein line, the decisive battle was to be fought out behind the British front in a form in which the greater aptitude of our troops for mobile warfare and the high tactical skill of our commanders could compensate for our lack of material strength. Separated from their supply depots, the British would be left with the option of either fighting it out to the end in their line or breaking out and falling back to the west, thus relinquishing their hold on Egypt.

Summing up, the success of the operation depended—the supply question apart—on the following factors:

(*a*) The effectiveness with which our move into the assembly areas was concealed.

(*b*) The speed with which the break-through of the British line and the thrust into their rear could be achieved—in other words, on the accuracy of our reconnaissance.

At the end of August, the ammunition and petrol which had been promised us by the Commando Supremo had still not arrived. The full moon, indispensable to our operation, was already on the wane. Any further delay would have meant giving up all idea of ever again resuming the offensive.

However, Marshal Cavallero informed me that the tankers would arrive under heavy escort in a matter of hours, or at the latest next day.

In the hope that this promise would be fulfilled and trusting to Field Marshal Kesselring's assurance that he would fly across up to 500 tons of petrol a day in an emergency—but above all, in the certainty that if we did not act during this full moon our last chance of an offensive

would be gone for ever, I gave the order for the attack to open on the
night 30-31 August.

30 Aug. 1942

DEAREST LU,

To-day has dawned at last. It's been such a long wait worrying
all the time whether I should get everything I needed together to
enable me to take the brakes off again. Many of my worries have
been by no means satisfactorily settled and we have some very grave
shortages. But I've taken the risk, for it will be a long time before
we get such favourable conditions of moonlight, relative strengths,
etc., again. I, for my part, will do my utmost to contribute to success.

As for my health, I'm feeling quite on top of my form. There are
such big things at stake. If our blow succeeds, it might go some way
towards deciding the whole course of the war. If it fails, at least I
hope to give the enemy a pretty thorough beating. Neurath has seen
the Fuehrer, who sent me his best wishes. He is fully aware of my
anxieties.[1]

[1]*Note by General Bayerlein.* . . . Professor Horster states that Rommel left his sleeping
truck on the morning of the attack with a very troubled face. "Professor", he said,
"the decision to attack to-day is the hardest I have ever taken. Either the army in
Russia succeeds in getting through to Grozny and we in Africa manage to reach the Suez
Canal, or. . . ." He made a gesture of defeat.

CHAPTER XIII

NOW OR NEVER—ALAM HALFA

DURING THE night 30-31 August, the infantry with the motorised group of the Panzer Army moved to the attack against the southern bastions of the British El Alamein front.

Shortly after passing the eastern boundary of our own minefields, our troops came up against an extremely strong and hitherto unsuspected British mine belt, which was stubbornly defended. Under intensely heavy artillery fire, the sappers and infantry eventually succeeded in clearing lanes through the British barrier, although at the cost of very heavy casualties and a great deal of time—in many cases it needed three attempts. The minefields, which contained an extraordinary number of mines (according to our estimate there were 150,000 in the sector where we attacked), were of great depth and protected by numerous booby-traps.

Before long, relay bombing attacks by the R.A.F. began on the area occupied by our attacking force. With parachute flares turning night into day, large formations of aircraft unloosed sticks of H.E. bombs among my troops.

The Army staff spent most of the night on the telephone, with reports pouring in in a continual stream. Even so there remained considerable uncertainty about the situation, although it gradually became clear that things could not have gone altogether as planned. The first report from the Afrika Korps reached me at about 08.00 hours in the neighbourhood of Jebel Kalakh. Owing to the great strength of the enemy minefields, the Corps had been unable to reach its appointed objectives. By dawn, its leading units, with the reconnaissance group, had reached a point some eight to ten miles east of our minefields. The British had defended their strong positions with extraordinary stubbornness and had thereby delayed our advance. This had given the enemy units in the threatened sectors time to send alarm messages and situation reports back to British Headquarters, and had enabled the British commander to take the necessary counter-measures. Such a respite was of immense value to the enemy, for he only needed to hold his line long enough to allow his mobile forces to take up a position from which immediate counter-action could be taken against any German-Italian forces which broke through.

News arrived a few minutes later that General von Bismarck, commander of the 21st Panzer Division, had been killed by a mine and that General Nehring, commander of the Afrika Korps, had been wounded in an air attack.

My plan for the motorised forces—to advance 30 miles east by moonlight and then strike north at dawn—had not worked. The assault force had been held up far too long by the strong and hitherto unsuspected mine barriers, and the element of surprise, which had formed the basis of the whole plan, had been lost. In these circumstances, we were now in two minds whether or not to break off the action. We no longer had the advantage of the time which the British would have needed, in the event of a quick break-through in the south, to reconnoitre the situation, make their decisions and put them into effect—a period during which there would have been no need to expect serious counter measures to our moves. The enemy now knew where we were. I decided to make the decision dependent on how things stood with the Afrika Korps.

Soon afterwards I heard that the Afrika Korps, under the fine leadership of its Chief of Staff, Colonel Bayerlein, had overcome the British mine belt and was about to move on to the east. I discussed the situation with Bayerlein and we decided that the attack should go on.

General Bayerlein had taken over acting command of the Afrika Korps after General Nehring had been wounded.

With the British armour now assembled for immediate action, it was impossible for us to continue with our wide sweep to the east, as our flanks would have been under a constant threat from the 7th Armoured Division in the south and the 1st and 10th Armoured Divisions in the north. This compelled us to decide on an earlier turn to the north than we had intended.

The objectives of the attack were now set as Hill 132 for the Afrika Korps and Alam Bueit-Alam Halfa for XX Italian Corps. According to our air reconnaissance, this ridge was now heavily fortified; it was also, as we later discovered, held by 44th British Infantry Division, newly arrived from Great Britain. From our experience in similar situations we knew that the battle for the [*Alam Halfa*] ridge, which was the key to the whole El Alamein position, would be very severe. Field Marshal Kesselring was accordingly asked to attack it heavily from the air during the next few days.

After the Afrika Korps had refuelled and taken on ammunition, which consumed a great deal of time, the advance was resumed at about 13.00 hours. The attack, which was made in a heavy sandstorm, went well forward at first, and carried the Italian Littorio Armoured Division along with it. Unfortunately, the Ariete and Trieste were still delayed in clearing lanes through the minefields and threading their units through the British defence system. The XX Motorised Corps, as a result, was

unable to begin its advance until 15.00 hours, and from the outset hung
somewhat behind on the left of the Afrika Korps.

From Afrika Korps H.Q., where I had again been discussing the
situation and our plans with Bayerlein, I drove to the Italian divisions
and urged them to hurry.

Meanwhile, the vehicles and tanks of the Afrika Korps were painfully
grinding their way through the soft sand covering their line of march.
Driving sandstorms blew on and off all day, making the lives of my
men a misery—although they did, at the same time, prevent the British

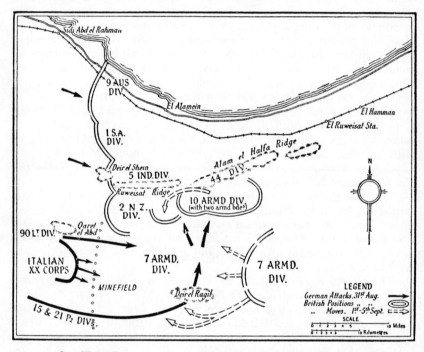

16. THE BATTLE OF ALAM HALFA, SEPTEMBER 1942

air forces making any heavy attacks on my units. Due to the heavy
going, the Afrika Korps' petrol stocks were soon badly depleted and at
16.00 hours we called off the attack on Hill 132. The XX Italian Corps
was still a considerable way behind, but the 90th Light Division had
reached its assigned position. Protection to the east and south-east was
provided by the reconnaissance battalions.

After nightfall our forces became the target for heavy R.A.F. attacks,
mainly on the reconnaissance group, but also—though less severe—on
other units. With one aircraft flying circles and dropping a continuous

succession of flares, bombs from the other machines, some of which dived low for the attack, crashed down among the flare-lit vehicles of the reconnaissance units. All movement was instantly pinned down by low-flying attacks. Soon many of our vehicles were alight and burning furiously. The reconnaissance group suffered heavy casualties.

Meanwhile, the promised petrol had still not arrived in Africa, added to which our supply traffic through the lanes in the enemy minefields was being seriously disturbed by the British armour south of our salient (7th Armoured Division). Consequently, on the morning of the 1st September, I found myself compelled to give up any attempt at major action for the moment; all large-scale movement of the motorised forces had to be avoided, and the most we could permit ourselves was a few local, limited objective attacks.

Acting on this decision, the Afrika Korps attacked on the morning of the 1st September with the 15th Panzer Division only; after shooting up a number of British heavy tanks, the division's main force managed to reach the area just south of Hill 132, where, with their petrol almost exhausted, they were forced to call off even this local advance.

The Afrika Korps continued to be assailed throughout the day by heavy R.A.F. bomber attacks. In the bare and coverless country, with the bomb-bursts frequently intensified by rock splinters, we suffered severe casualties. Seven officers were killed from the Afrika Korps' staff alone.

Next morning, after disposing of a few command matters, I drove through the area occupied by the Afrika Korps. Between ten and twelve o'clock we were bombed no less than six times by British aircraft. On one occasion I only just had time to throw myself into a slit trench before the bombs fell. A spade lying on the soil beside the trench was pierced clean through by an 8-inch splinter and the red-hot metal fragment fell beside me in the trench. Swarms of low-flying fighter-bombers were coming back to the attack again and again and my troops suffered tremendous casualties. Vast numbers of vehicles stood burning in the desert.

In the afternoon, I shifted my command post, and, in view of the bad supply situation, again considered whether to break off the battle.

The non-stop attacks of the British bomber formations continued the whole day through. The British artillery was also very active and fired vast quantities of ammunition—about ten shells were answering every one of ours. The movement of major formations and the establishment of timed march schedules now seemed to be ruled out. Our badly out-numbered fighters hurled themselves again and again towards the British bomber squadrons, but rarely succeeded in penetrating to their targets, for they were intercepted every time and engaged in combat by the tremendously strong fighter escorts of the " Party Rally " bomber squadrons.

Rommel is here referring to the perfect formation-flying of the British bomber squadrons, comparing them with formations performing a fly-past at the Nuremberg Party Rally celebrations.

Thus these bomber formations, flying almost undisturbed, were able to area-bomb our ranks with immense salvoes of bombs no less than twelve times on that one day alone.

Still no drop of the promised petrol had arrived in Africa. That evening, the Panzer Army had only one petrol issue left, and one issue, even with the greatest economy, could only suffice to keep our supply traffic going for a very short time.

An issue of petrol was equivalent to the quantity required by the units to travel 100 kilometres (62½ miles) over normally good going—i.e. terrain that was not particularly difficult.

By the 2nd September, out of the 5,000 tons of petrol which had been due to arrive by the 3rd, 2,600 tons had already been sunk and 1,500 tons were still in Italy.

From 23.00 hours onwards, right into the morning of the 2nd September, we were again attacked by relays of aircraft dropping bombs of all sizes. Once again they came crashing round my command post. A vehicle was set alight not ten yards from my slit trench.

After that night, I decided to call off the attack and retire by stages to the line El Taque-Bab el Qattara. My reasons were the serious air situation and the disastrous state of our supplies. Our offensive no longer had any hope of success, partly because we had no petrol and insufficient fighter cover and partly because the battle had now reached a stage where material strength alone would decide the issue. Had the attack on the plateau round Hill 132 been continued, it could only have developed into a battle of material attrition.

Meanwhile the British had assembled powerful armoured forces between Alam Halfa and Bab el Qattara and had then remained stationary in their assembly areas. Repeated local attacks followed, but these were easily beaten off. The impression we gained of the new British commander, General Montgomery, was that of a very cautious man, who was not prepared to take any sort of risk.

Montgomery had taken steps to prepare a strong counter-stroke, and even to organise a pursuit force. But in the end he decided to be content with restoring the line and " to proceed methodically with my own preparations for a big offensive later on." Accordingly, he refrained from, and restrained, efforts to cut off Rommel's retreat.

In the evening I conferred with Field Marshal Kesselring and gave him a detailed account of the effect of the British air attacks, in particular of their " bomb-carpets " in an area covered with tanks, guns and vehicles. He promised to do all he could to help us.

But that night again (2-3 September), the Afrika Korps, part of the Italian armoured divisions and the 90th Light Division were once more subjected to non-stop pounding by powerful British bomber formations. A steady succession of parachute flares kept the whole of the desert bathed in a brilliant light. Magnesium incendiaries, impossible to extinguish, lay flaring on the ground, lighting up the whole neighbourhood. Meanwhile, vast quantities of H.E. and fragmentation bombs, even some land-mines, dropped into the territory occupied by my troops. Many of the 88-mm. A.A. guns, which had previously scored an occasional hit, were now picked out by the British, attacked from a great height and destroyed. Hundreds of our vehicles were destroyed or damaged.

Next day, the withdrawal proceeded as planned. The British made only isolated attacks and, apart from these, let the air force and artillery take their toll. Kesselring informed us that he would send every aircraft he could raise to attack the British forces north of our break-through, where they were apparently entertaining ideas about launching an attack in our flank.

That night, while the R.A.F. made only small-scale sorties over our front, the attack of our air force on the 10th Indian Division, which was preparing for a thrust against the Brescia Division and the Ramcke Brigade, appeared to bring about the dispersal of the enemy approach march. All attacks against our flank made by other formations, especially the New Zealanders, were too weak to make any penetration and were easily beaten off.

A night attack on the X Italian Corps cost the British particularly heavy losses, including many dead. We took 200 prisoners, among them Brigadier Clifton, commander of 6th New Zealand Brigade.

Next morning I had a talk with Brigadier Clifton. He said that he was ashamed to have to admit to having been taken prisoner by the Italians. He had been in the act of persuading them to surrender by telling them of the strong British armour assembled in front of their position, and they had, in fact, already started taking the bolts out of their rifles, when to his disgust a German officer had come along and ruined the whole affair. He seemed very disgusted about it all. I tackled him about various acts contrary to international law for which the New Zealanders had been responsible. Repeated cases had occurred of prisoners and wounded being massacred by this particular division. He said it was probably due to the large number of Maoris which the division contained. For the rest, he expressed an absolute certainty of victory, understandable now that our attack had been repulsed. One of the veteran " Africans " of the other side, he had commanded troops against us ever since 1940, and had taken part in the fighting in Greece and the winter campaign in 1941-42.

He gave the impression of being a courageous and likeable man. He asked particularly that he should become a prisoner of the Germans and not be sent to Italy. I tried to grant his wish and, contrary to standing instructions, sent him back to a German depot in Mersa Matruh. However, the O.K.W. later gave orders for him to be handed over to the Italians.

The evening before he was due to be handed over, Clifton asked to be taken to the lavatory, where he climbed out of the window and vanished without trace. All troops were immediately warned by radio. A few days later several of my staff officers were out hunting gazelles when they suddenly spotted a weary figure plodding across the desert carrying what looked like a jerry-can of water. Closer inspection revealed him as the much sought-after Clifton, whereupon they straightway picked him up and brought him in again. I had a talk with him shortly afterwards and expressed my appreciation of his exploit. Such a trek through the desert is not everybody's meat and, not surprisingly, he looked completely exhausted. To put a stop to any further nonsense of the kind I had him sent straight across to Italy.[1] Later I heard that he had escaped from an Italian prisoner-of-war camp disguised as a Hitler Youth leader, complete with shorts and insignia, and in this garb had crossed the frontier into Switzerland.[2]

4 Sept. 1942

DEAREST LU,

Some very hard days lie behind me. We had to break off the offensive for supply reasons and because of the superiority of the enemy air force—although victory was otherwise ours. Well, it can't be helped. Made a quick call at H.Q. for the first time to-day, even had my boots off and washed my feet. I'm still hoping that the situation can be straightened out. All my wishes to you and Manfred.

P.S.—Bismarck killed. Nehring wounded.

The British showed little desire to make a real fight of it; there was indeed no need for them to do so, since time—as far as material was concerned—was working in their favour.

A number of statements made by British officers and men who were captured during this battle agreed in saying that the British command had been aware of our intention to attack on or about the 25th August. Several prisoners even went so far as to say that the British H.Q. had been informed by a senior Italian officer of our plan to attack on the southern part of the front.[3]

[1]*Note by General Bayerlein.* Professor Horster, who was present at all conversations between Rommel and Brigadier Clifton, draws attention to an interesting point.

During his conversation with Clifton, Rommel had suggested that Britain had overlooked the fact that the real danger to Europe lay in Asia.

When Clifton escaped from Mersa Matruh, Rommel was very alarmed that his statement about Asia (i.e. including also the Japanese) might have unfortunate political results. Consequently every possible measure was taken to ensure Clifton's recapture.

[2]Rommel's information was inaccurate. Clifton did in fact escape in Italy at his fifth attempt, but was caught near Como just before reaching the Swiss frontier. He was dressed externally as a merchant sailor, not as a Hitler Youth leader. He finally got away at his ninth attempt, from Germany—despite having been badly wounded in his eighth attempt.

[3]*Note by General Bayerlein.* This statement has so far received no confirmation from either side.

On the morning of the 6th September we completed our withdrawal and my troops went over to the defensive, utilising the strong British positions we had captured. With the failure of this offensive our last chance of gaining the Suez Canal had gone. We could now expect that the full production of British industry and, more important, the enormous industrial potential of America, which, consequent on our declaration of war, was now fully harnessed to the enemy cause, would finally turn the tide against us.

THE THIRD DIMENSION

Our offensive had failed because:

(a) contrary to our reconnaissance reports, the British positions in the south had been constructed in great strength.

(b) non-stop and very heavy air attacks by the R.A.F., whose command of the air had been virtually complete, had pinned my army to the ground and rendered any smooth deployment or any advance by time-schedule completely impossible.

(c) the petrol, which was an essential condition for the fulfilment of our plan, had not arrived. Some of the ships which Cavallero had promised had been sunk, some delayed and others not even dispatched. In addition, Kesselring had unfortunately been unable to keep his promise to fly over 500 tons a day to the front in an emergency.

General Westphal, in his book, says that Kesselring did actually send these 500 tons of petrol, but that it " consumed itself " on the way up to the front.

Our casualties had been very severe, caused mainly by the bombing and low-flying attacks of the R.A.F. They totalled, German and Italian together, 570 dead, 1,800 wounded and 570 prisoners—in all, nearly 3,000 men. On the material side, the main feature was our vehicle losses, which totalled 50 tanks, 15 field guns and 35 anti-tank guns, and 400 lorries.

According to formation reports we had taken 350 prisoners and knocked out or captured 150 British tanks and armoured cars. We had also destroyed 10 field guns and 20 heavy anti-tank guns.

The British losses, as given in Alexander's dispatch, were 1,640 men killed, wounded and missing; 68 tanks, 18 anti-tank guns, but no field guns.

The British " estimated " the enemy's loss in killed and wounded as 4,500— nearly double the figures that Rommel gives—but took prisoner only 300. They collected from the battlefield 51 tanks (of which 42 were German), 30 field guns and 40 anti-tank guns.

We had learnt one important lesson during this operation, a lesson which was to affect all subsequent planning and, in fact, our entire future conduct of the war. This was that the possibilities of ground action, operational and tactical, become very limited if one's adversary commands the air with a powerful air force and can fly mass raids by heavy bomber formations unconcerned for their own safety.

This battle was known to the troops for ever after as the " Six-day Race "[1]—from the fact that it had lasted six days from the opening of the offensive until our retreat into our new positions.

British ground forces, as has been shown, had hardly put in an appearance during the offensive. Montgomery had attempted no large-scale attack to retake the southern part of his line; and would probably have failed if he had. He had relied instead on the effect of his enormously powerful artillery and air force. Added to this, our lines of communication had been subjected to continual harassing attacks by the 7th Armoured Division. There is no doubt that the British commander's handling of this action had been absolutely right and well suited to the occasion, for it had enabled him to inflict very heavy damage on us in relation to his own losses, and to retain the striking power of his own force.

According to our estimate, some 1,300 tons of bombs had been dropped on the area occupied by my army's assault force during the six days of the battle. Although this was not very great compared with the quantity that was to be showered on us during the Alamein battle, it was far greater than anything that had so far been known during the African campaign.

In any case, two points were already clear:

(a) the paralysing effect which air activity on such a scale had on motorised forces; above all, the serious damage which had been caused to our units by area bombing.

(b) The British bid to secure complete command of the air and to exercise it to the full.

We were in no doubt that the forthcoming increase in British strength —the 100,000-ton convoy expected for the beginning of September had already arrived in Suez—would apply equally to their air force. From this we concluded that the R.A.F. would employ many times more aircraft against us in the coming battle than in the one just fought. This being so, we had to expect the following results:

The enemy would fight the battle of attrition from the air. His bombs would be particularly effective against motorised forces standing without cover in the open desert; their vehicles, tanks and guns—whether on the march, in assembly areas, or in the attack itself—would offer a wonderful target for bombers and low-flying aircraft. The enemy would be in a

[1] *Translator's note.*—After a famous German cycle race—the *Sechstagerennen.*

position to batter our forces so severely as to render them in time virtually unfit for action, and this without any appreciable expenditure of his own strength.

From the command point of view he would gain the following advantages:

(a) Through his total command of the air, he alone would have access to complete and unbroken reconnaissance reports.

(b) He would be able to operate more freely and boldly, since, if an emergency arose, he would be able, by use of his air-power, to break up the approach march and assembly and indeed every operation of his opponent, or alternatively delay them until he himself had had time to take effective counter measures.

(c) As a general rule, any slowing down of one's own operations tends to increase the speed of the enemy's. Since speed is one of the most important factors in motorised warfare, it is easy to see what effect this would have.

Moreover, whoever enjoys command of the air is in a position to inflict such heavy damage on the opponent's supply columns that serious shortages must soon make themselves felt. By maintaining a constant watch on the roads leading to the front he can put a complete stop to daylight supply traffic and force his enemy to drive only by night, thus causing him to lose irreplaceable time. But an assured flow of supplies is essential; without it the army becomes immobilised and incapable of action.[1]

All this provided us with inescapable conclusions. What we really needed was parity, or at least something approaching parity, in the air. This would have required a vast reinforcement of Kesselring's air force, especially in pursuit and fighter planes, but above all, would have needed the addition of a number of heavy bomber squadrons.

A balance of power in the air would have made the old rules of warfare valid again, although, of course, with certain tactical restrictions imposed by the intense aerial activity on both sides.

Anyone who has to fight, even with the most modern weapons, against an enemy in complete command of the air, fights like a savage against modern European troops, under the same handicaps and with the same chances of success. And since there was no foreseeable hope, with the German Luftwaffe so severely stretched in other theatres, of Kesselring receiving aircraft reinforcements in any way comparable with those

[1]*Note by General Bayerlein.*—This argument is of great importance. Rommel founded many of his later decisions on his experience in this and the subsequent Alamein battle, above all, his decision in 1944 to oppose the expected Allied invasion on the coast instead of risking an approach march from the French hinterland, which would have been operationally correct in normal conditions.

flowing to the British, we had to face the likelihood of the R.A.F. shortly gaining absolute air supremacy.

We therefore had to try to put our defence against the forthcoming British attack into such a form that British air superiority would have the least effect. For the first and most serious danger which now threatened us was from the air. This being so, we could no longer rest our defence on the motorised forces used in a mobile role, since these forces were too vulnerable to air attack. We had instead to try to resist the enemy in field positions which had to be construtced for defence against the most modern weapons of war.

We had to accept the fact that, by using his air-power, the enemy would be able to delay our operations at will, both in the daytime and —using parachute flares—at night. For no man can be expected to stay in his vehicle and drive on under enemy air attack. Our experience in the " Six-day Race " had shown us that any sort of time-schedule was now so much waste paper. This meant that our positions had henceforth to be constructed strongly enough to enable them to be held by their local garrisons independently and over a long period, without even the support of operational reserves, until reinforcements—however much delayed by the R.A.F.—could arrive.

The fact of British air superiority threw to the winds all the tactical rules which we had hitherto applied with such success. There was no real answer to the enemy's air superiority, except a powerful air force of our own. In every battle to come the strength of the Anglo-American air force was to be the deciding factor.

CHAPTER XIV

BATTLE WITHOUT HOPE—ALAMEIN

WITH THE failure of our offensive against the British Alamein line, a new phase opened which was eventually to lead to the final collapse of our North African front. In the period from the 6th September to the 23rd October the battle of supplies was waged with new violence. At the end of the period it had been finally lost by us and won by the British—by a wide margin.

Our feelings at the failure of our offensive can be imagined. The supply ships which Cavallero had promised would reach us in time for our offensive at the end of August or the beginning of September, in fact arrived in North Africa on the 8th September. Meanwhile, the supply situation had attained crisis proportions, largely because the quantities sent to us had never once come up to the agreed target; during the first eight months of 1942 we had received approximately 120,000 tons—only 40 per cent of our absolute minimum needs.

It was, of course, true that with the intense activity of the British strategic air force and Royal Navy in the Mediterranean, the difficulties had now considerably increased. Enemy aircraft were making attack after attack on our ports and destroying one supply installation after the other. More and more tonnage was being lost and less and less ships were being provided by the Italians for the Africa run. New construction of shipping —compared with the 1,300,000 tons or so which Italy had lost up to the beginning of October 1942—was pitifully small. Sinkings were going up steadily. Ten ships had been sunk by enemy action on the Africa run in the period from February until the end of July; between the end of July and the middle of October it was twenty. In fact, the question now was whether the supply problem could be solved at all even with the utmost efforts. The errors and omissions of the past had brought our supply organisation to such a pass that we had now very little hope of ever attaining tolerable supply conditions again.

Eighteen months before, senior officers of the German General Staff had declared that maintenance of the African theatre was an insoluble problem. The fact that this opinion was shared in the highest circles of

Wehrmacht command made it possible for the people in Italy and Europe who were lying down on the job to continue in their posts, because at the top level their arguments always fell on receptive ears and were accepted. Their estimate of the transport situation was—at any rate, up to the late summer of 1942—completely without foundation; it was the product of obsolete opinions and betrayed the tendency of the academic mind to evade all difficulties and prove them insurmountable. We should have swept away all old prejudices and preconceived ideas from the start.

There often occurred to me the difference between the Professor of Economics and the business man, as judged by their financial success. The business man may not perhaps be on the same intellectual plane as the professor, but he bases his ideas on real facts and puts the whole power of his will behind their realisation. The professor, on the other hand, often has a false conception of reality and although perhaps having more ideas, is neither able nor anxious to carry them out; the fact that he has them is satisfaction enough. And so the business man has the greater financial success.

The same difference can often be found between the academic and fighting soldier. One of the most important factors—not only in military matters, but in life as a whole—is the power of execution, the ability to direct one's whole energies towards the fulfilment of a particular task. The officer of purely intellectual attainments is usually only fitted for work as an assistant on the staff; he can criticise and provide the material for discussion. But a conclusion intellectually arrived at needs the executive power of the commander to follow it up and force it to realisation.

These remarks can be equally applied to the supply question. The malady from which we were suffering had its cause—apart from the weaknesses I have already described—in the lack of a sense of reality and an absence of all initiative and drive. In illustration of this I should perhaps indicate some of the things which might have been done:

(a) It never proved possible to get major Italian naval units used for the protection of convoys or the transport of urgent supplies. Of course, the fuel could not then have been used for the Rome taxis.

(b) It never proved possible to get an attack organised and mounted on Malta. I had offered to carry out this enterprise myself and am convinced that, given the number of troops for which I asked and proper support from the sea and air, I would have succeeded in taking the island fortress. With Malta in our hands, the British would have had little chance of exercising any further control over convoy traffic in the Central Mediterranean. Malta has the lives of many thousands of German and Italian soldiers on its conscience.

(c) It never proved possible to get quantity production of lighters and coastal vessels started in Italy or to organise a satisfactory service of coastal shipping under appropriate naval protection.

(d) It never proved possible to get new landing places with dock installations constructed along the coast, or to have the unloading capacity of the existing ports increased quickly enough.

I in no way underestimated the difficulties of organising our supply —as was always maintained by certain people in the Fuehrer's H.Q. I simply saw them in their true perspective. At the end of 1942, after the battle of El Alamein, maintenance of the African theatre of war quite clearly became an impossibility. But there is no doubt that secure convoy traffic could have been established in the spring and summer of that year. This would have enabled us to conquer the whole of the Mediterranean coast-line, and after that traffic across the Mediterranean would have presented no problem. But there was no understanding in the Fuehrer's H.Q. of the art of creating strategic centres of gravity at the decisive point.

Immediately after our abortive offensive, I reported to the Fuehrer's H.Q. and Commando Supremo in the following words:

" The German troops of the Panzer Army Africa, who are bearing the brunt of the war in Africa against the finest troops of the British Empire, must be provided with an uninterrupted flow of the supplies essential for life and battle, and every available ship and transport aircraft should be employed for that purpose. Failing this, the continued successful maintenance of the African theatre of war will be impossible and the army will sooner or later run the danger, when the British launch a major offensive, of suffering the same fate as befell the Halfaya garrison."

Meanwhile, the British were growing steadily stronger. By about the 11th September, they had five infantry divisions and one armoured division in the front, two infantry and two armoured divisions behind the front as army reserve, and a further two infantry divisions in the Nile Delta. Our anxiety was therefore continually increasing. We demanded substantial reinforcements of heavy anti-tank guns, to compensate at least in some measure for the tremendous British superiority in armour. We also asked for early reinforcement by another division.

Rations, too, were beginning to be a problem, now that we were coming to the end of the stocks we had captured in the Marmarica. On my visits to the front I was continually hearing of growing sick parades caused by the bad rations. Casualties from this cause were particularly heavy in divisions which contained troops who had been too long in Africa, or who had not been tested for fitness for tropical service.

I again pointed out the seriousness of the situation to the Fuehrer's H.Q. and stated that our supply problem must be solved at all costs by the use of every available scrap of shipping space; either that, or the German-Italian Panzer Army would in no circumstances be able to hold out for long in North Africa.

I demanded as a minimum the shipment of 30,000 tons during September and 35,000 tons during October, after the arrival of the 22nd Air Landing Division.[1] I also demanded the shipment across of every vehicle which was being held in Germany and Italy for the Panzer Army. We sent back accurate and detailed reports of the effect of British attacks on our troops and demanded a considerable reinforcement of our air force, particularly in fighter strength. But it soon became obvious that we need entertain little hope that our demands would be met.

I regarded the following stocks as indispensable requirements for a defence against the forthcoming British attack:

> AMMUNITION: eight daily issues.
> PETROL: 2,000 miles per vehicle.
> RATIONS: 30 days' stock.

I stated categorically that it would only be possible to guarantee a successful defence if these requirements were met.

9 Sept. 1942

DEAREST LU,

My health is now fairly well restored and I hardly think anybody would notice anything. However, the doctor is pressing me hard to have a break in Germany and doesn't want me to postpone it any longer. But Stumme must first arrive and be installed in his job.

On the one hand, I'm overjoyed at the prospect of getting away for a while and seeing you, but on the other I fear I shall never be free of anxiety about this place, even though I won't be able to get to the front myself. I know Churchill is supposed to have said that he will only be able to hold Egypt a few months longer, but I'm more inclined to think that he's considering launching a new offensive with superior forces in four to six weeks' time. A victory for us in the Caucasus is the only thing that would stop him.

Now Gause is unfit for tropical service and has to go away for six months. Things are also not looking too good with Westphal, he's got liver trouble [*jaundice*]. Lieut.-Col. von Mellenthin [*Ic.*] is leaving to-day with amoebic dysentery. One of the divisional commanders was wounded yesterday, so that every divisional commander and the Corps Commander have been changed inside ten days.

---

[1] *Note by General Bayerlein.*—The 22nd Air Landing Division, which was a motorised infantry division, had been withdrawn from Russia after a long period in action on that front. Its movement to North Africa was planned but never carried out.

11 Sept. 1942

I'm quite well so far. It goes up and down. It's high time I got out for a few weeks. The British seem to be having great anxieties in India and to be very worried about the Caucasus front. I hope to be the one to benefit. It was blowing sand again yesterday, but didn't get up to a real storm. I've received Manfred's letter of the 31st. I was very pleased with it.

It's quite likely that my letters will now arrive after I do. However, I'll go on writing; one never knows.

How are things looking in Wiener Neustadt? I'm very excited to see how I'll find everything. Manfred must have grown a tremendous lot in seven months and have practically caught me up.

In the early hours of the 14th September, after relay bombing attacks by 180 aircraft on the port and surroundings of Tobruk, the British attempted to land strong forces in the fortress area. According to documents which fell into our hands, their mission was to destroy the dock installations and sink the ships in the harbour.

The A.A. batteries on the peninsula immediately opened a furious fire on the British. German and Italian assault groups, which were quickly formed up, succeeded in enveloping the landed enemy troops. Fearing that the British were planning to capture Tobruk, we immediately set a number of motorised units in march for the fortress. But the local forces soon succeeded in restoring the situation. The British suffered considerable losses in killed and prisoners and—according to reports from the A.A. batteries—three destroyers and three landing or escort vessels were sunk. Next day our air force caught the British again and reported the sinking of one cruiser, one more destroyer and several escort vessels. A number of British ships were damaged by bombs.

On the 15th September I flew over to Tobruk myself and expressed my appreciation to the troops of the well-conducted defensive action they had fought. The report of the British attack had actually caused us no little alarm, for Tobruk was one of our most vulnerable points. I was afraid that the enemy might attempt another such operation at the start of his offensive, and instructed Vice-Admiral Lombardi and General Deindl to do everything they could to make the defence of the fortress secure.

16 Sept. 1942

DEAREST LU,

Arrived back last night from Tobruk. You'll no doubt have been pleased to hear the special communiqué about the abortive landing. Everything seems to be under control again now. Stumme is arriving in Rome to-day. I hope to start in a week's time.

Kesselring came this morning, after I'd seen and talked to him yesterday in Tobruk. He'd come from the Fuehrer's H.Q. The battle for Stalingrad seems to be very hard and is tying up a lot of forces which we could make better use of in the south.

I hear that Field Marshal List is retiring. I thought particularly highly of him, as you know.

This was the heaviest attack which the British made on our rear areas. Generally, minor operations of this kind were undertaken by the Commandos under the command of Colonel Stirling.[1] These Commandos, working from Kufra[2] and the Qattara depression, sometimes operated right up into Cyrenaica, where they caused considerable havoc and seriously disquieted the Italians. They tried again and again to incite the Arabs against us—fortunately, with little success, for there is nothing so unpleasant as partisan warfare. It is perhaps very important not to make reprisals on hostages at the first outbreak of partisan warfare, for these only create feelings of revenge and serve to strengthen the *francs-tireurs*. It is better to allow an incident to go unavenged than to hit back at the innocent. It only agitates the whole neighbourhood, and hostages easily become martyrs. The Italian commander shared my view, and so the occasional Arab raid was usually overlooked.

Meanwhile, in spite of the excellent care of the good Professor Horster, my health had grown so bad after an uninterrupted eighteen months in Africa, that it had become essential for me to embark on a long course of treatment in Europe without further delay. General Stumme was to deputise for me as Army Commander during my absence. He arrived at my headquarters on the 19th September. Later the same day a conference took place between Marshal Cavallero, Lieut.-Col. Otto (my Quartermaster) and myself. Otto and I complained of the frightful state of our supplies and especially about the Italian action in shipping across more formations destined for Tripolitania. These formations were of no earthly use at the front but merely required the use of shipping space which was already in great enough demand for the fighting troops. The Duce had actually given orders for two further divisions, additional to the Pistoia, to be brought to Tripolitania. At the same time, men of the Panzer Army's Italian formations who had been more than two years in Africa were being withdrawn, without any replacements forthcoming. As usual Cavallero promised to look after our interests.

On the 21st September, I flew with Gause and Bayerlein to inspect the German-Italian garrison at the Siwa oasis, where we were given an enthusiastic welcome by the Arab population. We presented gifts to the

[1] It is interesting to see that Rommel was unaware that a variety of special raiding forces were employed in these operations. Thus he used the term " Commandos " to embrace the S.A.S. (Special Air Service Regiment), the L.R.D.G. (Long Range Desert Group), and other guerrilla-type forces.

[2] The Kufra Oasis is some 500 miles south of Tobruk, deep in the Sahara Desert.

local chiefs and photographed the tribesmen in their magnificent coloured robes. I was presented with an envelope on which was stuck every postage stamp issued in the oasis, stamped with that day's postmark.

Next day I handed over command of the Panzer Army to General Stumme. He was rather put out when he heard that I proposed to cut short my cure and return to North Africa if the British opened a major offensive. He supposed that I had no confidence in him. But that was by no means the case; it was merely that I was convinced that even the most skilful Panzer General would be unable to take the right decisions in an emergency on the Alamein front unless he were familiar with the British. Words alone cannot impart one's experience to a deputy. On the Alamein front, there was a very great difference between quiet and critical days.

It was with a heavy heart that I set off for Derna next day (23rd) to fly to Italy. I intended to bring it home once more to the Italians that if we were to hold out in Egypt for any length of time, a quite extraordinary effort would have to be made in the field of supply.

On the 23rd September I reached the following agreements with the Italians: The Italians in Libya were to provide 3,000 men immediately to build a road behind the front. Continued driving over unmetalled tracks, mostly covered with deep sand and pitted with holes up to eighteen inches deep, was ruining our vehicles, especially as our drivers usually drove like the devil and without any regard for their vehicles. The spare part situation was so bad that we could no longer afford this wastage.

The Italians agreed to ship 7,000 tons of rails and sleepers to Africa for the construction of railway communications.

The Italians further undertook to attack and capture Kufra in order to put a stop to the sabotage raids for which it was forming a base.

It is interesting to compare Cavallero's promises with what was actually done by about the middle of October.

When General Barbassetti received the demand for 3,000 men, he declared that he was not in a position to provide that number and that the most he could spare was 400. Of these 400 only a little over 100 actually arrived and so the road could never be built.

Similarly, there arrived neither rails nor sleepers. The only work that was done on the railway was by men of the 90th Light Division.

When it came to the point, neither Barbassetti nor Cavallero was willing to attack, or in fact did attack, the Kufra oasis. Everything stayed as it was, and the threat of the British Commandos remained.

It is probable that Marshal Cavallero merely wanted to keep me quiet, and thought that it would be bound to be some time before I could be effective in Africa again.

On the 24th September I discussed the situation with the Duce. I left him in no doubt that unless supplies were sent to us at least on the scale I had demanded we should have to get out of North Africa. I think that, for all I said, he still did not realise the full gravity of the situation. All through the past two years I had myself informed him again and again of our supply difficulties, without any noticeable improvement resulting—except during the spring of 1942. Yet, in spite of this lack of response, things had never actually gone wrong. Of course people had no idea in Europe what difficult decisions had often faced us out there. We were always told: " You'll pull it off all right "—but unless the material conditions had first been created I could not pull off anything. The confidence everybody had in us was certainly very gratifying, but we in Africa quite frankly placed a great deal more value on an adequate supply. We in no way overestimated ourselves, but knew that any success we scored was due to natural causes.[1]

At any rate, I was pleased to hear that the German and Italian supply authorities were proposing to put a considerable quantity of French shipping into service in the near future. In addition the very efficient Gauleiter Kaufmann, an extremely talented man in organisation and technical matters, was to take our maintenance in hand. So in spite of everything there was at least a glimmer of light.

Several days later I reported to the Fuehrer. His headquarters had obviously been very impressed by the Panzer Army's successes and now wanted to force a decision in the Mediterranean area.

I outlined to the Fuehrer the course of our attack on the Alamein Line and the cause of its failure. I laid particular stress on the tremendous superiority of the British in the air, and described the effect of the new R.A.F. bombing tactics, above all, the limitations which they brought on the employment of motorised forces, caused by the extreme vulnerability of these forces to air attack. I also said that the only way to overcome the enemy air superiority was by the immediate dispatch to Africa of strong air forces of our own.

I dealt very thoroughly with the bad supply situation and, as with the Duce, made no secret of the fact that we would be unable to keep going unless a radical improvement was made. I described in detail the possibilities that existed for improving our supply. I also demanded that the ratio of the German supply quota to the Italian should be raised, pointing out that the strength of the German fighting formations far exceeded that of the Italian. I stated once more that the transport across the Mediterranean of 30,000 tons in September and 35,000 tons in October was an indispensable condition for a successful defence against the forthcoming British attack.

I concluded my report with the following words:

" I quite realise that, with the present strategic sea and air situation in the Mediterranean, a very great effort will be required to ensure a safe

[1]*Note by General Bayerlein*—By " natural causes ", Rommel apparently meant the absolute minimum of petrol, ammunition and material necessary for making war in the desert.

and uninterrupted German supply to Africa. It will make the utmost demands of all German and Italian transport services and will require the reinforcement of the transport fleet. But it is only by the fulfilment of the conditions I have stated that the German troops, who are bearing the main brunt of the fighting in Africa, will be able to maintain their hold on this theatre against the finest troops of the British Empire."

During the conference I realised that the atmosphere in the Fuehrer's H.Q. was extremely optimistic. Goering in particular was inclined to minimise our difficulties. When I said that British fighter-bombers had shot up my tanks with 40-mm. shells, the Reichsmarschall, who felt himself touched by this, said: "That's completely impossible. The Americans only know how to make razor blades." I replied: "We could do with some of those razor blades, Herr Reichsmarschall."

Fortunately, we had brought with us a solid armour-piercing shell which had been fired at one of our tanks by a low-flying British aircraft. It had killed almost the entire tank crew.

The Fuehrer promised that our supplies would be considerably increased during the next few weeks by the use of large numbers of *Siebelfaehren*. [*Flat ferries designed by a German engineer named Siebel.*] These were vessels of such shallow draught that torpedoes passed underneath them. They also carried several A.A. guns and were thus relatively invulnerable to air attack. One disadvantage of them was that they could not be used in a heavy sea, but heavy seas are not very frequent in the Mediterranean. I was shown production figures which held out a hope that much of our supply difficulty could be overcome in the near future —provided, of course, that it was not then too late.

While at the Fuehrer's H.Q. I was assured that a Nebelwerfer [*multiple rocket-projector*] Brigade of 500 rocket tubes was shortly to be sent to Africa. Forty Tiger tanks and self-propelled guns were also to be sent over as early as possible in *Siebelfaehren* and Italian transports.

Later it transpired that many of these promises had been given in a moment of over-optimism and on the basis of incorrect production figures, for it was neither possible to realise the building programme for *Siebelfaehren* on the scale provided for, nor to send the stated number of Nebelwerfer or of Tiger tanks to the African theatre.

During these days I found myself reluctantly compelled to face representatives of the Press in order to dispel a number of rumours which were in circulation about myself. With things as they were I could not, of course, give a true picture of the situation. In any case, by giving an optimistic account I hoped to bring about some postponement of the British offensive.

After this I went off to the Semmering[1] to clear up my liver and blood-pressure trouble. Before my departure from Africa, Professor Horster had insisted on my making an extended stay in Europe. He had already

[1]A mountain resort near Vienna.

kept me under continual observation during the " Six-day Race." Up on the Semmering I was completely cut off from the outside world, except for the radio, newspapers and occasional letters from General Stumme and Colonel Westphal. But with my army in such a plight I was of course incapable of attaining real peace of mind. I followed the operations of our submarines in the Atlantic with particular anxiety.

By declaring war on America, we had brought the entire American industrial potential into the service of the Allied war production. We in Africa knew all about the quality of its achievements. Now, during my stay in Europe, I obtained for myself some figures on American productive capacity. It was many times greater than ours. The battle which was being fought in the Atlantic was deciding whether the Americans would be able to go on carrying their material to Europe, Russia and Africa. I realised that there would be little hope left for us if the Americans and British succeeded in eliminating, or reducing to tolerable proportions, the U-boat threat to their convoys. But if we could strangle their sea routes, then the entire industrial capacity of America would avail the Allies little. As things turned out, of course, the Americans succeeded, several months later, in sinking so many of our submarines by the use of location devices and helicopters, as to render the further use of this weapon virtually impossible.[1]

The news I received from Africa was not very cheering. The British air force was becoming increasingly active and the Eighth Army was growing steadily stronger.   The Panzer Army lived in constant expectation of a major British attack. They thought that the attack would be launched at several points simultaneously, and that the British would subsequently throw in their whole strength at the point where a break-through seemed most likely to succeed.

According to our estimates, the British had a two to one superiority in tanks. This figure included on our side the 300 Italian tanks, the fighting value of which was very small. We still had only very few tanks armed with a 75-mm. gun, whereas the British had many hundreds equipped with heavy guns.[2] Of our 210 German tanks only 30 or so

[1]Rommel was so profoundly impressed by the tremendous war-potential of the U.S.A.—which, he felt, had fatally turned the scales against Germany—that he was apt to ascribe any powerful new development to the Americans without discrimination. That tendency was increased, naturally, by the way that the balance of qualitative superiority in tanks turned against him with the advent of the Grants and Shermans. But, in fact, the principal location device—the radar instrument known as H₂S—that eventually changed the course of the submarine war, as well as the war in the air, was a British invention.

[2]Rommel here understates rather than overstates the relative situation. The British superiority in tank numbers was nearly $2\frac{1}{2}$ to 1 over the combined German and Italian tanks, and about $5\frac{1}{2}$ to 1 over the German tanks.

A still more preponderant factor was that the British numbers included more than 500 tanks armed with a 75-mm. gun—some 400 of which were Shermans, and the remainder Grants and Lees. Rommel had only 38 tanks armed with a 75-mm. gun.

were Panzer IVs; the majority were Panzer IIIs, half of which were of the short-barrel type and hence very out of date.[1] As for the 300 Italian tanks—apart from their technical deficiencies which I have mentioned several times already—most of them were decrepit, and barely fit for action. Supplies were not being maintained at anything like the required level, so immense shortages existed in almost every field.

At this time, only four fast motor-ships, aggregating 19,000 tons, and seven large but slow transports of together 40,000 tons, were in use for the Panzer Army. Eight ships, totalling 40,000 tons, were in dock undergoing repairs.

My deputy, General Stumme, was on the move continually, both by car and aircraft, trying to bring our defence preparations up to the standard I required. He, too, had now come to realise the full extent of the supply deficiencies, on which the whole Africa problem turned. The longer things went on, the more obvious it became that, despite all the efforts of the army, the supply situation could no longer be improved. It was now too late.

THE DEFENCE PLAN

The Alamein line lay between the sea and the Qattara depression, which our reconnaissance had finally established as being impassable for major vehicle columns. Thus it was the only front in North Africa, apart from the Akarit position, which could not be turned at its southern end. All other positions could be collapsed by tying them down frontally and outflanking them to the south. Everywhere else it was possible to make a surprise sweep with motorised forces round the southern end of the line in order to seek a decision in mobile warfare in the enemy's rear. This fact of the open flank had led repeatedly to completely novel situations.

But at Alamein it was different. This line, if solidly held by infantry throughout its length, completely ruled out any chance of a surprise enemy appearance in one's rear. The enemy had first to force a breakthrough, which meant that the defence had a chance of holding its line long enough to enable the mobile reserve to come up and join the battle.

At El Alamein, therefore, we were presented with yet another set of tactical conditions. The defence was here at a certain advantage because it could dig in and protect itself with mines, while the enemy had to make his attack exposed to the fire of the dug-in defence. And the attacker had no choice but to assault and overcome the defender's line. Elsewhere—at Sollum, for instance, in 1941-42, and at Gazala in the

---

[1]The Panzer IV was armed with a 75-mm. gun and the Panzer III with a 50 mm. In both types there was an older short-barrelled model and a later one with a long barrel. The greater length of barrel gave a considerable increase in the range and penetration of the gun.

summer of 1942—the battle had been conducted in a wholly mobile form, with neither side deriving any initial advantage from its position, since the tanks and vehicles of both combatants stood equally unprotected in the desert. There had perhaps been a slight disadvantage for the attack, in that the defence had in both cases held a line extending to the south. For us at Sollum this was right, for the units employed in the Sollum-Halfaya line were non-motorised and thus only suitable for use in fixed and fortified positions. But it was not right for the British at Gazala, since all the British divisions in the Gazala line were fully motorised, and the small supply difficulties they were able to create for us did not make up for their absence from the battlefield of Knightsbridge-Acroma. As I have already explained, it is the extent to which one can concentrate one's forces, both in space and time, that counts in motorised warfare.

In the open desert, we were—as all previous actions had shown—considerably superior in training and command to the British. Although we could expect that the British had learnt many tactical lessons from the large number of battles and skirmishes we had given them, they could not have removed all their shortcomings, since these had their cause less in their command, than in the ultra-conservative structure of their army, which although excellently suited for fighting on fixed fronts, was far from suitable for war in the open desert.

Nevertheless, we still could not take the risk of putting the main weight of our defence on to operations in the open desert, for the following reasons:

(a) The relative strengths in motorised divisions had become too unequal; while our opponents were receiving a steady flow of motorised reinforcements, we received only non-motorised, which were as good as useless in the open desert. Consequently, we were forced to choose a form of warfare in which they, too, could play their part.

(b) The British air superiority, together with the new air tactics of the R.A.F., created severe limitations on the tactical use of motorised forces, of which a detailed explanation has already been given.

(c) We were permanently short of petrol. I did not want to get myself again into the awkward situation of having to break off a battle because we were out of petrol. In a mobile defensive action, shortage of petrol spells disaster.

For all these reasons, we now had to try to base our defence on a fortified and infantry-held line.

This meant that the British would first have to try for a break-through. We had no doubts about the suitability of the British Army for such a task, for its entire training had been based on the lessons learnt in the battles of material of the First World War. And, although technical developments had left their mark on this form of warfare, they had brought about no revolution. Although the tactical consequences of motorisation and armour had been pre-eminently demonstrated by British military critics,[1] the responsible British leaders had not taken the risk either of using this hitherto untried system as a foundation for peace-time training, or of applying it in war. But this failure, which had told so heavily against the British in the past, would not affect the issue of the approaching battle of position and break-through, because the extensive minefields would rob the armour of its freedom of movement and operation, and would force it into the role of the infantry tank. In this form of action the full value of the excellent Australian and New Zealand infantry would be realised and the British artillery would have its effect.

We, for our part, had to prevent the British from breaking through our line at all costs, since, for the reasons already given, we could not face having to fight a mobile defensive battle. Our motorised formations would hardly suffice to cover a withdrawal of the infantry from a front some 40 miles long—and, in any case, the infantry themselves might by that time have become so involved in the action that disengagement would be unthinkable.

This brought us to two inescapable conclusions:

(a) Our position had to be held at all costs.
(b) Any penetration would have to be cleaned up by immediate counter-attack to prevent it being extended into a break-through, for it was my opinion that if a break-through occurred, the British would throw their whole striking power into the breach.

We constructed our defence system to meet these requirements. We saw to it that the troops were given such firm positions, and that the front was held in such density that a threatened sector could hold out against even the heaviest British attack long enough to enable the mobile reserve to come up, however long it was delayed by the R.A.F.

Coming down to more detail, the defences were so laid out that the minefields adjoining no-man's land were held by light outposts only,

[1]*Publisher's Note.*—The following footnote was written by General Bayerlein for the German edition *Krieg ohne Hass* and indicates why the Rommel family were particularly anxious that Captain Liddell Hart should write an Introduction to, and edit, the English edition:—

Note by General Bayerlein.—Rommel was here referring to Captain Liddell Hart and General Fuller. In his opinion the British could have avoided most of their defeats if only they had paid more heed to the modern theories expounded by those two writers before the war. During the war, in many conferences and personal talks with Field-Marshal Rommel, we discussed Liddell Hart's military works, which won our admiration. Of all military writers, it was Liddell Hart who made the deepest impression on the Field-Marshal—and greatly influenced his tactical and strategical thinking. He, like Guderian, could in many respects be termed Liddell Hart's " pupil."

with the main defence line, which was two to three thousand yards in depth, located one to two thousand yards west of the first mine-belt. The panzer divisions were positioned behind the main defence line so that their guns could fire into the area in front of the line and increase the defensive fire-power of their sector. In the event of the attack developing a centre of gravity at any point, the panzer and motorised divisions situated to the north and south were to close up on the threatened sector.

A very large number of mines was used in the construction of our line, something of the order of 500,000, counting in the captured British mine-fields. In placing the minefields, particular care was taken to ensure that the static formations could defend themselves to the side and rear as well as to the front. Vast numbers of captured British bombs and shells were built into the defence, arranged in some cases for electrical detonation. Italian troops were interspersed with their German comrades so that an Italian battalion always had a German as its neighbour. The Italian armament was unfortunately so inefficient that it had to be distributed evenly over the whole front, thus ensuring that German arms were also available in every sector.

Our outposts were provided with dogs to give warning of any British approach to the minefields. We wanted to ensure that the work of clearing the minefields proceeded at the slowest possible speed and not until after our outposts had been eliminated. Most of the mines available in Africa were unfortunately of the anti-tank type, which infantry could walk over without danger. They were, therefore, comparatively easy to clear.

Thus the army was put on the defensive along these lines during my absence. But all our efforts were to prove unavailing against the immensely superior British forces—not because of mistakes we had made, but because victory was simply impossible under the terms on which we entered the battle.[1]

THE STORM BREAKS

An outline of the British plan is required as a preliminary to Rommel's account of the battle, for its fuller understanding. Attacking on a front where the scope for manœuvre was restricted, Montgomery used his infantry to open the way for his armour. He also chose to concentrate the weight of his attack in the northern sector.

The main attack here was delivered by Leese's XXX Corps with four infantry divisions—from right to left, the 9th Australian, 51st Highland, 2nd New

[1] *Note by General Bayerlein.*—It has been repeatedly stated by different writers that General Stumme did not plan the defences at El Alamein in the way that Rommel would have done. To this is must be clearly stated that Rommel issued orders for the construction of the defences before his departure from Africa, and that Stumme merely executed them.

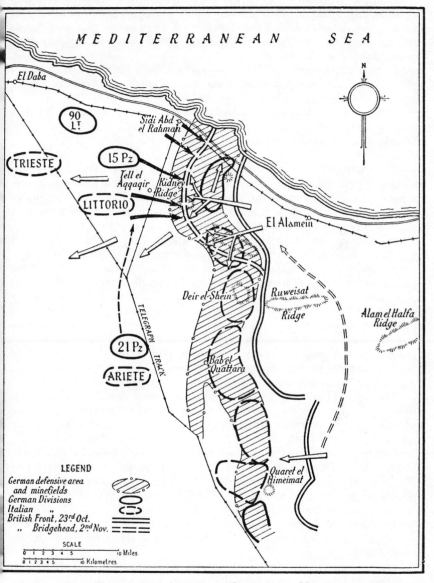

17. THE BATTLE OF ALAMEIN, OCTOBER—NOVEMBER 1942

Zealand, and 1st South African. The 4th Indian Division was to create a local diversion. After two corridors had been driven through the enemy minefields, the 1st and 10th Armoured Divisions of Lumsden's X Corps were to pass through, take up a position at the far end, and repulse the anticipated counter-attack of the enemy's armour before trying to drive on.

In the south, Horrocks' XIII Corps—44th and 50th (Infantry) Divisions and 7th Armoured Division—attempted a diversionary attack to distract the enemy's attention and pin down his reserves—particularly the 21st Panzer Division.

Although the Eighth Army comprised only three armoured divisions, it had three additional armoured brigades, making six in all, as well as a light armoured brigade—against two German, and two Italian.

The battle which began at El Alamein on the 23rd October 1942 turned the tide of war in Africa against us and, in fact, probably represented the turning point of the whole vast struggle. The conditions under which my gallant troops entered the battle were so disheartening that there was practically no hope of our coming out of it victorious.

Something over 200 German and about 300 Italian tanks faced qualitatively superior British armour to the strength of over 1,000 tanks. True, we had a fair number of guns, but many of these were obsolete Italian types, many of them captured guns and all of them terribly short of ammunition. In addition, the British had now gained complete air supremacy over the Mediterranean and, by bombing our ports and maintaining close air observation over our sea routes, supplemented by intense naval activity, were in a position virtually to paralyse our sea traffic. As a result, our stocks of supplies were so low that shortages of every kind were evident even at the beginning of the battle, with effects which will be clearly seen in the following account.

The 23rd October passed just like any other day on the Alamein front—until the evening, when, at 21.40 hours, a barrage of immense weight opened over the whole line, eventually concentrating on the northern sector. Such drum-fire had never before been seen on the African front, and it was to continue throughout the whole of the Alamein battle. Apart from the divisional artillery of the attacking and holding divisions, Montgomery had concentrated 15 heavy artillery regiments[1]—representing a total of 540 guns of a calibre greater than 105 mm.—in the northern sector between Hill 35 and Deir el Shein. The British bombarded our known positions with extraordinary accuracy, and enormous casualties resulted. R.A.F. bombers also took part in the preparatory barrage.

Our communication network was soon smashed by this drum-fire, and reports from the front virtually ceased. Our outposts fought to the last round and then either surrendered or died.

---

[1] By " heavy artillery " Rommel here means what, in the British Army, is classified as " medium artillery." In all some 1,200 guns were used in the opening bombardment.

Under the impact of the terrible British artillery fire, which grew to World War I proportions, part of the Italian 62nd Infantry Regiment left their line and streamed back to the rear. Exposed to this tornado of fire in their partially completed defence positions, their nerve had failed. By 01.00 hours the British had overrun our outposts and penetrated to our main defence line over a width of six miles. Our infantry resisted bitterly, although most of their heavy weapons had been smashed by the enemy artillery fire. Again and again the British brought up tanks. Soon they overran the remains of the 62nd Italian Infantry Regiment and broke into our line, where they were finally stopped by concentrated artillery fire. Two battalions of the 164th Infantry Division were also wiped out during the early hours of the morning by the concentric fire of the British guns.

The offensive as a whole made less progress, and went slower, than the British Command hoped. That was largely due to the density of the minefields. Dawn came before even one of the corridors was cleared sufficiently for the armour to pass through, and when it tried to push on beyond in daylight it was soon held up. In the other corridor the armour was still hung up in the minefield. It was not until the following morning, after fresh night attacks by the infantry, that the deployment was completed. The four armoured brigades of the X Corps, with their 700 tanks and strong artillery, then took up a position covering the mouth of the six-mile breach, ready to deal with the German armoured counter-attack which Montgomery hoped to provoke.

Back in H.Q.—which was sited on the coast only a few miles behind the front—General Stumme heard this tornado of fire, but because of the meagre stocks of ammunition in Africa, did not authorise the artillery to open fire on the British assembly positions. This was a mistake, in my view, for it would have at least reduced the weight of the British attack. When the artillery did finally open fire it was unable to have anything like the effect it might have had earlier, for the British had by that time been able to install themselves in the defence posts they had captured during the night. When dawn broke on the 24th of October, headquarters had still only received a few reports, and there was considerable obscurity about the situation. Accordingly General Stumme decided to drive up to the front himself.

The acting Army Chief of Staff, Colonel Westphal, pressed him to take an escort vehicle and signals truck as I had always done. But he refused to take any escort apart from Colonel Buechting; he intended to go no farther than the headquarters of the 90th Light Division and considered it unnecessary to take any other vehicles.

Concentric artillery fire began again in the early hours of the 24th, this time on the southern sector, where the British soon attacked with infantry and about 160 tanks. After overrunning our outposts they were brought to a halt in front of the main defence line.

Here, in the XIII Corps sector, the 7th Armoured Division got through the

first minefield on the opening night, but was stopped in front of the second by heavy
defensive fire. A narrow penetration was made on the next night, but when the
armour tried to go through it was again blocked by fire. As losses were rising,
Montgomery discontinued the attack in the south, for he wanted to preserve the
7th Armoured Division for further action elsewhere.

On the afternoon of the 24th, I was rung up on the Semmering by
Field Marshal Keitel, who told me that the British had been attacking
at Alamein with powerful artillery and bomber support since the previous
evening. General Stumme was missing. He asked whether I would be
well enough to return to Africa and take over command again. I said
I would. Keitel then said that he would keep me informed of developments, and would let me know in due course whether I was to return to
my command. I spent the next few hours in a state of acute anxiety,
until the evening, when I received a telephone call from Hitler himself.
He said that Stumme was still missing—either captured or killed—and
asked whether I could start for Africa immediately. I was to telephone
him again before I actually took off, because he did not want me to
interrupt my treatment unless the British attack assumed dangerous
proportions. I ordered my aircraft for seven o'clock next morning and
drove immediately to Wiener Neustadt. Finally, shortly after midnight,
a call came through from the Fuehrer. In view of developments at
Alamein he found himself obliged to ask me to fly back to Africa and
resume my command. I took off next morning. I knew there were no
more laurels to be earned in Africa, for I had been told in the reports I
had received from my officers that supplies had fallen far short of my
minimum demands. But just how bad the supply situation really was
I had yet to learn.

On arriving at Rome at about 11.00 hours (25th October) I was met
at the airport by General von Rintelen, Military Attaché and German
General attached to the Italian forces. He informed me of the latest
events in the African theatre. After heavy artillery preparation, the
enemy had taken part of our line south of Hill 31; several battalions of
164th Division and of Italians had been completely wiped out. The
British attack was still in progress and General Stumme still missing.
General von Rintelen also informed me that only three issues of petrol
remained in the African theatre; it had been impossible to send any more
across in the last weeks, partly because the Italian Navy had not provided
the shipping and partly because of the British sinkings. This was sheer
disaster, for with only 300 kilometres worth of petrol per vehicle between
Tripoli and the front, and that calculated over good driving country, a
prolonged resistance could not be expected; we would be completely
prevented from taking the correct tactical decisions and would thus suffer
a tremendous limitation in our freedom of action. I was bitterly angry,
because when I left there had been at least eight issues for the Army in
Egypt and Libya, and even this had been absurdly little in comparison

with the minimum essential of thirty issues. Experience had shown that one issue of petrol was required for each day of battle; without it, the army was crippled and could not react to the enemy's moves. General von Rintelen regretted the situation, but said that he had unfortunately been on leave and had consequently been unable to give sufficient attention to the supply question.

Rommel was justifiably incensed at the fact that virtually nothing had been done by the German authorities in Rome towards supplying the Panzer Army for the forthcoming battle. Rommel's reproach, however, should have been aimed at General von Rintelen's deputy rather than Rintelen himself, who had been absent on sick leave.

Feeling that we would fight this battle with but small hope of success, I crossed the Mediterranean in my Storch and reached headquarters at dusk (25th October). Meanwhile, General Stumme's body had been found at midday and taken to Derna. He had apparently been driving to the battlefield along the Alarm track when he had suddenly been fired on in the region of Hill 21 by British infantry using anti-tank and machine-guns. Colonel Buechting had received a mortal wound in the head. The driver, Corporal Wolf, had immediately swung the car round, and General Stumme had leapt out and hung on to the outside of it, while the driver drove at top speed out of the enemy fire. General Stumme must have suddenly had a heart attack and fallen off the car. The driver had noticed nothing. On Sunday morning the General had been found dead beside the Alarm track. General Stumme had been known to suffer from high blood-pressure and had not really been fit for tropical service.

We all deeply regretted the sudden death of Stumme. He had spared no pains to command the army well and had been day and night at the front. Just before setting off on his last journey on the 24th of October, he had told the acting Chief of Staff that he thought it would be wise to ask for my return, since with his short experience of the African theatre, and in view of the enormous British strength and the disastrous supply situation, he felt far from certain that he would be able to fight the battle to a successful conclusion. I, for my part, did not feel any more optimistic.

General von Thoma and Colonel Westphal reported to me that evening on the course of the battle to date, mentioning particularly that General Stumme had forbidden the bombardment of the enemy assembly positions on the first night of the attack, on account of the ammunition shortage. As a result the enemy had been able to take possession of part of our minefield and to overcome the occupying troops with comparatively small losses to himself. The petrol situation made any major movement impossible and permitted only local counter-attacks by the armour deployed behind the particular sector which was in danger. Units of the 15th Panzer Division had counter-attacked several times on the 24th and 25th October, but had suffered frightful losses in the terrible British artillery fire and non-stop R.A.F. bombing attacks. By the evening of the 25th, only 31 of their 119 tanks remained serviceable.

There were now only very small stocks of petrol left in North Africa and a crisis was threatening. I had already—on my way through Rome —demanded the immediate employment of all available Italian submarines and warships for the transport of petrol and ammunition. Our own air force was still unable to prevent the British bombing attacks, or to shoot down any major number of British aircraft. The R.A.F.'s new fighter-bombers were particularly in evidence, as is shown by the fact that every one of the captured tanks belonging to the *Kampfstaffel* had been shot up by this new type of aircraft.

Our aim for the next few days was to throw the enemy out of our main defence line at all costs and to reoccupy our old positions, in order to avoid having a westward bulge in our front.

That night our line again came under a heavy artillery barrage, which soon developed into one long roll of fire. I slept only a few hours and was back in my command vehicle again at 05.00 hours [*26th October*], where I learnt that the British had spent the whole night assaulting our front under cover of their artillery, which in some places had fired as many as five hundred rounds for every one of ours. Strong forces of the panzer divisions were already committed in the front line. British night-bombers had been over our units continuously. Shortly before midnight the enemy had succeeded in taking Hill 28, an important position in the northern sector.[1] He had then brought up reinforcements to this point ready to continue the attack in the morning with the object of extending his bridge-head west of the minefields.

Attacks were now launched on Hill 28 by elements of the 15th Panzer Division, the Littorio and a Bersaglieri Battalion, supported by the concentrated fire of all the local artillery and A.A. Unfortunately, the attack gained ground very slowly. The British resisted desperately. Rivers of blood were poured out over miserable strips of land which, in normal times, not even the poorest Arab would have bothered his head about. Tremendous British artillery fire pounded the area of the attack. In the evening part of the Bersaglieri Battalion succeeded in occupying the eastern and western edges of the hill. The hill itself remained in British hands and later became the base for many enemy operations.

I myself observed the attack that day from the north. Load after load of bombs cascaded down among my troops. British strength round Hill 28 was increasing steadily. I gave orders to the artillery to break up the British movement north-east of Hill 28 by concentrated fire, but we had too little ammunition to do it successfully. During the day I brought up the 90th Light Division and the *Kampfstaffel*, in order to press home the attack on Hill 28. The British were continually feeding fresh forces into

---

[1] Called by the British " Kidney Ridge "—from the shape of the ring contour on the map.

their attack from Hill 28 and it was clear that they wanted to win through to the area between El Daba and Sidi Abd el Rahman. I therefore moved the Trieste into the area east of El Daba. Late in the afternoon German and Italian dive-bomber formations made a self-immolating attempt to break up the British lorry columns moving towards the north-west. Some 60 British fighters pounced on these slow machines and forced the Italians to jettison their bombs over their own lines, while the German pilots pressed home their attack with very heavy losses. Never before in Africa had we seen such a density of anti-aircraft fire. Hundreds of British tracer shells criss-crossed the sky and the air became an absolute inferno of fire.

British attacks supported by tanks tried again and again to break out to the west through our line south of Hill 28. Finally, in the afternoon, a thrust by 160 tanks succeeded in wiping out an already severely mauled battalion of the 164th Infantry Division and penetrated into our line towards the south-west. Violent fighting followed in which the remaining German and Italian tanks managed to force the enemy back. Tank casualties so far, counting in that day's, were 61 in the 15th Panzer Division and 56 in the Littorio, all totally destroyed.

Following on their non-stop night attacks, the R.A.F. sent over formations of 18 to 20 bombers at hourly intervals throughout the day, which not only caused considerable casualties, but also began to produce serious signs of fatigue and a sense of inferiority among our troops.

Fatigue and depression were also evident on the British side, and there was a widespread feeling that the offensive might have to be broken off. While the German and Italian armour had suffered heavy losses in their attacks on the 25th and 26th, the British armour also lost heavily when they in turn tried to attack on the 26th. Both sides, indeed, successively provided an object lesson in the cost and futility of the " direct approach "—the offensive spirit unguided by subtlety of mind. On the British side, the commanders of the armour felt increasing doubts about the way it was being used to batter a way through. The infantry too, were also very tired, and depressed by their losses.

Montgomery decided that it would be wise to pause and change the plan, giving the bulk of his troops a rest while he was regrouping—and bringing up the 7th Armoured Division from the south. Frontal pressure was kept up meantime by minor attacks, on the 27th and 28th, and even in these one almost complete armoured brigade was used up.

The supply situation was now approaching disaster. The tanker *Proserpina*, which we had hoped would bring some relief in the petrol situation, had been bombed and sunk outside Tobruk. There was only enough petrol left to keep supply traffic going between Tripoli and the front for another two or three days, and that without counting the needs of the motorised forces, which had to be met out of the same stocks. What we should really have done now was to assemble all our motorised units in the north in order to fling the British back to the main defence line in a concentrated and planned counter-attack. But we had not the petrol to do it. So we were compelled to allow the armoured formations in the northern part of our line to assault the British salient piecemeal.

Since the enemy was operating with astonishing hesitancy and caution, a concentrated attack by the whole of our armour could have been successful, although such an assembly of armour would of course have been met by the heaviest possible British artillery fire and air bombardment. However, we could have made the action more fluid by withdrawing a few miles to the west and could then have attacked the British in an all-out charge and defeated them in open country. The British artillery and air force could not easily have intervened with their usual weight in a tank battle of this kind, for their own forces would have been endangered.

But a decision to take forces from the southern front was unthinkable with the petrol situation so bad. Not only could we not have kept a mobile battle going for more than a day or two, but our armour could never have returned to the south if the British had attacked there. I did, however, decide to bring the whole of the 21st Panzer Division up north, although I fully realised that the petrol shortage would not allow it to return. In addition, since it was now obvious that the enemy would make his main effort in the north during the next few days and try for a decision there, half the Army artillery was drawn off from the southern front. At the same time I reported to the Fuehrer's H.Q. that we would lose the battle unless there was an immediate improvement in the supply situation. Judging by previous experience, there was very little hope of this happening.

26 Oct. 1942

DEAREST LU,

Arrived 18.30 yesterday. Situation critical. A lot of work! After my wonderful weeks at home it's not easy to acclimatise myself to the new surroundings and the job in hand. There's too big a difference.

Relays of British bombers continued their attack throughout the night of the 26th. At about 02.00 hours a furious British barrage by guns of every calibre suddenly began in the northern sector. Soon it was impossible to distinguish between gun-fire and exploding shells and the sky grew bright with the glare of muzzle-flashes and shell-bursts. Continuous bombing attacks seriously delayed the approach march of the 21st Panzer Division and a third of the Ariete. By dawn the 90th Light Division and the Trieste had taken up position round the southern side of Sidi Abd el Rahman.

That morning [*27th October*] I gave orders to all formations to pin down the British assault forces during their approach by all-out fire from every gun they could bring to bear.

The tactics which the British were using followed from their apparently inexhaustible stocks of ammunition. Their new tank, the General Sherman, which came into action for the first time during this battle, showed itself to be far superior to any of ours.

Attacks against our line were preceded by extremely heavy artillery barrages lasting for several hours. The attacking infantry then pushed forward behind a curtain of fire and artificial fog, clearing mines and removing obstacles. Where a difficult patch was struck they frequently switched the direction of their attack under cover of smoke. Once the infantry had cleared lanes in the minefields, heavy tanks moved forward, closely followed by infantry. Particular skill was shown in carrying out this manœuvre at night and a great deal of hard training must have been done before the offensive.

In contact engagements the heavily gunned British tanks approached to a range of between 2,000 and 2,700 yards and then opened concentrated fire on our anti-tank and anti-aircraft guns and tanks, which were unable to penetrate the British armour at that range. The enormous quantities of ammunition which the enemy tanks used—sometimes they fired over 30 rounds at one target—were constantly replenished by armoured ammunition carriers. The British artillery fire was directed by observers who accompanied the attack in tanks.

27 Oct. 1942

Dearest Lu,

A very hard struggle. No one can conceive the burden that lies on me. Everything is at stake again and we're fighting under the greatest possible handicaps. However, I hope we'll pull through. You know I'll put all I've got into it.

YARD BY YARD

In the early hours of the 27th of October, the British attacked again towards the south-west at their old break-in point south of Hill 28. At about 10 a.m. I went off to Telegraph Track. Two enemy bomber formations, each of 18 aircraft, dropped their bombs inside ten minutes into our defence positions. The whole front continued to lie under a devastating British barrage.

Local counter-attacks were due to be launched that afternoon by the 90th Light Division on Hill 28 and by the 15th and 21st Panzer Divisions, the Littorio and a part of the Ariete, against the British positions between minefields L and I.

At 14.30 hours I drove to Telegraph Track again, accompanied by Major Ziegler. Three times within a quarter of an hour units of the 90th Light Division, which had deployed and were standing in the open in preparation for the attack, were bombed by formations of eighteen aircraft. At 15.00 hours our dive-bombers swooped down on the British lines. Every artillery and anti-aircraft gun which we had in the northern sector concentrated a violent fire on the point of. the intended attack. Then the armour moved forward. A murderous British fire struck into our ranks and our attack was soon brought to a halt by an immensely powerful anti-tank defence, mainly from dug-in anti-tank guns and a large number of tanks. We suffered considerable losses and were obliged to withdraw. There is, in general, little chance of success in a tank attack over country where the enemy has been able to take up defensive positions; but there was nothing else we could do. The 90th Light Division's attack was also broken up by heavy British artillery fire and a hail of bombs from British aircraft. A report from the division that they had taken Hill 28 unfortunately turned out to be untrue.

That evening further strong detachments of the panzer divisions had to be committed in the front to close the gaps. Several of the 90th Light Division's units also went into the line. Only 70 tons of petrol had been flown across by the Luftwaffe that day, with the result that the army could only refuel for a short distance, for there was no knowing when petrol would arrive in any quantity and how long the divisions would have to get along with the few tons we could issue to them. The watchword " as little movement as possible " applied more than ever.

In the evening we again sent S O S s to Rome and the Fuehrer's H.Q. But there was now no longer any hope of an improvement in the situation. It was obvious that from now on the British would destroy us bit by bit, since we were virtually unable to move on the battlefield. As yet, Montgomery had only thrown half his striking force into the battle.

28 Oct. 1942

DEAREST LU,

Who knows whether I'll have a chance to sit down and write in peace in the next few days or ever again. To-day there's still a chance.

The battle is raging. Perhaps we will still manage to be able to stick it out, in spite of all that's against us—but it may go wrong, and that would have very grave consequences for the whole course of the war. For North Africa would then fall to the British in a few days, almost without a fight. We will do all we can to pull it off. But the enemy's superiority is terrific and our resources very small.

Whether I would survive a defeat lies in God's hands. The lot of the vanquished is heavy. I'm happy in my own conscience that I've done all I can for victory and have not spared myself.

I realised so well in the few short weeks I was at home what you two mean to me. My last thought is of you.

Next day [*28th*] I was forced to decide on bringing further units

north, at the cost of almost completely denuding the southern front of
heavy weapons and German units. They were replaced by the third part
of the Ariete which had previously been engaged on the northern front.
During the morning the British made three attacks against our northern
front, but were thrown back to their starting point each time by our panzer
units. Unfortunately, we again lost heavily in tanks.

As on the previous days, ceaseless bombing attacks hammered down
on the German-Italian forces. The Luftwaffe tried all it could to help
us, but could achieve little or nothing against the tremendous numerical
superiority of the enemy.

The supply situation remained disastrous. In Italy, auxiliary cruisers
and destroyers were being mobilised in order to satisfy our urgent needs
for ammunition and petrol. Unfortunately only a few of the ships we
had been promised were coming to Tobruk; most were bound for
Benghazi. We knew from experience that transport from these ports to
the front took several days, and there was, therefore, little hope of these
supplies reaching us before it was too late.

Since midday on the 28th the existence of strong concentrations of
British armour had become apparent in minefield I. We assumed that
the British were about to launch what they intended to be their decisive
break-through and accordingly prepared ourselves, so far as our
diminished strength allowed, to meet the attack. Because of the heavy
casualties which had been suffered by the German-Italian infantry
divisions, the whole of the Afrika Korps had to be put into the line.

I again informed all commanders that this was a battle for life or
death and that every officer and man had to give of his best.

At about 21.00 hours a tremendous British drum-fire started to pound
the area west of Hill 28. Soon hundreds of British guns concentrated
their fire into the sector of the 2nd Battalion, 125th Regiment, north of
Hill 28.

*This was the opening of the new British offensive. It took the form of a right-
angled thrust northward to the coast, delivered from the broad wedge that had been
driven into Rommel's front. The aim was to pinch off the now projecting northern
flank of his position, and create an opening for a follow-up drive along the coast road,
towards Daba and Fuka.*

*The initial northward thrust was delivered by the 9th Australian Division with
part of the 23rd Armoured Brigade. It was only a partial success and the tanks
suffered very heavily.*

The British launched their assault at about 22.00 hours. The weight
of this attack was something quite exceptional. However, by concentrating
every gun in the area, we managed to break up the British attacks, which
were mainly made from Minefield I. Farther to the north, in the gap
between Minefields I and H, British tanks and infantry succeeded in
making a penetration. The battle raged at this point with tremendous
fury for six hours, until finally II/125th Regiment and XI Bersaglieri

Battalion were overrun by the enemy. Their troops, surrounded and exposed to enemy fire from all sides, fought on desperately.

Army H.Q. had meanwhile been moved farther to the west. I spent the whole of that night with a number of my officers and men on the coast road roughly in line with the old H.Q. site, from where we could see the flash of bursting shells in the darkness and hear the rolling thunder of the battle. Again and again British bomber formations flew up and tipped their death-dealing loads on my troops, or bathed the country in the brilliant light of parachute flares.

No one can conceive the extent of our anxiety during this period. That night I hardly slept and by 03.00 hours [*29th October*] was pacing up and down turning over in my mind the likely course of the battle, and the decisions I might have to take. It seemed doubtful whether we would be able to stand up much longer to attacks of the weight which the British were now making, and which they were in any case still able to increase. It was obvious to me that I dared not await the decisive break-through but would have to pull out to the west before it came. Such a decision, however, could not fail to lead to the loss of a large proportion of my non-motorised infantry, partly because of the low-fighting power of my motorised formations and partly because the infantry units themselves were too closely involved in the fighting. We were, therefore, going to make one more attempt, by the tenacity and stubbornness of our defence, to persuade the enemy to call off his attack. It was a slim hope, but the petrol situation alone made a retreat which would inevitably lead to mobile warfare, out of the question.

If retreat were nevertheless forced upon us, the principal aim of the Army would have to be to get as many tanks and weapons away to the west as it could. On no account could they be allowed to await their complete destruction in the Alamein line. So I decided that morning that if British pressure became too strong I would withdraw to the Fuka position before the battle had reached its climax.

This rearward line ran south from Fuka on the coast and terminated, like the Alamein line, in the Qattara depression.

29 Oct. 1942

DEAREST LU,

The situation continues very grave. By the time this letter arrives, it will no doubt have been decided whether we can hold on or not. I haven't much hope left.

At night I lie with my eyes wide open, unable to sleep, for the load that is on my shoulders. In the day I'm dead tired.

What will happen if things go wrong here? That is the thought that torments me day and night. I can see no way out if that happens.

On the morning of the 29th the British continued their attack against

II/125th Regiment under cover of heavy artillery fire. An attack by the 90th Light Division, aimed at relieving the battalion or, at any rate, reducing the pressure on it, was met by devastating British drum-fire. However, the remnants of II/125th Regiment were able to disengage under cover of this attack and fight their way back to the neighbouring units. The rest of them had either been killed or wounded and taken prisoner.

But the expected major attack did not come that day. It was the calm before the storm. At 07.00 hours Colonel Bayerlein returned from Europe and, after a short conference, set off for the Afrika Korps, where his presence was urgently required.

When it was found that Rommel had shifted the 90th Light Division to the coastal sector, thus blocking the prospects of a rapid break-through there, Alexander and Montgomery thought that the best course was to revert to the original axis, now that the opposition there had been thinned. The reorientation involved fresh re-grouping, so that the new attack, Operation Supercharge, was not ready for delivery until the night of the 1st November.

At about half-past eleven I received the shattering news that the tanker *Louisiana*, which had been sent as a replacement for the *Proserpina*, had been sunk by an aerial torpedo. Now we really were up against it. The ill-humour in which this news left me vented itself on the head of General Barbassetti, who arrived at my H.Q. shortly afterwards to represent Marshal Cavallero, who was detained in Rome. What riled me most was that heavily armed Italian auxiliary cruisers and other vessels, carrying cargoes intended for the front, were still being sent to Benghazi in order to keep them out of range of the torpedo-carrying British aircraft.

It was clear that it had now dawned on them even in Rome that the Army was facing annihilation unless its mobile formations could immediately be supplied with sufficient petrol. All at once it was decided to press submarines, warships, civilian aircraft and additional shipping space into service. If only this had been done after the fall of Tobruk, we would not have been sitting in front of El Alamein at the end of October. But now it was becoming steadily clearer that it was too late.

The 29th of October came and went and still the British had not launched their big attack. They were obviously regrouping. I was in course of discussing the details of the Fuka plan with Colonel Westphal, when suddenly the alarming news broke upon us that two British divisions had advanced through the Qattara depression and reached a point 60 miles south of Mersa Matruh. We were aghast, because we had virtually no defence against such a move. Several units stationed in the rear were immediately set in march for the threatened area. Next morning, however, we discovered that the whole story, which had come to us from the Commando Supremo, was a pure invention.

30 Oct. 1942

Dearest Lu,

Situation a little quieter. I've had some sleep, am in good spirits and hope to pull it off even yet.

The front continued comparatively quiet except for heavy artillery fire and air attacks hammering at our northern sector. That day the R.A.F. concentrated their attack on the coast road, where many of our vehicles were shot up by low-flying aircraft. Much to our relief, the petrol situation was slightly improved by the arrival of an Italian ship carrying 600 tons.

That day we had the Fuka position reconnoitred. The army had been so badly battered by the British air force and artillery that we could not now hope to stand up for long to the British break-through attempt, which was daily or even hourly expected. In the open desert, the Italian infantry formations would be so much dead weight, for they had practically no transport. At the time of our retreat from Cyrenaica in 1941-42, the Italians besieging Tobruk had been far enough west of the battlefield for them to be easily moved out behind a screen of motorised and armoured forces. Here, however, any withdrawal of the infantry would open up the centre and southern sectors of the front to the powerful British motorised forces standing ready there. The only thing for us was to try to whip out the infantry unexpectedly under cover of darkness, load all the units we could on to transport columns and then, after forming a wide front with the motorised forces, beat a fighting retreat to the west. But first we had to wait for the British to move, to ensure that they would be engaged in battle and could not suddenly throw their strength into a gap in our front and thus force a break-through.

Orders were given for the 21st Panzer Division to be withdrawn from the front line west of Minefields K and L during the night of the 30th and become mobile; it was to be replaced by the Trieste Division. These moves were proceeding in the darkness when suddenly a violent British barrage dropped on the sector held by the 125th Infantry Regiment in the north. Our army and A.A. artillery immediately engaged the British assembly areas south of Minefield H, but were unable to break up the dense concentration of British infantry and armoured formations in this sector. After an hour's barrage, the Australians opened their attack by pinning down the 125th Regiment at the front and assaulting its flank from the south. At the same time a strong force of British armour rolled north from the area north of Hill 28, and overran a light artillery battalion of the XXI Italian Corps, whose men, after a gallant resistance, either died or fought their way through to the neighbouring sector.

By next morning, the 31st October, a force of 30 heavy British tanks had reached the coast road and attacked part of the 361st Grenadier

Regiment, which was holding the second line. With the 21st Panzer Division still in process of handing over to the Trieste, the only unit immediately available for the counter-attack was the 580th Reconnaissance Battalion. I immediately drove up to Sidi Abd el Rahman and set up my command post east of the mosque. Meanwhile, the enemy had forced their way through to the coast and cut off the 125th Infantry Regiment. General von Thoma, who appeared at my command post with Bayerlein about 10.00 hours, was given command of our counter-attack, which was to be undertaken by troops of the 21st Panzer and 90th Light Divisions. It was to be preceded by heavy dive-bomber attacks and a barrage from all the artillery in that sector.

31 Oct. 1942

DEAREST LU,

Position very grave again, otherwise all well with me personally. I've got accustomed to the difficult situation. A week ago I was still with you, all unsuspecting.

Our attack went in at about 12.00 hours but failed to penetrate, as the enemy broke up and scattered our tanks and infantry with concentrated artillery fire and air attacks. However, contact was restored with 125th Regiment. Later we were able to relieve both battalions when a renewed attempt by the striking group under General von Thoma succeeded next day in throwing the enemy back across the railway line to the south.

Early in the afternoon of the 1st November, I went to Hill 16 with General von Thoma, General Sponeck and Colonel Bayerlein to inspect the country over which this action had been fought. Visibility was excellent. A Red Cross flag was flying from the railway station " The Hut " [*close to Tell el Eisa and to what the British called Thompson's Post*]. Seven wrecked tanks lay around " The Hut " alone, and farther on we could see another 30 or 40 destroyed British armoured vehicles. The British were obviously getting their wounded out, and our artillery had accordingly ceased fire.

That day waves of British aircraft, each of 18 to 20 bombers, attacked our front north of Hill 28 no less than 34 times. The air was filled with hundreds of British fighters, and large numbers of R.A.F. fighter-bombers spent the day shooting-up our supply vehicles on the coast road.

The supply situation remained as wretched as ever, although petrol showed a slight improvement as a result of increased supplies brought across by air to Tobruk. The ammunition situation was as bad as it could be. Only 40 tons had reached the African coast since the beginning of the British offensive and we were being forced to the strictest economy. We were compelled to issue orders that British assembly areas were to be engaged by harassing fire only and not by concentrated fire.

The British had so far used only a few divisions in their front line and still disposed of some 800 tanks, which were now assembled before our line in the northern sector for a decisive attack. We, on our side, had only 90 German and 140 Italian tanks to put in the battle. But how the situation appeared in Rome is best shown by a signal from Cavallero which reached us on the evening of the 1st November.

For FIELD MARSHAL ROMMEL
    The Duce authorises me to convey to you his deep appreciation of the successful counter-attack led personally by you. The Duce also conveys to you his complete confidence that the battle now in progress will be brought to a successful conclusion under your command.

UGO CAVALLERO

It was soon to be shown that the Fuehrer's H.Q. was no better informed over the situation in Africa. It is sometimes a misfortune to enjoy a certain military reputation. One knows one's own limits, but other people expect miracles and set down a defeat to deliberate cussedness.

Meanwhile, the reconnaissance reports had come in on the Fuka position. Steep declivities rendered its southern end proof against tanks, so that we could always hope to hold on there in an emergency until the British brought their artillery up, which might give time for reinforcements of some kind to be sent across.

Probably a hint of what we were doing percolated through some channel to the Fuehrer's H.Q. Anyway, it was already known there—as I was to learn later—that we had worked out a time-table for this operation.

Sunday, 1 Nov. 1942

DEAREST LU,
    It's a week since I left home. A week of very, very hard fighting. It was often doubtful whether we'd be able to hold out. Yet we did manage it each time, although with sad losses. I'm on the move a lot in order to step in wherever we're in trouble. Things were very bad in the north yesterday morning, although it was all more or less cleaned up by evening. The struggle makes very heavy demands on one's nervous energy, though physically I'm quite well. Some supplies are supposed to be on their way. But it's a tragedy that this sort of support only arrives when things are almost hopeless.

"TO VICTORY OR DEATH"

The expected British major attack came on the night of the 1st November. For three hours, shells from hundreds of British guns burst in our main defence line, while relays of night bombers attacked the German-Italian troops. Then massed British infantry and tanks advanced westward to the assault behind a moving curtain of fire. First came a heavy thrust against the 200th Infantry Regiment on either side of Hill 28. The British soon made a penetration and moved on with tanks and armoured cars to the west. After some heavy fighting we succeeded in halting this advance by throwing in the 90th Light Division's reserves. The enemy steadily strengthened his forces in the wedge he had driven into our line.

The British XXX Corps' attack was on a narrow front (4,000 yards), but made in great depth, by relays, to give it impetus. Two infantry brigades supported by the 23rd Armoured Brigade drove a lane 4,000 yards long through the enemy's new position, clearing the minefields as they advanced. Then the 9th Armoured Brigade passed through with the aim of advancing 2,000 yards farther and penetrating Rommel's gun-screen before daylight. It was followed up by the 1st, 7th and 10th Armoured Divisions. Alexander's dispatch says: "General Montgomery issued firm instructions that should XXX Corps not reach its objectives, the armoured divisions of X Corps were to fight their way through." But those instructions proved unavailing in their immediate application.

Soon afterwards, massed British formations broke through the 15th Panzer Division's front south-west of Hill 28. New Zealand infantry and powerful British armoured units—according to captured documents, there were between 400 and 500 tanks—advanced to the west, overran a regiment of the Trieste and a German Grenadier Battalion, in spite of a gallant resistance, and by dawn reached a point west of Telegraph Track.

According to reports from my artillery observers, there were another 400 British tanks standing east of the minefields. Isolated groups of British tanks and armoured cars succeeded in breaking out to the west and started hunting down our supply units.

2 Nov. 1942

DEAREST LU,
    Very heavy fighting again, not going well for us. The enemy, with his superior strength, is slowly levering us out of our position. That will mean the end. You can imagine how I feel. Air raid after air raid after air raid!

In the early hours of the morning [*2nd November*] the Afrika Korps counter-attacked and achieved some success, although at the cost of severe losses in armour, as our tanks were simply no match for the heavy British vehicles. The 4,000 yard British penetration—in which the enemy command had placed, besides the tanks already mentioned, fifteen artillery regiments with inexhaustible ammunition—was sealed off. It was only by the desperate fire of all available artillery and anti-aircraft guns, regardless of the ammunition shortage, that a further British penetration was prevented.

It was now extremely difficult to obtain any clear picture of the situation, as all our communication lines had been shot to pieces and most of our wireless channels were being jammed by the enemy. Complete chaos existed at many points on the front.

The 21st and 15th Panzer Divisions—those parts of them that were not already committed in the front—were now put in from the north and south respectively to pinch out the enemy wedge. Violent tank fighting followed. The British air force and artillery hammered away at our troops without let-up. Inside an hour at about midday seven formations, each of 18 bombers, unloaded their bombs on my troops. More and more of our 88-mm. guns, which were our only really effective weapons against the heavy British tanks, were going out of action. Although every air protection A.A. gun within reach had been brought up to the front we still had only 24 of these guns available for use that day. Soon, almost all our mobile forces were committed in the front. We had already squeezed every possible reinforcement out of the administrative units, yet our fighting strength was now only a third of what it had been at the start of the battle. I drove repeatedly to the front and watched the course of the battle from a hill.

The British were shooting up one after the other of the Littorio's and Trieste's tanks. The Italian 47-mm. anti-tank gun was no more effective against the British tanks than our own 50-mm., and signs of disintegration were beginning to show among the Italian troops. Units of the Littorio and the Trieste were on the run to the west and were no longer in the hands of their officers.

In the early afternoon the gravity of the situation in the north forced us to the decision to bring the Ariete up to the north along Telegraph Track and thus denude the southern front completely. After some delay I succeeded in making contact with Colonel Bayerlein, via the Chief of Staff, and notified him of this decision. The Ariete set off for the north later that afternoon, bringing with it a large part of the artillery from the southern front. I also decided that the time had come to shorten the front by pulling the 125th Regiment out of its positions and re-deploying it with its front to the east, in line with Telegraph Track.

In the evening I received reports on the Panzer's Army's supply situation. It was absolutely desperate. That day we had fired off 450 tons of ammunition; only 190 tons had arrived, brought by three destroyers to Tobruk.

The British now had what amounted to complete command of the air and sea up to a point beyond Tobruk, and were repeatedly attacking the town and harbour from the air. Several ships had been sunk in the harbour in the past few days. Due to our increased movement, the petrol situation was also becoming critical again. And we still had the heaviest fighting in front of us.

That evening it became clear that the British were concentrating their second-line armour at their point of penetration. So our final destruction was upon us. The Afrika Korps had only 35 serviceable tanks left.

Things looked different on " the other side of the hill." The 9th Armoured Brigade lost 75 per cent of its strength, having 87 tanks destroyed, and although the 2nd and 8th Armoured Brigades came up through the lane to reinforce it the attack was brought to a standstill by the combination of anti-tank guns ahead and tank threats on both flanks. The advance was still hung up throughout the next day, the 3rd November—thus providing Rommel with a good chance to slip away.

This then, was the moment to get back to the Fuka line. Some of our rear installations had already been carried off to the west. During the night the southern front was pulled back to the positions we had occupied before our offensive at the end of August. The 125th Regiment was moved into the area south of Sidi Abd el Rahman. The 90th Light Division, the Afrika Korps and XX Italian Corps were now to withdraw slowly enough to enable the foot divisions to march or be transported away. Seeing that the British had so far been following up hesitantly and that their operations had always been marked by an extreme, often incomprehensible, caution, I hoped to be able to salvage at least part of the infantry.

The army's strength was so exhausted after its ten days of battle that it was not now capable of offering any effective opposition to the enemy's next break-through attempt, which we expected to come next day. With our great shortage of vehicles an orderly withdrawal of the non-motorised forces appeared impossible. Added to that, the mobile forces were so firmly locked in battle that we could not expect to be able to disengage all of them. In these circumstances we had to reckon, at the least, with the gradual destruction of the army. I reported in these terms to the Fuehrer's H.Q.

Our intention for the 3rd of November was to withdraw before the British pressure to an area running south from a point some 10 miles east of El Daba. Our disengagement in the central and southern sectors passed unnoticed, although with no vehicles available and most of the heavy weapons having to be manhandled, the move went very slowly. However, in spite of all difficulties, the southern divisions were in their new positions by morning.

3 Nov. 1942

DEAREST LU,

The battle is going very heavily against us. We're simply being crushed by the enemy weight. I've made an attempt to salvage part of the army. I wonder if it will succeed. At night I lie open-eyed, racking my brains for a way out of this plight for my poor troops.

We are facing very difficult days, perhaps the most difficult that a man can undergo. The dead are lucky, it's all over for them. I think of you constantly with heartfelt love and gratitude. Perhaps all will yet be well and we shall see each other again.

The 3rd November will remain a memorable day in history. For not only did it become finally clear on that day that the fortunes of war had deserted us, but from that day on the Panzer Army's freedom of decision was continually curtailed by the interference of higher authority in its conduct of operations.

Already in the morning I had an uncomfortable feeling that in spite of our unequivocal situation reports, our higher command had not drawn the proper conclusions from the conditions we were facing, and I therefore decided to send my A.D.C., Lieutenant Berndt, to report direct to the Fuehrer. Berndt was to leave the Fuehrer's H.Q. in no doubt about our situation and was to indicate that the African theatre of war was probably already lost. He was to demand the fullest freedom of action for the Panzer Army. I wanted at all costs to avoid playing into the hands of the British in their efforts to surround and destroy us. I intended to fight delaying actions in as many intermediate positions as possible, forcing the enemy to bring up his artillery each time, and to avoid any decisive battle until either we had grown strong enough for it or the bulk of the African Army had been carried across to Europe, with only a small part left in Africa to cover the retreat.

At nine in the morning I drove east along the coast road as far as Forward H.Q. Large numbers of vehicles, mainly Italian, were jammed up on the road, but surprisingly there were no British fighter-bombers about. At about 10.00 hours General von Thoma and Colonel Bayerlein reported that the British were lying in a semicircle in front of the Afrika Korps, which still possessed 30 serviceable tanks. The British were making only probing and local attacks and appeared to be reorganising and supplying their formations. The moment seemed propitious, and I gave orders for part of the Italian formations to march off. Despite our frequent reminders, the vehicles promised by Barbassetti had still not arrived, and so the Italians had to march. Dense columns of vehicles were already streaming westwards. The Italian infantry marched off and soon the road was full of traffic. But the British soon spotted our move and attacked the coast road with about 200 fighter-bombers. Their bomber squadrons were also extremely active that day. The Afrika

Korps alone was attacked no less than eleven times during the morning by strong formations of bombers.

At about midday I returned to my command post, only just escaping, by some frantic driving, a carpet of bombs laid by 18 British aircraft. At 13.30 hours an order arrived from the Fuehrer. It read in roughly the following words:[1]

To Field Marshal Rommel

In the situation in which you find yourself there can be no other thought but to stand fast and throw every gun and every man into the battle. The utmost efforts are being made to help you. Your enemy, despite his superiority, must also be at the end of his strength. It would not be the first time in history that a strong will has triumphed over the bigger battalions. As to your troops, you can show them no other road than that to victory or death.

Adolf Hitler

This order demanded the impossible. Even the most devoted soldier can be killed by a bomb. In spite of our unvarnished situation reports, it was apparently still not realised at the Fuehrer's H.Q. how matters really stood in Africa. Arms, petrol and aircraft could have helped us, but not orders. We were completely stunned, and for the first time during the African campaign I did not know what to do. A kind of apathy took hold of us as we issued orders for all existing positions to be held on instructions from the highest authority. I forced myself to this action, as I had always demanded unconditional obedience from others and, consequently, wished to apply the same principle to myself. Had I known what was to come I should have acted differently, because from that time on, we had continually to circumvent orders from the Fuehrer or Duce in order to save the army from destruction. But this first instance

[1]Rommel gives a shortened version of the order. The full version reads as follows:

To Field Marshal Rommel

It is with trusting confidence in your leadership and the courage of the German-Italian troops under your command that the German people and I are following the heroic struggle in Egypt. In the situation in which you find yourself there can be no other thought but to stand fast, yield not a yard of ground and throw every gun and every man into the battle. Considerable air force reinforcements are being sent to C.-in-C. South. The Duce and the Commando Supremo are also making the utmost efforts to send you the means to continue the fight. Your enemy, despite his superiority, must also be at the end of his strength. It would not be the first time in history that a strong will has triumphed over the bigger battalions. As to your troops, you can show them no other road than that to victory or death.

Adolf Hitler

of interference by higher authority in the tactical conduct of the African war came as a considerable shock.[1]

Movements in progress to the west were stopped and everything possible was done to strengthen our fighting power. To the Fuehrer we reported that any further stand in the positions which the Panzer Army was then holding would mean the inevitable loss of the army, and thus of the whole of North Africa.

The order had a powerful effect on the troops. At the Fuehrer's command they were ready to sacrifice themselves to the last man. An overwhelming bitterness welled up in us when we saw the superlative spirit of the army, in which every man, from the highest to the lowest, knew that even the greatest effort could no longer change the course of the battle.

Not until the afternoon did the British follow up the X Italian Corps' withdrawal in the southern sector, having spent the morning pouring artillery fire into the abandoned positions. Attacks on the corps' northern flank were beaten off. This corps suffered particularly badly from the activities of enemy armoured cars behind our front.[2] A considerable number of these vehicles had broken through our line and were harassing our supply traffic, rendering the supply of X Corps' troops, even with the barest minimum of water and rations, almost an impossibility. Finally, we had to use Italian armoured cars to protect our supply convoys.

The Bologna Division was already on the march to the west and Italian staff officers had great trouble in getting it back to the front, for its march columns were almost impossible to locate.

3 Nov. 1942

Dearest Lu,

The battle still rages with unspent fury. I can no longer, or scarcely any longer, believe in its successful outcome. Berndt flies to the Fuehrer to-day to report.

Enclosed 25,000 lire that I've saved.

What will become of us is in God's hands. ..

P.S.—Have Appel exchange the lire. Currency regulations!

In the evening I sent Lieutenant Berndt off to the Fuehrer's H.Q. He was to report that if the Fuehrer's order were upheld, the final destruction of the German-Italian Army would be a matter of days only,

---

[1] *Note by Manfred Rommel.*—The existence of such passages as this caused my father to decide, in 1944, to burn that part of the manuscript dealing with El Alamein. His death on 14th October of that year prevented him carrying out his design.

[2] The Royal Dragoons' armoured cars had slipped through the German anti-tank screen in the dawn mist on the 2nd, and were followed later by the 4th South African Armoured Car Regiment.

and was to add that we had already suffered immense harm because of it. Later that night Berndt informed me from Mersa Matruh that hundreds of low-flying aircraft had attacked the densely crowded road, packed with two lines of traffic, continuously from nightfall at about 17.00 hours until his arrival in Mersa Matruh at 21.00 hours. The road was blocked at many points by burning vehicles and vast traffic jams had developed. In many cases drivers and men had abandoned their vehicles and fled westwards on foot. Abandoned tanks and vehicles stood at many points on the road.

The night of the 3rd November also passed without any particular move from the British. This was all so much lost time for us, for we could meanwhile have got the whole of our force back to Fuka—in all probability with only small casualties. I had not dared hope that the British commander would give us such a chance. And now it was passing unused.

On the morning of the 4th November, the Afrika Korps under General von Thoma, adjoining the 90th Light Division under General von Sponeck, held a thin semicircular line on either side of Tell el Mampsra, extending to a point some 10 miles south of the railway line, where it linked up with the Italian Armoured Corps, consisting of the Ariete and the remnants of the Littorio and Trieste. The south was held by the Italian Trento Division, Parachute Brigade Ramcke, and X Italian Corps.

After about an hour's artillery preparation, the British opened their attack at about 8 a.m. By throwing in all their strength, the Afrika Korps—which General von Thoma commanded in the front line—and the 90th Light Division succeeded in beating off enemy attacks supported by about 200 tanks, which went on till midday. The German Panzer Corps had only 20 serviceable tanks left.

Alexander's dispatch states: " *Our casualties were a negligible factor as far as the pursuit was concerned; on 4th November the Eighth Army could put in the field very nearly six hundred tanks against eighty German.*"

The number of German tanks left fit for action was fewer even than was supposed. More than 500 British tanks had been disabled in the struggle, nearly three times as many as the Germans had lost, but the British could afford it, and the adverse rate of attrition had been highly profitable on balance. It ensured ultimate victory provided that the commanders' resolution and their troops' endurance did not fail. That was the crux of the issue.

Field Marshal Kesselring arrived at my H.Q. during the morning. As I imagined that the Fuehrer had based his decision on optimistic situation reports sent back by the Luftwaffe, some angry words passed between us. Kesselring thought that the Fuehrer had learnt from his experience in the East that, in circumstances like these, the front must be held at all costs. I said to him very clearly: " So far I've always taken it for granted that the Fuehrer left the command of the army to me.

This crazy order has come like a bombshell. He can't just blindly apply experience he's gained in Russia to the war in Africa. He really should have left the decision here to me."[1]

In actual fact, the Fuehrer's order had been based on other, quite different grounds—as was to become increasingly clear as time went on. Paradoxical though it may sound, it was the custom at the Fuehrer's H.Q. to subordinate military interests to those of propaganda. They were simply unable to bring themselves to say to the German people and the world at large that Alamein had been lost, and believed they could avert its fate by a "Victory or Death" order. Until this moment we in Africa had always had complete freedom of action. Now that was over.

After the conference with Kesselring, I drove to Afrika Korps H.Q. which was housed in a dugout a few miles west of the front. Before leaving I had telephoned Bayerlein to tell him that the 90th Light Division was now bulging badly to the east and that the Afrika Korps should only withdraw slowly if British pressure became too strong. On my arrival at Corps H.Q. their Ia reported that the British had not yet brought artillery up to the Afrika Korps' front, and that all their attacks so far appeared to have been halted.

I now heard by telephone from my Chief of Staff, Westphal, that the British had broken through the XXI Corps' front south of XX Corps, and that units of the XXI Corps were retreating westwards. The Italian anti-tank guns were simply useless against the heavy British tanks. At about 10.00 hours a powerful force of British armour had appeared in front of the XX Corps and shortly afterwards the Italian divisions, their artillery in particular, had come under intensely heavy artillery fire and continuous R.A.F. bombing attacks. Westphal added that the situation was very serious and that a violent armoured battle was now in progress.

At about 13.00 hours, Bayerlein arrived back at Afrika Korps' H.Q. from the front, and reported on the Korps' situation. The Korps' *Kampfstaffel*[2] had been holding the centre of the line at Tell el Mampsra, with 21st Panzer Division to its north and 15th to its south. The two divisions had managed to dig in reasonably well. But Bayerlein went on to say that the *Kampfstaffel* had been wiped out and that it had been impossible to persuade General von Thoma to leave the front line, where he had probably sought his death. Bayerlein had escaped on foot at the last moment just as the British tanks were preparing to overrun the hill Tell el Mampsra—where the vehicles and equipment of the shattered *Kampfstaffel* were burning—and break through to the west.

Enormous dust-clouds could be seen south and south-east of head-

[1] *Note by Manfred Rommel.*—Kesselring did, in fact, discuss with my father the possibility of circumventing Hitler's order. Kesselring gave it as his view that Rommel, as the man on the spot, should do what he thought was right.

[2] As earlier mentioned this was a combat unit of about company strength, which had originally been formed to protect Corps H.Q., but was always employed on special combat tasks.

quarters, where the desperate struggle of the small and inefficient Italian tanks of XX Corps was being played out against the hundred or so British heavy tanks which had come round their open right flank. I was later told by Major von Luck, whose battalion I had sent to close the gap between the Italians and the Afrika Korps, that the Italians, who at that time represented our strongest motorised force, fought with exemplary courage. Von Luck gave what assistance he could with his guns, but was unable to avert the fate of the Italian Armoured Corps. Tank after tank split asunder or burned out, while all the time a tremendous British barrage lay over the Italian infantry and artillery positions. The last signal came from the Ariete at about 15.30 hours:

" Enemy tanks penetrated south of Ariete. Ariete now encircled. Location 5 km. north-west Bir el Abd. Ariete's tanks in action."

By evening the XX Italian Corps had been completely destroyed after a very gallant action. In the Ariete we lost our oldest Italian comrades, from whom we had probably always demanded more than they, with their poor armament, had been capable of performing.

A view over the battlefield from Corps' H.Q. showed that strong British tank formations had also broken through the Afrika Korps and were pressing on to the west.

Thus the picture in the early afternoon was as follows: on the right of the Afrika Korps, powerful enemy armoured forces had destroyed the XX Italian Motorised Corps, and thus burst a 12-mile hole in our front, through which strong bodies of tanks were moving to the west. As a result of this, our forces in the north were threatened with encirclement by enemy formations twenty times their superior in tanks. The 90th Light Division had defended their line magnificently against all British attacks, but the Afrika Korps' line had been penetrated after a very gallant resistance by their troops. There were no reserves, as every available man and gun had had to be put into the line.

So now it had come, the thing we had done everything in our power to avoid—our front broken and the fully motorised enemy streaming into our rear. Superior orders could no longer count. We had to save what there was to be saved. After a preliminary talk with Colonel Bayerlein, who had now assumed command of the Afrika Korps again, I issued orders for the retreat to be started immediately. General von Thoma had tried to prevent the British break-through with his *Kampfstaffel* and, as we heard later over the British news service, had been taken prisoner after the destruction of his force.

This decision could at least be the means of saving the motorised part of the Panzer Army from destruction, although the army had already lost so much as a result of the 24-hour postponement of its retreat—including practically the whole of its infantry and large numbers of tanks, vehicles and guns—that it was no longer in a position to offer effective opposition to the British advance at any point. Orders for the retreat went out at 15.30 hours, and the movement began immediately.

There was now no chance of getting order into our columns, for nothing short of a quick retreat could save us from the British air attacks, which reached a climax that day. Anything that did not immediately reach the road and race off westwards was lost, for the enemy followed us up over a wide front and overran everything that came in his path.

Next morning—far too late—signals arrived from the Fuehrer and the Commando Supremo authorising the withdrawal of the army to the Fuka position.

CHAPTER XV

ALAMEIN IN RETROSPECT

WE HAD lost the decisive battle of the African campaign. It was decisive because our defeat had resulted in the loss of a large part of our infantry and motorised forces. The astonishing thing was that the authorities, both German and Italian, looked for the fault not in the failure of supplies, not in our air inferiority, not in the order to conquer or die at Alamein, but in the command and troops. The military career of most of the people who aimed these accusations at us was notable for a consistent absence from the front, on the principle of " *weit vom Schuss gibt alte Krieger* "—" far from the battle makes old soldiers."

It was even said that we had thrown away our weapons, that I was a defeatist, a pessimist in adversity and therefore largely responsible. My refusal to sit down under this constant calumny aimed at my valiant troops was to involve me later in many violent arguments and rows. Our old ill-wishers particularly—men who had always resented our success —drew from our defeat the courage to vilify us, where previously they had had to keep silent. The victim of it all was my army, which, after my departure from Tunis, fell to a man into British hands, while highly qualified armchair strategists were still entertaining ideas about operations against Casablanca.

The fact is that there were men in high places who, though not without the capacity to grasp the facts of the situation, simply did not have the courage to look them in the face and draw the proper conclusions. They preferred to put their heads in the sand, live in a sort of military pipe-dream and look for scapegoats whom they usually found in the troops or field commanders.

Looking back, I am conscious of only one mistake—that I did not circumvent the " Victory or Death " order twenty-four hours earlier. Then the army would in all probability have been saved, with all its infantry, in at least a semi-battleworthy condition.

To leave future historians in no doubt as to the conditions and circumstances under which both troops and command had to labour at El Alamein, I give the following summary:

The first essential condition for an army to be able to stand the strain of battle is an adequate stock of weapons, petrol and ammunition. In fact, the battle is fought and decided by the Quartermasters before the shooting begins. The bravest men can do nothing without guns, the guns nothing without plenty of ammunition, and neither guns nor ammunition are of much use in mobile warfare unless there are vehicles with sufficient petrol to haul them around. Maintenance must also approximate, both in quantity and quality, to that available to the enemy.

A second essential condition for an army to be able to stand in battle is parity or at least something approaching parity in the air.[1] If the enemy has air supremacy and makes full use of it, then one's own command is forced to suffer the following limitations and disadvantages:

> By using his strategic air force, the enemy can strangle one's supplies, especially if they have to be carried across the sea.
>
> The enemy can wage the battle of attrition from the air.
>
> Intensive exploitation by the enemy of his air superiority gives rise to far-reaching tactical limitations (already described) for one's own command.

In future the battle on the ground will be preceded by the battle in the air. This will determine which of the contestants has to suffer the operational and tactical disadvantages detailed above, and thus be forced, throughout the battle, into adopting compromise solutions.

In our case, neither of the conditions I have described were in the slightest degree fulfilled and we had to suffer the consequences.

As a result of British command of the air in the Central Mediterranean, and of other reasons I have already given, the army's supplies were barely sufficient to keep life going, even on quiet days. A build-up for a defensive battle was out of the question. The quantity of material available to the British, on the other hand, far exceeded our worst fears. Never before in any theatre of war had such a vast quantity of heavy tanks, bombers and artillery, with inexhaustible supplies of ammunition, been engaged on so short a front as at El Alamein.

British command of the air was complete. On some days they flew 800 bomber sorties and 2,500 sorties of fighters, fighter-bombers and low-flying aircraft. We, on the other hand, could fly at the most 60 dive-bomber and 100 fighter sorties.[2] And this number continually decreased.

---

[1] Rommel's conclusion here would seem to be brought in question by the successes he achieved under conditions of air inferiority. At the same time the effect of the handicap becomes very clear in studying his account—the much increased demands on tactical skill and also the much-increased risks.

[2] This figure refers to the German air force only. The Italians also flew about 100 sorties. See page 335 for German figures.

The principles of British command had on the whole not altered; method and rigid adherence to system were still the main feature of their tactics. But on this occasion the British principles actually helped the Eighth Army to victory, for the following reasons:

(a) There was no open desert fighting, as our motorised forces were drawn to the front to support the frontally engaged infantry divisions.

(b) The British had such superiority in weapons, both in quality and quantity, that they were able to force through any and every operation.

The methods which the British employed for the destruction of my force were conditioned by their overwhelming material superiority. They were based on:

Extreme concentrations of artillery fire.

Continuous air attacks by powerful waves of bombers.

Locally limited attacks, executed with lavish use of material and manifesting an extremely high state of training, fully in line with previous experience and the conditions under which the battle was fought.

For the rest, the British based their planning on the principle of exact calculation, a principle which can only be followed where there is complete material superiority. They actually undertook no operations[1] but relied simply and solely on the effect of their artillery and air force. Their command was as slow as ever in reacting. When we embarked on our retreat on the night of the 2nd November, a long time elapsed before the British forces started their pursuit—and, but for the intervention of that unfortunate order, we would probably have been able to escape to Fuka with the bulk of our infantry. Their command continued to show its customary caution and lack of resolute decision. Thus they repeatedly allowed their armoured formations to attack separately, instead of throwing in the 900 or so tanks, which they could safely have committed on the northern front, in order to gain a quick decision with the minimum of effort and casualties. In fact, only half that number of tanks, acting under cover of their artillery and air force, would

[1]The term " operations " has a more specific meaning in German military language than in English—covering the intermediate sphere between strategy and tactics, and being applied to generalship in the handling of forces *in the field*. The German sense is best expressed in the now little-used term " grand tactics." In the German Army, the distinctive sense given to " operations " and " operational " helped to develop the idea of manœuvre in contrast to battering-ram tactics—to sheer massing of superior weight in men and weapons. But it tended to overshadow the importance of strategy, and the extent to which action in the field is subject to factors of a wider kind.

have sufficed to destroy my forces, which frequently stood immobile on the battlefield. These piecemeal tactics also caused the British themselves very high casualties. In all probability their command wanted to hold back its armour for the pursuit, as their assault formations could not apparently be regrouped quickly enough to follow up.[1]

In the training of their armoured and infantry formations the British command had made excellent use of the experience they had gained in previous actions with the Axis forces—although, of course, the new methods they used were only made possible by their vast stocks of ammunition, material and new equipment. These methods are described in detail in the following:

Tank Tactics

Here the new British methods were made possible by the use of new tanks, more heavily gunned and armoured than ours (including the Grant, Lee and Sherman; the heavy Churchill is also said to have put in an appearance[2]), and their inexhaustible supplies of ammunition.

With the light tanks sent out in advance, the heavier, gun-carrying tanks remained more and more in the rear. The task of the light tanks was to draw the fire of our anti-tank and anti-aircraft guns and armour. As soon as our guns and tanks had given away their positions, the heavier British tanks opened a destructive fire on all the targets they had located, from a range of up to 2,700 yards and, if possible, from the rear slope of a hill. Their fire seemed always to be directed by the commander of the squadron. The vast quantities of ammunition which this system needed were continually fed forward in armoured machine-gun carriers. By this means the British shot up our tanks, machine-gun nests and anti-aircraft and anti-tank gun positions at a range at which our own guns were completely incapable of penetrating their heavier tanks and could not, in any case, have afforded the ammunition they would have needed to shoot themselves in.

Artillery Tactics

The British artillery once again demonstrated its well-known excellence. A particular feature was its great mobility and tremendous speed of reaction to the needs of the assault troops. The British armoured units obviously carried artillery observers to transmit the needs of the front back to the artillery in the shortest possible time. In addition to the advantage given by their abundant supplies of ammunition, the British benefited greatly from the long range of their guns, which enabled them to take the Italian artillery positions under fire at a range at which the Italian guns, most of which were limited to 6,000 yards, were com-

[1]Rommel's impression was mistaken. See note on page 342.
[2]Four of the Churchill tanks were present in this battle.

pletely unable to hit back. As by far the greater part of our artillery was made up of these obsolete Italian guns, this was a particularly distressing circumstance for us.

Infantry Tactics

When our defence had been shattered by artillery, tanks and air force, the British infantry attacked.

With our outposts pinned down by British artillery fire—their positions had been located long before by air reconnaissance—highly-trained British sappers, working under cover of smoke, cleared mines and cut broad lanes through our minefields. Then the tanks attacked, followed closely by infantry. With the tanks acting as artillery, British storming parties worked their way up to our defence posts, suddenly to force their way into our trenches and positions at the point of the bayonet. Everything went methodically and according to a drill. Each separate action was executed with a concentration of superior strength. The artillery followed up close behind the infantry in order to crush any last flickers of resistance. Success was not usually exploited in any depth but was confined to occupation of the conquered positions, into which reinforcements and artillery were then brought up and disposed for defence. Night attacks continued to be a particular speciality of the British.[1]

Was there an Alternative?

As I have already explained at length, our own dispositions at the outset of the battle were guided by the experience we had gained in previous actions. Having once installed our infantry in the Alamein line, we were bound to accept battle there in spite of the enemy's immense superiority in artillery and ammunition. Had we withdrawn immediately, we would have had to abandon all the ammunition we had piled up at Alamein—having no transport to move it back—without having any worthwhile supplies in the rear to replace it. Quite apart from the heavy losses which the non-motorised infantry would probably have suffered during the retreat, we would also have lost the advantage of prepared

[1]This development had an interesting background. The value of attacking under cover of darkness was urged by one or two military thinkers after World War I, but disputed by most soldiers on the score that the risks of confusion were too great. Eventually the argument for night attack convinced a War Office Committee appointed in 1932, but the recommendations of this committee were still resisted or neglected by the majority of commanders. One of the few exceptions was Sir Frederick Pile, a dynamic tank leader who was then commanding an infantry brigade in Egypt. He took up the theory enthusiastically and developed an intensive system of night attack training in the desert. At that time Montgomery was one of his battalion commanders, and, although at first sceptical, was converted by experience of these trials. When Montgomery returned to Egypt in 1942 to take over command of the Eighth Army, he made the fullest use of night attacks in all his offensives—as his key method of breaking into the enemy front.

positions, for no defences had yet been constructed at Fuka. As it was, the British suffered considerable losses in our minefields and we managed to shoot off at them almost all the ammunition we had stored in the Alamein line.

Our tactical reactions during the battle were guided by the needs of the situation and the extent of our material resources, which were small enough.

After the battle, with all the experience it had brought us, I had an idea for a plan which might have enabled us to put up a more successful defence of Western Egypt against an enemy with the material strength of Montgomery's army, attacking from Alexandria. Not that we, of course, could ever have put the plan into effect; our petrol shortage would have seen to that. Moreover, we had tied up too much of our material—material which was now irreplaceable—in the construction of the Alamein line. However, I mention the plan here because it contains one or two points of substance.

It would first have been necessary to establish the non-motorised infantry in the Fuka line, using the maximum possible number of mines and with positions constructed similarly to those at El Alamein. The line at Fuka, like that at El Alamein, rested in the south on the Qattara depression and thus could not be turned. It had the additional advantage that steep declivities rendered some twelve miles of it in the south impassable to tanks and vehicles.

The El Alamein line would have been held by motorised formations and reconnaissance units, while the motorised forces located between Alamein and Fuka would have been grouped for a mobile defence.

On the British launching their attack, the action would probably have developed on something like the following lines: The British motorised forces would have thrust forward into open country, following up our reconnaissance and motorised forces, which would have withdrawn from the Alamein line. Then, in a position favourable to ourselves, battle would have been joined between our mobile forces and the British, who would now have been without the protection of their artillery regiments. In this battle, which would have been fought in front of the Fuka line, our armour would not, of course, have been capable of standing up to the powerful British striking groups for long. However, experience indicated that we would probably have been able to force the over-cautious British into more than one difficult tactical situation and to inflict considerable losses on their striking forces. When the moment came, as it was bound to come, that the British had concentrated their forces on the battlefield and were threatening to get the upper hand—in other words, when there was a danger that a continuation of the mobile battle would work more to their advantage than to ours—we would have had to extricate our motorised forces from the battle and bring them back behind the German-Italian line before their losses had become too great. The sole purpose of this mobile fighting in front of the Fuka line would have been to soak up some of the British striking power.

In the absence of their massive artillery support, a British attack at Fuka against a line similarly constructed to that at El Alamein, would have met with a bloody rebuff. They would have been forced to bring up their artillery, and this would have meant moving all their installations forward. Thus we would have been given a reprieve during which many things could have happened. The Nebelwerfer regiment might have come across, we might indeed have actually received our " Tigers "— at the very least, somebody might have done something to improve the supply situation. Even so, it is still very doubtful whether we could have held out in the African theatre any longer than we actually did. I only include these notes because several of my later plans and actions in Tripolitania and Tunisia were based on principles which had been formed out of our experience at El Alamein.

I have said that our defence plan was a compromise. There was no real redress either for our inferiority in the air or for the supply situation; nor was it possible to motorise the infantry. It was left to the command in Africa to cope with these problems as best it could.

Such a compromise can be no ideal solution. We simply did what we could, with our very meagre resources, to come to terms with the unalterable disadvantages under which we suffered. It was a matter of getting the best out of a hopeless situation. Armed with a pitch-fork, the finest fighting man can do little against an opponent with a tommy-gun in his hands.

No one can say that we had not given warning, months before the British offensive, that the army would be unable to fight a successful defence, unless a minimum specific build-up was created in Africa and unless certain specific quantities of reinforcements and replacement material reached African soil. That this was not done, was very well known to the people who later flung the most mud. To quote only one example —instead of the thirty issues of petrol I had demanded, we had had three. The figure I had given for our material requirements had been based on the anticipated increase in British strength. I could not of course have foreseen just how great the strength of the British was actually to be.

In these circumstances, there was never any chance of the army achieving success at El Alamein. Our sole advantage, compared with the many afforded to the enemy, was the possession of prepared positions; but these were soon stormed, after a terrible artillery and air bombardment, by British infantry, who gnawed their way yard by yard into our defence system. One sector after another of the northern front fell into British hands, until finally the Axis troops lost the whole of the northern part of their line. A further stand at El Alamein was then senseless, for not only were the defending forces exposed to the full weight of the enemy's non-stop air attacks in roughly improvised positions, but also the vehicle assemblies were being obliterated by the torrential British artillery fire. That way lay destruction.

Our counter-attacks early in the battle could not be made with a concentration of strength, as British assembly areas in the southern sector gave us good cause to fear that if we drew off all the motorised forces they would attack there as well. And the shortage of petrol would never have allowed us to move the Ariete and 21st Panzer Division back there again. At that stage of the battle, therefore, it was too great a risk to draw off all our motorised forces from the southern front to the north.

There is another very important point to be taken into account. Any formation we employed on the northern front was ground away by the British bombing and drum-fire far more quickly than were the attacking British by our defensive fire. The units which remained in their starting positions mostly had their vehicles dug in and were comparatively seldom attacked. But the northern sector was like a mill. Everything that went into it, regardless of quantity, was ground down to dust.

The bravery of the German and of many of the Italian troops in this battle, even in the hour of disaster, was admirable. The army had behind it a record of eighteen magnificent months, such as has seldom been equalled, and every one of my soldiers who fought at Alamein was defending not only his homeland, but also the tradition of the Panzer Army " Afrika". The struggle of my army, despite its defeat, will be a glorious page in the annals of the German and Italian peoples.

SORTIES BY THE GERMAN LUFTWAFFE DURING THE BATTLE OF EL ALAMEIN[1]

Date	Total Sorties	Fighter Sorties	Tons of Bombs Dropped
24/10/42	107	69	5.0
25/10/42	140	49	22.0
26/10/42	113	63	28.1
27/10/42	147	78	29.1
28/10/42	163	106	20.2
29/10/42	196	129	29.1
30/10/42	200[2]	125[2]	30.5[2]
31/10/42	242	128	43.3
1/11/42	141	80	12.8
2/11/42	175	111	20.7

[1]These figures were given to Rommel by General Seidemann, Commander of the Luftwaffe in Africa.

[2]Figures for 30/10/42 are estimates only.

BATTLE STRENGTH, ACCORDING TO RETURNS, OF
GERMAN-ITALIAN ARMOURED FORMATIONS DURING
THE BATTLE OF EL ALAMEIN

Nature of Action	Date	No. of Tanks held by German and Italian Formations		
		PANZER II, III, IV	M-TANK	L-TANK
	24/10/42	219	318	21
	25/10/42	154	270	21
	26/10/42	162	221	21
	27/10/42	137	210	21
Defence and counter attacks with limited objective	28/10/42	81	197	21
	29/10/42	109	190	21
	30/10/42	116	201	21
	31/10/42	106	198	21
	1/11/42	109	189	21
	2/11/42	32	140[1]	15[1]
	3/11/42	24	120[1]	0[1]
Decisive break-through	4/11/42	12	0	0

[1]Estimates only.

CHAPTER XVI

THE GREAT RETREAT

ON THE night of the 4th November, the army retreated to Fuka. The movement was made over a broad front, mainly through the open desert, as the coast road was continuously bathed in the brilliant light of British flares and under non-stop R.A.F. attack. It was a race between the British armour and ourselves, both striving for the same goal.

The 1st and 10th Armoured Divisions, after breaking out, were told to drive north-westwards and get astride the coast road at Daba and Galal, west of Daba. The 7th Armoured Division and the New Zealand Division, with armoured troops attached, were sent on a wider circuit through the desert, and directed on Fuka.

On the evening of the 4th November these pursuit forces were well in rear of Rommel's battered army, whose retreat had been delayed by Hitler's intervention. Yet by the following afternoon the bulk of the remaining German troops, who were motorised, had managed to slip through the series of " trap doors," and had regained a good chance of escaping. It is not easy to see how they succeeded—especially in view of the disorder and congestion on the coast road—in running the gauntlet of air and ground attack.

After the event, the failure to block their escape was ascribed to the intervention of sudden rain—Montgomery said, in his account, " only the rain on 6th and 7th November saved them from complete annihilation." The downpour that began on the evening of the 6th helped the later stages of Rommel's " get-away," but by then its prospects were already becoming better. The most crucial stage of the pursuit was during the day and night of the 4th. During that period, escape looked hardly possible. But while Rommel's troops were spurred on by desperation, Montgomery's were slowed down by the natural reaction that followed their hard and prolonged efforts in the battle. The magic of Rommel's reputation, particularly for table-turning ripostes, also induced caution. Moreover, the most promising of the initial cut-off strokes were retarded by halting for the night, for fear of confusion in the dark, instead of driving on to block the coast road.

In the next stage, the pursuit suffered not only from the impeding mud but from lack of sufficient petrol to maintain the momentum.

Many of my units were so short of vehicles that they had to be made dependent on the transport of the armoured formations. Even so, they were frequently hard put to it to save their men, as the distance to Fuka

was 60 miles. The paratroopers and Italians in the south had to march.
It had, as I have already said, been impossible to provide proper maintenance for the troops in the south for some days, due to the activities
of British armoured cars which had penetrated our line and disturbed
our supply traffic. As a result these formations suffered severely from
petrol and water shortage.

When all the necessary orders had been issued, my headquarters also
moved off shortly after nightfall from the area south-west of El Daba
and drove back to Fuka along the southern side of the railway. It was a
pitch-dark night and the vehicles often drove off the track and up to
their axles into sand-drifts, from which they had to be hauled out each
time and man-handled by all hands back to the track. It brought to my
mind the desperate attempt we had made to get to Alexandria after our
victory at Tobruk. Then my troops, exhausted after their long battle
but nevertheless afire with enthusiasm, had crossed this self-same stretch
of country to grasp at our one and only chance of finally seizing the
initiative in Africa. But our supplies had let us down and now we were
reaping the consequences. Thoughts were bitter on that night of defeat.

Towards morning [5th November] we reached the wire round the
Fuka airfield where we had to halt. The coast road to our right was still
brilliant with the light of flares and British bombs were still falling among
our lorry columns. After stopping for several hours on the airfield we
drove on again at dawn to a hill two miles to the south-west, where we
set up the Panzer Army's H.Q.

The authorisation for the retreat, which had now arrived—far too
late—from the Fuehrer and Duce, charged us with the duty of extricating
all German and Italian troops, especially the non-motorised units. We
could do nothing but shrug our shoulders, for extricating the infantry
was precisely what the original order had prevented us from doing.
Moreover, had we waited for the authorisation we would have lost not
only the infantry but also the armoured and motorised divisions. Now
only Fate could show whether the British would permit us to stay at
Fuka long enough for the Italian and German infantry to catch up.

It was my intention to hold on there with the motorised forces until
either the infantry withdrawal was complete, or until the British, who at
that time had complete command of the situation and could dictate the
speed of our retreat, were poising themselves to strike the final blow at
our motorised forces. If it came to the latter, I would have to try to save
all there was to be saved and would no longer be in a position to worry
about the infantry; otherwise, the entire army would be destroyed and
not a man of it would cross the frontier at Sollum. The reason why I
have dwelt on this point is that we were afterwards accused by stupid
people, who knew nothing of conditions in Africa, of having left the
Italian infantry in the lurch at El Alamein.

During the 5th November, a large part of the Afrika Korps, the 90th

Light Division, and elements of the Italian motorised forces reached the area round Fuka. Fresh British forces from their second line, consisting of approximately 200 tanks and 200 armoured troop-carriers, were pressing hard on the heels of the Afrika Korps' rearguard. The X Italian Corps and 1st Parachute Brigade succeeded in reaching the area south-west of El Daba during the night. The long march on foot, in conditions of acute water shortage, was severely taxing the strength of these formations.

As early as midday, violent fighting began at Fuka between our motorised forces and greatly superior British armour. Sandstorms frequently reduced visibility to zero. Soon a powerful British outflanking column advanced against our open southern flank and it became obvious that we would have to sound the retreat before everything was lost.

There was wild confusion on the coast road between Fuka and Mersa Matruh. Vehicle columns, their lorries full of stragglers, jammed up and choked the whole road, while overhead the R.A.F. reigned supreme, flying one attack after the other against every worthwhile target. I first visited the front on the coast road and then drove south to the Afrika Korps, which at that time—it was still morning—was already engaged in heavy fighting. By the time I returned to my staff the British outflanking column had already been reported.

Shortly afterwards two bombing attacks were made on the Panzer Army's H.Q., which the British had apparently located through its wireless traffic. Westphal and I lay in a slit-trench and let the carpet of bombs pass over. There was little damage. Shortly afterwards several Sherman tanks came in sight and opened fire on everything they could see. We apparently no longer had any troops between us and the British.

With the Afrika Korps broken through between the 15th and 21st Panzer Divisions and no more reserves left, I gave orders—with a heavy heart, because of the German and Italian formations still on the march—for the withdrawal to Mersa Matruh.

When the orders were out, we too, moved off. It was a wild helter-skelter drive through another pitch-black night. Occasional Arab villages loomed up and dropped behind us in the darkness, and several vehicles lost contact with the head of the column. Finally, we halted in a small valley to wait for daylight. At that time it was still a matter of doubt as to whether we would be able to get even the remnants of the army away to the west. Our fighting power was very low. The bulk of the Italian infantry had been lost. Of the XXI Corps, part had been destroyed after a stiff resistance against the overwhelmingly superior British, and part had been overtaken in its retreat and taken prisoner; the vehicles which we had repeatedly demanded for them from the Italian Supply H.Q. had not arrived. The X Italian Corps was on the march south-east of Fuka, short of water and ammunition, and, to be quite frank, with no hope of escaping to the west. Of these formations only the transport echelons were on the coast road, choking it with their traffic as they slowly trickled west. There was little we could do to get order into the columns; it would have taken time and all we had to do was to get the move over as quickly as possible.

As for the XX Italian Motorised Corps, it had been practically wiped out on the 4th November—no more than a few companies and detachments remained in the hands of the Corps' staff. Tanks and vehicles had been dispersed and scattered and could not be brought into action.

The only forces which retained any fighting strength were the remnants of the 90th Light Division, the Afrika Korps' two divisions—now reduced to the strength of small combat groups, the Panzer Grenadier Regiment Africa and a few quickly scratched together German units, the remains of the 164th Light Division. Tanks, heavy A.A. guns, heavy and light artillery, all had sustained such frightful losses at El Alamein that there was nothing but a few remnants left.[1]

At dawn on the 6th November, we tried to reassemble and get some order into the Panzer Army's staff—a far from easy task, as our vehicles were scattered all round the country. Our first find, when we attempted to gather our little force together, was a coloured British soldier who had crept into hiding near my vehicle. Shortly afterwards several lorries north of us went up in flames. After some difficulty we eventually succeeded in rounding up our vehicles and during the morning filtered them through the mined area south of Mersa Matruh as far as a point 1,000 yards to the east, where we set up Army Headquarters.

Conditions on the road were indescribable. Columns in complete disorder—partly of German, partly of Italian vehicles—choked the road between the minefields. Rarely was there any movement forward and then everything soon jammed up again. Many vehicles were on tow and there was an acute shortage of petrol, for the retreat had considerably increased consumption.

While the 15th Panzer and 90th Light Divisions succeeded in reaching their allotted stations south-west of Mersa Matruh, the 21st Panzer Division was forced to form a hedgehog with the Army's last tanks south-west of Quasaba; the petrol which had come up was only sufficient for one of the Afrika Korps' divisions. The Voss Group,[2] which had remained behind as a decoy in the Fuka position, had apparently been outflanked during the night by a strong force of British armour. At about 10.00 hours on the 6th November, this force launched an attack with 60 tanks against the almost completely immobilised 21st Panzer Division. The division defended itself desperately and, by gathering together all its strength, succeeded in beating off the attack. The Voss Group, on its way back

---

[1] See appendix preceding chapter for battle strength of German and Italian armoured formations during El Alamein.

[2] Captain Voss, Commander of 580th Reconnaissance Battalion, formerly A.D.C. to Rommel.

from Fuka, took the British force in the rear and inflicted considerable
casualties on them. Then it took up position south-west of 21st Panzer
Division with the object of preventing any British attempt to encircle
the division, whose tanks were by that time completely immobilised.
The petrol columns which were dispatched did not get through. The
enemy launched attack after attack against the 21st Panzer Division, until
finally, in the afternoon, the division destroyed all immobilised tanks
where they stood and fought its way westwards with the wheeled transport.
But after a few miles it was again forced to form a hedgehog. Finally, we
managed to get a little petrol up to this remnant of the division during
the night, thus enabling it to move off westwards at last into its allotted
position.

Meanwhile, our columns were steadily streaming westwards and
were now approaching Sollum. In the afternoon the Italian General
Gandin appeared on behalf of Marshal Cavallero to inquire about
our situation and plans. This suited me very well. I gave him a detailed
account of the battle, laying particular stress on the effects of the supply
crisis and the Fuehrer's and Duce's order. I told him point-blank that
with the present balance of forces there was not a chance of our making
a stand anywhere, and that the British could keep on going right through
to Tripolitania, if they chose to. We could never accept battle, but would
have to confine ourselves to trying to delay the British long enough to
allow our columns, in which the utmost confusion reigned, to get across
the Libyan frontier. There could be no attempt to restore any semblance
of order until they arrived in Libya, because so long as they were this
side of the frontier they were in constant danger of being cut off. Speed,
therefore, was the one thing that mattered. We could attempt no
operation with our remaining armour and motorised forces because of
the petrol shortage; every drop that reached us had to be used for getting
our troops out. Gandin left my H.Q. visibly shaken. It was clear that
to the Commando Supremo war was simple. When, for instance, during
the July crisis at Alamein, I had told Marshal Cavallero that in the event
of a British break-through threatening, only two possibilities would exist
—either to stay in our line and be forced to surrender in two or three
days by lack of water, or to beat a fighting retreat to the west—Cavallero
had said he could give no guidance for such an event; one simply should
not contemplate it. That was no doubt an easy way out.

During that day, we succeeded in forming a fairly firm front and
beat off all enemy attacks. Although the enemy must have been aware
of our weakness, he still continued to operate with great caution. All
German troops everywhere, and some of the Italian units, made a very
disciplined and good impression and appeared to be firmly in the hands
of their officers. It was a personal blow to every man to have to give up
all this territory we had conquered with such high hopes during the
summer.

The petrol situation was disastrous, in spite of the fact that ships had reached Benghazi on the 4th November with 5,000 tons—an unprecedented quantity. The news of our collapse had apparently even galvanised Rome into action. But what was the good of petrol in Benghazi? We needed it at the front, where our columns were waiting. Incidentally, 2,000 of the 5,000 tons had already been destroyed during British air raids on Benghazi. We tried our hardest to persuade the Italians and Kesselring to bring the petrol straight to the front.

Torrential rain fell during this period, making many tracks impassable and forcing us to rely almost solely on the coast road, which became hopelessly jammed up with traffic at many points. But the British, also, had their difficulties and were unable to send their columns through the desert fast enough to outflank us. The result was a considerable slowing up of speed on both sides.

The effect on the British outflanking moves through the desert was worse than Rommel realised. The heavy downpour on the night of the 6th November turned their desert routes into a morass. The lorry-borne New Zealand Division, the lorried infantry brigades of the armoured divisions, and their supply echelons became stuck. The tanks themselves were slowed down, but hampered even more by the way their supporting troops and supplies were held up.

The earliest exponents of armoured warfare in the 1920s had urged that the new-model forces should be completely on a tracked vehicle basis, while emphasising the drawbacks of incorporating, and making them dependent upon, wheeled vehicles. In the autumn of 1941, the German Army had forfeited its chance of decisive victory in Russia because the wheeled portion of their Panzer divisions became bogged. Now the British Army, in turn, provided another object lesson.

That, however, was not the only cause of failure in the pursuit. The 1st Armoured Division, after its first turn-in at Daba, had swung out again to block Rommel's line of escape west of Mersa Matruh. It moved fast—outstripping Rommel's retreat along the congested coast road. But on the 6th, before the rain became serious, its armoured brigade was twice brought to a halt by lack of petrol— the second time when within close reach of Rommel's escape road. That was the more galling because the divisional commander, General Briggs, had urged—before the break-out—that one armoured division at least should be loaded up with sufficient petrol for a prolonged pursuit. But caution had prevailed, and ammunition for the battle had been treated as the prime requirement.

The outcome of the hold-up was that on the following day the outflanking pursuit was only carried on by an armoured-car regiment and some elements of the 4th Light Armoured Brigade—which proved too weak to cut off or pin down the retreating forces. The 10th Armoured Division, which had been halted at Fuka, was then ordered to push on to Matruh along the coast road. But that direct pursuit only served to push Rommel's rearguards back, along the road they were taking, and gave them the best chance of keeping the pursuers in check.

With this general reduction of tempo I hoped to have a chance of getting at least a little order into the motorised forces, to enable them to hold on to Mersa Matruh for a few more days and thus gain time for some defences to be constructed at Sollum. In the morning [*7th November*], I conferred with Stefanis, commander of the XX Italian Motorised Corps, and his Chief of Staff, Ruggeri. There was now little hope left of any further major bodies of their troops getting away. Many stragglers were still being collected up and, of the whole Corps, there now remained a little over a battalion and about ten tanks. The reserve tanks which had been held for the Corps in Mersa Matruh were already worn out from long desert driving. Some we had to destroy, others were carried back to the rear on transporters. I ordered the Italians to move on to Buq Buq and Capuzzo, where they were to collect up their stragglers and form them into units.

We discovered during the morning that British movements were not being as badly hampered by the going as we had at first expected, and it was possible that the enemy would reach our line that day. I therefore conferred with Bayerlein at Afrika Korps H.Q. as to our next move. We decided under no circumstances to accept battle, as that must inevitably result in the destruction of the remainder of our motorised units. After yesterday's bad affair with the 21st Panzer Division, Bayerlein was trying desperately to get his petrol up. The 21st Panzer Division had unfortunately been very badly knocked about. Of the 30 tanks it had salvaged from El Alamein, only four now remained intact. And that was not all, for during yesterday's incident, when the division had been attacked by the British in an almost completely immobilised state, it had lost almost all its guns.

After this conference I issued orders for the army to hold its line as long as possible and to lay down a concentrated fire on all enemy attack preparations. It was on no account to allow itself to be drawn into a battle from which it could not easily disengage, but, if pressure became serious, was to fall back slowly to a rearward position.

At about 10.00 hours, General Ramcke reported in with some 600 men of his brigade. Having heard that the British had caught up with the retreating Italian X Corps at about the level of Fuka and, after a brief action, taken them all prisoner, we had given up hope of ever seeing Ramcke and his men appear out of the desert again. The march of these paratroopers was a very fine achievement. They had been equipped with very few vehicles, but had ambushed some British lorries and made themselves mobile. Ramcke must have led them extremely well. The brigade had never been very popular with us, because, following the normal Luftwaffe practice, they had always been demanding special treatment. They had wanted, for instance, units taken out of line in order to husband their special troops. Now they were angry again because we had not provided them with vehicles for the retreat. But it had been impossible—for one thing, because we had had no vehicles, and secondly, because we could not have carried off all the German troops and left the Italians completely in the lurch. However, we now had them picked up by passing vehicles and taken back to the rear for rest and recovery.

All that day, powerful formations of British bombers and close-support aircraft attacked the coast road and inflicted serious casualties on our columns. The British launched attack after attack against our rearguard—formed by the 90th Light Division—but came off worst. Three outflanking attacks, each by infantry with tank support, were beaten off. In the afternoon, a strong British force moved west over hard and stony ground, where they were able to make rapid progress relatively unhampered by the rain.

It is not clear what force Rommel means, unless it be part of the 4th Light Armoured Brigade—which was not a " strong force." The main force was reorganised after the hold-up on the 7th, when it became evident that Rommel was slipping out of reach, and that the follow-up would be a long race, not a short one. To diminish the supply problem it was obviously necessary to reduce the scale of the pursuit force, and this was now constituted only of the 7th Armoured Division and the New Zealand Division (with attached armour). This force, under the command of X Corps, moved off afresh on the 8th November with the frontier as its first objective, and Tobruk as the next. The New Zealand Division followed the coast road, while the 7th Armoured Division took the inland route on top of the escarpment. The task of striking at Rommel's rearguards was entrusted primarily to the air force, which operated from forward landing grounds that were often ahead of the main ground advance.

After the frontier positions had been gained the New Zealand Division stopped there to reorganise, while the 1st Armoured Division went forward to replace it in the advance.

It was now decided to move Army H.Q. back to the Sidi Barrani district. We first tried to get through south of the coast road, but found that the rain had covered the tracks with deep mud. Several vehicles stuck fast and had to be dragged out at the cost of much toil and sweat. After that we decided to continue the journey along the coast road and a few hours later the new H.Q. was set up near the Sidi Barrani airfield. Shortly afterwards the Quartermaster brought us a report from the frontier. Apparently a vast column of vehicles, thirty to forty miles long, was jammed up this side of the Halfaya and Sollum passes, and the retreat over the hills, which lay under continual R.A.F. low-flying and bomber attacks, was probably going to take a week. It was very unlikely that the enemy would grant us all that grace, so I gave orders for movement through the passes to be speeded up by co-opting large numbers of officers for traffic control duties. Driving was to continue day and night, regardless of bombing and low-flying aircraft. A.A. barrages over the area had already been ordered. The Luftwaffe commander had meanwhile informed me that German fighters were up over the threatened area. We hoped to hold the Sollum-Halfaya front against the British spearheads long enough to enable us at least to reorganise our columns behind it and form up new fighting units.

With the shipping situation so difficult, we could expect no replacements to speak of from Europe in the near future. Hence, if the British continued the pursuit, the evacuation of Cyrenaica would become inevitable and we would be unable to think of making another stand before Mersa el Brega. I hoped that by the time we arrived there, more material would have been shipped out to Tripolitania, so that we would face the British striking columns better armed and be able to take any opportunities that offered of beating up partial enemy forces.

As the British now appeared to be bringing an armoured division round the south of Mersa Matruh, I gave orders for all forces to evacuate the area during the night and retire to Sidi Barrani with 90th Light Division as rearguard. During the night of the 7th the British, correctly, turned north in an attempt to cut off our retreat. But the trap was empty; all they netted was a small number of burnt-out vehicles, which we had had to destroy because of petrol shortage. There is never any point in attempting an outflanking movement round an enemy force unless it has first been tied down frontally, because the defending force can always use its motorised forces—assuming it has petrol and vehicles —to hold up the outflanking columns while it slips out of the trap.

That night, enemy bombers flew non-stop attacks against the Sollum-Halfaya position. At that time the two burning problems of our retreat were, firstly, whether we should be able to get our columns through the passes soon enough, and secondly, our petrol supply. So long as these enormous columns were still jammed up on this side of the passes, the motorised combat groups would have to go on trying, by every means open to them, to delay the enemy. Next morning there was still a 25-mile queue of vehicles waiting to get through the passes. Traffic had moved very slowly during the night, as a result of the incessant attacks of the R.A.F.

At about 08.00 hours [*8th November*] I met Bayerlein and informed him that a convoy of about 104 ships was approaching Africa, and it was possible that the British and Americans were about to strike at us from the west. At about 11.00 hours this was confirmed. The Anglo-Americans had, in fact, landed in North-West Africa during the night— as I heard shortly afterwards from Westphal. This spelt the end of the army in Africa.

At about midday, I drove to the west and met the Quartermaster, who brought with him the new Engineer Commander, General Buelowius, and Lieutenant Berndt. Major Otto reported that the movement of our vehicles would take another two days, and that traffic blocks on the road were making it extremely difficult to bring supplies up to the fighting troops—as the railway could only cope with a few tons a day. I therefore decided to send back the XX Italian Corps, 3rd Reconnaissance Battalion and later the Afrika Korps via Habata, in order to relieve the pressure on the road and leave the passes free for the 90th Light Division as rearguard. Without delaying I turned round and drove back to inform the various formations of this decision. At Buq Buq I met General Stefanis and Major von Luck and put them in the picture.

Shortly after 14.00 hours I met Colonel Bayerlein and discussed the consequences for us of the British and American landing in the west. On the subject of my order to use the Jebel ascent north of Habata for the retreat of the Afrika Korps, Bayerlein demurred—for, as he said, the Afrika Korps' vehicles were not up to such a cross-country journey. I told him that I was well aware of this difficulty, but that as things stood we had no choice. However, I decided to leave the final decision until the 9th November.

Meanwhile numerous British vehicles and scout-cars were being sighted on our southern flank, where we were keeping a very close watch. Accordingly, the Voss Group and 3rd Reconnaissance Battalion put out a number of reconnaissance detachments south of the railway line, in order to give warning of a British thrust in good time for the necessary counter-measures to be taken. In the coastal sector the enemy made no attempt to press us hard with major forces that day, but merely maintained contact with armoured cars.

Our columns were now flowing comparatively smoothly over the passes—as I saw for myself that evening. Traffic was being controlled by numerous officer-manned traffic posts and control teams. There was now a hope that all the lorry columns would be across by midday on 9th November, which would enable the Afrika Korps to use the road. With petrol so short and many vehicles on tow, this would mean a great easing of the situation. It is a great mistake in circumstances like these to attempt to get order into supply troops which have panicked and lost their organisational structure, until it can be done in peace and quiet. One should simply allow them to run and try to channel their flight gradually into ordered routes. After a few days of this, the troops' self-confidence and urge to discipline will begin to assert themselves again and reorganisation can then be undertaken without difficulty.

Orders had come from the Duce for the Sollum line to be held. That it was impossible to do this for long is evident from the fact that we now had no battle-worthy armoured or anti-tank units large enough to contain a powerful armoured thrust through the open desert south of Sidi Omar. Thus it could on no account be considered. Casualties in the German motorised forces had certainly been heavy in killed and wounded, but had not been too serious in terms of total man-power, not at any rate, in comparison with the number of men which the fully motorised Eighth Army had lost during the summer. The vital thing now was to get every German and Italian soldier and as much material as possible away to the west to enable us either to make a stand somewhere farther back, or to ship them back to Europe. Meanwhile, the Italians had moved elements of the Pistoia Division and some other battalions up to the Libya-Egypt frontier, and were wanting to place them under my command. I was forced to decline, however, as I no longer had the necessary equipment for either their communications, their transport or their supply.

On the morning of the 9th November there were about a thousand of our vehicles left on the coastal plain east of the pass. The move through the passes had gone off more quickly than we had expected. Several low-flying attacks were made on our columns again during the morning and my escort vehicles did not escape unscathed, although the damage was not serious. I notified Bayerlein that the Afrika Korps would, after all, be able to use the coast road over the passes. In view of the improved situation on the Sollum Pass, I also gave orders for the area west of Sidi Barrani to be evacuated.

The Army's total strength at this time was roughly as follows:

For manning the Sollum front we had 2,000 Italian and 2,000 German fighting troops with 15 German anti-tank and 40 German field guns, and a few Italian anti-tank guns and several Italian field guns.

For the mobile reserve we had 3,000 German and 500 Italian fighting troops with 11 German and 10 Italian tanks, 20 German anti-tank guns, 24 anti-aircraft guns and 25 field guns.

It was obvious that with these forces we could not afford to await an attack by hundreds of British tanks and several motorised infantry divisions.

The "Young Fascist" Division, which should really have been brought up from the Siwa Oasis to Sollum, could never have arrived there in time and was accordingly diverted to Mersa el Brega. To accept a British attack in the Marmarica was unthinkable, painful though it was to us all to have to give up territory so hardly won. But courage which goes against military expediency is stupidity, or, if it is insisted upon by a commander, irresponsibility.

9 Nov. 1942

Dearest Lu,
I'm well. Thanks for letter. Heartfelt greetings.

10 Nov. 1942

I've had no chance to write since the enemy break-through at Alamein, but you're to have a few lines to-day. Things go badly with an army which has been broken through. It has to fight its way out and lose what's left of its fighting power in the process. We can't go on like that for long, for we have a superior enemy after us.

Physically I'm all right. For the rest I must do my best to keep going to the end. Seiderer has arrived, also Buelowius. They are both pretty shattered by the conditions here.

THE EVACUATION OF CYRENAICA

Meanwhile, we had heard that the Axis powers had landed troops in Tunisia and were trying to meet the threat from the west. Nevertheless, there was still a possibility that the British and Americans would be able to mount an operation against the Panzer Army from that quarter. In that event, I felt that our best action would be for the Panzer Army to hold the hill country on either side of Cirene and get its men away to Europe from that area by means of aircraft, submarines and small ships, ultimately evacuating North Africa altogether.

During the night of the 10th November, hundreds of British fighter-bombers ranged the area round Capuzzo by the light of flares, causing a considerable amount of damage.

Late the following morning, the British launched an energetic attack along the coast; we also detected armoured car concentrations in the south. Accordingly the 90th Light Division received orders to withdraw at around midday along the road through Sollum. The move went according to plan and was completed by the afternoon, after the road through the passes had been blown up behind the rear vehicles.

The administrative echelons, with scattered men and detached units, were now all pouring back into Cyrenaica. Formations which still retained any fighting strength disposed themselves for a delaying defence. We could not even make a stand in the Gazala line, because that, too, would have needed mobile support which we had not the forces to provide—as the figures already given will show. We did not yet know how many troops there were with the administrative echelon in the rear.

In view of the situation in Tunisia, I asked Marshal Cavallero and Field Marshal Kesselring to come to North Africa. I wanted to get from them a precise statement on the prospects of Tunisia being held, and, in spite of the demands of the Tunisian front, to obtain at least some reinforcements for my army in the Mersa el Brega line. The situation demanded a strategic decision and, while tactical decisions tend to require a certain boldness, a strategic decision such as this should only be taken after meticulous examination of all possible consequences, and should, as a matter of principle, satisfy the need for 100 per cent security.

Yet neither Cavallero nor Kesselring considered it necessary to come to Africa. I therefore decided to send Lieutenant Berndt to the Fuehrer's H.Q. next day to report the position. When he returned several days later, Berndt reported that he had met with little understanding. The Fuehrer had instructed him to inform me that I should leave Tunis out of my calculations and simply act on the assumption that the bridgehead would be held. This was typical of the attitude of our highest command. It was to be characteristic of, and at the same time to determine, the coming series of reverses. Excellent as our tactical achievements were in all theatres of war, they lacked the solid strategic foundation which would have directed our tactical skill into the right channels. In other respects too, Berndt reported, " the master " had been far from amiable. Although he had sent me an assurance of " his very special confidence ", he had apparently been noticeably out of temper. He had promised active support in the matter of supplies, and had said that we should notify our requirements in all fields as quickly as possible—nothing would be denied us. The Mersa el Brega position was to be held at all costs, for it was to be the spring-board for a new offensive.

Meanwhile, the retreat through Cyrenaica continued. We had been able to refuel for another 60 or 100 miles just before Sollum, but that was the last petrol there was in Cyrenaica. It was virtually impossible to bring up the petrol stored in Benghazi because of the heavy burden which the non-motorised troops, the sick and the wounded were placing on our lorry columns. Also many of our columns were still in a bad state of disorganisation. We were thus faced with very serious problems, when, on the 10th November, we had to prepare the evacuation of the Marmarica. I informed higher authority in no uncertain terms that major loads of war material for the Panzer Army should be shipped across to Tripoli now, while it was still possible, for in a very few weeks British aircraft would be able to take off for Tripoli from the Sirte coast.

It was proving particularly difficult to filter our troops through the narrow lanes in the Tobruk and Gazala minefields, as these were menaced both by fighter and bomber aircraft and by enemy armoured car units.

The British had now launched an armoured division [*the 7th*] round the south of Sidi Omar in an attempt to overtake us and we accordingly pulled back to the level of Tobruk. During his follow-up on the 11th November the enemy unfortunately succeeded in overpowering a battalion of the Pistoia and three batteries of the German Army Artillery in the Halfaya position.[1] Our columns were still on the road from Bardia to Tobruk, with the rearguard located between Sollum and Bardia, when British forces were suddenly reported south of the Gambut airfield. I was very worried lest they should move north and cut off the road to the west. Fortunately, they kept south and the withdrawal was able

[1]*Note by General Bayerlein.*—The British took the Halfaya Pass during the night, after the surrender of the Italian battalion holding it, and then passed an armoured brigade through to the plateau behind it by dawn. This brigade then pushed on west at first light. Lying in rest positions in the country behind the passes was 90th Light Division. During the morning General von Sponeck happened to be driving east where he suddenly saw the dust cloud stirred up by the approaching British armoured brigade. There was only just time to alert his division and get it out of the British reach at the last moment.

to proceed more or less smoothly. British air activity was also less intensive than on the previous day. By using our last petrol reserves from airfields and stores we succeeded in reaching the El Adem-Tobruk line at about midday. Not until then did the British push through to the road, by which time there was nothing left of our forces east of their road-block.

We intended to stand as long as possible at Tobruk, in order to get away at least part of the 10,000 tons of material which were still lying there. By the 11th November, despite our requests that nothing but petrol should be flown across, our transport squadrons had brought across 1,100 men. These troops had not the slightest value in action, for they had not been properly fitted out for battle. Neither had they any vehicles of their own, which meant that they were nothing more than an encumbrance on our transport.

We received one wireless message after the other calling on us to gain as much time in our retreat as possible. But the speed of the retreat was now dictated solely by the enemy and our petrol situation.

There was again a large vehicle jam in the Gazala bottle-neck on the 12th which made it essential for us to go on holding the Tobruk front until evening. Hundreds of vehicles were on tow, some with engine trouble, others out of petrol. Discipline everywhere was now good. The panic which had reigned in the German-Italian columns was now over, and they were all convinced that they would be able to get away. The petrol situation was as gloomy as ever, as the Luftwaffe, with many of its transport groups tied up in Tunisia, could no longer fly across more than 200 tons a day.

There now being signs that the British intended to launch an out-flanking drive round through Acroma to approach Tobruk from the west, we were forced to the decision to evacuate the fortress. Tobruk now possessed only symbolic value. Militarily it could not be held in the situation at that time, without delivering up a large part of the Army to certain sacrifice. We did not intend to repeat the mistake which the British had made in 1942. Thus the enemy was able to occupy it, virtually without fighting, on the night of the 12th, after its evacuation by the 90th Light Division.

Throughout our retreat we called on all our resources of imagination to provide the enemy with ever more novel booby traps and thus to induce the maximum possible caution in his advance guard. Our Engineer Commander, General Buelowius, one of the best engineers in the German Army, did a splendid job.

On the following evening it became evident that the British were making another attempt to outflank us by a thrust in considerable strength on Segnali. Air reconnaissance reported over 1,000 vehicles moving west.

13 Nov. 1942

Dearest Lu,

The battle in [*French*] North Africa[1] is nearing its end. This will put the odds even further against us. Here, too, the end will not be long for we're being simply crushed by the enemy superiority. The army is in no way to blame. It has fought magnificently.

At about midday on the 13th November, the first contingent of the Panzer Army reached the Mersa el Brega line. In spite of considerable traffic jams in the defiles, the movement of our columns went more or less according to plan.

Unfortunately, it again proved impossible to bring petrol east over the choked roads from Benghazi or to bring it up by rail to Barce, since the Italians had already blown the track. We were, therefore, compelled to ask the Luftwaffe to come to our assistance with transport aircraft.

After the British had overcome the Gazala line, our position became particularly difficult, as they now had numerous possibilities for out-flanking movements aimed at enveloping the whole of Cyrenaica. The closest watch was necessary over the tracks round Mechili to ensure that our motorised forces could be dispatched early enough to intercept the British assault columns. The evacuation of Cyrenaica also had to go ahead now at full speed. It had repeatedly been shown in the various African battles that the Gazala line was the critical point in any retreat to the west. Although we had been able, by skilful manœuvring, to get away in 1941-42 without serious losses, Bergonzoli's troops, hampered by their non-motorised infantry, had been trapped there.

Rommel is here referring to the Italian retreat through Cyrenaica in the winter of 1940-41, after their shattering defeat at Sidi Barrani.

14 Nov. 1942

Dearest Lu,

Heading west again. I'm well in myself, but you won't need to be told what's going on in my mind. We have to be grateful for every day that the enemy does not close in on us. How far we shall get I cannot say. It all depends on the petrol, which has yet to be flown across to us.

How are you both? My thoughts—even with so much on my mind—are often with you. What will become of the war if we lose North Africa? How will it finish? I wish I could get free of these terrible thoughts.

Next day, we were faced with a grave petrol crisis, when the Luftwaffe flew across only 60 tons instead of our full day's demand of 250, which

[1]The Allied forces which had landed in Algeria were pushing eastward, and on the 12th the port of Bone, 50 miles from the Tunisian border, was seized by British parachute troops and Commandos. The general advance, however, was slow.

Kesselring had promised. As a result of this crisis and the fact that heavy rain had softened the tracks we had been intending to use to ease the load on the road, we were unable that day to reach our objectives. It was, of course, extremely exasperating to have such a hold-up in the difficult situation I have described, in which speed was everything. Fortunately, the enemy was also prevented from using the cross-desert tracks and his movement was equally delayed.

Marshal Cavallero had been in Libya since the 12th November, but had not, of course, thought it necessary to come and confer with me, although I had several times asked him to. He sent me instead, via Ritter von Pohl (German Air Attaché), an order on behalf of the Duce to stand fast in Cyrenaica for at least another week. The same order also required us to hold on to the Mersa el Brega position at all costs, as the fate of the Axis forces in Africa depended on it. It would have been very much better if Marshal Cavallero had applied this zeal he was now asking from us to the task of supplying the Panzer Army before Alamein, or, indeed, if he had now begun to do so. We had always done our share, and the courage of my troops had overcome difficulties far worse than anything the supply staffs had had to meet. It was time that our higher authorities demanded the same expenditure of energy from themselves as we had made our norm. Marshal Cavallero belonged to the type of the intellectually fairly well-qualified, but weak-willed office-chair soldier. The organisation of supplies, the command of men, anything in any way constructive requires more than intellect; it requires energy and drive and an unrelenting will to serve the cause, regardless of one's personal interests. Academic soldiers mostly look on war as a pure intellectual problem and demand energy and drive only from those whom they somewhat contemptuously refer to as " Troupier ",[1] but from themselves, never. They rest content with their professional qualifications, which are attested for them by others of the same ilk, and regard themselves as the source of all good and the " Troupier " as the source of all evil. It is time that a clean sweep was made of this mentality, both in Germany and Italy.

On the 15th November the petrol crisis took an even more acute turn when several petrol ships on the way to Benghazi were turned back, and a tanker left Benghazi with 100 tons of petrol still on board. Added to this, the Luftwaffe was still flying only very small quantities across. Lack of petrol prevented the Afrika Korps from getting under way until midday and by evening it was halted again without a drop in its tanks. The 90th Light Division still had a small supply. On the morning of the 15th I informed Ritter von Pohl, in no uncertain terms, that in future I wanted to receive the proper amount and not to be promised 250 tons and receive 60. The road was still hopelessly blocked with traffic and

---

[1] A term, usually of scorn, used to denote the field commander with few or no staff or academic qualifications.

very little ammunition could be brought up to the Afrika Korps. On top of all else, some over-zealous people had blown up the ammunition dump at Barce along with the ammunition we were most short of. The British were again very active in the air that day, shooting up large numbers of our vehicles in the bottlenecks. Otherwise, they appeared to be organising their supplies before resuming the pursuit. The premature departure of the Italian ships from Benghazi prevented us from getting out as much of our stores as we might otherwise have done. Every possible expedient should have been used to get at least the ammunition away before the port was given up.

Rain continued to fall during the night of the 15th. The British were slow in following up our movements and our sappers found the time and leisure to prepare all kinds of neat little surprises for them. Once again the war was moving across the beautiful country of Cyrenaica, in whose gigantic rubble heaps the splendour of the former corn-growing colony could still be detected. In Cyrenaica, as in Tripolitania, the Italians had performed great feats of colonisation. Its former occupants, the Arabs, had let the land go to rack and ruin, lacking the means, both financial and technical, to cultivate it. Many new settlements had been created, particularly in the Barce district and the surroundings of Beda Littoria—the area which was now serving the 90th Light Division as a rearguard line—by the hard and unremitting toil of the Italian farmers, who had wrested the land yard by yard from the desert.

I had the layout of these settlements explained to me in detail. The country had formerly been desert grassland nourishing only a few Arab sheep and cattle, with a few patches here and there planted with barley. The irrigation systems, which in many places still existed from Roman times, had sanded up and gone to ruin. The cultivation of wheat in the clayey Cyrenaican soil had been an unknown craft to the Arabs. The first Italian settlers who had attempted to carve a new life out of Africa had been pressed very hard by the rebellious Senussi until 1929, and it was not until after the Italian Government had proceeded against the hostile Arabs that Italian settlers had begun to flow to Cyrenaica in any quantity. There is no doubt that Mussolini deserves the greatest possible credit for what was done in Libya. He created generous financial credits and had settlements constructed with community wells and irrigation systems. Thousands of houses were built in Cyrenaica and Tripolitania, and a considerable return of wheat had already been achieved, when the war came and destroyed the work of years. During our retreat the settlers suffered severely at the hands of the Arabs. Their fields were devastated and their houses plundered. The rebirth of Cyrenaica as the " granary of Rome " now seemed very far off.

16 Nov. 1942

DEAREST LU,

Another good step back. To cap it all it's now raining, which makes it all the more difficult to move. Shortage of petrol! It's enough to make one weep. Let's hope the British are having equally bad weather.

The Afrika Korps was still immobilised. The Italian Supply H.Q. had been overcome by a perfect frenzy of destruction. Ammunition dumps were blown up and water-points destroyed, all of which were urgently needed for the maintenance of the fighting troops. It was only at the last moment that we managed to stop them demolishing the water and electricity works in Benghazi.

Next morning, although the going was still bad, the British followed up with strong forces hard on the heels of the 90th Light Division and also appeared in considerable strength on our flank near Msus. This meant that we now had to get out of Cyrenaica as fast as we could if the Army was not to be cut off and destroyed in the area round Benghazi. As usual, of course, we were up against it for petrol. Italian warships, which we had been promised several days before would bring it across to us, simply did not arrive.

To our good fortune, the Luftwaffe soon reported that the British outflanking column at Msus was being badly held up by floods caused by the torrential rain. Petrol was now so short that we would have been unable to meet a British thrust at that point with our motorised forces.

This flank move was carried out, however, by merely a couple of armoured car regiments with some supporting arms. Alexander's dispatch says:

" *The enemy was withdrawing through the Gebel and it was a great temptation to imitate our previous strategy by pushing a force across the desert to cut him off at or near Agedabia. General Montgomery was determined, however, not to take any chances, especially in view of the difficulties of the maintenance situation, and X Corps was instructed to dispatch only armoured cars by this route. Later, however, when it appeared that the enemy's retreat had actually been brought to a temporary standstill by lack of fuel, X Corps was ordered to strengthen, if possible, the outflanking force; this proved impracticable in the then existing circumstances.*"

At dawn on the 18th November, British armoured cars and tanks probed forward from Msus against our covering force but were beaten back. The morning brought us the news that the destroyers bringing petrol to us were being turned back. Shortly afterwards a British convoy of 15 transport vessels with an equal number of escort craft, was reported north-east of Derna en route for the west. We assumed that this meant a British landing in Benghazi, and, in spite of heavy seas, ordered all barges laden with tanks and material to put out to sea. All other war material left in Benghazi was destroyed. Most of the barges sank during the next few hours and we were thus unable to salvage more than a very small part of our stores from the Cyrenaican port. Harbour and dock installations were demolished and the utmost confusion reigned among Benghazi's civil population. This sorely-tried town was changing hands for the fifth time in the war.

The advanced guard of the Afrika Korps now withdrew with great difficulty as far as the district round Zuetina, where it was regrouped for defence to the east. Hundreds of vehicles were on tow. In spite of the acute danger from the enemy and the terrible shortage of material, exemplary order was maintained and everything went more or less according to plan. Again and again the British outflanking column west of Msus was thrown back by the 33rd Reconnaissance Battalion. Early in the morning of the 19th November the 90th Light Division evacuated Benghazi. During the day the whole of the Afrika Korps arrived in its new position, and the 90th Light Division established itself in Agedabia. The evacuation of Cyrenaica was complete.

The retreat from Gazala to Agedabia had been fraught with particular danger, because the British had all the time had the possibility of cutting us off by a thrust through Mechili. Sections of my force had stood choking the roads without petrol for days on end, and the British air force had flown attack after attack against the 60-mile column, with considerable success. The quantity of petrol we had received, while very considerable from the Luftwaffe point of view—it had been carried almost exclusively in transport aircraft—had not sufficed to fill the needs of the Army. Nevertheless, we had succeeded in making a planned withdrawal. From Tobruk to Mersa el Brega we had lost scarcely a man.

When we arrived in Agedabia, we had virtually no petrol left. There were 500 tons lying in Tripoli and another 10 tons in Buerat, but even the latter was still 250 miles away. The principal cause of this crisis was the fact that the front was now out of reach of transport aircraft from Italy. That day an Italian tanker carrying 4,000 tons of petrol was sunk off Misurata, although a smaller tanker with 1,200 tons aboard succeeded in reaching Tripoli. Every supply lorry that would run was immediately sent off to Tripoli to bring it up. It was an ugly situation to have to stand immobilised for any length of time in the desert. Marshal Bastico said he would do all he could to help us and would bring the 500 tons which had already been unloaded in Tripoli up to Agheila as quickly as possible.

Meanwhile, work had been going forward at full pressure—so far as our limited resources permitted—on the Mersa el Brega line. The line as such was very well situated. A few miles south of the coast it abutted on a salt marsh approximately 10 miles across, beyond which there was a long stretch of very heavy going for vehicles. Thus any enemy attacking from the east and wishing to outflank the position and take the defence in the rear was bound to haul off a long way to the south. And the farther one has to pull out to the south in North Africa, the riskier the

operation is. Nevertheless, defence of even the Mersa el Brega line needed
the use of motorised forces at least strong enough to take on the enemy's
outflanking column. In any action at this point between two forces of
more or less equal strength, the attacking force could not fail to find
itself in a difficult tactical position throughout the battle, for its supply
route, reaching well down to the south, would inevitably be very vulnerable
to interference by the motorised defence. The main points for the defence
plan in this circumstance would be to bar the defile at Mersa el Brega,
secure the Sebcha [*salt marsh*] crossing and hold a mobile force provided
with sufficient petrol and ammunition ready behind the front. Without
this force, or without the petrol, the Mersa el Brega position could never
be held.

It soon became clear that we were in for another mutual build-up of
strength at the Mersa el Brega position. The British needed to organise
their supplies. The outcome of the battle would depend on whether or
not we were able to obtain some sort of reinforcement by motorised forces
and secure a supply of ammunition and petrol for them before the enemy
was ready to attack.

Meanwhile, the Italian Divisions " Young Fascist," Pistoia and Spezia
(only part of the last two had been brought across to Africa) had been
installed in the Mersa el Brega line and had started with its construction
under the direction of Marshal Bastico. Units of the newly-arrived
Centauro Armoured Division had been deployed behind the line. The
paratroopers, the 164th Light Division and the remnants of the XXI
Italian Corps had also been assembled and were being formed up near
Mersa el Brega. As soon as I arrived in the area I pointed out that
fortifications, however strong, could not help us, as the enemy could
outflank the whole line—even though with some difficulty. And then,
I said, the non-motorised Italian formations, like their comrades at
Alamein, would become easy prey for the British armoured and motorised
brigades, to whom they would be able to offer no serious resistance in
the open desert.

To rouse some understanding of the tactics of this situation in our
higher command I sent General de Stefanis (as Marshal Cavallero would
not come to see me) to report to the Duce and Marshal Cavallero in
Rome. De Stefanis, who was an intelligent officer, well informed in
matters of tactics, was fully aware of the shortcomings of the Italian Army.
He was to lay particular stress on the serious limitations which a commander has to suffer in his freedom of decision, when, having no stocks
of supplies to draw on, he is forced to live from hand to mouth and can
never be certain what the next day will bring. It was now too late to alter
the course of events which had been started at El Alamein. The only
thing to do was to look facts in the face and try to get the best out of the
situation in the greater long-term interest. This being so, there could be
no question of accepting battle at Mersa el Brega.

Perhaps an hour after I had instructed General de Stefanis on his mission and he had left for Rome, I drove off to see General Navarrini, who was now commanding the XXI Italian Corps, comprising the Pistoia, Spezia and Young Fascist Divisions. He, too, fully realised that to accept battle with the existing balance of strength would mean the destruction of his force, and I promised him that I would see to it that we did not lose the Italian infantry a second time.

Looking back over the events at the beginning of 1942, we discussed the possibility of repeating our surprise attack on the British in front of Agedabia and destroying the partial forces which they had there. In reality there was, of course, never a hope of our putting this purely academic discussion into effect, as we had neither the petrol nor sufficient tank destruction units for such a scheme. The flow of supplies could not now be concentrated at Tripoli—as it had been at the end of 1941—but had to be directed to Tunisia, thus making it impossible for us to assemble the necessary stores and replacement equipment for such an undertaking.

This apart, the situation was very similar to the one we had faced in the winter of 1941-42. The British had again followed up with partial forces, leaving their main body in the rear. Even with the excellent British supply organisation, their whole force could not yet be maintained at Agedabia. In fact, provided the Cyrenaican ports have been effectively destroyed, the area round Agedabia must always be a critical point for a force attacking from the east, for the maintenance of an army over such distances cannot be improvised immediately by road alone. Consequently, a large part of it has to remain behind in the Marmarica. The defence, with an adequate supply base behind it in the west, can fall on and destroy the enemy's vanguard before other formations can arrive. Even if reinforcements are drawn from Cyrenaica, it is quite likely that they will arrive too late and find the battle already decided. Then they, too, will be open to attack and destruction by a superior enemy.

If I were advancing from the east, I would never accept a counter-attack at Agedabia, but would pull back and not join battle until I had linked up with other formations, as Wavell had done in 1941.

In January 1942, we had succeeded—for the reasons I have described —in falling upon and smashing the British vanguard with locally superior forces before effective help could reach them. This had brought about the final collapse of Ritchie's offensive. This time, however, any such scheme had to remain theoretical. It could never be realised, because— contrary to 1941-42—the necessary conditions were not fulfilled. What made this so galling was that the British dispositions were excellently suited for such an operation.

The great retreat had been the result of our defeat at El Alamein. Once we had got over the first disorganisation, the behaviour of the troops, both German and Italian, had been exemplary. Our losses, apart from those suffered at El Alamein itself, had not been great.[1] Of the 90,000 or so German troops (including Luftwaffe and Navy), which we must have had before Alamein, 70,000 had been saved, not including the thousands of sick and wounded who had been flown to Europe.

We had still received no strategic decision from the supreme German and Italian authorities on the future of the African theatre of war. They did not look at things realistically—indeed, they refused to do so. What we found really astonishing was to see the amount of material that they were suddenly able to ship to Tunisia, quantities out of all proportion to anything we had received in the past. The urgency of the danger had at last percolated through to Rome. But the British and Americans had meanwhile multiplied their supply shipments many times over and were steadily increasing their strategic command over sea and air. One Axis ship after the other was going down beneath the waters of the Mediterranean, and it was becoming obvious that even the greatest effort could no longer hope to effect any decisive improvement in the supply situation; we were up to our necks in the mud and no longer had the strength to pull ourselves out.

The mismanagement, the operational blunders, the prejudices, the everlasting search for scapegoats, these were now to reach the acute stage. And the man who paid the price was the ordinary German and Italian soldier.

[1]*Note by General Bayerlein.*—The casualties of the Panzer Army from the beginning of the battle of El Alamein up to its arrival at the Mersa el Brega line amounted to: German troops, 1,100 killed, 3,900 wounded and 7,900 prisoners; Italian troops (approximations only, figures cannot be guaranteed), 1,200 killed, 1,600 wounded, and 20,000 prisoners. (Figures obtained from *Offizieller Bericht des Oberkommandos Afrika.*)

CHAPTER XVII

CONSULTATION IN EUROPE

IN THE weeks ahead, far greater difficulties were caused us by the lack of understanding of our higher authorities than by any activities of the British. There was, as I have already shown, only one course open to us —never to accept battle. A successful defence against a British outflanking drive—however ardently our masters may have desired it—was beyond all hope.

We now had left only a third of the fighting power that we had had before Alamein. We had neither supply dumps nor stocks, and lived, in the truest sense of the word, from hand to mouth. Very little was arriving in Tripoli. Tankers in particular were falling victim one after the other to British torpedo-carrying aircraft and submarines. My suggestion that they should be disguised as merchant ships was not acted on by the relevant authorities. In attacking our petrol transport, the British were able to hit us in a part of our machine on whose proper functioning the whole of the rest depended.

At that time I fondly believed that the attitude adopted by higher authority towards the Army arose out of a mistaken appreciation of our situation and prospects, probably caused by somewhat peculiar reporting on the part of the Italians and the Luftwaffe. I hoped to be able to arouse in them in course of time a realisation of the true facts of the situation. But I was to learn that people in our higher commands were sometimes not prepared to accept unpalatable truths; they put their heads in the sand and only gave in before the force of events.

While General de Stefanis was away in Italy, a signal arrived from the Fuehrer confirming the Duce's order that the Mersa el Brega line was to be held at all costs. Large reinforcements of tanks and guns, both anti-tank and anti-aircraft, were promised, but we knew from long experience what these promises meant. We were also made subordinate to Marshal Bastico again, " to satisfy purely formal considerations."

Rommel had already been subordinate to Bastico before the Panzer Army's advance into Egypt. During the El Alamein fighting, however, he had been responsible direct to the Commando Supremo and the Fuehrer's H.Q.

I had already decided to use the breathing space which we expected during the British build-up to drive the facts of the situation home to the Commando Supremo and the Fuehrer's H.Q. and to insist on the proper conclusions being drawn.

I have already indicated some part of my plan; but will give it in connected form for greater clarity.

(a) In the existing conditions of supply, which permitted us neither the months' overdue replacements of tanks, vehicles and weapons, nor the build-up necessary to sustain a mobile battle, we could not hope to make a stand against a heavy British attack anywhere in Tripolitania. The reason was that every possible position could be outflanked in the south and would thus require the main burden of the defence to be put on the motorised forces.

It was therefore necessary to think from the outset in terms of evacuating Tripolitania completely in order to make a last withdrawal to Gabes—where a line could be held bounded on the south-west by the Shott el Jerid—and there finally make our stand.

This line is 120 miles west of the Tunisian frontier, and midway between Tripoli and Tunis. It covers the narrow 12-mile stretch between the sea and the chain of lakes and marshes known as the Shott el Jerid (or Fejaj).

Two things would matter in carrying out this withdrawal from Mersa el Brega to Tunisia, firstly, to gain the maximum possible time, and secondly, to execute the operation with the minimum losses of men and material.

Our great problem was the non-motorised Italians. The slowest formation, assuming that one is not prepared to abandon it, always determines the speed of retreat of the whole army. This is a disastrous disadvantage in the face of a fully-motorised and superior enemy. It was therefore going to be absolutely essential for us to move the Italian divisions into new positions farther west before the British attack opened, leaving the motorised forces at Mersa el Brega to tie down the British, mine the roads and use every opportunity that offered to inflict damage on the enemy vanguard. The British commander had shown himself to be overcautious. He risked nothing in any way doubtful and bold solutions were completely foreign to him. So our motorised forces would have to keep up an appearance of constant activity, in order to induce ever greater caution in the British and make them even slower. I was quite satisfied that Montgomery would never take the risk of following up boldly and overrunning us, as he could have done without any danger to himself. Indeed, such a course would have cost him far fewer losses in the long run than his methodical insistence on overwhelming superiority in each tactical action, which he could only obtain at the cost of his speed.

The retreat to Tunisia would need to be made in a number of stages, in order to force the British into as many approach marches as possible. This was another gamble on the caution of the British commander, which later turned out to be well justified. The first stop was to be made at Buerat and the second at Tarhuna-Homs. We had no intention of accepting battle even at these points, but planned to get the infantry away before we were attacked, while the mechanised formations lightly engaged the British and delayed their advance. Finally, in the Gabes position—which, like that at El Alamein, could not be outflanked to the south—we would make our stand.

(b) At Gabes, we would be able to put the main weight of the battle on the non-motorised infantry. The position did not lend itself to attack by motorised forces, and could only be broken by a tremendous concentration of material. Montgomery would therefore need several months to transport sufficient material up through the whole of Libya to enable him to attack the Wadi Akarit [*this obstacle spans the Gabes defile*] with an assured prospect of success.[1] And during these months, our motorised forces would be refitted with material brought into Tunis while the retreat was going on. Together with the Fifth Panzer Army, which had meanwhile landed in Tunis, we would then have the chance of creating a real punch.

The great danger for us was the wide-open western front in Tunisia, which offered the British and Americans excellent possibilities for an offensive. It was therefore essential for us to strike first and launch a surprise attack with the whole of our motorised forces, destroying part of the Anglo-American formations and driving the rest back into Algeria. Meanwhile, Montgomery would be unable to do anything against the Gabes line without large-scale stocks of artillery ammunition.

When the Anglo-American forces in western Tunisia had been defeated and deprived of their striking power, the quickest possible reorganisation would be necessary to enable us to attack Montgomery, throw him back to the east and delay his deployment. This operation would, of course, be fraught with considerable difficulty, due to the unfavourable nature of the terrain.

(c) In the long run neither Libya nor Tunisia could be held, for, as I have already said, the African war was being decided by the battle

---

[1]*Note by General Bayerlein.*—Rommel has not expressed himself very clearly here. He obviously meant that it would take several months to organise the supply of an army over a distance as far as from Port Said to Mareth. He did not mean that Montgomery would need several months for his build-up after he arrived at Mareth.

of the Atlantic. From the moment that the overwhelming industrial capacity of the United States could make itself felt in any theatre of war, there was no longer any chance of ultimate victory in that theatre. Even if we had overrun the whole of the African continent, with the exception of a small strip of territory providing the enemy with good operational possibilities and permitting the Americans to bring in their material, we were bound to lose it in the end. Tactical skill could only postpone the collapse, it could not avert the ultimate fate of this theatre.

Hence our object in Tunisia would again have to be to gain as much time as possible and get out as many as we could of our battle-tried veterans for use in Europe. We knew by experience that there would be no hope of supplying and equipping an Army Group in Tunisia, which meant that we would have to try to reduce the fighting troops there to fewer but well-equipped formations. If a major, decision-seeking offensive were launched by the Allies, we would have to shorten the front step by step and evacuate increasing numbers of troops by transport aircraft, barges and warships. The first stand would be in the hill country extending from Enfidaville round Tunis, the second in the Cap Bon peninsula. When the Anglo-American forces finally completed their conquest of Tunisia, they were to find nothing, or at the most only a few prisoners, and thus be robbed of the fruits of their victory, just as we had been at Dunkirk.

(d) From the troops evacuated to Italy, a striking force would be formed. These troops, in both training and battle experience, were the best we had to oppose the British and Americans. My relations with them were such that on that score alone they were worth far more under my command than their actual numbers represented.

During the coming weeks I discussed my ideas with all our superior commands and hoped—vainly, as it turned out—to get them ultimately adopted. On the 22nd November, I had a meeting with Marshal Bastico. I developed the arguments given above and emphasised that the moment had now come when we had to give effect to the order to " resist to the end in Mersa el Brega," which meant the certain destruction of the army unless the order were revoked in time.

" We either lose the position four days earlier and save the army, or lose both position and army four days later." With this and similar arguments I tried to drive the facts of the situation home. Navarrini also did all he could to convince Marshal Bastico—who, though probably himself aware that the course we proposed was the only possible one, outwardly still held out against it. But there was not much he could say, because we too had no illusions about the great disadvantages which would accrue from the evacuation of Tripolitania; however, there was simply nothing else for it. Finally, he promised to represent our view as objectively as he could to higher authority.

21 Nov. 1942

DEAREST LU,

The last few days have been quiet as far as actual fighting is concerned. It's been pouring with rain on and off, which hasn't made life particularly comfortable, especially as I've been camping out in my car.

To-day I've a roof over my head again, and a table. That is great luxury. I've written you some thoroughly miserable letters, which I'm now sorry for. Although a favourable turn in the situation is almost more than I dare hope for now, nevertheless miracles do sometimes happen.

On the 24th November, Field Marshal Kesselring and Marshal Cavallero at last came to Africa for the meeting which I had so long been seeking. It took place at Arco dei Fileni,[1] on the frontier between Cyrenaica and Tripolitania; Kesselring, Cavallero, Bastico and I were present.

To put something of a damper on the over-optimistic mood in which Cavallero and Kesselring both appeared, I opened the meeting by describing the course of the fighting since Alamein, stressing the fact that the appalling supply conditions before the battle had been the cause of the whole sorry story. The troops had fought magnificently. We had lost practically all our heavy equipment, partly in the Alamein line and partly during the retreat, although every vehicle had had another in tow in order to get back as much material as possible. The remains of the army represented in fighting strength approximately one weak division. I added that the armament of the three Italian infantry divisions was practically unusable and that they could on no account be allowed to cross swords with the British. It was therefore completely impossible to hold the Mersa el Brega line. I again put forward my ideas on the subject of evacuating Tripolitania. Here, however, I came up against the solid opposition of Kesselring and Cavallero. The former looked at everything from the standpoint of the Luftwaffe, and thought principally of the consequences which the move would have on the strategic air situation in Tunisia. As for the latter, he lived in a world of make-believe.

I told them both that it would be too late to think of a retreat in two or three weeks' time when the British moved against our line with 800 armoured vehicles, 400 guns and 550 anti-tank guns. We had to make up our minds now. If they really wanted to hold the Mersa el

[1]Known to the Eighth Army as " Marble Arch."

Brega line, then the following equipment with crews would have to be sent to the front within a week:

> 75-mm. anti-tank guns—50
> Long-barrelled Panzer IVs—50
> Field guns of 100-150 mm. calibre—78
> Transporters and ample ammunition for the above
> At least 4,000 tons of petrol and 4,000 tons of ammunition

We would also need a considerable reinforcement of the air force.

Judging by experience, there was not a chance of these demands being satisfied, so that there was only one solution—back to the west. Ultimately neither of them could advance any logical argument against this reasoning. When I asked their views on the tactical action to be taken in the event of a British outflanking thrust, neither said a word. They had not come with any intention of learning from events and thus forming a rational judgment; they believed the fault lay with us and thought they could improve our fighting spirit with bombastic and magniloquent phrases. Me, they regarded as a pessimist of the first order, and they were probably the source of the legend which later went the rounds back in the rear—and was swallowed whole by certain office-chair soldiers only too anxious to delude themselves—that I was " cock-a-hoop in victory, but a prey to despair in defeat." In any case, it was quite obvious that neither of the Marshals would ever support my case.

The reader should bear in mind that Rommel's account was written shortly after the bitter end of the African campaign, and that he had no opportunity to revise it. His harsh comments on Kesselring, in particular, should not be taken as a considered opinion. There is a significant difference in the view he took later, as expressed in the final chapter written in 1944, shortly before he died, when he saw the African events in better perspective. They show a far higher appreciation of Kesselring's qualities.

The supply situation was still very serious. Instead of the 400 tons a day we needed, 50 tons was all we could bring overland up to the front, due partly to our shortage of vehicle space and partly to the great distance of Tripoli from the front. The result was to be seen in deficiencies of every possible kind.

On the 26th November we received the reaction to the meeting with Kesselring and Cavallero. While Kesselring required us to detach troops to protect the town of Tripoli, the Duce maintained his demand for the Mersa el Brega line to be held. On top of that Mussolini wanted us to launch an attack on the British as soon as possible, in which we would receive the support of a strongly reinforced Luftwaffe. What that support would amount to we knew only too well from our experience. In the event of a British attack, Marshal Bastico was to decide whether or not a retreat was necessary. Moreover, the Commando Supremo had im-

pressed on the Marshal that in order to stiffen my back he was to give
no such order except in the direst emergency. Rather decently, Bastico
immediately got in touch with me to enable some preliminary arrangements to be made.

I was extremely indignant at these orders. Hitherto it had always
been the Panzer Army's command which had again and again managed
to pull our fortunes out of the morass into which they would inevitably
have sunk if things had been left to the Commando Supremo. Now
that the impossibility of getting any sense into Rome had again been
demonstrated, I decided to fly to the Fuehrer. I wanted to ask him
personally for a strategic decision and to request, as a long-term policy,
the evacuation of North Africa. I intended to lay before him the operational and tactical views of the Panzer Army, as I have already described
them, and get them accepted.

We took off on the morning of the 28th November and reached
Rastenburg in the afternoon. The first talks opened at about 16.00
hours between Keitel, Jodl, Schmundt and myself. The two former were
extremely wary and reserved.

At about 17.00 hours I was ordered to the Fuehrer. There was a
noticeable chill in the atmosphere from the outset. I described all the
difficulties which the army had had to face during both the battle and
the retreat. It was all noted and the execution of the operation was
described as faultless and unique.

Unfortunately, I then came too abruptly to the point and said that,
since experience indicated that no improvement in the shipping situation
could now be expected, the abandonment of the African theatre of
war should be accepted as a long-term policy. There should be no
illusions about the situation and all planning should be directed towards
what was attainable. If the army remained in North Africa, it would be
destroyed.

I had expected a rational discussion of my arguments and intended
to develop them in a great deal more detail. But I did not get as far,
for the mere mention of the strategic question worked like a spark in a
powder barrel. The Fuehrer flew into a fury and directed a stream of
completely unfounded attacks upon us. Most of the F.H.Q. staff officers
present, the majority of whom had never heard a shot fired in anger,
appeared to agree with every word the Fuehrer said. In illustration of
our difficulties I mentioned the fact that only 5,000 of the 15,000 fighting
troops of the Afrika Korps and 90th Light Division had weapons, the
remainder being completely unarmed. This provoked a violent outburst
in which we were accused, among other things, of having thrown our
arms away. I protested strongly against charges of this kind, and said in
straight terms that it was impossible to judge the weight of the battle
from here in Europe. Our weapons had simply been battered to pieces
by the British bombers, tanks and artillery and it was nothing short of

a miracle that we had been able to escape with all the German motorised forces, especially in view of the desperate petrol shortage, which had allowed us to retreat at a rate of only tens of kilometres a day. I stated that all other armies would suffer the same fate if the Americans ever succeeded in setting foot on the continent.

But there was no attempt at discussion. The Fuehrer said that his decision to hold the eastern front in the winter of 1941-42 had saved Russia and that there, too, he had upheld his orders ruthlessly. I began to realise that Adolf Hitler simply did not want to see the situation as it was, and that he reacted emotionally against what his intelligence must have told him was right. He said that it was a political necessity to continue to hold a major bridgehead in Africa and there would, therefore, be no withdrawal from the Mersa el Brega line. He would do everything possible to get supplies to me. The Reichsmarschall [*Goering*] was to accompany me to Italy. He would be vested with extraordinary powers and was to negotiate with the Italians and all responsible authorities. We, however, had had experience enough of these ventures.

After leaving the Fuehrer's H.Q., Goering and I travelled in a rail-car as far as Gumbinnen where we changed to Goering's special train for the journey to Rome. I was angry and resentful at the lack of understanding displayed by our highest command and their readiness to blame the troops at the front for their own mistakes. My anger redoubled when I was compelled to witness the antics of the Reichsmarschall in his special train. The situation did not seem to trouble him in the slightest. He plumed himself, beaming broadly at the primitive flattery heaped on him by imbeciles from his own court, and talked of nothing but jewellery and pictures. At other times his behaviour could perhaps be amusing—now, it was infuriating.

Goering also possessed inordinate ambition and had no scruples about the means he used to advance it. Thus he thought that there were easy laurels to be earned on the African front and was angling to manœuvre the Luftwaffe into control of it. Units of his Praetorian Guard, the Panzer Division " Hermann Goering," were already on their way to Tunis.[1] His estimate of the possibilities offered by the African theatre was to prove a disastrous fallacy. I do not think that there has been any other front where we have been opposed by a command with such excellent qualities and by such well-trained troops—not to mention their equipment and armament—as the British and later the Americans in North Africa. Our only advantage over them was our more modern conception of war, and this was of no avail once the material conditions

---

[1]*Note by General Bayerlein.*—This remark is interesting. Rommel was firmly convinced that Goering was pursuing the intentions he describes and various signs, in fact, pointed to it. Rommel, for his part, always bitterly opposed the raising of S.S. and Luftwaffe Field Divisions. He several times suggested to Hitler in 1943 that a single unified army should be formed again, without these " Praetorian Guards".

for it no longer existed. It was consequently madness to underestimate our Western enemies in the slightest degree.

During the whole of this period my bitterest enemy was Goering. I think he wanted to get me sacked in order to realise his own plans in North Africa. He dismissed every appreciation of the situation which I sent to the Fuehrer's H.Q. as mere pessimism. He gave birth to the absurd idea that I was governed by moods and could only command when things went well; if they went badly I became depressed and caught the " African sickness". From this it was argued that since, to win battles, it needed a general who believed in victory and since I was a sick man anyway, it was necessary to consider whether to relieve me of my command. On the subject of the " moods", I should perhaps say that we at the front were naturally not particularly pleased when the situation approached disaster. The Reichsmarschall, on the other hand, sat through it all in his saloon carriage. Thus the angle of approach was a little different.

To avoid wasting the opportunity altogether, I instructed my A.D.C., Lieutenant Berndt, a man with a very persuasive tongue, to make the Gabes plan [*a retreat into Tunisia and defence of the Gabes line*] palatable for Goering. I myself found his opinions so infuriating that sooner or later I would have been bound to speak out, which would have finished any chances I might have had.

By displaying all its advantages in the most exaggerated form, Berndt did, in fact, succeed in rousing Goering's enthusiasm for the plan. He made a particular point of the propaganda effect which an offensive into Algeria by the combined motorised forces of the two armies would have on world opinion. Goering beamed his approval and decided to give the idea his support.

But the success was short-lived, for when we arrived in Rome, Kesselring came out against the plan because of the increased air threat it would mean to Tunisia. I pointed out that we did not really have any choice, for the retreat would sooner or later be forced on us. We should exploit the advantage of the concentration of strength at a moment particularly favourable for us. But the Reichsmarschall considered that the disadvantage given by an air triangle Malta-Algiers-Tripoli outweighed the advantages of the plan. So a retreat to Gabes was out of the question, and no further thought should be given to it. I had on my lips the argument that it was nonsense to be talking of an air triangle when it was all the same to us in the end where the British aircraft which bombed our ports came from; however, I realised the futility of the whole discussion and kept quiet.

In the conference with the Duce, Goering declared that I had left the Italians in the lurch at Alamein. Before I could make a worthy reply to this monstrous statement, Mussolini said: " That's news to me; your retreat was a masterpiece, Marshal Rommel."

On this occasion the Italians were far more reasonable than our own higher command and began by supporting my recommendation to retire to the Gabes position. However, no real agreement was reached. I had, meanwhile, issued orders to my army that if the British attacked, the Mersa el Brega line was to be held to the last man, and had referred to the Fuehrer's order. The Italians saw quite clearly that this must lead to the inevitable destruction of the army, and I did, therefore, manage to get permission from the Duce to begin with the construction of the Buerat line and to take steps to move the non-motorised Italian infantry back there in good time. The motorised forces also received authority to withdraw in the event of a British attack. That was at least something.

On the morning of the 2nd December, a conference took place in the Commando Supremo on supply matters. I had already drawn attention to the fact that practically the whole of our shipping space was being used for the Fifth Panzer Army [*in Tunisia*] and that my army was not even receiving the necessities of life, although it was carrying the main burden of the fighting. The most likely reason for this was the interest that the Luftwaffe and various other Rome authorities had in supplying the Fifth Army for an offensive to the west.

At the outset of the conference, Goering stated that I must at all costs hold on indefinitely at Buerat, but that if possible I should already begin attacking the enemy from Mersa el Brega.

The discussion then turned to a number of technical points concerning the method of carrying supplies to Tripoli. In particular, Goering suggested that we might lay a mine-barrier after the British example, which would keep the seaways between Tunis and Italy safe from submarines from both sides. Adequate quantities of sea-mines were available in Germany. The Italian Navy, of course, opposed any such scheme and put forward all manner of objections.

I found all this talk very embittering. If our highest authorities had only occupied themselves with the subject a little earlier, and put these ideas into practice months before, victory in Africa would have been ours. Most people do not seem to exert themselves until the water is lapping round their shins.

I was not best pleased when it came out that Kesselring had diverted to Tunis a number of the latest type of 88-mm. guns, which the Fuehrer had promised us and which we urgently required. It was unfortunate but true that in matters of supply Kesselring behaved in a very uncomradely spirit towards us and thought only of himself. Finally, Kesselring gave orders for these ships to be diverted back to Tripoli.

Particularly interesting was Goering's political attitude towards the Italians in relation to the difficult situation in Africa. Although we had always been forbidden to say a word to the Italians about the shortcomings of their Army and State, or to demand improvements, Goering now began to talk to Cavallero about really fundamental questions, such as the poor Italian armament, their sea strategy and similar thorny subjects. The only result, of course, was that he put their backs up without having any hope of getting anything put right. I have already drawn attention in an earlier chapter to the unsatisfactory political basis on which the Italo-German alliance was founded. It was the source of most of the trouble and faults which led to the loss of the African war. A war of alliance always causes difficulty and friction between the allies, as each country tries to work for its own ends rather than the other's. The right thing in these circumstances is to air all differences openly and not to cover them with a cloak of silence. Many Italians felt very deeply that the Axis was a sham, and consequently believed that in final victory we would have scant regard for their interests.

It was generally felt that if Tripolitania were lost, Mussolini would be threatened by a political crisis in Italy. His position may well have been still further weakened by Goering's sudden heavy-handed behaviour. A great many Italians had had enough of the war and were considering how best they could get out of it.

Flying back to Africa I realised that we were now completely thrown back on our resources and that to keep the army from being destroyed as the result of some crazy order or other would need all our skill.

CHAPTER XVIII

BACK TO TUNISIA

My STAFF in Africa were profoundly shocked when they heard what little appreciation our highest command had shown for our position.

Meanwhile, the British had not been idle. Artillery had been brought into position and supply dumps established, and they were now very active with reconnaissance. Now that we were out of range of air transport from Sicily, our petrol situation had grown even worse. In fact, we were to all intents and purposes completely immobilised. With petrol so short, the Luftwaffe was having to confine itself to only the most essential of sorties.

Although 5,000 tons of petrol had arrived in Africa for the Panzer Army during November, no less than 8,100 tons had been sunk by the British on the way. The scale of these sinkings and the quantity of petrol lost by them is made even more clear when it is realised that the greater part of the 5,000 tons which did arrive was flown over by the Luftwaffe.

In these circumstances it had now become a matter of doubt whether we would ever be able to get our formations back as far as Buerat. The major British attack was expected for mid-December and we had to be out by then. When I talked over the situation with Marshal Bastico on the 3rd December we decided to go on doing all we could to get the facts across to our higher authorities. For the rest we were completely dependent on the arrival of the promised petrol ships.

But the petrol situation did not improve during the next few days. Our first idea had been not to attempt a withdrawal until enough petrol was available to get the whole force back. But we soon had to give that up, since on the 5th December it became increasingly evident that the British attack would not be long delayed. So we began to shift the Italians back on the night of the 6th. In spite of the need for secrecy —I was certain that if the British once got wind of our intentions they would attack immediately—the Italians made an atrocious din and some of their vehicles even drove back through the moonlit night with blazing headlights.

Thus the Italians were carried away night by night to the west.

Their move swallowed up practically all the meagre amount of petrol we did receive, and transport of ammunition to the front virtually ceased. The armoured and motorised forces were all but immobilised and could never have reacted to British attacks. S O S after S O S was dispatched to Europe. With the enemy concentrating his air reconnaissance—also part of his ground reconnaissance—in the south, it was obvious that he was preparing a wide hook through the desert to outflank our line. It therefore became every day more urgent to get ourselves mobile again.

8 Dec. 1942

My dear Manfred,

It's time that I sent you my congratulations on your 14th birthday. My wishes must not arrive too late.

The war is very hard and it looks doubtful whether I shall be permitted to return to you. You know what a difficult struggle we're having with the British at present, how great their superiority is and how small our supplies. If it goes on like this, we shall be crushed by the enemy's immense superiority. It is a bitter fate for my soldiers and me to have to go through this at the end of so heroic and victorious a struggle. We will do our very utmost to avoid defeat.

Now, to you, Manfred, dear. . . . You're going to be 14, and school will soon lie behind you. You must realise the seriousness of the situation and learn as much as you can at school. You are learning for yourself. It is not impossible that you might soon have to stand on your own feet. The times could become very, very hard for all of us. Be guided by your mother, who always has your best interests at heart. I am not pleased that the Hitler Jugend makes such heavy demands on your time and that school has to suffer as a result. It's probably too much for you. . . .

11 Dec. 1942

Dearest Lu,

Not much news. Things have livened up a little at the front. Our supply troubles are as bad as ever and are causing me a lot of headaches. I wonder if you could have an English-German dictionary sent to me by courier post. It would come in very useful.

I'm terribly looking forward to seeing your letters and especially the first one. Nehring has been relieved of his command and a Colonel-General has taken over. I wonder if he'll do any better?[1]

Christmas will be here in a few days. I wish you both, from my heart, a very happy Christmas.

On the night of the 11th December, after laying down heavy artillery fire on several of our strong points, the British opened an attack along

[1] Nehring, the former commander of the Afrika Korps, had been sent to command in Tunisia, but was there superseded by von Arnim.

the coast road in the north. Shortly afterwards my troops succeeded in engaging a British scouting party which had the task of reconnoitring road conditions near Merduma. Thus Montgomery's intentions were finally clear. The British made attack after attack against our strong-points in the north and soon there was no more doubt—the enemy offensive had opened.

The withdrawal of the non-motorised German and Italian troops was now complete. It being essential to avoid getting our forces too closely engaged in battle in the Mersa el Brega line we sounded the retreat in the evening and, from 7 o'clock onwards, an unbroken stream of fighting troops and transport moved off to the west. There was no hope of opposing a British outflanking thrust with the motorised forces; we had too little petrol. It would therefore have been suicide to have remained in the position any longer.

Montgomery had intended to launch his attack on the 16th December, but hastened it when he saw signs, at the beginning of the month, that Rommel was about to withdraw. His plan was to make a frontal attack with the 51st Highland Division, with the 7th Armoured Division advancing on its left flank, while the 2nd New Zealand Division carried out a much wider outflanking move with the aim of getting astride Rommel's line of retreat—at the Wadi Matratin, near Merduma, sixty miles west of Agheila. The attack as a whole was conducted by XXX Corps (Leese) which had taken over from X Corps.

The New Zealand Division was concentrated round El Haseiat by the 9th December, and started its outflanking move from that rearward position on the 12th. Montgomery ordered that large-scale raids by the 51st Division should open on the night of the 11th, to occupy the enemy's attention, and that the frontal attack proper should be launched on the 14th. But these preliminary raids were taken by Rommel to be the start of the attack, and thus led him to hasten his intended withdrawal— an effect that spoilt Montgomery's plan.

Our petrol was only enough to carry the motorised group back to the El Mugtaa district—where, provided the British did not advance round the flank into the Merduma area, we intended to make a preliminary halt and await the renewed attack.

The British commander's planning had contained one mistake. Experience must have told him that there was a good chance that we would not accept battle at Mersa el Brega. He should not, therefore, have started bombarding our strong-points and attacking our line until his outflanking force had completed its move and was in a position to advance on the coast road in timed co-ordination with the frontal attack.

Meanwhile, on the 10th December, the Fifth Panzer Army Command had been formed in Tunis under Colonel-General von Arnim. Unfortunately, very little co-ordination existed between this new command and ourselves. We badly felt the need during this period of a single authority on African soil which could have welded together under a common command the two armies whose fates were so closely dependent on each other.

THROUGH THE SIRTE

Once again my troops were moving through the arid and monotonous wastes of the Great Sirte, westwards—and probably for the last time. The retreat went as planned during the night, with the British obviously noticing nothing, for next morning, the 13th, they put down a violent barrage on our old positions. British fighter-bombers attacked the bottleneck at El Mugtaa all that day.

Late in the morning, a superior enemy force launched an attack on Combat Group Ariete, which was located south-west of El Agheila, with its right flank resting on the Sebcha Chebira and its left linking up with 90th Light Division. Bitter fighting ensued against 80 British tanks and lasted for nearly ten hours. The Italians put up a magnificent fight, for which they deserved the utmost credit. Finally, in the evening, the British were thrown back by a counter attack of the Centauro's armoured regiment, leaving 22 tanks and 2 armoured cars burnt out or damaged on the battlefield. The British intention of cutting off the 90th Light Division had been foiled.

Throughout that day I had reconnaissance forces out in the Merduma area to prevent a surprise attack on the coast road by an enemy outflanking column.

That day the British sank a tanker and two fast ships laden with a total of 3,500 tons of petrol. This was a heavy blow for us, particularly in view of the British threat from the south, which made a speed-up in the operation essential.

Air reconnaissance, which had been specially ordered because of the anxiety we felt for our flank, very soon reported the advance of powerful British forces on Merduma. This meant that we now had to use our last drop of petrol to get out of the sack. It was infuriating for me to have to stand idly by and watch the wonderful opportunities which the enemy offered us for effective counter-moves. For example, the British commander used a column of only about 2,000 vehicles for his southern hook, and it would have been simple enough, if only we had had the petrol, to have left a small force holding the Mugtaa defile while the bulk of our motorised forces attacked and destroyed the enemy outflanking column. As things were, however, the situation presented us with deadly peril.

So that night the retreat was resumed. Next morning, the 21st Panzer Division held the Mugtaa defile as rearguard. At about 10.00 hours, I moved Army H.Q. back to a point some 30 miles east of Nofilia, where, during the afternoon, I received news from the Luftwaffe commander that the British had reached a point 20 miles south-east of

Merduma. This was bad news indeed, because there was then very little petrol left at the front and we had to get some up over the road. Meanwhile, the 3rd Reconnaissance Battalion, which was screening our southern front, was being slowly forced back to Merduma by the greatly superior enemy force.

At about midday a British bomber formation flew over, the first for a long time, and chose my H.Q. as a target for its bombs, probably attracted by General Seidemann's highly conspicuous Storch. The Ic truck was burnt out and several other vehicles were damaged.

During the afternoon the 15th Panzer Division, with a combat group of 21st Panzer Division, moved in front of Merduma to hold the Via Balbia open for the main body of the 21st Panzer Division, which was still heavily engaged at Mugtaa. To avoid the forces at Mugtaa fighting themselves to a standstill, I at length gave the order for a retreat to the level of Arco dei Fileni.

In the evening the British broke through the 3rd Reconnaissance Battalion's screen near Merduma and a considerable force moved off west towards Nofilia in an attempt to outmarch us.

I now decided to deploy all troops within reach in the district round Nofilia. The Afrika Korps moved off to its new positions during the night, with the 90th Light Division remaining as rearguard at Wadi Matratin. Dawn found the 21st Panzer Division on the march to Nofilia, but the 15th Panzer Division's petrol was late in getting up and the division was still standing fast at Merduma.

In the early hours of the 16th, British infantry succeeded in taking a commanding height in front of the 90th Light Division's rearguard line. By the time the 15th Panzer Division arrived at the Via Balbia, with the main body of the enemy following up hard on its heels, the British vanguard had already crossed the road. However, the division succeeded in scattering the British vanguard and fighting its way through towards Nofilia with very few casualties. With the British main body following it up so closely it was now impossible for the division to hold the rearguard line on the 90th Light Division's southern flank, as had originally been intended. This made the 90th Light's position untenable and they, too, had to be brought back to Nofilia.

16 Dec. 1942

DEAREST LU,

We've made camp in flower-decked meadows. But we're on the way back, alas, and there's no prospect of the situation improving. Eight more days to Christmas. I wonder where we'll be then.

The British columns in the south now made another attempt to cut us off. A Cairo Radio broadcast announced that we were in a bottle which the British commander was about to cork. When we heard this I said to my officers that the bottle would soon be empty if only we could get our tanks full. Our petrol was only just enough to get us back to Nofilia, and, with no substantial supplies in sight, I found myself compelled to face the prospect of holding on in the Nofilia area for another day, in spite of the threatened encirclement. To prevent the enemy making a quick dash to the coast road and cutting it beyond us, our formations were ordered to deploy in depth along the road to the west. Thus the screen formed by the Afrika Korps round Nofilia was to be continued west along the road by the 33rd and 580th Reconnaissance Battalions, the Panzer Grenadier Regiment "Afrika", and the 90th Light Division in that order. The Sirte area was held by the "Young Fascist" Division and Combat Group Ariete.

During the night our forces moved into the areas assigned to them and by morning they were in position, but again out of petrol. In the course of the morning [*17th*] the British attacked at a point 6 to 10 miles south-west of Nofilia and a violent action started with units of the Afrika Korps and the 33rd Reconnaissance Battalion, all of which were immobilised. The battle drew steadily closer to the coast road. Finally, after a few tons of petrol had at long last arrived, a counter-attack was launched by elements of the Afrika Korps and the 3rd Reconnaissance Battalion, and 20 British tanks were shot up in heavy fighting. This held the road open and, when the petrol ration came through, the units which had been threatened with encirclement streamed back along it to the west.

At nine o'clock that morning I left my H.Q. to persuade Marshal Bastico to join with me in contesting the order to hold on at any price to the Buerat position. I regarded it merely as an intermediate stop; I wanted to force the British to a lengthy halt, but intended to withdraw to Tarhuna-Homs when they renewed their attack. It was clear by this time that the Commando Supremo would go on giving authority to retreat at the last possible moment, that is to say, when the danger to the army was so great that it could even be seen from the perspective of Rome. But that could be too late. The withdrawal to Gabes could have been planned far more systematically and far more to our advantage, if people had acted consistently with the end in view, instead of repeatedly allowing themselves to be forced into making emergency decisions at the last moment under the impact of enemy pressure.

On the way I discussed the matter with General Navarrini. He was not very optimistic and thought it doubtful whether, with petrol so short, we would ever get back that far. I pointed out that the main thing for us was on no account to accept a decisive battle and to do everything in our power to avoid the British pinning down our forces frontally. It was, of course, true that our speed of retreat would be determined by the small amount of petrol which could be brought up in any one day.[1]

---

[1]This point deserves emphasis, since it has a constant bearing on any strategical and tactical deductions about the course of the operations during the British advance through Tripolitania.

But I thought that there was still a hope that the British would not throw their main effort into an outflanking drive round the south. Had they done so, then our escape would more than once have been a matter of grave doubt.

At about 12.00 hours I went into conference with Marshal Bastico at Buerat. After I had once again stressed the importance of starting to think now about the evacuation of Tripolitania, we eventually decided to wireless a joint appreciation of the situation to the Commando Supremo and to ask once again for decisions. I was to prepare the appreciation. During the conversation Marshal Bastico explained in some detail the results which would ensue from the evacuation of Tripolitania. But with supply conditions in such a state, these results were inevitable. A soldier must learn to accept facts.

Bastico himself was fully aware of the fact that we would not be able to hold on to Buerat. I asked him to look on the Tarhuna-Homs line as our next stop. Immediately after the conference was over I dictated my appreciation, in which I asked permission to evacuate the non-motorised infantry by stages from the Buerat position. I also asked that on the wider issue all operational thinking should be directed towards executing the Gabes plan. My appreciation was endorsed by Marshal Bastico in all essential points.

The Panzer Army's supply situation did not improve. Of ten large ships destined for Tripoli, nine were sunk by the British and the tenth carried no petrol.

To add to our worries, we were in a continual state of anxiety about Tunisia. We received virtually no comprehensive information on which we might have formed a judgment of the situation on that front. Both armies were supposed to assume that the other could maintain its position and to act accordingly. My main fear was that the British and Americans might take their correct operational decision and attack the Gabes bottle-neck from Southern Tunisia, thus driving a wedge between the two armies. It was, in fact, partly this that made me in such a hurry to get back to the west and if it had been left to me and I had had more petrol, I would probably have moved across into Tunisia far earlier than I actually did.

18 Dec. 1942

DEAREST LU,

We're in heavy fighting again, with little hope of success, for we're short of everything. One's personal fate fades into the background in face of the bitter fate of the army, and the consequences and effects it will have.

Bastico was also very depressed yesterday. The situation in the west seems to be no better, particularly in the ports. We are hoping to be able to carry on for a few days yet. But petrol is short, and without petrol there's nothing to be done.

On the 18th December I inspected the Buerat position, the construction of which had meanwhile been going ahead under the direction of Westphal, so far as our very limited resources permitted. 80,000 mines had been laid, most of them, however, anti-personnel mines. At several points along the front an anti-tank ditch had been dug by German and Italian labour units.

Meanwhile, the British had announced that they had closed the ring round Nofilia and were about to mop up its contents. Several of our units were said to be inside and making vain attempts to break out. In fact, only one platoon had been left inside and even that succeeded in breaking out.

On the afternoon of the 19th of December, a Duce order arrived in reply to the appreciation which Marshal Bastico and I had sent jointly to the Commando Supremo. Judged in relation to the circumstances at that time, its wording was pretty bombastic. It read roughly as follows:

" Resist to the uttermost, I repeat, resist to the uttermost with all troops of the German-Italian Army in the Buerat position."

How did Mussolini imagine such actions were fought? I had really done all I could to arouse some understanding of the art of desert warfare in our higher commands and had particularly emphasised that to concern oneself with territory was mere prejudice. The all-important principle was to keep on the move until a tactically favourable position for battle was found and then to fight. In the conditions we were facing, that position was the Gabes line. Nevertheless, orders were once again issued to the troops to " resist to the uttermost".

I immediately wirelessed Marshal Cavallero and asked him what we were to do if the enemy outmarched us in the south and simply chose not to do battle with the Buerat garrison.

Marshal Cavallero replied that the battle should be so conducted that the Italian troops were not sacrificed again. I thereupon instructed General Mancinelli to drive personally to Marshal Bastico and inform him that I could not " resist to the uttermost " in the Buerat position and at the same time get the Italians away. He had to make up his mind which it was to be. Bastico replied evasively.

His position was extremely unpleasant. He was very well aware of the difficulties we were facing and, as I have already said, ultimately realised the impossibility of making a lengthy stand at any point this side of Gabes. But as Governor of Libya he did not feel he could come out in favour of evacuating Tripolitania. Besides, he knew that Cavallero and his clique were only just waiting for an occasion to get rid of him as a scapegoat for their own mistakes.

I was, in fact, very much afraid at that time that the British commander might continue his attempt to outmarch us in the south. If he had done so, then the Buerat position would have collapsed without a shot.

Montgomery could not continue a large-scale advance for administrative reasons. So he preferred to wait until he had built up sufficient stocks to carry the advance right through to Tripoli without a pause. " I was also concerned with ensuring the correct balance in the rear areas and, in planning the next phase of our advance, was anxious to bring forward a corps to occupy the El Agheila position when XXX Corps moved on again to the west." X Corps was to be brought up—comprising the 1st Armoured, 50th, and 4th Indian Divisions. Its move up, however, was delayed by supply complications arising from damage to the port of Benghazi in heavy gales on the 4th and 5th of January.

Characteristically also, the Luftwaffe tried to have another go at us. Kesselring declared that we had improperly used petrol intended for the front in the rear areas, and that it was because of this that we were unable to undertake any counter-moves with our motorised forces. There was not the slightest truth in this accusation and the only purpose of it was probably to provide a story to account for the small quantities of petrol which were reaching us. Actually, 95 per cent of the petrol we had received had been used in withdrawing the front and getting up petrol to the fighting formations. The only people who had taken petrol without authority were Luftwaffe units. For days past hundreds of supply lorries had stood stationary on the road with empty tanks, and the troops had now barely enough ammunition to keep the enemy at bay. We were, therefore, intensely angry at this story and immediately sent Kesselring a signal telling him what we thought about it.

The British now seemed to be undertaking large-scale supply operations in preparation for a more complete outflanking drive. Endless columns of vehicles were moving west down the Via Balbia from Tobruk and Benghazi and unloading was going on at top speed in both the ports.

Intensive operations were being conducted against our supplies by the Long-Range Desert Group, working to a well-thought-out plan. They succeeded again and again in shooting up supply lorries behind our lines, laying mines, cutting down telephone poles and similar nefarious activities. Their parties were extremely difficult to catch, for they made only the briefest of appearances and then vanished without trace back into the desert.

While the motorised troops continued to hold their position at Sirte, tremendous efforts were made to build up the Buerat position. We laid every mine we had. In case the Duce should really decide to hold a fixed front at Buerat we at least wanted to be prepared. It would, of course, have been better to have used all our resources in pushing ahead with the Tarhuna-Homs line, where the non-motorised Italians could have been used to far better advantage.

Soon the Buerat front was strong enough to resist a fair-scale British break-through attempt—that is, of course, assuming that they chose to attack it frontally. Like almost every other position in North Africa, the enemy could make a hook round the south to attack the Via Balbia, without even making contact with the fortified line. If he decided to throw several divisions into such a move the battle would be decided by the motorised forces alone. And in motorised forces we were hopelessly inferior—quite apart from the fact that our petrol would not possibly run to a mobile battle. Non-motorised forces cannot create a centre of gravity quickly enough, and they thus lack the quality which matters most in mechanised warfare. Because of their lack of speed the enemy can take them on one after the other, each time with locally superior forces, and destroy them piecemeal without suffering undue casualties himself.

During the next few days I repeatedly pointed out that the British might choose to make no frontal assault on the Buerat position, but instead go round its southern flank. I asked for instructions for such an event. On each occasion I received an answer referring me to the Duce's order. Everybody in Rome was scared to death of making an independent decision and invariably tried to unload the responsibility on to somebody else. I decided on no account to let up until I had been given an answer which did justice to my question. I had no wish to be the scapegoat for the armchair strategists in Rome.

24 Dec. 1942

DEAREST LU,

To-day my thoughts are more than ever with you two at home. To you, Manfred, once more all the best for your 15th year. I expect you will already have received my birthday letter. And I wish you both a very happy Christmas. God will help us as in the past.

... I'm going off very early this morning into the country and will be celebrating this evening among the men. They're in top spirits, thank God, and it takes great strength not to let them see how heavily the situation is pressing on us.

Kesselring was here yesterday. New promises were made, but it will be the same as it ever was. They can't be kept because the enemy puts his pencil through all our supply calculations.

On the 24th December we set off at 07.00 hours on a beautiful sunny morning to inspect the country south of our front. First we drove along the Via Balbia and then—with two Italian armoured cars as escort—through the fantastically fissured Wadi Zem-Zem towards El Fashia. Soon we began to find the tracks of British vehicles, probably made by some of Stirling's people [*actually, the Long-Range Desert Group*] who had been round there on the job of harassing our supply traffic. The tracks were comparatively new and we kept a sharp look-out to see if we could catch a "Tommy." Near El Fashia I suddenly spotted a lone vehicle. We gave chase, but soon found that its crew was Italian. Troops from my *Kampfstaffel* were also in the area. They had surprised some British Commandos the day before and captured maps marked with British store dumps and strong points. Now they were combing through the district also hoping to stumble on a " Tommy."

During the return journey our Christmas dinner trotted up to us in the shape of a herd of gazelles. Armbruster [*an interpreter on the staff of the Panzer Army*] and I each succeeded in bringing down one of these speedy animals from the moving cars.

When I arrived back at H.Q. I learnt that the British had meanwhile launched an attack south of Ssrte with 4,500 vehicles and were now moving on to the west. In Sirte itself, the men of the 15th Panzer Division had just got together for their Christmas celebration when the attack came and they had to pack up and hastily evacuate the district. At about 17.00 hours General Bayerlein and I joined the H.Q. Company's Christmas party, where I received a present of a miniature petrol drum, containing, instead of petrol, a pound or two of captured coffee. Thus proper homage was paid to our most serious problem even on that day. At 20.00 hours I invited several people from my immediate staff to share a meal off the gazelles we had brought in that morning.

During next day [*the 25th of December*] the British halted their advance and seemed to be waiting for reinforcements and stores to be brought up. The 90th Light Division and 580th Reconnaissance Battalion, who were holding the rearguard line, were pulled back step by step behind the Buerat position.

I took this opportunity to inspect the Buerat position from the enemy's side, mainly to find out how effective our decoy installations were. At El Alamein, the British had concentrated a tornado of shells on our 88-mm. gun positions, in order to neutralise from the outset the guns which were most dangerous to them.   So this time we were making extensive use of dummies to disperse the effect of the British artillery.

By the 29th of December all troops had withdrawn behind the Buerat line.

28 Dec. 1942

Dearest Lu,
    Our fate is gradually working itself out. Supplies have been very short and it would need a miracle for us to hold on much longer. What is to happen now lies in God's hands. We'll go on fighting as long as it's at all possible. I saw this coming when we were last together and discussed the most important things with you.

    In these hard days my thoughts are more than ever with you. I have to keep telling myself that it will all come right again some day. Keep your chin up and I'll do the same.

30 Dec. 1942

The battle has now been joined. I haven't the slightest doubt
about its outcome, the forces are too unequal. Supplies have almost
entirely dried up. So now we must surrender ourselves to the inevitable
and hope that God will yet prosper our cause. I was at the front
yesterday and am going again to-day.

31 Dec. 1942

Kesselring is coming again to-day and there is a hope that the
situation may change " slightly " in our favour. Not much, but still
a little. One can't, of course, expect anything very great.

At midday I'm having a meeting with Bastico, who is more and
more feeling himself as C.-in-C. That's something one simply has
to swallow. Anyway, it does mean that he shares the responsibility. . . .

. . . I'm badly worried about the heavy fighting going on in the
East [*Stalingrad*]. Let's hope we'll come through it all right. The
army here is in the best of spirits. It's a good thing the men don't
know everything.

BUERAT RESPITE

To our surprise, the enemy halted at Buerat and thus granted us yet
another reprieve, which we immediately used to plead once again for
the withdrawal of the Italian troops to Tarhuna. If we were to escape
envelopment from the south, then the non-motorised Italians had to get
out—as at Mersa el Brega—while the going was good.

Only light forces had followed up Rommel's retreat to the Buerat line. Mont-
gomery was planning to launch his attack on that line, with the XXX Corps, on
the 15th January.

Accordingly, on the 31st of December, yet another conference took
place between Marshal Bastico and myself. The Commando Supremo
had apparently now decided, after a long shilly-shally, not to risk the
possible destruction of the army at Buerat. But they still wanted to have
it both ways and thought that I should hold the Buerat position to the
extreme limit of resistance and, if destruction threatened, retire to the
west. They said it was essential to maintain resistance in Tripolitania for
at least another month or two. I replied at once that the length of our
stay in Tripolitania would be decided by Montgomery and not by the
Commando Supremo, and that the non-motorised troops must be moved
back immediately. It would be too late once the British had launched
their attack. I drew particular attention to the fact that the enemy
had hitherto always tried to outflank us outside the range of our fire.

Marshal Bastico thereupon asked whether I was prepared to order
the withdrawal of the non-motorised forces myself. This, of course,

would have been a way out, but it would have brought me into even worse odour with the Commando Supremo, with results which would have hit the whole army. They would, moreover, have doubtless taken the first opportunity of sending me another Duce order. It was thus a matter of principle. I therefore replied that I must insist on receiving Marshal Bastico's formal authority for the withdrawal of the infantry divisions, but would decide myself when they would actually move off.

It is always a bad sign in an army when scapegoats are habitually sought out and brought to sacrifice for every conceivable mistake. It usually shows something very wrong in the highest command. It completely inhibits the willingness of junior commanders to take decisions, for they will always try to get chapter and verse for everything they do, finishing up more often than not with a miserable piece of casuistry instead of the decision which would spell release. The usual result is that the man who never does more than supinely pass on the opinion of his seniors is brought to the top, while the really valuable man, the man who accepts nothing ready-made but has an opinion of his own, gets put on the shelf.

Marshal Bastico was a fundamentally decent man with a sober military understanding and considerable moral stamina. He saw the position as I did, in its true light, but had the misfortune to be charged by the Commando Supremo with the task of representing the Duce's point of view to me. As this was usually fallacious he was always on bad ground in the argument which followed. He did, in fact, always take my part, and by his efforts at mediation contributed greatly to the fact that the retreat through Tripolitania, in spite of the senseless obstinacy of our superiors, was a success.

So on this New Year's Eve we sat together in the operations truck in a mood of grim humour. As far as possible we kept off the military situation and so managed to stay in reasonably good spirits.

1 Jan. 1943

DEAREST LU,

The old year did not pass without some easing of our situation. So I enter 1943 with new hope. That's at least something.

My most heartfelt wishes for the New Year to you and Manfred. Bayerlein, Bonin and I sat cosily round in our small command vehicle till midnight and our thoughts turned frequently towards home. . . .

A few days later, the order arrived from Marshal Bastico to start shifting the Italian troops back to the Tarhuna-Homs line. But there was still a string attached to it, for it charged us with the task of holding up the British in front of the Tripoli defences for at least six weeks. I have already shown how pointless it was to fix such targets. Of course I tried to gain as much time as I could, but it never occurred to me to commit myself to definite dates. I immediately reported to this effect through Bastico to the Commando Supremo.

During the lull at the beginning of January 1943, I kept continually on the move with Bayerlein, trying to gain a picture of the country over which the forthcoming battle would be fought, and to have the battlefield, as it were, imprinted on my mind. We took this opportunity to visit the old Roman city of Leptis Magna, the ruins of which were still standing. An Italian professor acted as our guide and explained the features of the place in excellent German. But our thoughts were more with Montgomery than with ancient ruins. Moreover, the strain and lack of sleep of the past few days were beginning to tell, and my A.D.C., Lieutenant von Hardtdegen, particularly distinguished himself by falling asleep between two pieces of feminine statuary. Bayerlein photographed him there.

5 Jan. 1943

DEAREST LU,

Nothing new to report from here. The enemy still doesn't risk an attack. I wonder how long it will be? I wrote to Helene and Gertrud yesterday. It's still cold and windy. The only time it gets tolerably warm is when the sun comes through for a bit at midday. That's something I'm not used to in Africa. I've had a letter from von Luepke, who was taken prisoner a year ago. He was in South Africa, escaped and trekked north with another man for four months. Finally, a Zulu handed him over to the British again.

There's very little post coming through at the moment; most of what comes is from November. There's probably a whole lot at the bottom of the sea. I'm in a slightly better humour again, there being now some hope that we'll be able to make a stand somewhere.

7 Jan. 1943

Kesselring and Cavallero have been here, also Gause. But they're not even making promises now. We've got to manage as best we can. Gause will be ringing up to ask you to get a couple of pairs of Marshal's epaulettes with batons. It's still quiet here, our friends are very cautious.

8 Jan. 1943

Nothing new. Our opponents are taking their time over things, which means a more orderly existence for us. I went a long way inland yesterday and am going off on another reconnaissance to-day.

How are things with you? The field post, like supplies generally, is working wretchedly. Did Manfred ever receive my birthday letter? He doesn't mention it.

Meanwhile, the British moved farther up, obviously still intending to put the main weight of their attack on the south. British bomber activity was also increasing again, and they were attacking our supply installations day and night. Thirty tons of ammunition reached the front between the 1st and ·8th January, as against 50 tons used. During the same period we used 1,900 tons of petrol; 800 arrived.

On about the 10th January, the threat of an Anglo-American attack from Tunisia on the Gabes defile [*mid-way between Tripoli and Tunis*] became particularly acute. This operation would have divided the two armies. Marshal Cavallero accordingly asked me whether I could move a division across there. As this defile represented a lifeline for us, I suggested sending over the 21st Panzer Division and supplying it from Tunis. The division moved off to the west on the morning of the 13th.

13 Jan. 1943

DEAREST LU,

Now we're getting on the move again. You can imagine my anxieties. My thoughts rest with you, in these long and wakeful nights.

14 Jan. 1943

It's Bayerlein's birthday and he's just being serenaded. The Afrika Korps has a particularly high regard for him and has much to thank him for. There's no important change yet in the situation. There was a sand-storm yesterday and our movements went unobserved. Things in the east seem to be on the mend again, which is a great relief. But how they'll go here will depend in the long run entirely on supplies. And I need not tell you what they're like. The enemy air force is already very active.

We now learnt, through our wireless interception service, that the enemy would complete his preparations and be ready to attack on January 15. We had already established the presence of 400 to 500 British aircraft on the forward airfields—not many, it is true, compared with their numbers at El Alamein, but more than double those of the German-Italian air force, which also included no heavy bombers. The line-up of forces on the 15th was approximately as follows:

	British	Axis
TANKS	approximately 650[1]	36 German, 57 Italian
GUNS	,, 360	72 German, 98 Italian
ANTI-TANK GUNS	,, 550	111 German, 66 Italian
ARMOURED CARS	,, 200	17 German, 16 Italian

[1]The actual number of tanks that Montgomery brought up for this thrust was 450. The plan of attack was that the 51st Division would push along the coast road, with the 23rd Armoured Brigade on its left flank to develop local leverage, while the 7th Armoured Division and 2nd New Zealand Division carried out a wider manœuvre. Montgomery took personal command of the coastal thrust, so that Leese might be more free to conduct the outflanking operation—which was to drive towards Tripoli by way of Beni Ulid and Tarhuna.

In the event the British pushed their artillery forward on the night of the 14th. The first attacks followed at first light on the 15th, launched in the southern sector by the 7th Armoured Division and elements of the 2nd New Zealand Division. They first made a thrust on Fortino with about 140 tanks and 100 armoured cars, and then went straight on to attack the 15th Panzer Division. There they were brought to a halt. After bringing up artillery they continued their attack in the early afternoon and a violent tank battle ensued which went to our advantage. The British left 33 tanks lying on the battlefield. We lost two.

The British were now moving up over the whole of the rest of the front and it was obvious that they would continue their attack with all their strength, concentrating the main weight in the south. We had neither the petrol nor the ammunition to guarantee a defence in such a battle, and so orders went out to retire to the west. All troops, German and Italian, moved off during the night.

15 Jan. 1943

DEAREST LU,

Our movement has begun. How fast it will go will depend on the pressure. I'm not feeling too good, for obvious reasons. Berndt has been away again and is expected back to-morrow.

Physically I'm well so far. Of course the nervous strain is particularly severe just now and I have to keep a real grip on myself.

THE END IN TRIPOLITANIA

Next day, the 16th January, the British followed up closely and soon a strong British force with a total of 100 fighting vehicles launched an attack against the thirty of 15th Panzer Division. With nothing on its flanks, either north or south, the division was in a far from comfortable position. The British drove recklessly into their fire and lost another 20 tanks in heavy fighting. The 90th Light Division threw back the 51st [Highland] Division after it had already penetrated into the outpost positions of the rearguard line.

The petrol shortage now began to make itself felt again, for consumption had, of course, gone up considerably with the increased movement. Partly for this reason and partly because of the steadily increasing enemy strength we were not going to be able to keep up the fight in open country much longer and so had to avoid becoming too closely involved in the battle.

17 Jan. 1943

DEAREST LU,

The second day of the battle lies behind us. It was tough going on the southern flank, and it will be a miracle if we can hold out for long against this overwhelming onslaught. I've seen this coming, as you know, even though other people have until recently taken a much more favourable view of our situation. In the fighting ahead we will do our duty as our country expects of us.

On the 17th January rearguard fighting developed near Beni Ulid, in which the mass of 7th Armoured Division moved as if to outflank and cut off our units. Accordingly the 90th Light Division also now made a fighting withdrawal.

This front, with its wide-open southern flank, could not, of course, be held for long without running the risk of losing a considerable part of our force. I therefore gave orders for the retreat to the Tarhuna-Homs line to begin on the night of the 17th January. To make quite certain of the safety of the Italian infantry, I also gave orders for their transport back to the Tripoli defence line to begin immediately the motorised forces arrived in the Tarhuna-Homs line.

At midday on the 17th, I informed the Chief of Staff of the Italian Command in Libya that in face of the enormous superiority of the enemy there could be no thought of holding the Tarhuna-Homs line. We had to be prepared to see the British arrive in front of Tripoli as early as the 20th January.

While the Italians were being carried off to the west, the British followed up with strong forces and moved up to our line. The Italian High Command had informed me that the Tarhuna-Homs line was difficult to outflank. In other respects, too, the defensive possibilities were extremely good, for any British attack from the south or south-east had to be made over sandy and adverse country. In fact, there is no doubt that given a somewhat better stock of supplies, we could have kept the enemy at bay here for a very considerable time.

19 Jan. 1943

DEAREST LU,

The fighting continues with undiminished violence. We're now in fairly hilly country where we hope to make something of a stand. But there's no compensating for the inequality between the two forces. Berndt has arrived back, Kesselring has supplanted him in the Fuehrer's favour. His journey was certainly very useful and timely, but whether the expectations can be fulfilled is another matter. So much has already been overtaken by events and we still have the worst to come. Berndt brought me the warmest greetings from the Fuehrer, whose unbounded confidence I still enjoy. And indeed we are doing all that is humanly possible in this situation. But whether success will be granted us is of course more than doubtful.

The times have grown very grave (in the East also). There's going to be total mobilisation of labour for every single German without regard for place of residence, status, property or age. You should keep your eyes open in good time for something suitable. Manfred, too, will soon have to stand behind a work bench or an anti-aircraft gun. It is, as you know, a matter of life or death for the German people. I'm writing this to you because I want to tell you quite openly what is likely to happen. It's better to get used to the idea early, for then it's easier to adapt oneself. Of course things are not so rosy either for our enemies, especially the Russians. For a long time now they've been brutally forcing the last ounce of work out of every section of their people. It is only by this that their latest successes can be explained.

On the 19th January about 200 British tanks pushed on along the road to Tarhuna in an attempt to overrun my troops in their first rush. But they were halted, with very severe losses, by the concentrated fire of our artillery.

On the same morning I set up my H.Q. in a settler's farm on a hill north-west of Tarhuna, from where we could see dust-clouds stirred up by British vehicles moving along the Tarhuna-Garian road, south of Tarhuna. On arriving a few hours later at the 15th Panzer Division, I discovered that the British were on the point of launching a thrust on Garian with a whole armoured division. This was a particularly threatening move and I threw in the whole of our artillery to meet it. Immediate regrouping became necessary. The 164th Division, units of the Parachute Brigade and the Reconnaissance Group were deployed in a screen to the west to prevent a British attack on the Tarhuna-Castel Benito road. Soon the enemy brought his artillery up and poured shells into our positions near Tarhuna. The British commander was now conducting his operations far more energetically than he had done in the past.

Meanwhile, no fighting of any consequence took place in the northern sector, and we were able to complete the disengagement of the forces still in the Homs area according to plan.

In the evening the British intention became finally clear—to bind down our forces by heavy attacks at Homs and Tarhuna, while at the same time carrying out an outflanking movement on a major scale through Garian. Thousands upon thousands of British vehicles were concentrated in the south. During the day the Luftwaffe tried all they could to hold up the advance of the southern British column, but with little success; by evening the column had reached a point some 30 miles from Garian and had crossed the Tarhuna-Garian road. When this news came in I was forced to decide to give up Tarhuna immediately in order to release a large enough striking group with which to oppose the enemy advancing deep in our flank. It was also necessary to speed up the withdrawal of the Italians still remaining in the Homs area.

All moves were carried out as planned in the night of the 19th January, and by morning our dispositions were as follows:

(a) During the night the 90th Light Division had relieved the Italian Infantry at Homs and taken up positions as rearguard.

(b) The 164th Division was holding the defile west of Tarhuna with the Parachute Brigade deployed in depth behind it to prevent a British attack on the road.

(c) The 15th Panzer Division and Reconnaissance Group Luck were located in the area round Azizia to parry a thrust up from Garian to the north.

(d) The " Young Fascist " Division and Combat Group Centauro were positioned south of Sorman to meet any British attacks still farther west.

In the early hours of that morning gigantic explosions from the direction of Tripoli announced the demolition of the port installations. All the more important depots were destroyed, there now being no further hope of retaining our hold on the port.

20 Jan. 1943

Dearest Lu,

We got through yesterday very well, but the supply position is making our situation more difficult every day. The enemy is trying hard to shift the fighting to the west as quickly as possible. . . .

. . . Paulus is perhaps even worse off than I am. He has a more inhuman enemy. We can only hope that God does not desert us altogether. [*Paulus was commanding the forces at Stalingrad which had now been cut off and surrounded by the Russians.*]

In the early morning [*of the 20th*], a signal arrived from Marshal Cavallero, sent by him on instructions from the Duce, in which the latter stated that my decision to withdraw our forces from the Tarhuna-Homs line and position them to meet the expected major attack in the Azizia-Sorman area was contrary to his instructions to hold the Tarhuna-Homs line for at least three weeks. The situation was not serious enough to justify my action, which had been over-hasty. A stand simply must be made, as otherwise the Mareth line could not be properly built up. For the rest, Cavallero referred me expressly to the Duce's directives and demanded my compliance.

We gasped when we received this signal. A position which has been broken through or outflanked is valueless unless there are mobile forces available to throw back the enemy outflanking column. The best strategic plan is useless if it cannot be executed tactically.

I immediately wirelessed the Commando Supremo to this effect but had an opportunity the same afternoon of speaking to Marshal Cavallero in person, in the presence of Field Marshal Kesselring and Marshal Bastico. I gave my views on the signal we had received that morning and stated forcibly that the time limits I had been given had come from Mussolini and Cavallero; I had never accepted them. At the conclusion of the discussion, which became very stormy, I demanded a specific Commando Supremo decision as to whether we were to do battle with the British at Tarhuna-Homs and thereby deliver up the army to certain destruction, or whether we were to move off to Tunisia. " You can either hold on to Tripoli a few more days and lose the army, or lose Tripoli a few days earlier and save the army for Tunis. Make up your mind," I said in the end to Marshal Cavallero. During the meeting the bad news came in that British torpedo-boats had sunk ten out of fourteen petrol barges west of Tripoli.

Next day [*the 21st*], the enemy attacked sharply at all points of the front. Strong British columns worked their way through the wadis between Garian and Tarhuna, which the Italians had described as completely impassable, and threatened to cut off the 164th Division's rear-guard, west of Tarhuna. I sent a combat group under General Frantz to meet this move.

Meanwhile, other British forces made an attempt from the east to take the pass held by troops of the 164th Division west of Tarhuna, but without success. The enemy's strength in this sector was steadily increasing and, in view of the acute danger to our right flank, I was compelled to order the withdrawal of the non-motorised infantry from the Tripoli defence line and their transport back to the Zavia area. Marshal Cavallero, on behalf of the Duce, avoided giving a clear-cut decision on my question whether or not Tripoli should be defended to the last. He instructed me that the army must be preserved, but that as much time was to be gained as possible.

Incidentally, the events of that day fully confirmed the correctness of my judgment on the 19th January and justified the removal of the motorised forces into the Sorman-Azizia area. Had we stayed in the Tarhuna-Homs line, as the Duce was insisting from his seat in Rome, the army with all its infantry would have been surrounded and destroyed.

22 Jan. 1943

DEAREST LU,

I couldn't write yesterday. There was too much doing from morning till night. Severe rebuke from Rome because we're not holding out any longer against the enemy pressure. We do what we can. Yesterday's developments have completely justified my course of action. With the supply difficulties we're having, it's a question of whether we'll manage to carry on the struggle at all for long. We intend to fight and will fight as long as it is possible. I have my troubles with our Allies, that I need not tell you. That they should now become saucy, on top of everything else, was only to be expected. I don't think they'll be with us much longer. People and nations don't change.

The movement west continued until the 22nd, by which time the enemy had brought up 6,000 vehicles to Tarhuna and was expected to attack on the 23rd. Consequently, I now found myself compelled to order the evacuation of Tripoli, after all its installations had been destroyed.

The appointed moves were completed during the night, under heavy enemy pressure and non-stop fighter-bomber attacks. Our success in getting almost all our material and stores away from Tripoli was a considerable feat on the part of our Quartermaster, as only 7 per cent could be taken by sea, the remaining 93 per cent having to go by road. Food which we had to leave behind was handed over to the Prefect for distribution to the civil population.

23 Jan. 1943

Dearest Lu,

I hope to make a good job of the manœuvre in progress now. There is very lovely country round here, one would like to travel through it at ease in peace-time. Will that ever be?

Starting from midday on the 23rd January, the British launched strong forces against the Tripoli defence line, but were beaten off. Our 30,000 Italian infantrymen were now to be moved back immediately to assist in the construction of the Mareth line. To secure their withdrawal against a surprise attack, the remaining forces were again grouped in a screen along the road far to the west. In the afternoon I managed to take a look round the Roman ruins at Sabratha.

The Eighth Army entered Tripoli three months to the day after launching its attack at Alamein—having advanced 1,400 miles.

After the fall of Tripoli, the British allowed themselves a short pause to regroup and bring up supplies. This suited us very well for it gave us time at least to carry away the supplies we had stored in the Zuara area.

25 Jan. 1943

Dearest Lu,

Yesterday went as planned. I simply can't tell you how hard it is for me to undergo this retreat and all that goes with it. Day and night I'm tormented by the thought that things might go really wrong here in Africa. I'm so depressed that I can hardly do my work. Perhaps someone else would see a little more light in the situation and be able to make something of it. K. [*Kesselring*], for example, is full of optimism. Maybe he sees in me the reason why the army has not made a longer stand. He can have no idea of the true value of my troops, especially the Italians, or of the balance of strength which is weighted even more heavily against us by the excellent motorisation of the enemy, his establishment of tanks and armoured cars and his favourable supply situation. I'm waiting anxiously to see what's going to happen. I shall hold on here as long as I can. K. is now my superior.

Note by General Bayerlein.—At that time, Rommel's recall was being pressed by the Italians, C.-in-C. South and the Fuehrer's H.Q., on the grounds that he had given up the Tarhuna-Homs position against the Fuehrer's and Duce's orders. Rommel was deeply distressed at first by these attempts.

On the 26th January, we shifted Army H.Q. into the district west of Ben Gardane [*across the Tunisian frontier*]. On the way we saw the railway which was under construction between Tunis and the Libyan frontier. If only we could have held the front at Sirte for three months, this railway would probably have been completed between Tunis and Sirte. It was greatly to our disadvantage that the Italians had not built a line along the North African coast before the war, as a supply route several hundred miles long is really only tolerable if the bulk of the goods can be carried either by rail or sea. Road transport is relatively uneconomic due to the large amount of petrol it consumes.

At midday on the 26th I received a signal from the Commando Supremo informing me that on account of my bad state of health, I was to be released from my command when we reached the Mareth line, the actual date being left to me. An Italian Army Command was to be formed under General Messe, who had led the Italian Expeditionary Corps in Russia. After my experience during the retreat, I had little desire to go on any longer playing the scapegoat for a pack of incompetents and requested the Commando Supremo to send General Messe to Africa as soon as possible, so that he could be initiated into his new command.

28 Jan. 1943

DEAREST LU,

In a few days I shall be giving up command of the army to an Italian, for the sole reason that " my present state of health does not permit me to carry on." Of course it's really for quite other reasons,[1] principally that of prestige. I have done all I can to maintain the theatre of war, in spite of the indescribable difficulties in all fields. I am deeply sorry for my men. They were very dear to me.

[1] Passage doubtful. It is partially illegible in original hand-written text.

Physically, I am not too well. Severe headaches and overstrained nerves, on top of the circulation trouble, allow me no rest. Professor Horster is giving me sleeping draughts and helping as far as he can. Perhaps I'll have a few weeks to recover, though with the situation as it is in the East what one would like is to be in the front line.

At about 15.00 hours [*on the 26th*] I went off to inspect the Mareth front and form a judgment as to its value. The front lay [*80 miles inside the frontier of Tunisia*] between the sea and the Matmata Hills and consisted of a line of antiquated French block-houses which in no way measured up to the standards required by modern warfare. Added to that they had been completely disarmed after the Armistice with France. They could, therefore, serve little purpose in action other than as cover against artillery fire, and the defence proper would have to be fought from field positions lying between the French block-houses. The southern part of the line could be regarded as completely proof against tanks. Its centre was given some protection against tanks by a steep wadi, but this obstacle could be overcome by well-trained tank crews. Its northern end was covered to the front by a salt marsh, but most of this was negotiable by vehicles. The siting of the line was also bad, for it lay immediately behind some high ground, which denied any long-range artillery observation to the defence, and at the same time provided the attacking force with excellent opportunities for fire control. So these hills, too, had to be held by our troops, which meant a serious division of our strength.

Strategically, the choice of this line by the Commando Supremo held a big snag, as it was capable of being outflanked—though it is true, with some difficulty. In 1938, the French Generals Catroux and Gautsch had made a trial outflanking march with a Sahara Company loaded on lorries in order to establish whether or not such an operation was possible, and had, in fact, decided that it was not. But the British under Montgomery were far better motorised than the French desert troops had been. If they undertook such an operation, then the occupation of the Mareth line and all the construction that had been done on it would avail us nothing. I therefore issued a warning in good time against the possibility of such an enemy move.

In view of this weakness, I demanded occupation of the Akarit line between the Shott el Jerid and the sea. This line [*40 miles behind the Mareth line*] could not be outflanked and would have therefore enabled us to make effective use of the non-motorised infantry. I emphasised that our motorised forces were not strong enough to hold fronts at El Hamma on one side and Gafsa on the other, and at the same time provide support for the Mareth line. But our superiors could not see it. In the event, of course, the British did actually carry through an extremely well-planned outflanking movement, which rendered the Mareth line completely worthless. Although Bayerlein, in fact, succeeded in leading his mobile forces back to Akarit in a reasonably intact condition in spite of the break-through threatening from three sides, it would have been far better if we had concentrated our fortifications at Gabes in the first place.

Rommel does not mean at the town of Gabes, but at the defile 15 miles westward—across which ran the Wadi Akarit. He sometimes speaks of this as the Gabes line and sometimes as the Akarit line.

On the 31st January, Marshal Bastico laid down his command and returned to Italy. There had more than once been friction between us, but it had almost always been as a result of some directive or other from the Commando Supremo. In general, we had worked well together and he had often supported me. It was to a great extent to his credit that in spite of the peculiar ideas of our higher authorities, the army did manage to get back to Mareth reasonably unscathed and did not fall victim on the way to some order or other to fight to the end.

But the dismissal of Marshal Cavallero, which occurred at about the same time, came as welcome news. It would have been better if that man had been replaced long before by somebody a little more competent.

By about the 1st February, the British had already begun to get a lively traffic passing through the port of Tripoli, using several light tankers. Our air reconnaissance also reported the presence of a number of larger ships. Of course the Luftwaffe was in no position to hinder the enemy at all in this work. The British approach march began in the east and we could soon expect the Eighth Army to be moving against us in all its old strength.

At about this time Messe arrived in Africa. Like most people who came from Russia, he looked on things with considerable optimism. I did not intend to hand over the army until I could feel that its position was reasonably firm for some time ahead.

2 Feb. 1943

DEAREST LU,
    Nothing much new. The calm before further operations. It seems —from what has been said—that the change in command was planned long ago. The Italians have always laid claims to it, of course.

During January, a number of our A.A. gunners succeeded in surprising a British column of the Long-Range Desert Group in Tunisia and captured the commander of 1st S.A.S. Regiment, Lieut.-Col. David Stirling. Insufficiently guarded, he managed to escape and made his way to some Arabs, to whom he offered a reward if they would get him back to the British lines. But his bid must have been too small, for the Arabs, with their usual eye to business, offered him to us for 11 pounds of tea— — a bargain which we soon clinched. Thus the British lost the very able and adaptable commander of the desert group which had caused us more damage than any other British unit of equal strength.

On the 15th February 1943. the rearguard of the 15th Panzer Division finally withdrew into the forefield of the Mareth line and the great retreat from Alamein to Tunisia was over. The fighting spirit of the troops was unbroken, which was little short of a miracle after such a series of reverses and was ultimately due to the fact that they did not feel themselves to have been defeated by anything but sheer weight of material.

7 Feb. 1943

DEAREST LU,

Dr. Horster came to see me yesterday and advised me to begin my treatment as soon as possible. My whole being cries out against leaving the battlefield so long as I can stand on my feet.

8 Feb. 1943

I've decided only to give up command of the army on orders, regardless of the state of my health. With the situation as it is, I intend to stick it out to the limit, even against the doctor's advice. You will understand my attitude. The successor that Rome has sent for me will have to wait his turn.

12 Feb. 1943

It's two years to-day since I arrived on African soil. Two years of heavy and stubborn fighting, most of the time with a far superior enemy. On this day, I think of the gallant troops under my command, who have loyally done their duty by their country and have had faith in my leadership. I have endeavoured to do my duty, both in my own sphere and for the cause as a whole. . . . We must do our utmost to beat off the mortal dangers which beset us. Unfortunately it's all a matter of supplies. I hope that my decision to remain with my troops to the end will be confirmed. You will understand my attitude. As a soldier one cannot do otherwise.

FROM ALAMEIN TO MARETH—RETROSPECT

In mechanised warfare, retreat offers a commander, even with numerically inferior forces, considerable tactical opportunities, provided always that certain conditions are fulfilled. These conditions are:

(*a*) That his force must remain intact and retain its fighting power.
(*b*) That each fresh assembly area during the retreat must be provided with adequate stocks of petrol, ammunition, rations and replacement equipment.

The farther the enemy advances and the longer his supply route becomes, the more troops he must leave behind, if he is to be able to maintain himself. During an advance, the supply route is lengthened, during a retreat it is shortened. The retreating army always has its strength concentrated. Hence the moment must eventually come when the retreating force is locally superior to its enemy. If at that moment it has access to an adequate supply of petrol and ammunition, it has a wonderful opportunity. It can turn and strike at the advancing enemy force, and destroy it—assuming that the enemy is foolish enough to stand and give battle. Such an operation must be executed at great speed to ensure that the enemy is given no chance to bring up reinforcements.

With this in mind it had been our intention to break off the Alamein battle before it had reached its climax. We had suffered throughout the battle from considerable command limitations, caused by the presence of the strong German and Italian non-motorised formations. And these limitations, we knew, would become far worse during the retreat, when the motorised forces would be repeatedly compelled to stand up to the British long enough to permit the Italian withdrawal to be completed.

But then events took charge. On orders from the Fuehrer and Duce, we were compelled to go on doing battle with the British on the 3rd and 4th November. And these two days decided our future fate, for they cost us very nearly 200 tanks [*including the Italians*]—almost all our remaining armour—and a large part of the Italian formations. They robbed us of all chance of engaging in mobile warfare during the retreat, for the army was now so shattered that there was nothing for it but continued withdrawal. The most we could hope to do was to force the enemy into repeated approach marches and deployments and thus gain as much time from him as we could. This we succeeded in doing. Nowhere— either at Mersa el Brega or Nofilia, at Buerat or Tripoli—was Montgomery able to destroy us. But a counter-attack by our motorised forces was unthinkable.

This was particularly deplorable, as the enemy presented us repeatedly with excellent tactical opportunities for such a move. Montgomery had an absolute mania for always bringing up adequate reserves behind his back and risking as little as possible. The speed of reaction of the British command was comparatively low. In the earlier stages of the retreat their outflanking column was too weak and we could have attacked and destroyed it on several occasions if only we had had the petrol. Montgomery should have put his main weight behind his outflanking drives, as these had the greatest chance of bringing us to battle. At Buerat and Tripoli, on the other hand, the British commander showed real stature and had obviously overcome his urge for exaggerated caution. He went out for a decision with energy and vigour and it needed a great effort from us to save the situation.

I can claim the credit for having correctly assessed the supply possibilities for my army, and for having arrived, on the basis of that assessment, at the correct strategic conclusions. All things considered, we had managed to make the best of the situation. Tactically, the retreat had not run its course according to the British plans, which had intended the destruction of my army, but according to mine. The army had been able to cope with all its difficulties, even with the German and Italian higher commands, who, from their distant European vantage-points had again and again sought a panacea in resistance to the last round. It would have been resistance to the last drop of water. Gratitude and admiration were due to the troops, who, despite the constant retreating, the bad rations, and the tremendous strain, had not failed even in the most appalling situations and had showed a fighting value no less than on the day they had captured Tobruk.

The fact that our higher authorities had refused to think from the outset in terms of a final unavoidable evacuation of Tripolitania had cost us much time and material. Thus the entire work of fortifying the Buerat line had in the end been useless; likewise the fortifications at Tarhuna-Homs. If only the Italian infantry had gone straight back to the Gabes line and begun immediately with its construction, if only all those useless mines we had laid in Libya had been put down at Gabes, all this work and material could ultimately have been of very great value.

CHAPTER XIX

BETWEEN TWO FIRES

WITH THE move into Mareth we were once again able to work on different strategic principles. By exploiting our " interior lines," we were now in a position to concentrate the mass of our motorised forces for an attack on the British and Americans in Western Tunisia, and possibly to force them to withdraw. We had no need to expect any effective diversionary attack by Montgomery during this operation, for any such attack, launched without powerful artillery and bomber support, was certain to come to a halt in the Mareth line, with a heavy cost in casualties to the British. We first intended to eliminate the threat of the two armies being divided by an Anglo-American thrust from Gafsa to the sea, by smashing the enemy assembly areas. This done, our striking force was to double back to Mareth to attack Montgomery. We proposed to give up the Medenine [*20 miles east of Mareth*] and Ben Gardane areas to the British shortly before this attack, in order to prevent them opposing us in prepared defences.

As a prelude to these operations, the 21st Panzer Division, which was under Fifth Army Command and had meanwhile been brought up to strength again, attacked the Faid Pass [*80 miles north of the Gabes defile*] on the 1st February, with the object of gaining it as a starting point for a thrust on Sidi Bouzid and Sbeitla [*15 miles west and 35 miles north-west, respectively, of the Faid Pass*]. The pass was stormed in an outflanking attack and 1,000 prisoners were taken.

The greatest operational danger for the Tunisian bridgehead was an American attack from Gafsa [*70 miles north-west of the Gabes defile*] through to Gabes, which would have divided the two Axis armies. Consequently, our first aim had to be to break up the American assembly areas in south-west Tunisia. Accordingly, the 21st Panzer with elements of the 10th Panzer Division was ordered to attack the Americans at Sidi Bouzid and Sbeitla, with the object of breaking up and as far as possible destroying their concentrations. At the same time, a combat group formed by my army was to dispose of the American garrison in Gafsa. No further operational objectives were fixed for the moment.[1]

[1]The operations are comprehensively called the Battle of Kasserine.

On the 14th February, the 21st Panzer Division moved forward from its bridgehead at the Faid Pass in an enveloping attack against 2nd U.S. Armoured Division,[1] which was stationed in the Sidi Bouzid area. With the enemy formations pinned down frontally, one armoured group advanced round the northern sector deep into the American flank, while another went forward to Sidi Bouzid and attacked them in the rear, thus forcing the enemy into an extremely difficult tactical situation. A violent tank battle developed in which the inexperienced Americans were steadily battered down by my tankmen—veterans of hundreds of desert battles—and soon large numbers of Grants, Lees and Shermans were blazing on the battlefield. The bulk of the American force was destroyed and the remainder fled to the west.

At this success, I urged the Fifth Army, which was in charge of the operation, to push straight on during the night, keep the enemy on the run and take Sbeitla. Tactical successes must be ruthlessly exploited. A routed enemy who, on the day of his flight, can be rounded up without much effort, may reappear on the morrow restored to his full fighting power.

However, the 21st Panzer Division did not follow up the retreating Americans until the night of the 16th. On the morning of the 17th February, the division was in position in front of Sbeitla. But the delay had enabled the Americans to organise some sort of a defence and they now fought back skilfully and bitterly. If Ziegler,[2] who was commanding the 21st Panzer Division's operation, had only followed up his success at Sidi Bouzid immediately on his own initiative, he would not have had to fight so hard for Sbeitla. However, enemy resistance was overcome by evening. In those few days the 2nd U.S. Armoured Division had lost 150 tanks[3] and 1,600 men captured. The 21st Panzer Division's losses had been very small.

The Americans had as yet no practical battle experience, and it was now up to us to instil in them from the outset an inferiority complex of no mean order.

Following on the 21st Panzer Division's success at Sbeitla, the Americans had withdrawn their garrison at Gafsa on the night of the 14th, before my combat group had been able to launch its attack. Elements of the Afrika Korps and the Centauro were thus able to occupy Gafsa on the afternoon of the 15th February without a fight.

Driving along the road to Gafsa on the morning of the 16th, we

---

[1] It was the 1st U.S. Armoured Division. The German stroke came as a surprise because the Allied Command had been expecting that the attack was coming towards Fondouk, forty miles farther north. General Bradley remarks in his war memoirs: " This belief came to be a near-fatal assumption."

[2] Lieut.-General, deputy commander of the Fifth Panzer Army.

[3] The same figure was given to war correspondents at Eisenhower's headquarters. Alexander, in his dispatch, states that the American losses included 86 medium tanks, but does not mention the number of light tanks lost.

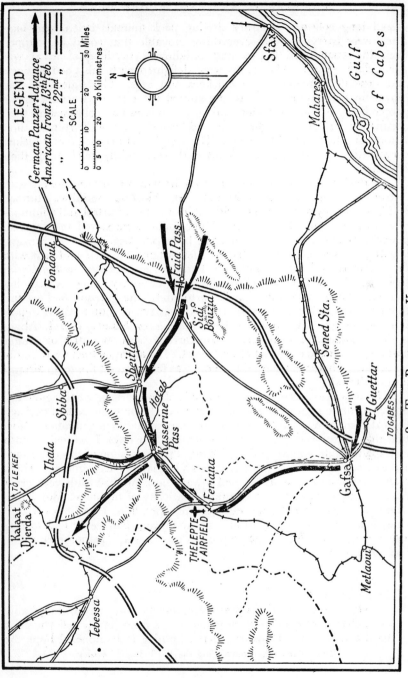

LEGEND

German Panzer-Advance
American Front, 13th Feb.
        "   22nd   "

SCALE

18. THE BATTLE OF KASSERINE

passed long columns of Arabs driving pack animals laden with loot. They were carrying away everything movable that could be stripped from the abandoned houses and buildings. Anything of wood was particularly prized. The Arabs were delighted with this good business and presented my men with chickens and eggs. The Americans had blown up their ammunition in the citadel without any warning to the people living in the neighbourhood and 30 houses had collapsed on their occupants. The bodies of 30 Arabs had been dug out of the ruins of their houses, and 80 were still missing. The people were consequently feeling very bitter towards the Americans and were noisily celebrating their liberation.

Meanwhile, my *Kampfstaffel* was on its way to the south-west with instructions to get through to Metlauoi and blow up the railway tunnel. In Metlauoi they captured a considerable quantity of petrol and a number of railway trucks. 200,000 tons of phosphate were stored in the area, material which could no doubt have been put to good use in Europe, if only we could have got it there. Liebenstein,[1] whom I had sent with the Afrika Korps' combat group to Feriana [*40 miles north-west of Gafsa*] took that important centre on the 17th February, after overcoming stubborn American resistance. Unfortunately, the garrison had set fire to their stores. We also heard from reconnaissance that Allied depots were already burning even in Tebessa [*80 miles north-west of Gafsa*]. About a dozen American armoured troop-carriers with mounted or trailer 75-mm. guns were captured or destroyed. The advance then went boldly on towards Thelepte, where the enemy was forced to set fire to 30 aircraft on the airfield.

The Americans seemed to be pulling back to Tebessa. Their command appeared to be getting jittery and they were showing the lack of decision typical of men commanding for the first time in a difficult situation. Now that the operation had gone successfully for four days, I wanted to push forward with all our strength to Tebessa, take possession of this important airbase, supply and transport centre, and strike on deep into the Allied rear. The situation in Africa had always been implicit with very great risks for me, because of the constant inferiority of my force. But I had never gambled; even in the most daring operation, I had always kept enough in hand to deal with any situation, and had never had to fear losing everything. But in the position as it was now, a rather greater risk had to be taken.

18 Feb. 1943

DEAREST LU,

My health is bearing up at the moment. But there will probably be a change of command very shortly. I need hardly tell you how hard this hits me. However, there's nothing to be done. I hope the

[1]Major-General, commanding the 164th Light Division.

treatment I will be having will put me back on form and restore my old vigour, so that I can get going on full power again.

No doubt the operation we were planning would have been fraught with great dangers for us if the Anglo-American command had made its correct operational move and launched the mass of its force against our long flank, with the object of taking our supply bases and leaving our striking force high and dry. But commanders whose battles have so far all been fought in theory tend as a rule to react directly rather than indirectly to the enemy's moves.[1] Beginners generally lack the nerve to take decisions based on military expediency alone, without regard for what is weighing most heavily on their minds.

I was convinced that a thrust beyond Tebessa by the combined armoured and motorised forces of the two armies would force the British and Americans to pull back the bulk of their forces to Algeria, thus greatly delaying their offensive preparations. The essential conditions for the stroke to succeed were that it should be made at once and that the striking force should be strong enough to overcome any reviving enemy resistance rapidly and break through to the open road. The thrust northwards had to be made far enough behind the enemy front to ensure that they would not be able to rush their reserves to the passes and hold up our advance. I was satisfied that by holding a number of passes and strategic points on the roads we would be able to contain the attacks we could expect on our flank. But whether or not the enemy main body would lose the race with my striking force was nevertheless open to question.

Colonel-General von Arnim was not prepared to recognise the possibilities of the proposed operation, probably because he wanted to keep the 10th Panzer Division in his sector for a small private show of his own. Consequently, he pronounced firmly against the plan, although he was in no position to have any real grasp of the situation, for he had had little or no battle experience with our western enemies and hence had no means of knowing anything of the weaknesses of their command.

I accordingly decided to transmit my proposals at once to the Commando Supremo and Commander-in-Chief South. Bayerlein managed to convince General Seidemann (Commander of the Tunisian Air Force) of the possibilities which the operation offered. I put my faith in the habitual over-optimism of Kesselring [*C.-in-C. South*] and the Italians, and expected them to give their unqualified agreement now that it was a question of going forward again. For one thing, the Duce badly needed a victory to bolster up his internal political position.

In the evening Kesselring informed me that he agreed to my plan and would report accordingly to the Commando Supremo. So we sat

[1]This observation is another example of Rommel's shrewd grasp of the psychological basis of the " strategy of indirect approach".

down in a fever of impatience to await the decision. Nothing had happened by midnight and it was obvious that the Italians were in no hurry. We therefore sent a further message pointing out that the decision must be reached quickly as otherwise too much time would be lost and the success of the undertaking would be jeopardised.

At last, at about 01.30 hours on the 19th of February, a signal arrived giving the Commando Supremo's authority for the operation, but with the all-important modification that the thrust was not to be made to Tebessa but via Thala to le Kef.[1] This was an appalling and unbelievable piece of shortsightedness, which did, in fact, ultimately cause the whole plan to go awry. A thrust along that line was far too close to the front and was bound to bring us up against the strong enemy reserves.

At other times our higher authorities were so wildly over-optimistic that they hardly knew what to demand of us next; now, however, when a little boldness really was required, they lacked the guts to give a whole-hearted decision. But there was no time for argument, otherwise no effective operation, capable of breaking up the American assembly areas, would materialise at all.

Accordingly the Afrika Korps' combat group was immediately put on the road for the Kasserine Pass, north-west of Kasserine [*20 miles west of Sbeitla, and the same distance east of Feriana*]. The 21st Panzer Division received orders to thrust up a neighbouring valley to Sbiba [*25 miles north of Sbeitla*]. Units of the 10th Panzer Division were brought up in its wake to Sbeitla, from where they could either be thrown in to join the 21st Panzer Division at Sbiba or to help the Afrika Korps' group at Kasserine, according to how the situation developed.

Meanwhile, the Allies had put all the forces they could raise in Northern Tunisia on the march for the threatened front in the south-west. The forces available at that moment for the protection of their southern flank were comparatively weak.

While the Afrika Korps' group was deploying in the area round Kasserine, the 3rd Reconnaissance Battalion was thrown forward in an attempt to rush the pass, but the enemy fought back fiercely and the attempt failed. [*The 34th U.S. Division was holding this sector.*]

---

[1]This meant that the thrust had to be made northwards against the Allies' immediate rear instead of north-westwards towards their communications as Rommel had proposed and planned.

Rommel's revelation of the way he was overruled by the Italian Supreme Command is the more interesting because Mr. Churchill, in Volume IV of his war memoirs, assumes that the northward direction was Rommel's choice. General Alexander, who took command in the crisis, conveys in his dispatch that he expected Rommel to take the northward route, where the going was easier, and therefore " ordered General Anderson to concentrate his armour for the defence of Thala." (From his view of Rommel, Alexander also thought it likely that Rommel would seek " a great tactical victory "— the Tebessa move would have been strategical rather than tactical.)

Thus the Allied forces would have been caught off balance if Rommel had gone the way he wished.

An attack by Panzer Grenadier Regiment " Menton," after achieving some initial success, also collapsed. The trouble was that they had gone the wrong way about it. After fighting for so long in the desert, the officers had suddenly found themselves confronted with a terrain not unlike the European Alps. The hills on either side of the pass ran up to some 5,000 feet and were held by American troops accompanied by artillery observers. Menton had unfortunately confined his attack to the valley, probably having underestimated the Americans. He should have combined hill and valley tactics and should have taken possession of the hills on either side of the pass in order to eliminate the enemy artillery observers and get through to the enemy's rear.

At about 13.00 hours on the 19th February, I drove to the headquarters of the Afrika Korps group to obtain an exact picture of the situation. At intervals along the road we passed American vehicles, their drivers dead at the wheel—obviously victims of our air attacks. Numerous small groups of scattered Americans were still being brought in. I dispatched General Buelowius with a combat group to make an outflanking attack on the Kasserine Pass. Then I went on to the 21st Panzer Division, which unfortunately had also been taking its time, but was now getting ahead rather better. I was as yet undecided to whom to send the 10th Panzer Division.

However, the 21st Panzer Division also soon came to a halt in front of Sbiba. After being badly held up by the state of the roads, which were waterlogged after the continuous heavy rains, they ran up against a dense minefield, which was strongly defended by the enemy. [Here, the 1st Guards Brigade.]

The first mine barriers were overcome after a fierce struggle, but there the division finally came to a stop. They had made the same mistake of attacking frontally in the valley instead of striking off across the hills.

The bad weather, despite the difficulties it gave us, was actually very much to our advantage, as it prevented the enemy from bringing the full weight of his air force to bear, the effect of which, in the deep, ravine-like valleys, would have been very severe.

What I had feared had now happened at both our points of attack. The enemy had had a chance of installing his reserves in hill positions which were difficult to assault, and was gaining time to bring up further reinforcements. In an offensive against Tebessa, we would probably have got well under way before meeting serious resistance, whereas here we had collided very early with an enemy who had not been disorganised by a headlong race to the front and had had time to make his preparations in peace.

In the belief that the Allies were weaker at Kasserine than at Sbiba, I decided to focus the weight of our attack in the Kasserine sector and bring up the 10th Panzer Division.

At 07.00 hours on the 20th of February, I drove to Afrika Korps H.Q.

in Kasserine, where I met General von Broich, commander of the 10th Panzer Division. Unfortunately he had brought only half his force, von Arnim having held back part of it in the north for his own purposes. The division's motor-cycle battalion was already on the move and I passed it on the way.

All Menton's attacks had been brought to a halt by extremely well-placed American artillery and mortar fire from the hills. Now 10th Panzer Division's motor-cycle battalion was to join in the battle. Unfortunately, we heard and saw nothing of it for almost the whole of the morning. When I inquired from von Broich what all the delay was, he told me that he had detailed a different unit for the assault, as he wanted to reserve the motor-cycle battalion for the pursuit. The assault unit was still on its way up to the front. Once again valuable time was being squandered. I was extremely angry and ordered the commanders to take themselves closer to the front where they could get a proper view of the situation. I had the motor-cyclists brought forward immediately, for the Americans were growing stronger every hour and our position consequently more difficult.

From midday onwards the attack was resumed in fierce hand-to-hand fighting. *Nebelwerfer* were brought into action for the first time in Africa and proved very effective.

Finally, at about 17.00 hours, the pass was at last in our hands. The Americans had fought extremely well and Menton's losses had been considerable. During the evening we discovered an enemy armoured formation on the other side of the pass. It was partially formed up in a side valley and was apparently intended to come to the aid of the Kasserine defenders. I immediately passed an armoured group forward through the pass. This advance, made over the quickly rebuilt bridge across the Hatab river, took the enemy completely by surprise; they were pressed back against the mountains and soon destroyed by the veteran tankmen of the 8th Panzer Regiment. The action took place at point-blank range, and the enemy soon abandoned his tanks and vehicles and tried to escape on foot over the hills. We captured some 20 tanks and 30 armoured troop-carriers, most of which were trailing a 75-mm. anti-tank gun. The Americans were fantastically well equipped and we had a lot to learn from them organisationally. One particularly striking feature was the standardisation of their vehicles and spare parts. British experience had been put to good use in the American equipment.

Expecting the enemy to counter-attack next day, I decided to hold the Afrika Korps' column and the 10th Panzer Division (or the part of it we had received) round Kasserine for the time being, to enable us to take effective measures against whatever move the enemy might make.

During the night of the 20th, however, our columns moved on from Kasserine, northwards along the Kasserine-Thala road and westwards towards Tebessa. The enemy had withdrawn.

Next morning, the 21st February, I drove up to the Kasserine Pass to inspect the destroyed American tanks. A long column of captured armoured troop-carriers was moving back through the pass, some of them still filled with American prisoners. Three completely shattered enemy troop-carriers lay on the road, where they had driven on to their own mines. Buelowius told me that the *élan* of the Bersaglieri had served us very well during the attack. Their commander had unfortunately been killed.

The enemy's plan now appeared to be to fight delaying actions in new positions and to stay on the defensive. On this assumption, I decided to press on immediately into his rear. At about midday the 10th Panzer Division moved off towards Kalaet Jerda, where they were to cut the road junction and railway and render them unusable. The Afrika Korps' group was to throw back the enemy at El Hamra and take the summit of the pass on the road to Tebessa. The 21st Panzer Division was to hold its line. By deploying troops at several danger spots I hoped to split the enemy forces far more than our own. Meanwhile, the Fifth Army was to try to pin down the enemy by frontal attacks in their sector and prevent them from throwing further reinforcements into the southern front.

By 13.00 hours, the 10th Panzer Division was advancing in great strides towards Thala [*35 miles north of Kasserine*]. En route it overran a British anti-tank company—the advanced troops of an approaching formation. I had gone forward to the 10th Panzer Division with Bayerlein and Horster at about midday. The division was not getting forward fast enough, and I had to be continually at them to keep the speed up; they did not seem to realise that they were in a race with the Allied reserves. To form my own judgment of the situation I drove forward to the leading scouts to see what was happening. I found them lying in a cactus grove close beside an Arab village. Heavy artillery fire was falling in the village and confusion was complete, with every living creature, bird and beast, scattering in all directions. Bayerlein collected up eggs which some hens had dropped. Then we, too, had to get into cover, and Bayerlein crawled amongst the cacti carrying his precious booty. We came to no harm— neither, fortunately, did the eggs.

We now moved off to a hill about 500 yards away, from where we watched the course of our attack. Seventeen destroyed tanks lay in front of us—they were Mark VIs, so it was small wonder that they had come down so quickly from the north. We also saw to our amazement that they were now fitted with a 75-mm. gun.[1] Our artillery soon joined

[1]Rommel was mistaken. The British Mark VI (Crusader), a very speedy tank, had only been armed with a 2-pounder (40 mm.) gun when it appeared in 1941, while the later model in 1942 had a 6-pounder (57 mm.). It was never rearmed with a 75-mm. gun. But close-support Crusaders of the original model mounted a 3-inch howitzer (76 mm. approx.). These were probably what Rommel saw.

battle with the enemy guns and shortly afterwards we ourselves came under the fire of the tank attack and had to make another getaway. On the way we saw the bodies of several British soldiers lying beside some destroyed anti-tank guns. Arabs had plundered the bodies and robbed them of their clothing. There was nothing to be seen of these ghouls, which was fortunate for them, for they would otherwise have had something to remember us by. Shortly afterwards I drove forward again to the infantry east of the road and called on them to speed up their advance. I gave General von Broich orders to have the Panzer Grenadiers follow up the tanks lorry-borne. It would be time enough for them to dismount when they came up against enemy positions.

At about 19.00 hours, the 10th Panzer Division succeeded in penetrating into Thala, which was already held by the enemy. During our entry a British battalion allowed itself to be overrun by the tank spearheads before opening fire. Our tanks wheeled about, attacked the enemy in the rear and drove them out of their positions, 700 prisoners falling into our hands. However, we were soon forced to leave Thala again, after the enemy had brought up more units of the 6th British Armoured Division and other Allied formations.

Before the start of the operation, we had asked von Arnim to send us the 19 Tiger tanks[1] which were with the Fifth Panzer Army. If we had had these tanks at Thala, we might have been able to push on farther. But von Arnim had refused our request, saying that all the tanks were under repair, a statement which we later discovered to have been untrue. He had wanted to hold on to the detachment of Tigers for his own offensive.

Driving back from the 10th Panzer Division in the late afternoon of 21st February, I could see a heavy artillery duel going on in the direction of the Afrika Korps' attack. It looked as though their column had made little progress and this impression was confirmed by the reports which awaited me at H.Q. After some initial success, the division's advance had steadily slowed down in the face of continually stiffening resistance. Unfortunately it, too, had kept to the valley bottom and had not simultaneously advanced over the hills on either side in order to reduce the positions in the pass by an attack round their flank. This was the third time this mistake had been made. Here again the right course would have been to have put the main weight of the attack on the hills, bearing in mind, however, that the use of tanks would have been impossible in view of the wooded terrain. The American defence had been very skilfully executed. After allowing the attacking column to move peacefully on up the valley, they had suddenly poured fire on it from three sides, quickly bringing the column to a halt. Buelowius's

---

[1]These new heavy tanks (56 tons) mounted an 88-mm. gun, and had thus a much stronger punch than any yet introduced on either side, while they also had thicker armour (102 mm. in front).

men had been astounded at the flexibility and accuracy of the American artillery, which had put a great number of our tanks out of action. When they were later forced to withdraw, the American infantry followed up closely and turned the withdrawal into a costly retreat.

Next morning, the 22nd February, I drove up to Thala again, where I was forced to the conclusion that the enemy had grown too strong for our attack to be maintained.

Later, at about 13.00 hours, I met Field Marshal Kesselring, who arrived at my H.Q. with Westphal and Seidemann. We agreed that a continuation of the attack towards Le Kef held no prospect of success and decided to break off the offensive by stages.

Accordingly, the 10th Panzer Division and the Afrika Korps' group were drawn back to Kasserine during the night, where they took up positions north-west of the pass. The 21st Panzer Division [*the easterly prong*] was to remain at Sbiba for the moment, but was to be prepared to receive orders to mine the road and withdraw.

Kesselring asked me whether I would like to take over command of the Army Group. Apparently, as a result of the Kasserine offensive, I had ceased to be *persona non grata*, and had become acceptable again, in spite of my defeatism. After what I had been through in the last few months, however, and knowing, in any case, that the Fuehrer had already earmarked Colonel-General von Arnim for command of the Army Group, I declined the offer. Anyhow, I had no great wish to hold a command under the Luftwaffe and Commando Supremo and to have to go on suffering their interference in tactical questions. Field Marshal Kesselring, his undoubted merits aside, had no conception of the tactical and operational conditions in the African theatre. He saw everything through rose-coloured glasses and had now been further strengthened in his self-delusion by our successes over the Americans. He thought that many more such opportunities would occur and that the fighting value of the Americans was low. Although it was true that the American troops could not yet be compared with the veteran troops of the Eighth Army, yet they made up for their lack of experience by their far better and more plentiful equipment and their tactically more flexible command. In fact, their armament in anti-tank weapons and armoured vehicles was so enormous that we could look forward with but small hope of success to the coming mobile battles. The tactical conduct of the enemy's defence had been first class. They had recovered very quickly after the first shock and had soon succeeded in damming up our advance by grouping their reserves to defend the passes and other suitable points. Not all their troops, however, had come up so quickly and I firmly believe that if we had gone for Tebessa we would have been able to thrust far beyond it to the north before meeting any serious resistance.

The last of our formations was withdrawn behind the Kasserine Pass line on the 23rd February. The bad weather now ended and from midday onward we were subjected to hammer-blow air attacks by the U.S. Air Force in the Feriana-Kasserine area, of a weight and concentration hardly surpassed by those we had suffered at Alamein. Aircraft of all kinds maintained a ceaseless attack by cannon fire and bombs against my troops retreating through the valley bottoms, and observation planes directed the fire of numerous batteries on all worthwhile targets throughout the zone. Within fifteen minutes 104 enemy aircraft were seen over Kasserine alone. While I was on my way to forward H.Q. at about 16.00 hours, 18 bombers laid a bomb carpet 100 yards ahead of our column. The attacks lasted until nightfall and gave an impressive picture of the strength and striking power of the Allied air force.

And so ended the battle of Sbeitla-Kasserine. It had begun with a great victory for the German armour over the " green " Americans, an advantage which should have been exploited by a thrust deep into enemy territory to collapse the whole of their Tunisian front. Unfortunately, the orders which the Commando Supremo had sent us for the use of our striking column took no account of this great aim, and the attack was directed into the reach of the Anglo-American reserves. The stubborn American defence of the Kasserine Pass and the delayed arrival of the Fifth Army's forces prevented us from making a surprise break-in to the enemy hinterland, and the enemy was thus given time to organise his defence in the rear and bring his reserves up to the critical spot.

Clumsy leadership by certain German commanders, and the absence of the forces which had been held back by the rivalry of Fifth Army, led to a premature check in our attack. We failed to clear the Americans off the Hamra Plateau and were thus unable to free our western flank.

23 Feb. 1943

DEAREST LU,

I've been unable to write until to-day. I've stood up well so far to the exhausting days of battle. Unfortunately we won't be able to hold the ground we've gained for long.

ARMY GROUP " AFRIKA "

On the evening of the 23rd February, an order arrived from the Commando Supremo stating that to satisfy the urgent need for a unified command in Tunisia, Army Group " Afrika " was to be formed under my command. I received the news with mixed feelings. On the one hand, I was glad to feel that I would again be able to have some wider influence over the fate of my men—General Messe having shortly before assumed command over the Mareth front; on the other hand, I was not very happy at the prospect of having to go on playing whipping-boy for the Fuehrer's H.Q., the Commando Supremo and the Luftwaffe.

24 Feb. 1943

Dearest Lu,

I've moved up a step in command and have given up my army as a result. Bayerlein remains my Chief of Staff. Whether it's a permanent solution is doubtful. I'm tolerably well, although the last few days have been pretty exhausting.

Communiqués from the East now sound a little better again. That's a ray of light after such bad times.

On the 24th February, I held a conference with the Ia of Fifth Army to discuss their plans. Von Arnim was planning an outflanking attack to destroy the enemy forces which had assembled in the area round Medjez el Bab [*40 miles west of Tunis*]. I agreed the scheme, but could not accept their further plan to evacuate the plain of Medjez el Bab after the operation and return to their starting point. This area was an ideal place for motorised forces to assemble for an attack on Tunis, and consequently represented an " Achilles' heel " for our front.

In the evening I met Colonel Westphal at the Luftwaffe Commander's Headquarters. He asked me, on behalf of Field Marshal Kesselring, to hold on to our rearguard positions at Kasserine for another few days and to co-operate if required with Fifth Army in its advance on Beja. This was the first I had heard of Beja, or of Fifth Army's plan. I was far from taken with it, as its objective was set much too high for the small force available. In any case, the operation should have been started on the day we attacked Thala.

It was unfortunately impossible to leave the 10th Panzer Division at Kasserine, as its withdrawal had already started and we were expecting a heavy enveloping attack on the division's present positions during the next few days, which could not have been warded off without major casualties.

It was typical of the small minds in the Commando Supremo that they lacked any kind of sense of reality by which they might have formed a rational judgment of the military situation. They did not base their plans on the real possibilities of the situation, but allowed the wish to father the thought. Although these people in Rome considered themselves competent to take tactical decisions affecting Tunisia, they had not even been capable of co-ordinating Fifth Army's attack on Beja with ours on Thala, by which the chances of both operations might have been materially increased.

The Fifth Panzer Army's offensive opened on the 26th February. The attack appeared to take the enemy completely by surprise and was thus able to achieve a comparatively easy break-through. But soon the enemy was launching heavy counter-attacks. The wet weather in which the attack was made was in some ways a disadvantage, as it provided our attacking forces with great difficulty in getting up their heavy weapons.

The attack continued for several more days. It could never, at the best, have achieved any major success, and the losses suffered by our forces were of greater moment than those we were able to inflict on the enemy. Nowhere did it develop into a smooth-running tactical manœuvre; it was, in fact, a mere waste of strength. It made me particularly angry to see how the few Tigers we had in Africa, which had been denied us for our offensive in the south, were thrown in to attack through a marshy valley, where their principal advantage—the long range of their heavy guns—was completely ineffective. The heavy tanks either stuck fast in the mud, or were pounded into immobility by the enemy. Of the 19 Tigers which went into action, 15 were lost. It was the same with all the other tanks that went into that narrow valley, large numbers of which were destroyed by the British. I very soon gave orders to Fifth Army to put a stop to the fruitless affair at the earliest possible moment. Unfortunately, the attack was continued at a later date, after my departure from Africa, under precisely the same conditions. Hill after hill was stormed and the same rigid tactical picture emerged as had become familiar in the battles of material of the First World War.

26 Feb. 1943

DEAREST LU,

. . . But we're absolutely delighted by the better news from the East. Things seem to be going up again after all.

If only we could win a major victory here. I rack my brains night and day to find a way. Unfortunately, the conditions for it don't exist. Everything depends on supplies—and has done for years.

My health has kept going so far. Heart, nerves, and rheumatism are giving me a lot of trouble. But I intend to stick it out as long as is humanly possible.

From Captain Alfred Ingemar Berndt

26 Feb. 1943

DEAR FRAU ROMMEL,

At the beginning of February the physical and mental condition of your husband had reached such a state that Professor Horster considered an immediate course of at least eight weeks' treatment to be indispensable. The latest date for this was given to the Fuehrer's H.Q., through C.-in-C. South, as the 20th February.

An aggravating factor contributing to your husband's condition was the unresolved command situation. The Italians had sent his successor, without any statement or any orders for his recall having come from the German side. They were waiting for a sick report. He, for his part, took the very proper view—which I passed on—that he would never report sick. He belonged to his men and if he himself had determined the time of his departure and something had happened a few days later, he would have been accused of lack of foresight and of having left a few days too early.

Meanwhile certain operations, which could not be postponed, had to be undertaken against the west. Troops of both armies were to take part. When he saw there was jealousy he stood back and gave up the command in favour of the others. But when its success was not exploited either according to his ideas or quickly enough, he intervened with a very audacious proposal—which, by the way, was watered down—and received command. It was mobile operations again. That evening he ordered a bottle of champagne, and said he felt like an old war-horse that had heard the music again. During the next few days his condition improved to such an extent that one might easily have taken him for his old self. Professor Horster diagnosed an improvement and raised no objections to his continuing his operational plans for a few weeks before starting on his course of treatment.

I reported accordingly—though the Marshal must not know this—to the Fuehrer and C.-in-C. South. Right in the middle of our successful operations we received the decision—Army Group "Rommel", with both Armies under command. It was a further great confirmation of the Fuehrer's and Duce's confidence. I brought this about, in order to renew his belief that he still enjoyed the fullest confidence, even after the retreat. He was always persuading himself to the contrary. Confidence could not have been more clearly stated.

Whether he will return to Africa, after his sick leave, will depend on how the situation develops. If it is possible for the fight to be continued offensively, I should say he would. If not, then the Fuehrer, who has described the Marshal as his best offensive general, will certainly post him elsewhere for a major offensive task. Of course, the burden of his even greater responsibilities weighs very heavily on him at the moment, but it has also given him the fillip he needed. So it has turned out well. He can rely blindly on all his staff.

It was wonderful to see the joy of his troops during the last few days, as he drove along their columns. And when, in the middle of the attack, he appeared among a new division which had not previously been under his command, right up with the leading infantry scouts in front of the tank spearheads, and lay in the mud among the men under artillery fire in his old way, how their eyes lit up. What other commander has such a wealth of trust to draw upon.

The house on the Semmering has been cancelled. But I think he will still be coming in the second half of March, possibly at the end of the month. He will then bring a small staff with him—something like 2 officers and 6 N.C.O.s and men—to write his battle report.

I hope this letter has put you in the picture.

With best wishes and *Heil Hitler*,

I am, Yours sincerely,

BERNDT

27 Feb. 1943

DEAREST LU,

A very difficult time lies behind me and possibly still more difficult ahead. I hope to have the strength to go through it all. My nerves have never let me down yet, and they must go on standing up to it. If only I had what one needs to make war here. But the supply line is too difficult.

1 March 1943

It's still doubtful whether I shall start on my treatment. It's not easy for me to get away from here.

3 March 1943

I may have the Army Group now, but the worry is no less. Schmundt has written me a very nice letter. The Fuehrer is worried about me. But I can't get away for the moment. I'll just have to go on for a bit. I wouldn't mind having a different job. I'm dictated to by Rome in every single thing, yet the full responsibility is mine. That I find intolerable. I often think my nerves will snap. One is continually having to take paths which lead very close beside the abyss. If it goes wrong, the consequences will be incalculable. It's spring outside, blossoming trees and meadows, sunshine. The world could be so beautiful for all men. Such infinite possibilities exist to make them contented and happy. There is so much that could be done— especially here in Africa with its wide-open spaces.

4 March 1943

I'm expecting Gause this evening. He is now to be Chief of Staff. Arnim—situation permitting—is to deputise for me during my sick leave. I don't see it happening, though. I can't get away from here. We're facing decisive events. . . .

5 March 1943

Before I go off on a new and daring operation on orders from above, my dearest love to you and the boy.

Meanwhile, orders had been received, on the 23rd February, for the attack which I had proposed against the British positions at Medenine. It was a particularly difficult operation, but if it failed in its object of breaking up the Eighth Army's assembly areas and thereby postponing

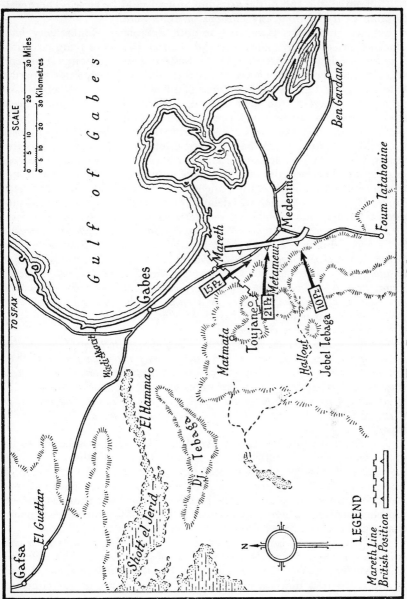

19. THE BATTLE OF MEDENINE

Map labels:
Gafsa
El Guettar
TO SFAX
Wadi Akarit
Shott el Jerid
El Hamna
Dj. Tebaga
Gabes
Gulf of Gabes
Mareth
Matmata
Toujane
15Pz
21Pz
Metameur
Hallouf
10Pz
Jebel Lebaga
Medenine
Ben Gardane
Foum Tatahouine

SCALE
0   5   10   20   30 Miles
0 5 10   20   30 Kilometres

N

LEGEND
Mareth Line
British Position

their offensive, the end of the army in Africa would be close. There was no point in harbouring any illusions on that score.

Shortly before this date, on the 20th February, Montgomery had attacked the southern front of the 15th Panzer Division's rearguard line in order to relieve the pressure on the western Tunisian front. A violent struggle had raged all day between my men and overwhelmingly superior British armour. Only with the greatest of difficulty and by counter-attacking again and again with their 20 available tanks had the division been able to hold its retreat road open. The division, which had fought splendidly, had then been withdrawn during the night behind the outposts of the Mareth line, which had allowed Montgomery to move into the area in which we intended to fight, rather earlier than we had bargained for. It was, therefore, time that we were getting under way.

As a result of the Fifth Army's offensive, the move of the 10th and 21st Panzer Divisions to Mareth was delayed by a few days, which gave Montgomery further time to build up the defences in his newly-won position.

Montgomery was also allowed time to reinforce his strength at Medenine. By the 26th February he had brought up the whole of the 51st Division to reinforce the 7th Armoured Division. By the 6th March, when Rommel eventually launched his attack, Montgomery had also brought up the New Zealand Division, the 201st Guards Brigade, and two additional armoured brigades. His defensive dispositions were complete by the evening of the 4th March. Besides 400 tanks he had over 500 anti-tank guns in position. Thus in the interval Rommel's chance of striking with superior strength had vanished.

General de Guingand, the Eighth Army's Chief of Staff, speaking of the situation a week earlier, says in his memoirs: " Montgomery frankly admitted to me that, for once, through his action to assist First Army, he now found himself unbalanced. So we worked feverishly to prepare ourselves to meet this attack when it came. . . . By March 5th we were ready for the attack, and a very strong force was ready to receive it. Rommel had missed his opportunity, and we all breathed freely again."

An attack against the Eighth Army at Medenine was bound to be an extremely difficult undertaking, not only because of the great battle experience of Montgomery's troops, but also because of the nature of the terrain, which offered a very small choice of tactical possibilities— that is unless large quantities of petrol were to be consumed in the approach march. There was little chance of coming upon the enemy at any point where he would not be expecting an attack.

Our whole enterprise was therefore built on the hope that the British would not have had time to complete the organisation of their defences in the Medenine area. The decision to make the attack at all was based on the realisation that we only had two choices open to us—either to await the British attack in our own line and suffer a crushing defeat, or to attempt to gain time by breaking up the enemy's assembly areas.

Heated discussion raged round the method of executing the attack.

Finally, we accepted a proposal by General Messe, whereby one Panzer division was to deploy on the road, another behind the Jebel Tebaga, and only one was to be brought across the mountains. Although the ground near the Jebel Tebaga was too open for tanks to attempt a break-through at that point, the plan nevertheless had advantages over the others we had considered.

Several of my staff suggested putting the whole thing off until the next full moon—a suggestion which I could not accept, for by that time the enemy preparations would be certain to be complete.

All these delays caused a further postponement of the attack, but finally the date was fixed for the 6th of March. On the 5th, I moved up to Forward H.Q. on Hill 715 south of Toujane [*the southern end of the Mareth line, 20 miles inland*], and conferred with the commanders of the attacking formations. The view from this hill was remarkable, ranging far beyond Medenine.

Next morning the sky was cloudy and the whole battle ground shrouded in mist. Like a hammer-blow the artillery opened fire on the stroke of six. *Nebelwerfer* bombs lobbed through the layers of mist into the valley below. The 10th Panzer Division had meanwhile moved up through Hallouf without interference from the enemy.

The attack began extraordinarily well but soon came up against strong British positions in hilly country, protected by mines and anti-tank guns. The enemy had constructed a strong defence line facing towards the south-east. Attack after attack was launched, but achieved no success. Dive-bombers which tried to take a hand ran into an A.A. screen of hitherto unparalleled intensity over the Metameur hills. As there was now nothing more to be seen from Hill 715 I took myself up farther forward, where it soon became clear that the attack had failed and there was nothing more to be done about it. At about 17.00 hours I gave orders to discontinue the action, hold the captured territory and recover damaged vehicles. During the evening I was forced to decide to break off the operation altogether.

The attack had bogged down in the break-in stage and the action had never had a chance of becoming fluid. The British commander had grouped his forces extremely well and had completed his preparations with remarkable speed. In fact, the attack had been launched about a week too late. The operation had lost all point the moment it became obvious that the British were prepared for us. We had suffered tre-mendous losses, including 40 tanks totally destroyed.[1]

But the cruellest blow was the knowledge that we had been unable

[1]Montgomery states that 52 German tanks were left behind on the battlefield. No British tanks were lost, and only one squadron was engaged in the fighting.

Just as Alam Halfa paved the way for victory at Alamein, so Medenine paved the way for Montgomery's successful attack on the Mareth Line. De Guingand aptly remarks: " When studying Montgomery's campaigns it is interesting to see how his greatest offensive victories were each preceded by a defensive success."

to interfere with Montgomery's preparations. A great gloom settled
over us all. The Eighth Army's attack was now imminent and we had
to face it. For the Army Group to remain longer in Africa was now
plain suicide.

THE END IN AFRICA

At the end of February I had instructed the two commanders, Colonel-
General von Arnim and General Messe, to draw up their appreciation
of the situation in Tunisia. Both documents drew attention to the
untenability of the positions which the Army Group was having to hold.
I summarised their reports as follows:

> " At present the two Armies in Tunisia are holding a front about
> 400 miles long, with centres of gravity at two points, one in the area
> west and south-west of Tunis and the other in the Mareth line between
> the coast and the mountains. Some 350 miles of this line are only
> very lightly held and, in some places, owing to our lack of troops,
> not held at all. The greater part of the Fifth Panzer Army's front is
> mountainous, but even in the mountains an enemy infantry attack
> could open almost any of the weakly held passes from the rear.
> Between the two Armies there is a large gap on either side of the
> Shott el Jerid, which, in the dry season, will offer excellent oppor-
> tunities for operations by the enemy motorised forces."

I calculated the size of the force, including Americans, British and
French, with which the Army Group would be faced at the moment of
the Allied attack, and arrived at the following results:

> 1,600 tanks
> 1,100 anti-tank guns
> 850 guns
> Approximately 210,000 fighting troops

I assumed that the Allies would take their correct action and attack
the bridgehead with all their forces simultaneously. Our front was
completely incapable of meeting such an attack and the infantry screens
would very soon be penetrated. Before long all operational reserves
would be committed at crisis points.

I demanded that the following conclusions should be drawn:

> " A front of 400 miles, is, in the long run, impossible to hold, and
> it should be shortened to 100 miles. As a possible new front I suggest:
> The Fifth Army's front as far as Jebel Mansour and from there
> across the mountains to Enfidaville. It would be an advantage to
> force the enemy out of the Medjez el Bab and Bou Arada areas and

across the mountains to the west. This proposal would, of course, mean giving up a large part of Tunisia, including some airfields. It would also provide the enemy with overland communications between his Eastern and Western Groups. However, the shortened front would have the advantage that it could probably be held longer than the front as it exists at the moment. If this long front collapses, the First Italian Army will receive no further supplies and the two Armies will be defeated one after the other. It would then be impossible to shorten the front as we would no longer have the forces to do it. That would mean the total loss of the African bridgehead."

I then dealt with the supply situation and stated that to create the build-up necessary for a defence against a major attack would need an increase in our monthly shipments to 140,000 tons. As far as could humanly be foreseen, and judging by the experience of the last few years, this figure was now unattainable.

My report concluded with the following words:

" In view of the gravity of the situation I request that an early decision be reached on the plan for the future long-term conduct of the campaign in Tunisia. We can expect the enemy's offensive to open with the next full moon."

The decision on my proposals was very slow in arriving, but after sending many reminders, I finally heard from Kesselring that the Fuehrer was unable to agree with my judgment of the situation. Attached to the reply was a statement comparing the forces available on either side, made up by regiment numbers, irrespective of their state of motorisation, equipment or strength of personnel. The intention of this comparison was to prove that we were nowhere near as inferior in strength as we were always maintaining.

Of course we could have defended the great expanse of Tunisia with the forces we had, if they had been properly motorised, armed with modern weapons and provided with adequate stocks of supplies. But of this there was no chance and so the only possibility was to base our defence on well-fortified and thickly held positions, and to use our small motorised forces solely for the purpose of ironing out enemy penetrations in our front. For the non-motorised forces to hold the front in any density, the longest it could be was 100 miles, never 400.

It was clear that our higher authorities were building illusions for themselves on the strength of our increased shipments at this time. Certainly they were very large compared with what we had known. In January the figure was 46,000 tons, including 50 tanks, 2,000 vehicles and 200 guns; in February it was 53,000 tons, with 50 tanks, 1,300 vehicles and 120 guns. But they should have remembered that the British and American armament was now more up-to-date and efficient than it had been, and that their units now had larger establishments of guns and anti-tank guns. The quantity of material now being shipped to the Allies was many times greater than ever Auchinleck had received in Egypt.

It was with these thoughts in mind that I drove back to Beni Zelten on the 7th March, where I took leave of General Ziegler and Colonel Bayerlein. Bayerlein had been appointed to General Messe's staff as German Chief of Staff; I was certain that he would make the best that could be made out of any situation. Above all, we had to ensure that no disaster could occur as a result of some failure on the part of the Italians. During the morning I finally decided to fly once again to the Fuehrer's H.Q. I felt it my duty to do all in my power to rouse a true understanding in the highest quarters of the practical operational problems of Tunisia. More especially I at least had to see to it that the troops were saved. I accordingly asked General von Arnim, who was to take over command of the Army Group as my deputy to come to my H.Q., only to learn that he and General von Vaerst had been called that morning to Rome. I was furious and at once told Kesselring over the telephone what I thought about it, whereupon he cancelled his conference. I handed over the Army Group to von Arnim next day and on 9th March took off for Rome.

On arrival I drove first to the Commando Supremo and had a talk with Army General Ambrosio. I soon realised that the Italians were not expecting me to return to Africa and thought that the Fuehrer would order me to take sick leave. This was far from being my idea, for I hoped to get my plans accepted and then to continue for some little while yet in command of the Army Group.

I then drove with Ambrosio and Westphal to the Duce, with whom we talked for about twenty-five minutes. I told Mussolini briefly and plainly what I thought of the situation and explained the conclusions that I wanted drawn. But he, too, seemed to lack any sense of reality in adversity and spent the whole time searching for arguments to justify his views. Among other anxieties he feared a considerable shock to opinion in Italy if Tunis were to fall. I declined his offer to send another Italian division to Tunis, saying that he should rather equip those already there so that they could be expected to do battle with the British. The whole tone of the Duce's conversation, which he made in German, was very cordial, although it began to become a little more acrimonious towards the end. In fact, I heard later from Berndt that the Duce had been intending that day to award me the Italian Gold Medal for Military Valour.[1] But he held his hand, apparently annoyed by my " defeatist " attitude. Nevertheless, he thanked me for our great achievements in the African campaign and assured me of his undiminished confidence.

Actually, I had always had a great regard for the Duce. He was

[1] Medaglia d'Oro al Valor Militare.

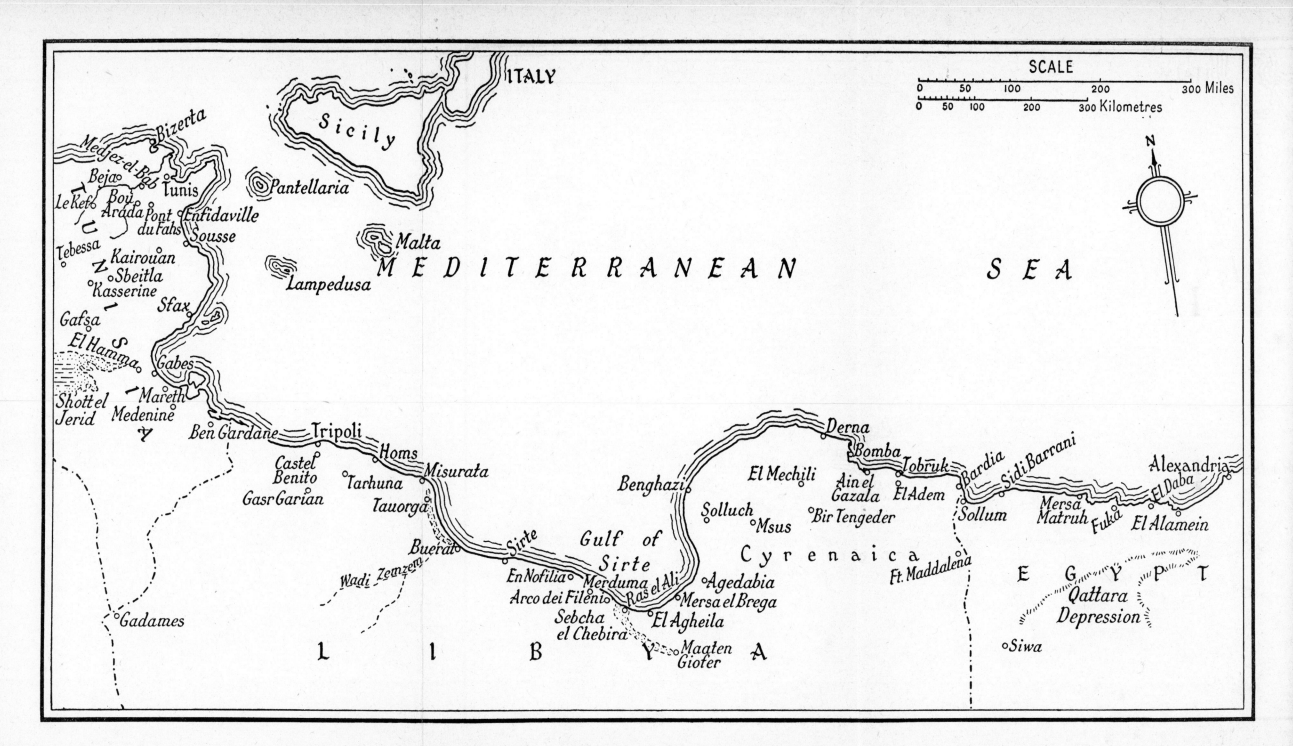

The coast of North Africa from Alexandria to Tunis

probably a great actor, like most Italians. He was certainly no Roman, though he tried to act the part. Although of a high intellectual capacity he was far too dependent on his emotions to be able to carry through his ambitious plans. Yet there can be no doubt that the Italian people owe him a great deal. The draining of the Pontine marches, the colonisation of Libya and Abyssinia, none of these would have happened without him. Unfortunately, many of his associates did not look on things in the same idealistic light, and ran a good line in organised graft. Now the Duce saw his dreams crumbling. It was a bitter hour for him, and he was quite incapable of shouldering the consequences. Perhaps I should have spoken differently to him at the end, but I was so heartily sick of all this everlasting false optimism that I just could not do it.

When I inquired, at about midday, whether the Reichsmarschall, who happened to be in Rome at the time, wished to see me he sent word that I should travel to the Fuehrer's H.Q. with him in his special train. Hermann Goering seemed to be noticeably anxious to come with me to the Fuehrer's H.Q. I declined the offer, as I wanted to make my report to the Fuehrer without Goering's continual interjections, which, being invariably of an optimistic tinge, were too attractive.

On the afternoon of the 10th March I arrived at the Fuehrer's H.Q., somewhere in Russia. The same evening I received an invitation to take tea with Hitler and was thus able to talk to him in private. He seemed very upset and depressed about the Stalingrad disaster. He said that one is always liable to look on the black side of things after a defeat, a tendency which can lead one into dangerous and false conclusions. He was unreceptive to my arguments and seemed to pass them all off with the idea that I had become a pessimist. I emphasised as strongly as I could that the " African " troops must be re-equipped in Italy to enable them to defend our southern European flank. I even went so far as to give him a guarantee—something which I am normally very reluctant to do—that with these troops, I would beat off any Allied invasion in southern Europe. But it was all hopeless. He instructed me to take some sick leave and get myself put right so that I could take command again later for operations against Casablanca.[1] It simply never occurred to him that things could go wrong in Tunisia. Nor would he hear of the front being shortened, for then it would be impossible to take the offensive again. My request to be permitted to continue in command of the Army Group for a few weeks, during which time it would be shown whether the Americans really were going to take the offensive, he refused. He did, however, seem to realise the necessity for removing the infantry immediately from Mareth to Gabes and for beginning with the construction of the Gabes line.

[1] As Casablanca is on the Atlantic coast, it is evident that Hitler was picturing a counter-offensive that would throw the Allies completely out of Africa. That is remarkable evidence of his state of delusion.

Goering appeared at H.Q. next day, bringing with him a wave of unfounded optimism. The Fuehrer decorated me with the Oakleaves with Swords and Diamonds;[1] but other than that everything remained as before. All my efforts to save my men and get them back to the Continent had been fruitless. I flew back to Wiener Neustadt and then went off to the Semmering to start my treatment.

There was not long to wait for the Anglo-American offensive to open. Although the Fuehrer had at first given orders for the move back to the Akarit position, these orders were very soon countermanded. Apparently Kesselring had also flown to the Fuehrer's Headquarters and, being the bearer of better tidings, had found a willing ear. It was particularly important for him that the Mareth line should be held, for it was he and the Commando Supremo who had got us into that particular mess. During a subsequent conference with von Arnim he said that I had neglected to embody the Gabes position into the Mareth line and to fortify them together, which was what the Fuehrer had had in mind. This makes it quite clear that he failed to recognise the real problem. It was impossible, with the forces we had, to deal with one British attack on Mareth, another at El Hamma [*on the inland approach to the Gabes defile*] and an American attack on [*the rear of*] Gabes at one and the same time. All the work which had been expended on the Mareth line would not have availed us in the slightest if the British and Americans had broken through to the coast west of our front. An eventual retreat to Akarit would then have become inevitable, without the Italian infantry having had a chance of exercising their full effect in the Mareth line. Whether this triangle were fortified or not, to defend solely the bulge up to Mareth was absurd. Incidentally my arguments were to be completely justified by the unhappy events to come.

Orders were issued by the Fuehrer's H.Q. to maintain the utmost secrecy concerning my recall. My military reputation was still to serve as a deterrent. But, since the strategic situation was now hopeless, not even a Napoleon could have done anything about it. Optimism could not help, nor energy—however ruthless. Troops have to shoot and move, and for that they need ammunition and petrol. But for adequate supplies of these two commodities we waited in vain. Von Arnim's position was far from enviable and he did everything that was humanly possible to make our higher authorities see reason, but all in vain.

As we had anticipated, Montgomery sent his X Armoured Corps round the Matmata Hills and threw it against the Mannerini sector,[2] simultaneously attacking the Mareth line in the north. The Americans

[1] See footnote on page 39.

[2] The sector between the Shott el Jerid and the inland end of the Mareth Line (which rested on the Matmata Hills), covering the army's flank to the south. It was held by Italian troops under the command of General Mannerini.

moved forward at the same time from Gafsa with approximately one armoured division. Strategically their operation was very well conceived and we were forced, mainly by the effective co-ordination of the attacks on the Mareth line with those in the Mannerini sector, to constant tactical makeshifts. Heavy demands were made on the officers' powers of improvisation and it was a relief to me to know that General Messe had Bayerlein beside him.

In spite of it all, it did prove possible to get the army back from Mareth to the Wadi Akarit and retain a considerable part of its fighting power. But the troops were given no time to install themselves in their new positions and Montgomery was soon able to make a deep penetration into our line, thus rendering the Akarit position untenable. The Italians had now practically ceased to exist as a fighting force. A large part of the First Italian Army's artillery, both German and Italian, had been lost in the Mareth line without having had a chance of materially affecting the issue. The 10th Panzer Division had meanwhile succeeded in preventing an American break-through to [the rear of] Gabes, although at a heavy cost to itself. The remnants of the First Italian Army, together with the 10th Panzer Division, now retired to the Enfidaville line, the construction of which had been ordered while I was still in Africa and been continued by von Arnim. In spite of all our heavy reverses, Eisenhower[1] had not succeeded in his primary operational aim of dividing the First Italian from the Fifth Panzer Army. He had not made his right wing strong enough and had flung his troops against our strongly-held hill positions in the north at a frightful cost in blood. He could have avoided all this if he had massed his forces in accordance with the strategic requirements. Thus he should first have thrown his weight into south-west Tunisia in order to divide the First Italian from the Fifth Panzer Army, following this up by destroying the First Army in conjunction with Montgomery. Then he should have switched his effort to Pont du Fahs or Medjez el Bab in order to destroy Fifth Army. All this storming of mountains in the north availed the Americans nothing.

The Enfidaville position was now very thinly held. The infantry and artillery of the First Italian Army were largely unfit for action. Their motorised forces had also been worn away in the open south. Supplies to Africa had as good as ceased and every single man knew that the end was near—all, in fact, except our highest command. From my hospital in the Semmering, I demanded that a start should be made in bringing the troops away—of course without result. Then I asked that at least the irreplaceable people should be got out, people such as Gause, Bayerlein and Buelowius. But still no move was made. (In the event General Gause was saved by von Arnim, who sent him off to a conference in Italy;

[1]General Eisenhower had been placed in supreme command of all the Allied forces in North Africa at the beginning of February, but General Alexander was given operational command of the fighting front.

Bayerlein was sick and also flown to Italy; General Buelowius fell into enemy hands.)

Finally, on the 6th May, the Americans[1] advanced to the kill at Medjez el Bab. Under a rolling artillery barrage and massive Allied bomber attacks, they quickly won a deep penetration into our line and extended it to a break-through after the almost complete annihilation of the 15th Panzer Division. The front collapsed, there were no more arms and no ammunition and it was all over. The Army surrendered.

This was followed in the Fuehrer's H.Q. by an extraordinary collapse of morale. It was a complete surprise to them. This will be incomprehensible unless it is realised how certain people at these highest levels were waging their struggle for power on the backs of the fighting troops. Goering was particularly busy just then trying to get the better of the Army. His Luftwaffe field divisions were a beginning. He probably wanted to introduce his scheme with a great military victory, which would be placed to the credit of the Luftwaffe. As a suitable site for this victory he chose North Africa, thinking that victories came relatively easily there. With virtually no military experience behind him, it probably all looked terribly simple.

It cannot be denied that Goering had considerable talent for organisation and an intelligence above the average. But he was too fond of his comforts to put his whole strength behind the realisation of his plans.

Characteristically, Goering also had a finger in the Stalingrad pie. I was told that when the Fuehrer decided to send the commander of Sixth Army orders to break away to the west, Goering said to him:

" But surely, my Fuehrer, you're not going to weaken! We'll supply Stalingrad from the air."

Terrible as it was to know that all my men had found their way into Anglo-American prison camps, even more shattering was the realisation that our star was in decline and the knowledge of how little our command measured up to the trials which lay ahead. The moment the first Allied soldier set foot on Italian soil, Mussolini was finished and the dream of the rebirth of the Roman Empire was probably over for good.

---

[1]This may be an instance of Rommel's tendency to use the term " Americans " for the Allies as a whole, or may be simply due to a slip of the pen—he says " Anglo-American " in his concluding paragraph.

In the final attack, the main blow was delivered, in the Medjez el Bab sector by the British IX Corps under General Horrocks—with the 4th British and 4th Indian (Infantry) Divisions opening the way for the 6th and 7th Armoured Divisions' drive into Tunis. A powerful flank leverage was applied by the U.S. II Corps under General Bradley—with 1st, 9th, 34th, and 1st Armoured Divisions—which had been pushing forward in the north, and entered Bizerta on the 7th May, almost simultaneously with the British entry into Tunis.

Part Four

ITALY

CHAPTER XX

ITALY, 1943

By Manfred Rommel

It was the middle of March 1943. I stood on the big airfield just outside Wiener Neustadt waiting for my father, having been forewarned by wireless of his return from the Fuehrer's H.Q. At last the twin-engined yellow and green mottled Heinkel bomber touched down on the grey runway. The hatch under the fuselage opened and my father climbed slowly down the thin aluminium ladder to the ground.

"The Fuehrer won't let me go back to Africa again," he said, as we clasped hands. "Von Arnim is taking over the Army Group."

A day or two later my father left Wiener Neustadt with my mother to continue the medical treatment he had interrupted at the beginning of the battle of El Alamein. I stayed at home to avoid interrupting my schooling, and was only able to visit my parents by train at week-ends.

I was fourteen years old at the time and am naturally not in a position to give an exact record of all that my father said during those weeks. But a few events of the period so impressed themselves on me that they are still quite fresh in my memory.

Thus, I can remember to this day how astonished I was when my father told me that he'd "fallen into disgrace and could expect no important job for the present." His contacts with the Fuehrer's H.Q. during this period were, in fact, far from good. He received no information beyond the press and radio communiqués and occupied himself with writing his African memoirs.

As the battle raged round the Mareth line and the Akarit defences, my father paced restlessly up and down the big study which had been provided for him by the hospital authorities. He had no doubts about its outcome. He was bitter in his criticisms of the Supreme Command, without sparing even Hitler himself, which I, as a then enthusiastic member of the Hitler Jugend, heard with mixed feelings. A few days before the German and Italian Africa divisions assembled to march off into the Allied P.-o-W. camps, my father suddenly received a telephone call from the Fuehrer's H.Q. ordering him to report to Hitler.

On that day a new phase began in my father's military career, a phase during which he saw Hitler's political and military leadership at close quarters for the first time, and obtained experience which was to lead to his final break with the Nazi system.

Unfortunately, he wrote no connected account covering the period from the 10th May 1943 until the day when he was commanded to undertake an inspection of the Atlantic Wall. The only documents which exist are private letters and a diary in note form, dated the 9th May to 6th September 1943, in which is included the shorthand record of numerous conferences. From this material and from the memories of my mother and myself, the following account has been prepared.

On the 10th May 1943, the crisis had reached alarming proportions on all fronts. The Sixth Army, with 320,000 German troops, had been shattered in the ruins of Stalingrad, 230,000 of its men had been killed and the other 90,000 taken prisoner. Similar disaster was shaping for another 130,000 German troops in Tunisia.

This was the situation when my father landed at Tempelhof airport in the early afternoon of the 10th May. He was taken at once to head-quarters, where he met Hitler, pale and restless, his self-confidence shaken.

" I should have listened to you before," the Fuehrer said, so my father told us later, " but I suppose it's too late now. It will soon be all over in Tunisia."

Within a few days, press and radio announced the capitulation of Army Group " Afrika ". Later in the war, when hundreds of thousands of German troops had been senselessly sacrificed by Hitler, my father found comfort in the knowledge that his " Africans " were prisoners-of-war of the Western Powers. But the letters he wrote home after the capitulation in Tunisia show how deeply it affected him at the time.

15 May 1943

Dearest Lu,

Dined with Zeitzler (Halder's successor) this evening and had a very pleasant conversation. Our views coincide in everything.

I hear that Arnim is being very decently treated by the British. So I hope that Buelowius, Seiderer, Kolbeck and all the rest of the brave boys will also find a bearable fate. . . .

18 May 1943

. . . Gause is coming to-day. I'm terribly pleased, for it will mean the end of this unbearable loneliness. More officers of our old staff will probably soon be joining us and then there'll be plenty to do.

Physically, I'm very well. But this loneliness and the last stages in Tunis have left a bad scar. However, it will pass.

24 May 1943

Arrived here yesterday safely and quickly.[1] Gause turned up from the opposite direction two minutes after us. Now we're going to get down to work. As always and everywhere in life, there are many difficulties to be overcome. However, I'm confidently hoping that we'll pull it off. I'm feeling much more cheerful now that there's work to be done. One forgets all the past troubles.

Our short time together was lovely. See that Manfred makes the most of his remaining time at home. I can't get used to the idea yet that this $14\frac{1}{2}$-year-old lad will be in barracks in a few months. For you the parting will be particularly hard. . . .

When my father wrote, " I'm confidently hoping we'll pull it off," he was presumably referring to the war as a whole, as he had no specific assignment at that time. But his words must not be misunderstood and taken to mean that he still thought that Germany could achieve total victory. He did, however, still think that the military capacity of the German people was sufficient to force their enemies to conclude a tolerable peace.

My father communicated his views on this subject to Hitler, but soon learned that the Supreme War Leader took a very different view of his responsibilities towards the German people from that which he had always assumed was the case. Two conversations which he had with Hitler during 1943 particularly impressed him. He talked of them to my mother and myself. Concerning the first, he said that it took place after a long talk which he had with Hitler about the material strength of the British and Americans. It was at a time when Hitler was very worried about Italy, which appeared to be about to collapse at any moment. My father felt that this was the time to give Hitler his views on the general war situation.

He pointed out that special communiqués were becoming more and more infrequent and that upwards of 30 U-boats were being lost every month. It could not go on like that for long. Things were looking bad in the east, and in Italy. Germany would, of course, produce more arms and ammunition as a result of the total mobilisation of labour which was being introduced in 1943. " But even then," he asked, " can we keep pace with the whole world? "

Hitler listened to it all with downcast eyes, my father said. Suddenly he looked up and said that he, too, was aware that there was very little chance left of winning the war. But the West would conclude no peace with him—certainly not the people who were then at the helm. And the people who would have been prepared to negotiate with him had no

[1]In accordance with German security regulations, Rommel did not indicate where he was, but it is evident that this letter was written from Rastenburg, in East Prussia, the site of Hitler's Headquarters at the time.

power. He had never wanted war with the West. But now the West would have their war—have it to the end.

My mother has told me that my father later expressed the view that Hitler realised in 1943 that the war was lost. Yet the more the disasters piled up and the more criticism he saw directed at himself the more desperately he clutched at every straw and tried to persuade himself of victory.

While fronts cracked, while thousand of German troops took the march into the grave, while the vapour trails of powerful enemy bomber formations patterned the sky over Germany, Hitler whipped himself up into a pathological impotent hatred, which allowed the demoniac side of his personality to emerge, the side which had remained hidden in the days of his success. The change took place in the course of a few months.

My father told my mother that one evening at the end of July 1943, he was witness of a second utterance by Hitler on the subject of the end of the war, which he had found no less shattering.

" If the German people are incapable of winning the war," Hitler had said, " then they can rot." In any case, the best were already dead. If he was to be beaten, he would fight for every house, nothing would be left. A great people must die heroically—it was a historic necessity.

"Sometimes you feel that he's no longer quite normal," my father commented, when he spoke of this incident.

Having grown up in the old European officer tradition my father was deeply imbued with the principle of unconditional obedience. His fundamental attitude on this subject can be seen from a letter which he wrote me at Christmas 1943.

25 Dec. 1943

Dear Manfred,

 ... In a fortnight you'll be leaving home to enlist as a Luftwaffe auxiliary, and a new life will begin for you. . . . You must learn to obey the orders of your superior quickly and without argument. Often there'll be orders which you don't like, often you won't understand the point of them. Obey without question. A superior cannot go into a long palaver about his orders with his subordinates and there's no time to give reasons. . . .

However, my father now began to recognise more and more clearly that there are limits to the obedience of even a high ranking commander. On the one side there were Hitler's orders, the orders of a man who wanted to drag his whole people down with him into the pit of disaster; on the other there were eighty million Germans—eighty million people fighting, not to be senselessly sacrificed in the glowing embers of their own homes, but for existence. In the later months of 1943, my father felt the time for decision approaching him.

We have often been asked when my father made up his mind to intervene in Hitler's plan to drag Germany down to destruction with him.

Perhaps some clue may be given by a conversation I had with him in December 1943. I remember this conversation particularly well as it concerned primarily my own affairs.

There was, at that time, a great propaganda drive going on all over Germany to persuade young men to opt for the Waffen-S.S. rather than the army. Brightly-coloured placards blazed out on every street corner. It was well known that the S.S. troops were far better equipped than the army, and they had a more handsome uniform. So one day I decided to opt for the Waffen-S.S. and told my father of my decision in order to get his consent.

He reacted strongly. " That's out of the question," he said. " You'll join the same force as I've served in for over thirty years."

My father normally used to leave me a great deal of freedom in matters of this kind, and so I began to argue my point of view. But this time he cut me short. While, he said, he perfectly well recognised the quality of the S.S. troops, under no circumstances did he want me to be under the command of a man who, according to his information, was carrying out mass killings.

" Do you mean Himmler? " I asked.

" Yes," he answered, and instructed me to maintain absolute silence about the whole affair. The war was not going at all well and he had heard that people like Himmler were trying, by actions of this kind, to burn the bridges of the German people behind them. I think he was not at all certain at that time whether Hitler knew anything about what was going on, for no mention of the mass executions had ever been made at the Fuehrer's H.Q. And perhaps he would never have brought himself to the decision to end the war—by a revolt if necessary—if he had not received further information in the early months of 1944 which confirmed these crimes and gave some idea of their extent. From that moment on, all my father's inner allegiance to Adolf Hitler, whom he had once admired, was destroyed, and he brought himself, from his knowledge of the Fuehrer's crimes, to act against him.

But before these developments in the political field, military events of great significance had been taking place in Italy. These, my father was able to observe—when he was not himself one of the leading actors—from close quarters during the whole of 1943.

On the night of the 9th July Allied landing forces launched an attack on Sicily.[1] The Italians, although having very nearly 300,000 men and

[1]The Allied landings took place in the early hours of the 10th July. They were made on a wide stretch of the south-east coast, by Montgomery's British Eighth Army and Patton's Seventh Army. The Italian coast-defence divisions collapsed immediately, and almost the whole burden of the defence then fell on the two German divisions that lay in reserve. These made a stubborn fighting withdrawal towards the Straits of Messina, in the north-east corner of Sicily. With the aid of two more German divisions, hastily dispatched there, they managed to delay the Allies' complete clearance of the island until the 17th August. But the Allies' success in the landing, and menacing approach to

1,500 guns on the island, put up virtually no resistance and from the outset the main brunt of the fighting fell on the two (later four) German divisions in Sicily. At the same time the old struggle over the question of command flared up between the Army and Luftwaffe. The first entries in my father's diary show his attitude to this question.

15/7/43
. . . Evening, situation conference with Fuehrer. General Hube to take command in Sicily.

16/7/43
. . . Midday, situation conference. Goering wants General Stahel as Commander-in-Chief instead of Hube. I got Hube agreed, and suggested General Bayerlein as Chief-of-Staff. The Fuehrer agreed. Heavy Russian tank losses in the East. The break-through at Briansk is being sealed off. Phoned General Bayerlein, but could not reach him.

Evening, situation conference with Fuehrer. Hube being ordered to take offensive. Of the German paratroops sent in, only 300 succeeded in fighting their way through to our lines. So much for Luftwaffe command!

18/7/43
To the Fuehrer at noon. F. M. von Kluge present. Russians attacking in the East over whole front. Attacks contained for the moment. No chance of pulling any divisions out. I hear the Fuehrer has been advised not to give me command in Italy as I am adversely disposed towards Italians. I imagine the Luftwaffe is behind this. So my move to Italy is again put right back. The Fuehrer probably meeting the Duce.

Although my father managed to get his way over the appointment of General Hube in command of the German forces in Sicily, the Luftwaffe succeeded in preventing his own appointment, which had been planned, as C.-in-C. Italy.

But shortly before, a document had been found on the body of a British courier which had drifted ashore in Spain, indicating that an invasion of Greece was being planned.[1] Hitler decided to appoint my the mainland of Italy, accentuated the Italian people's desire for peace and produced the downfall of Mussolini.

[1] This had been a " plant " by the British, intended to distract German attention from the next Allied operation—the invasion of Sicily. The disclosure here that, a fortnight *after* this invasion, Rommel was despatched to the Balkans is significant. It suggests that, besides the deceptive effect prior to the invasion of Sicily, the British " plant " continued to influence Hitler's planning, and thus " sold the dummy " again in aid of the next Allied move, on to the Italian mainland—by making the Germans fear that the attack on Sicily was only a strong feint and that the main assault would be made on Greece with exploitation through the Balkans. The story of how this cover plan was ingeniously planted on the Germans has recently been revealed by the Hon. Ewen Montagu who was responsible for its conception and execution—while readers of Duff Cooper's novel, *Operation Heartbreak*, will recognise the source of his plot.

father to be C.-in-C. South-East, with command over all German and Italian forces in that theatre. But after only twenty-four hours a change occurred in the situation which necessitated my father's immediate recall. Two diary entries, written in note form, tell more or less all there is to betold about this Balkan interlude.

23/7/43
    . . . Long discussion with the Fuehrer. I am to report in detail and direct to him on conditions in Greece. Forces there, besides Eleventh Italian Army, include only one German armoured division (1st Panzer Division) and three infantry divisions.

25/7/43
    Left Wiener Neustadt 08.00 hours by air. Arrived Salonika 11.00 hours. Terrific heat.
    17.00 hours conference with Colonel-General Loehr. Loehr described the situation as being dependent upon supplies. It seems to me a great deal of work remains to be done before Greece can be regarded as a fortress. Will fly round to-morrow before taking over command, in order to get to know the country. General Gause also doesn't take a very rosy view of the situation here.
    21.30 hours. General Warlimont phoned and reported that Eleventh Italian Army will be definitely under command. I want to get the German divisions directly under my command by interpolating a German Corps H.Q.—instead, as was suggested at the Fuehrer's H.Q., of having them under Italian command. 23.15 hours, a call from O.K.W. reversed everything. Duce in protective custody. I am recalled to the Fuehrer's H.Q. Situation in Italy obscure.

As can be seen from these diary entries, the Italian *coup d'état* came as a complete surprise to Hitler. Wild excitement reigned in the Fuehrer's H.Q. The situation was still completely obscure and everybody waited avidly for news. My father received orders to assemble troops in the Alps and prepare a possible entry into Italy. His diary again gives the atmosphere of those days:

26/7/43
    12.00 hours arrived Rastenburg. Went straight to *Wolfschanze* [*Wolf's lair—the name of Hitler's H.Q.*]. Situation conference with the Fuehrer. All the leading men of the Services, State and Party present (including Grand-Admiral Doenitz, Foreign Minister von Ribbentrop, Reichsfuehrer S.S. Himmler, Reichsminister Doctor Goebbels; etc.) F. M. von Kluge was there to report on situation in

the east. The break-through at Orel still not cleaned up. The Americans have meanwhile occupied the western half of Sicily and have broken through.

Situation in Italy still obscure. Nothing is yet known of the circumstances of Mussolini's downfall. Marshal Badoglio has taken office as head of the Government on command of the King. In spite of the King's and Badoglio's proclamation, we can expect Italy to get out of the war, or at the very least, the British to undertake further major landings in northern Italy.[1]

Lunched with the Fuehrer after the conference. The Italian Minister Farrinaci is expected. He managed to escape.

In Rome it has apparently got to the point of actual violence against members and property of the Fascist Party, although nothing has yet happened, apart from minor friction, between Germans and Italians. Farrinaci informs us that we can expect Italy to make armistice proposals in a week or 10 days. The British may then land at Genoa and Leghorn. Contact still exists with our own troops.

I hope to be sent to Italy soon.

Evening, talked with Guderian.

27/7/43

Situation conference with Fuehrer. F. M. von Weichs taking over command in Greece. In spite of the fact that the Italians have two Armies stationed in the north and are obviously going to turn traitor, it is impossible for me to march into Italy, for political reasons. However, everything is being prepared and I have the job of supervising the German concentration.

28/7/43

I am to prepare the entry into Italy—as discussed with the Fuehrer —without being myself allowed, for the present, to cross the old 1938 frontier. . . . Some further facts have now come out about the situation in Italy. The Fascist Grand Council, which had been convened by Mussolini, declared itself in disagreement with his course of action. In the discussion which followed, 18 voted against, 8 for and 2 abstained. Mussolini is then reported to have gone to the King, but to have been taken into protective custody by some officers on the

---

[1]This is of particular interest and significance in showing that both the German and Italian Supreme Commands shared Kesselring's view that the Anglo-American forces would exploit their superiority in sea-power by landing high up the leg of Italy, rather than landing on and near the foot—as they did. Moreover, throughout the many months when the Allies were laboriously pushing up the length of the peninsula, the German Command continued to expect a landing in the north, to by-pass its own defence lines. It failed to realise the Allies' limitations in landing-craft, and their cautious aversion to the risks of landing far outside the reach of land-based air cover.

way. Apparently Badoglio was then charged with forming a new
cabinet. They say there is a general " Fascist Hunt " going on under
Badoglio. . . .

At 16.45 hours General Feuerstein and Colonel Sigel came for a
conference. Feuerstein is in command of the combat group which is
to open up the Brenner in the event of trouble.

Next day, the 29th July, a conference took place between my father,
General Feuerstein—a stocky, black-moustached man, regarded as a
first-class mountain specialist—and Hofer, Gauleiter of the Tyrol. The
record of the discussion, which was taken down in shorthand, shows the
basic tactical problems with which the German High Command was
confronted at that time.

> *Hofer:* This is what I ask you to do. To-day you can walk across
> the Brenner into Italy, to-morrow you will have to fight your way
> across, and if that happens, there'll be demolitions that will make
> the railway unusable for at least six months.
> *Feuerstein:* The Gauleiter wants to get things moving.
> *Hofer:* Yes. The whole stretch of line is prepared for demolition,
> and so I say make a surprise dash across it, no matter with how
> many troops.
> *Rommel:* The O.K.W. has reserved its decision on that.
> *Hofer:* You shouldn't have put anything on the frontier unless you
> were prepared to march immediately. The Italians have noticed
> it. . . . If we do intervene, we must make a job of it. It's high time.
> A couple more days and we won't be able to. The road will be
> blown up and hundreds of pill-boxes will be manned. As from
> to-day the Italians are manning their second and third lines. . . .
> They've been working for years on nothing else but their " Wallo
> Alpino del Littorio".
> *Rommel:* I know all this. Rather to-day than to-morrow. But we
> have to wait. It's political necessity.
> *Hofer:* Field Marshal, I'm not asking you frivolously and as an
> amateur. What I'm thinking is you won't get across the Brenner
> unless you tread on it as hard as you can. I beg you to move.
> *Rommel:* I must wait for the Fuehrer's orders. I can't jump the gun.
> *Rommel to Feuerstein after Hofer had gone:* You know what I think is
> happening? I think Churchill has rejected the Italian Govern-
> ment's advances and that they're trying to stick it out. But the
> internal situation in Italy will force them to make peace.

As the following letters show, my father was equally in the dark at
first as to the true intentions of the new Italian Government, though he
did suspect that Badoglio was aiming at an independent capitulation.

What he most feared was a sudden move by the Italians with Allied paratroop assistance to close the passes and hold them until the Allies had occupied the whole of Italy. To ensure that this did not happen, my father gave General Feuerstein orders on the 30th July to cross the Brenner and occupy the threatened passes. He, himself, however, on Hitler's personal instructions, was not yet allowed to set foot on Italian soil.

29 July 1943

DEAREST LU,

I am in Munich for a few days with my H.Q. This job is much more to my liking than the one in the South-East. Not that it's going to be easy. It's not difficult to see what's in the Italians' mind now that Mussolini has gone—cross over to the other side, bag and baggage. But it's not so certain that they'll find a way across. The new people aren't finding it all that easy. There'll probably be chaos first. In the east, the Russian offensive seems to be slowly weakening, except round Orel, where there is still heavy fighting.

30 July 1943

The situation in the south seems to be stabilising and clarifying. It is not impossible that the new Italian Government will continue the fight on our side. True, anti-Fascist elements are becoming very much in evidence. Even the Pope is now wanting to lean on us— we appearing to him no doubt as the lesser evil. I still have no entry permit.

3 Aug. 1943

I can't get away at the moment and probably won't be able to get home very soon, as the new job is already under way and the troops moving. I myself am still not allowed—for certain reasons— to go into Italy, not even to cross the old 1938 frontier. It's not a very pleasant situation, but I'll just have to lump it. Anyway, Kesselring will be played out in Italy sooner or later.

Things have been very critical for the last few days, although we have managed to get a reinforced division across the frontier into South Tyrol, in spite of Italian protests. I hope they'll now keep in line and help us to defend their country. It'll be a war area either way, that can't be altered. Why did they start the war with their miserable armament? It's better to fight the war in Italy than here at home.

I met Schoerner[1] yesterday in Mittenwald, where I had a con-

---

[1]*Note by Manfred Rommel.*—Schoerner, later Field-Marshal, was at that time commanding the German troops in Northern Norway. Feared on account of his ruthless severity in dealing with his subordinates of all ranks, he was given the nickname *Schrecken*

ference. He's very well, the old " Terror of the Arctic Passage ", fat
and lively. Talks incessantly.

Operations in northern Italy continued on 31st July and a further
conference took place between my father and Feuerstein, the shorthand
record of which provides valuable evidence of the impression which the
Italians made on the advancing German troops.

Feuerstein: The entry of our troops is going smoothly. We're getting
co-operation from the Italian Prefect in Bolzano. But you can't
entirely trust these Italians and we'll have to go on holding the
Brenner.

Rommel: Quite, but under the heading of air defence and anti-
sabotage precautions.

Feuerstein: The Italian barracks are stiff with troops—they could
muster a whole Army Corps. Their attitude towards the German
officers is better than to their own. The middle-ranking officers
are no use.

Rommel: Because they have no understanding for their men.

Feuerstein: Incidentally, we found all the demolition chambers empty
and haven't come across any mines.

Rommel: . . . Will the Italian attitude remain like this?

Feuerstein: It could be reversed at any moment on orders from Rome.

Rommel: That's something we must protect ourselves against.

Feuerstein: A German Intelligence Bureau has been set up to keep a
check on Italian troop movements to the north. Part of an Alpine
division is on its way to Milan at this moment. They're said to
have only 10 rounds per man—due apparently, to the ammunition shortage.

Rommel: That's quite possible. Their industry has never really
functioned properly.

Feuerstein: We've had a lot of trouble with the Tigers on the concrete
roads. Two have been lost, one burnt out, the other overturned.
I've even asked for workshops, stores and petrol. The depots are
all full, yet the people in charge have to ask permission from
Rome first.

Rommel: The same old delaying tactics. They never take a decision.
How did the Brenner crossing go?

der Eismeerstrasse—" Terror of the Arctic Passage ". In 1944 Schoerner had an unparalleled rise in his career, commanding first an army, then Army Group " South
Ukraine". Later he became C.-in-C. Army Group " Kurland " and finally C.-in-C.
Army Group " Central ", which held Czechoslovakia until May 1945. He grew still more
brutal, and more hated, in the last phase. After the armistice Schoerner left his men and
tried to make his way through to American-held territory in civilian clothes. He succeeded,
but the American command delivered him back to the Soviet Union together with
160,000 German troops who had belonged to the Eastern Army. Various returned
prisoners of war report that Schoerner is to-day training Soviet mountain troops.

Feuerstein: We opened up the barriers and haven't closed them again. No more crossing permits are being made out and traffic is now flowing smoothly.

After the Italian troops had at first—under protest—allowed the Germans to pass, Italo-German relations suddenly became strained during the next few days. But the situation then righted itself again. " Will they fight on our side? " was the question occupying everybody's mind in the south. It was impossible to get any clear idea of Italian intentions.

When all the passes on Italy's frontier were firmly in German hands, the advance was halted. My father still had the feeling, contrary to the German authorities in Rome, that the Italian negotiations with the British and Americans had come to a standstill, and that it was because of this fact alone that they had not provoked a final breach.

Gradually tempers subsided. Soon Italian and German troops were playing football together. But, meanwhile, unknown to the officers and men stationed in Italy, the political temperature was rising to boiling point.

My father's diary and letters have the following to say about how the situation was viewed from Army Group B:[1]

2/8/43

General Feuerstein reports that a critical situation developed on the Brenner at about midday yesterday, when the Italians tried to hold up the advance of 44th Infantry Division. General Gloria had given orders for fire to be opened if 44th Division attempted to continue their march. The order was not carried out by the subordinate Italian units on the Brenner and 44th Division's march proceeded smoothly, the Italians for the most part withdrawing to the south.

[1] This was the H.Q. organ which Rommel had taken over on being momentarily appointed to command the Balkan theatre. When, after Mussolini's overthrow, Hitler hastened to reinforce his southern flank and prepare for a move into Italy, Rommel moved to Munich with the staff of Army Group B, and troops were allotted to it. Rommel officially took over supreme command in Northern Italy on the 15th August. On the 12th September, after Italy had changed sides, the H.Q. moved to Lake Garda. When, in November, Hitler decided to give Kesselring supreme command of the whole Italian theatre, Rommel handed over half his staff (of Army Group B) along with his troops. He was then appointed by Hitler to inspect and improve the defences on the North Sea and Atlantic coasts from Denmark to the Pyrenees, and his nucleus staff was temporarily called Army Group B.z.b.v. (" for special purposes "). This move brought him into the sphere of Field Marshal von Rundstedt, the Commander-in-Chief West, and with an ill-defined role that inevitably produced a difficult situation. A partial solution was contrived, early in 1944, by giving operational command of the main stretch of the " invasion " front—between the Dutch-German border and the Loire— to Rommel's Army Group B, while this in turn came under Rundstedt. The staff of Army Group B was then enlarged, but it was not given a Quartermaster's department of its own—administration remained with Rundstedt's H.Q.

In the evening, propaganda marches by Italian troops took place in Bolzano. Later the tension eased off again. According to General Feuerstein, reconnaissance has reported the presence of strong troop concentrations in the Verona—Bolzano area—about 60,000 men.

3/8/43
Situation easing off. Even newspaper reports indicate that the Italians now want to co-operate. Since six o'clock S.S. L.A.H. [*S.S. Leibstandarte Adolf Hitler*] has been crossing the Brenner.

4/8/43
The *Generalquartiermeister*, General Wagner, arrived, and stayed to lunch. He told us that production will greatly increase as from the autumn and that this will see us through the trough. He said that ammunition expenditure in the east is astonishingly high (and so, we may hope, by the same token, are the Russian losses).

Consul-General Baron von Neurath[1] arrived in the afternoon. He claims to know of the Italian intention to get out of the war and of negotiations between Eisenhower and Badoglio. He also says that the British are intending to land at Trieste and Genoa. " In the negotiations with Eisenhower, the latter firmly rejected the Italian demand for the German troops to be allowed to withdraw, and insisted on the unconditional surrender of all German and Italian troops and all war material. Badoglio did not accept this, but new contacts have been established through the Navy, which has Anglophile tendencies. America and Britain are pursuing their negotiations separately, as each is trying to gain supremacy. In the event of either an Italian revolution or a surrender, landings can be expected at Trieste and Genoa, with the main weight at Trieste. . . ."

A document found in my father's diary notes that Colonel Christ, Chief of Staff to Field Marshal von Richthofen, reported on 5th August 1943. He stated that out of a total of 240 bombers 120 were fit to take the air. Eighty fighters were available in the Italian theatre of war.

He said that Field Marshal von Richthofen's opinion of the Italians was that they were not to be trusted, even though they had good intentions towards the Germans at the moment. They were, in fact, finished, as they had no material. However, something could perhaps be done with them if they became incorporated into German units.

My father stated that this was in complete accordance with his own ideas and that he did not know who had given him the dangerous reputation of being an Italian-hater.

[1]Son of the former Foreign Minister.

On the subject of the political attitude of the Italians, Colonel Christ said that they were glad to have got rid of Fascism, and took it amiss that the Fuehrer treated exclusively with Mussolini and not with the King.

6 Aug. 1943

DEAREST LU,

My Army Group is slowly getting moving. The main thing is that there's a good flow going across the Italian frontier, which should take away the enemy's taste for major operations.

The Italians seem to want to go along with us. Mussolini is not likely to come back. The party was very corrupt, it seems, and was swept away in a matter of hours. I hear that Mussolini failed in everything towards the end. It suits us in some ways, of course, to have only one big man running things in Europe. . . .

7/8/43

Yesterday's conference at Tarvisio between the O.K.W. and leading Italians was conducted by the Italians as a delaying action. Meanwhile, they have moved elements of the " Trentina " and " Julia " divisions and part of the Alpine division to various locations on the Brenner.

8/8/43

An S.S. scouting troop sent out to reconnoitre towards La Spezia was unable to get beyond Aulla because of road-blocks. The Italians obviously want to prevent German troops occupying the naval base at La Spezia.

9/8/43

10.45 hours, General von Vietinghoff reported back from the Fuehrer, having been given command of both Corps in southern Italy. The Fuehrer intends to evacuate southern Italy and " will not be happy until the divisions in southern Italy and Sicily are standing south of Rome." He does not anticipate a British landing in southern Italy (because of the malaria danger). He no longer trusts the Italian promises.

Co-operation between Kesselring and von Vietinghoff will probably not be easy, as Kesselring's idea is to push as many German troops down south as possible. The Fuehrer is still unwilling to allow me into Italy, as he imagines that this would be tantamount to a declaration of war, " since the Italians hold it against me that I am the only General who has led them to victory." The Fuehrer intends to leave

all discussion of the question of Fascism in Italy until a later date.
I have spoken to Jodl and asked again for heavy anti-tank guns to
be provided. The Italian Navy is showing more activity and has
attacked the harbour at Gibraltar.

11.05 hours. Oberfuehrer [S.S. Brigadier] Ostendorf, Chief of
Staff of II S.S. Panzer Korps (Commander—Gruppenfuehrer Hauser)
reported. I instructed him on the situation and drew his attention to
the fact that it was the Fuehrer's wish that we should take up our
position in Italy on the basis of good understanding. . . .

9 Aug. 1943

DEAREST LU,
I have to fly to the Fuehrer's H.Q. in a day or two, but only for
a short time. The situation with these unreliable Italians is extremely
unpleasant. To our faces they protest their truest loyalty to the
common cause, and yet they create all kinds of difficulties for us and
at the back of it all seem to be negotiating. Unfortunately, I'm not
allowed to go into Italy and talk to the blighters openly. Berndt has
written. He's having a lot of work with the evacuation of Hamburg
and Berlin. The casualties in Hamburg must have been very high.
This must simply make us harder. . . .

9/8/43
Roatta has sent General Feuerstein an impudent letter, in which
he complains of Feuerstein's attitude towards the Italians as being
one not customary between Allies. Another clever Italian reversal
of the facts. All friction would disappear immediately if only they
would send their divisions to the southern front. Then we would be
able to move our divisions south and would not have to worry about
our supply lines.

According to American reports, the Russians are inclining towards
peace negotiations. If this is true, it opens out undreamed-of
possibilities for us.

10/8/43
The Italians are still opposing the securing of the Alpine passes
by German troops. They feel themselves bound to distrust us and
won't acknowledge the importance to us of our supply routes. We
daren't take the risk of one day finding the passes blocked by Italian
or Anglo-American troops, and so can't give way. I'm certain that
a bomb on one of the passes would cure them of their obstinacy.

11/8/43
09.30 hours. Flew to Fuehrer's H.Q. in spite of early warning
[*preliminary warning of approaching air raid*]. Arrived just in time for

situation conference at midday. Goering, Doenitz, Student and Himmler were present.

In the East, heavy fighting near Kharkov, major Russian breakthrough west of the city. Near Leningrad a battle of attrition, drumfire lasting all day.

Concerning Italy, the Fuehrer and I are in agreement on our judgment of the situation. The Fuehrer seems to intend to send me in soon. Like me, he doesn't believe in the sincerity of the Italians. I said I considered that the time had come to make clear demands on Italy, in order to provide a basis for a common prosecution of the war. The Italians had done nothing yet towards defence and it was time that preparations were made. The Fuehrer said that all that the Italians were doing was trying to gain time, so as to get out of the war in the end. The probable purpose of the Churchill-Roosevelt meeting [*the Quebec Conference*], particularly in view of the fact that the Italians were obviously taking part, was to persuade the Italians to turn traitor, in which case the Allies would no doubt impose easier conditions.

The Fuehrer clearly intends to stick to the old plan—reinstatement of Fascism—because, as he says, it is the only guarantee of unconditional Italian loyalty. He sharply criticised the work of Mackensen, von Rintelen and Kesselring, on the grounds that they are still completely misreading the situation—especially Kesselring—and are putting their full confidence in the new Italian Government.

Goering said that the Fuehrer is the only person who can guarantee the Italian King's throne for him. The Fuehrer spoke against this and said that the new King doesn't want his throne secured by him (Hitler) and, in any case, Kings were finished. Added to that he was in British pay. . . .

Conference with Jodl before dinner. He had a plan worked out, based on a proposal of ours, whereby command would extend over northern Italy. My new proposal: command to extend over the whole of Italy; two armies (southern and northern) with Italians under command; Army Group H.Q. to be in the vicinity of Rome so as to exercise an influence over the Commando Supremo and the Government. Jodl agreed, after his objections had been overcome.

11/8/43

Evening situation conference. Von Ribbentrop present. He put Consul-General von Neurath at my disposal. I said I feared that the conference with the Italians would lead to nothing, as they were intending to betray us. My proposal—to fight delaying actions in Sicily and not to withdraw to Italy except under enemy pressure; also to construct four defence lines: (1) Cosenza-Taranto; (2) Salerno; (3) Cassino; (4) a rearward line in the Apennines—was approved. The Fuehrer raised the objection that the airfields in Calabria would have to be pushed farther forward because of the defence line running north of Cosenza. They would have to be put down in the Catanzaro neck. He, too, believes that the plan will never come to anything, because of Italian opposition. He instructed me to represent him at a conference to be arranged with the Italian command with the object of clarifying the Italian attitude. Jodl is also to take part.

During the evening conference, the Fuehrer kept studying air photographs of Ventotene,[1] the island where Mussolini is held prisoner. He kept Doenitz and Student back to discuss the liberation of Mussolini. I hope this job won't be put on my plate. I can see no good in it.

In accordance with Hitler's instructions, my father and Jodl went to Bologna on the 15th August in order to clarify the whole situation in a conference with General Roatta, the Chief of Staff of the Italian Army. The preliminaries to the conference did not augur well, for my father was informed that the Italians intended to use the occasion either to get rid of him by mixing poison with his food or to have him seized by Italian troops. He accordingly took a company of German grenadiers with him to occupy the conference building and take post alongside the Italian sentries.

According to the minutes of the conference, a dispute occurred at the outset between Jodl and Roatta concerning the surprise withdrawal of Italian occupation troops from France. When Jodl asked what had been Italy's purpose in making this move, Roatta replied: " Simply to gain forces for the defence of Italy. The situation is that only 24 Italian divisions out of a total of 62 are stationed in the motherland and of these 24, only 11 can be really said to be battle-worthy. Anyway, all these troops are for use against the common enemy, the British and Americans."

The Italian Chief of Staff having thus demonstrated the weakness of the Italian Army, my father and Jodl asked him to explain why there was such a large flow of Italian troops to the north. Roatta replied that only one Alpine division was involved. This division had come back from Russia badly cut about and had been moved south at the change

---

[1]After Mussolini's overthrow and arrest on the 25th July, he was taken to the Island of Ponza, which lies near Ventotene—in the Gulf of Gaeta, west of Naples. But after a few days he was moved for safer custody to the island of Maddalena off the north coast of Sardinia. Just as Hitler had planned a rescue attempt it was discovered that Mussolini had been flown back to Italy and placed in a heavily guarded ski-ing hotel on a high peak in the Abruzzi Mountains—a spot that was reached only by funicular. However, a small glider-borne detachment under Skorzeny's leadership audaciously landed on the peak during the night of the 8th September, bluffed the guard into surrendering, and carried off Mussolini in a little Storch plane.

of Government for political reasons. The division was now being returned
to its former garrison duties in the Alps. Following this division, a second
one was being moved, but solely with the object of securing the railways
against sabotage and British attacks. General Roatta continued in these
words: " The sole task of these two divisions is to secure the railway line.
In any case, the Commando Supremo, quite apart from the fact that it
has no unfriendly intentions whatever towards Germany, is not so stupid
as to suppose that these two divisions, in process of refitting, would be
capable of defending the Italian frontier against a German invasion."

General Roatta then went over to the counter-attack. " The Commando Supremo," he said, " cannot tolerate doubts being cast on the
integrity of directives and orders given by Italy. Every doubt of this kind
is a gross insult. The Commando Supremo does not wish any further
discussion of these details. Direct protection of the soil of Italy must be
left to Italians, just as the guard at the Royal Palace can only be undertaken by Italians. The Germans can take over air defence. The Italian
frontier defences will not be manned, except possibly where two or three
men may be found in certain of the defence works on maintenance duties.
In any case, most of these fortifications are unarmed."

When Jodl tried to put forward the Italian revolution as grounds for
the German intervention, Roatta broke in at once: " No revolution has
taken place in Italy, merely a change of Government. The old Government committed suicide. The circumstances attendant on this have now
been overcome and there are no grounds for distrust."

General Jodl, however, stated that Germany must insist on the
defence of her own supply lines being in the hands of German troops.

No agreement was reached on this point, as ultimately both parties
to the conference were in no doubt as to the real reasons for the occupation.

The discussion finally came round to the grouping of German and
Italian troops for the defence of Italy against the British and Americans.
Roatta put forward the view that the S.S. Leibstandarte should be sent
to Sardinia and that the remaining German troops should be employed,
as far as possible, in southern Italy. The Command would clearly have
to remain in the hands of the Commando Supremo. And that included
Field Marshal Rommel, who would also have to be subordinate to the
Commando Supremo. Of course my father and Jodl could not agree to
these proposals. Thus the conference ended in a complete failure. The
Axis was broken. My father summed up the result of the meeting in the
following laconic diary entry:

15/8/43
    The Italians are refusing to give way on certain of their demands,
as for example, exclusive Italian defence of the railways and Italian
command over all troops in Italy. They declare our demands to be
a vote of no confidence and feel themselves touched in their honour.

At this point it should be noted that it was on the 15th August that Italy made her first approach to the Allies on the subject of an armistice. A note sent by Roosevelt and Churchill to Stalin on the 16th August 1943 begins with the following sentences: " The British Ambassador in Madrid reported to us on August 15th that General Castellano, representing Badoglio, had arrived there bearing a letter of introduction from the British Minister at the Vatican. Castellano declared that he had authorisation from Badoglio to state Italy's willingness to surrender uncon-ditionally, if she could thereupon join the Allies. This seems to be a firm offer, the British Minister at the Vatican having confirmed that Badoglio had stated in writing that he had given authorisation to Castellano . . ."[1]

One outcome of the Bologna conference is described in my father's diary entry of 18th August 1943.

18/8/43
. . . A letter arrived from General Rintelen saying that Roatta has made a complaint about the alleged cordonning off of the building during the conference in Bologna. I am having him reply that it happened without my knowledge.

Hitler's plans for the post-war period were discernible to my father, if at all, in only the haziest of outlines. It seemed, indeed, as if Hitler's own ideas on the subject changed as the war went on.

After the defeat of France in 1940 my father had the impression that Hitler was aiming at a European solution. The words read on Hitler's behalf by Field Marshal Keitel to the French Armistice Commission in the Forest of Compiégne on the 21st June 1940 seemed to indicate that the National Socialist Government was intending to follow a reasonable policy. " After a heroic resistance, France has been defeated in one series of bloody battles, and has collapsed. Against so brave an enemy Germany does not intend to give the armistice conditions or armistice negotiations the character of a humiliation."

We knew from my father that he repeatedly proposed to Hitler during the African campaign that Germany should make France a partner in the war against Britain, and should conclude a peace treaty with her and guarantee her overseas possessions.

Hitler refused, although the French—according to my father's information—would not have looked unkindly on such a solution in 1941 or 1942. The Fuehrer gave as the reason for his view the difficulties which a German-French military alliance would cause with Spain and Italy, as both these countries were out to annex large areas of France's North African possessions. He did not underestimate the value of such an alliance, but it simply could not be done.

[1]Sherwood, *The White House Papers*, Vol. II, page 741.

My father gave me his personal views on the problem of Europe in a walk which we took shortly before his death.

He said that in his opinion—I quote his words approximately—Europe's tragedy was that Napoleon's policies had been incapable of maintaining the unification of European peoples which his campaigns had enforced. Had this not been the case, every European country would have been spared great suffering—one has only to think of the wars of 1866, 1871, 1914-18. The tragedy of Germany was that she had not known how to bring about the unification of Europe during this war. The world would then have had to deal with 300 million Europeans instead of 80 million Germans, and Germany's war aims would not have clashed with the vital interests of other peoples. My father said that he had put these ideas to Hitler as late as 1943, but had received a negative reply. It is probably this incident which is referred to in the following diary entry concerning a conference which took place at the Fuehrer's H.Q. on 4th September 1943, the day after the first Allied landing in southern Italy.

4/9/43

The Fuehrer gives the impression of quiet confidence. He intends to send me to the King of Italy very shortly. He agreed my ideas for the conduct of operations in Italy—envisaging defence on the coasts —in spite of Jodl's objections, which are not valid for modern warfare. The Fuehrer regards union of European states as premature.

Situation in the East has grown critical. Russia has forced a major break-through. . . . The British are not to be attacked in Calabria, but instead the area is to be evacuated.

20.30. Dinner with the Fuehrer. He advised me to be cautious in my dealings with the Italian King.

During the next week the Allied troops which had landed in Calabria thrust forward as far as the River Sangro. On the 9th September 1943, the day on which Eisenhower's landing craft ran on to the Salerno beaches, Italy's capitulation became known in Germany.

My father's diary covering this period was unfortunately lost in the confusion of the post-war years. But one can turn to other sources and to his private letters to learn something of what followed.

First to General Westphal, who in his book, *The German Army in the West*, tells of the visit of Admiral de Courten, Italian Minister of Marine, to the headquarters of C.-in-C. South on the 7th September 1943:

" Admiral de Courten explained that according to all the signs an Allied landing on the mainland was imminent, and that the Italian Navy did not want to remain idle in harbour while this vital struggle was in progress. They did not wish to be the victims of another ' Scapa Flow '.

Therefore, the Navy's heaviest units would shortly make a surprise sortie from La Spezia to steam around the western cape of Sicily and seek an engagement with the British Fleet, which would end either in victory or on the sea's bed. This move must remain secret until the very last minute, and the German Air Liaison party would therefore only be taken on board a short while before weighing anchor. The emotion with which de Courten made his statement, his tears and his invocation of the German blood that flowed in his veins from his mother's side, did not fail to make a deep impression. Neither to Kesselring nor myself did the thought occur that this was most probably all a ruse to lull German suspicions of the impending cruise of the Italian Fleet to internment in Malta."

On the 8th September 1943, General Westphal was invited to a conference in General Roatta's H.Q. in Monte Rotondo. In his book he gives his account of this conference:

" In the middle of the talk there came a German phone call from Rome: the conclusion of an armistice agreement had just been given out over the wireless. Roatta said that this was just a trick of the enemy. The conversation ended by his expressing the hope that in the future our mutual collaboration would be even closer than before. Our return through the turbulent and wildly happy crowds of Rome showed us that the Italian capitulation was a reality.

" On the following night," Westphal continues, " Roatta sent me a telephone message saying that at the time of our conversation he had had no knowledge of the Italian surrender. For the truth of this he pledged his word of honour."

Now to my father's letters:

9 Sept. 1943

DEAREST LU,

So Italian treachery is now a fact. Our judgment of them was right. My plans are going well so far. But this turn of events has made the whole situation very difficult. However, all we can do to save it will be done. . . .

10 Sept. 1943

The events in Italy have, of course, long been expected and the very situation has now arisen which we have done all we could to avoid. In the south, Italian troops are already fighting alongside the British against us. Up north, Italian troops are being disarmed for the present and sent as prisoners to Germany. What a shameful end for an army! . . .

Before operations were concluded, my father was unexpectedly taken ill with appendicitis, to which he referred in the following letter to me:

24 Sept. 1943

DEAR MANFRED,

Thank you for your letter of 13th September. I'm horrified to hear that you're still on holiday. I hope you won't forget all you've learnt. My appendix operation went off well. It all happened very suddenly. At eight o'clock in the evening I felt perfectly all right. An hour and a half later I had a raging pain on the right side of my stomach and was sick. Unfortunately, it did not ease up and I was in great pain all night until finally I got some sleep with the help of a doctor. I was operated on next morning.

Everything's gone well here so far. The traitors have been disarmed and most of them have already been carted off. I've put two stamps for you in the thick white envelope between the letters. . . .

When the German Wehrmacht had completed the disarming of the Italian Army, Hitler planned to give my father the high command in Italy and to transfer Kesselring to a command in Norway.

As my mother and I well remember, Hitler discussed with my father the possibility of launching a counter-offensive to retake southern Italy and possibly also Sicily. My father saw not the smallest chance of this, but was rather of the opinion that the defence of Italy with the available forces was a problem which he could not guarantee to solve. His particular fear was that the Allies would tie down frontally the mass of the German forces engaged in Central Italy and then make a surprise landing by Marines and paratroops in the Po valley, in order to cut off the German forces and thus collapse the entire southern front of the " Fortress of Europe ".

My father therefore proposed to give up southern and central Italy and make a final stand in the Apennine line south of the Po valley. This would shorten the coastal front and enable it to be more thickly held. Kesselring, on the other hand, was of the opinion that it was well within the bounds of possibility to maintain resistance south of Rome for quite some time. We can see how the situation appeared to Kesselring's staff, in General Westphal's account:

" . . . Rommel's opinion was likewise asked for. He, however, considered that the amphibious capabilities of the enemy were such that a line too far to the south would be in great danger and that there was a risk that the whole army group might be trapped by a landing higher up the coast. He would not wish to answer for this risk, although he admitted that the line south of Rome could be held by half the number of troops which would be necessary in the Apennines. Hitler vacillated for a long time. . . . In the middle of November he ordered Rommel to take over the command of Kesselring's forces as well as his own. Whilst the cable was still being transmitted, he changed his mind and ordered Field Marshal

Kesselring to take over the supreme command of the Italian war theatre from November 21, 1943."

The last letter which my father wrote from Italy deals with these events.

26 Oct. 1943

DEAREST LU,

The job was *not* confirmed. By all accounts the Fuehrer changed his mind after all. In any case, he didn't sign the order promulgating the appointment. Of course I know no more than that. Maybe I aroused no great hopes that the position would be held, maybe my delay in taking over command was the cause. There may again, of course, be entirely different reasons. So, for the moment, Kesselring remains. Perhaps I'll be posted away. Anyway, I'll take it as it comes.

The situation in the East is very critical. It looks as though we shall have to give up the great Dnieper bend under very difficult conditions. In that case we'll probably not be able to hold the Crimea either. There, too, it seems, the enemy superiority is just too great. I wonder where we'll go from there.

I received Marshal Graziani to-day. He's an impressive personality, quite different from all the other Italian officers I've known. Of course he has no sort of authority at the moment. Even the Italian police can exert no authority to-day. We have to help them. The Japanese Ambassador was also here. These people seem to have quite a regard for me. . . .

On my trip to the Adriatic coast yesterday, I visited the small state of San Marino, which is neutral. After a quick look round the town, and buying a number of stamps, I was just about to leave when a minister came up to me on behalf of the Regent and said that the Regent would be glad of the pleasure of meeting me. So back we went to the castle again. . . .

. . . Of course the state wanted an assurance that its neutrality would be respected by the German Reich. Well, we'll see. San Marino has not been involved in a war since 1600. Napoleon wanted to enlarge it and give it a port and some guns. But the Regents refused, they preferred to stay small. One can't become a national of San Marino. . . .

On the 21st November 1943, my father stepped into his aeroplane on the Villafranca airfield to leave Italy for good. He flew off to a new task. He was returning to the undulating, close-hedged hills of Normandy, through which his road to fame had passed in 1940 and which were to be the scene of his last military defeat.

Part Five

INVASION

CHAPTER XXI

INVASION, 1944

By Lieut.-General Fritz Bayerlein

My FIRST meeting with Field Marshal Rommel after the African campaign was at the Fuehrer's Headquarters in East Prussia in July 1943. He was living in the half-timbered house of the former Army C.-in-C. We had both previously attended one of the Fuehrer's conferences. It was a few days after the collapse of the Byelgorod—Kursk offensive [*Hitler's last bid for victory on the Eastern front—L. H.*],[1] in which our attacking forces had become bogged down in the Russian anti-tank screens and defences, and the bulk of our latest tanks had been lost. And with that had gone all hope of a new summer offensive in Russia.

After the conference Rommel and I sat in his study and talked about the general military situation. He had, in the interim, adjusted himself to the completely changed strategic situation and was full of ideas for the future conduct of the war. As this conversation is the only evidence of Rommel's views on the war situation at this period, I will quote it to the best of my memory.

" You know, Bayerlein," he said, " we have lost the initiative, of that there is no doubt. We have just learnt in Russia for the first time that dash and over-optimism are not enough. We must have a completely new approach. There can be no question of taking the offensive for the next few years, either in the West or the East, and so we must try to make the most of the advantages which normally accrue to the defence. The main defence against the tank is the anti-tank gun; in the air we must build fighters and still more fighters and give up all idea for the present of doing any bombing ourselves. I no longer see things quite as black as I did in Africa, but total victory is now, of course, hardly a possibility."

I asked him how he imagined the defence would be carried out in practice.

" We must fight on interior lines," he replied. " In the East we must

---

[1]Footnotes and notes inserted in the text throughout this chapter are by General Bayerlein, unless followed by the initials *L. H.*

withdraw as soon as possible to a suitable, prepared line. But our main effort must be directed towards beating off any attempt of the Western Allies to create a second front, and that is where we must concentrate our defence. If we can once make their efforts fail, then things will be brighter for us. We'll soon be producing an enormous amount of war material. A few days ago the Fuehrer told me that by the beginning of 1944 we can expect to have an output of 7,000 aircraft and 2,000 tanks a month. If we can only keep the Americans and British off for two more years, to enable us to build up centres of gravity in the East again, then our time will come; we'll be able to start drawing blood from the Russians once more, until they allow the initiative to pass more and more back to us. Then we'll be able to get a tolerable peace."

Rommel now went on to talk about the tactics of defence. He said (I am again quoting from memory):

" You remember, Bayerlein, how difficult we found it to attack the British anti-tank screens in Africa. It needed first-class, highly-trained troops to achieve anything at all against them. Now I've made a careful study of our experiences in Russia. The Russian is stubborn and inflexible. He will never be able to develop the well-thought-out, guileful method with which the Englishman fights his battles. The Russian attacks head on, with enormous expenditure of material, and tries to smash his way through by sheer weight of numbers.

" If we can give the German infantry divisions first fifty, then a hundred, then two hundred 75-mm. anti-tank guns each and install them in carefully-prepared positions, covered by large minefields, we shall be able to halt the Russians. The anti-tank guns can be quite simple; all that is necessary is that they should be able to penetrate any Russian tank up to a reasonable range and at the same time be usable as an infantry gun.

" There is not the slightest hope of our keeping pace with the enemy in the production of tanks, but we certainly can in anti-tank guns, if the enemy is having to produce tanks for his attack. For every one tank that is made, it's possible to turn out perhaps ten anti-tank guns.

" Now, let us suppose that the Russians attack in a heavily-mined sector where our anti-tank guns are forming a screen, say six miles deep, then—for all their mass of material—they are bound to bog down in the first few days and, from then on, they'll have to gnaw their way through slowly. Meanwhile we shall be installing more anti-tank guns behind our screen. If the enemy makes three miles' progress a day, we'll build six miles, depth of anti-tank screen and let him run himself to a standstill. We'll be fighting in the cover of our positions, he'll be attacking in the open. We'll lose anti-tank guns and he'll lose tanks. To move the guns we can use Russian horses or any other makeshift we can lay our hands on. That's what the Russians do and we must adopt their methods. Once it becomes clear to the troops that they can hold their ground, morale will go up again. . . . Tanks, precision anti-tank guns and all kinds of other things will have to be cut down. Our last chance in the East lies in equipping the army thoroughly for an unyielding defence.[1]

" But the West is the place that matters. If we once manage to throw the British and Americans back into the sea, it will be a long time before they return. . . ."

This conversation came back to my mind when I heard that Field Marshal Rommel had been given the task of organising the defence against invasion in France. In France also—and in the East—he believed that victory could no longer be gained by mobile warfare—not merely because of the British and American air superiority, but also because the German armaments industry was no longer capable of keeping pace with the western Allies in the production of tanks, guns, anti-tank guns and vehicles. The solution he arrived at is described in a report which he made to Hitler, dated 31st December 1943, on his tour of inspection of the Atlantic coast. He began by discussing the probable location of the Allied landing, and it is interesting to see that his first opinion on this point was different from that which he advanced later.

" The focus of the enemy landing operation," he wrote, " will probably be directed against Fifteenth Army's sector (the Pas de Calais), largely because it is from this sector that much of our long-range attack on England and central London will be launched. With difficult sea conditions, it is likely that the enemy's main concern will be to get the quickest possible possession of a port or ports capable of handling large ships. Furthermore, he will probably endeavour to capture the area from which our long-range attack is coming as quickly as possible.

" . . . It is most likely that the enemy will make his main effort against the sector between Boulogne and the Somme estuary and on either side of Calais, where he would have the best support from his long-range artillery, the shortest sea-route for the assault and for bringing up supplies, and the most favourable conditions for the use of his air arm. As for his airborne forces, we can expect him to use the bulk of them to open up our coastal front from the rear and take quick possession of the area from which our long-range missiles will be coming.

" . . . The timing of the enemy attack is uncertain, but he will make every effort to launch the operation before the start of our long-range

---

[1]These arguments were also formulated in a diary entry dated 6th August 1943 which reads: " The necessity for reorganising infantry companies so as to provide a greater establishment of anti-tank weapons at company level is becoming increasingly apparent. Quadruple A.A. guns should also be supplied to infantry companies, if possible on self-propelled mountings. Fire-power must be increased at the expense of the rifleman."

There is no doubt that the German successes at the beginning of the war were only made possible by the fact that the French, British and Russian infantry were virtually helpless in the face of a massed tank attack, due to their weakness in anti-tank weapons. However, it came to be shown on all fronts towards the end of the war that the fundamental superiority which previous wars had shown, of a well dug-in defence, equipped with modern weapons, still held good.

attack on England. If, due to bad weather or unfavourable sea conditions, he fails in this, he will launch his attack either at the beginning or shortly after the beginning of our long-range campaign. For the longer our attack on England goes on, the more will its effect be felt, with inevitable damage to the morale of the British and American troops. Thus, by launching our long-range attack at the beginning of a period of weather unfavourable for a landing, we have the chance of creating particularly adverse conditions for the enemy's attack.[1]

". . . The landing will probably be preceded by very heavy attacks from the air and be made under cover of a smoke-screen and of intense fire from numerous warships, with simultaneous heavy-bomber attacks. In addition to the seaborne landing, airborne troops will probably be dropped close behind the coastal defences in the main attack sectors, in order to break up the defences from the rear and create a major bridge-head in the shortest possible time.

" On the coast, our defence line, thin as it is at present, will suffer severely from the enemy bombing and artillery bombardment and it seems very doubtful whether, after this battering, it will be capable of beating off the enemy, whose forces will be approaching over a wide front, in hundreds of armoured assault craft and landing-craft and under cover of darkness or fog. But if the landing is not beaten off, our thinly held and shallow front will soon be pierced and contact will be established with the airborne troops behind.

" We can hardly expect a counter-attack by the few reserves we have behind the coast at the moment, with no self-propelled guns and an inadequate quantity of all forms of anti-tank weapons, to succeed in destroying the powerful force which the enemy will land. We know from experience that the British soldier is quick to consolidate his gains and then holds on tenaciously with excellent support from his superior air arm and naval guns, the observers for which direct the fire from the front line.

" With the coastline held as thinly as it is at present, the enemy will probably succeed in creating bridgeheads at several different points and in achieving a major penetration of our coastal defences. Once this has happened it will only be by the rapid intervention of our operational reserves that he will be thrown back into the sea. This requires that these forces should be held very close behind the coast defences.

" If, on the other hand, our principal reserves have to be brought

[1]General Speidel, in his book, *We Defended Normandy*, tells us that Rommel was constantly inquiring into the latest state of development of the new weapons. Both Frau Rommel and her son remember him telling them, after the invasion, that he had recommended using the V-weapons against the invasion ports on the south coast of England before the Allied landing, in order to bring about a postponement of the Allied operation. Hitler, however, had refused, with the statement that the VI could not be used against a target smaller than London, and that, in any case, he did not want to start using the V-weapons until he could produce them in large enough quantities.

up from well back inland, the move will not only require a great deal of time—time which the enemy will probably use to reinforce himself at his point of penetration and either organise his forces for defence or press the attack farther inland—but will also be under constant danger from the air. Bearing in mind the numerical and material superiority of the enemy striking forces, their high state of training and tremendous air superiority, victory in a major battle on the continent seems to me a matter of grave doubt. British and American superiority in the air alone has again and again been so effective that all movement of major formations has been rendered completely impossible, both at the front and behind it, by day and by night, and our own air force has only on very rare occasions been able to make any appearance in support of our operations."

The conclusions which Rommel drew from these arguments are highly instructive. He had to ensure, with the resources available to him, that his ill-equipped and badly-armed infantry divisions were capable of inflicting a defeat upon the British, with all their modern armament. He continues:

". . . I therefore consider that an attempt must be made, using every possible expedient, to beat off the enemy landing on the coast and to fight the battle in the more or less strongly fortified coastal strip. This will require the construction of a fortified and mined zone extending from the coast some five or six miles inland and defended both to the sea and to the land. The existing minefields, fenced in with wire, present little or no obstacle and wide lanes would be cleared through them in a very short while. The proposed mined zone would consist of numerous minefields, each several kilometres wide and deep, constructed according to a planned layout, between the coast and a line six miles inland. I fully realise the enormous number of mines which such a scheme would require. For the present, however, it would suffice if the fields were mined at the coastal and inland fronts only, with the remainder laid out as dummies.

" Certain strips within this mined zone, mainly parallel to the coast and along the roads leading up to it, would have to be kept clear for our counter-attack. We have learnt in our engagements with the British that large minefields with isolated strong points dispersed within them (field positions) are extremely difficult to take. Moreover, mined zones of this kind lend themselves particularly well to garrisoning by auxiliary troops or reserve formations.

" Hence the divisions employed on the coast will have two tasks, to defend the coast against the enemy sea landing forces, and to hold the land front five or six miles inland against airborne troops. If it happened that the enemy dropped his airborne troops within the mined zone, they would not be too difficult to destroy there.

" One thing which is necessary, even if it is only to reduce the effectiveness of the enemy bomber attacks and sea bombardment, is to increase the depth of the defended area. The commander of a coast-defence division will need to have his command post in the middle of his mined zone, as he will, in a sense, be fortress commandant of the zone.

"In the event of one of these zones escaping attack, the division holding it could easily be pulled out and be replaced, circumstances permitting, by auxiliary or holding units. Even when only thinly held, these mined zones still possess great defensive strength.

". . . The number of anti-tank weapons and rapid-fire machine-guns in the forward sector of the main coastal battle area is far too small. Since everything must be directed towards destroying the enemy landing force while it is still on the water, or at the latest during the landing itself, the defensive strength in the forward part of the divisions' main battle areas must be made much greater than at present. For defence is a comparatively simple matter so long as the enemy assault boats and landing-craft are on the water. Once they have beached and disembarked their troops and weapons, their fighting power multiplies many times over.

"It will therefore be necessary, in the worst-threatened sectors, to have heavy anti-tank guns, self-propelled guns and anti-aircraft combat troops standing ready in the forward part of the defence zone, whence they can be rushed up to the coast to engage the enemy while he is still disembarking.

". . . I regard it as urgently necessary to have two reserve divisions held a short distance to the east of the coastal defences, along the worst-threatened stretch of coast between Boulogne and the mouth of the Somme, so that they can intervene in support of the coast-defence divisions, as soon as possible after the main centre of the enemy attack has been identified, and thus prevent the creation of any enemy bridgehead. It will be less a question of a formation action than of the piecemeal destruction of the disembarking or disembarked enemy by small combat groups. The battle for the coast will probably be over in a few hours and, if experience is any judge, the rapid intervention of forces coming up from the rear will be decisive. One condition for the success of this counter-attack by the reserves will be for all available Luftwaffe tactical air forces to support the attack and, above all, fight off the enemy bomber formations."

The methods which Rommel used to exploit the resources at his disposal were characteristic of his gift for improvisation and grasp of technicalities. The new defence plan showed once again his complete independence of orthodox doctrine and systems. He was the last to "become rigidly fixed in the admiration of his own ideas". The following is a brief description of the main technical details of his scheme, based on documents which he himself issued.

Minefields

"In the two-year campaign in Africa," wrote Rommel in a memorandum, "I had the opportunity of testing the importance of mining in all the various forms of warfare, and became particularly familiar with the mass use of mines by the enemy. Our resources, in comparison, were unfortunately very small. After the happy outcome of the heavy fighting in the Marmarica and Cyrenaica in the winter of 1941-42, the British made the maximum possible use of mines in constructing their new line, which extended from Ain el Gazala 50 miles south into the desert. In this line and in the foreground of Tobruk they laid over a million mines in two months and constructed inter-connecting minefields, of a depth, in places, of several thousand yards.

". . . In the fighting which followed, round Bir Hacheim, for the Ain el Gazala line, for the foreground of Tobruk and finally for Tobruk itself, we again and again found ourselves in the position of having to overcome an enemy who had established himself with large numbers of anti-tank guns, and in some places even tanks, deep in the mined zone. This fighting was of extreme severity, although, thanks to the courage of our troops and the tenacity and flexibility of officers of all ranks, it was in fact brought to a successful conclusion. It certainly taught me the value of the British large-scale mining. Had there been German troops holding those British positions, they could hardly have been taken."

Thus, as a result of his experience in Africa, Rommel believed that large minefields would provide conditions in which the ill-equipped German infantry divisions[1] would be able to take on the U.S. and British forces.

The following extract from a letter written by General Meise, the Engineer Commander of Army Group B, on 17th March 1944, shows the scale of Rommel's mine-laying plans.

". . . For the first stage, that is a thousand-yard strip along the coast and a similar strip along the land front, 10 mines a yard will be required, making a total for the whole of France of 20,000,000 mines. For the remainder of the zone (8,000 yards), France will require in all some 200,000,000 mines. . . ."

Although Rommel made tremendous efforts to get the mining completed, they came too late to be fully effective. It is, however, possible that if Hitler had charged Rommel with organising the defence of the Atlantic and Channel coasts in the summer of 1943, the invasion battle would have gone in Germany's favour. Rommel organised the manufacture of mines in France, where sufficient captured explosive was lying unused to make 20,000,000 anti-personnel mines. The following note from the War Diary of Army Group B shows what he achieved:

" Up to 20th May 1944, 4,193,167 mines were laid on the channel

---

[1] At the end of January, for example, the Seventh Army possessed over 32 different weapons with 252 different types of ammunition, of which 47 types were no longer produced. The entire army had only 170 75-mm. anti-tank guns and 68 88-mm. anti-tank/anti-aircraft guns. (War Diary, Army Group B.)

coast, 2,672,000 of them on Rommel's initiative, and most of them after the end of March. In the same short period, also at Rommel's initiative, 1,852,820 mines were improvised in the early stages of production."

How Rommel imagined the battle in these minefields is shown in the following extract from a paper which he wrote:

"Between and around the stationary tanks, strong point groups, strong points and resistance nests, minefields of great depth will be laid. These minefields will contain mines of all kinds and are likely to be highly effective. If the enemy should ever set foot on land, an attack through the minefields against the defence works sited within them will present him with a task of immense difficulty. He will have to fight his way through the zone of death in the defensive fire of the whole of our artillery. And not only on the coast, for numerous and extensive minefields will also exist round our positions in the rear areas. Any airborne troops who attempt to penetrate to the coast from the rear will make the acquaintance of this mined zone."

Foreshore Obstacles[1]

Concerning the purpose of these obstacles, Rommel wrote:

". . . Since the end of January, the construction of foreshore obstacles has been in progress along the whole of the Atlantic coast and, at the more important points, is now steadily approaching completion. It will be asked why the work was not started earlier, for that would have enabled a far stronger barrier to be built. The answer is that this form of obstacle was not thought of earlier. There is even an advantage in having begun the work so late, for the enemy will have to adapt himself at the last moment to this new form of defence, which is certain to take a heavy toll of his landing-craft. It is, in fact, possible that these new obstacles have contributed towards the long postponement of the enemy offensive. . . .

"The object of these new underwater obstructions is not only to halt the enemy's approach to the beaches—which will be made in hundreds of landing boats and ships, in amphibious vehicles and in waterproofed and underwater tanks, all under cover of darkness or artificial fog—but also to destroy his landing equipment and troops. They consist of a wide

---

[1]Obstacles laid under the surface of the water, to act as " artificial reefs " to stop or destroy shore-bound ships. They consisted in their essentials of:
  (1) Stakes driven into the sea bottom, many carrying an anti-tank mine at the tip.
  (2) Concrete tetrahedrons, also equipped at the apex with either steel blades or anti-tank mines.
  (3) Various other devices such as captured anti-tank obstacles.
  (4) Rommel's proposed " nutcracker mine." This consisted of a stake let into a concrete housing containing a heavy shell. A landing-craft striking the stake would, by lever action, cause the other end to press against the fuse and detonate the shell.
  (5) Beach-lighting was also provided to illuminate the approaching enemy.

variety of obstacles armed by mines or shells. Every effort will be made
to have them installed in depth and make them effective at all states
of the tide. Recent Anglo-American invasion exercises have been timed
for the landing to be made two hours after low tide, after artillery and
bombers have previously attempted to destroy dummy foreshore obstacles.
We all know how difficult it is to destroy barbed wire obstructions by
artillery fire. How much more difficult then, will it be to do enough
damage to a wide and deep belt of such stoutly constructed obstacles as
to make a trouble-free landing possible across them? Immense quantities
of ammunition and bombs will be necessary and thus a long period of
preparation. And if the enemy, contrary to expectations, does succeed
in destroying the under-water obstacles, we will know where he is coming
and be able to prepare our defence and bring up reserves.

" The more time the enemy gives us, the stronger will be the obstacles,
and we may sooner or later expect all battalions to be in a position to
report that their barriers are dense, deep and armed, i.e. supplied with
thousands of mines and shells. . . ."

According to General Meise, four belts of under-water obstacles were
to be provided. An extract from a letter dated 17th May 1944 described
them as:

1. A belt in six feet of water at mean high tide.
2. A belt in six feet of water at half-tide of a twelve-foot tide.
3. A belt in six feet of water at low tide.
4. A belt in twelve feet of water at low tide.

When invasion day came, the first two belts had been completed in
most sectors, particularly in Normandy, but too little time had been
available to install the lower belts, although Rommel had already made
extensive preparations towards their construction.

The size of Rommel's achievement can be assessed from the following
note from the War Diary of Army Group B:

" Up to the 13th May 1944, a total of 517,000 foreshore obstacles
were constructed along the Channel front, 31,000 of which were fitted
with mines."

Air-Landing Obstacles

Here, too, Rommel explains the purpose of the scheme and the
method of execution.

" I come now to security against airborne troops. It is possible that
the enemy will commit everything he has, at the outset of his attack, in
order to gain a quick victory and secure a wide foothold at some point
along the coast. The enemy powers dispose of a large number of very
powerful and highly-trained airborne formations. We must therefore be
prepared for these forces to be used against the coastal defence zones,
either in a sudden surprise attack or after a short but intense aerial

bombardment. Parachute troops could be dropped in very large numbers, by moonlight or at dawn or dusk, either along the coast or a few miles inland. Or airborne troops at divisional strength with load-carrying gliders could land behind our coastal front and attempt to break through the defences from the rear. It is also possible that the enemy might put down his airborne formations far back in the hinterland for use in an operational role, or he might scatter them in small combat groups all over France in order to bring about a quick mobilisation of the *Armée Secrète* [*the Maquis*]. But so long as we go on holding the coast, we are bound to be able to wipe out, sooner or later, either operationally employed airborne troops or formations dropped in groups deep in the hinterland.

". . . Hence the important thing is to ensure that all territory which might conceivably be used for landing airborne troops is treated in such a manner that enemy aircraft and gliders will break up while landing, and the enemy as a result suffer severe losses in men and material —in addition to those caused by the quick opening of our defensive fire. . . . All divisions will take the necessary steps, as early as possible, to have the area between the land and sea fronts thoroughly staked out."

The obstacles which Rommel planned consisted of stakes approximately 10 feet high driven into the ground at 100 feet spacing. He realised, of course, that the stakes alone would present no lethal obstacle to troops landing with gliders and consequently gave orders for a high proportion of them to be fitted with captured shells at the top and for them all to be inter-connected by wire. The shells were to be so arranged that they would be detonated by a pull on the wire. Experiment showed that a glider landing in territory treated in this manner could not fail to suffer heavy losses, and would, in fact, have little hope of success. Only a few days before the invasion, Rommel succeeded in obtaining the release of a million captured shells for arming these obstacles, but it was too late—there was no time left to install them.

ROMMEL'S LETTERS FROM THE WEST

December 1943—June 1944

While we have Rommel's views on defence against the invasion in considerable detail, there exists, unfortunately, no connected account by him covering this period, from which we might have learned his more personal concerns. The only remaining authentic source is to be found in the letters which he wrote to his wife and son during these months, the most interesting passages from which are given in the following annotated extracts:

During Rommel's tour of inspection along the Danish coast

8 Dec. 1943

DEAREST LU,

We're off again to-day up to the northernmost point. The round trip will be over in a couple of days and then the paper work will begin. Hard fighting still in the east and south. I need not tell you with what feelings I look on from a distance.

I hear that the call-up is going to be extended to the 14-year-olds. The lads will be sent to labour service or defence according to their size and physique.

11 Dec. 1943

We're now back from the capital [*Copenhagen*]. A few days' written work and then the job will continue.

You can still buy everything you want here in Denmark. Of course the Danes will only sell to their own compatriots. I've bought a few things for Christmas, so far as the money went. [*Rommel, in common with all German officers, was only allowed a certain amount of Danish money.*]

After Arrival in France

15 Dec. 1943

. . . Arrived safely yesterday. I've found myself a lovely billet in a chateau [*at Fontainebleau*] which once belonged to Madame de Pompadour. But I won't be here long. I'm already off on a trip to-morrow—as to-day's news announced. It seems that they can't tell the British and Americans soon enough that I'm here.

I lunched with R. [*Rundstedt*] to-day. He seems very pleased and I think it's all going well, but I must first get a picture of the situation and see how things are.

The old chateau is a lovely place. The French built very generously and spaciously for their upper classes two centuries ago. We're absolutely provincial in comparison.

25 Dec. 1943

It was grand that the telephone call worked so well last night and that I now know that things are all right with you both. The big news was Manfred's call-up on the 6th January. He is sure to be pleased, but for us, and above all, for you, it's painful to see the youngster leave home, and it will take us a long time to get used to the idea.

I wish you both a happy Christmas. Enjoy the time you still have together. . . . I spent yesterday evening with the officers of my staff and afterwards with the men, though it's difficult to be really cheerful at the moment.

19 Jan. 1944

Returned to-day from my long trip. I saw a lot and was very satisfied with the progress that has been made. I think for certain that we'll win the defensive battle in the West, provided only that a little more time remains for preparation. Guenther's going off to-morrow with a suit-case. He's to bring back my brown civilian suit and lightweight coat with hat, etc. I want to be able to go out without a Marshal's baton for once. . . .

. . . Situation in the East: apparently stabilised.

. . . In the South: severe fighting and more heavy attacks to be met.

. . . In the West: I believe we'll be able to beat off the assault.

21 Jan. 1944

I've been a dog owner since yesterday, when the O.T.[1] presented me with two dachshunds. One of them (a dog) is a year old, long haired with a proper moustache. The other is only three months. The younger one was very affectionate immediately, but the older one is not so forthcoming. The two of them are now lying beneath my writing-desk. The older one barks whenever anyone comes. They both howl occasionally at night. Probably they're homesick for their previous owner.

26 Jan. 1944

The job's being very frustrating. Time and again one comes up against bureaucratic and ossified individuals who resist everything new and progressive. But we'll manage it all the same. My two hounds had to be separated, after the older one had well nigh killed the younger with affection.

29 Jan. 1944

The situation in the East is still very tense and serious, although we are shooting up masses of enemy tanks, 860 in the last three days, which they'll have a job to replace.

The situation in Italy has developed as I always feared it would. The open, unprotected flanks were a great danger. However, I feel certain that we'll manage to restore the situation.

I'm having a new coat made in Paris. My old one is too tight and too thin. . . .

[1]Organisation Todt. This organisation, named after Franz Todt, the builder of Germany's *Autobahnen*, was responsible for the construction of bridges, roads, pill-boxes, railways, etc., in the front area.

31 Jan. 1944

DEAR MANFRED,

I was particularly pleased with your first letter as Luftwaffe auxiliary, because you have settled in so well to your new conditions. It is not easy for an " only child " to leave home. Perhaps you'll be getting a few days' leave in February and then you must give us a full report. There's still an endless amount of work here before I'll be able to say that we're properly prepared for battle. People get lazy and self-satisfied when things are quiet. But the contrast between quiet times and battle will be tough and I feel it essential to prepare for hard times here.

I'm out on the move a lot and raising plenty of dust wherever I go.

All the best to you and warmest greetings,

YOUR FATHER

31 March 1944

DEAREST LU,

No news of importance. Stalin seems to have made all manner of demands to his Allies, such as supplying him with a fleet of strength equivalent to the former Italian Mediterranean Fleet (to come out of the present naval resources of America and Britain), provision of three Mediterranean ports (Taranto, one in Palestine and one in North Africa), a third of the Arabian oil and a definite date for the second front in western Europe. If the conditions are not fulfilled, Stalin will regard himself as no longer bound by his previous agreements with the Allies. It would be fine if it were true. I saw plenty to cheer me here yesterday. Although we've still a lot of weaknesses, we're looking forward full of confidence to what's coming.

27 April 1944

It looks as though the British and Americans are going to do us the favour of keeping away for a bit. This will be of immense value for our coastal defences, for we are now growing stronger every day—at least on the ground, though the same is not true for the air. But even that will change to our advantage again some time.

My little dog is touchingly affectionate and loves sweet things. He sleeps in my room now, underneath my luggage stand. He's going to be inoculated soon against distemper. Went riding again yesterday, but I'm feeling my joints pretty badly to-day.

Guderian is due here this afternoon. The affair with Geyr von Schweppenburg[1]—with whom I recently had to be very rough

[1]This was a conflict of views as to the disposition of the Panzer divisions, and is related on page 466, *et seq.*—L. H.

because he would not give way to my plans—has all been cleared up now by orders from above and decided as I wanted it.

8 May 1944

The O.T. have now sent me a big, brown, smooth-haired hunting dog. It's young, good at following and affectionate, and has soon settled down to its new life. Elbo [*the younger of the dachshunds— Rommel had sent the elder home to his wife but it had been run over by a car*] looked aggrieved at first, but he now has lots of fun with his play-fellow. It was at feeding time that Elbo suffered badly at first. Anyway, the two of them got me up the hill four times yesterday. I shall either send Elbo to you shortly or get you to look out for a dog for yourself. It's strange what a distraction these creatures can be, and how they can take your mind off your troubles.

15 May 1944

The middle of May already and still nothing doing, although a pincer attack seems to have started in Italy, which may well be the prelude for the great events of the spring or summer. I've been away for a couple of days, talking to the officers and men. It's quite amazing what has been achieved in the last few weeks. I'm convinced that the enemy will have a rough time of it when he attacks, and ultimately achieve no success.

19 May 1944

I telephoned to the Fuehrer for the first time a couple of days ago. He was in the best of humours and did not spare his praise of the work we've done in the West. I now hope to get on a little faster than we have been doing.

The weather is still cold and it's raining at last. The British will have to be patient for a bit. I'm waiting to see whether I shall be able to get away for a couple of days in June. It's out of the question at the moment. Unfortunately, things have not gone very well in Italy. The enemy's tremendous superiority in artillery, and even more in the air, has broken our front open.

21 May 1944

Things were very lively in the air again yesterday. We ourselves were left alone. It's quieter to-day so far. The enemy successes in Italy are very unfortunate. Strength on the ground was not un-favourable to us. It's simply that their superiority in the air and in ammunition is overwhelming, the same as it was in Africa. I hope things will go better here in the West. There's been no real air preparation so far. The damage caused some days ago has long since been put right. . . .

. . . Rundstedt paid us a visit here yesterday. In the afternoon I
had a talk with a captured British officer who was quite reasonable.

HIGH COMMAND PREPARATIONS FOR THE INVASION

In an address delivered on the 20th March 1944 to the Commanders-
in-Chief of the three armed services in the West, Hitler gave his views
on the role of the Western theatre of war. In the course of this address
he said:
  ". . . It is evident that an Anglo-American landing in the West will
and must come. How and where it will come no one knows. Equally,
no kind of speculation on the subject is possible. Whatever concentrations
of shipping may exist, they cannot and must not be taken as any evidence,
or any indication, that the choice has fallen on any one sector of the long
Western front from Norway to the Bay of Biscay, or on the Mediterranean
—either the south coast of France, the Italian coast or the Balkans. Such
concentrations can be moved or transferred, at any time, under cover of
bad visibility, and will obviously serve as feints. At no place along our
long front is a landing impossible, except perhaps where the coast is
broken by cliffs. The most suitable and hence the most threatened areas
are the two west coast peninsulas, Cherbourg and Brest, which are very
tempting and offer the best possibilities for the formation of a bridgehead,
which would then be enlarged systematically by the mass use of air
forces and heavy weapons of all kinds.
  ". . . By far the most important thing for the enemy will be to gain a
port for landings on the largest possible scale. This alone gives a wholly
special importance to the west coast ports and orders have therefore
been issued designating them 'Fortresses', in which the Commandant
alone will be responsible for the training and operations of all three
services. He has the task of doing everything possible to make the
fortress impregnable. He is personally responsible for ensuring that the
fortress is held to the last round of ammunition, the last tin of rations,
until every last possibility of defence has been exhausted.
  ". . . The enemy's entire landing operation must under no circumstances be allowed to last longer than a matter of hours or, at the most,
days, with the Dieppe attempt as a model. Once the landing has been
defeated it will under no circumstances be repeated by the enemy. Quite
apart from the heavy casualties he would suffer, months would be needed
to prepare for a renewed attempt. Nor is this the only factor which would
deter the Anglo-Americans from trying again. There would also be the
crushing blow to their morale which a miscarried invasion would give.
It would, for one thing, prevent the re-election of Roosevelt in America
and, with luck, he would finish up somewhere in jail. In England, too,
war-weariness would assert itself even more greatly than hitherto and

Churchill, in view of his age and his illness, and with his influence now on the wane, would no longer be in a position to carry through a new landing operation. We could counter the numerical strength of the enemy—about 50 to 60 divisions—within a very short time, by forces of equal strength. The destruction of the enemy's landing attempt means more than a purely local decision on the Western front. It is the sole decisive factor in the whole conduct of the war and hence in its final result.

" The 45 divisions which we now have in Europe, excluding the Eastern front, are needed in the East, and will and must be transferred there so as to effect a fundamental change in that situation as soon as the decision in the West has been reached. Thus, on every single man fighting on the Western front, as representing the decisive front of the war, depends the outcome of the war and with it the fate of the Reich. This realisation of the decisive importance of each individual's effort must at all costs become part and parcel of the thought process of every officer and man."

Not the least significant point emerging from this address of Hitler's, which was recorded in shorthand, is the lack of decision which prevailed in the Fuehrer's H.Q. Though there were several points where a landing was particularly likely, they refused at that stage to be persuaded by these signs to create concentrations at them. Hitler was actually undecided between two schools of thought, that represented by Field Marshal von Rundstedt and Geyr von Schweppenburg on the one hand, and Rommel on the other.

General Geyr von Schweppenburg, who, at that stage, was only responsible for the training of the armoured formations in France, wanted to form a Panzer Group under his own command to contain all the panzer divisions stationed round Paris. In support of his case he laid particular stress on the possibility of an Allied airborne landing of an operational character in the country round Paris. He also considered that the British and Americans should be allowed to land and make a penetration, so that their forces could then be destroyed and thrown back into the sea by a counter-offensive on the grand scale.

Even though his first argument was rejected by all the experts, his second fell on fruitful ground, as the majority of the senior German officers had hitherto fought only in the East and only knew war in its two-dimensional form. These officers were unable to have any idea of the effect that the British and American command of the air had had on the southern theatre of war. Moreover, they regarded the British and Americans as comparatively incompetent at mobile warfare and considered that our Western enemies could not possibly be any sort of match for the German Eastern front veterans.

As can be seen from Rommel's account, a wealth of experience had been gained in North Africa of the most up-to-date and advanced methods of war. Not one of the officers who opposed Rommel's views in France had ever fought against such a skilful enemy, or with such tactical refinements, as had Rommel during his two years in Africa. The suggestion that his wish to move the available panzer divisions to the most threatened part of the coast arose out of his ignorance of the principles of strategy, is not upheld by the evidence. In fact, the main reason for his successes in the mobile warfare in Africa had been his understanding of the art of concentrating the maximum possible force on each occasion at the right place and the right time. He had had more experience of this than any of the others, especially General Geyr von Schweppenburg.[1]

A further point is that Rommel did in fact ask for another six to eight panzer divisions and five to seven motorised divisions to be sent from Germany for deployment as an operational reserve in the Paris area.[2] On the 17th May I myself had a long talk with Rommel at La Roche Guyon [*Rommel's headquarters in France*] on the differences which existed between the East front generals and the men with African experience. As we strolled in the park, Rommel spoke in roughly the following terms:

" Our friends from the East cannot imagine what they're in for here. It's not a matter of fanatical hordes to be driven forward in masses against our line, with no regard for casualties and little recourse to tactical craft; here we are facing an enemy who applies all his native intelligence to the use of his many technical resources, who spares no expenditure of material and whose every operation goes its course as though it had been the subject of repeated rehearsal. Dash and doggedness alone no longer make a soldier, Bayerlein; he must have sufficient intelligence to enable

---

[1]Immediately after his removal from his command at the beginning of July, when his armoured forces had been shattered one after the other by the R.A.F. and U.S. Air Force, even under the cover of the bushes and hedges of Normandy, von Geyr wrote to Rommel:

DEAR FIELD-MARSHAL, 6 *July* 1944
    On relinquishing my command, may I be permitted to add a few words to my official leave-taking. The recent battles in a theatre of war more exacting than any I had hitherto experienced have, in addition to providing me with my posting to Army Group B and uniting me in purpose with yourself, wrought an inner change in me. Your soldierly qualities and experience have transformed the temper of my obedience into something different and finer than the effort of will it had hitherto been.
    I feel I may ask you, Herr Field Marshal, to accept my thanks for the confidence which you placed in me and my troops in those brief hard days of battle which we went through together. Since I regard my military career to be at an end, I think that I can say this without fear of misinterpretation.
                I am, Herr Field Marshal,
                            Yours obediently,
                                    FREIHERR VON GEYR

[2]General Speidel, *We Defended Normandy*, Chapter IX.

him to get the most out of his fighting machine. And that's something these people can do, we found that out in Africa."

From the experience I had recently gained in the East I could do nothing but agree. What told against us so heavily in Russia was that an inferiority complex had grown up there, born of the poor equipment of our men and of the bad conduct of operations by the O.K.W., which had repeatedly cost us heavy and pointless casualties. Added to that there was the fear of falling prisoner into Russian hands and being delivered up to this inhuman opponent. These aggravating factors apart, however—although they can hardly be overestimated—it was the African theatre of war which had always made the greater demands on the intellect.

" You have no idea," I remember Rommel saying, " how difficult it is to convince these people. At one time they looked on mobile warfare as something to keep clear of at all costs, but now that our freedom of manœuvre in the West is gone, they're all crazy after it. Whereas, in fact, it's obvious that if the enemy once gets his foot in, he'll put every anti-tank gun and tank he can into the bridgehead and let us beat our heads against it, as he did at Medenine. To break through such a front you have to attack slowly and methodically, under cover of massed artillery, but we, of course, thanks to the Allied air forces, will have nothing there in time. The day of the dashing cut-and-thrust tank attack of the early war years is past and gone—and that goes for the East too, a fact, which may, perhaps, by this time, have gradually sunk in."

During these weeks Rommel did all he could to get his view accepted. But Headquarters vacillated and, in the question of the major reserves, would not come down on either side. Hitler's approval of Rommel's scheme for defending France on the coast had obviously not been given out of sympathy with Rommel's line of thought, but simply because he could always find pleasure in the idea of massive fortifications. On the question of the operational reserves, Hitler and his staff were more inclined to accept Geyr von Schweppenburg's proposals, as they, too, did not believe that the enemy air force could exercise so great an influence over the movement of troops.

The following extract from a letter which Rommel wrote on the 23rd April 1944 to Colonel-General Jodl is most revealing on this point:[1]

" If, in spite of the enemy's air superiority, we succeed in getting a large part of our mobile force into action in the threatened coast defence sectors in the first few hours, I am convinced that the enemy attack on the coast will collapse completely on its first day. Very little damage has

---

[1] On the 21st March, Rommel had succeeded in convincing Hitler of the necessity of stationing reserves near the coast, but Hitler, a mere 24 hours later, had reversed this decision. It was during this period that Rommel coined the saying: " The last out of his door is always right."

so far been done by the heavy enemy bombing to our reinforced concrete installations, although our field positions, dugouts and communication-trenches have in many places been completely obliterated. This shows how important it is to get concrete over all our positions, even those, such as artillery, anti-aircraft and reserve positions, which are located behind the front.

" My only real anxiety concerns the mobile forces. Contrary to what was decided at the conference on the 21st March, they have so far not been placed under my command. Some of them are dispersed over a large area well inland, which means that they will arrive too late to play any part in the battle for the coast. With the heavy enemy air superiority we can expect, any large-scale movement of motorised forces to the coast will be exposed to air attacks of tremendous weight and long duration. But without rapid assistance from the armoured divisions and mobile units, our coast divisions will be hard put to it to counter attacks coming simultaneously from the sea and from airborne troops inland. Their land front is too thinly held for that. The dispositions of both combat and reserve forces should be such as to ensure that the minimum possible movement will be required to counter an attack at any of the most likely points, whether in the Low Countries, in the Channel area proper, in Normandy or in Brittany, and to ensure that the greater part of the enemy troops, sea and airborne, will be destroyed by our fire during their approach.

" Contrary to myself, General Geyr von Schweppenburg, who may well know the British in peacetime but has never yet met them in battle, sees the greatest danger in an operational airborne landing deep inside France, and so wishes to be in a position to mount a quick counter-operation. His forces have been located mainly with that end in view. Furthermore, he does not wish to take his armoured divisions to an area behind the land front of the coastal defences, where the enemy could make an airborne landing. I, on the other hand, see the greatest danger in the enemy using every weapon he has, especially airborne troops, to break through our coastal defences over a wide front, and thus gain a foothold on the continent. To my mind, so long as we hold the coast, an enemy airborne landing of an operational nature must, sooner or later, finish up in the destruction of the troops who have landed. In our experience, moreover, enemy airborne forces have in the past always been wiped out wherever the landing has been made in areas held by our troops. I believe airborne troops can be destroyed in this way at far less cost in bloodshed than by mounting an attack from outside against an already landed enemy, who could have large numbers of anti-tank guns ready for action within a few minutes, and could then be supported by his bomber formations. I have disagreed very violently with General von Geyr over this question and will only be able to execute my ideas if he is put under Army Group command early enough.

" The most decisive battle of the war, and the fate of the German people itself, is at stake. Failing a tight command in one single hand of all the forces available for defence, failing the early engagement of all our mobile forces in the battle for the coast, victory will be in grave doubt. If I am to wait until the enemy landing has actually taken place, before I can demand, through normal channels, the command and dispatch of the mobile forces, delays will be inevitable. This will mean that they will probably arrive too late to intervene successfully in the battle for the coast and prevent the enemy landing. A second Nettuno,[1] a highly undesirable situation for us, could result. . . ."

Rommel again had no success. In May he called attention to the threat to Normandy and requested the dispatch of an entire A.A. Corps into the district between the Orne and Vire, a Nebelwerfer brigade into the country south of Carentan, the 12th S.S. Panzer Division into the Cotentin peninsula and the Panzer Lehr Division[2] to the neighbourhood of Avranches. In addition, he asked that the navy should immediately start with the mining of the Bay of the Seine. [*The navy was then mining the Bay of Biscay.*] None of these demands, which he hoped would make up in part for the small size of the occupying force and weak fortifications in Normandy, was met.

The following extract appears in Rommel's diary[3] for the 3rd June:

" Afternoon with C.-in-C. West [*Rundstedt*]. C.-in-C. [*Rommel*] is planning a trip to Germany.

" 5th–8th June 1944. Fears of an invasion during this period were rendered all the less by the fact that tides were very unfavourable for the days following, and the fact that no amount of air reconnaissance had given the slightest indication that a landing was imminent. The most urgent need was to speak personally to the Fuehrer on the Obersalzberg, convey to him the extent of the man-power and material inferiority we would suffer in the event of a landing, and request the dispatch of two further panzer divisions, an A.A. corps and a Nebelwerfer brigade to Normandy. . . ."

After receiving von Rundstedt's authority for the trip and telephoning General Schmundt, Hitler's adjutant, to notify him of his coming,

---

[1] The Allies' landing at Anzio and Nettuno, close to Rome on the 22nd January 1944 is commonly called " Anzio " by the Allies, but " Nettuno " by the Germans. Kesselring succeeded in bottling up the force that had landed here, but it remained a threatening wedge in the rear of the main German front astride the Italian peninsula—and broke out at the end of May following the Allies' renewed advance from the south. That dual stroke forced the Germans to abandon the whole of Central Italy including Rome, and to retreat to the Gothic Line in the Apennines north of Florence.—*L. H.*

[2] This was commanded by General Bayerlein.—*L. H.*

[3] The personal diary from which this entry has been taken was maintained by Rommel's A.D.C. Rommel himself dictated no entries for this diary, either during the invasion or in the days immediately preceding it. It seems likely that the entry here quoted was written some time after the landing had taken place.

Rommel left his headquarters at La Roche Guyon by car on the morning of the 5th June.

INVASION DAY

The night of the 5th June was dark. Only occasionally did the moon break through the low blanket of cloud to pour her cold light over the Normandy coast. The sentries in the isolated defence posts paced with steady steps up and down their beats.

Shortly after nightfall, the monotonous drone of Allied bombers began again and soon the crash of bursting bombs could be heard from various points along the coast. Night bombing was not exactly a rarity in Normandy, but that night it increased from hour to hour and soon reached an unprecedented intensity. Further large formations made landfall after midnight and suddenly large areas of country behind the coast were marked out by " Christmas trees " dropped by pathfinder aircraft. Then from one o'clock onwards, thousands of parachutists dropped into the marked areas, while hundreds of gliders, carrying guns, vehicles and men, planed down and landed. The anti-glider stakes which Rommel had had installed were ineffectual in preventing the landing, as they had neither been wired together nor fitted with mines. They did cause severe damage to the gliders, but the loads of men and equipment mostly reached the ground unharmed.

The commanders of the nearby German posts raced to the field telephone and reported the landing, whereupon the whole machinery of command went into action.[1] Soon the battle inland was in full fury, for the Allied parachute troops at once advanced on the coast in order to break open the coast defences. And soon the first soldier fell in the battle that was to seal the fate of the German Reich.

The radar stations along the Bay of the Seine were out of action, having been destroyed from the air a few days before. Because of bad weather, the German air force had carried out no reconnaissance flights over the Channel, and the German outpost ships had remained in harbour. Consequently, the German Command completely failed to notice that a gigantic Allied Armada had crossed the Channel, passed the line of the German outpost ships ten hours before and formed up in the Bay of the Seine. The first they knew of it was at 05.30, when a broadside from the Allied Fleet burst at one blow over the German positions. Shell now followed shell, and the guns of six battleships, 23 cruisers and 104 destroyers began a bombardment without parallel, while a stream of Allied bomber squadrons followed each other in over Normandy and laid one bomb carpet after the other.

[1] Its functioning, however, was badly disjointed by the Allies' widespread and continuous air attacks.—L. H.

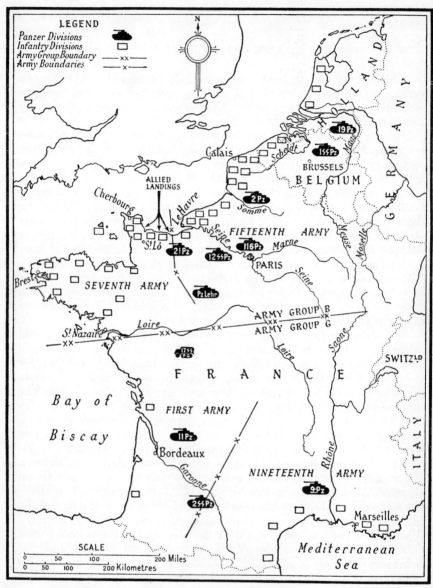

20. THE LAY-OUT OF GERMAN DEFENCES ON D-DAY

Under the fire of their warships, American and British special service troops drew near to the beach, leapt from their small armoured boats and began to demolish the beach defences which the low tide had left exposed. This would have been impossible if the lower obstacles, below the low water line, had been installed. Soon afterwards, while the guns of the warships continued their efforts to hold the defence down, great numbers of landing boats drove up on to the beach.

The German soldiers who had survived the tornado of fire, now saw their chance. Regardless of the inferno raging round them, most of them remained by their weapons until either they fell, or their weapons were destroyed. At some points they even succeeded in preventing the landing, although the greater part of the thinly held and shallow line was impossible to hold. American and British infantry moved on from the beaches, infiltrated between the isolated defence posts and linked up at several points with the parachute troops who had dropped behind the front. Amphibious and disembarked tanks reached the beach, thus enabling the infantry to carry forward the principal attacks with strong armoured support, against which the Germans had no defence, apart from mines, a few *Panzerfaeuste*[1] and some isolated anti-tank guns.

The divisions' few reserves were quickly thrown in at crisis points, and achieved some success wherever they came into action at the moment of landing. But the marching columns were attacked again and again by whole swarms of fighter-bombers. To the division commanders it was like a battle against a spring tide, which one knows with absolute certainty will soon sweep away the last pitiful resistance and flood inland. Soon all the reserves were committed and there were no more troops available. The front began to crumble at many points and by the afternoon it was clear that the Allied landing had succeeded.

The sole armoured formation lying on the invasion coast was the 21st Panzer Division, under the command of Lieut.-General Feuchtinger, which was located near Caen. The division possessed some 150 tanks, 60 assault and self-propelled guns and approximately 300 armoured troop-carriers. On the morning of the 6th June, Feuchtinger formed up part of the division for a counter-attack against the British parachutists east of the Orne. His troops were already on the move to the assembly area when an order arrived from Seventh Army instructing the division to launch its counter-attack on the *west* bank of the Orne. Feuchtinger immediately amended his orders accordingly, but irretrievable time had been lost and all that now materialised was an attack west of the Orne by one battle group,[2] which did, in fact, get through to the coast. But the British commander, in face of this danger, dropped parachute troops

[1]Literally " tank fists "—anti-tank rocket projectors.

[2]This battle-group consisted of about 50 tanks and a battalion of Panzer grenadiers.— L. H.

in the rear of the group, forcing it to break off the attack and withdraw in order to avoid being cut off.[1]

On the evening of the 6th June, therefore, the situation did not look very encouraging. On the right of the German front the British had gained a bridgehead some 20 miles wide and three to six miles deep, and on the left the Americans had gained two footholds. The intervening territory had been held and the Anglo-American penetrations sealed off. But all available reserves had been thrown into the battle and the commanders now watched impatiently for the arrival of the main armoured force, hoping it would soon come and throw the enemy back into the sea. But nothing came. Ammunition was running low and economy was necessary all along the front. Among the staffs, so far as they had not already been killed, that feeling of hopelessness, which was to be so characteristic of the forthcoming battle, began to spread.

But what had been happening in the rear all this while? During the night of the 5th, Field Marshal von Rundstedt had alerted the Panzer Lehr Division and the S.S. Panzer Division Hitler Jugend (both these divisions would have already been on the coast if Rommel had had his way), but the O.K.W. had informed him that it was not yet certain whether the landing in Normandy was in fact the main landing, and that he would therefore have to wait. Further delays occurred and it was not until the evening of the 6th June that elements of the two divisions began to move towards the coast. Rommel had been recalled to France by his Chief of Staff, General Speidel, with whom he worked in a rarely found harmony.

How Rommel viewed the situation in the first days of the battle can be seen from a document which he wrote on the 10th June 1944:

" The course of the battle in Normandy to date gives a clear indication of the enemy's intentions:
  (a) to gain a deep bridgehead between the Orne and Vire, as a springboard for a powerful attack later into the interior of France, probably towards Paris;
  (b) to cut off the Cotentin peninsula and gain possession of Cherbourg as soon as possible, in order to provide himself with a major port of large landing capacity. (There seems also to be a possibility, as things are developing, that the enemy will dispense with

---

[1]This, actually, was the evening arrival of the glider-borne remainder of the 6th Airborne Division, as originally planned, to reinforce the two parachute brigades that had landed before dawn. At the same time a large quantity of parachutes were dropped, but these carried containers of stores, not troops.

The timely appearance of this later airborne wave had such an upsetting effect on the German panzer troops that they very naturally regarded it as an overhead counter-stroke to their ground counter-stroke—an impression that persists in many of the later accounts from the German side.—L. H.

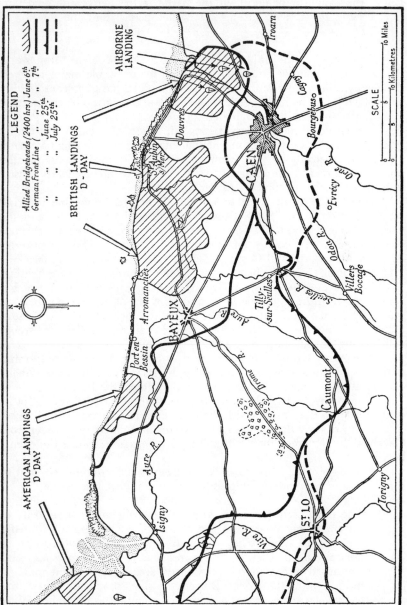

21. BATTLES ROUND CAEN

LEGEND

Allied Bridgeheads (2400 hrs.) June 6th
German Front Line (" ") " 7th
" " " June 25th
" " " July 25th

AIRBORNE LANDING

BRITISH LANDINGS
D-DAY

AMERICAN LANDINGS
D-DAY

SCALE
To Kilometres
To Miles

Troarn
Caen
Bourgebus
Caen
Évrecy
Odon R.
Orne R.
Villers Bocage
Douvres
St Aubin
St Hey
Aromanches
Port en Bessin
BAYEUX
Tilly-sur-Seulles
Seulles R.
Aure R.
Drôme R.
Caumont
Isigny
Aure R.
Vire R.
ST LO
Torigny

N

the Cotentin peninsula if the battle is too fierce, and make an early thrust with all his available means, into the interior of France.)

" As a result of the stubborn defence of the coast defence troops and the immediate counter-attacks launched by the available major reserves, the enemy attack, despite the strength of his effort, has gone considerably more slowly than he had hoped. The enemy also seems to be committing more forces than he had originally planned.

" Under cover of his very strong air force, the enemy is visibly reinforcing himself on land, and neither our air force nor our navy is in a position, especially by day, to offer him any hindrance. Consequently, the enemy forces in the bridgehead are growing at a considerably faster rate than reserves are flowing to our front.

" Due to the enemy's air superiority, it proved impossible to bring 1st S.S. Panzer Corps, 7th Nebelwerfer Brigade, the A.A. Corps and the Corps " Meindl " up to the Orne and Vire fast enough to enable them to counter-attack the enemy forces after the landing. The Nebelwerfer Brigade, A.A. Corps and Corps " Meindl " are still on the way forward; 1st S.S. Panzer Corps has been forced on the defensive in severe fighting.

" For the present the Army Group must content itself with forming a continuous front between the Orne and Vire out of the forces which are gradually arriving, and allowing the enemy to move up to it. Unfortunately, it will not be possible, in these circumstances, to relieve the troops still holding out at many points along the coast.

" The Army Group is endeavouring to replace the armoured formations now in the line as soon as possible by infantry, so that the armour can be used to form mobile reserves again behind the front.

" The Army Group also intends to shift the centre of gravity of its operations into the Carentan-Montebourg area during the next few days, in order to destroy the enemy in that sector and divert the danger from Cherbourg. Not until then can any attack be made against the enemy between the Orne and Vire.

" Our operations in Normandy are tremendously hampered, and in some places even rendered impossible, by the following factors:

(a) The immensely powerful, at times overwhelming, superiority of the enemy air force. As I and officers of my staff have repeatedly experienced (and as field commanders, including Obergruppen-fuehrer[1] Sepp Dietrich, have reported) the enemy has total command of the air over the battle area up to a point some 60 miles behind the front. During the day, practically our entire traffic—on roads, tracks and in open country—is pinned down by powerful fighter-bomber and bomber formations, with the result

[1]Obergruppenfuehrer—Lieutenant-General of the S.S.

that the movement of our troops on the battlefield is almost completely paralysed, while the enemy can manœuvre freely. Every traffic defile in the rear areas is under continual attack and it is very difficult to get essential supplies of ammunition and petrol up to the troops.

" Even the movement of minor formations on the battlefield —artillery going into position, tanks forming up, etc.—is instantly attacked from the air with devastating effect. During the day, fighting troops and headquarters alike are forced to seek cover in wooded and close country in order to escape the continual pounding from the air. On the 9th June, the situation in the battle area behind the S.S. Corps, was that large numbers of enemy fighter-bomber squadrons circled the battlefield continuously, while powerful bomber formations dropped a very heavy weight of bombs on troops, villages, bridges and crossroads, with complete disregard for the civilian population. Neither our anti-aircraft nor the Luftwaffe seems capable of imposing any check on the paralysing and destructive effect of the enemy air force (27,000 sorties in one day)[1]. The troops—Army and Waffen S.S.—are putting up as good a defence as they can with the means available to them, but ammunition is short and can only be replaced under the most difficult conditions.

(b) The effect of the heavy naval guns. Up to 640 guns have been used. The effect is so immense that no operation of any kind is possible in the area commanded by this rapid-fire artillery, either by infantry or tanks. Yet, despite this heavy bombardment, the garrisons on the coast and the units who counter-attacked in the Montebourg area, have held their positions with extreme stubbornness. But we can expect the enemy warships—unless they are put out of action by the navy and air force—to continue to intervene in the land fighting—above all, on the Cotentin peninsula—with the most lavish expenditure of ammunition.

(c) The material equipment of the Americans, with numerous new weapons and war material, is far and away superior to that of our divisions. The enemy armoured formations—as Obergruppenfuehrer Sepp Dietrich has informed me—appear to fight their actions at a range of as much as 2,500 yards, using vast quantities of ammunition and with magnificent air support. (This was already the case at El Alamein.) Also in evidence is their great superiority in artillery and outstandingly large supply of ammunition.

(d) Parachute and airborne troops are employed in such numbers and with such flexibility, that the troops they engage are hard put to

[1] This is an overestimate. Even on D-day the total number of sorties flown by the Tactical and Strategic Air Forces was only 10,585.—*L. H.*

it to fight them off. Where they drop into territory not held by our troops, they dig in immediately and can no longer be dislodged by infantry attacking with artillery support. We must expect more airborne landings, particularly in territory which is not held by our forces. Our air force has unfortunately not been able to intervene against these formations, as was originally intended. Since the enemy is able, with his air force, to pin down our mobile forces for days at a time, while he is all the while carrying on operations with mobile forces and reconnaissance troops, our situation is becoming extremely difficult.

" The troops of all services are fighting with the greatest doggedness and the utmost pugnacity, despite the immense material expenditure of the enemy. I request that the Fuehrer be informed. . . ."

But Hitler vetoed Rommel's plan to move against the American bridgehead in the Carentan-Montebourg area and gave orders instead for Army Group B to mount an attack against the British bridgehead from the Caen area, using the reinforcements with which it had been supplied. Yet the American bridgehead in the Cotentin was not only potentially more dangerous than the British one—as it could be the base for a move to cut off the entire Cotentin peninsula—but it also contained fewer troops at first. However, nothing came of the attack which Hitler ordered at Caen, as the British troops were reinforced far more quickly than ours, and were able to seize the initiative almost from the outset.

In his book, *We Defended Normandy*, General Speidel tells us that after the landing, the O.K.W. prohibited C.-in-C. West and C.-in-C. Army Group B from drawing off any divisions from north of the Seine, and reserved to itself the decision concerning each single division. They also sent the headquarters of Army Group B and C.-in-C. West one intelligence document after the other indicating that the Allies had retained sufficient troops in the British Isles to mount a second landing. Rommel himself declared to his son, shortly before his death, that he, too, had at first considered that if the bulk of the German troops had been drawn off from the Pas de Calais, an Allied landing there would have been quite within the bounds of possibility. An Allied plan to engage all the German forces in Normandy, destroy the Seine bridges by air attack and then land in the Pas de Calais and thrust into the Ruhr could not have been dismissed as absurd. He had later realised, however, that it had been a decisive mistake to leave the German troops in the Pas de Calais.

During the invasion battle, two conferences took place between Hitler, von Rundstedt and Rommel. At the first of them, which was held on 17th June 1944 near Soissons, Rommel opened the conference by giving a report on the situation, in which he described how impossible were the conditions under which the German soldier was being forced to fight. With von Rundstedt's support, he asked Hitler to come to the front and get an accurate picture of the situation for himself by talking direct to the field commanders. It had meanwhile become known to the Army that Churchill had, as so often before, paid a visit to the British troops in the bridgehead front, and the German troops in the west were very disappointed that the Fuehrer had not so far visited them. The record of Rommel's closing words throws interesting light on the plan which he proposed for one more attempt to do battle with the Allies. He said later to his family that the attempt would probably have failed, but that it nevertheless did offer a one-in-four chance of success, whereas continued persistence in rigid warfare was bound, with deadly certainty, to lead within a few weeks to the destruction of Army Group B.[1]

" C.-in-C. Army Group B cautioned against undertaking any major clean-up of the front by offensive methods, as this would expend the strength of the Panzer divisions. Proposal: Infantry divisions to be put into the Orne sector. Panzer divisions at present committed to remain west of Caen and reserve formations to be assembled on the flanks. After completion of the approach march, a limited withdrawal to be made southwards, with the object of launching an armoured thrust into the flank of the advancing enemy and fighting the battle outside the range of the enemy's naval artillery. . . ."

But next morning, after an errant V1 had dived to earth near his headquarters, Hitler turned straight round and made off back to the Reich, leaving the Western front to its fate. Nothing came of the operation which Rommel had proposed. Victory was to be gained by " holding fast tenaciously to every square yard of soil."

Finally, on the 29th June 1944, von Rundstedt and Rommel went to Hitler again, this time at Berchtesgaden, in order to learn the views of the highest command on the situation on the invasion front. Hitler's statement to his Field Marshals, which was recorded in a point-by-point summary, gives a fair impression of the confused state of his ideas at that time.

". . . After a detailed appreciation of the situation, in which particular reference was made to the enemy command of the air, to the effect of the enemy's naval artillery and finally to the systematic and inflexible conduct of operations on the part of the British, using the maximum of material, the Fuehrer gave the following directive for the continuation of the struggle:

(a) As point one, the Fuehrer stated that the first essential is to bring the enemy attack to a halt as a pre-condition for subsequently cleaning up the bridgehead.

[1]The passages quoted here have been taken from conference notes which were incorporated with the entries for the relevant dates in the diary kept by Rommel's A.D.C.

(b) The Luftwaffe is to create a constant state of unrest over the enemy bridgehead by the use of the latest types of aircraft (jets and rocket bombers) which are to engage and destroy enemy aircraft over the bridgehead.

(c) Sea-mining is to continue, both in order to hit at the enemy's supplies and to render the enemy warships' stay in coastal waters as uncomfortable as possible.

(d) Special bombs to be employed for the engagement of battleships. On this point, the Fuehrer made it clear that he regarded the destruction of the enemy's battleships as of outstanding importance.

(e) The creation of anti-aircraft nests on supply roads. To this end old aircraft cannon and other anti-aircraft weapons will be installed in nests along the supply roads between Paris and the battle zone, in order to make road strafing impossible for the enemy.

(f) The immediate provision of 1,000 fighters[1] from new production, in order to achieve air superiority over a limited area for at least a few days a week. By flying three sorties a day with the fighters then available, a total of up to 1,500 sorties a day could be flown.

(g) Employment by the navy of all available naval units, including torpedo boats, 'E' and 'U' boats as well as midget craft. According to a report by Grand Admiral Doenitz, however, the number of craft which can be committed is extremely small. The following are available:

> 1 Torpedo boat in Le Havre
> 12 'E' boats
> 8 'U' boats with 'Schnorkel' apparatus

Von Rundstedt and Rommel now gave their views on the situation. Rommel asked Hitler, among other things, how he imagined the war could still be won.

As a result of this argument, both Field Marshals—von Rundstedt and Rommel—expected to be relieved of their posts. Surprisingly, however, Rommel remained in office and only von Rundstedt was recalled, to be replaced by Field Marshal von Kluge. Von Kluge had already been influenced against Rommel at the Fuehrer's H.Q. by Hitler, Jodl and Keitel, who had spoken of him as independent, defeatist and disobedient. In addition, the military situation had been represented to von Kluge as not unfavourable. Consequently, he arrived at Rommel's H.Q. full of that exaggerated optimism which was shown by most Eastern front

---

[1]Hitler had talked repeatedly of these 1,000 jet fighters, even before the invasion. In reality the jet fighter was at this time not yet ready for action, and, in fact, no quantity use was ever made of these aircraft although 1988 of them were produced by German industry before the end of the war.

commanders on the day they first entered the Western theatre, and administered a severe censure to Rommel. The latter was not prepared to accept the accusations made against him and accordingly addressed the following letter to von Kluge:

H.Q. 5 July 1944

To C.-IN-C. WEST.
HERR GENERALFELDMARSCHALL VON KLUGE.

I send you enclosed my comments on military events in Normandy to date.

The rebuke which you levelled at me at the beginning of your visit, in the presence of my Chief of Staff and Ia, to the effect that I, too, " will now have to get accustomed to carrying out orders", has deeply wounded me. I request you to notify me what grounds you have for making such an accusation.

(Signed) ROMMEL
Generalfeldmarschall

In the document enclosed with this letter, which Rommel had already forwarded to Hitler, he stated once again, in all clarity, his criticism of the conduct of the war in Normandy.

COMMANDER-IN-CHIEF
ARMY GROUP B.   *MEMORANDUM*   *H.Q. 3 July 1944*

The reasons why it has been impossible to maintain a lasting hold on the Normandy coast, the Cherbourg peninsula and the fortress of Cherbourg, are set out below:

(1) The garrison forces stationed in Normandy were too weak and in some cases badly over-age (e.g. 709th Division, where the average age was 36); their equipment was inadequate for modern requirements, ammunition stocks were too small, constructional work on fortifications was in arrears and the supply situation was utterly inadequate.

(2) Repeated requests for reinforcements made by Army Group B before the invasion—above all, at the end of May, when the threat to Normandy became apparent—were refused. Most important of these was a request for the 12th S.S. Panzer Division *Hitler Jugend* to be moved into the Lessay-Coutances area to enable it to launch an immediate and overwhelming counter-attack on an enemy landing on either the west or east coast of the Cotentin. To bring the 12th S.S. Panzer Division up from its station south of the Seine, in the expected conditions of enemy air superiority, would have required at least two days and would have been bound to involve them in heavy losses. Colonel-General Jodl was aware

of this fact, for shortly before the enemy invasion he again had me asked through General Buhle, how long the 12th S.S. Panzer Division would require to get into action in Normandy. However, my persistent demands for the dispatch of this division were turned down and all I received was a promise that in the event of an enemy attack it would be put under my command immediately.

(3) My suggestion to position the Panzer Lehr Division where it could intervene rapidly in a coastal battle in either Normandy or Brittany was also not fulfilled, due to fears of a possible enemy airborne landing in the neighbourhood of Paris.

(4) The Army Group requested that strong anti-aircraft forces should be deployed by the end of May, above all, at those points where the enemy has already been making heavy and unhindered air attacks against our battery positions and fortifications. On the advice of G.O.C. 3rd A.A. Corps, I proposed that the entire A.A. Corps should be stationed as a formation between the Orne estuary and Montebourg [*18 miles S.E. of Cherbourg*], as this area was showing signs of being particularly threatened by the enemy activity. The request was not complied with and the A.A. Corps was instead deployed in a mobile role, with one of its four regiments on either side of the Somme and one weak regiment between the Orne and the Vire. This division of the A.A. Corps' strength— so prejudicial to the defence of Normandy—was justified on the grounds of shortage of petrol. Thus two regiments remained in the vicinity of the V2 launching points to provide protection for them when fire was opened.

(5) Since it was to be expected that the forward movement of reinforcements would present great difficulty after the attack had opened, I suggested that the Normandy defences should be strengthened by moving 7th Nebelwerfer Brigade into the area south of Carentan. This request was also not approved, and the brigade was not put under my command until after the landing. Consequently, it did not go into action during the first days of the invasion.

(6) To deny the enemy good landing conditions I pressed repeatedly for the Bay of the Seine to be mined in good time by the navy and air force, using the latest type of mines. This bay, with its shallow waters, is particularly suited for mining. This request also was not acted upon. Mine-laying did not start until after the enemy landing had taken place and then under conditions of extreme difficulty and mainly from the air.

(7) Orders were given by the Quartermaster-General for stocks of ammunition in Normandy to be cut during May, as part of the scheme for withdrawing ammunition from C.-in-C. West's command in order to build up reserve stocks in Base and Army

Ammunition Depots. This would have made holdings of ammunition even smaller than they already were. The Army Group, however, on the initiative of General Marcks,[1] succeeded in resisting this measure.

(8) Despite the existence of the railway network and sea routes, supply conditions, especially in Normandy, were already becoming difficult even before the invasion, due to the heavy bombing of railway installations.

(9) After the enemy had succeeded in gaining his foothold on the Continent, it was the intention of Army Group B when its reinforcements had arrived, first to wipe out the bridgehead north of Carentan, thus eliminating all danger to the Cotentin peninsula and the fortress of Cherbourg, and not until then to launch an attack on the enemy between the Orne and the Vire. The O.K.W., however, did not agree and gave orders for our main weight to be shifted to the eastern flank at the Orne estuary.

(10) The advance elements of 12th S.S. Panzer Division Hitler Jugend, did not arrive in the area north-west of Caen until 09.30 hours on the 7th June, after a 75-mile approach march, during which they sustained substantial losses from low-flying aircraft. There being then neither the time nor the space for a formation operation, its attack could not be driven home.

Panzer Lehr Division had 110 miles to cover, and its leading elements did not arrive at the battle front west of Caen until 13.00 hours on the 7th June. They, too, were hindered in their advance by low-flying aircraft, and the wheeled units became separated from the tracked. As a result, their attack could no longer be put in; they were, in fact, hard put to it to maintain their position against the enemy, who had by that time grown strong. An unfortunate result of this was that the division failed to establish contact with, and provide support for, the units of 352nd Infantry Division which were still fighting at Bayeux.

The leading elements of 2nd Panzer Division, which had to be brought up from its station on either side of the Somme (160 miles as the crow flies), arrived on the 13th June. A further seven days were needed before it could go into action as a division.

3rd Parachute Division required six days for its approach march from Brittany to its battle area north-east of St. Lô (135 miles as the crow flies), during which time it was under constant threat from the air. By the time it arrived, the attack it was due to launch on Bayeux was no longer possible, as strong enemy forces had already taken possession of the Forest of Cerisy.

77th Division required six days before it could intervene with

[1] Commanding the 84th Corps, which covered the invasion sector in Normandy.—L. H.

substantial forces in the fighting in the north of the Cotentin peninsula.

All the reserves that came up arrived far too late to smash the enemy landing by counter-attacks. By the time they arrived the enemy had disembarked considerably stronger forces and himself gone over to the attack under cover of powerful air and artillery support.

(11) Support by our air force was not forthcoming on the scale originally foreseen. The enemy had command of the air over the battle-ground up to a point some 60 miles behind the front. In sorties of immense strength he smashed the defence installations in the coastal zones and effectively opposed the approach march of our reserves and the supply of our troops, principally by damage to the railway system.

(12) Naval activity was also not on the scale that had originally been promised. (Only 6 U-boats, for example, instead of 40.) Due to adverse weather conditions no outpost ship watch was kept on the Bay of the Seine on the night of the 5th June. U-boat activity against the landing fleet was on a relatively small scale. As a result of the enemy air attack on le Havre on the 12th June, the navy lost a large part of its craft suitable for use against the landing fleet.

The mining of the Bay of the Seine, which was undertaken immediately after the invasion, has also shown no noticeable success to date. Landings are still taking place on the very largest scale and the daily bombardment by naval guns, " on a scale hitherto unknown " (Report by 2nd S.S. Panzer Corps), is causing serious difficulties for our front.

(13) The Army Group has had no part in the machinery of supply. It has no Quartermaster staff of its own and had at first no authority to give instructions to the Quartermaster at Headquarters West.

(14) Channels of command were unsatisfactory. At the start of the invasion, the Army Group had no control over the mobile formations of Panzer Group West (see above), nor over the Nebelwerfer Brigade. On the " direction " of the A.A. Corps, etc., I have already given my views in a report. Only unified, close-knit command of all services, after the pattern of Montgomery and Eisenhower, will vouchsafe final victory.

(Signed) ROMMEL
Generalfeldmarschall

Hardly had von Kluge inspected the front in Normandy, when he changed his views completely. He also acknowledged the justice of the words which Rommel had written to the Fuehrer's H.Q. at the end of

June: " The enemy's command of the air restricts all movement in terms of both space and time, and renders calculation of time impossible. For armoured or motorised troops in divisional strength upwards, it limits the possibilities of command and manœuvre to night or bad weather operations, which cannot as a rule develop into anything more than operations with limited objective. Daylight action is, however, still possible—given sufficient A.A. defence—for a small armoured combat group."

Nothing now is revealed by Rommel's papers concerning his part in the July 20th affair, principally because he destroyed everything which might have been incriminating for himself or other people. There are, however, one or two points which should be cleared up.

Rommel's view that it might be necessary, in an emergency, to arrive at a reasonable peace even against Hitler's will, dated from the summer of 1943. But from what he said later to his wife and son, he appears to have felt that a *coup d'état* against Hitler, before the invasion, would have been a mistake. He gave the following reasons for his view:

(1) Until the invasion, Germany's only front was in the East. A *coup d'état* might have caused a collapse of the Eastern front and made it possible for the Russians to flood over Central Europe without the British or Americans being in a position to stop them.

(2) In the spring of 1944 the psychological conditions for a military revolt did not exist, for the troops and most of the officers in France were convinced that the British and Americans could be beaten off and that Germany would finally halt the Russians by means of her new weapons (jet fighters, secret weapons and new tanks).

(3) If Germany had, in fact, succeeded in beating off the invasion, the British and Americans would then have foregone their demand for unconditional surrender, in the fear of either a Russian occupation of the whole of Europe or of Germany taking the offensive again in Russia. This last chance of forcing a conditional peace on the enemy was one that Germany could not afford to miss.

Rommel's idea was that if the invasion were repelled, the West would eventually come round to the idea of fighting side by side with a new Germany in the East. He regarded it as completely unthinkable that the Western Allies would give such support to Bolshevism as, in fact, they did. Supported by General Speidel, his able and loyal Chief of Staff, he had already made contact with various headquarters before the invasion, and discussed the possibilities of such a move.

Although after the 20th July Rommel commented to his family and various officers that " Stauffenberg had bungled it and a front-line soldier would have finished Hitler off ", yet it must be remembered that these words sprang from the anger he felt at the callousness with which Hitler had had the generals and politicians hanged who had taken part in the affair. Rommel, in fact, had never known of the attempt to be made on Hitler's life and would not have approved it if he had. Shortly before his death he said to his son Manfred:

" The attempt on Hitler was stupid. What we had to fear with this man was not his deeds, but the aura which surrounded him in the eyes of the German people. The revolt should not have been started in Berlin, but in the West. What could we have hoped to achieve by it? Only, in the end, that the expected forcible American and British occupation of Germany would have become an unopposed ' march-in', that the air attacks would have ceased, and that the Americans and British would have kept the Russians out of Germany. As for Hitler the best thing would have been to have presented him with an accomplished fact."

It was probably this argument that brought Rommel and Speidel to the decision to open independent peace negotiations with the Western Allies, after they had been finally forced to the realisation that the German front in France would collapse within a few weeks. Everything had been prepared and von Kluge and many others won over, when, on the 17th July, fate intervened and Rommel was severely wounded and rendered *hors de combat* by Allied low-flying aircraft near Livarot.

Shortly before this happened, he had sent to Hitler the following last report, the purpose of which was to state his case clearly and in all urgency, so that it could never be said that he had stabbed anyone in the back.

C.-IN-C. ARMY GROUP B   *H.Q. 15 July*
The situation on the Normandy front is growing worse every day and is now approaching a grave crisis.

Due to the severity of the fighting, the enemy's enormous use of material—above all, artillery and tanks—and the effect of his un-restricted command of the air over the battle area, our casualties are so high that the fighting power of our divisions is rapidly diminishing. Replacements from home are few in number and, with the difficult transport situation, take weeks to get to the front. As against 97,000 casualties (including 2,360 officers)—i.e. an average of 2,500 to 3,000 a day—replacements to date number 10,000, of whom about 6,000 have actually arrived at the front.

Material losses are also huge and have so far been replaced on a very small scale; in tanks, for example, only 17 replacements have arrived to date as compared with 225 losses.

The newly arrived infantry divisions are raw and, with their small establishment of artillery, anti-tank guns and close-combat anti-tank weapons, are in no state to make a lengthy stand against major enemy attacks coming after hours of drum-fire and heavy bombing. The fighting has shown that with this use of material by the enemy, even the bravest army will be smashed piece by piece, losing men, arms and territory in the process.

Due to the destruction of the railway system and the threat of the enemy air force to roads and tracks up to 90 miles behind the front, supply conditions are so bad that only the barest essentials can be brought to the front. It is consequently now necessary to exercise the greatest economy in all fields, and especially in artillery and mortar ammunition. These conditions are unlikely to improve, as enemy action is steadily reducing the transport capacity available. Moreover, this activity in the air is likely to become even more effective as the numerous air-strips in the bridgehead are taken into use.

No new forces of any consequence can be brought up to the Normandy front except by weakening Fifteenth Army's front on the Channel, or the Mediterranean front in southern France. Yet Seventh Army's front, taken over all, urgently requires two fresh divisions, as the troops in Normandy are exhausted.

On the enemy's side, fresh forces and great quantities of war material are flowing into his front every day. His supplies are undisturbed by our air force. Enemy pressure is growing steadily stronger.

In these circumstances we must expect that in the foreseeable future the enemy will succeed in breaking through our thin front, above all, Seventh Army's, and thrusting deep into France. Apart from the Panzer Group's sector reserves, which are at present tied down by the fighting on their own front and—due to the enemy's command of the air—can only move by night, we dispose of no mobile reserve for defence against such a break-through. Action by our air force will, as in the past, have little effect.

The troops are everywhere fighting heroically, but the unequal struggle is approaching its end. It is urgently necessary for the proper conclusion to be drawn from this situation. As C.-in-C. of the Army Group I feel myself in duty bound to speak plainly on this point.

(Signed) ROMMEL

Events quickly bore out Rommel's warning of a forthcoming break-through on Seventh Army's front. While Montgomery executed his pincer attacks in the Caen area, pressure in the St. Lô sector increased daily. As this was the sector where Army Group B was expecting the Allied offensive to come, Panzer Lehr Division (which was under the

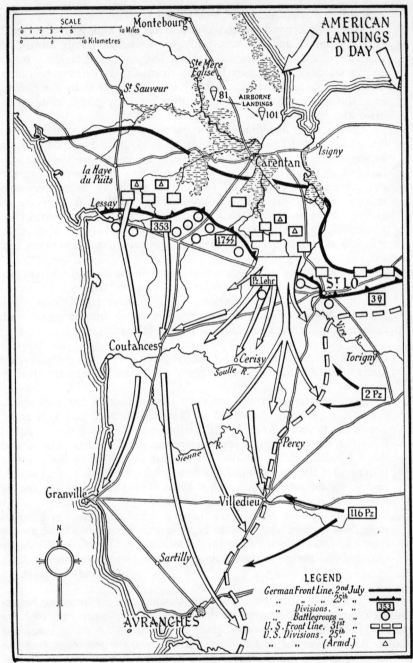

SCALE

AMERICAN
LANDINGS
D DAY

Montebourg

Ste Mère
Eglise

St Sauveur

81

AIRBORNE
LANDINGS

101

la Haye
du Puits

Carentan

Isigny

Lessay

353

17ss

St LO

3 ⊘

Pz.Lehr

Coutances

Cerisy

Soulle R.

Torigny

2 Pz

Sienne R.

Percy

Granville

Villedieu

116 Pz

N

Sartilly

LEGEND
German Front Line, 2nd July
  „   „   „ 25th „
  „   „ Divisions „ „
  „   „ Battlegroups „
U.S. Front Line, 31st „
  „   „ Divisions 25th „
  „   „   „ (Armd.)

353

AVRANCHES

22. BATTLES IN THE CHERBOURG PENINSULA

writer's[1] command) was moved across there from the British sector. On the 18th August 1944 I made a report to Army Group on the battle which ensued. A copy of this report which I sent to Rommel was found among his papers and provides the basis of the account that follows.

After the heavy fighting my division had been through, only 50 per cent of its original strength remained. To make matters worse, I had to leave half my remaining armour behind in my old sector as support for the infantry division which had taken over from us.

By about the 23rd July, U.S. troops had gained suitable jump-off positions for their offensive and had taken St. Lô. Panzer Lehr Division held a 6,000-yard sector west of the town and, by allocating only weak reserves, had formed a defence zone of 4,000 yards in depth. The 50 or 60 tanks and self-propelled anti-tank guns still remaining to the division were deployed in static positions as armoured anti-tank guns and the Panzer Grenadiers were well dug-in on their field positions.

On the 24th July, 400 American bombers attacked our sector, but without doing much damage. My A.A. battalion even managed to shoot down ten of their aircraft. The expected ground attack did not come.

But on the next day, there followed one of the heaviest blows delivered by the Allied air forces in a tactical rôle during the whole of the war. I learnt later from American sources that on the 25th July a force consisting of 1,600 Flying Fortresses and other bombers, had bombed the Panzer Lehr's sector from nine in the morning until around midday. Units holding the front were almost completely wiped out, despite, in many cases, the best possible equipment of tanks, anti-tank guns and self-propelled guns. Back and forth the bomb carpets were laid, artillery positions were wiped out, tanks overturned and buried, infantry positions flattened and all roads and tracks destroyed. By midday the entire area resembled a moon landscape, with the bomb craters touching rim to rim, and there was no longer any hope of getting out any of our weapons. All signal communications had been cut and no command was possible. The shock effect on the troops was indescribable. Several of the men went mad and rushed dementedly round in the open until they were cut down by splinters. Simultaneous with the storm from the air, innumerable guns of the U.S. artillery poured drum-fire into our field positions.

During this time I myself was located at a regimental sector command post near La Chapelle-en-Juger, in the centre of the bombardment. Housed in an old Norman chateau, with ten-foot walls, we were rather better protected than the others. Again and again the bomb carpets rolled towards us, most of them passing only a few yards away. The ground shuddered. Quick glimpses outside showed the whole area shrouded by a pall of dust, with fountains of earth spewing high in the

[1]General Bayerlein.—L. H.

air. For many hours we were unable to leave the cellar and it was afternoon before I was able to get out of the chateau and ride back on my motor cycle to Division H.Q. (I had long since learned to prefer a motor cycle to a car, having had six cars shot up during the invasion battle and several drivers killed.) We were repeatedly troubled by fighter-bombers on the way back.

When I arrived at Division H.Q. the first reports were just coming in of enemy infiltrations into the bombed area. Resistance was offered by the few surviving detachments of my division, but most of these groups were wiped out by the tactical air support rolling forward in front of the attack. Some weak reserves from other sectors tried to halt the avalanche by counter-attacks, but their attempts were smashed by the enemy artillery and air force in the forming-up stage and came to nothing. By the following morning, the American break-through was complete.

The Americans continued their advance south all the morning, using infantry with bomber and fighter-bomber support, and then in the afternoon brought their tank packs up into the lead. In the course of this move they overhauled the last pitiful remnants of my division, which had fallen back, together with the divisional staff, to the south. I lay with my headquarters in a Norman farmhouse, set in typical Normandy country, criss-crossed with hedges, low hills and sunken roads, when suddenly scouts reported U.S. tanks advancing in our immediate neighbourhood. Soon the tanks were rolling past us. On sighting our vehicles, which we had parked a little way off in the bushes, the American tankmen opened fire and shot every one of them into flames. The front room of our house was immediately hit by an H.E. shell. I lay with five men in the next room. It was impossible to leave the house, for American machine-gun fire was swishing past the house door. The window at the back was barred and so we were caught like rats in a trap. Gradually the tanks moved on and the firing ceased. We were now behind the American lines. Evening brought a chance to slip away to our own troops. For hours I trekked back through sunken roads, until at about midnight I came across a stray vehicle of my division, which carried me on to the rearward elements of my otherwise annihilated formation.

But the Americans were now pouring through into the open country with nobody to stop them—just as Rommel had predicted. After turning west to Coutances they sealed off and annihilated our forces fighting in the Cotentin peninsula, leaving a vast hole torn in the German front, through which Patton's army poured into the heart of France. That was the beginning of the end. The thrust on Avranches, with which the O.K.W. planned to cut Patton off, was smashed during its assembly by massed American bomber attacks and never got started. Without the U.S.A.A.F. and the R.A.F. this attack could have been launched earlier and would almost certainly have resulted in a resounding victory. Hence, like the invasion battle itself—and this was the opinion of Rommel and most of his leading commanders—this battle was lost only because of the total supremacy which the Allies enjoyed in the air.

The personal burdens which Rommel and the other responsible commanders in the west had to bear during the invasion battle were tremendous, for on this front was being decided the final fate of the German people; here was being decided whether or not the Soviet hordes would march through Berlin, whether the last German towns would be preserved or would crumble to dust and ashes. Those of Rommel's letters of this period that have survived, tell us something of his feelings:

10 June 1944

DEAREST LU,

. . . It is a hard fight that the army is having to withstand. I was up at the front yesterday and am going again to-day. The enemy's air superiority has a very grave effect on our movements. There's simply no answer to it. It's quite likely to start at other places soon. However, we do what we can.

13 June 1944

The telephone line yesterday was really terrible, but it was better than nothing. The battle is not going at all well for us, mainly because of the enemy's air superiority and heavy naval guns. In the air 300-500 sorties of ours face 27,000 of theirs. I reported to the Fuehrer yesterday. Rundstedt is doing the same. It's time for politics to come into play. We are expecting the next, perhaps even heavier blow to fall elsewhere in a few days. The long-husbanded strength of two world powers is now coming into action. It will all be decided quickly. We are doing what we can. I often think of you at home, with heartfelt wishes and the hope that everything can still be guided to a tolerable end.

14 June 1944

Very heavy fighting. The enemy's great superiority in aircraft, naval artillery, men and material is beginning to tell. Whether the gravity of the situation is realised up above, and the proper conclusions drawn, seems to me doubtful. Supplies are getting tight everywhere. How are you both? Still no news has arrived.

15 June 1944

Was up forward again yesterday, the situation does not improve. We must be prepared for grave events. The troops, S.S. and Army alike, are fighting with the utmost courage, but the balance of strength tips more heavily against us every day. Our air force is playing a very modest part over the battle area. I'm well so far. I have to keep my head up in spite of it all, even though many hopes are having to be buried. You can no doubt imagine what difficult decisions we will soon be faced with, and will remember our conversation in November 1942.[1]

18 June 1944

There's a chance of sending you a quick letter to-day by one of the men. I saw the Fuehrer yesterday, who is at present in the west. I gave him a detailed report and clarified everything. If the O.K.W. at first had the idea that the troops at the front were not fighting well, this idea has now been revised. Our opponents themselves have provided my army with the best of all possible testimonials. Of course large forces of ours were overwhelmed by the immense weight of the enemy bombing and naval barrage, but every man still living fought like the devil. If people had listened to me we would have counter-attacked with three divisions on the first evening, and would probably have beaten off the attack. Frightful delays were caused by the panzer divisions having to travel between 250 and 400 miles to the front and in many places the battle was going badly. Much of this has now sorted itself out and I am looking forward to the future with less anxiety than I did a week ago. The long-range action[2] has brought us a lot of relief. A number of generals fell in the first few days of battle, among them Falley, who was killed on the first night —the 5-6th June.

. . . A quick enemy break-through to Paris is now hardly a possibility. We've got a lot of stuff coming up. The Fuehrer was very cordial and in a good humour. He realises the gravity of the situation. . . .

23 June 1944

Militarily things aren't at all good. The enemy air force is dealing extremely heavily with our supplies and at the moment is completely strangling them. If a decisive battle develops, we'll be without ammunition. You can imagine how worried I am. Even Cherbourg will not be able to hold out for long in these circumstances. We must be prepared for grave events.

24 June 1944

Now it's started in the East.[3] I hope things at least go well there.

---

[1]Following on a meeting which he had had with Hitler and Goering in November 1942—shortly after the battle of El Alamein—Rommel had said to his wife in Rome that the war was lost and that an attempt would have to be made as soon as possible to arrive at a compromise peace.

[2]Rommel presumably refers here to the V1 attack on England.—*L. H.*

[3]The Russians opened their summer offensive of 1944 on the 23rd June, and launched it against the Vitebsk sector, north of the Pripet Marshes. The German commanders had proposed to forestall it by withdrawing to the line of the Beresina before the blow fell, but Hitler forbade any step back. Bursting through the overstretched German front,

Cherbourg can hardly hold out for long despite the heroic struggle of its defenders. Given a sufficient weight of bombs and heavy shells the enemy can make any place ripe for assault. The tragedy is that we can't reply in the same terms. I'm going off to the front now, as I do almost daily.

24 July 1944[1]

I'm now in hospital and being very well looked after. Of course I must keep quiet until I can be moved, which will be a fortnight yet. My left eye is still closed and swollen, but the doctors say it will get better. My head is still giving me a lot of trouble at night, though I feel very much better in the daytime. The attempt on the Fuehrer, coming on top of my accident, has left me very badly shattered. We must thank God that it passed off as well as it did. I sent up my views on the situation shortly before it happened.[2]

I'm terribly grieved about Daniel [*Rommel's driver*], he was an excellent driver and a loyal soldier.

All my love and best wishes to you and Manfred.

Several weeks later Rommel had himself transported back to Germany in order to avoid falling wounded into Allied hands. He did not know that he thereby sealed his own fate, for Hitler had probably by that time already decided on his death—although he had telegraphed to Rommel on the 24th July:

" Accept, Herr Field Marshal, my best wishes for your continued speedy recovery.

" Yours,

ADOLF HITLER"

the Russians drove 150 miles deep in a week and got across the Minsk-Warsaw highway. By mid-July they had advanced deep into Poland and Lithuania. The Russian armies south of the Pripet Marshes joined in the offensive, and by the end of July the combined drive had reached the Vistula near Warsaw and crossed the San in the south—an advance of up to 450 miles in five weeks. Here at last they were brought to a halt, and paused to rebuild communications before renewing their offensive on this central front in January 1945—when they swept forward to the Oder, barely 60 miles from Berlin. Meanwhile, the Russian left-wing armies pushed through Rumania, Yugoslavia, and Hungary in a gigantic wheeling movement which reached the outskirts of Budapest by the 4th November, although the city did not fall until the 13th February. During the autumn too, the Russian right-wing armies overran the Baltic states, and the Germans' northern army group—which clung on there by Hitler's orders—was cornered in the Courland peninsula.—*L. H.*

[1] Rommel's first letter after he was wounded. He dictated it but could not sign it. His letters between the 24th June and the 17th July are missing.

[2] Rommel was bound to express some sort of opinion in this letter. He had previously demanded, in a wireless message to Hitler, that the proper conclusions should be drawn from the inevitable collapse of the West.

Concerning the last few months of Rommel's life, there are again no papers of his in existence, but his son, Manfred, then a fifteen-year-old boy, was posted home and attached to his father's staff where he naturally learned a great deal of his views from daily conversations.

CHAPTER XXII

THE LAST DAYS

By Manfred Rommel

ONE day in the middle of August 1944, on the gun-site where I was serving on the outskirts of Ulm, I received a telephone call from my battery commander. "Your father has arrived in Herrlingen and you have been posted to his staff. You will be collected to-day."

A command car carried me to Herrlingen, drove through the garden gate and stopped in front of the house. The maid opened the door. I threw my rucksack to the floor with a clatter of mess-tins, hurriedly washed my hands and then went into the study. My father, his left eye covered with a black bandage, sat in an armchair beside a low coffee-table. The left half of his face had been crushed by the weight of the blow it had received. He raised himself shakily to his feet and we exchanged greetings. "I'm getting along pretty well so far," he said in reply to my question. "I still get headaches and my left eye is closed and won't move. But it will all get better."

We sat down and my father's face grew grave as he turned towards my mother and continued talking of his experiences in Normandy. I quote this, as all other conversations, to the best of my memory.

"My functions in Normandy," he said, "were so restricted by Hitler that any sergeant-major could have carried them out. He interfered in everything and turned down every proposal we made. The British and Americans had only two bridgeheads to begin with, a weak one on the Cotentin peninsula and a somewhat stronger one near Bayeux. Naturally, we wanted to attack the weak one first. But no; Hitler thought otherwise. The half-hearted dispersed attack which resulted was simply nipped in the bud. If we pulled a division out, Hitler ordered us to send it straight back. Where we ordered 'Resistance to the last round', it was changed from above to 'Resistance to the last drop of blood'. When Cherbourg finally surrendered, they sent us a court-martial adviser. That was the sort of help we got.

"The troops behaved splendidly. During the first few days they fought among themselves for possession of the *Panzerfaeuste* [*anti-tank rocket projectors*]. But then came the feeling of hopelessness; that there was nothing to be done. After only a few days, one of the corps commanders remained in his car when it was attacked by British low-flying aircraft. He fell back into his seat badly wounded. His A.D.C. tried to get him out before the second attack. But he held on to his seat and said: 'Leave me here. I'd rather have it that way.' The next burst of fire killed him."

My father stood up shakily and gazed out of the window for a while. Then he went on: "But all the courage didn't help. It was one terrible blood-letting. Sometimes we had as many casualties on one day as during the whole of the summer fighting in Africa in 1942. My nerves are pretty good, but sometimes I was near collapse. It was casualty reports, casualty reports, casualty reports, wherever you went. I have never fought with such losses. If I hadn't gone to the front nearly every day, I couldn't have stood it, having to write off literally one more regiment every day." Suddenly he turned with a jerk and leant on the window-seat. "And the worst of it is that it was all without sense or purpose. There is no longer anything we can do. Every shot we fire now is harming ourselves, for it will be returned a hundred-fold. The sooner it finishes the better for all of us."

We looked at each other. Then I said: "Perhaps there are new weapons that will still turn things in our favour."

"Rubbish," he replied. "Nobody has any such weapons. The only purpose of these rumours is to make the ordinary soldier hang on a bit longer. We're finished, and most of the gentlemen above know it perfectly well, even if they won't admit it. Even they aren't so stupid that they can't recognise facts that anybody could work out on the fingers of one hand."

The doctors begged my father to keep to his bed for a few weeks. But he did not heed their advice. He was too restless. Early each morning I would hear him slowly making his way downstairs and I would follow shortly afterwards to read to him. Usually a long discussion started over breakfast. For me—a fifteen-year-old Luftwaffe auxiliary—there was still an aura of glory round the personage of Hitler, despite all I had heard. So, when my father began with his criticism, I usually tried to say something in favour of the régime. He would analyse his arguments to me with touching patience. "War," he said once, "has seldom brought anything for any of the people engaged in it. But the people aren't usually asked. Once war has begun, you go on fighting simply to get the best you can out of it. But what when there is no more to be got? Then it's better to stop it at once. And that, you see, is our position to-day, except that we are fighting an enemy in the East before whom there can be no surrender. There it's a matter of fighting for our lives, and that complicates the issue. What we should do now is to see to it that our

Western enemies occupy the whole of Central Europe and keep the Russians outside our borders."

When my father heard of troops being sent from the Eastern to the Western front, he exploded. " These fools! " he cried out once when he heard that a panzer division had been sent from Poland to Holland. " They think of nothing but their own skins. What good is it to them to prolong their miserable lives by a few more months? The Eastern front will simply crack and the next Russian push will bring them into German territory. We all know what that means."

Up to that time I had heard nothing of my father's attempts to bring about a separate peace in the West and it had never entered my head that there could have been any connection between him and the officers who were arrested after the 20th of July. I was all the more astonished, therefore, when we heard one day that some Gestapo men were hanging round the neighbourhood and taking a great interest in all that went on in our house. At about that time my father and I had taken to walking together almost daily through the wood near our house. One morning I was sitting with him in his room, when he suddenly said: " Look here, Manfred, it's possible that there are certain people round here who would like to do away with me quietly and without too much fuss—by an ambush in the wood, for instance. But I don't intend to let it put me off my walk. So for the time being, we'll take pistols. You can have my 8 mm. These individuals don't hit anything with their first shots. If shooting does start, the thing to do is to fire blind towards where it's coming from, and they'll almost always go for cover or aim badly."

I did not at first quite take in the implication of this instruction of my father's, until he said to me one day: " Tell me, Manfred, what do you young chaps think when Hitler suddenly hangs a whole lot of people who have persuaded themselves—not wholly without reason—that the war is lost and that we should make an end of it at last? "

" I don't know," I replied, " they're all really pretty sick of the war up at the gun-site, but most of them still believe we can win it somehow or other."

" But it's already lost," my father broke in. " What if I, too, had declared myself ready to end it, even against Hitler's will? "

" Why do you ask that? " I inquired.

" Oh, let's leave it for now," he said. " Anyway, one thing is quite clear, it's intolerable that the fate and welfare of a whole nation should depend on the whim of a small group. There must be some limit, otherwise, the most fantastic things can happen without anyone noticing."

From that day on, I, too, had the feeling of approaching disaster.

At that time, my father was firmly convinced that war was bound to come within a few years between Russia and the Western Powers and, contrary to most officers of the same mind who came to see us, was equally convinced of a victory of the Western world, even in the more distant future. In this connection I remember with particular clarity a conversation which took place about a month after my father's return from France. It was about ten o'clock in the evening in his big study at Herrlingen. My father, wearing his brown, single-breasted civilian suit, sat opposite me in an armchair. He was at that time already very active and impulsive again, although his left eye was still swollen as a result of his wound. The other eye had for many years been very long-sighted and I had therefore been posted home temporarily to read documents to him. That evening it was a statistical book concerning the distribution of raw materials which was interesting him, but the book already lay closed on the table and we talked of the future, which at that time looked very dark.

"Russia and the West are like fire and water," my father said. "There will be friction and probably war. Perhaps not immediately after our collapse, for the whole world is tired of war. The danger will come after a few years."

"A poor prospect for the British and Americans, don't you think?" I asked. "Russia's land forces are on an altogether different scale from those of the West."

"That isn't what will decide the issue," my father replied. "Have our better tanks and élite divisions in Normandy been of any avail? No, young man, the Americans have got command of the air and they'll keep it. That is a sentence of death for any land army, however large, that has to fight without adequate air cover."

"Perhaps the Russians will wait until after the war," my mother interrupted; "until the Americans have disarmed. The Western peoples want a high standard of living and their industries will be converted to civilian production."

"Even then America and Britain will win," he replied; "even if Europe succumbs to the storm from the East. We mustn't forget that Britain and America have sea-power and can carry their war material to any point on the face of the globe which is accessible to the sea. Here is French North Africa," he said, pointing to the map which I had brought at his request, "with many large ports and first-class railway communications. But between the Caucasus and Egypt, there are only occasional stretches of railway and even those have a smaller gauge than the Russian system, so they wouldn't be much good to them. Between Libya and Tunisia, there is no railway at all for 2,000 miles or so, so the Russians would have to carry supplies for their mass army by lorry over several thousand miles, and that is a practical impossibility. A lorry of this kind requires a gallon of petrol for every seven miles, that is about 280 gallons for a 2,000-mile trip, plus another 280 for the journey back—about 120 cans in all. So the greater part of the load of each lorry would have to be its own petrol. Another thing is that the modern tank-motor won't stand up to such distances. So would the Russians be dangerous after

Rommel with Field Marshal Rundstedt at La Roche Guyon, May, 1944

Rommel with General Speidel in France, 1944

After his death Rommel's body was taken to the hospital in Ulm. Two days later it was brought back to his home. On October 18th the coffin was carried from the house, past a guard of honour, and placed on a gun carriage on which it was borne in state through the streets of Ulm. (Below) Hitler's wreath

two or three thousand miles? Of course not." He gave his own answer.
" And in Africa a small, well-equipped force could maintain a delaying
resistance for months."

" Then again," he went on, " we've just heard that Britain and the
United States are producing about four times as much as Russia. Now,
there can be no doubt that in an emergency these two countries could
assemble a force in French West Africa unmolested. From there they
would slowly wrest command of the air and become stronger month by
month. Then they would begin to move forward as they are now doing
in the West. Their bomber fleets would cut off the Russian Army from
its supply bases, pin it to the ground and destroy it. Then they would
move on step by step, with their ships carrying their supplies without
effort to any place on earth, to Tobruk, to Suez or to Basra, according to
how the operation progressed. And once the oil areas on the Caspian
Sea came in range of their bombers, Russia's Achilles' Heel would lie
open."

While my father was occupying himself with these ideas, Hitler's
bloodhounds were busy seeking the threads that ran from the Bendler-
strasse [the War Ministry] to the headquarters on the Western front.
General von Stuelpnagel, military commander in France, fell into the
hands of the Gestapo, following an abortive suicide attempt. Field Marshal
von Kluge, who had replaced von Rundstedt as C.-in-C. West after the
latter's dismissal on account of his defeatist outlook, had disappeared
weeks before. One day, my father had a long talk with a courier officer
who had brought news from France. When I heard the courier's
car drive off, I went into my father's study. He sat at his desk, his face
grave.

" Kluge is dead," he said. " We now know what happened to him.
Hitler sacked him and gave orders for him to return to the Reich. On
the way he poisoned himself in his car. When the driver turned round
after they had been going some time, he saw a dead body in the back.

" When von Kluge arrived in France," my father continued; " he
greeted me with the words: ' Now you, too, will have to learn to obey
orders.' The Fuehrer's headquarters had put him up to it. Of course
there was immediate trouble, but a brief visit to the front was enough
to convince him that I was right, and he, too, came round to the view
that the war must be ended independently. But on the 20th July he
knew nothing about the revolt until Hitler's message was read over the
radio. Then, of course, it was too late."

There is no doubt that the possibility had already occurred to my
father that he, too, could fall victim to Hitler's terror, but he could hardly
have had any suspicion that he would die by the same means as von
Kluge.

At the beginning of September, we received the news that General

Hans Speidel had been relieved of his office as Chief of Staff of Army Group B. A few days later he came to see my father in Herrlingen. They talked for many hours. General Speidel was due to report to the Fuehrer's H.Q. a day or two later and they agreed to take the opportunity to launch yet another peace proposal through General Guderian, then Chief of the General Staff.

But it was not to happen.

My father's case presented a particularly difficult problem for Hitler, for the news that even Field Marshal Rommel regarded the war as lost and was advising a separate peace would have been tantamount to a declaration of military bankruptcy. That is why Hitler held his hand so long after learning of my father's efforts to conclude a separate peace. On the 7th September, he had General Speidel arrested and the last act of the drama began. Speidel's arrest was whispered from mouth to mouth and former friends of my father suddenly became remarkably silent. " The rats are leaving the sinking ship," he said, with a smile, when he noticed it. But he was very worried about Speidel's fate and although he had not yet been informed officially of the arrest, tried by every means available to him to obtain his release. Finally, he sat down and wrote his last letter to Adolf Hitler.[1]

1 Oct. 1944

Mein Fuehrer,

Unfortunately my health is not yet as I could have wished. The quadruple fracture of the skull, the unfavourable development of the situation in the west since I was wounded, and not least the removal from his post and arrest of my former Chief of Staff, Lt.-Gen. Speidel —of which I learnt only by chance—have made demands on my nerves far beyond endurance. I no longer feel myself equal to further trials.

Lt.-Gen. Speidel was assigned to me as Chief of Staff in the middle of April 1944, in succession to Lt.-Gen. Gause. He was very well reported on by Col. Gen. Zeitzler and by his former Army Commander, Gen. Wöhler. Shortly before taking up office with the Army Group he had been awarded the Knight's Cross by you, and had been promoted to Lt.-General. In his first weeks in the west, Speidel showed himself to be an outstandingly efficient and diligent Chief of Staff. He took firm control of the staff, showed great understanding for the troops and helped me loyally to complete the defences of the Atlantic Wall as quickly as possible with the available means. When I went up to the front, which was almost every day, I could rely on Speidel to transmit my orders—as discussed beforehand—to the

---

[1]The reader should bear in mind that this letter was written at the peak period of the bloodthirsty purge that followed the plot against Hitler—and that, in Rommel's endeavour to save the life of a cherished assistant and friend, his prime concern must have been how he could best appeal to, and allay the suspicions of, the vengeful tyrant.

L.H.

Armies, and to carry on all talks with superior and equivalent formations along the lines I required.

When the battle in Normandy began, Speidel did not spare himself to bring success in the struggle with the enemy, who set us a heavy task, above all with his air superiority, his heavy naval guns and his other material superiority. Up to the day when I was wounded, Speidel stood loyally at my side. Field Marshal von Kluge also seems to have been satisfied with him. I cannot imagine what can have led to Lt.-Gen. Speidel's removal and arrest. *Oberstgruppen-fuehrer* Sepp Dietrich and Speidel were good friends and met frequently.

Unfortunately it proved impossible to fight the Normandy battle in such a manner that the enemy could be destroyed while still on the water, or at the latest at the moment of landing. The reasons for this I gave in the attached report, which Gen. Schmundt no doubt placed before you while he was still with you.

When Field Marshal von Kluge assumed command in the west an acrimonious scene took place at Army Group B in the presence of my Chief of Staff and Ia. I did not take silently the charges levelled against me, but spoke my mind in private to Field Marshal von Kluge, and asked him, moreover, on the following day, to let me know what grounds he had for making them. The charges were withdrawn verbally in the course of a conversation in which I pressed Field Marshal von Kluge, with all urgency, always to report the situation at the front to you quite openly and not to conceal unpleasant facts; for only by such service could you, *mein Fuehrer*, be enabled to see clearly and arrive at the right decisions. My last situation report went to C.-in-C. West the day before I was wounded and was—as Kluge later told me—sent on to you with a supplementary note by him.

You, *mein Fuehrer*, know how I have exerted my whole strength and capacity, be it in the Western campaign 1940 or in Africa 1941-43 or in Italy 1943 or again in the west 1944.

One thought only possesses me constantly, to fight and win for your new Germany.

Heil, mein Fuehrer,

E. ROMMEL

But General Speidel's whereabouts remained shrouded in darkness. Shortly after his arrest his name was mentioned, together with my father's, before the Army Court of Honour. But the " Rommel Case " was not discussed officially.

On the 7th October a signal arrived in Herrlingen. Field Marshal Keitel asking my father to go to Berlin for an important conference on the 10th October. A special train would fetch him from Ulm. " I'm not that much of a fool," my father said when he saw it. " We know these people now. I'd never get to Berlin alive." He spoke openly of the matter to Professor Albrecht, the brain specialist at Tuebingen University, under whose care he was, whereupon the Professor immediately certified him as unfit to travel. He also tried to persuade my father to go into his clinic, where he would not be so easy to get at. My father said he would keep the offer in mind.

But events moved rapidly. My father's refusal to go to Berlin lengthened his life by only four days.

Oskar Farny, the landowner, had been a friend of my father's ever since they had been subalterns together in Weingarten. As a former Centre Party Reichstag Deputy, Farny had always regarded the National Socialists with considerable distrust, and in the second half of the war had had long conversations with the former Ministers, Fehr and Gessler, concerning the possibility of making an end of the war and of the Nazi régime.

Fehr and Gessler were arrested on the 13th October 1944, and Farny, when my parents visited him later the same day, was expecting the Gestapo to come for him at any moment. "But Hitler will never dare do anything to you," he said to my father, "you're too popular, it would attract too much attention." My father answered as if he already had foreknowledge of his death. "You're wrong," he said, "Hitler wants to get rid of me and he'll leave no stone unturned to do it."

When my parents arrived back at Herrlingen again after the long car journey, they found a telephone message awaiting them to the effect that two Generals were coming next day to talk to my father about his "future employment".

My battery, to which I had returned several weeks before, had given me leave for the 14th October. I left the gun position very early in the morning and arrived at Herrlingen at 7.00 a.m. My father was already at breakfast. A cup was quickly brought for me and we breakfasted together, afterwards taking a stroll in the garden.

"At twelve o'clock to-day two Generals are coming to see me to discuss my future employment," my father started the conversation. "So to-day will decide what is planned for me; whether a People's Court or a new command in the East."

"Would you accept such a command," I asked.

He took me by the arm, and replied: "My dear boy, our enemy in the East is so terrible that every other consideration has to give way before it. If he succeeds in overrunning Europe, even only temporarily, it will be the end of everything which has made life appear worth living. Of course I would go."

Shortly before twelve o'clock, my father went to his room on the first floor and changed from the brown civilian jacket which he usually wore over riding-breeches, to his Africa tunic, which was his favourite uniform on account of its open collar.

At about twelve o'clock a dark-green car with a Berlin number stopped in front of our garden gate. The only men in the house apart from my father, were Captain Aldinger,[1] a badly wounded war-veteran corporal and myself. Two generals—Burgdorf, a powerful florid man, and Maisel, small and slender—alighted from the car and entered the house. They were respectful and courteous and asked my father's permission to speak to him alone. Aldinger and I left the room. "So they are not going to arrest him," I thought with relief, as I went upstairs to find myself a book.

A few minutes later I heard my father come upstairs and go into my mother's room. Anxious to know what was afoot, I got up and followed him. He was standing in the middle of the room, his face pale. "Come outside with me," he said in a tight voice. We went into my room. "I have just had to tell your mother," he began slowly, "that I shall be dead in a quarter of an hour." He was calm as he continued: "To die by the hand of one's own people is hard. But the house is surrounded and Hitler is charging me with high treason. 'In view of my services in Africa,'" he quoted sarcastically, "I am to have the chance of dying by poison. The two generals have brought it with them. It's fatal in three seconds. If I accept, none of the usual steps will be taken against my family, that is against you. They will also leave my staff alone."

"Do you believe it?" I interrupted.

"Yes," he replied. "I believe it. It is very much in their interest to see that the affair does not come out into the open. By the way, I have been charged to put you under a promise of the strictest silence. If a single word of this comes out, they will no longer feel themselves bound by the agreement."

I tried again. "Can't we defend ourselves ..." He cut me off short.

"There's no point," he said. "It's better for one to die than for all of us to be killed in a shooting affray. Anyway, we've practically no ammunition." We briefly took leave of each other. "Call Aldinger, please," he said.

Aldinger had meanwhile been engaged in conversation by the General's escort to keep him away from my father. At my call, he came running upstairs. He, too, was struck cold when he heard what was happening. My father now spoke more quickly. He again said how useless it was to attempt to defend ourselves. "It's all been prepared to the last detail. I'm to be given a state funeral. I have asked that it should take place in Ulm. In a quarter of an hour, you, Aldinger, will receive a telephone call from the Wagnerschule reserve hospital in Ulm to say that I've had a brain seizure on the way to a conference." He

---

[1]Hermann Aldinger, captain on the Reserve, a wiry Wuerttemberger of about 45 and a landscape architect in civilian life, had been on friendly terms with my father ever since the First World War. My father, whom he had already accompanied in 1940 in France and 1941 in North Africa, had summoned him to his staff again when he returned to Germany in August 1944 after he had been wounded.

looked at his watch. " I must go, they've only given me ten minutes."
He quickly took leave of us again. Then we went downstairs together.

We helped my father into his leather coat. Suddenly he pulled out
his wallet. " There's still 150 marks in there," he said. " Shall I take
the money with me? "

" That doesn't matter now, Herr Field Marshal," said Aldinger.

My father put his wallet carefully back in his pocket. As he went
into the hall, his little dachshund which he had been given as a
puppy a few months before in France, jumped up at him with a whine
of joy. " Shut the dog in the study, Manfred," he said, and waited in
the hall with Aldinger while I removed the excited dog and pushed it
through the study door. Then we walked out of the house together.
The two generals were standing at the garden gate. We walked slowly
down the path, the crunch of the gravel sounding unusually loud.

As we approached the generals they raised their right hands in
salute. " Herr Field Marshal," Burgdorf said shortly and stood aside
for my father to pass through the gate. A knot of villagers stood outside
the drive. Maisel turned to me, and asked: " What battery are you
with? "

" 36/7, Herr General," I answered.

The car stood ready. The S.S. driver swung the door open and stood
to attention. My father pushed his Marshal's baton under his left arm,
and with his face calm, gave Aldinger and me his hand once more before
getting in the car.

The two generals climbed quickly into their seats and the doors were
slammed. My father did not turn again as the car drove quickly off up
the hill and disappeared round a bend in the road. When it had gone
Aldinger and I turned and walked silently back into the house. " I'd
better go up and see your mother," Aldinger said. I went upstairs again
to await the promised telephone call. An agonising depression excluded
all thought.

I lit a cigarette and tried to read again, but the words no longer
made sense. Twenty minutes later the telephone rang. Aldinger lifted
the receiver and my father's death was duly reported. That evening we
drove into Ulm to the hospital where he lay. The doctors who received
us were obviously ill at ease, no doubt suspecting the true cause of my
father's death. One of them opened the door of a small room. My father
lay on a camp-bed in his brown Africa uniform, a look of contempt on
his face.

It was not then entirely clear what had happened to him after he
left us. Later we learned that the car had halted a few hundred yards up
the hill from our house in an open space at the edge of the wood. Gestapo
men, who had appeared in force from Berlin that morning, were watching
the area with instructions to shoot my father down and storm the house
if he offered resistance. Maisel and the driver got out of the car, leaving

my father and Burgdorf inside. When the driver was permitted to return ten minutes or so later, he saw my father sunk forward with his cap off and the marshal's baton fallen from his hand. Then they drove off at top speed to Ulm, where the body was unloaded at the hospital; afterwards General Burgdorf drove on to Ulm Wehrmacht Headquarters where he first telephoned to Hitler to report my father's death and then to the family of one of his escort officers to compose the menu for that night's dinner. General Burgdorf, who was hated for his brutality by 99 per cent of the Officer Corps, ended his own life in Berlin in April 1945, after staggering round drunk with Bormann for several days in the Fuehrer's bunker.

Perhaps the most despicable part of the whole story was the expressions of sympathy we received from members of the German Government, men who could not fail to have known the true cause of my father's death and in some cases had no doubt themselves contributed to it, both by word and deed. I quote a few examples:

In the Field
16 October 1944

Accept my sincerest sympathy for the heavy loss you have suffered with the death of your husband. The name of Field Marshal Rommel will be for ever linked with the heroic battles in North Africa.

ADOLF HITLER

Fuehrer's Headquarters
26 October 1944[1]

The fact that your husband, Field Marshal Rommel, has died a hero's death as the result of his wounds, after we had all hoped that he would remain to the German people, has deeply touched me. I send you, my dear Frau Rommel, the heartfelt sympathy of myself and the German Luftwaffe.

In silent compassion, Yours,

GOERING, Reichsmarschall des
Grossdeutschen Reiches

Berlin
17 October 1944

MY DEAR FRAU ROMMEL

On the occasion of the unhappy loss which you have suffered through the death of your husband, my wife and I send you an expression of our warmest sympathy. In Field Marshal Rommel the German Army loses one of its most successful commanders, whose name will be for ever linked with the heroic two-year struggle of the

---

[1]It is curious that Goering's telegram should have been dispatched ten days after Hitler's.

Afrika Korps. Please be assured of our deepest sympathy in your grief.
Heil Hitler,
Reichsminister DR. GOEBBELS and FRAU GOEBBELS

While these men were seeking, by their hypocrisy, to give the last touch of realism to the farce, thousands of German soldiers were dying in the north, south, east and west, with little hope, but with belief in the integrity of their command.

CHAPTER XXIII

THE SKY HAS GROWN DARK

These striking reflections on the campaigns in Africa and Normandy were written by Rommel while he was at home recovering from his injuries in Normandy. It was only a rough draft, and he had no chance to revise it, as he would certainly have done if he had lived. That must be borne in mind when considering occasional loose ends in the argument and sweeping comments on individuals. His concluding tribute to Kesselring is an example of the way he often came to take a juster view of men with whom he was for a time in hot disagreement.

The capitulation at Tunis wrote " Finis " to the campaign in North Africa. As at Stalingrad it was the baleful influence of Hermann Goering that sealed the Army Group's fate. The result was that 130,000[1] German soldiers who were badly needed for the defence of southern Europe—among them my troops, men who simply could not be replaced—marched into Anglo-American captivity.

The war in North Africa was decided by the weight of Anglo-American material. In fact, since the entry of America into the war, there has been very little prospect of our achieving ultimate victory. Some hope did remain so long as our submarines were able to maintain their mastery of the Atlantic, for the greatest production of tanks, guns and vehicles would have availed America nothing if she could not have carried them across the seas. But this " Battle of the Atlantic", which in all probability decided the whole war, was soon lost by us with frightful casualties among our U-boats. All else was dependent on this fact, and we were now doomed to inevitable defeat at any place which was accessible to the Anglo-American transport fleets.

Hence, in an Anglo-American invasion, the main question for the invaders was whether they would be able to clear a bridgehead of

[1] It is interesting to note in comparison with this figure that from the beginning of 1941 to the evacuation of Tripolitania in 1942-43, the casualties of the German element of the Panzer Army Afrika amounted to 5,200 killed and 14,000 prisoners.—*F.B. In this chapter footnotes by General Bayerlein are followed by the initials F.B.; those by Captain Liddell Hart by the initials L. H.*

sufficient depth to enable them to bring in and unload their material undisturbed. Once they had succeeded in this, there could no longer be any hope of victory for us.

But even the Allies could not simultaneously land twenty divisions with all their equipment and stores on a defended coast, but needed some time to bring them in one after the other. Hence, as in all landing operations, the first few days were bound to be the critical period.

There were then two possible ways in which a landing could be defeated, either (a) by creating a concentration of strength at the threatened point during the first few days and throwing the enemy back into the sea or (b) by extending the critical period of the landing until the requisite force had been assembled for the counter-blow. In other words, by making the local defending force at the point of landing strong enough to enable it to prevent an extension of the enemy bridgehead during the few days when it was on its own.

As our forces in France were not strong enough to perform both functions simultaneously—of holding the coast in strength and maintaining an adequate operational reserve inland—we were faced with an " either, or ". Either we could have a more or less strong coastal garrison in the threatened areas by drawing on the operational reserve, or we could have a strong operational reserve by taking troops from the coastal defences.

Field Marshal von Rundstedt, a soldier of very considerable strategic calibre, planned to put himself in a position to combat any of the possible moves open to the enemy, by placing his panzer and motorised divisions in Central France, whence they could have been rapidly dispatched to the battlefield and could thus have achieved a heavy local superiority during the first day or two of the landing. This plan, despite the weakness of the coastal garrison which it entailed, would have been the correct solution in normal circumstances and would have provided 100 per cent certainty of success. But Field Marshal von Rundstedt could have no conception of the extent of the Anglo-American air superiority or of the operational and tactical restrictions which this would force on us.

In an approach march by so many panzer and motorised divisions, which, because of the weakness of the coastal garrison, would have to be completed in the minimum possible time, close adherence to a time-schedule would be absolutely essential. From my experience in Africa, I doubted—rightly, as the event showed—whether it would be possible to carry out such a plan in the time available.

We in Africa had had opportunity enough at El Alamein of studying the effect of Anglo-American bombing tactics on our motorised formations. And we could expect that the air forces which the Allies would use in France on invasion day would be many times greater than those they had used in North Africa. In France, moreover, contrary to the African desert, there were only a few roads over which the approach march could be made, and these ran across rivers and through towns. This meant that the opportunities for effective action by the Allied air fleets would be considerably greater there than in the desert.

I therefore drew the attention of Field Marshal von Rundstedt in particular to the following points:

(a) Anglo-American fighter-bombers would cover the approach roads both by day and—using flares—by night, and stop all traffic.

(b) Allied bomber squadrons would smash all bridges and towns too, if by so doing they could hope to close the approach roads for a few days. This would result in important roads being put completely out of use.

(c) The motorised forces would suffer tremendous casualties from air attack while still on the march.

(d) Thus the maintenance of time-schedules would be totally impossible, and extensive reorganisation would become necessary. It is, of course, comparatively easy to regroup two or three divisions, but it is a very different matter to reorganise an approach march by ten divisions and takes a lot of time, especially if the men are not accustomed to improvisation.

(e) It would be ten days or a fortnight before the striking force could arrive on the field and be regrouped for action, during which time the Americans would have overpowered our weak coastal garrisons fighting without tank support, thrust inland and built up supplies in their bridgehead. Once this had happened, the attack of our striking force, already decimated during its march to the front, would have no hope of success. Of course it would always have been possible to split off several formations and get them to the front quickly by forced marches, but that would have been the end of the single offensive concentration, which was the principal advantage of the Rundstedt plan.

I therefore held firmly to my own plan, which in the circumstances could not possibly be anything more than a compromise. In the first place, the coast was to be fortified as strongly as possible. The infantry was to take up position on the beaches and the tanks deploy close behind so that their guns would also be effective on the beaches. By having the strongest possible local force on the spot at the points most seriously threatened, I intended to achieve the following:

(a) The defences would get the utmost advantage out of the period of greatest technical difficulty in a landing, i.e. the moment when the invading troops are approaching the beach in their landing-craft and ships. Low water obstructions, beach mines and the concentrated fire of all arms on the landing forces would multiply the difficulty of the manoeuvre many times over.

(b) Our local forces would prevent the invaders extending their bridgehead to an area large enough to enable them to maintain their supply. Meanwhile, armoured and motorised forces would be drawn off from other sectors and assembled behind the threatened front, whence they would launch a counter-attack to clean up the enemy footholds. I hoped to make up for the time which the motorised forces could be expected to lose as a result of enemy air attack, by a rather stronger occupation of the coastline.

Unfortunately, it proved impossible in the time available to fortify the coastline to the extent required, although we did everything we could to expedite the work. Moreover, neither the Fuehrer's H.Q. nor the Commander-in-Chief West was prepared to recognise the threat to Normandy, as both imagined that the better strategic possibilities offered by a bridgehead in the Pas de Calais would induce the Allies to land in that sector.[1] But the fulfilment of the enemy's strategic plans was entirely dependent on the success of their landing, and, while success was unlikely in the Pas de Calais, it was far from unlikely in the lightly fortified Normandy area. Their primary consideration, therefore, was the success of the actual landing operation; the strategic disadvantages of Normandy compared with the Pas de Calais were of less importance. The Allies had time and material enough.

Thus it happened that two demands which I made—namely, the mining of the Bay of the Seine, and the dispatch to Normandy of certain forces, viz. several Panzer Divisions,[2] an A.A. Corps, a Nebelwerfer Brigade, and parachutists—were neither of them fulfilled before the invasion. This placed us under a disastrous handicap from the start.

Nevertheless, it is my belief that even if we had had these forces at the scene of the landing, we would still have lost the battle, as our counter-attacks would have been smashed by the Allied naval guns and air force, and our artillery and Nebelwerfer positions would have been put out of action one after the other by the fantastic Allied barrage. Added to this

[1]This statement is a little confusing, as the Fuehrer's H.Q. several times drew attention to the special threat to Normandy and it was von Rundstedt who thought primarily in terms of an Allied landing in the Pas de Calais.
    Leaving aside the possibility of a slip in writing, Rommel may have wanted to indicate that the Fuehrer's H.Q. was not sufficiently convinced of the invasion in Normandy as to give any support to the attempts he was making to have several panzer divisions and other formations moved there before the Allied landing.—F.B.
[2]Rommel means here the Panzer Lehr Division and 12th S.S. Panzer Division Hitler Jugend. Had this proposal been acted on, armoured forces in the following strength would have come into action in the early hours of the Allied landing: 520 armoured fighting vehicles, 120 assault and self-propelled guns and 1,200 armoured troop-carriers. (In the event only 21st Panzer Division was available on the 6th June, with the following strength: 150 tanks, 60 assault and self-propelled guns and some 300 armoured troop-carriers.) In addition, several hundred A.A. guns and a great number of Nebelwerfer would have been able to take their toll of the Allied landings.—F.B.

we lacked the extensive mining and large-scale construction of shallow water obstacles which we had planned. We had had far too little time for the work to start with, and then the tremendous destruction which Allied strategic bombing had caused to communications—especially in Normandy—even before the invasion, had not exactly helped to hasten it. Ultimately it was shown that no compromise of any kind can make up for total enemy air and artillery superiority.

For the rest, my predictions concerning the move of the motorised forces to the front were confirmed. After days of marching (actually, the greater part of it had to be done by night), the divisions arrived at the invasion front, having already suffered severe casualties on the way.

One thing is certain, that with the invasion battle we lost the last chance of gaining that strategic vantage point which a victory on the coast would have given us, and which would have been of such inestimable value as a basis for developments in the political field.

But it was in North Africa that a really great opportunity was missed, owing to the failure of our highest authorities to appreciate correctly the strategic possibilities of the African theatre. Disastrous blunders and mistakes finally led to the surrender of the Axis troops in Tunis. I feel that perhaps I should summarise the possibilities which the African theatre offered us and the reasons why they were not exploited. It was the most important and at the same time most tragic feature of this campaign that its character and possible strategic significance were recognised too late by the responsible men. And when they did see it, they refused to acknowledge that their realisation had come too late, and that the strategic situation in the Mediterranean area had then deteriorated so far that a further maintenance of the African theatre was out of the question.

Over a period of several years, the Near East was held by a comparatively small British force, amounting in its best days to no more than 12 divisions. One devastating defeat after another was inflicted on these divisions, yet the Axis forces were never strong enough to embark properly on the strategic exploitation of their successes. But the British Army Group in the Near East was the sole protection for vast territories, which were of the most immense importance to the Allies, as the following will show:

The areas withheld from the Axis grip by the British Army Group " Near East " [*actually called "Middle East", L.H.*] included:

(*a*) The Suez Canal, Egypt, and East Africa. The Suez Canal itself had less strategic importance in this war than is generally supposed, owing to the fact that the Italians were able to bar the Mediterranean at Sicily.

(b) Syria, Mesopotamia and Persia. Three factors made this area of
particular importance to the Allies.

   (i) In 1939, Persia and Irak together provided in all some 15
million tons of mineral oil, compared with Rumania's 6.5
million tons. Possession of this territory would have permitted
the Axis to put far more of its army on wheels and would thus
have created the conditions for victory in the Russian plains.
We could also have greatly increased our air force and made
more liberal use of it.

  (ii) The principal flow of American arms and material aid to
Russia passed through Basra in the Persian Gulf, where tens
of thousands of vehicles and thousands of tanks were unloaded
on their way to the Russians. Axis possession of this area
would have meant the re-routing of American shipping to
Murmansk, a route on which the Americans were exposed—
up to the beginning of 1943—to great danger from German
submarines and aircraft, due to the fact that their convoys
had to pass along a large stretch of the Norwegian coast.

 (iii) If Axis troops had succeeded in taking the whole of the
Mediterranean coastline and Mesopotamia, they would have
been provided with an excellent base for an offensive against
the southern Russian front. It would no longer have been
possible for the British to threaten or interfere with German-
Italian transport across the Mediterranean and there would
thus have been virtually no more supply difficulties.

This, therefore, was how the strategic situation in the Mediterranean
basin must have appeared to the British. The possibilities which this
situation in fact offered to the Axis powers are discussed below.

The most important question to be asked in relation to the African
war is whether it would have been possible, by a better distribution of the
total German forces, to have gained mastery of the Mediterranean air
and guaranteed a safe supply line for the Axis Army in North Africa.

A second, and scarcely less important question is whether it would
have been possible, by a better distribution of the total German forces,
to have released mobile formations from unimportant sectors elsewhere
and moved them to North Africa.

Colonel-General Halder told me in 1941 that the Army High Command regarded the North African theatre as a lost cause and that they
were setting the German troops no other task but to delay the collapse
of Italian resistance in Libya for as long as possible. Herr Halder tried
to justify his view by asserting that it would be impossible to keep an
army of more than two or three divisions supplied in North Africa for
long. He only held this opinion, incidentally, while I remained in

command of the army. As early as June 1941, General Gause appeared in North Africa on an O.K.W. mission to study the possibility of employing larger forces in that theatre under another command. Nothing, however, came of the scheme.

Concerning the overall strategic situation in the Mediterranean area, the O.K.W. and O.K.H. showed a passivity nothing short of irresponsible. Our supply difficulties were in reality far easier to overcome than those which the British were facing, for they had to carry all their material over a 12,000-mile sea route round the Cape. The following steps were all that would have been necessary to release sufficient troops for North Africa, and to safeguard their transport to Libya and their supply:

(a) The creation of an adequate air concentration in the Mediterranean area, by moving Luftwaffe formations from France, Norway and Denmark. (Taken in relation to the total war effort, the establishment of air mastery over the Mediterranean would have more than compensated for a weakening of German air power in the countries concerned.)

(b) Transfer to the North African theatre of several of the armoured and motorised formations which were lying idle in France and Germany. (There was no serious danger at that time of any large-scale Allied invasion of France or any other country.)

(c) Malta should have been attacked and taken.

(d) The appointment of one man to take charge of supplies, with full powers over all Wehrmacht authorities concerned in their handling and protection. He would have required full support at all times on political matters.

These measures had nothing extraordinary about them and would have been quite normal action to take, yet they would have conclusively decided the war in Africa in our favour.

It was not until the news of the African collapse penetrated to Europe that people began to realise the importance of Africa and to increase their efforts, just as small-minded people always need crisis and danger to enable them to see beyond their own noses. All at once it was found possible to ship anything up to 60,000 tons a month to Tunis, in spite of the fact that the British and Americans then had a far tighter grip on the Mediterranean than they had had in 1941-42.[1] But it was too late.

We in North Africa had drawn attention again and again to the possibilities of the African theatre, but had been fobbed off each time by

---

[1]One must, however, remember that the sea trip from Naples to Tunis was far shorter than that from Naples to Tripoli, Benghazi or Tobruk.—*F.B.*

the High Command with the most threadbare of arguments. No opportunity had been missed of propagating our ideas, but it had all been in vain.

Given more motorised formations and a secure supply line, this is approximately what we could have achieved between the beginning of 1941 and the summer of 1942:

(a) We could have defeated and destroyed the British Field Army, and that would have opened the road to the Suez Canal. The British would then have required at least two months to bring up fresh troops to the Near East, two months during which we could have undertaken whatever operation we chose. (It is fair to assume that the British would not in that event have sent any further contingents of troops to the Near East.)

(b) With the entire Mediterranean coastline in our hands, supplies could have been shipped to North Africa unmolested. It would then have been possible to thrust forward into Persia and Irak in order to cut off the Russians from Basra, take possession of the oilfields and create a base for an attack on southern Russia. The Russians could hardly have conjured up in a hurry a motorised force which would have been anything like a match for ours in the open plains either organisationally or tactically.

(c) While building-up in Mesopotamia in preparation for a major offensive against the south Russian front, it would have been necessary to cut Murmansk off from the rest of Russia and if possible take possession of it by a thrust from Finland. This would have entailed the use of motorised and armoured formations in the far north, which would undoubtedly have made very heavy demands on our transport system, but such an undertaking would have been well worth while in any event. Russia would then have been virtually isolated from America, for the Japs would have hunted down the American freighter fleet in the Pacific, while the two most important ports, Basra and Murmansk, would have been closed to the Americans. The only port left to the Russians would have been Archangel, and that is ice-bound for many months of the year and is in any case very badly situated.

(d) Our final strategic objective would have been an attack on the southern Caucasian front aimed at the capture of Baku and its oilfields. This would have struck the Russians in a vital spot. A great part of their armour, which was carrying the main burden of the fighting on their side, would have been out of action for lack of petrol. Their air force would have been crippled. They could no longer have expected any further effective American help.

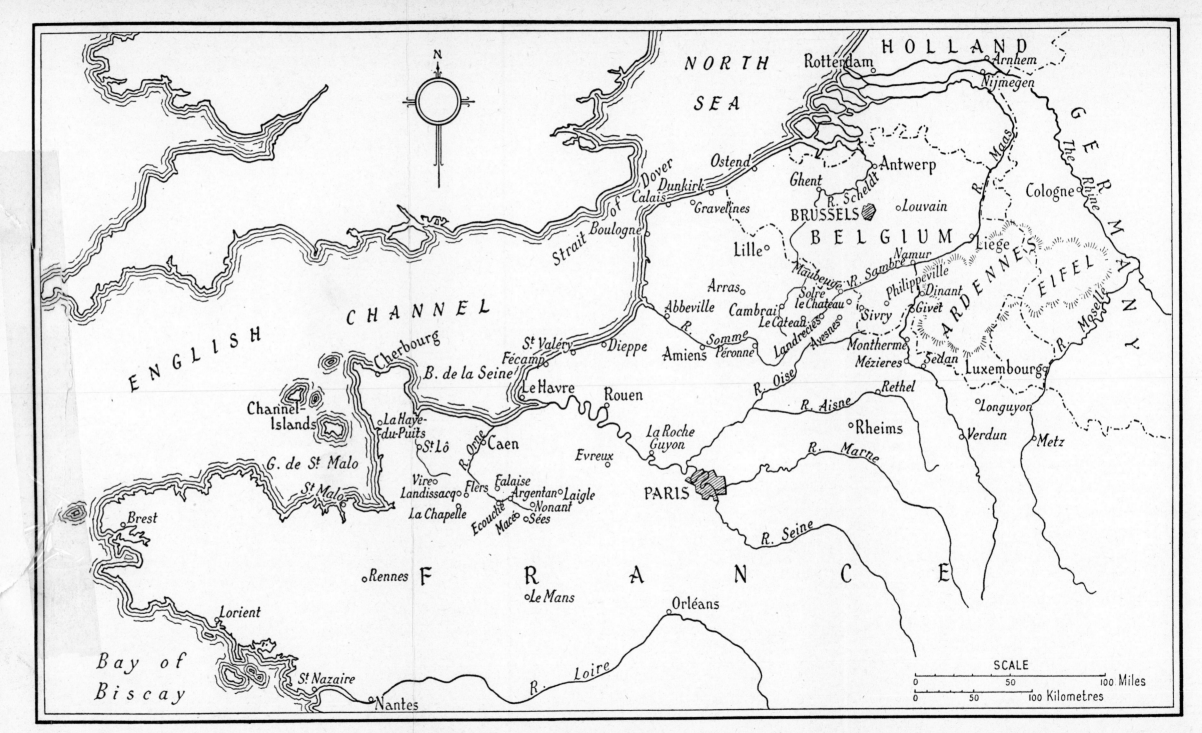

NORTHERN FRANCE

Thus the strategic conditions would have been created for us to close in from all sides and shatter the Russian colossus.

When I put this plan forward in its essential features, it was turned down by people of limited vision as a complete fantasy. But in no single point was it based on unfounded suppositions or unjustifiable hypotheses. It would have given the 100 per cent certainty which at other times they always demanded.[1] Anyone who fights a whole world must think in continents. It mattered nothing how many million square miles of territory lay behind the thin barrier which the Eighth Army had set up in the Libyan desert. What mattered was to break through that line and flow like a tidal wave over the unprotected country behind.

The O.K.W.'s approach to this whole question reflected an attitude typical of certain sections of the Wehrmacht, especially the General Staff.[2] These people always behaved as though the whole field of strategy was their exclusive prerogative. Their caution was not Montgomery's, who obviously considered that insistence on 100 per cent certainty was to be preferred to a policy of boldness, which is true in questions of strategy, although certainly not in tactics. These people's caution was fear of responsibility. On the one hand, they were perfectly ready to work out operations which were nothing less than strategic gambles, with but small chance of success—provided it was done over somebody else's signature. But on the other, they were always very shy of suggesting operations on their own initiative, even when they contained no shadow of risk and held out a promise of great success. As I hold the opinion that this attitude had also caused a great deal of harm elsewhere, I should like to go rather more deeply into the whole question.

[1]The argument here seems a little incomplete and poses a number of other problems, such as, for instance, the possibility that the Allies might, in fact, have landed in France if the motorised formations for Africa had been drawn from there. We would, in fact, probably have had to draw them from the Eastern Front and stayed on the defensive there. The relative importance which the Allies attached to these two theatres can be seen from a memorandum which Roosevelt wrote for Hopkins on the 16th July, after the fall of Tobruk (Sherwood, *The White House Papers*):

" The Middle East should be held as strongly as possible, whether Russia collapses or not. I want you to take into consideration the effect of losing the Suez Canal."—*F.B.*

[2]It is already possible, without necessarily taking a partisan view, to establish two points:

(1) Rommel's criticism of the arrangements for supplying his army were largely justified. There is no doubt that, if greater attention had been given to the problem, the African theatre could have been supplied tolerably well up to the summer of 1942.

(2) Rommel's strategic plan seems more sensible than the O.K.W.'s method of driving endlessly into Russia and leaving the West to lie fallow. If there is anything to be said against the scheme it is that it was neither militarily nor economically possible for Germany, Italy and Japan to survive in a war against the whole world.—*F.B.*

MODERN MILITARY LEADERSHIP

In the last quarter of the nineteenth century, all the major European powers began to fill their General Staffs with officers of the more intellectual type, who had been brought up to regard war as a science. Schlieffen's conception of the Commander-in-Chief as the brain of the Army found universal acceptance, and officers came to be assessed on their intellectual qualifications alone. This greater intellectual training of officers was a necessity and arose from the following facts:

(a) The introduction of universal conscription, which led to a great increase in the size of armies.

·(b) The steadily growing number of new technical devices, applicable both to supply and battle, which necessitated planning of a far more elaborate nature, both in its conception and preparation. Though the basic theme of the battle remained simple—since the brunt of the fighting was still borne by the infantryman—its execution became more and more intricate.

(c) The fact that the conduct of war, both strategy and tactics, had developed into a science.

The idea of the *Feldherr*—the great military leader—and the current doctrines of war, deeply rooted in the Officer Corps, completely satisfied the demands made on the officer class by World War I.

Every European nation has a strong tendency to be tied by tradition, even in matters of science. It was not, therefore, surprising that after World War I, in which the respective commands had exploited the then existing means of war to their uttermost limit, many of the European General Staffs became rigidly doctrinaire in their outlook. While unquestioningly accepting the views of great men in matters of principle, they themselves became lost in the detail, tangled it all up into a dreadful complexity, turned warfare into an exchange of memoranda and stuck to their ideas through thick and thin. Soon they were unable to see even the simplest possibilities of a situation, and they never failed to find in their followers and fellow-thinkers a sounding-board for their theories.

In Germany, development of the air and tank arms was interrupted by the Versailles Treaty. This was perhaps an advantage, since our theories were able to develop in an atmosphere of far greater freedom than they could have done if they had been directed into set channels by the existence of armoured formations with an established organisation and a predetermined tactical rôle. National Socialism, moreover, gave the *avant garde* in the General Staff the upper hand in many questions of principle. Elsewhere in Europe, in France and England, for example, where military development was neither interrupted nor revolutionised by an internal upheaval, this was not the case and there grew up a tremendous rigidity and adherence to system which could in no way meet the requirements of modern warfare. We, on our side, would have had very little advantage over the French and British in 1940, even with our up-to-date tank and air arms, if these arms had not been matched by equally up-to-date organisation, training and tactical doctrines.

Nevertheless, even the German Officer Corps was by no means completely free of the old prejudices. There was a particular clique that still fought bitterly against any drastic modernisation of methods and clung fast to the axiom that the infantry must be regarded as the most important constituent of any army. This may be true for Germany's eastern army as it is fighting to-day[1] in Russia, but it will not be true in the future—which is where our attention should be concentrated—when the tank will be the centre of all tactical thinking. The African campaign and the new aspects of warfare which it brought were never understood by men like General Halder.[2] They stuck to their established methods and precedents, even though these often showed themselves to be outdated and hence false. The consequence was that Goering and Himmler thought they knew better how to make war, and often caused great harm by their dilettantism, while the senior military commands, with their professional staffs, were increasingly overruled.

My staff and I gave no regard whatever to all this unnecessary academic nonsense, which had long been overtaken by technical development. Consequently, many officers of the academic type, steeped in their ancient theories, failed to understand us and so took us for adventurers, amateurs and the like. Not that I would have let this worry me unduly, had it not been for the disastrous effect which it had on the course of the war in Africa.

The fact of the mechanisation of all human existence is equally valid for the science of war. The tactical leader of the future, who will decide the battle—for the main emphasis of future battles will be on the tactical destruction of the enemy's fighting power—will need not only mental gifts of a high order, but also great strength of character if he is to be a match for his task. Because of the great variety of tactical possibilities which motorisation offers it will in future be impossible to make more than a rough forecast of the course of a battle. This being so, the issue will be decided by flexibility of mind, eager acceptance of responsibility, a fitting mixture of caution and audacity, and the greater control over the fighting troops. I give a few points on which special emphasis will have to be laid in the future training of an Officer Corps:

[1]Written before the end of the war.

[2]Colonel-General Halder, who was without doubt a reliable judge in matters concerning the European theatre of war, had little understanding for the mobile warfare in Africa. On many subjects his view was completely contrary to Rommel's. However, one must hear Halder's case, of course, before arriving at an objective judgment.—*F.B.*

(a) Fundamental to the training of senior officers will be the most comprehensive instruction possible in technical and organisational matters. The object of this instruction will be to induce a certain independence of mind, so that particular value will need to be laid on teaching officers to think critically on questions of basic principle. Respect for the opinion of this or that great soldier must never be allowed to go so far that nobody dares to discuss it. A sure sense of reality must be aroused. Given a well-founded knowledge of basic principles, any man of reasonably cool and logical mind can work out most of the details for himself, provided he is not inhibited in his thinking.

(b) Mental conception must be followed by immediate execution. This is a matter of energy and initiative. What the soldier needs is a combination of realist intellect and energy. Whatever is attempted must be carried through. The young officer must understand from the outset of his training that just as much energy is required of him as mental ability. The sensational victory is, more often than not, largely a victory for the energy of the officers.

(c) One point which is overlooked by most military theorists is the psychology of the troops. Average performance is everywhere accepted as satisfactory. It is tremendously important to realise the attitude of the soldier to war. A man leaving his home and family to-day, to do his duty under the most terrible conditions at the front, does so in a fine spirit of idealism, and commanders of men must be under no illusions about this. Officers must, therefore, do all they can to maintain and preserve this idealism in their men.

By skilful psychological handling, in which personal example plays the principal part, the performance of troops can be increased enormously. This provides the commander with the superior instrument, enables him to accomplish far more tactically than his opponent, and thus places him at an advantage throughout the action.

The commander must try, above all, to establish personal and comradely contact with his men, but without giving away an inch of his authority. When an attack is ordered, the men must never be allowed to get the feeling that their casualties have been calculated in advance according to the laws of probability, for that is the end of all enthusiasm. The soldier must continually receive fresh justification for his confidence, otherwise it is soon lost. He must go into battle easy in mind and with no doubts about the command under which he is fighting.

This precept was frequently disregarded in Russia, where whole divisions and armies were delivered up, often pointlessly, to the terrible enemy. The understandable result was that officers and men no longer went into battle with a light heart, but kept one eye on their neighbours and never took a chance. When one is forced to fight against such an enemy, more than ordinary care must be taken to ensure that no unit is ever left in the lurch. Only thus can the effects of fear and anxiety be minimised. This point of the proper psychological handling of troops cannot be too highly stressed to all officers.

(d) When two armies meet on the battlefield, each of the opposing commanders has his own particular plan according to which he intends to engage his enemy, and the battle develops out of the two opposing plans. Only rarely in history has a battle gone completely according to the plan of either side and then usually because either the victor has had absolute quantitative or qualitative superiority or the loser has been utterly incompetent. In modern mobile warfare over flat and open country, battles are no longer decided in a matter of days, and the struggle for the initiative may rage over the same tract of country for weeks on end. In these circumstances, it is extremely important for the commander to know his opponent and be capable of assessing his psychological reactions. Senior officers should be closely informed on the psychological stresses to which a commander is exposed during battle and should be provided with the necessary psychological equipment to enable them to turn this knowledge to advantage.

(e) The greatest efforts must be made in the field of training to counteract the separatist tendencies of the various services and arms of the services. It happens again and again that the air force or army begins to play its own private political game. This struggling for power is rather like sawing off the branch on which one is sitting. One must be particularly vigilant to ensure that no kind of corps ambition develops. Anything which may deflect from unity of purpose, from the will to pull together, must be utterly eradicated.

AFRICA IN RETROSPECT

Victory in battle—save where it is brought about by sheer weight of numbers, and omitting all question of the courage of the troops engaged—never comes solely as the result of the victor's planning. It is not only the merits of the victor that decide the issue, but also mistakes on the part of the vanquished. This rule can be applied to the African theatre of war. It was the British mistakes, dating back in many cases to before the war, that made our victories possible. The following is a brief résumé of the reasons for the Eighth Army's defeats:

Whereas in Germany, as I have already said, the elements of modern armoured warfare had already crystallised into doctrine before the war —thanks mainly to the work of General Guderian—and had found practical expression in the organisation and training of armoured formations, the British had remained conservative and their responsible quarters had almost entirely rejected the doctrine of mechanised warfare that had been so brilliantly set forth by some of their own countrymen. At the beginning of the war, Britain had for all practical purposes not gone beyond the stage of the infantry tank plus the light reconnaissance tank.[1] Training paid little heed to the requirements of mechanised warfare—as yet, of course, only hypothetical—including in particular speed of movement, flexibility and close contact between command and troops. An exception was to be found in the British reconnaissance units, whose training was first class.

The British commanders were certainly quick to realise what was wrong, but motorisation alone, however excellent, could not put the trouble right, for neither the re-training of officers and commanders nor the adaptation of the machinery of command—a terribly cumbersome structure in Britain—could be carried out quickly enough. The range of the British tank and anti-tank guns was far too short, and remained so until the summer of 1942. Infantry tanks were at first not even provided with H.E. ammunition, but only with solid shell. It is also my belief that most senior British officers have a certain tendency to think along established lines. The only one who showed a touch of genius was Wavell. Auchinleck was a very good leader, but he usually left control of tactical operations to his subordinate commanders, who soon allowed me to call the tune, and who reacted more frequently than they acted, often without real necessity. Neither Cunningham nor Ritchie were tank specialists and they were, therefore, unable to introduce any far-reaching modernisation into British training. What is more, they rarely managed to commit their forces correctly according to the tactical requirements of mobile warfare. At Alamein [in July], however, Auchinleck took the initiative himself and executed his operations with deliberation and noteworthy courage. Every time I was on the point of forcing a breakthrough with my German motorised formations, he launched an attack on the Italians elsewhere, scattered them and either penetrated uncomfortably close to our supply area or threatened a break-through in the south. On each occasion I was forced to break off my own attack in order to hurry to the help of the threatened sector.

[1]Two armoured divisions had been formed in England (as well as one in Egypt), but even the first of these was not sent to France until after the German offensive was launched in May 1940. The delay in its arrival was unfortunate for the outcome. It also caused the British Army's practical development to appear more backward than it actually was.
                                                                                     L. H.

Montgomery was in a position to profit by the bitter experience of his predecessors. Moreover, while supplies on our side had been cut to a trickle, American and British ships were bringing vast quantities of material to North Africa, many times greater than either Wavell or Auchinleck had ever had.

Montgomery did not leave the slightest detail out of his calculations. He discounted all academic theorising and let himself be guided by experience alone. He showed himself very advanced in his thinking when, on arriving at El Alamein, he worked out the essential rules of the front for himself and proceeded to shape his method of attack accordingly. His principle was to fight no battle unless he knew for certain that he would win it. Of course that is a method which will only work given material superiority; but that he had. He was cautious—to my mind, excessively so—but then he could afford to be. But where he was most to be envied was in having men behind him who threw the whole weight of their personality into the scales to provide him with the material he needed.

Montgomery was undoubtedly more of a strategist than a tactician. Command of a force in mobile battle was not his strong point, although, as far as one could see, he was fully alive to the fact that certain tactical principles must prevail. In the field of higher strategic planning he must be credited with outstanding achievements, not least during the invasion battle, which was fought under his command. It would be difficult to accuse Montgomery of ever having made a serious strategic mistake.

It was indeed the general rule that the higher ranking British officers thought more in terms of strategy than tactics. As a result the majority of their responsible officers made the error of planning operations according to what was strategically desirable, rather than what was tactically attainable.

Viewed as a whole, it was a great mistake for the British to be continually replacing their Commander-in-Chief, and thus forcing the new man to learn the same bitter lessons all over again. The British commanders were capable soldiers; it was merely that some of them had preconceived ideas—like those which many German generals brought with them to Africa—which they would certainly have discarded after their first reverses. But they were always relieved of their command before they had the chance.

What was astonishing was the speed with which the Americans adapted themselves to modern warfare. In this they were assisted by their extraordinary sense for the practical and material and by their complete lack of regard for tradition and worthless theories. An intellect directed to practical ends, initiative and the urge for material wealth have combined to make America, economically, the strongest power in the world. For what matters to-day is not which nation has the oldest tradition or which is the most ready to make sacrifices, but which commands the greatest production of coal and steel.

In Europe, some people waste a great deal of their energy on things which bring them perhaps some inner satisfaction, but no real benefit. They are singularly inept at coping with life and derive little help from their intellect. Inside the mechanism of an army, incidentally, such people can be a terrible clog on the wheels and the best thing to do is to get rid of them.

Colin Ross,[1] in his book *The Western Hemisphere*, gives what is probably an excellent character study of the Americans. It is men such as he describes who will be best qualified to take command in a world where the struggle for existence is waged, not in the quiet retreat of the scholar, but in the industrial areas, in the research laboratories and on the battlefield.

The leaders of the American economy and the American General Staff have achieved miracles. The organisation, training and equipment of the U.S. Army all bear witness to great imagination and foresight, and, above all, to the positive determination of the American people to act in unison and create a war machine with real striking power. Starting from scratch an army has been created in the very minimum of time, which, in equipment, armament and organisation of all arms, surpasses anything the world has yet seen. Though we may perhaps still retain some lead over them in the quality of certain items of our equipment, yet the general balance of American organisation and the steady development they have achieved in equipment and armament are things we have not yet been able to equal.[2]

Technically and strategically the landing in Normandy was a brilliant achievement of the first magnitude. It showed that the Americans had the courage, at any rate in the technical field, to employ a multitude of devices hitherto untried in action.[3] European generals of the old school

[1] A popular German travel writer.

[2] Rommel's opinion of the Americans was clearly influenced by the deep impression which the apparatus of the Anglo-American invasion army—complete to the last detail —had made on him.

What impressed Rommel most were the artificial harbours which were brought up by the British and Americans and sunk before the invasion battle to save them from the necessity of immediately capturing a port. The initiative for these harbours came from the British.—*F.B.*

[3] Rommel was evidently unaware of the large extent to which the new invasion devices were of British conception and design—above all, the "specialised armour" which played so important a part in the success of the invasion. This embraced D.D. (swimming) tanks, "flail" mine-clearing tanks, flame-throwing tanks, and armoured engineer vehicles for several purposes. These new units had been developed and trained by a large-scale experimental formation (known as the 79th Armoured Division) under General Hobart, with strong support from Montgomery and others. The American High Command was more hesitant about employing these untried instruments in the landing, and the contrast was seen in the lesser success and heavier losses of the initial landings on the American sector. *L.H.*

could certainly have executed the invasion with the forces available, but they could never have prepared it—neither technically, organisationally, nor in the field of training. The functioning of the Allied fighting machine, with all its complexity, surprised even me, and I already had a fairly high opinion of their powers.

In Tunisia the Americans had to pay a stiff price for their experience, but it brought rich dividends. Even at that time, the American generals showed themselves to be very advanced in the tactical handling of their forces, although we had to wait until the Patton Army in France to see the most astonishing achievements in mobile warfare. The Americans, it is fair to say, profited far more than the British from their experience in Africa, thus confirming the axiom that education is easier than re-education.

Probably our most fundamental and important advantage over the enemy in North Africa was that when my army arrived in Africa in 1941, it was in a better position to benefit from further training on modern lines than were the British. My officers, particularly the younger commanders and General Staff Officers, were up to date in their thinking and not hampered by the conservatism of the British officer.

From the outset it was our endeavour to turn our army into an instrument for the most rapid improvisation and to accustom it to high speed of manœuvre. Officers who had too little initiative to get their troops forward or too much reverence for preconceived ideas were ruthlessly removed from their posts and, failing all else, sent back to Europe. With the lower-ranking staff officers, I was less concerned about their knowledge of strategy (for how often does a junior staff officer have to think in terms of strategy?) than that they should bring with them a good grounding in tactics, to enable them to cope with the many tactical problems which faced us in the African campaign. I tried all possible methods of establishing close signal communication with the fighting troops and concluded that a headquarters near the front, equipped with radio and protected by a strong bodyguard, gives the best results. From my officers, I demanded the utmost self-denial and a continual personal example, and as a result, the army had a magnificent *esprit de corps*. There was never any collapse of morale among the German fighting troops, never any surrender due to apathy or fatigue. Discipline was always maintained and never had to be enforced even in the most terrible situations.

The experience of this magnificent and entirely spontaneous loyalty between officers and men kept hope alive even through the darkest hours of the African war. Even in Tunis, the troops retained full confidence in their command—probably a unique phenomenon after a retreat of 1,200 miles. But a bitter fate denied them any escape to Europe. I have evidence[1] that even in captivity my men have borne their lot with the same spirit of loyalty that distinguished the Panzer Army during two years of African war.

Our opportunities in North Africa were squandered and thrown away by the supreme commands of Germany and Italy. As a result of the senseless sacrifice of so many German and Italian troops in Tunisia, it became impossible to beat off the landings in southern Italy. The Allied experiment was successful and this gave them the confidence they needed to risk a landing in France. Only through the courage of our troops and the splendid leadership of Kesselring and Westphal has the collapse of the Italian front so far been prevented. But the disaster in Tunisia completely undermined the Duce's prestige and put an end to his dream of an " Imperium Romanum".

The British and Americans were halted in the mountains of Italy, but soon afterwards landed powerful forces in Normandy and shattered my formations with their artillery, tanks and air force. My men went to their death in their thousands, without hesitation, in a battle that could not be won.

No longer could we carry the burden of three fronts. The Russians broke through our line in the east, destroyed many of our divisions and are pushing westwards. Only with great difficulty and by using our last reserves have we been able to improvise new fronts, both east and west. The sky over Germany has grown very dark.

[1]Rommel received many letters from his officers and men in British and American prisoner-of-war camps.—*F.B.*

APPENDIX

[see illustration facing page 258]

ROMMEL'S PLAN OF ATTACK ON THE NILE

Note by Manfred Rommel.—This plan had been drawn up before the battle of Alam Halfa and was to be put into operation after Montgomery's army had been destroyed at the El Alamein position. A special problem for the German Staff was the crossing of the Nile. General Gause (who himself had been a sapper at one time) had worked out, even before the attack on El Alamein, the number of pontoon bridges required for the passage of the Nile and mentioned, as soon as my father spoke about Alexandria and Cairo, that there was not a single German pontoon bridge in Africa. My father, however, was relying on his being able to capture several Nile bridges by a *coup-de-main*. He intended, once the decisive engagement with Montgomery's front-line troops had begun, to throw his reconnaissance units and paratroops forward to a lightning attack on the Nile bridges in Cairo and Alexandria. By means of this operation, he not only intended to secure the bridges, but wanted to undermine the 8th Army's power of resistance with the news that " the Germans have reached the Nile." It was my father's view that there was small likelihood of the British having prepared the bridges for demolition at this time. It was also planned that the moment the first German paratroops and reconnaissance units appeared in and around Cairo and Alexandria, the Egyptians would be called upon to support the Axis forces. It was known from Egyptian officers who were in touch with the Germans that such a revolt was contemplated.

INDEX

INDEX

INDEX TO EDITORIAL NOTES

By GENERAL BAYERLEIN

By CAPTAIN LIDDELL HART

By MANFRED ROMMEL

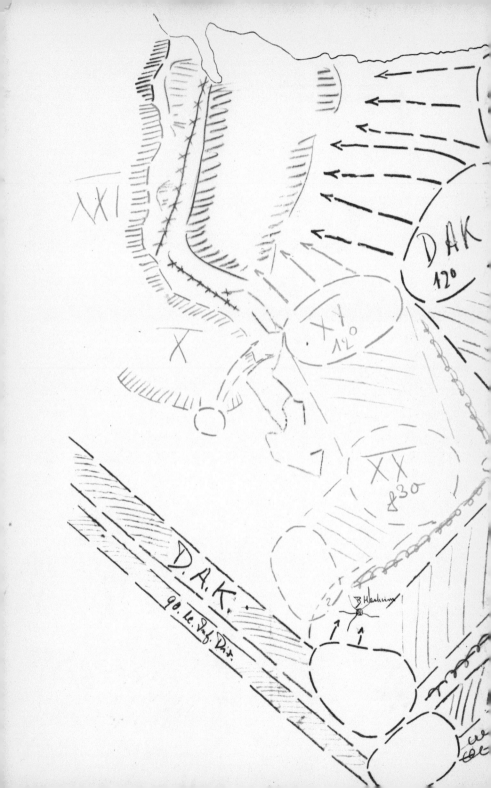